AF574438

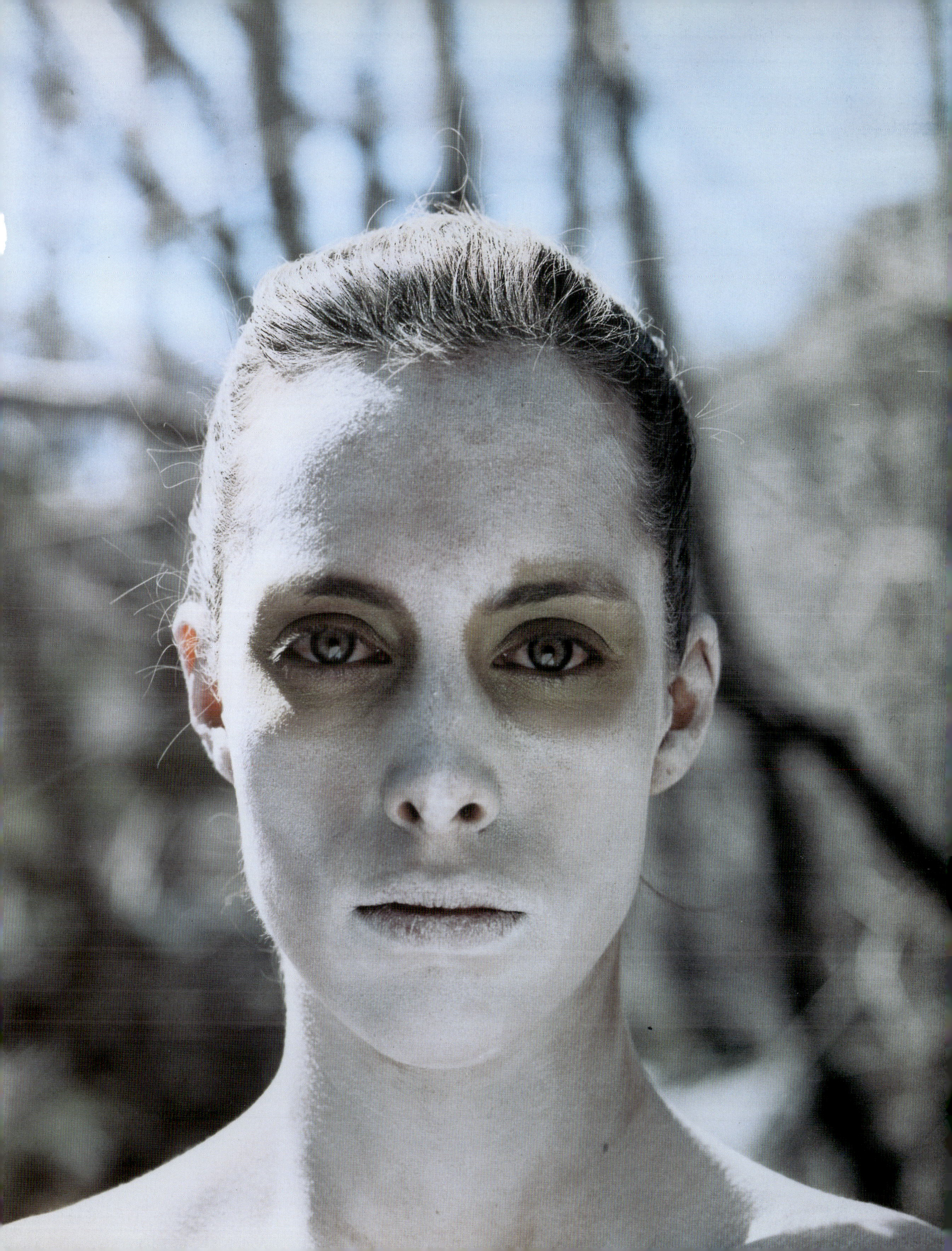

ENRIQUE MARTINEZ CELAYA

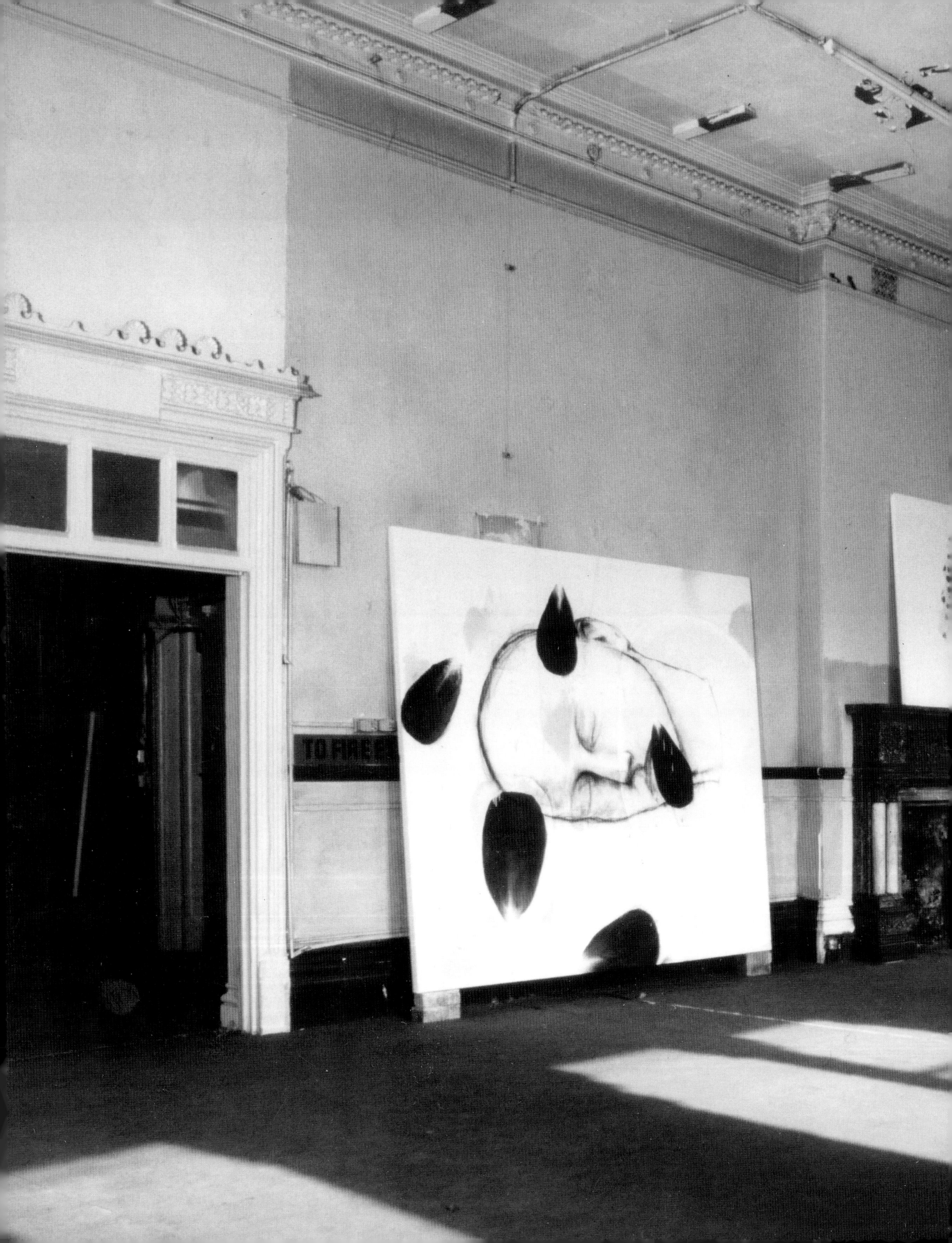
TO FIRE

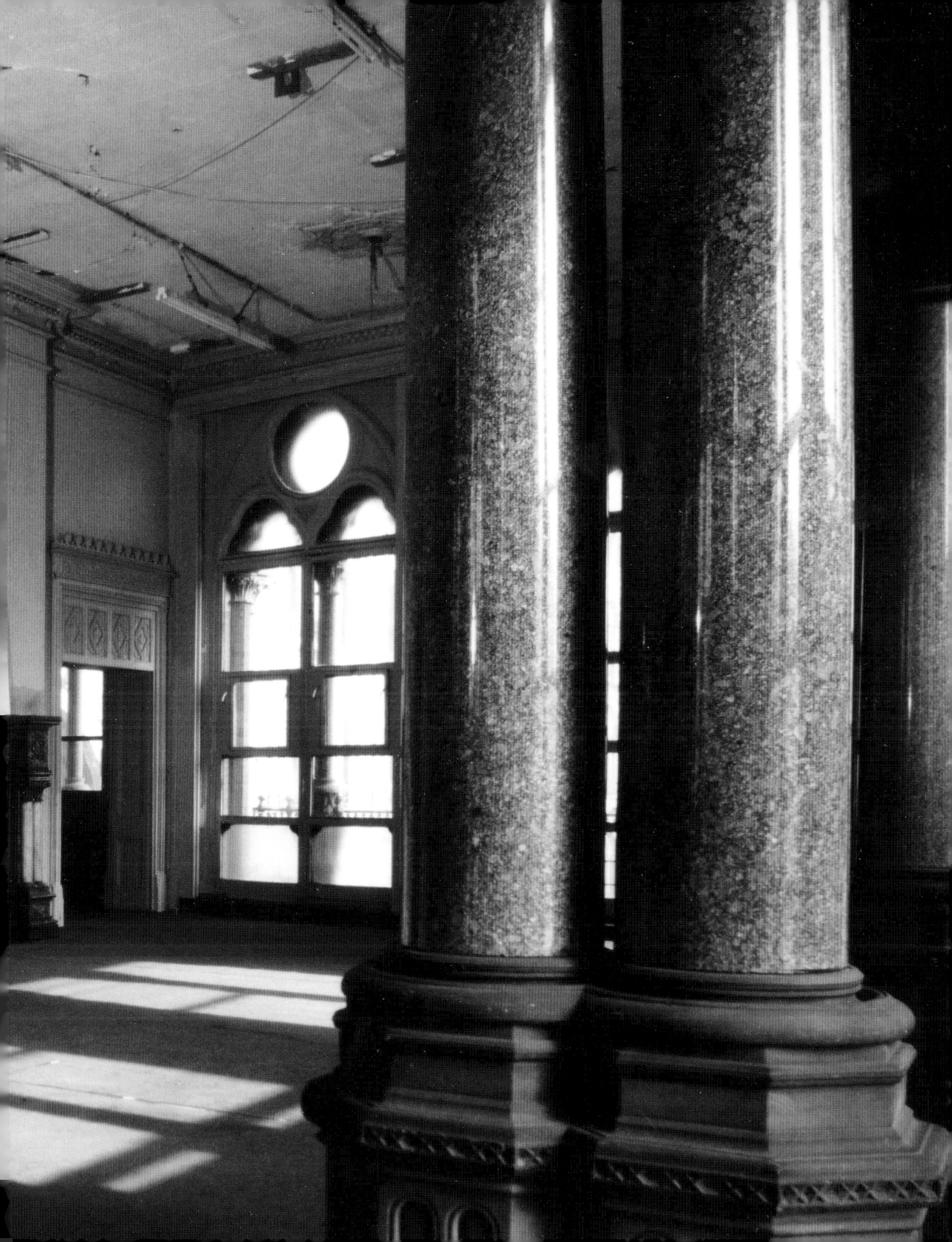

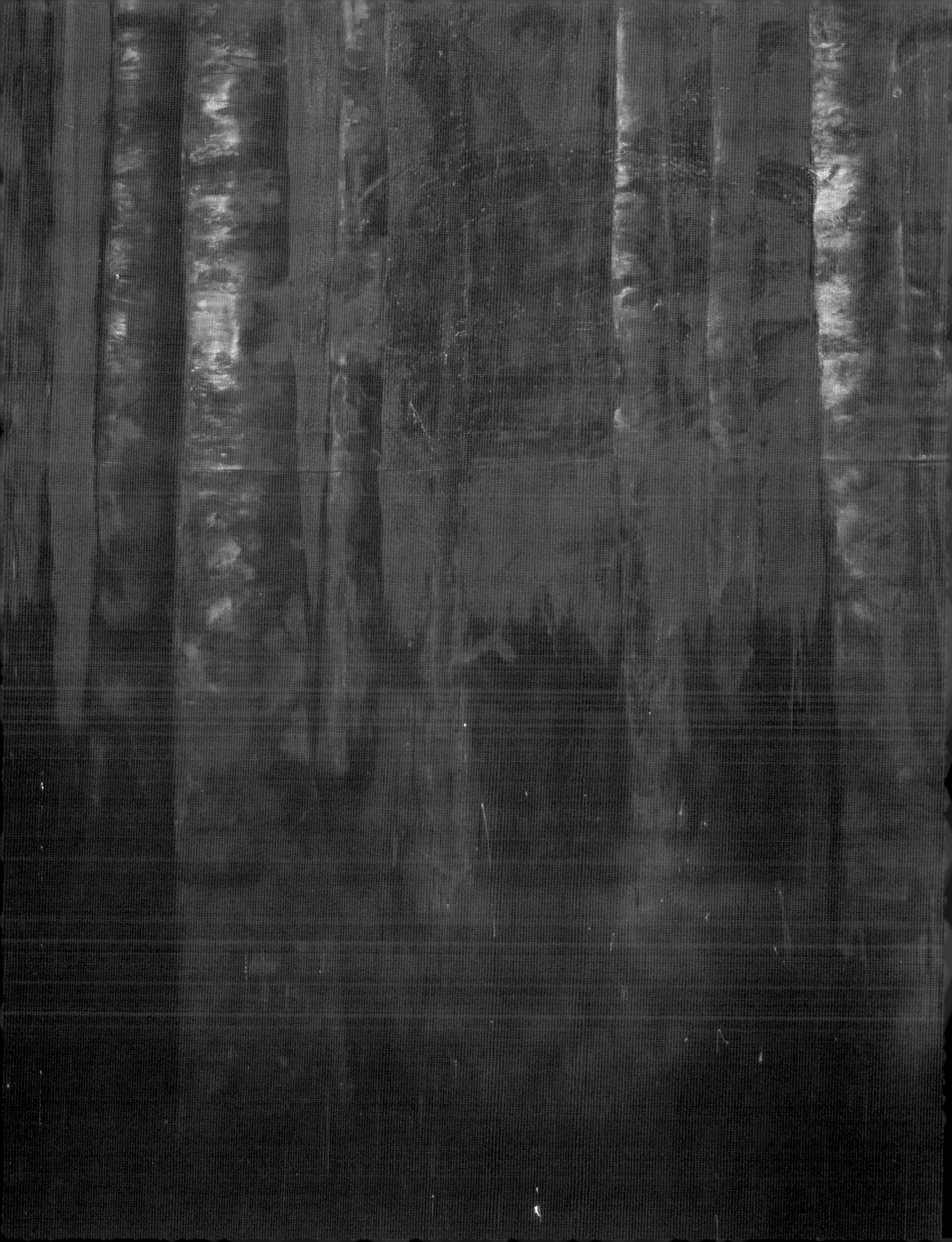

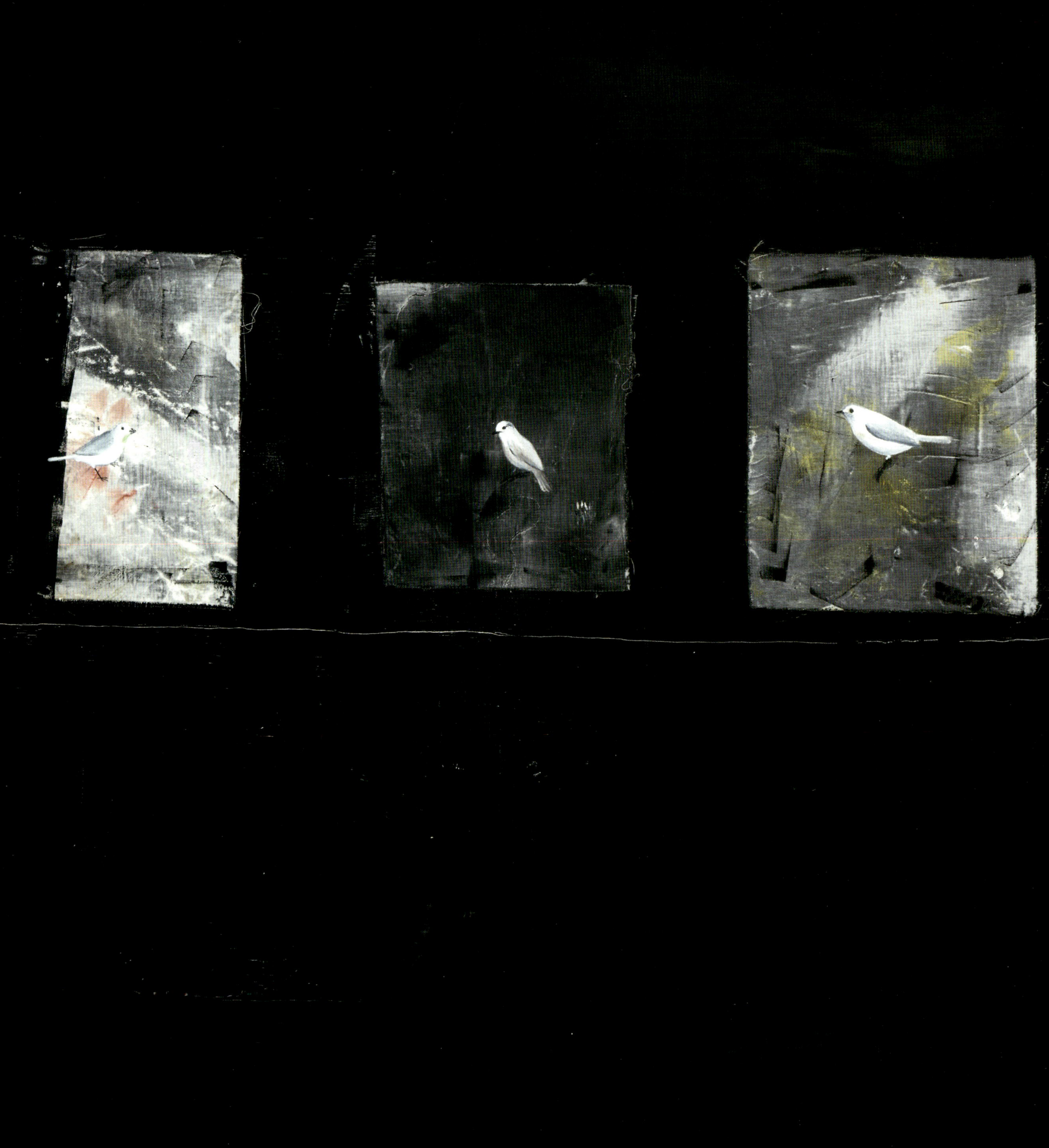

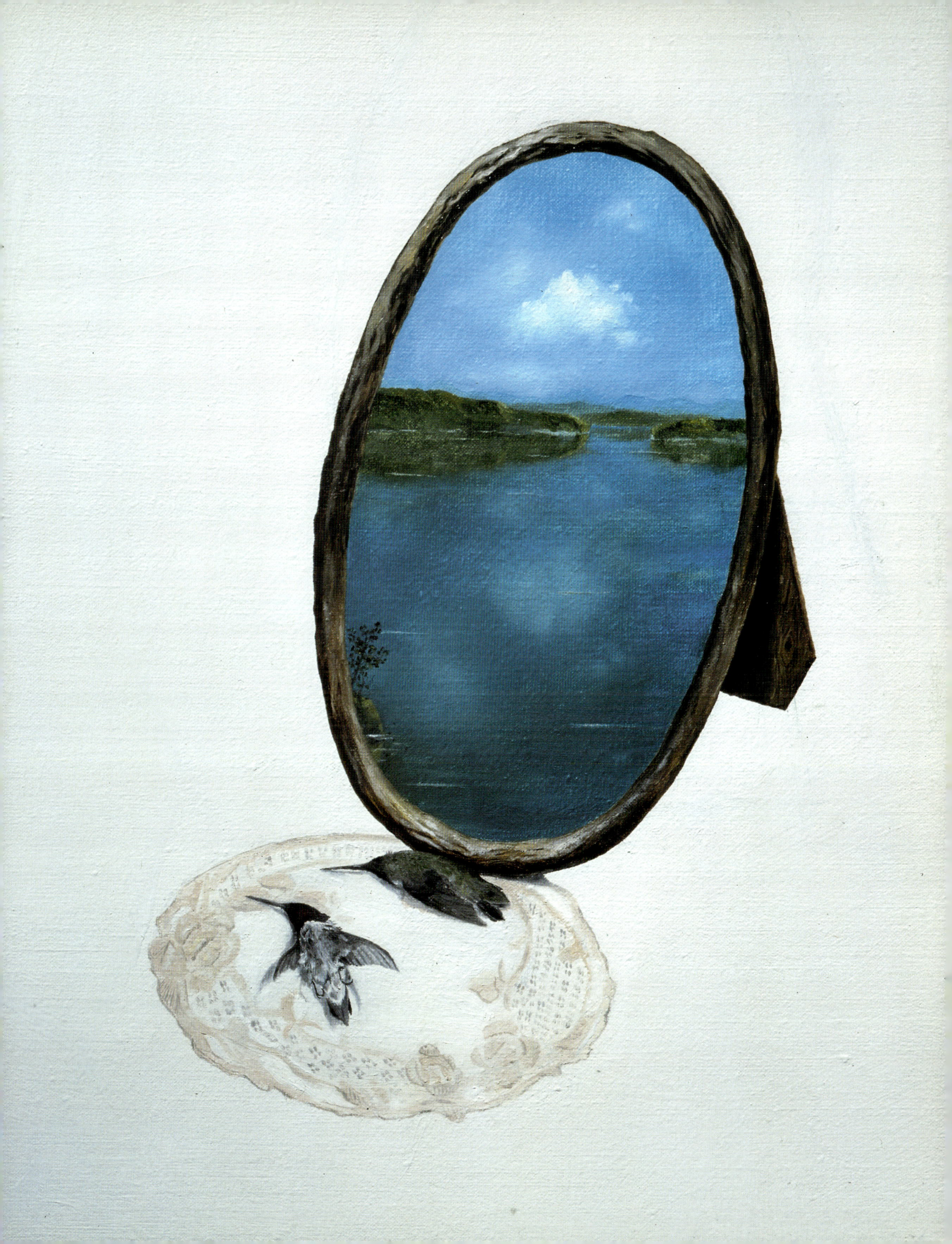

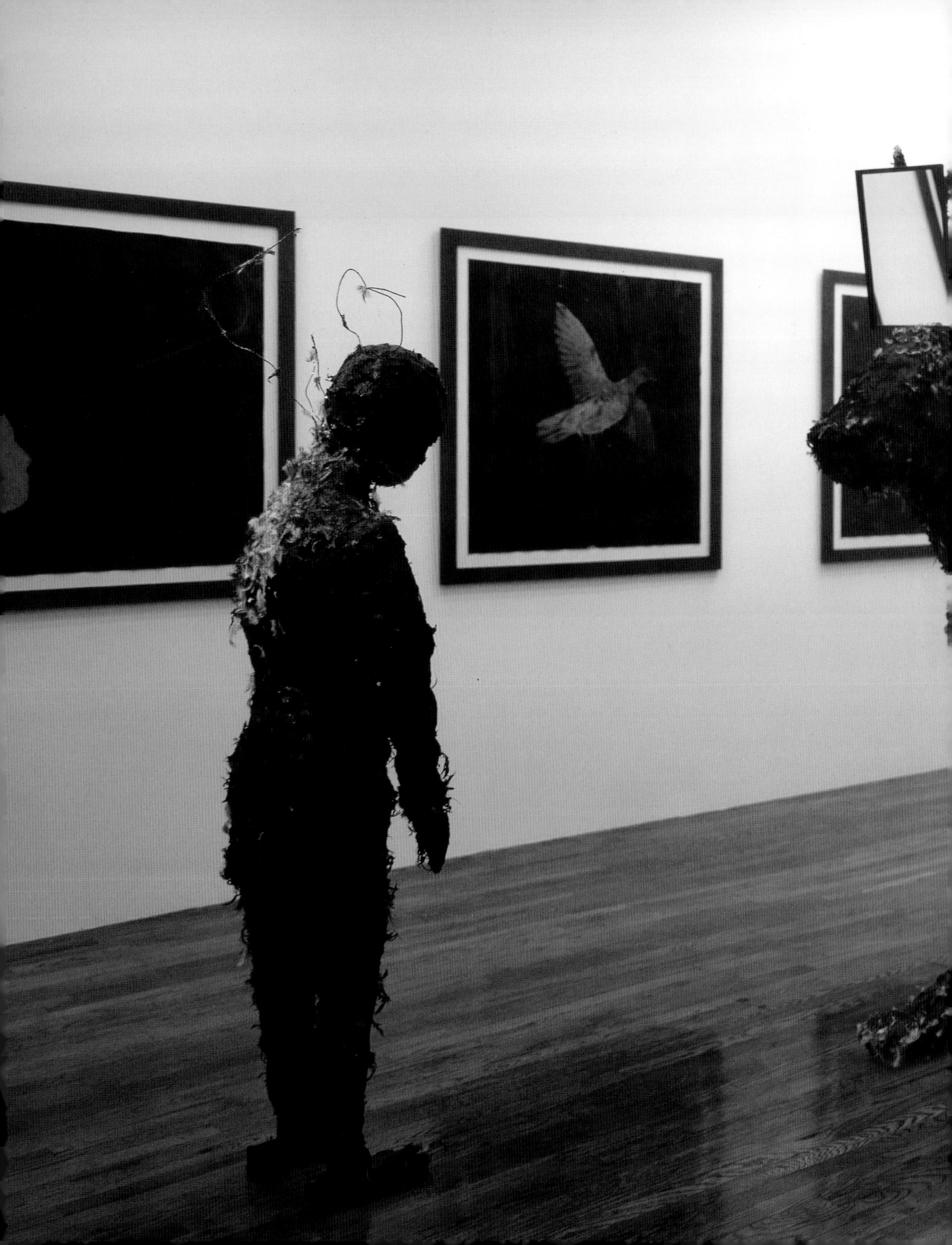

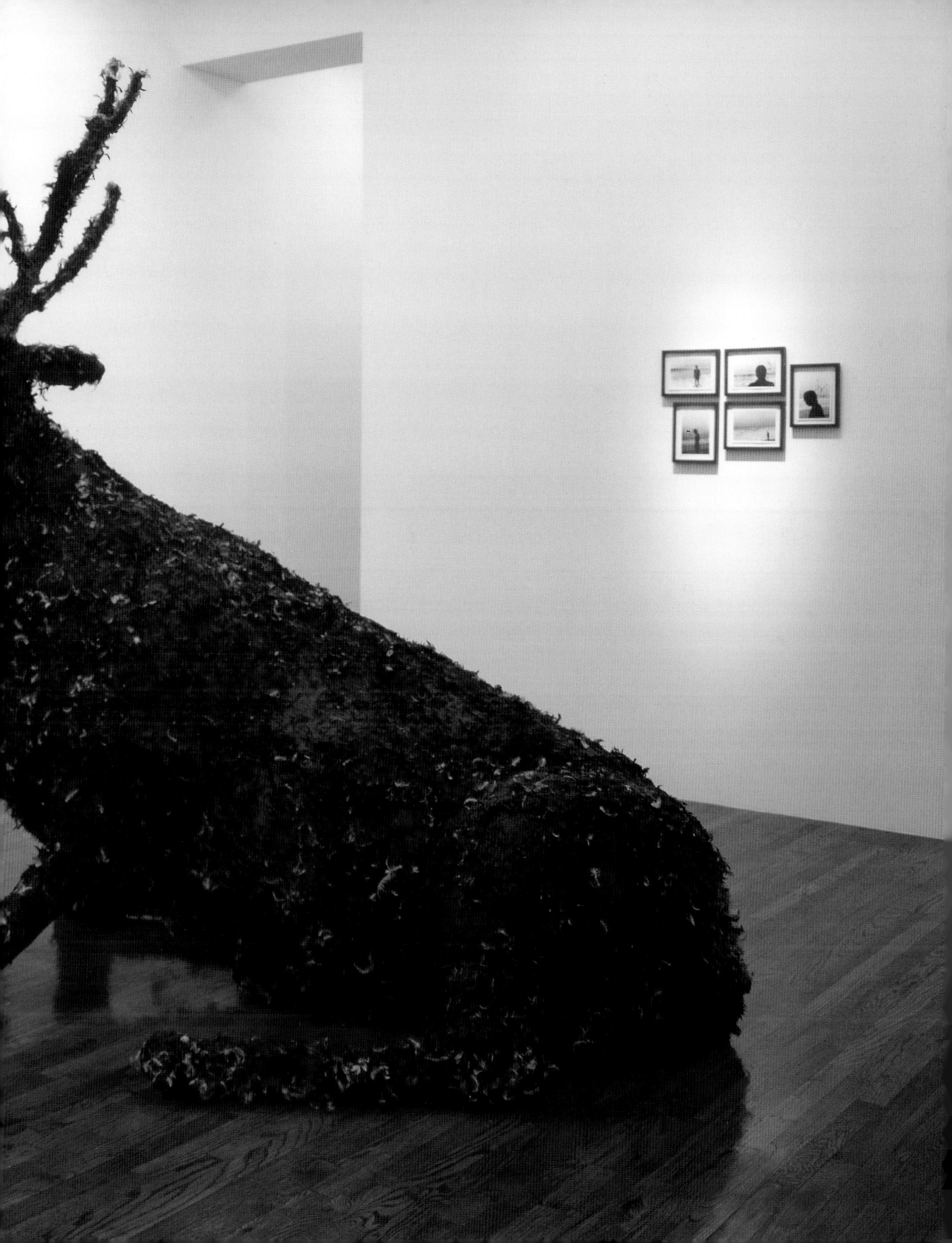

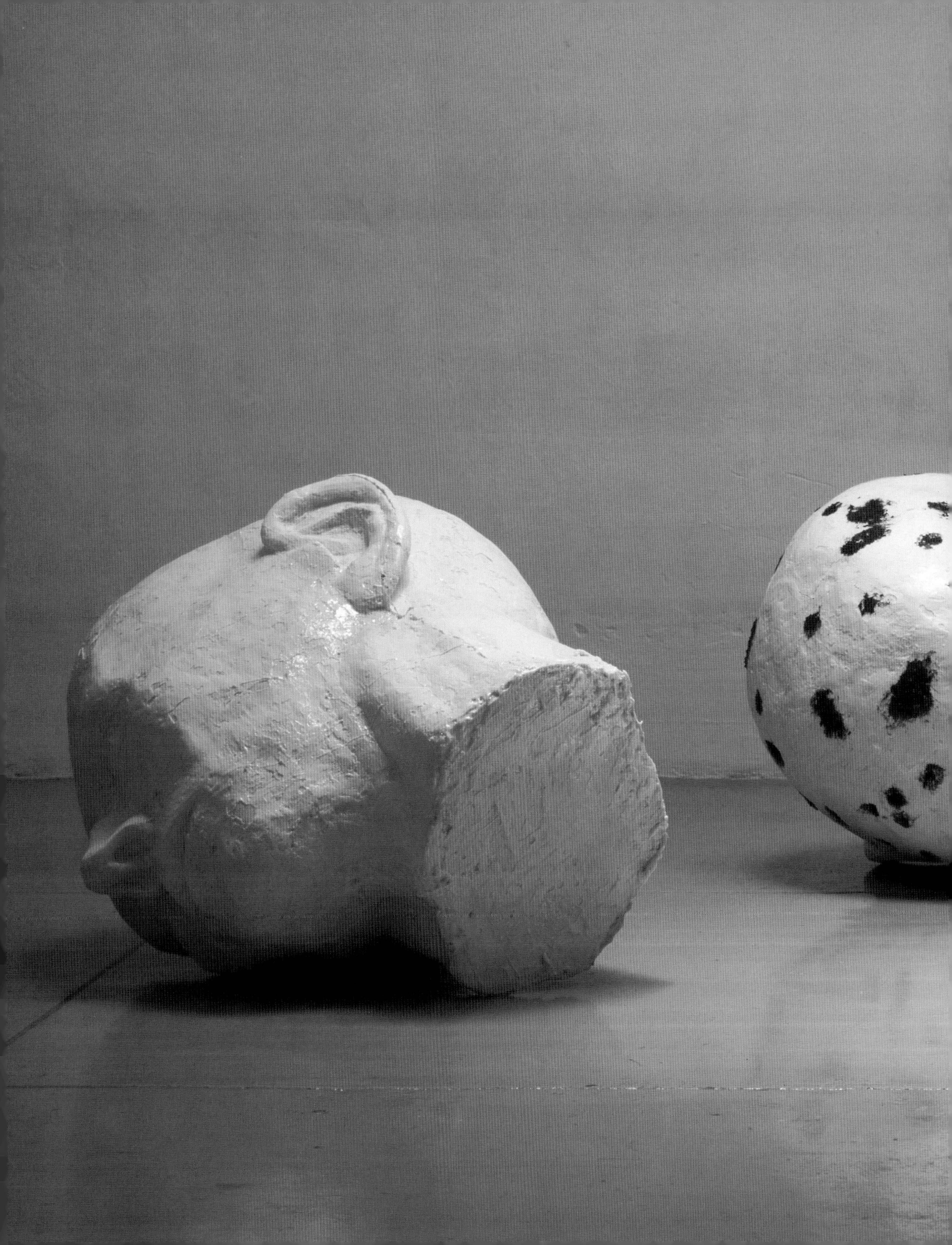

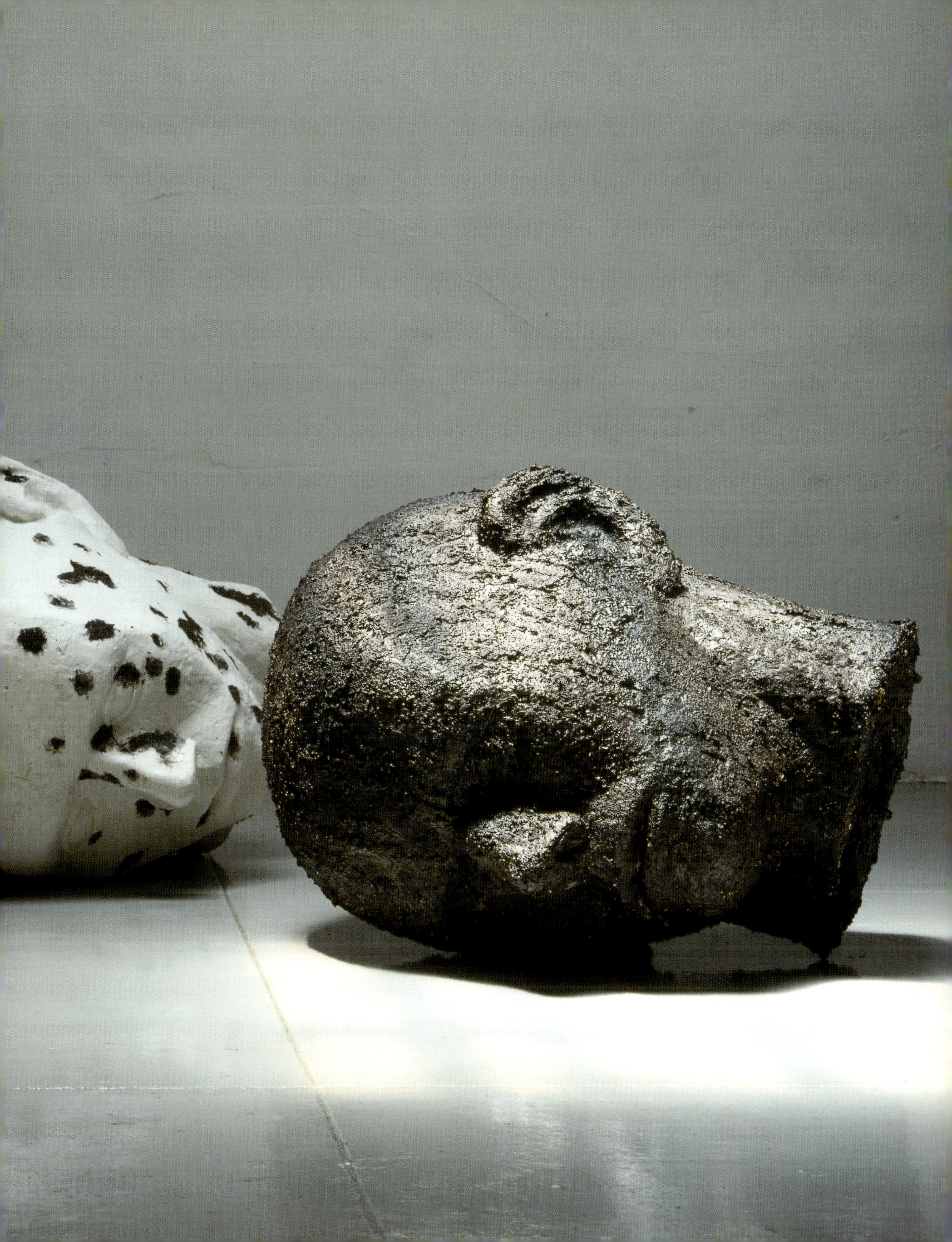

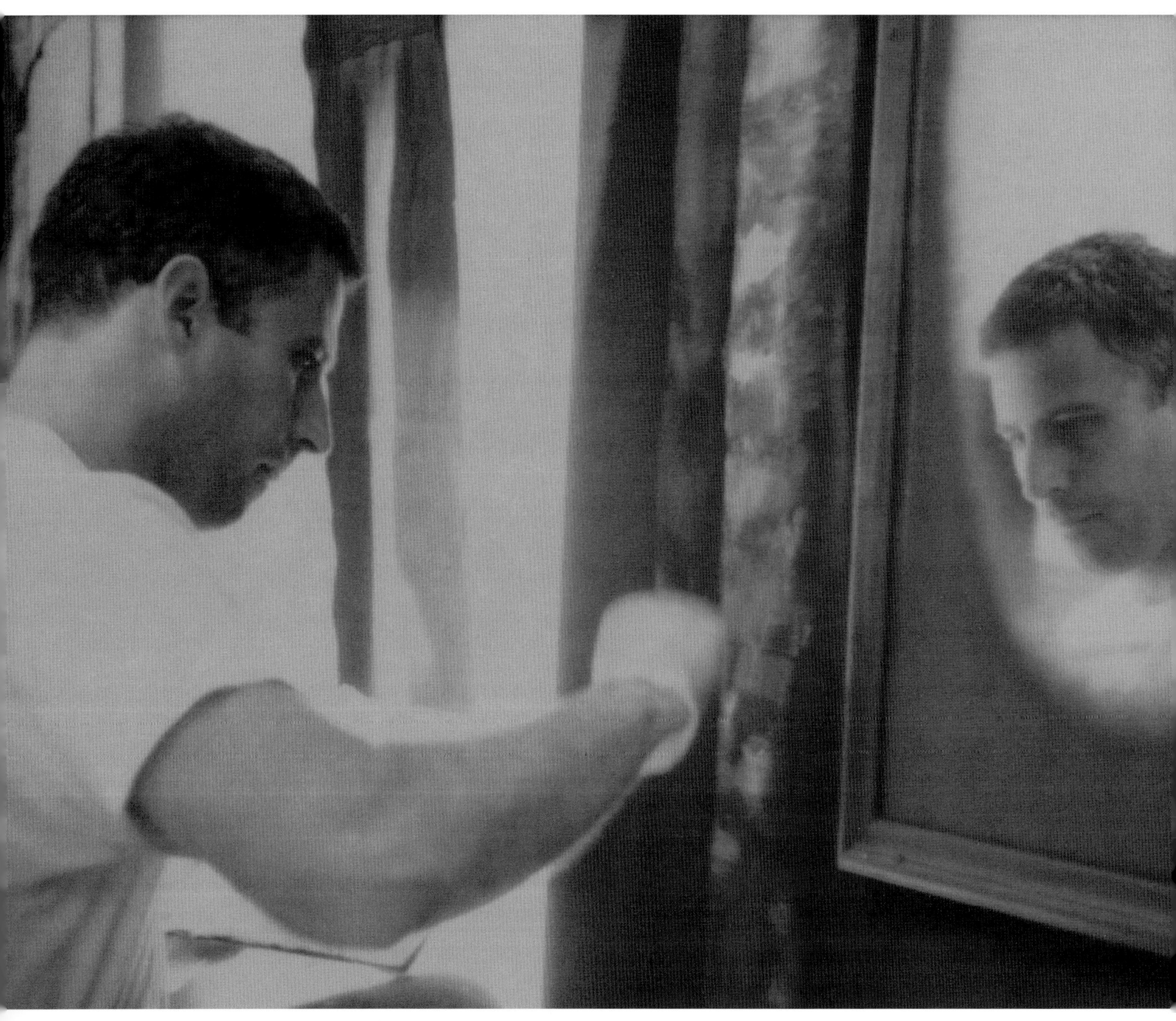

ENRIQUE MARTINEZ CELAYA

1992–2000

The Contemporary Museum, Honolulu

WIENAND

This monograph is published on the occasion of the exhibition *Enrique Martínez Celaya, 1992–2000*, organized by James Jensen, Associate Director/Chief Curator at The Contemporary Museum, Honolulu, Hawaii.

Exhibition Schedule:
The Contemporary Museum, Honolulu, Hawaii
August 24–October 21, 2001

Orange County Museum of Art, Newport Beach, California
November 11, 2001–February 3, 2002

Sandra and David Bakalar Gallery
Massachusetts College of Art, Boston, Massachusetts
February 22–March 30, 2002

Die Deutsche Bibliothek – CIP-Einheitsaufnahme

Enrique Martínez Celaya : 1992–2000 ; [on occasion of the Exhibition Enrique Martínez Celaya, 1992–2000 ; exhibition schedule: the Contemporary Museum, Honolulu, Hawaii, August 24–October 21, 2001 ; Orange County Museum of Art, Newport Beach, California, November 11, 2001–February 3, 2002 ; Sandra and David Bakalar Gallery, Massachusetts College of Art, Boston, Massachusetts, February 22 – March 30, 2002] / [ed. David Minnery. Transl. Alexandra Bootz ...]. – Köln : Wienand, 2001
ISBN 3-87909-765-8

Design Concept/Layoutkonzept
Enrique Martínez Celaya

Design/Graphik
Whale and Star

Editor/Redaktion
David Minnery

Copy Editor/Lektorat
Emil Hübner

Design Assistant/Mitarbeit Graphik
Adrienne Ponting, Christina Guerrero, Michael Parker

Translations/Übersetzungen
Alexandra Bootz, Susanne Schmidt, Sabine G. Shurter, Corinna Schreiber, Inga Funck

Copy Editor of the Translations/Lektorat der Übersetzungen
Uta Hasekamp

Publishing Coordinator/Koordination
Beatrice Foessel

Publishing Coordinator Wienand/Koordination Wienand
Christian Roussel

General Production/Gesamtherstellung
Druck- und Verlagshaus Wienand GmbH, Köln

www.martinezcelaya.com
www.tcmhi.org
www.wienand-koeln.de
www.whaleandstar.com

ISBN 3-87909-765-8

Printed in Germany

CONTENTS/INHALT

DIRECTOR'S FOREWORD

Georgianna M. Lagoria

In 1997, The Contemporary Museum acquired a work on paper by Enrique Martínez Celaya. Entitled *The End of Tragedy*, this mysterious work with oil, graphite, varnish, and collage on layers of translucent paper holds the blood-red image of a lion at its center, the ghost-like shape of a hummingbird hovering behind/beyond, and a tiny drawing of a toothpick in its cellophane wrapper. This spare yet powerful and intensely beautiful work was the first most in Hawaii had seen by this young artist from Los Angeles. I thank James Jensen, our Associate Director/Chief Curator, for bringing Martínez Celaya to our attention, into our collection, and for conceiving of and organizing the artist's first one-person museum exhibition for The Contemporary Museum, Honolulu.

The Contemporary Museum is a relatively young organization–operating barely twelve years since opening in late 1988 at its Makiki Heights site. To develop an in-depth presentation of work by a mainland-based artist, publish a major monograph, and tour the exhibition to the continental United States is no small feat and requires the resources of many. I extend my heartfelt gratitude to Jennifer and Royce Diener, Dieter and Si Rosenkranz, Carol Salisbury, Cade Roster and Wailea Davis, Persis Corporation, Neuberger Berman, LLC Fund at The New York Community Trust, Pomona College, the Hawaii State Foundation on Culture and the Arts, CSX Lines, and Aston Hotels & Resorts for providing the means with which to realize this vision. Thanks as well to the collectors and institutions lending works to the exhibition and to the staff of The Contemporary Museum for their care and expertise in handling the loaned artwork.

To the brilliant Enrique Martínez Celaya, thank you for entrusting us with the task of shaping your extraordinary body of work into a public offering for Hawaii's community and beyond. It is a pleasure and a privilege to be among the first group of art museums to recognize not only your achievements to date, but the promise of the future, as well.

VORWORT DER DIREKTORIN

Georgianna M. Lagoria

1997 erwarb das Contemporary Museum eine Papierarbeit von Enrique Martínez Celaya mit dem Titel *The End of Tragedy/Das Ende der Tragödie.* Im Zentrum dieses geheimnisvollen Werkes aus Öl, Graphit, Lack und einer Collage aus Schichten durchscheinenden Papiers steht die blutrote Gestalt eines Löwen. Im Hintergrund ist schemenhaft ein flatternder Kolibri zu sehen und daneben ein kleiner gezeichneter Zahnstocher, der noch in seiner Zellophanhülle steckt. Diese karge und doch kraftvolle, wunderschöne Arbeit war die erste des jungen Künstlers aus Los Angeles, die auf Hawaii zu sehen war. Mein besonderer Dank gilt unserem Co-Direktor und Chefkustos James Jensen, dafür dass er uns auf Martínez Celaya aufmerksam machte, unsere Sammlung mit seinen Arbeiten bereicherte und die erste Einzelausstellung des Künstlers in einem Museum für das Contemporary Museum in Honolulu konzipiert und organisiert hat.

Das Contemporary Museum wurde erst Ende 1988 auf Makiki Heights eröffnet und ist mit seinen zwölf Jahren eine relativ junge Institution. Eine umfassende Ausstellung über einen Künstler vom amerikanischen Festland zu entwickeln, ihre Reise in die Vereinigten Staaten zu organisieren und eine umfangreiche Monographie herauszugeben, ist eine nicht unbeachtliche Leistung und konnte nur mit der Unterstützung zahlreicher Helfer gelingen. Mein herzlicher Dank gilt daher Jennifer und Royce Diener, Dieter and Si Rosenkranz, Carol Salisbury, Cade Roster und Wailea Davis, der Persis Corporation, Neuberger Berman, dem LLC Fund at The New York Community Trust, dem Pomona College, der Hawaii State Foundation on Culture and the Arts, CSX Lines und den Aston Hotels & Resorts, die die Mittel zur Verfügung stellten, mit denen diese Idee verwirklicht werden konnte. Ebenso danken wir den Sammlern und Institutionen, die uns Werke aus ihrem Besitz zur Verfügung gestellt haben, sowie allen Mitarbeitern des Contemporary Museum für ihren sorgfältigen und fachkundigen Umgang mit den Leihgaben.

Nicht zuletzt möchte ich Enrique Martínez Celaya danken, der uns mit der Aufgabe betraut hat, sein außergewöhnliches Oeuvre den Menschen auf Hawaii und darüber hinaus vorzustellen. Es ist eine Freude und eine Auszeichnung, zu den ersten Kunstmuseen zu zählen, die nicht nur die bisherigen Leistungen sondern auch das Zukunftspotenzial dieses vielversprechenden Künstlers erkennen und würdigen.

LENDERS TO THE EXHIBITION/LEIHGEBER

Patrick Aroff, Santa Monica
Steven Baigelman, Los Angeles
Ramis Barquet, New York
Bilbao/Mekis Collection, Coconut Grove, Florida
Ross Bleckner, New York
Stephen Cohen, Los Angeles
Stephen Cohen Gallery, Los Angeles
Ike and Marsha Coron, Malibu
The Contemporary Museum, Honolulu
Davenport Museum of Art, Iowa
Amy and Roger Faxon, New York
Danny First, Los Angeles
Frederick R. Weisman Art Museum, University of Minnesota, Minneapolis
Galeria Ramis Barquet, New York
Sara Nemeth Goodman, Los Angeles
Jocelyn Grayson, Woodstock, Vermont
Achille Murat-Guest, Virginia
Griffin Contemporary, Venice, California
William Griffin, Venice, California
Scott Dean Harrington, Los Angeles
The Manfred Heiting Collection, Amsterdam
Christopher and Tracy Keys, Laguna Beach, California
Andrea King, Los Angeles
Los Angeles County Museum of Art
Enrique and Alexandra Martínez Celaya, Los Angeles
Michael and Christine McCullough, Newport Beach
The Museum of Fine Arts, Houston
Neuberger Berman Collection, New York
Mary Paeng, San Francisco
Tom Peters, Los Angeles
RBC Dain Rauscher, Minneapolis
Michael Rank, North Carolina
Dieter and Si Rosenkranz, Berlin
Willy J. Salet, Aspen
Heidi Schneider, New York
Sheldon Memorial Art Gallery And Sculpture Garden, University of Nebraska, Lincoln, Nebraska
Joyce and Ted Strauss, Solana Beach, California
Julien J. Studley, Inc., Los Angeles
J. H. Theodoracopulos Collection, New York
And private collectors who wish to remain anonymous./Und private Sammler, die nicht namentlich genannt werden wollen.

PREFACE AND ACKNOWLEDGMENTS

James Jensen

I first encountered the work of Enrique Martínez Celaya in the fall of 1995 in an exhibition at the Dorothy Goldeen Gallery in Santa Monica, California. I was immediately intrigued by the dazzling white spareness of similar related paintings with isolated small passages of drawn, painted or collaged imagery. Despite their visual economy, the canvases nevertheless seemed to be profoundly ambitious. The expansive white fields spoke both of absence and of potential. While the representation or incorporation of recognizable objects from the real world admitted the possibility of narrative interpretations, the juxtaposition of disparate elements also allowed for more symbolic and open-ended readings of these austere yet beautiful paintings.

I again saw Martínez Celaya's work in 1997 in an exhibition at Burnett Miller Gallery in Santa Monica. The range and disparity of the works on view, which included a sculpture of a woman mounted on the wall and painted head to feet with a landscape of a river under a cloud-filled sky, a series of tiny paintings of hummingbirds, a painting of a hand done on transparent fabric, and a large pale canvas of a head, evidenced a significant shift in Martínez Celaya's way of working–away from focusing on aesthetic and stylistic relationships between his works, as in the earlier white paintings, to a more conceptual approach in which works in different media interacted in and with a space, as well as with each other, to form a coherent, cogent entity or whole.

Since then I have followed the evolution of Martínez Celaya's career as he has developed a significant and compelling body of work comprising paintings, drawings, sculpture, photographs, and installations. As his art gains wider recognition and receives increased critical attention, it is a pleasure and an honor for The Contemporary Museum, which was among the first institutions to purchase his work, to organize Martínez Celaya's first one-person museum exhibition, tracing his development and achievement from his early mature images, the black paintings of 1992–93, to his recent body of work exhibited in 2001, an installation purchased in its entirety by Dieter and Si Rosenkranz, Berlin, Germany. This exhibition and its accompanying publication provide an opportunity at this important juncture in Martínez Celaya's career for a fuller examination and deeper understanding of this highly regarded young Los Angeles artist.

Martínez Celaya is a prodigiously independent-minded artist who cannot be categorized by a repeated use of a style, medium or format. He possesses a restless, multifarious intellect and moves easily from painting to sculpture to drawing to photography. The disparate aspects of Martínez Celaya's art are connected by an evolving vision shaped by circumstances, experiences, memories–of his youth spent in Cuba, Spain and Puerto Rico, his education in physics and art, and influential figures such as his father, Marcos Martínez, and Bartoldo Mayol, the artist to whom he was apprenticed at age eleven and who instilled in Martínez Celaya a love for the process of making art.

Martínez Celaya has explored notions of symbolism, hermeticism, displacement, fragmentation, time, remembrance, mortality and identity, examined ideas attached to concepts of beauty, and questioned the nature of the art objects he presents, as well as the possibilities of visual media and the limitations–perhaps inadequacy–of representation itself. The unfolding of these concerns is reflected in the organization of the exhibition and the plates in this publication into five sections focusing on the progression of a number of central themes and abiding images that have appeared in his work.

Martínez Celaya is also a poet, and his art works have a link to literary concerns and practices. Artists, like poets, work within certain fixed conventional structures where they seek their own distinctive and unique vision. For artists and poets, metaphor is their common 'language;' equivalence is the context for disclosing the essence of one's thoughts either in words or in visual terms. Further, the improvisatory quality of Martínez Celaya's work, the ambiguity of its juxtaposed elements, are akin to William S. Burroughs' use of the 'cut-up,' in which various texts are separated into parts with scissors and reassembled in a kind of automatic writing into new texts with fresh potential for meaning.

Looking at Martínez Celaya's works, one readily senses that for him the mental and physical act of making is paramount, for the process/progress of his mind and hand are often plainly visible in the marks and changes, the drips and floods of pigment spilling across canvas and paper. The push and pull between the subjective and objective in his work finds an analogue in the tension he establishes between the tactile and the visual. The process of making art is for Martínez Celaya a dialogue with himself that is both conscious and instinctive. He lets flow a stream of consciousness as he works, reworking, adding, removing, seemingly responsive to trying almost anything, never hesitating but always pressing forward, not accepting his first solution as final. What emerges is an impassioned and very personal vision of exceptional beauty and voice–mysterious, elegiac, poetic, psychologically charged, deeply concerned with meaning.

•

This exhibition and publication have been made possible by the involvement and assistance of numerous individuals and organizations to whom I am most grateful. First and foremost is Enrique Martínez Celaya, whom it has been my pleasure in the course of this project to come to know as an artist and a friend. Throughout this endeavor he has been an active collaborator in every aspect, and I have enjoyed my many visits and dialogues with him. His thoughtful intelligence and his spirit of warmth, integrity and patience have made our collaboration exciting and rewarding. To him I extend my wholehearted appreciation and admiration.

This publication is enhanced and enriched by the contributions of several individuals. The essays by Abigail Solomon-Godeau, Charles Merewether, and Rosanna Albertini broaden our context for understanding and appreciating Martínez Celaya's work. In his conversation with Martínez Celaya, Howard N. Fox, poses stimulating questions that bring the voice of the artist into the dialogue offered here. The commentaries on the works by Judson Emerick and Arden Reed, based on extensive discussions with the artist, provide added insights into Martínez Celaya's vision and process. Colette Dartnall has produced a biography that provides insight into the artist's life, and Peter Kirby has provided an extraordinary video of the artist at work.

This exhibition could not have happened without the generosity of the lenders who graciously agreed to share works from their collections. Appreciation and thanks are extended to all of them for their cooperation. I would also like to express my gratitude to those individuals who made it possible to secure loans from museum and corporate collections: Michelle Robinson, Curator of Collections and Exhibitions at the Davenport Museum of Art; Andrea Rich, President and Director, and Howard Fox, Curator of Modern and Contemporary Art, at the Los Angeles County Museum of Art; Peter C. Marzio, Director, and Anne Wilkes Tucker, Gus and Lyndal

Wortham Curator of Photography, at The Museum of Fine Arts, Houston; Jan Driesbach, Director, and Dan Siedell, Curator, at the Sheldon Memorial Art Gallery, University of Nebraska-Lincoln; Lyndel King, Director, and Patricia McDonnell, Curator, at the Frederick R. Weisman Art Museum, University of Minnesota, Minneapolis; Don McNeil, Consultant for RBC Dain Rauscher, Minneapolis; and I. Michael Danoff, Director of the Art Program, and Heidi Schneider, Executive Vice President, Private Asset Management, at Neuberger Berman, New York.

The dedicated efforts of Griffin Contemporary in Venice, California have been crucial to the realization and success of this project. Bill Griffin devoted considerable time, energy and resources to ensure that needs were met and things could go forward smoothly. He and his gallery staff, Meredith McDaniel, Director, and Melissa Beaver, Registrar, made the gallery's archives and records freely available to me and were extremely helpful in locating works, researching information and providing photographic documentation. Their enthusiasm and encouragement have been invaluable. I would also like to thank Rena Bransten and the staff of her gallery in San Francisco, particularly Walter Maciel and Calvert Barron, and Ramis Barquet and the staff of his gallery in New York, particularly Virgilio Garza, for their assistance in the course of this endeavor.

Following its premiere in Honolulu, this exhibition will travel to the Orange County Museum of Art in Newport Beach, California and the Sandra and David Bakalar Gallery at the Massachusetts College of Art in Boston, thus extending its reach and impact by making the artist's work available to a larger audience. I am grateful to Naomi Vine, Director of the Orange County Museum of Art, and Jeffrey Keough, Director of Exhibitions at the Massachusetts College of Art, for their interest and support in bringing the Martínez Celaya exhibition to their institutions. I would like to additionally recognize Elizabeth Armstrong, Deputy Director of Art and Chief Curator, and Sarah Vure, Curator, at the Orange County Museum of Art, and Lisa Tung, Exhibitions Curator at the Massachusetts College of Art, for their roles in coordinating the presentations of the exhibition at their respective venues.

This exhibition and publication have been made possible through the generosity of several donors. I would like to add my thanks to that of Director Georgianna Lagoria for the major support provided by Jennifer and Royce Diener, Dieter and Si Rosenkranz, Carol Salisbury, Cade Roster and Waileia Davis, Persis Corporation, Neuberger Berman, LLC Fund at The New York Community Trust, Pomona College, the Hawaii State Foundation on Culture and the Arts, as well as in-kind support from CSX Lines and Aston Hotels & Resorts.

The success of any exhibition is dependent upon the careful and proficient work of the staff that supports the curator. I would like to express my appreciation and gratitude to Georgianna Lagoria, Director, for her ongoing encouragement and support; Kathy Hong, Director of Development, for her assistance in obtaining funding for this project; Allison Wong, Assistant Curator, and Katherine Love, Exhibitions Assistant, for their diligent attention to many aspects of this project; Stephanie L'Heureux, Registrar, for her expert handling of the many tasks associated with gathering the loans and coordinating the packing and transportation for this traveling exhibition; Sanit Khewhok, Collections Manager, John Koga, Chief Preparator, and Brian Koga and Cynthia Takamiya, Preparators, for their careful unpacking/packing, handling and installation of the works in the exhibition; Nancy Conley, Librarian, for assembling materials on the artist for public use in the museum's Cades Library; Louise Lanzilotti, Curator of Education, and Elizabeth Train, Museum Educator, for their development of interpretive materials, programs and activities to help make the experiencing of the exhibition more accessible and more meaningful for museum visitors. To these and other staff, docents and volunteers I would like to say thank you for your cooperation and assistance.

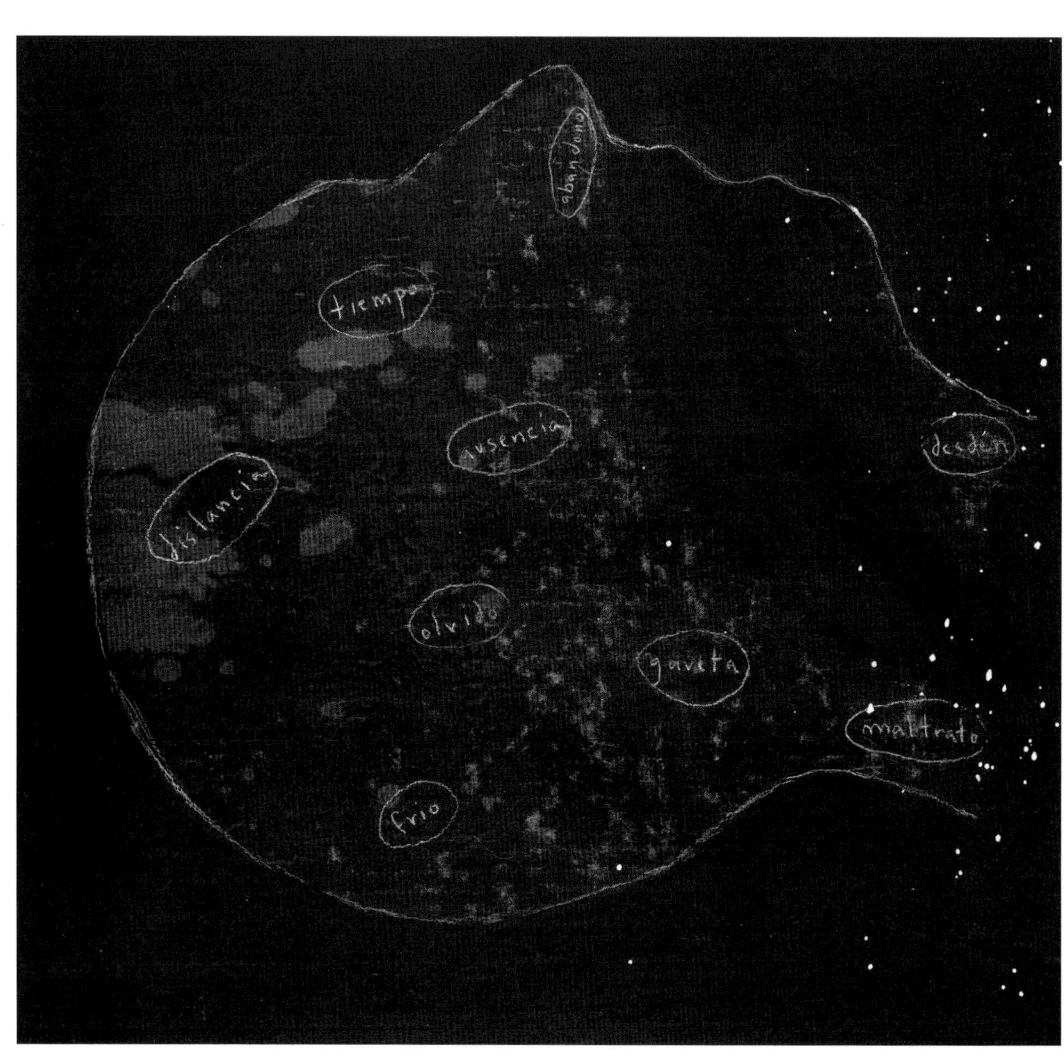
abandono
tiempo
ausencia
desdén
distancia
olvido
gaveta
maltrato
frio

VORWORT UND DANKSAGUNG

James Jensen

Ich habe Enrique Martínez Celayas Arbeiten zum ersten Mal 1995 in der Dorothy Goldeen Gallery in Santa Monica, Kalifornien, gesehen. Die strahlend weiße Kargheit der einander ähnlichen, miteinander korrespondierenden Gemälde, die nur hie und da durch gezeichnete, gemalte oder collagierte Motive unterbrochen wurde, faszinierte mich sofort. Denn trotz ihrer visuellen Ökonomie erweckten die Arbeiten den Eindruck enormen Anspruchs. Die ausgedehnten weißen Flächen erzählten von Abwesenheit und Potenzial zugleich. Und während die Darstellung und Einbeziehung von Objekten aus der Wirklichkeit eine narrative Interpretation ermöglichte, forderte die Nebeneinanderstellung einzelner, disparater Elemente eine eher symbolische, offene Deutung dieser strengen, aber wunderschönen Bilder.

Meine nächste Begegnung mit Martínez Celayas Werk war 1997 bei einer Ausstellung in der Burnett Miller Gallery in Santa Monica. Die Verschiedenartigkeit der Exponate – unter anderem eine an der Wand befestigte Frauenskulptur, die von Kopf bis Fuß mit einer Landschaft (ein Fluss unter einem wolkenverhangenen Himmel) bemalt war, eine Serie kleinformatiger Kolibribilder, eine Arbeit auf transparentem Stoff, die eine Hand zeigte, und eine große Leinwand mit dem blassen Bild eines Kopfes – ließ auf eine signifikante Veränderung der Arbeitsweise des Künstlers schließen. Das Interesse an ästhetischen und stilistischen Verhältnissen, das in den früheren, weißen Bildern zu beobachten ist, war einem eher konzeptuellen Ansatz gewichen: Die in unterschiedlichen Medien umgesetzten Werke interagierten in und mit dem Raum und gleichzeitig untereinander und bildeten dabei eine kohärente, überzeugende, eigenständige Entität.

Seither habe ich Martínez Celayas künstlerische Entwicklung genau verfolgt. Aus den zahlreichen Gemälden, Zeichnungen, Plastiken, Photographien und Installationen ist ein bedeutendes Werk entstanden. Angesichts der wachsenden Anerkennung und erhöhten kritischen Aufmerksamkeit, die Celayas Kunst entgegengebracht wird, freut sich das Contemporary Museum – das zu den ersten institutionellen Käufern seiner Arbeiten gehört – besonders, Martínez Celayas erste große Einzelausstellung in Museen organisieren zu dürfen, die den Zeitraum vom Beginn seines reiferen Werks, den schwarzen Gemälden von 1992/93, bis zu seiner jüngsten Arbeit aus dem Jahr 2001 umfasst, einer Installation, die bereits in den Besitz von Dieter und Si Rosenkranz in Berlin übergegangen ist. Die Ausstellung und die sie begleitende Publikation bieten die Möglichkeit, diesen interessanten aufstrebenden Künstler aus Los Angeles an einem entscheidenden Punkt seiner Karriere besser kennen zu lernen und zu verstehen.

Martínez Celaya ist ein absolut eigenständiger Künstler, der sich jeder Kategorisierung entzieht. Es gibt keinen Stil, kein Medium oder Format, den oder das er typischerweise verwenden würde. Er besitzt einen ruhelosen, komplexen Intellekt und springt mühelos zwischen Malerei, Skulptur, Zeichnung und Photographie hin und her. Verbindungsglied zwischen den disparaten Aspekten in Martínez Celayas Kunst ist eine Vision, die sich aus Erfahrungen und Erinnerungen entwickelte – seine Jugend in Kuba, Spanien und Puerto Rico, sein Physik- und Kunststudium und die Menschen, die ihn beeinflusst haben, wie sein Vater, der Maler Marcos

gegenüberliegende Seite

AUSENCIA (ABSENCE), detail
/AUSENCIA (ABWESENHEIT), Ausschnitt, 1998
Sammlung Enrique und Alexandra Martínez Celaya

Martínez, und Bartoldo Mayol, jener Künstler, der sein Lehrmeister wurde, als Martínez Celaya elf Jahre alt war, und der in ihm die Liebe für den künstlerischen Schöpfungsprozess geweckt hat.

Martínez Celaya untersucht in seiner Arbeit Vorstellungen von Symbolismus, Hermetismus, Deplatzierung, Fragmentation, Zeit, Erinnerung, Sterblichkeit und Identität. Er analysiert der Schönheit verhaftete Ideen, hinterfragt das Wesen der von ihm präsentierten Objekte, stellt die Möglichkeiten visueller Medien und die Grenzen – vielleicht gar die Unzulänglichkeit – von Darstellung an sich zur Diskussion. Die Entwicklung dieser Anliegen spiegelt sich sowohl in der Organisation der Ausstellung als auch im Bildteil dieser Publikation wider, die jeweils in fünf Bereiche aufgeteilt sind, welche zentrale Themen und deren Darstellung im Werk des Künstlers aufgreifen.

Martínez Celaya ist auch Dichter, und seine Kunst weist Bezüge zu literarischen Fragen und Praktiken auf. Ähnlich wie der Poet bedient sich auch der Bildende Künstler bestimmter fester Strukturen, um seine eigene unverwechselbare und einzigartige Vision zu finden. Die Metapher ist ihre gemeinsame „Sprache", Äquivalenz der Kontext, in dem sich die Essenz des eigenen Denkens offenbaren lässt, sei es durch das Wort oder durch das Bild. Darüber hinaus erinnern das Improvisierte in Martínez Celayas Werk und die Ambiguität der nebeneinander gestellten Elemente an die Art, wie William S. Burroughs das „cut-up" einsetzte: Verschiedene Texte werden mit der Schere auseinandergeschnitten und in einer Art automatischem Schreibprozess zu neuen Texten mit frischem Bedeutungspotenzial zusammengesetzt.

Ein Blick auf sein Werk verrät, dass für Martínez Celaya der mentale und physische Schöpfungsakt ausschlaggebend ist. Die Spuren von Veränderung, die Farbtropfen und -bäche, die sich über Leinwand und Papier ergießen, lassen oft deutlich erkennen, welchen Prozess, welchen Fortschritt die Gedanken und Hände des Künstlers vollzogen haben. Das Hin und Her zwischen dem Subjektiven und dem Objektiven findet seine Entsprechung in der Spannung zwischem dem Taktilen und dem Visuellen, die er in seinen Bildern aufbaut. Für Martínez Celaya ist der künstlerische Schaffensprozess ein Dialog mit sich selbst – bewusst und zugleich instinktiv. Er lässt sich von einem Bewusstseinsstrom tragen, überarbeitet, fügt hinzu, nimmt weg, ist offenbar bereit, alles auszuprobieren, ohne zu zögern, immer nach vorne drängend, stets auf der Suche nach einer besseren Lösung. So entstehen leidenschaftliche, sehr persönliche Visionen, außergewöhnlich in ihrer Schönheit und ihrem Tonfall – geheimnisvoll, elegisch, poetisch, psychologisch aufgeladen, zutiefst um Bedeutung bemüht.

•

Die Ausstellung und die vorliegende Publikation wurden durch das Engagement und die Hilfe zahlreicher Personen und Organisationen, denen ich sehr dankbar bin, erst ermöglicht. Mein größter Dank gilt Enrique Martínez Celaya, den ich im Laufe dieses Projekts als Künstler und als Freund schätzen gelernt habe und meine zahlreichen Treffen und Gespräche mit ihm haben mir viel Freude bereitet. Seine Aufmerksamkeit und sein wacher Verstand, seine Wärme, Integrität und Geduld haben unsere Zusammenarbeit aufregend und zufriedenstellend gemacht. Ihm gilt meine aufrichtige Wertschätzung und Bewunderung.

Die vorliegende Publikation lebt auch von den Beiträgen verschiedener Personen: Die Aufsätze von Abigail Solomon-Godeau, Charles Merewether und Rosanna Albertini stellen Martínez Celayas Werk in einen größeren Kontext, damit wir es besser verstehen und würdigen können. Mit seinen anregenden Fragen gibt Howard N. Fox dem Künstler Gelegenheit, selbst zu Wort zu kommen. Die Kommentare aus der Feder von Judson Emerick und Arden Reed, die auf intensiven Gesprächen mit dem Künstler beruhen, geben einen zusätzlichen Einblick in Martínez Celayas künstlerische Vision und Entwicklung. Und die Biographie von Colette Dartnall informiert über das Leben des Künstlers.

Ohne die Großzügigkeit der Leihgeber, die liebenswürdigerweise ihre Sammlungen für uns geöffnet haben, wäre die Ausstellung nicht möglich gewesen. Für ihre Mitarbeit möchten wir ihnen an dieser Stelle herzlich danken. Mein weiterer Dank gilt all jenen, die Leihgaben von

Museen und Unternehmen beschafft haben: Townsend D. Wolfe, Direktor des Arkansas Arts Center, Jenny Dixon, Leitende Direktorin, und Marysol Nieves, Chefkustodin des Bronx Museum of the Arts, Andrea Rich und Howard Fox, Präsidentin und Direktorin des Los Angeles County Museum of Art bzw. Kustos der Abteilung für Moderne und Zeitgenössische Kunst, sowie I. Michael Danoff und Heidi Schneider, Leiter des Art Program bzw. Vizepräsidentin und Manager Privatvermögen bei Neuberger Berman, New York.

Das große Engagement von Griffin Contemporary in Venice, Kalifornien, hat entscheidend zur Verwirklichung und zum Erfolg des Projekts beigetragen. Bill Griffin investierte enorm viel Zeit, Energie und Ressourcen, um alles Notwendige zur Verfügung zu stellen und einen reibungslosen Ablauf zu gewährleisten. Seine Mitarbeiterinnen Meredith McDaniel und Melissa Beaver, Direktorin bzw. Archivarin der Galerie, sorgten dafür, dass ich freien Zugang zu den galerieeigenen Archiven und Aufzeichnungen hatte, halfen mir Werke aufzuspüren und beschafften Informationen und Photomaterial. Ihre enthusiastische Mitarbeit war Gold wert. Des Weiteren möchte ich Rena Bransten und ihrer Galerie in San Francisco, hier insbesondere Walter Maciel und Calvert Barron, sowie Ramis Barquet und seiner Galerie in New York, dort vor allem Virgilio Garza, für ihre Unterstützung dieses Projekts danken.

Nach der ersten Ausstellungsstation in Honolulu wird die Ausstellung im Orange County Museum of Art in Newport Beach, Kalifornien, und schließlich am College of Art in Boston, Massachusetts, gezeigt. So wird sie Martínez Celayas Werk einem größeren Publikum zugänglich machen. Mein Dank gilt an dieser Stelle der Direktorin des Orange County Museum of Art, Naomi Vine, sowie Jeffrey Keough, Direktor der College of Art Galleries, die durch ihr Interesse und ihren Einsatz die Ausstellung an ihr Haus geholt haben. In diesem Zusammenhang möchte ich auch Sarah Vure und Lisa Tung, Kustodinnen am Orange County Museum of Art sowie am College of Art, erwähnen, die beide eine entscheidende Rolle bei der Koordinierung und Präsentation der Ausstellung an den jeweiligen Institutionen spielten.

Nur durch die Großzügigkeit einer Reihe von Spendern wurden die Ausstellung und die begleitende Publikation ermöglicht. Ich möchte mich deshalb Georgianna Lagoria anschließen und Jennifer und Royce Diener, Dieter un Si Rosenkranz, Carol Salisbury, Cade Roster und Waileia Davis, der Persis Corporation, Neuberger Berman, dem LLC Fund at The New York Community Trust, dem Pomona College, der Hawaii State Foundation on Culture and the Arts sowie CSX Lines und den Aston Hotels & Resorts für ihre generöse Unterstützung danken.

Der Erfolg einer jeden Ausstellung hängt von der Erfahrung und Sorgfalt der Menschen ab, die den Kurator unterstützen. Ich möchte daher folgenden Personen meinen tiefen Dank aussprechen: Direktorin Georgianna Lagoria, die nicht müde wurde, mich zu ermutigen und zu unterstützen; des Weiteren Kathy Hong, Leiterin der Museumsförderung, für ihre Hilfe bei der Mittelbeschaffung für das Projekt, Allison Wong, Kuratorische Assistentin, und Katherine Love, Ausstellungsassistentin, für ihre Gewissenhaftigkeit und Aufmerksamkeit für zahlreiche Aspekte des Projektes, Stephanie L'Heureux, Archivarin, für ihren großen Sachverstand bei der Koordinierung von Beschaffung, Verpackung und Transport der Leihgaben für diese Wanderausstellung, Sanit Khewhok, Verwalter der Sammlungen, John Koga und seinem Mitarbeiter Brian Koga und Cynthia Takamiya für ihre sorgfältige Arbeit beim Aus- und Verpacken und Aufstellen der Arbeiten in den Ausstellungsräumen, Nancy Conley, Bibliothekarin, für die Zusammenstellung von Material über den Künstler, das nun in der Cades Library des Museums für jedermann zugänglich ist, Louise Lanzilotti, Pädagogische Leiterin, und Elizabeth Train, Museumspädagogin, für die Entwicklung von Material, Programmen und Aktivitäten, die die Ausstellung für den Besucher leichter zugänglich und zu einer wirklichen Erfahrung machen sollen. Ihnen allen sowie den vielen anderen Mitarbeitern, Führern und freiwilligen Helfern möchte ich für ihre tatkräftige Unterstützung von Herzen danken.

Artist's Acknowledgments/Dank des Künstlers

I would like to dedicate my part in this exhibition to the memory of Jorge Luis Borges. When we met, he was eighty-three and I was seventeen. His lessons, presence and depth continue to be a source of strength and a beacon. The publisher has kindly included some illustrations that I prepared for his poem 'You are not the others' starting on page 268.

Many of my projects for the past few years benefited from the inspired hands of David Minnery and the support of William Griffin. I would like to thank both of them for their sensitivity to my sometimes difficult expectations. I would like to thank James Jensen for conceiving of this exhibition and the enthusiasm that he had showed for my work. I am grateful to Harley Baldwin, Ramis Barquet, Peter Bäumler, Rena Bransten, Stephen Cohen, Richard Edwards, Michy Maxuarch Burnett Miller, and Andrew Mummery for their belief in my work. Many projects would not have happened without the generosity of Katherine Priestley, Dieter and Si Rosenkranz, Heidi Schneider, Danny First, Dorothy Goldeen, Manfred Heiting, Andrea King, Peter Stanley and Pomona College. I also would like to thank Christina Guerrero, Adrienne Ponting, Michael Parker and Beatrice Foessel for their assistance. My deepest gratitude goes to my family, who supported me in countless ways. Most of all, I would like to thank my wife, Alexandra, who has enriched my life in so many ways and who has been by my side during the preparation of the museum exhibition and this book.

Ich möchte meinen Anteil an dieser Ausstellung dem Gedenken an Jorge Luis Borges widmen. Als wir uns kennenlernten, war er 83 und ich 17. Seine Lehren, seine Gegenwärtigkeit und sein Scharfsinn sind für mich noch immer eine Quelle der Stärke und ein Leitstern. Der Herausgeber war so freundlich, einige meiner Illustrationen zu Jorge Luis Borges' Gedicht „You are not the Others" (Du bist nicht die anderen) in die vorliegende Publikation aufzunehmen (ab Seite 268).

Viele meiner Projekte der letzten Jahre profitierten von der inspirierten Arbeit David Minnerys und der Unterstützung durch William Griffin. Ich möchte beiden für ihr Verständnis für meine manchmal schwer zu erfüllenden Erwartungen danken. James Jensen möchte ich für die Konzeption dieser Ausstellung danken und für den Enthusiasmus, den er meiner Arbeit entgegengebracht hat. Und ich bin Harley Baldwin, Ramis Barquet, Peter Bäumler, Rena Bransten, Stephen Cohen, Richard Edwards, Michy Maxuarch Burnett Miller und Andrew Mummery für ihren Glauben an meine Arbeit zu Dank verpflichtet. Viele Projekte wären ohne die Großzügigkeit von Katherine Priestley, Heidi Schneider, Danny First, Dorothy Goldeen, Dieter and Si Rosenkranz, Manfred Heiting, Andrea King, Peter Stanley und dem Pomona College nicht möglich gewesen. Außerdem möchte ich Christina Guerrero, Adrienne Ponting, Michael Parker und Beatrice Foessel für ihre Unterstützung danken. Meiner Familie bin ich für ihre uneingeschränkte Unterstützung zutiefst dankbar. Vor allem möchte ich meiner Frau Alexandra danken, die mein Leben auf so vielfältige Weise bereichert und die während der Vorbereitung der Ausstellung und dieses Buches an meiner Seite war.

Enrique Martínez Celaya

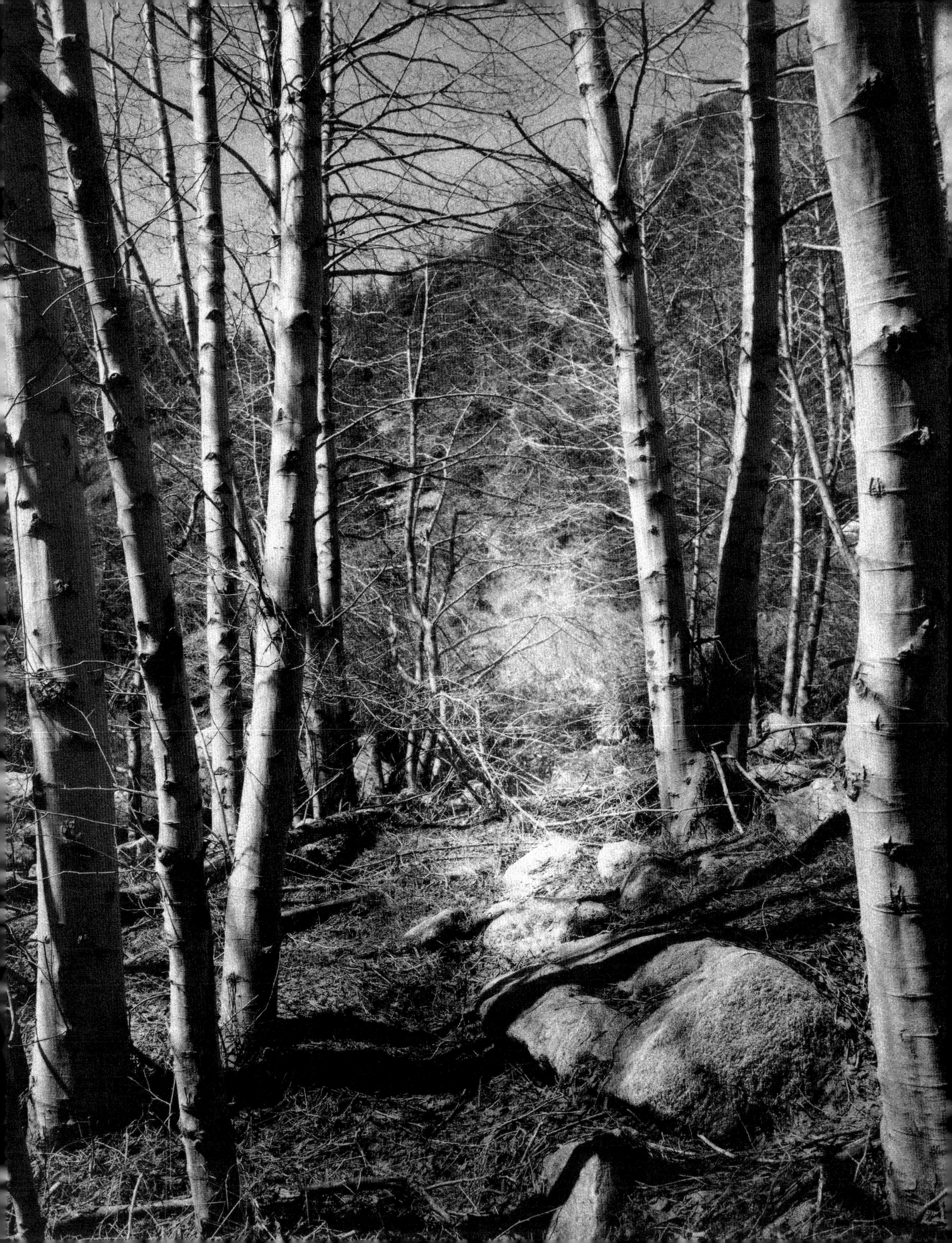

DEPARTURE WITHOUT RETURN

Charles Merewether

Fleeings, fleeings – on toward a
Darkness with no voice.
Nothing left to us and nothing
Yielding any trace

Sergei Esenin

In 1958 Paul Celan returned to the task of translating the work of the Russian poet Sergei Esenin. The overwhelming sense of deprivation and silence that permeates these few lines above characterizes what Celan himself was striving to articulate during this period. Shortly after, Celan opens the final poem *Stretto (Engführung)* of his 1959 volume of poems, *Sprachgitter (Speech-Grille),* with the lines: "Brought to / the region / with the infallible trace" and then "The place, where they lay, it has / a name–it has / none." Having found the terrain of those deported to the extermination camps, Celan leaves us deprived of speech, of naming: "Two mouthfuls of silence." The conditions of possibility for the text are grounded on impossibility, the impossibility to name after the event, an event of annihilation, trace but no trace. They are what can never be present but already past, untraccable. And yet, there is within this movement between one and another, between traces, a radical discontinuity or caesura that calls forth the poem.

Celan's poem opens itself beyond a historical moment towards a specifically modern experience of being in the world, a belonging that is more than a matter of place, an always elsewhere. The poem exists by virtue–if virtue it can be called–of this discontinuity. Celan writes within this still-point of destitution that falls between time, a place of dis-encounter, where "every place is elsewhere along the way."[1]

Yet, the question that will continue to haunt him is how to inhabit the uninhabitable place of exile: a no-man's land, a present that is neither future nor past, that is not only bound by the silent movement of recollection but opens towards a dialogue that is beyond itself, an unrecognizable future.

facing page

VANTAGE (AGUA REMOVIDA[MURKY WATER]), detail
/STANDPUNKT (BEWEGTES WASSER), Ausschnitt, 2000
Courtesy of Enrique Martínez Celaya

I

Threadsuns
Above the grey black wastes

Paul Celan

Such thoughts permeate the artistic work of Enrique Martínez Celaya. Over the past eight years of his artistic career he has been drawn to a Catholic iconography concerning martyrdom and the figures of saints such as Saint Joan or Saint Catherine. Placed under a sign of sacrifice, the

1. Paul Celan, *Collected Prose.* Translated by Rosemarie Waldrop. (New York: Sheep Meadow Press, 1986), 54.

figuration of these images oscillates, veering away from the iconic towards the indexical. They become allegorical. Fragments of the body become signs for a giving-up of the self; of a necessary sacrifice; of what must be left behind. Thinking about the origin of art, Georges Bataille has suggested how art reveals the sacred through the transgression of the profane. This sacramental element is the revelation of continuity through death. Sacrifice becomes a necessary measure of renewal. It is, as if in the making of these images, the artist is purging himself of an identity, a demand to estrange himself, to defamiliarize the familiar so that as Celan writes: "every place is elsewhere along the way." This can be seen in the work belonging to *Berlin, the Fragility of Nearness*, 1997–98, and *Berlin*, 1998, a book of poems and photographs of saints on graveyard tombs.[2] The images are like stars in the night, radiating out of the surrounding pools of darkness. The source or point of origin has disappeared: images become the afterlife on which one depends for orientation to move forward, surviving the contingencies and erasure of historical time. The stones outlive the presence of their subject, photography arrests life. Photography becomes the epitaph of the subject's life. There is no phenomenological presence, but distancing and death.

Martínez Celaya submits his work to explicit procedures of erasure, disfiguration and dismemberment: each turning around the necessary but impossible desire to recover an original moment of wholeness. Sacrifice remains central to Martínez Celaya's artistic project. And, we see its mark in earlier paintings such as *The Trouble with Memory*, 1993; *None of it Reminds Me of You*, 1995; *Acceptance of Longing*, 1997. The space of proximity towards the other demands an economy of sacrifice. It is given; it has always been there, inescapable. And yet iconicity seems only to expose even more the fragility of living on, as if abandoned to live in the aftermath of others, in the trace of their wake. The practice of art becomes both expiatory and restitutional.[3] Here in this liminal space, the 'vagabondage of the imagination' comes into play. As Julia Kristeva has remarked, the space of liberty offered to us by the image connects us with the sacred and, "with the terror that death and sacrifice provokes, with the serenity that flows from the identificatory pact between the sacrificed and the sacrificer, and with the joy of representation indissociable from the sacrifice, the only passage possible."[4] Kristeva's point reminds us of the pact between the sacrificed and sacrificer. What then are we to make of the autobiographical referent as it appears in the artist's series of self-portraits pictured as a severed head: the sacrificial object? Paintings and drawings such as *A Dry Bed*, 1998, *Quiet Night (Recollection) I*, 1999, and others are subjected to defacement, to dismemberment. There is, in the end, no comfort here, no sound of laughter associated with the transgressive act of sacrifice. There is no pact without losing oneself, of giving up the artistic self. Dispossessed by the gods of our own making, we are left to wander the borders of existence, desolate, mute, left with traces that no longer can be given a name.

What then are we to make of these traces with which we are left, traces that, like grains of sand, slip between the fingers? Do we make sense of the trace as a sign of something no longer and therefore a mark of absence around which memory gathers itself for what has been lost? Is it, in other words, something residual: a remainder that, like a fragment or ruin, survives? To view the image in such terms is to suggest that something remains: a memory or imprint to do with the past surviving in the present, which has a materiality and history that can be identified. For traces to be indicative would be to confer on them the status of signs. The problem is that, as a sign, our relation to the past is dependent upon the order of representation: an order that is not only posterior, but masters the past in the same way as memory controls that which

2. Enrique Martínez Celaya, *Berlin*. (Los Angeles: Stephen Cohen Gallery and William Griffin Editions, 1998).
3. See Abigail Solomon-Godeau, "Restitutional Fragments" in Enrique Martinez Celaya, *Berlin, the Fragility of Nearness*. (Venice: William Griffin Editions, 1998), 39–45.
4. This is a phrase from Julia Kristeva, *Visions Capitales*, cited in A. Solomon-Godeau, ibid., 45, fn.1.

preceded it. Or is the trace something less, insofar as its appearance is not a matter of survival or absence, but more like the hollowed–out imprint of an impression: a past that has never been present? This would be a past which no memory, no thing could resurrect, capture, represent as present.

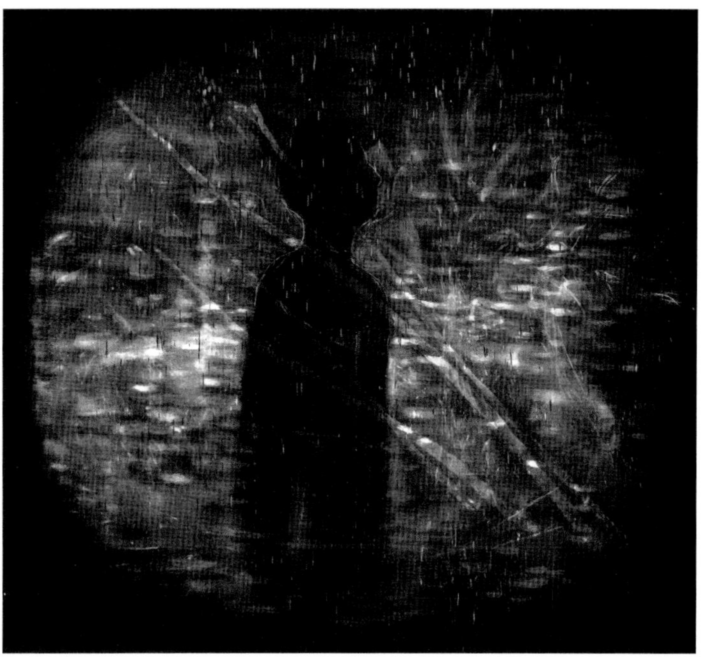

SPOKEN FOR (THE MERCIFUL)
/FÜRGESPROCHENE (DIE GNADENVOLLEN), 2000
Museo Extremeño Iberoamericano de Arte Contemporáneo (MEIAC), Badajoz, Spain

II

> Singable Remainder–trace
> of one who–mute,
> remote–broke out of bounds
> through sicklescripts of snow
>
> Paul Celan

The recent artistic projects of Martínez Celaya seek another way, another path across this fragile terrain of nomination. The artifice of representation is exposed as a fugitive substitute and meaning becomes transitory. In paintings from the series Pictures of Mercy, 2000; Drafts of a Landscape, 2000; and Coming Home, 2001, Martínez Celaya turns towards procedures of dispersal, disappearance, blankness as if seeking now to deny the referential, to purify art of its claim over naming, over the autobiographical or historical. Art becomes, following Stéphane Mallarmé, the elimination of things. The elimination of things makes possible the advent of art. No light shines the way, no path is given.

This is the language of paintings *Spoken For (The Merciful)*, 2000 and *Redemption*, 2000, from Drafts of a Landscape in which the self is exposed–an exposure to another that is constitutive of human experience and its ground. Yet that other is not present, but rather always past: those who are spoken for, those who are given redemption. It is we who always come after. It is the experience of immediacy that happens in the past and therefore a non-encounter. The encounter with the outside of the self is the self's origin and therefore, as Jacques Derrida observes, "I mark(s) first of all a division in what will have been able to appear in the beginning."[5] We might say that the work appears to gather its meaning by way of an estranged relation to itself. By neither repeating nor returning us to the place of origin, the use of the indexical in Martínez Celaya's work opens up an interval that is discontinuous with what has gone before. This is not a work of nostalgia, a re/turning in the sand as if symbolizing an experience of loss and desire to recapture the past or an identity of self through an origin. Rather, it marks a space between impression and imprint, neither present nor absent insofar as there is no plenitude either given or referred to as elsewhere.

We should perhaps view this body of work not in terms of sight, but of listening, nor in terms of presence, but of the trace. It is as if the estrangement of voice from language parallels the estrangement of the body from space. Language calls for voice, to breathe the air around it. Celan speaks of the poem as a 'turn of breath' thereby linking the body directly.[6] Breathing becomes a form of listening and attunement. It both breathes outwardly and takes in the air. It allows for the temporal moment of nearness and distance because it both speaks–it is an event of language–and acknowledges silently the other. It remains unvocalized, and is, in this sense, unsayable. This is the space of consciousness, of a coming into being through an awareness of what is outside the self, an exposure of the self.

5. Jacques Derrida, *Margins: Of Philosophy*, (Chicago: Chicago University Press, 1982), 275.
6. Paul Celan, *Collected Prose*, op. cit., 47.

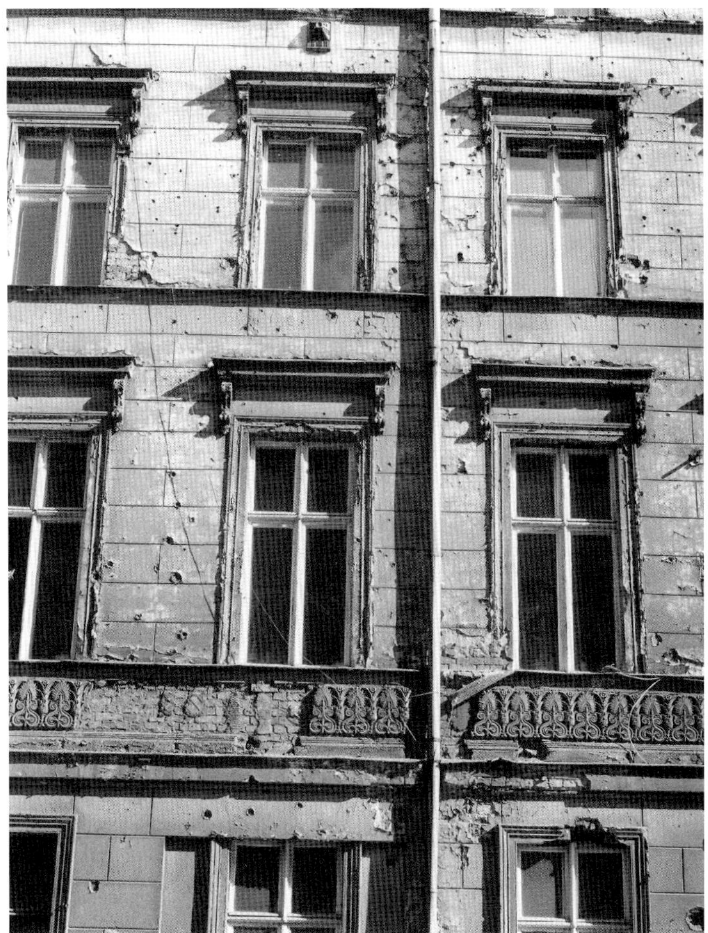

PHOTOGRAPH BY THE ARTIST OF BULLET HOLES IN A BERLIN BUILDING/KÜNSTLERPHOTO MIT KUGELLÖCHERN IN EINEM BERLINER GEBÄUDE, 1998

Emmanuel Lévinas wrote in his essay *Language and Proximity* that "one sees and hears like one touches."[7] For Lévinas this is a matter of sensibility rather than consciousness. Sensibility is the subject's relation to the elemental as in Martínez Celaya's paintings from the series Drafts of a Landscape: the forest in which the figure wanders, or the sound of the ocean that resides like a memory in the heart of the conch shell. This is the experience of proximity without being disclosed or revealed. The blanket of night offers the intimacy of proximity, the warmth that encloses without revealing, while the relation to the past, to what precedes, to the realm of memory, belongs to the order of the sign of its emptiness, its desolation. Absence becomes a force of effacement and reinscription. Again, Lévinas offers us a reading:

> The opening of the empty is not only the sign of an absence. The figure traced on the sand is not the element of a path but the very emptiness of the past. And that which has been withdrawn is not evoked, does not return to presence–not even to an indicated presence.[8]

We may say nothing is visible, that it remains opaque and consciousness of the other happens through listening, not sight. It is a listening that has to do with what has passed into memory. The black dense ground of Martínez Celaya's paintings in Drafts of a Landscape offer something both less and more than exposure. Nothing is clear. It is as if night has descended, vision itself is obscured, so that the ground becomes more present. Yet, in its discordant relation to the fragility of the line, it offers a density in which the figure appears still. Stillness pervades and one listens, not sees.

This is the Orphic tradition to which the work of Martínez Celaya belongs, a tradition that within modernity, both Mallarmé and Maurice Blanchot shape.[9] In the story of Orpheus, the poet descends to the underworld to recover his companion Eurydice who has accidentally died and entered the land of the dead. He presents himself to Hades and Persephone, seeking her release. The gods grant him his wish but only on the condition that he does not look at Eurydice during their return journey into the light of the world. Eurydice appears from amidst the ghosts and follows him through the dark passages of the underworld in total silence. But, Orpheus suffers a moment of forgetfulness and, seeking assurance, turns around to look upon her. At that moment Eurydice disappears.

Although stricken by grief, the sacrifice of Eurydice, of her perpetual invisibility, enables Orpheus' song to flourish. In wandering the earth, his music entrances others whom he meets along the way. However, one day Orpheus is approached by a group of Thracian maidens whereupon he spurns their advances. Enraged, they throw javelins and stones that his music dissipates. But Orpheus' music is drowned by their screams and he is seized upon. Tearing him apart, they severe his head and throw his body into the river Hebrus. Later, the fragments of his dismembered body are gathered up and buried. Here, in this place the nightingale sings its pure song.

As Blanchot writes, disappearance (in reference to Eurydice) "becomes the density of shadow that makes flesh more present, and makes this presence more heavy and more strange, without name and without form; a presence one cannot then call either living or dead, but out of which everything equivocal about desire draws its truth."[10] Not only does the sacrifice of Eurydice

7. Emmanuel Lévinas, *Collected Philosophical Papers* (Dordrecht: Martinus Nijhoff, 1987), 118.
8. Emmanuel Lévinas, *En Decouvrant l'Existence* avec Husserl et Heidegger (Paris: Vrin, 1949), 208.
9. See Maurice Blanchot, *The Gaze of Orpheus and other Literary Essays*. Translated by Lydia Davis. (New York: Station Hill Press, 1981). Having now invoked Celan, Lévinas and Blanchot, I should add that both Blanchot and Lévinas wrote of Celan.
10. Maurice Blanchot, *The Infinite Conversation*. (Minneapolis: University of Minnesota Press, 1993), 188.

become necessary, but also Orpheus dies for his singing. Writing begins with a certain sacrifice. Writing is on the side of disappearance, at the border between being and nothingness.

As Lévinas remarks, "The tracing of traces is accompanied by its simultaneous effacing–its own retreat" (and this trace) "disturbs the order of things in an irreparable fashion."[11] It is a re-marking that leaves a spectral trace. The trace leaves, the past is irreversible, there is not recourse, no return. This is the basis too for a critique of representation, of the evidential, of the insistence on showing or revealing, of everything brought into the light. This would correspond too with Sigmund Freud's notion of an originary site of repression and of its lifting or of bringing into light a memory, as if one may return to recover or restore that which has been lost. The trace cannot be converted in this way precisely because this would bring the other into the phenomenal and immanent and therefore within the economy of the same, of continuity. Lévinas proposes a concept of the trace that does not depend upon notions of revelation, unveiling or disclosure. The traces remain, if you will; they are constitutive or part of the fullness of the present but they remain invisible, at best the uncanny.

III

He speaks truly who speaks shadow
Paul Celan

The series of paintings, Coming Home, 2001, is composed of stone-gray images of light, the luminous light of the vast sky and its reflection on the ocean beneath. Between heaven and earth, between worlds, a solitary figure stands at the edge of the ocean, the dove dissolves in the light of morning and the reflection of the elk opens to "all sky unveiled, beyond mercy."[12] Exposed to the winds, the cold wind of winter is the experience of estrangement. There is no bright illumination, but shadows, no homecoming, but placelessness. Vision has become unreliable. One speaks from out of the darkness. We are in a foreign place. Dispossessed, in a neutral space one sees without seeing. Again it is as if there is an opening here towards something concealed, a listening that waits like the hunter in Kurosawa's film *Derzu Uzala*. The hunter no longer sees, but continues to hunt by way of listening. He belongs to the unforgiving landscape of survival, of living on. There is no clear horizon line, no place to rest the eye in this wandering. Where then do we find ourselves without these lines etched, these traces of recollection? These are not images of return, of arriving in the place long forgotten. We may say rather there is the desire to inhabit, to belong, of be/longing. This place beyond becomes then the destination of the image, or more precisely, of perception, that which is perceived and the experience of being perceived. There is a spacing here, an interval which the trace points onto between the referent and the horizon that exceeds it.

The distance is even greater than it seemed. We are offered glimpses through the veils of night, and gray blankness of dawn to which we are exposed. There is a forgetting here, a movement away from language as standing in for, as concealing in all its artifice and fabrication. Necessary and yet estranging, Martínez Celaya's work mimics the vain ambition to naturalize it. He places the mirror between the antlers reflecting the vast canopy of the sky above, or floats the sculpted head on the surface of the water, or places the sculpted boy gazing beyond at the edge of the shore.

11. Emmanuel Lévinas, *En Decouvrant l'Existence*, op. cit., 206, 208.
12. Cited in Enrique Martínez Celaya, *October* (Amsterdam: Cinubia, 2001), unpaginated.

The thickness of the air, resonant throughout the series Coming Home is breathless. In the 'vagabondage of the imagination' art has provided a place, but what place is this other than within the realm of art itself, an escaping that finds itself at the threshold of the spectral land of the uncanny, outside the human. The artifice of art becomes the uncanny of the human. If we have spoken of breathing as the advent of language, then we must now speak of the interruption of language, when breath is withheld. Perhaps, this approximates what Blanchot called *desouvrement*, a neutral space of stillness. Blanchot writes of it as an interval, an *entre-temps* between still future and already past, and the divided condition of the trace. This is, in other words, a caesura or spacing of belonging that does not belong to either past or future, is untraceable. That is why in Martínez Celaya's work there is something strangely suspended. To return to the story of Orpheus, it is that Eurydice was never present to him except as the figure of memory that he seeks to overcome. She appears to Orpheus as a ghost only to be overcome by a nocturnal desire to see what is invisible. He forgets the interdiction and she disappears into the shades of Lethe.

IV

> I follow my wandering senses into this new world of the spirit
> and come to know freedom.
> Paul Celan

There is no continuity in time that is history, no totality of past and future. Similarly, there is no essence to which one may appeal, nor identity, nor ground. It is rather a setting free of places, an outside. This outside, this undomesticated space has no name. What if we were to accept the groundlessness as the place from which to begin, a provisional site. In effect, there is no essence to which one can appeal. The trace neither reaches back nor carries forward, as if bound by and to the referent. It is not a sign insofar as it is purely indicative or stands in an empirical relation to an event or something once present. There is nothing residual here–no fragments, ruins, marks or evidence–so it does not seek (by way of pathos or nostalgia) an originating moment. Rather, while the trace offers a connection to the world insofar as it operates as a memorial form tied to the past, it is governed by structural possibility of its iteration or repetition, which itself is only possible by virtue of the absence of the repeated. It is retroactive, subject to a certain departure, to a leaving behind in order for memory to be produced and therefore opens itself to a future because it remains to be seen–can only be seen–and therefore understood, after the fact.

Yet, if the trace becomes something both less and more than the originating referent, is it properly speaking still a trace, unless it is a trace of a trace? Does this not, in some manner, split the figure of the trace and would not this split produce two halves antagonistic to one another? How do we delimit the trace except by what is inscribed, in effect, through the disappearance of what we may infer produced it? To think the trace is to pursue its trail either back or forward, to see it alternately as attachment or detachment, re-presentation or erasure, proximity or distance, a return or a leave-taking. This paradoxical condition constitutes the structure of the trace.

The step taken is not given. It is, rather, made possible by coming after the trace of that which has been erased. The trace is founded within a movement of erasure: an erasure because it is only a shadow or imprint of the impression made in the sand. Appearance is constituted by the erasure of such marks. Presence becomes the sign of an absent origin that has never been present, but is always a past to come. That is, a presence that in being predicated on absence exists only by virtue of coming after, by way of repetition. Materiality is not simply a given that bears traces but, rather, is itself defined, shaped and stabilized through processes of selection, exclusion and elaboration. The materiality that the trace assumes is then witness to the fracture of its own condition.

Falling on either side of this divide, the trace either informs and shapes the future by virtue of its ties to the past, or is bound by the future, always coming after, opening onto a horizon that exceeds its referent. As Lévinas asks in his essay *Phenomena and Enigma*:

> How refer to an irreversible past that is a past which the very reference would not bring back...like memory which retrieves the past, like signs which recapture the signified? What would be needed would be an indication that would reveal the withdrawal of the indicated instead of a reference that rejoins it. Such is the trace.[13]

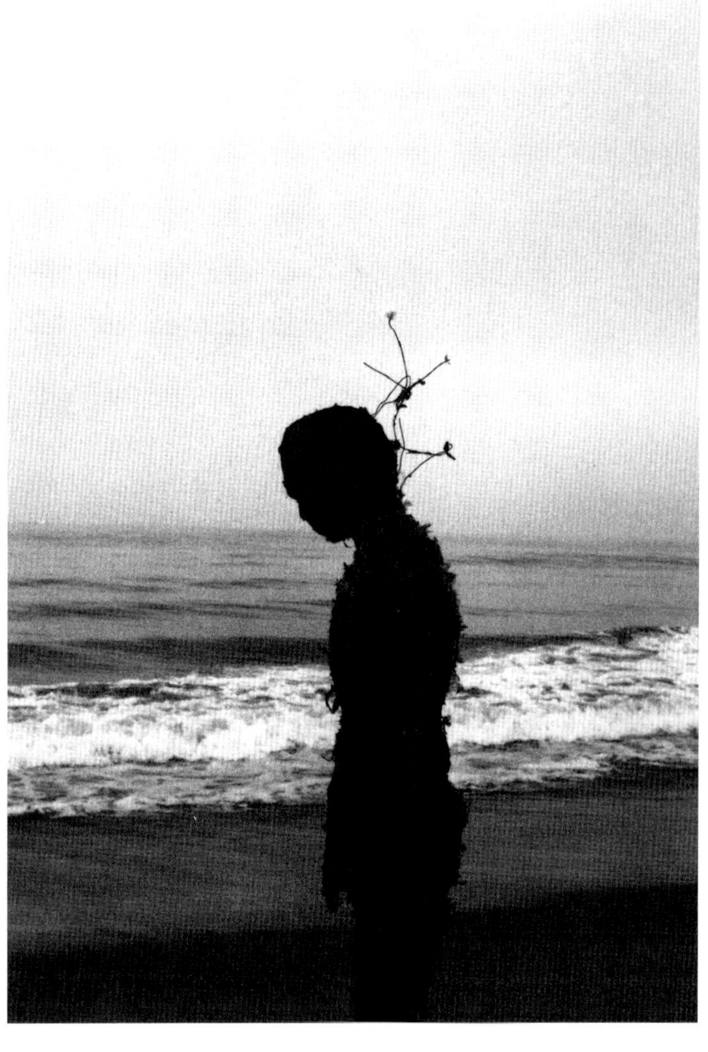

THE SHORE, III/DAS UFER, III, 2000
Private collection, Brussels, Belgium

In these terms, the past cannot be made present, brought back, resurrected or redeemed. This would be, as Lévinas remarks a "returning home to itself like Ulysses who through all his peregrinations is only on the way to his native land."[14] Belonging as it does to the epic cycle of Nostoi or nostalgia, the story is driven by a sense of lack or need, as Lévinas defines it, which is fulfilled by way of homecoming.[15] The nostalgic, needful nature of memory helps to explain its deep penchant for recapture and reproduction, for the re-presentation of the past. From this perspective, Martínez Celaya's work suggests that the relation between trace and memory is problematic precisely because memory is tied to recollection: a return to the same. Moreover, it is a past that has never been present. The images that occupy the work of this artist are, at best, fugitive, transitory, a memory before recollection. Taken in this way the trace remains loyal to the indexical. It no longer finds itself imprisoned within the confines of presence and absence, but is instead conditioned by its movement of repetition and difference. They have neither a phenomenal presence nor plenitude, but rather appear by virtue of erasure and division.

Against the myth of Ulysses–Lévinas proposes a departure without return, such as that of Abraham leaving his homeland for a destination unknown. Abraham's departure is also from the self and a sense of responsibility that exceeds self-reference and a perspective that always returns to the same, to an economy of the self rather than the other. Thrust into the openness, the more it belongs to the other, to what it is not. Celan spoke of "how the poem intends another, needs this other, needs an opposite. It goes toward it, addresses it. For the poem, everything and everybody is a figure of this other toward which it is heading."[16] To hold open this openness, demands a certain forgetting, and to contemplate with patience the darkness that surrounds us. This 'reaching out of recollection' characterizes the desire of Martínez Celaya's art.

13. Emmanuel Lévinas, "Phenomena and Enigma" in *Collected Philosophical Papers*, op. cit., 65.
14. Emmanuel Lévinas, *Totality and Infinity*, trans. Alphonso Lingis (Pittsburgh: Dusquesne UP, 1969), 346.
15. Emmanuel Lévinas, *Totality and Infinity*, ibid., 33.
16. Paul Celan, *Collected Prose*, op. cit., 49.

AUFBRUCH OHNE RÜCKKEHR

Charles Merewether

Fluchten, Fluchten – hin zu
stimmenloser Dunkelheit.
Nichts, was uns bleibt und irgendeine
Spur hinterließe

Sergei Jessenin

gegenüberliegende Seite

REMINDER, detail/MAHNUNG, Ausschnitt, 2001
Courtesy of Baldwin Gallery, Aspen, Colorado

1958 wandte sich Paul Celan wieder der Übertragung der Werke des russischen Dichters Sergeij Jessenin zu. Das übermächtige Gefühl von Verlust und Schweigen, das diese wenigen obigen Zeilen durchzieht, ist bezeichnend für das, was Celan selbst in jener Zeit auszudrücken suchte. Wenig später, 1959, begann Celan das letzte Gedicht „Engführung" seiner Gedichtsammlung „Sprachgitter" mit den Worten: „Verbracht ins / Gelände / mit der untrüglichen Spur", und dann: „Der Ort, wo sie lagen, er hat / einen Namen – er hat / keinen." Nachdem er so die in die Vernichtungslager Deportierten lokalisiert hat, nimmt uns Celan mit den Worten „zwei Mundvoll Schweigen" die Sprache und die Fähigkeit zu benennen. Die Voraussetzungen für die Möglichkeit des Textes bauen auf Unmöglichkeit auf, der Unmöglichkeit, nach dem Ereignis noch zu benennen, nach der Vernichtung – Spur und doch keine Spur –, die niemals gegenwärtig sein kann und trotzdem schon vergangen ist, unaufspürbar. Und dennoch gibt es innerhalb dieser Bewegung zwischen dem Einen und dem Anderen, zwischen den Spuren, eine radikale Diskontinuität oder Zäsur, durch die das Gedicht entsteht.

Celans Gedicht geht über den historischen Augenblick hinaus und öffnet sich einer spezifisch modernen Erfahrung des In-der-Welt-Seins, einer Zugehörigkeit, die mehr ist als eine Frage des Ortes, ein Immer-Anderswo. Das Gedicht existiert dank – sofern man hier von Dank reden kann – dieser Diskontinuität. Celan schreibt am Totpunkt des Fehlens, der zwischen die Zeiten fällt, einem Ort der Nichtbegegnung, an dem „jeder Ort anderswo längs des Weges ist".[1]

Dennoch wird ihn die Frage weiterhin verfolgen, wie der unbewohnbare Ort des Exils zu bewohnen ist: ein Niemandsland, eine Gegenwart, die weder Zukunft noch Vergangenheit ist, die nicht nur durch die stille Bewegung der Rückbesinnung gebunden ist, sondern sich einem Dialog öffnet, der über sie selbst hinausgeht, eine nicht erkennbare Zukunft.

I

Fadensonnen
über der grauschwarzen Ödnis

Paul Celan

Ähnliche Gedanken durchziehen die künstlerische Arbeit von Enrique Martínez Celaya. In den vergangenen acht Jahren seiner Künstlertätigkeit bediente er sich immer wieder einer katho-

1. Paul Celan, *Sprachgitter* (Frankfurt am Main: S. Fischer, 1959)

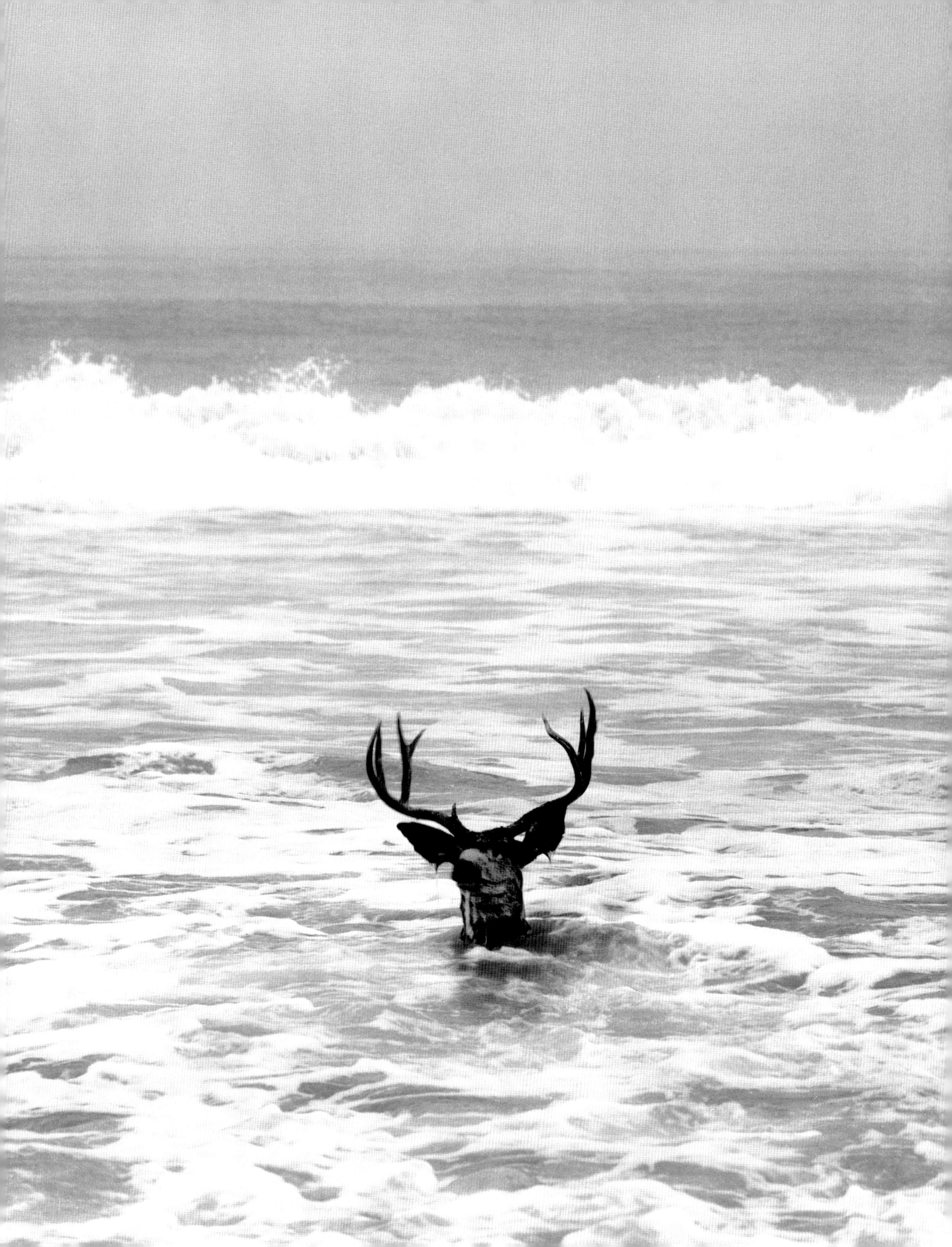

lischen Ikonographie, die das Märtyrertum und Figuren wie die Heiligen Johanna und Katharina aufgreift. Die unter dem Zeichen des Opfers stehende Figuration dieser Bilder oszilliert, wendet sich fort vom Ikonischen hin zum Indexikalischen und verleiht ihnen etwas Allegorisches. Körperfragmente werden zu Zeichen der Selbstaufgabe, eines notwendigen Opfers, zu Zeichen dessen, was es aufzugeben gilt. Im Zuge seiner Überlegungen über den Ursprung der Kunst hat Georges Bataille postuliert, die Kunst offenbare das Sakrale durch Transgression des Profanen. Dieses sakramentale Element ist die Offenbarung von Kontinuität durch den Tod. Das Opfer wird zu einem notwendigen Schritt der Erneuerung. Es ist, als reinige sich der Künstler durch das Erschaffen der Bilder von einer Identität, als folge er dem Verlangen sich zu entfremden, das Bekannte unbekannt zu machen, so dass nach Celans Worten „jeder Ort anderswo längs des Weges ist". Dies zeigen die Arbeiten zu *Berlin, the Fragility of Nearness/Berlin: Die Zerbrechlichkeit der Nähe*, 1997/98, und *Berlin*, 1998, ein Band mit Gedichten und Photographien von Heiligenfiguren auf Gräbern.[2] Die Bilder wirken wie nächtliche Sterne, erstrahlen aus Flächen von Dunkelheit. Die Quelle oder der Ursprungspunkt ist verschwunden: Die Bilder werden zu dem Leben im Jenseits, das man zur Orientierung braucht, wenn man sich voranbewegen will, sie überleben die Wechselfälle und Tilgungen der Geschichte. Die Steine überdauern die Gegenwart ihres Sujets, die Photographie hält das Leben fest und wird zum Epitaph des Lebens ihrer Sujets. Es gibt keine phänomenologische Gegenwart, sondern nur Distanzierung und Tod.

Martínez Celaya unterzieht seine Arbeiten explizit den Prozeduren der Tilgung, Entstellung und Verstümmelung: Jede von ihnen handelt von dem Notwendigen, aber Unmöglichen, ein Wunsch, einen ursprünglichen Moment der Ganzheit wiederzuerlangen. In Martínez Celayas künstlerischem Projekt bleibt das Opfer ein zentrales Anliegen, was auch in früheren Werken wie *The Trouble with Memory/Das Problem mit dem Gedächtnis*, 1993, *None of it Reminds Me of You/Nichts davon erinnert mich an Dich*, 1995, und *Acceptance of Longing/Akzeptanz der Sehnsucht*, 1997, zu erkennen ist. Der Zwischenraum der Nähe zum Anderen verlangt eine Ökonomie des Opfers. So ist es vorgesehen; so war es immer, unausweichlich. Dennoch scheint das Ikonische die Fragilität des Weiterlebens nur noch stärker zu offenbaren, so als sei es einem Leben in den Fußstapfen anderer überlassen, in der Spur ihres Kielwassers. Künstlerisch tätig zu sein wird zum Sühne- und gleichzeitig zum Wiederherstellungsakt.[3] Hier, in diesem Grenzbereich, kommt das „Schweifenlassen der Fantasie" ins Spiel. Julia Kristeva zufolge verbindet uns der Freiraum, den uns das Bild bietet, mit dem Sakralen und „mit dem ganzen Schrecken, den der Tod und das Opfer hervorrufen, mit der Heiterkeit, die aus dem Pakt der Identifikation zwischen Geopfertem und Opfernden fließt, und mit der Lust an der Repräsentation, die untrennbar mit dem Opfer verbunden, ja der einzig mögliche Weg seiner Durchführung ist".[4] Mit ihrer Feststellung erinnert Kristeva uns an den Pakt zwischen Geopfertem und Opferndem. Wie sollen wir demnach die autobiographische Referenz verstehen, die in Martínez Celayas Serie von Selbstporträts in Form eines abgetrennten Hauptes verbildlicht ist – als eine Opfergabe? Bilder und Zeichnungen wie *A Dry Bed/Ein trockenes Bett*, 1998, *Quiet Night/Stille Nacht*, 1999, und andere werden Entstellungen und Verstümmelungen unterzogen. Es bleibt hier letztendlich kein Trost, es geht kein Lachen einher mit dem transgressiven Akt des Opferns. Man kann keinen Pakt schließen, ohne sich selbst zu verlieren, das künstlerische Selbst aufzugeben. Verstoßen von den Göttern, die wir selbst erschufen, streifen wir entlang an den Grenzen der Existenz, verzweifelt, stumm, allein mit Spuren, die nicht mehr benannt werden können.

2. Enrique Martínez Celaya, *Berlin* (Los Angeles: Stephen Cohen Gallery and William Griffin Editions, 1998).
3. Siehe Abigail Solomon-Godeau, „Restitutional Fragments" im Katalog Enrique Martínez Celaya, *Berlin, the Fragility of Nearness* (Venice, Kalifornien: Griffin Editions, 1998), S. 39–45.
4. Julia Kristeva, *Visions Capitales*, zitiert in A. Solomon-Godeau, ibid., S. 45, Anm. 1 (von der Übersetzerin des Essays aus dem Französischen übertragen).

Wie sind also diese Spuren zu verstehen, auf die wir zurückgeworfen sind, Spuren, die so wenig greifbar sind wie zwischen den Fingern zerrinnende Sandkörner? Verstehen wir die Spur als Zeichen von etwas, das nicht mehr ist, und somit als Kennzeichen von Abwesenheit, um das herum sich die Erinnerung an etwas sammelt, das verloren ging? Ist sie sozusagen ein Rückstand, ein Überbleibsel, das wie ein Fragment oder eine Ruine überlebt hat? Das Bild in solchen Begriffen zu betrachten heißt davon auszugehen, dass etwas bleibt: eine Erinnerung oder ein Abdruck, der mit der Vergangenheit zu tun hat, die in der Gegenwart überlebt, die bzw. der also eine identifizierbare Materialität und Geschichte hat. Denn wären Spuren indikativ, hieße das, ihnen den Status von Zeichen zuzugestehen. Das Problem dabei ist, dass unser Verhältnis zur Vergangenheit als ein Zeichen von der Ordnung der Darstellung abhängt: eine Ordnung, die nicht nur im Nachhinein entsteht, sondern zudem die Vergangenheit so meistert, wie die Erinnerung beherrscht, was ihr vorausging. Oder ist die Spur doch insofern etwas Geringeres, als ihre Erscheinung nicht eine Frage von Überleben oder Abwesenheit, sondern eher dem ausgehöhlten Abdruck eines Eindrucks vergleichbar ist: eine Vergangenheit, die niemals gegenwärtig war? Dies wäre eine Vergangenheit, die keine Erinnerung und kein Ding wiederaufleben lassen, einfangen oder als Gegenwart darstellen könnte.

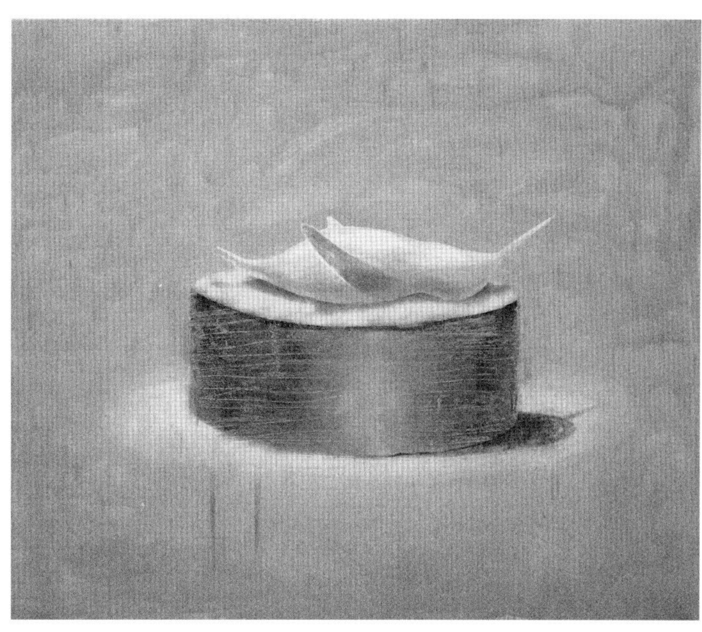

ACCEPTANCE OF LONGING/AKZEPTANZ DER SEHNSUCHT, 1997
Erworben duch das Los Angeles County Museum of Art, Modern and Contemporary Art Council, Art Here and Now

II

Sinbarer Rest – der Umriß
dessen, der durch
die Sichelsschrift lautlos hindurchbrach,
abseits, am Schneeort

Paul Celan

Martínez Celayas jüngste künstlerische Projekte suchen einen anderen Weg, einen anderen Pfad durch dieses fragile Terrain der Benennung. Der Kunstgriff der Darstellung wird als flüchtiger Ersatz offenbart, Bedeutung vergänglich. In Bildern aus den Serien Pictures of Mercy/Gnadenbilder, Drafts of a Landscape/Skizzen einer Landschaft und Coming Home/Heimkehr greift Martínez Celaya zu Mitteln wie der Verstreuung und dem Verschwinden oder Auslassen, so als versuche er nun, das Referenzielle zu verleugnen und die Kunst von ihrem Anspruch an Benennung, an Autobiographisches oder Historisches zu reinigen. Stéphane Mallarmé zufolge wird Kunst zur Eliminierung der Dinge, die die Entstehung von Kunst erst möglich macht: Kein Licht erhellt den Weg, kein Pfad ist vorgegeben.

Dies ist die Sprache der Bilder *Spoken For (The Merciful)/ Fürgesprochene (Die Gnadenvollen)*, 2000, und *Redemption/ Erlösung*, 2000, aus Drafts of a Landscape, in denen das Selbst offenbart wird – eine Offenbarung gegenüber einem Anderen, das konstitutiv und grundlegend für menschliche Erfahrung ist. Doch ist dieses Andere nicht gegenwärtig, sondern vielmehr stets Vergangenheit: Es sind die, für die gesprochen wird, denen Erlösung gewährt wird. Wir sind es, die immer später kommen. Es ist eine Erfahrung von Unmittelbarkeit, die in der Vergangenheit stattfindet, und somit eine Nichtbegegnung. Die Begegnung mit dem, was außerhalb des Selbst

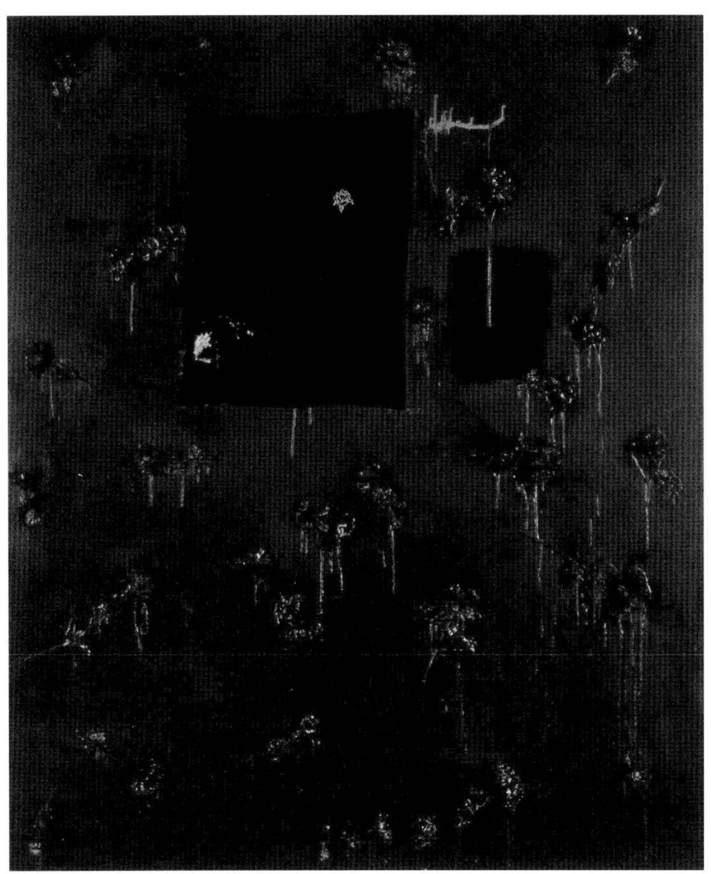

THE TROUBLE WITH MEMORY
/DAS PROBLEM MIT DEM GEDÄCHTNIS, 1993
Privatsammlung, London, Großbritannien

liegt, ist der Ursprung des Selbst und markiert deshalb, wie Jacques Derrida es formuliert, „in erster Linie eine Teilung in dem, was am Anfang zu erscheinen imstande gewesen sein wird".[5] Man könnte sagen, dass das Werk seine Bedeutung anscheinend durch ein entfremdetes Verhältnis zu sich selbst erlangt. Indem er den Ursprungspunkt weder wiederholt noch uns dorthin zurückführt, eröffnet Martínez Celaya durch Einsatz des Indexikalischen ein Intervall, das frei von Kontinuität zum schon Vergegangenen ist. Es ist also nicht etwa Nostalgie am Werk, keine Rück- oder Umkehr zu Vertrautem, es soll weder eine Verlusterfahrung noch die Sehnsucht symbolisiert werden, die Vergangenheit oder die eigene Identität durch Bezugnahme zum Ursprung wieder einzufangen. Vielmehr markiert Martínez Celaya einen Raum zwischen Eindruck und Abdruck, der weder gegenwärtig noch abwesend ist, da ein Anderswo, das vollkommen wäre, weder existiert noch angedeutet wird.

Wir sollten diese Werkgruppe womöglich weniger unter dem Aspekt des Sehens betrachten als dem des Hörens, und nicht unter dem Aspekt der Anwesenheit, sondern dem der Spur – so als geschähe parallel zur Entfremdung der Stimme von der Sprache auch eine Entfremdung des Körpers vom Raum. Sprache verlangt nach Stimme, will die Luft ringsum atmen. Celan spricht vom Gedicht als „Atemwende" und stellt damit eine direkte Verbindung zum Körper her.[6] Atmen wird zu einer Form des Zuhörens und der Einstimmung, atmet Luft – aus ebenso wie ein. Es erlaubt vorübergehend sowohl Nähe als auch Distanz, da es sowohl einerseits – als sprachliches Ereignis – spricht, als auch andererseits stillschweigend das Andere anerkennt. Es bleibt unvokalisiert und ist in diesem Sinne unsagbar. Dies ist der Raum des Bewusstseins, des Erlangens von Sein durch ein Bewusstwerden dessen, was außerhalb des Selbst liegt, eine Offenbarung des Selbst.

Emmanuel Lévinas schreibt in seinem Essay „Language and Proximity", dass „man so sieht und hört, wie man berührt".[7] Für Lévinas ist dies eher eine Frage der Sensibilität als des Bewusstseins. Sensibilität ist das Verhältnis des Sujets zum Elementaren, wie es in Martínez Celayas Bildern aus der Serie Drafts of a Landscape erscheint: der Wald, der Regen – der Wald, in dem die Figur umherschweift, oder der Klang des Ozeans, der tief im Gehäuse einer Meeresschnecke wohnt wie eine Erinnerung. Dies ist die Erfahrung von Nähe ohne Offenbarung oder Preisgabe. Der Mantel der Nacht bietet die Intimität der Nähe, die Wärme, die umschließt ohne zu offenbaren, während das Verhältnis zur Vergangenheit, zum Vorausgegangenen, zum Reich der Erinnerung, in die Kategorie des Zeichens seiner Leere, seiner Verlassenheit fällt. Abwesenheit erlangt die Bedeutung von Auslöschen und Neumarkieren oder -zeichnen. Auch zu diesem Punkt weiß Lévinas etwas zu sagen:

> Die Öffnung des Leeren ist nicht nur das Zeichen einer Abwesenheit. Die in den Sand gezeichnete Figur ist nicht Element eines Pfades, sondern tatsächlich die Leere der Vergangenheit selbst. Und das, was fortgenommen wurde, wird nicht evoziert, kehrt nicht in die Gegenwart zurück – nicht einmal in eine angedeutete Gegenwart.[8]

Man könnte sagen, dass nichts sichtbar ist, dass alles opak bleibt und das Bewusstwerden des Anderen durch Hören geschieht und nicht durch Sehen. Es ist ein Hören, das mit dem zu tun

5. Jacques Derrida: *Margins of Philosophy* (Chicago: Chicago University Press, 1982), S. 275 (frz. Originaltitel *Marges de la philosophie*, dt. Titel *Randgänge der Philosophie*).
6. Paul Celan, *Sprachgitter*, op. cit.
7. Emmanuel Lévinas, *Collected Philosophical Papers* (Dordrecht: Martinus Nijhoff, 1987), S. 118.
8. Emmanuel Lévinas, *En Decouvrant l'Existence avec Husserl et Heidegger* (Paris: Vrin, 1949), S. 208.

hat, was in die Erinnerung übergegangen ist. Der schwarze, dichte Grund in Martínez Celayas Bildern aus Drafts of a Landscape bietet etwas, das gleichzeitig weniger und mehr ist als Offenbarung. Nichts ist klar. Es ist, als habe sich die Nacht herabgesenkt, die Sicht als solche verdunkelt, so dass der Grund stärker gegenwärtig wird. Dennoch bietet er in seinem diskordanten Verhältnis zur Fragilität der Linie eine Dichte, in der die Figur still erscheint. Die Stille ist durchdringend und man hört, statt zu schauen.

Martínez Celayas Werk reiht sich in die orphische Tradition ein, die in der Moderne von Mallarmé und Blanchot geprägt wird.[9] In der Orpheuslegende steigt der Dichter in die Unterwelt hinab, um seine Gefährtin Eurydike zurückzuholen, die unerwartet gestorben und ins Totenreich eingegangen ist. Er spricht bei Hades und Persephone vor und bittet sie, Eurydike freizugeben. Die Götter gewähren ihm seinen Wunsch unter der Bedingung, dass er sich auf dem Rückweg in die Oberwelt nicht nach Eurydike umschaut. Eurydike tritt aus der Geisterwelt hervor und folgt ihm in völligem Schweigen über die dunklen Pfade der Unterwelt. Doch in einem unbesonnenen Moment blickt Orpheus unwillkürlich nach hinten, um nach ihr zu sehen. In diesem Augenblick verschwindet Eurydike. Orpheus ist zwar von Gram gebeugt, doch das Opfer von Eurydike, ihre ewige Unsichtbarkeit, lässt seinen Gesang erblühen. Er irrt durch die Lande, und seine Musik verzaubert alle, denen er begegnet. Eines Tages nähert sich ihm eine Gruppe thrakischer Mänaden, deren Annäherungsversuche er zurückweist. Erbost werfen sie Speere und Steine nach ihm, die seine Musik allerdings unschädlich zu machen vermag. Erst in ihrem Geschrei geht sein Gesang unter und die Frauen ergreifen Orpheus, zerreißen ihn und werfen seinen Kopf in den Fluss Hebros. Die Glieder seines verstümmelten Körpers werden später aufgesammelt und bestattet. An seinem Grab singt die Nachtigall ihre reine Weise.

Blanchot zufolge wird das Verschwinden (bezogen auf Eurydike) „zur Dichte des Schattens, der das Fleischliche gegenwärtiger und diese Gegenwart schwerer und fremdartiger macht, namen- und formlos, eine Gegenwart, von der man nicht sagen kann, ob sie lebendig oder tot ist, aber aus der alles Uneindeutige der Sehnsucht seine Wahrheit bezieht".[10] Es wird nicht nur das Opfer von Eurydike notwendig, sondern auch Orpheus muss für seinen Gesang sterben. Auch das Schreiben beginnt mit einem gewissen Opfer. Schreiben steht auf der Seite des Verschwindens, an der Grenze zwischen Sein und Nichts.

Nach Lévinas „geht das Aufspüren von Spuren einher mit seiner gleichzeitigen Auslöschung – seinem eigenen Rückzug" und diese Spur „stört die Ordnung der Dinge auf irreversible Weise".[11] Es ist ein Nach-Zeichnen, das eine immaterielle Spur hinterlässt. Die Spur räumt das Feld, die Vergangenheit ist irreversibel, es gibt keinen Regress, keine Rückkehr. Dies ist auch die Basis für eine Kritik der Darstellung, des Evidenziellen, des Beharrens auf dem Darstellen oder Offenbaren und all dessen, was ans Licht gebracht wird. Dies würde auch Sigmund Freuds Begriff eines originären Ortes der Repression entsprechen und der davon hoch- bzw. ans Licht gebrachten Erinnerung, so als dürfe man zurückgehen, um wiederzuerlangen oder -herzustellen, was verloren gegangen ist. Die Spur lässt sich nicht auf diese Weise konvertieren, eben weil dies das Andere in das Phänomenale und Immanente bringen würde und damit in die Ökonomie des Selben, der Kontinuität. Lévinas schlägt ein Konzept von Spur vor, das unabhängig ist von Begriffen wie Offenbarung, Aufdeckung oder Enthüllung. Die Spuren bleiben sozusagen; sie sind konstitutiv oder Teil der Fülle der Gegenwart, bleiben aber unsichtbar, bestenfalls unheimlich.

9. Siehe Maurice Blanchot, *The Gaze of Orpheus and Other Literary Essays*, engl. Übersetzung Lydia Davis (New York: Station Hill Press, 1981). Nachdem hier Celan, Lévinas und Blanchot angeführt wurden, wäre zu ergänzen, dass sowohl Blanchot als auch Lévinas über Celan geschrieben haben.
10. Maurice Blanchot, *The Infinite Conversation* (Minneapolis: University of Minnesota Press, 1993), S. 188 (frz. Originaltitel *L'entretien infini*, dt. Titel *Das Unzerstörbare: ein unendliches Gespräch über Sprache, Literatur und Existenz*).
11. Emmanuel Lévinas, *En Decouvrant l'Existence*, op. cit., S. 208, 206.

III

Der spricht wahr, der Schatten spricht
Paul Celan

Die Gemäldeserie Coming Home, 2001, besteht aus steingrauen Bildern von Licht, dem leuchtenden Licht des weiten Himmels und seiner Reflexion auf dem Ozean. Zwischen Himmel und Erde, zwischen den Welten, steht eine einsame Figur am Rande des Ozeans, die Taube löst sich im Morgenlicht auf und die Reflexion des Hirschs öffnet sich „dem gesamten entschleierten Himmel, jenseits der Gnade".[12] Den Winden ausgesetzt, ist der kalte Wind des Winters die Erfahrung der Entfremdung. Es gibt kein helles Licht, sondern Schatten, keine Heimkehr, sondern Heimatlosigkeit. Das Sehen ist unzuverlässig geworden. Man spricht aus dem Dunkeln. Wir befinden uns an einem fremden Ort. Verstoßen, sehen wir in einem neutralen Raum ohne zu sehen. Wieder scheint es so, als gebe es hier eine Öffnung zu etwas Verborgenem, einem Hören, das wartet wie der Jäger in Kurosawas Film *Derzu Uzala*. Der Jäger sieht nichts mehr, jagt aber mit Hilfe des Hörsinns weiter. Er gehört zur gnadenlosen Landschaft des Überlebens, des Weiterlebens. Es gibt keine klare Horizontlinie, keinen Ort, an dem das umherstreifende Auge ausruhen kann. Wo also befinden wir uns ohne diese tief eingegrabenen Linien, diese Spuren der Zurückbesinnung? Dies sind keine Bilder von Rückkehr, von Ankunft am längst vergessenen Ort. Man könnte eher von einer Sehnsucht nach einer Bleibe, nach Zugehörigkeit, von Verlangen nach Zugehörigkeit sprechen. Dieser jenseitige Ort wird also zum Ziel des Bildes, oder genauer gesagt der Wahrnehmung, dessen, was wahrgenommen wird, und der Erfahrung wahrgenommen zu werden. Hier besteht ein Zwischenraum, ein Intervall, auf das die Spur verweist, zwischen dem Bezeichneten und dem Horizont, der über es hinausgeht.

Der Abstand ist noch größer als gedacht. Wir dürfen kurze Blicke durch die Schleier der Nacht auf die graue Leere der Morgendämmerung erhaschen, der wir preisgegeben sind. Es gibt hier ein Vergessen, eine Bewegung fort von der Sprache als Ersatz für und Verschleierung von all ihrem Raffinement und ihrer Konstruiertheit. Zwangsläufig und doch entfremdet imitiert Martínez Celayas Arbeit die vergeblichen Versuche, sie zu naturalisieren. Er setzt den Spiegel zwischen die Geweihhälften, um den weiten Baldachin des hohen Himmels darin zu reflektieren, lässt die Plastik eines Kopfes auf der Wasseroberfläche treiben oder platziert die Skulptur eines in die Ferne starrenden Knaben unmittelbar am Ufer.

Die Dichte der Luft, die in der gesamten Serie Coming Home mitschwingt, ist atemlos. Im „Schweifenlassen der Fantasie" hat die Kunst zwar einen Ort zur Verfügung gestellt, doch dieser Ort ist nichts anderes als ein Ort innerhalb der Kunst selbst, eine Flucht, die sich an der Schwelle zum immateriellen Land des Unheimlichen, außerhalb des Menschlichen findet. Der Kunstgriff der Kunst wird zum Unheimlichen des Menschlichen. Wenn wir den Atem als Beginn von Sprache bezeichnet haben, dann müssen wir nun von einer Unterbrechung der Sprache sprechen, wenn der Atem angehalten wird. Es ist vielleicht annähernd das, was Blanchot als *desouvrement* bezeichnet, ein neutraler Raum der Stille. Blanchot beschreibt es als Intervall, als *entre-temps* zwischen noch Zukünftigem und schon Vergangenem, als geteilte Natur der Spur. Es ist sozusagen eine Zäsur oder ein Zwischenraum der Zugehörigkeit, der weder zur Vergangenheit noch zur Zukunft gehört, unaufspürbar ist. Deshalb besitzen Martínez Celayas Arbeiten auch etwas seltsam Schwebendes. Um zur Orpheus-Legende zurückzukehren:

12. Zitiert in Enrique Martínez Celaya, *October* (Amsterdam: Cinubia, 2001), unpaginiert.

Eurydike war für ihn nie anders gegenwärtig als in der Gestalt der Erinnerung, die er zu bewältigen sucht. Sie erscheint Orpheus als Geist, nur um von einer nächtlichen Sehnsucht überwältigt zu werden, zu sehen, was unsichtbar ist. Er vergisst das Verbot und sie verschwindet in Lethes Schattenwelt.

IV

> Ich folge meinen umherstreifenden Sinnen in diese neue Welt des Geistes und lerne die Freiheit kennen.
>
> Paul Celan

Geschichte als Kontinuität in der Zeit, Totalität von Vergangenheit und Zukunft gibt es nicht. Ebenso wenig gibt es eine Essenz, an die man appellieren könnte, weder eine Identität noch ein Grund. Es ist eher ein Hintergrund, frei von Orten, ein Außen. Dieses Außen, dieser undomestizierte Raum, trägt keinen Namen. Was wäre, wenn man diese Grundlosigkeit als Ausgangspunkt akzeptieren würde, als provisorischen Platz? Tatsächlich gibt es keine Essenz, an die man appellieren kann. Die Spur führt weder zurück noch nach vorn, so als sei sie durch und an das Bezeichnete gebunden. Sie ist kein Zeichen insofern, als sie rein indikativ ist oder in einem empirischen Verhältnis zu einem Ereignis oder zu etwas einst Gegenwärtigem steht. Es gibt hier keinerlei Rückstand – keine Fragmente, Ruinen, Merkmale oder Beweise –, so dass sie nicht (mit Pathos oder Nostalgie) nach einem originären Moment sucht. Vielmehr wird die Spur, die ja eine Verbindung zur Welt bietet, da sie als vergangenheitsgebundene Form der Erinnerung funktioniert, von der strukturellen Möglichkeit ihrer Iteration oder Wiederholung bestimmt, die ihrerseits nur durch die Abwesenheit des Wiederholten möglich ist. Sie ist retroaktiv, hängt von einem bestimmten Ausgangspunkt ab, einem Etwas-hinter-sich-lassen, so dass Erinnerung geschaffen wird, und öffnet sich damit selbst einer Zukunft, da sie erst nach dem Geschehnis zu sehen ist – gesehen werden kann – und zu verstehen ist.

Doch wenn die Spur zu etwas wird, das gleichzeitig weniger und mehr ist als das ursprünglich Bezeichnete, ist sie dann genau genommen noch eine Spur, wenn sie nicht Spur einer Spur ist? Spaltet dies nicht gewissermaßen die Gestalt der Spur in zwei Hälften auf, und würde diese Spaltung nicht zwei zueinander antagonistische Hälften erzeugen? Wie lässt sich die Spur eingrenzen außer durch das, was im Endeffekt durch das Verschwinden dessen markiert bzw. gezeichnet wird, von dem man annehmen darf, dass es die Spur hervorrief? Sich die Spur gedanklich vorstellen heißt ihren Pfad entweder vorwärts oder rückwärts verfolgen, sie wechselweise als Bindung und Loslösung sehen, als Vergegenwärtigung oder Tilgung, Nähe oder Distanz, Rückkehr oder Abschied. Dieser paradoxe Zustand konstituiert die Struktur der Spur.

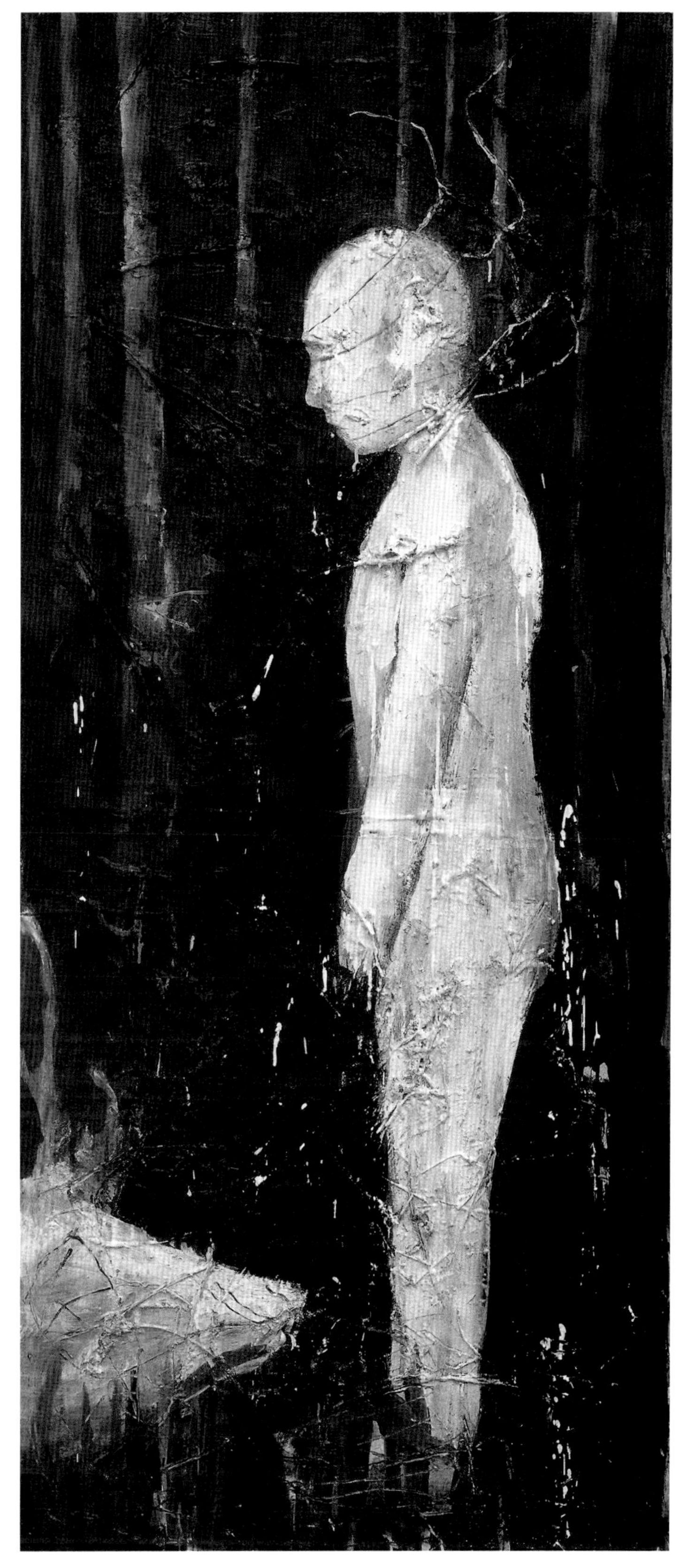

RE-INVENTORY/RE-INVENTUR, 2000
Sammlung Dieter und Si Rosenkranz, Berlin, Deutschland

Der getane Schritt ist nicht vorgegeben, sondern wird vielmehr möglich, indem er auf die Spur dessen folgt, was getilgt wurde. Die Spur entsteht in einem Moment der Tilgung: eine Tilgung, weil sie nur ein Schatten oder Abdruck des im Sand entstandenen Eindrucks ist. Erscheinung wird durch die Tilgung solcher Male konstituiert. Gegenwart wird zum Zeichen eines abwesenden Ursprungs, der niemals gegenwärtig war, ist aber immer eine zukünftige Vergangenheit. Mit anderen Worten, eine auf Abwesenheit beruhende Gegenwart existiert nur dank ihres Spätergeschehens, durch Wiederholung. Materialität ist nicht einfach etwas Gegebenes, das Spuren trägt, sondern wird vielmehr selbst durch Prozesse der Selektion, Ausschließung und Ausarbeitung definiert, gestaltet und stabilisiert. Die von der Spur angenommene Materialität ist also Zeugin des Bruchs ihres eigenen Zustands.

Je nachdem, auf welche Seite dieser Teilung die Spur nun fällt, fließt sie entweder in die Zukunft mit ein und gestaltet sie durch ihre Vergangenheitsgebundenheit, oder sie ist zukunftsgebunden, da sie immer im Nachhinein auftritt und sich auf einen Horizont öffnet, der über das von ihm Bezeichnete hinausgeht. So fragt Lévinas in seinem Essay „Phenomena and Enigma":

> Wie lässt sich über eine irreversible Vergangenheit sprechen, die eine Vergangenheit ist, die selbst die Referenz nicht zurückbringen würde ... wie die Erinnerung, die die Vergangenheit hervorholt, wie Zeichen, die das Bezeichnete wiedereinfangen? Man bräuchte einen Hinweis, der die Fortnahme des Angedeuteten offenbart, anstatt einer Referenz, die sich ihm wieder anschließt – so etwas wie die Spur.[13]

So gesehen lässt sich die Vergangenheit nicht gegenwärtig machen, zurückholen, wiedererwecken oder wiederherstellen. Dies wäre nach Lévinas' Worten „eine Heimkehr zu sich selbst, wie bei Odysseus, der bei all seinen Irrfahrten nur auf dem Weg zum Land seiner Geburt war".[14] Diese Geschichte, die zum Epenkreis der Nostoi (Heimkehr der Helden von Troja) gehört, lebt von einer Sehnsucht nach Fehlendem oder einem Bedürfnis, wie Lévinas es definiert, das durch die Heimkehr erfüllt wird.[15] Das nostalgische, von Bedürfnissen bestimmte Wesen der Erinnerung erklärt zum Teil ihren starken Hang dazu, wiedereinzufangen, zu reproduzieren und Vergangenheit zu vergegenwärtigen. Unter diesem Aspekt betrachtet, legt Martínez Celayas Werk nahe, dass das Verhältnis zwischen Spur und Erinnerung eben deswegen problematisch ist, weil die Erinnerung an Zurückbesinnung gebunden ist: eine Rückkehr zum Selben. Zudem ist sie eine Vergangenheit, die niemals gegenwärtig war. Die Bilder, die die Arbeit dieses Künstlers bestimmen, sind bestenfalls flüchtig, vorübergehend, eine Erinnerung vor der Zurückbesinnung. So gesehen bleibt die Spur dem Indexikalischen treu. Sie ist nicht länger innerhalb der Begrenzungen von Gegenwart und Abwesenheit gefangen, sondern wird durch ihre Bewegung der Wiederholung und der Andersartigkeit bestimmt. Die Bilder haben weder phänomenale Gegenwart noch Fülle, sondern erscheinen vielmehr durch Tilgung und Teilung.

Alternativ zum Mythos des Odysseus schlägt Lévinas einen Aufbruch ohne Rückkehr vor, wie etwa den von Abraham, der seine Heimat mit unbekanntem Ziel verließ. Abrahams Aufbruch verkörpert auch einen Abschied vom Selbst und ein Gefühl der Verantwortung, die über die Selbstbezüglichkeit und über immer wieder auf sich selbst zurückfallende Perspektiven hinausgeht, einen Aufbruch zu einer Ökonomie des Selbst anstelle des Anderen. Vorgestoßen in die Weite, gehört er umso mehr zum Anderen, zu dem, was er selbst nicht ist. Celan sprach davon, dass „das Gedicht etwas Anderes sagen will, dieses Andere braucht, einen Gegensatz braucht. Es geht auf es zu, spricht es an. Für das Gedicht ist alles und jedes eine Gestalt dieses Anderen, auf das es sich zubewegt."[16] Diese Weite offen zu halten erfordert ein gewisses

13. Emmanuel Lévinas, „Phenomena and Enigma", in *Collected Philosophical Papers*, op. cit., S. 65.
14. Emmanuel Lévinas, *Totality and Infinity* (Pittsburgh: Dusquesne UP, 1969), S. 346 (frz. Originaltitel *Totalité et infini, essai sur l'extériorité*, dt. Titel *Totalität und Unendlichkeit*).
15. Lévinas, *Totality and Infinity*, ibid., S. 33.
16. Celan, *Sprachgitter*, op. cit.

Vergessen und setzt voraus, dass man geduldig das Dunkel betrachtet, das uns umgibt. Dieses „Herausstreben aus der Zurückbesinnung“ ist charakteristisch für die Sehnsucht, die Martínez Celayas Kunst innewohnt.

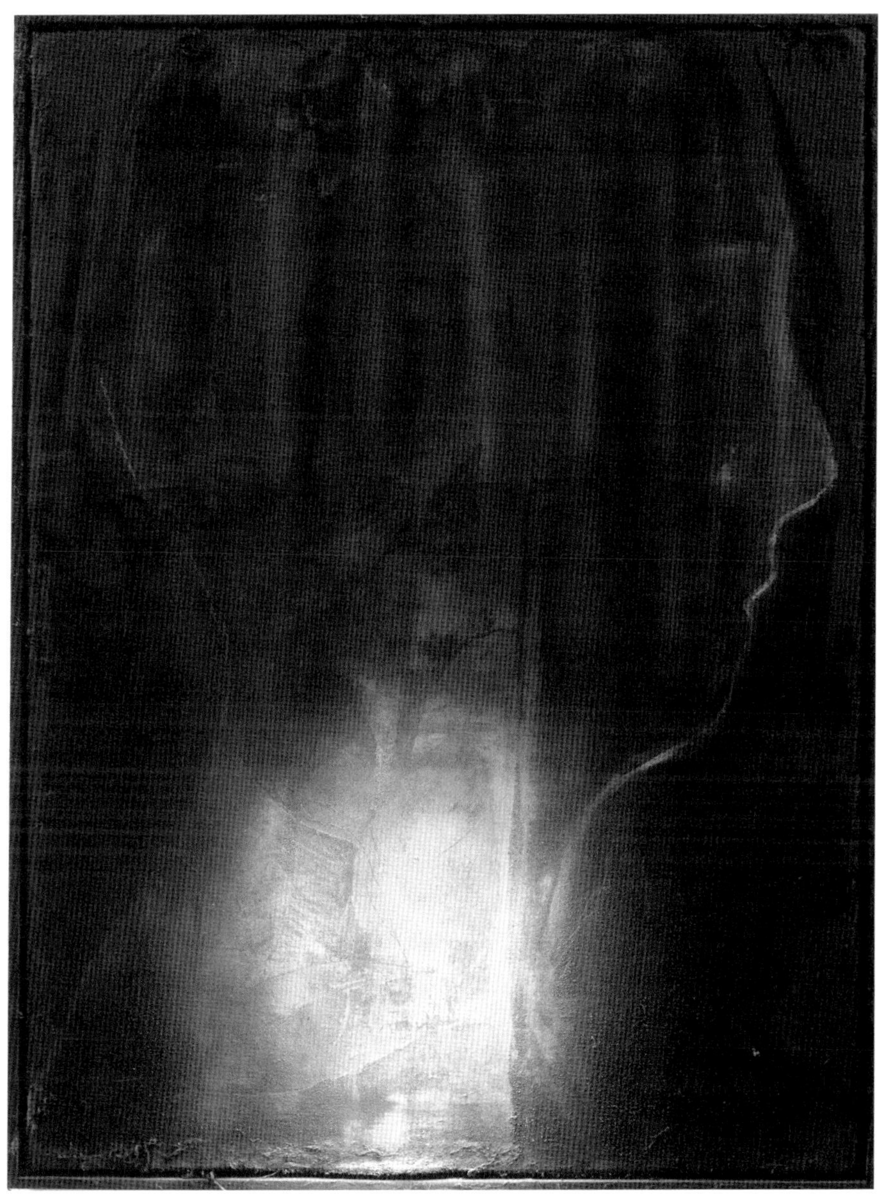

FIGURE (RESONANCE)/GESTALT (RESONANZ), 2000
Sammlung Jocelyn Grayson, Woodstock, Vermont

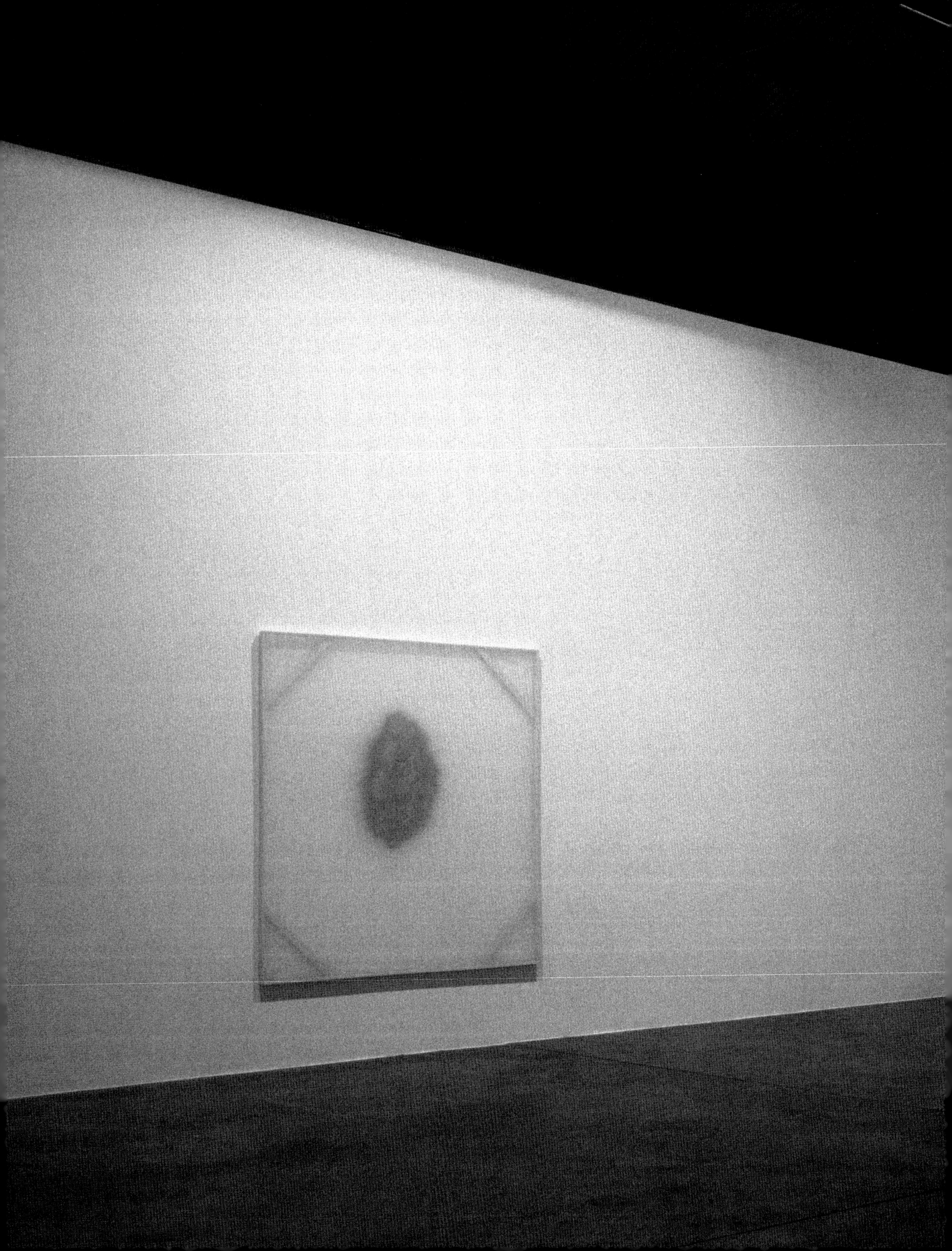

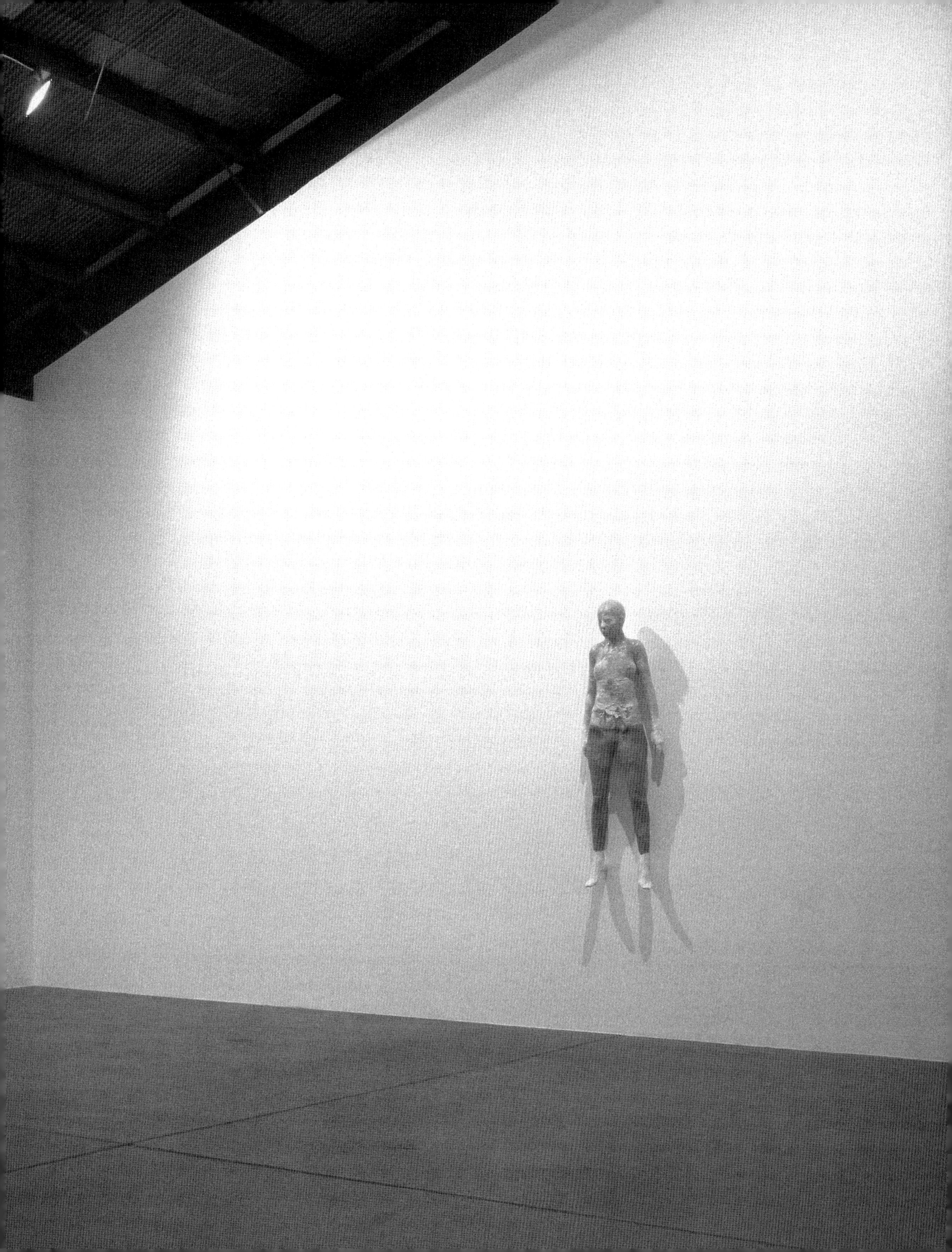

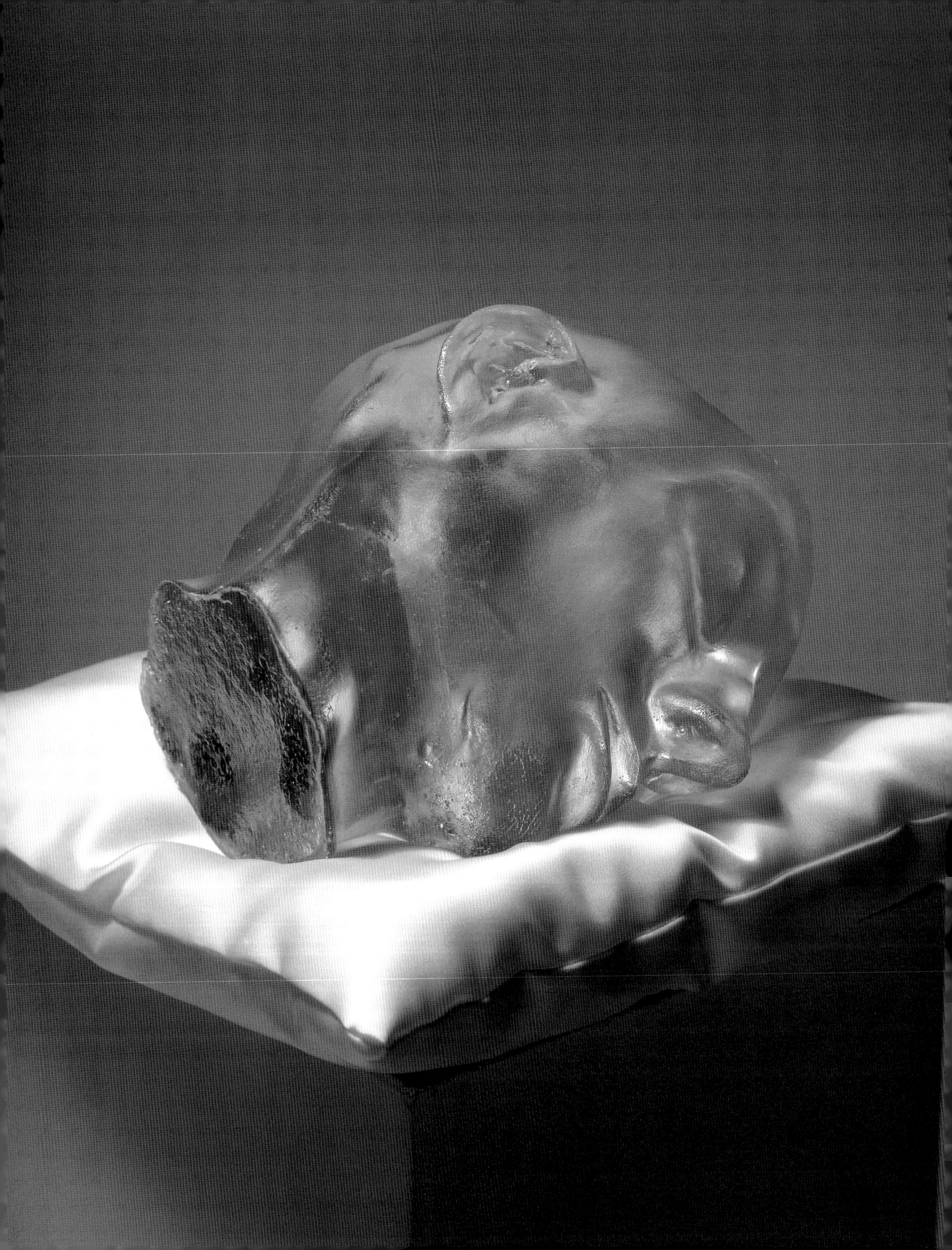

RESTITUTIONAL FRAGMENTS

Abigail Solomon-Godeau

> Sommes-nous fatalement de esclaves de l'image? Ce n'est pas sûr, répondent les philosophes, par métier incertains, l'image est potentiellement un espace de liberté: elle anéantit la contrainte de l'objet-modèle et lui substitue l'envol de pensée, le vagabondage de l'imagination. J'ajoute, et c'est mon parti pris, que l'image est peut-être le seul lien qui nous reste avec le sacré: avec l'épouvante que provoque le morte et le sacrifice, avec la sérénité qui découle du pacte d'identification entre sacrifié et sacrifiants, et avec la joie de la représentation indissociable du sacrifice, sa seule traversée possible.[1]
>
> Julia Kristeva, *Visions Capitales*

A translucent human head, approximately life size, seemingly bloodied at the point of severance, rests on a pristine white pillow like a strange votive offering. Reposing on a spare and elegant wooden base, it is positioned at waist height so that the spectator is compelled to gaze down upon it. Cast in a milky-colored light-reflecting resin, its features are serene, composed. Insofar as the head and face are generic rather than specific its gender is not visually apparent, but is made clear by its title–*Saint Catherine (Absolution)*, 1997.

What does it mean to make iconographic use of a religious figure–specifically, a female saint–in contemporary art? How is one to think about the deployment of Saint Catherine, on the very cusp of the twenty-first century, as subject or as motif? What might it mean to traffic in female effigies that were once devotional icons, and are now, for the most part, confined to the domain of religious kitsch? And what might it mean for a sophisticated, secular, and professionally trained artist to take as his saintly personage one whom even the Vatican has more or less disavowed? (Saint Catherine's Feast Day was eliminated in 1969, thereby implying some considerable doubt about her historical existence).

But the variations on the theme of the decapitated Catherine, patron saint of scholars and philosophers as well as wheelwrights and mechanics, that Enrique Martínez Celaya presented in an ensemble of works in 1997, were themselves outgrowths of a previous body of work. In this earlier series, Martínez Celaya made reference to another female saint–this one an actual historical figure–namely, Saint Joan of Arc, the Maid of Orleans. Here too was a hagiographic figure who experienced mystical visions, violent death and martyrdom. Because Saint Catherine, along with Saint Michael, was identified by Joan as one of her visionary apparitions, one may therefore assume that working thematically in 1996 with the martyrdom of Joan of Arc, prompted Martínez Celaya's subsequent interest in this second virgin martyr. Neither of these saints, apocryphal or real, would seem obvious choices for an artist like Martínez Celaya. In France, Joan of Arc is effectively 'owned' by the nationalist, xenophobic Right, for whom she functions as the reactionary pendant to the republican Marianne, the secular goddess of the French Revolution. Saint Catherine, as the Catholic Encyclopedia informs us, "is worthy to

facing page

ST. CATHERINE (ABSOLUTION)
/DIE HEILIGE KATHARINA (ABSOLUTION), 1997
Collection of Mary Paeng, San Francisco, California

1. "Are we inevitably the slaves of the image? One isn't sure, answer the philosophers, by trade uncertain: the image is potentially a space of liberty; it annihilates the limitation of the model-object and substitutes for it the free flight of thought, the vagabondage of the imagination. I [would] add, and it is my parti pris, that the image is perhaps the only connection with the sacred that remains to us: with the terror that death and sacrifice provokes, with the serenity that flows from the identificatory pact between the sacrificed and the sacrificer, and with the joy of representation indisassociable from the sacrifice, the only passageway possible." Julia Kristeva, exh. cat., (Paris: Musée du Louvre, 1998) 11
All translations from this text are my own.

watch over the virgins of the cloister and young women of the world." Interestingly, one of the reasons for Joan's execution for heresy was her stubborn insistence on her direct and unmediated relation to God (as opposed to the necessity of mediation or hierarchy of the church). In the (apocryphal) case of Catherine, it was her dazzling intellectual prowess in refuting her pagan interlocutors, and thus converting (so the story goes) even the wife of the emperor Maxentius, that made her so threatening to the status quo. It was these same qualities that made her the patron saint of scholars, rhetoricians and philosophers. Nevertheless, on the basis of the works themselves, it would seem that what preoccupies Martínez Celaya, in both suites of work, has less to do with the biographical particulars of either saint, or even with the legends that developed around them, than with more ecumenical, more general notions of sacrifice and redemption. But where the works that made up the 1996 ensemble New Works for Jeanne d'Arc included a plaster cast of an intact female body supine on the floor, the works in the 1998 series Berlin, the Fragility of Nearness, which focused on Saint Catherine iconographically, represent–more or less abstractly, more or less figuratively, and in both sculptural and two dimensional forms–only the severed head of Catherine. Even the instrument of her martyrdom, the spiked wheel which was to have killed her and which miraculously shattered, thereby necessitating her decapitation, is absent. We are given only this floating, disembodied head, hairless, bloodless, and almost featureless. A head, we could say, without qualities.

It should in any case be clear that the representation of figures from Christian history and hagiography in the work of a contemporary artist like Martínez Celaya, cannot be taken at face value, for all that, biographically speaking, Martínez Celaya is from a Cuban, Catholic family and has also lived in Spain. For good or for ill, it is no longer possible historically for a contemporary artist, whether or not he is a believer, to have the same relationship to Christian iconography as did the pre-modern image-maker. On the contrary, it seems far more plausible to consider Martínez Celaya's idiosyncratic iconography as functioning more on an allegorical than a literally referential level. Moreover, a severed head has meanings both cultural and psychoanalytical quite apart from the fate of an apocryphal saint. Thus, the image of the disembodied head, which has featured in Martínez Celaya's work since 1995, has at least one other iconographic history, one belonging to Surrealism and the concept of acephale–the condition of headlessness. Which is not to say that Martínez Celaya's imagery makes conscious homage to Surrealism, but rather, to indicate that like other recurring motifs in his work, Martínez Celaya's approach is more syncretic than symbolic. For Martínez Celaya, however, and in contrast to the surrealists, it is the disembodied head rather than the headless body that is regularly invoked. These include such painted and graphic works as *Soundless: Anywhere But In Between*, 1997; *The Secrets*, 1997; *Accumulation of Tiredness*, 1998; as well as those that are modeled or cast (e.g., the various heads of *St. Catherine (Artificer)*, 1997; *Quiet Night (Dirt)*, 1999, etc.). These have somewhat different implications from the acephale of the surrealists. For the latter, 'losing one's head' was not only emancipatory; it stood for the repudiation of what was perceived as the deadening and soul-killing rationalism, positivism and instrumentalism of modern industrial societies. The acephale functioned as well to contest the notion of the centered, self-knowing and sovereign subject, parallelling the celebration of the 'low', the abject, the irrational and the

THE WEDDING DRESS/DAS HOCHZEITSKLEID, 1996
Private collection, Paris, France

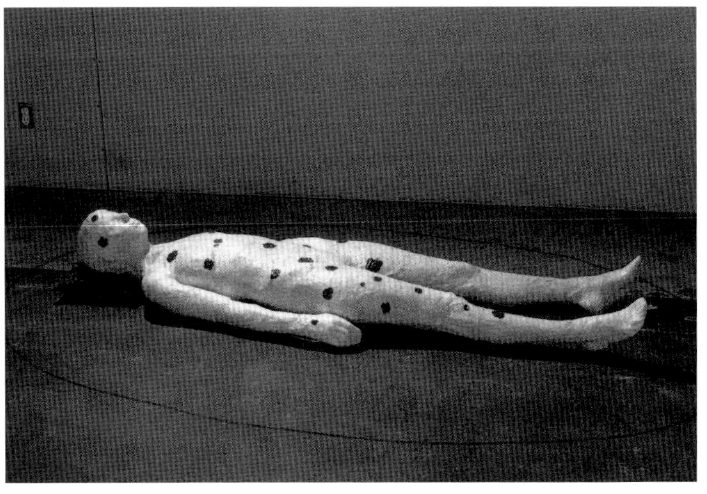

unconscious. Although in certain works, Martínez Celaya's use of the bodyless head is directly suggestive of decapitation (e.g., the bloody stump of neck in *Soundless*), just as the paintings and casts likewise suggest mutilation or amputation, in others, the head or limb is highly schematized, if not abstracted. In these instances (e.g., *A Boy in his Room*, 1997; *Powers and Dominions*, 1997), the representations are closer to the conventions of the ex-voto than they are to the sanguinary relic or depiction of a discrete body part. Given the range of iconographic associations and precedents, as well as its ostensibly religious reference, it would seem, therefore, that Martínez Celaya's iconography is better considered within the framework of postmodernist appropriation or re-appropriation than as an exclusively subjective and wholly personal lexicon. But unlike the practice of other postmodernist artists, however, we are dealing here neither with a directly citational mode of art-making, nor with the recuperative use of popular religious paraphernalia such as that which features in the altars of Amalia Mesa-Bains. But at the same time we need to acknowledge that there is often at work in Martínez Celaya's hybridized ensemble of objects, paintings, and mixed-media assemblages a nominal subject–i.e., the severed head of Saint Catherine, the hummingbird, the birch tree–which necessarily entails some consideration of the particular associations of each motif. We need also to attend to the possible meanings of Martínez Celaya's forms and materials, for these are as constitutive of meaning as is the subject itself. In other words, as with any body of work, we must attend to the work of the signifier as much as to the nature of the signified. In this respect, it is important to recognize that Martínez Celaya is in no simple or obvious way a 'painter' or for that matter, a 'sculptor.' On the contrary, although Martínez Celaya produces paintings and sculptures, he more accurately typifies the so-called post-studio artist, that is to say, an artist who uses whatever formal language and whatever form of material that best expresses his ideas. These might include sculptures, installations, painted objects, and assemblages, and poetry, as well as materials and substances from rose petals to tar to industrial resins. Most recently, he has produced a series of large-scale, variously manipulated photographs, a medium that has been theorized as the postmodern medium par excellence[2]. In this new corpus of work, entitled the Elegias Series, 2000–2001, the negative in some cases has been hand colored with ink; in another instance, a suturing bandage of tape surrounds the model's head, in others the background seems bleached away, in others, the image is itself tinted. It is this protean, and indeed often experimental working process, as well as the sheer variety of his conceptual and formal investigations, which make his art both complex, highly mutable, and often uncategorizable.

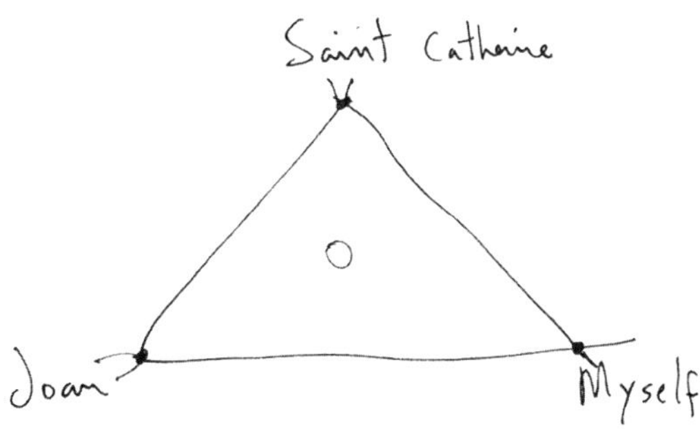

Sketchbook/Skizzenbuch, 1997

But what is of particular interest here, especially in the context of the work assembled under the collective title Berlin, the Fragility of Nearness, 1998, the Winter works on paper, 2000, or more recently, the photographic series, and the plaster cast of a standing woman (*The River*, 1997), is a kind of oscillation between his fabrication of art works that operate on the register of the indexical–for example, those works made from casting the living body or his photographic work–and those other, typically graphic works that operate on the register of the icon–that is, an image with only a conventional relationship to its referent. Hence, the sculptural heads

2. See, for example, Douglas Crimp, "The Photographic Activity of Postmodernism" in Crimp, *On the Museum's Ruins* (Cambridge: The MIT Press, 1996); Rosalind Krauss, "The Originality of the Avant-Garde" in Krauss, *The Originality of the Avant-garde and Other Modernist Myths* (Cambridge: The MIT Press, 1985); Craig Owens, "The Allegorical Impulse: Toward a Theory of Postmodernism, Part 2" in Owens, *Beyond Recognition: Representation, Power and Culture* (Berkeley and Los Angeles: The University of California Press, 1992).

and arms fabricated from plastic resin produce one form of perception, the large-scale photographs another, while the iconic works–the large canvases upon which the simplified and often ghostly heads appear to float, or those that feature his emblematic hummingbird–prompt a somewhat different reaction. In the former instance, the object is linked directly to the corporeal and thus prompts a nearly visceral response; in the latter, the affect is more mediated, more allusive, belonging as it does to the order of the pictorial.

Which is to say that the forms by which Martínez Celaya articulates his explorations of various subjects and motifs are as important as the meanings generated by the motifs themselves. Notwithstanding the fact that Martínez Celaya is what one would call a somewhat 'literary' artist, one whose work is suffused with iconography that is personal, even autobiographical, and for both reasons, idiosyncratic, there are nevertheless issues explored in his work that go beyond the purely personal or subjective. It is these latter works that are especially interesting to explore, and in what follows, I want to consider several aspects of Martínez Celaya's work of the past few years or so as an indirect way of considering how and why Martínez Celaya's multifaceted production should be understood within the presiding terms of postmodernity. What is at issue here is the way by which even the most earnest and searching attempts to invent a visual language of the 'authentic' self, an iconography at once subjectivized, personal, spiritual, and hermetic, is countered, if not foiled, by the sheer weight of accrued cultural meaning that attaches to all recognizable iconography. Like the severed head, or, for that matter, any of the objects or narratives that feature in one's dreams, signs and objects can be simultaneously personal–tied to an individual's history and subjectivity–and conventional, inscribed by meanings that are historical and cultural. It is, I would suggest, the tension between Martínez Celaya's concatenation of private meanings, allusions, and symbols with the pre-existing 'forest of signs' which shapes our conscious and unconscious minds and inevitably shapes our reception of art, that produces the characteristic effect of melancholy, loss and longing to which Martínez Celaya's audience so powerfully respond.

To a certain extent, this melancholy ambience is a pervasive feature of a great deal of postmodernist art, especially painting. This has been interpreted by many critics as signaling the 'impossibility,' as well as the atavism of the enterprise of painting, indeed of the traditional aspirations of high art in the new postmodern world of simulation and simulacra, of cyberspace, of a global culture of consumption and the colonization of consciousness by the juggernaut of commodity culture[3]. The aura of melancholy that inheres in so much of Martínez Celaya's work is, in this sense, to be understood as a condition of its production, not an effect. For if Martínez Celaya's work addresses itself to the sacred, it is nevertheless an address directed to a thoroughly secularized audience and culture (the art world is not for the most part populated with churchgoers); if it speaks to the sacrificial or ritualistic origins of the art object, it speaks however to a world whose totems are commodities; if it labors to provoke in the viewer some notion of the transcendental or the metaphysical, it cannot animate what is irretrievably lost. The very titles of Martínez Celaya's works allude to these contradictions and aporias–*The Acceptance of Longing*, 1997; *The Undeniable and Unfortunate Truths*, 1998; *The End of Tragedy*, 1995, among others. In what follows then, I want to consider certain distinctive features of Martínez Celaya's work, features that seem to have regularly informed his objects and paintings, but which also may be seen to relate to more general issues and tendencies in contemporary art.

3. The standard account of this epistemological transformation of culture and consciousness is Fredric Jameson. See Jameson, "Postmodernism or the Cultural Logic of Postmodernism," orginally published in *The New Left Review* 146 (July–Aug. 1984) and Jameson, "Postmodernism and Consumer Culture" in Hal Foster, ed., *The Anti-Aesthetic: Essays on Postmodernism* (Seattle: Bay Press, 1986). Discussions of the melancholy characteristics of postmodern art may be found in Yve Alain Bois, "Endgame" in *Endgame*, exh. cat., (Boston: ICA, 1984); Thomas Lawson, "Last Exit: Painting" in Brian Wallis, *Art After Modernism: Rethinking Representation* (Boston and New York: David Godine and The New Museum of Contemporary Art, 1986); Craig Owens, "The Allegorical Impulse, Parts I and II," in *Owens, Beyond Recognition*, op. cit.

The Body in Pieces

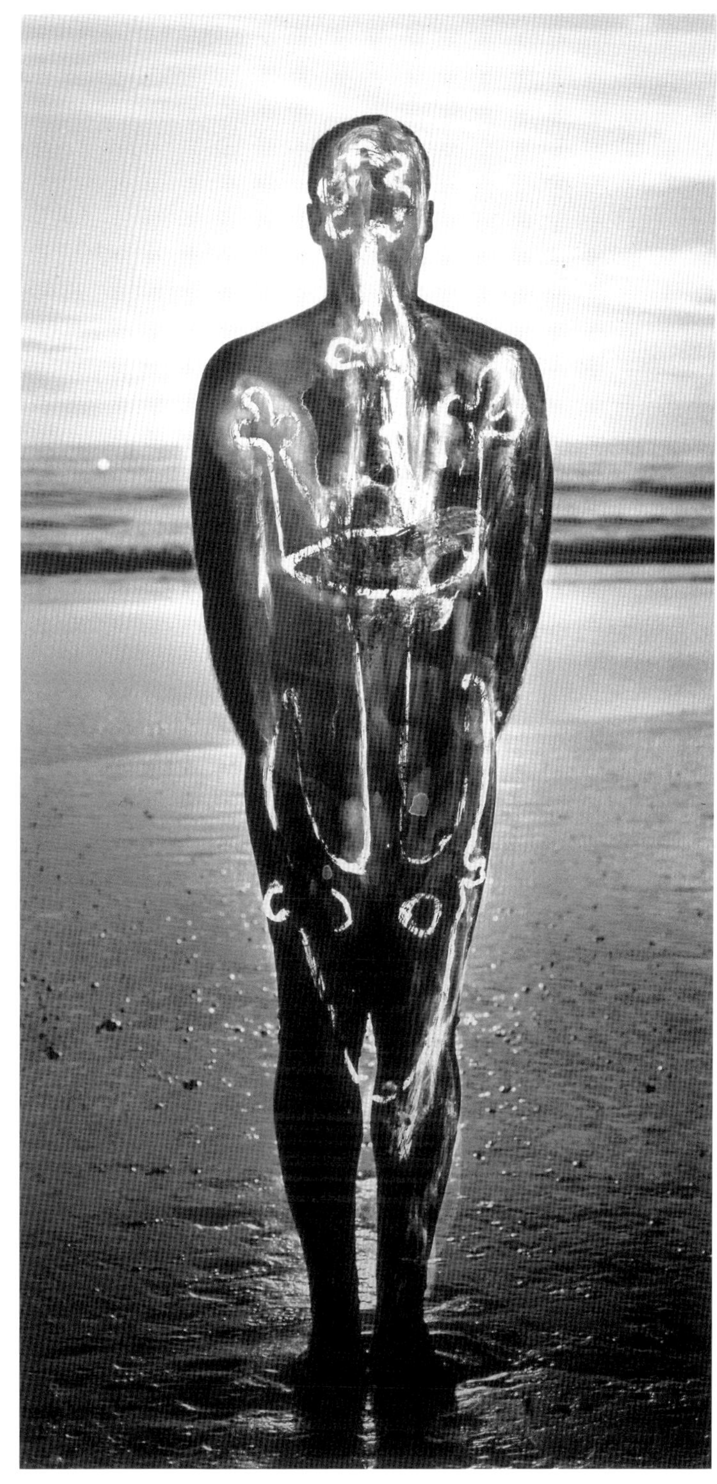

WATER AND FIGURE/WASSER UND GESTALT, 2000
Whitney Museum of American Art, New York, New York

"To decapitate = to castrate." So Freud wrote in his 1919 essay, *Medusa's Head*.[4] Given the frequency with which the severed head or disembodied arm appear in Martínez Celaya's work, and irrespective of their other meanings, might this motif not signal a specifically masculine anxiety about bodily integrity? Might it not also indicate some anxiety about the role and status of the artist in the wake of what Roland Barthes famously described as 'The Death of the Author.' For the most part (although with certain important exceptions), whole figures appear in Martínez Celaya's work only when they are female, or in certain cases, where the artist's own body is featured (typically in silhouette); even so, entire figures tend to be more the exception than the rule. More characteristic, for example, is the painting *Pena (Sorrow)*, 1997–1999, suggestive of a bleeding amputated wrist, just as certain of the generic heads (e.g., *Soundless: Anywhere But In Between*, 1997) or the silhouetted head in the pendant canvas *The Empty Garden*, 1999, with its blood-like streams of paint which evokes a violent decapitation. That the running lines and drips that flow from head and hand are not blood colored, but brown and black–the colors of the painted forms–suggest not only the mutilation of the body, but the painting itself as a site of mutilation; painting is revealed as a kind of wound. In this respect, the relationship between body and work is a venerable one; it is a relationship made explicit in language as when we speak of a body, or corpus of work. This implied equivalence between body and artwork recalls such precedents as Joan Miró's biomorphic paintings or, more recently, Fontana's violated and ruptured surfaces in which the canvas is either virtually or literally punctured, dimpled, slit; canvas as bodily membrane punctuated by orifices. Similarly, a work such as Martínez Celaya's *The Liar and the Thief*, 1996, with its cuts, slits, and crude stitching produces what might be perceived as a 'wounded' canvas. Such a reading returns us to the work of the signifier–the material construction of the painting itself. Which is to say that if the [human] body can no longer be imagined as whole, intact and perfect (as in the example of classical art), perhaps it is also the case that painting and sculpture (which are themselves classical media) must also be considered as fields of loss, injury and dispersal. Such a reading might well be augmented by consideration of the Freudian concept of castration, with the proviso that it be taken somewhat more broadly and allusively. In these terms, castration may be understood in its more fundamental sense, as a figuration of loss. Thus, the irretrievable loss of classical ideals of harmony, wholeness and autonomy (whether associated with the body as such or the sovereignty of the subject) is parallelled by the loss of authority and mastery once vested in the artist himself. Hence the melancholy and nostalgia to which Martínez Celaya frequently refers in his interviews and writing, and which virtually all his critics have perceived in his work, are akin to the loss of mastery that informs contemporary masculine subjectivity and much of its cultural production.[5] It is, in any case, evident that ours is an epoch

4. Sigmund Freud, "Medusa's Head" in Freud, *Writings on Art and Literature*, (Stanford: Stanford University Press, 1997).
5. See in this respect, Craig Owens' essay "Honor, Power and the Love of Women" in *Owens, Beyond Recognition*, op. cit.

that has not much belief in the wholeness, integrity or totality of the body (indeed, the cult of the gym and the health club argues more for acute anxiety than untroubled acceptance). Hence, to the degree that such a conception of an intact and inviolate body exists at all, it is as an unrealizable, even a lost ideal. Consequently, and in acknowledgment of the psychic and social realities of our uneasy *fin-de-siècle*, contemporary artists' renderings of the body have been typically oriented to the fragment, itself suggestive of mutilation or implied violence (for example, the work of Robert Gober or Kiki Smith), to the informe (John Miller) or to the monstrous (Charles Ray, Cindy Sherman). Martínez Celaya's work would seem to operate frequently on the first two registers. Obviously, the disembodied arms and severed heads that feature both in Martínez Celaya's two- and three-dimensional work are fully in keeping with the metaphorics of trauma, dismemberment, disintegration, and corporeal alienation that characterize such a significant part of contemporary subjectivity and it's cultural Imaginary. The informe–initially theorized by the French dissident surrealist Georges Bataille in the 1930s, and recently elaborated in the work of Yve Alain Bois and Rosalind Krauss[6]–makes its appearance in the densely worked surfaces composed of tar, mixtures of dirt and detritus, and variously distressed surfaces composed of canvas, paper, cloth or wall coverings. Sculptures such as *The Border of Night*, 1997, a crudely, almost brutally modeled head, disgorges from its gaping wound a profusion of balled-up socks; the 'low' as it were, erupting from the putatively high–the seat of reason, an eminently 'Bataillian' conceit. In many of the paintings, the surface becomes itself a ground of violence or abjection, in tension with that aspect of Martínez Celaya's iconographic lexicon that represents more anodyne, poetic associations (flowers, petals, birds, delicate bird wings, etc). This counter-pointing of the lyrical with the crude, the lapidary with the brutally gestural, is itself an essentially postmodernist strategy. Just as the coexistence of 'high' and 'low' elements within a single work signal the breakdown of traditional hierarchies of representation, so too does the mingling of expressive gesture and mimetic depiction function to indicate the conventionality of all marking and representational systems.

Kitsch

Similarly, the deployment of such materials as painting surfaces as brocade and black velvet, which he uses extensively in his Drafts of a Landscape works, 2000, or the use of such pictorial clichés as roses, hearts, and birds signal what might be called the promiscuity of postmodern art-making and thus the tacit acknowledgment that the gravitas of high modernism belongs to another age. How then can flowers and birds, saints and petals, degraded materials like black velvet grounds or flocked faux brocade wallpaper be made to transmit to the viewer meanings that are intended to be neither ironic nor parodic? Such a task is analogous to Martínez Celaya's deployment of his virgin martyrs. In both cases it would seem that what is at stake is the effort to excavate affective meanings that have been obscured precisely in the historical incorporation of both into the banality and abjection of kitsch. As Peter Schjeldahl has recently observed, "There is a tradition in modern thought which links evil with so-called kitsch."[7] Presumably, he is referring here to that argument in modernist aesthetics, one most prominently associated with the critic Clement Greenberg, that conceives of kitsch as the evil twin of high or elite modern culture.[8] But, as Schjeldahl argues, kitsch may be thought of as "the mass-franchise variant of

6. See in this regard, Yve Alain Bois and Rosalind Krauss, *Formless: A User's Guide* (Cambridge: Zone Books, 1997).
7. Peter Schjeldahl, "The Blooming Beast," *The New Yorker*, July 3, 2000. "Notes on the Problem of Kitsch" in Gillo Dorfles, ed., *Kitsch: The World of Bad Taste* (New York: Universe books, 1969) 76.
8. The standard essay on this subject is Clement Greenberg, "Avant-Garde and Kitsch" in Greenberg, *Art and Culture* (Boston: Beacon Books, 1962).

'good taste' itself, which a wit of my acquaintance defines as the residue of somebody else's privilege. I fail to detect a moral emergency in anyone's reliance on second- or even eleventh-hand aesthetics."[9] More to the point here, however, is the way by which kitsch may operate as a vehicle of authentic feeling, despite its inauthenticity in aesthetic terms. In one of Martínez Celaya's most spectacular mixed media works that traffics with kitsch elements, *The House of Arms*, 1998, an arm and hand cast made of wax and titanium oxide reposes on a coffin-like cradle of white velvet and plaster (p. 61). Photographed upon a ground of yellow, pink and red rose petals, the ensemble is at one and the same time redolent of low-rent gift shop display, reliquary, and wax museum. Upon the top surface of the arm, a section from one of Martínez Celaya's poems (*Berlin)* is roughly incised, graffiti-like: It reads as follows:

> All the treasures in the windows,
> all the ghosts that wave at me from your balconies,
> smiling, all those great lovers
> forever embracing in your rooms,
> all the mothers heating water,
> all the boys smelling of soap, all the girls of talc.

Here too, Martínez Celaya risks the sentimentality associated with ersatz, and thus with kitsch, but the wager is that the evocation of loss and longing will trump the conventionality of the sentiment.

It is of course the case that there exists a strand within modern and contemporary art, one that stretches from Joseph Cornell to Mike Kelley to Jeff Koons (I mention only a few) in which kitsch objects or materials make up the work or constitute an important element within it. In this respect, it seems evident that Martínez Celaya's use of kitsch is much closer to Cornell's, whose work is also tinged with melancholy and nostalgia, than it is to the aggressive cynicism of Koons. Martínez Celaya's use of materials such as silk flowers (e.g. *Strawberry*, 1994, or *Watering Can*, 1994), flocked velvet (e.g., *Map*, 1998) or garishly colored pillows of synthetic fabric upon which to cushion, and indeed formally present his saint's heads, his graphic renderings of hearts (e.g., *Destiny*, 1996) are collectively perhaps to be understood as constituting a redemptive gesture. Such a gesture might be considered as an elevation of debased materials or iconography that is intended to be poignant rather than ironic. Such objects, images or stuffs are in fact somber testimonials to the humble desire for the 'beautiful' that is the utopian impulse that underwrites the consumption (if not the production) of the most degraded and desolate forms of mass-produced kitsch. While certain of Martínez Celaya's critics have tended to identify his use of kitsch materials or emblems with the Latino and Hispanic cultures in which he spent his youth, there are more interesting ways to think about this aspect of their construction. Kitsch is, after all, one of the dominant forms of most contemporary religious paraphernalia; bleeding hearts of Jesus, light bulb-crowned plastic madonnas and the like. As objects of devotion and reverence, the kitsch icon is infused nonetheless with authentic feeling–piety, hope, yearning, whatever, thus transcending its debased substance. In much the same way that Martínez Celaya seeks to appropriate his saints for poetic ends, so too does he work to reprocess or redeem his kitsch material. Which is to say that like the choice of saints themselves as nominal subjects, the works are fabricated as a type of votive and redemptive offering, and it is the material stuff of their making, as well as their discrete elements derived from categories of the base (soil), the aesthetically privileged (the rose) and the industrial (plastic resins, chemical dye) that function as a form of subtle restitution.

9. Schjeldahl, op. cit., 76.

Restitution

Etymologically, the word restitution derives from the Latin *restituere*, meaning an act of restoration or a condition of being restored. In the original Latin, the word is formed as a compound with the prefix re-, but whose root is the word *statuere*. As it happens, *statuere* (which is also the root for the word statue) means to set up, to station. Accordingly, while restitution in its contemporary usage generally has a legal or practical meaning, its linguistic history links it with one of the most ancient of cultural practices, that is, the setting-up of relics, fetishes, and statues as sacred propitiatory offerings, surrogates for what was earlier effected by means of human sacrifice.

In this archaic meaning, the statue, like the work of art in general, has roots not merely in the cult, but in the ritual sacrifice. In this sense, the most ancient of cultural/religious artifacts are rendered–set up–not for the living, but for the dead. These thus become themselves sacrificial offerings and eventually, they come to function as intercessors, as in the devotional cult of Christian saints:

> Tournées vers les morts, destinées aux morts, ces créations devaient leur être resituées: renvoyées à l'invisible, elles étaient en ce sens et littéralement "sacrifiées". Mais, en mettant en acte le sacrifice, elles s'imprégnaient de la puissance à laquelle on sacrifiait, puissance de vie et de mort. Et même lorsqu'elle était exposée, l'œuvre sacrée n'était pas destinée à être goûtée par les yeux des vivants, comme il est de mise dans la culture désormais muséiforme de notre modernité. Quand il leur arrivait de prendre place dans le monde du paraître, les artefacts inventés par les hommes continuaient à intercéder auprès des pouvoirs invisibles, pour transposer leurs vertus aux vivants. Telle était leur logique sacrée.[10]

There is much in Martínez Celaya's work that alludes to or even makes explicit reference to this atavistic function. Indeed, the epigraphic text that introduces New Works for Jeanne d'Arc evokes both the expiatory and restitutional dimension of the offering: "One dress and one dove / for her marriage of fire / and four blankets to prevent / her from burning." There are as well those works whose titles make unambiguous reference to religious ritual (e.g., *Sacrifice*, 1995; *Ascension*, 1998; etc.). Here too, however, it is on the level of the signifier that the meanings are generated and in this respect, it is significant that Martínez Celaya produced, in the period 1992 to 1995, a series of works in which the surfaces of paintings and drawings were torn, mutilated, violated in different ways only to be subsequently sutured or otherwise provisionally rejoined by means of grommets, stitches or pasting. It is as though the work was itself staged as the sacrificial object and, at a second moment in its formation, made itself the object of restitution. In one of the resin versions of St. Catherine's head, the neck bears a suggestion of the severed arteries and viscera, only this has been indicated by the excrescences formed by the roses inserted in the severed neck and petrified in the heat of the process that congeals the resin itself. In a more recent work, *Auto retrato con dibujos (23 de abril)/Self Portrait with Drawings(April 23)*, 2000, he uses an image of his own head, where the mutilation is covered with drawings from his childhood. There is, to be sure, a kind of self-conscious re-enactment of ritual here. For if, as Walter Benjamin famously observed, the ancient origins of art lay in cult and ritual, the condition of all subsequent art marks the passage from cult value to exhibition value.[11] Once we no longer kneel in front of the fresco or altarpiece, we cede the sacred, and indeed the sacrificial, and are inescapably lodged in the world of exchange value, of the commodity, of the work of art as commodity fetish. For artists like Martínez Celaya who wish to reinvest the art object with some vestiges of its 'magic,' and for whom traditional media such as painting and sculpture are

10. "Facing the dead, destined for them, these creations were supposed to be restored to them: cast into invisibility, they were in this sense, literally sacrificed. But, in acting out sacrifice, they endowed themselves with the power to which they were sacrificed. They acquired the power of life and death. And even when they were displayed, this sacred oeuvre was not destined for the enjoyment of the eyes of the living as is now the custom museumorphology of our modernity. When it so happened that they took place in the world of appearances, the artifacts invented by men continued to intercede on their behalf with the invisible powers in order to transpose their virtues to the living. Such was their sacred logic." Kristeva, "Le crâne: culte et art" in Kristeva, op. cit., 19.

11. Walter Benjamin, "The Work of Art in the Age of Mechanical Reproduction" in Benjamin, *Illuminations*, trans. Hannah Arendt (New York: Harcourt, Brace, Jovanovich, 1969).

still viable options, the task is to demonstrate convincingly that 'hand-made' art still retains a power outside and independent of that dense network of meanings already known, already read, already seen. Thus, if on the one hand, Martínez Celaya acknowledges the conventionality of representational codes and practices ('gestural' painting as indicative of the artist's subjectivity; symbolism that can be tied to the artist's biography, etc), on the other, he wants to suffuse the works with a melancholy and elegiac effect that will communicate itself to the viewer, a restitution of value and presence whose very impossibility suffuses the works with their characteristic melancholy.

Castration

"To decapitate = to castrate". And as Kristeva observes, "La peur de l'organe génital féminine est dans tous les cas si intense que les artistes préhistoriques conjurent son pouvoir en le remplaçant par le crâne ou le visage féminin..."[12] Obviously, Freud did not mean to suggest that the real decapitation of actual historical figures necessarily enacts this equivalence. Within the Freudian model, moreover, women are, for all intents and purposes, perceived as already castrated (although Lacan makes explicit Freud's implicit notion that all human subjects are to be understood as castrated). Rather, Freud takes as his example an antique mythic female monster with a lengthy history of visual representation (is it necessary to specify by male artists?) as an instance by which the fear of castration, instated–inescapably–in the process of subject formation, becomes at one and the same time a figuration of castration and its simultaneous denial. Figuration is thus the crucial term; the image of Medusa figures (and manages) the psychic threat posed by the female body. Hence, on the one hand, the severed head-figure of castration; on the other hand, the profusion of phallic snakes that crowns the Gorgon; hence too, the subsequent, apotropaic petrification of the head, cut from its body by Perseus's sword.

In its essentials, and in its dialectical structure, the myth of Medusa echoes and reprises the dynamics of fetishism. "Contre la peur de la mort," writes Kristeva, "l'épouvante de la castration est cependant érotisable, jouable." She continues:

> C'e n'est pas la survie entière du corps qui est menacée, dit le fantasme de castration, il s'agit seulement du pouvoir phallique: celui qui manque à la femme et qui peut être enlevé à l'homme, s'il est châtié par un père ou par une mère tout-puissante. Pourtant, contre le risque terrifiant de la castration, le sujet dispose désormais des ressources de son érotisme et de son langage qu'il n'avait pas au temps de son impotence infantile. Séduction et répresentation viennent à la rescousse de la peur de la mort et du deul, et la mélancholie catastrophique peut être combattue par les délices de la perversité sadomasochiste.[13]

Representation, as Kristeva argues, is therefore itself a way by which the subject wards off its psychic perils. A comparable work is performed by the fetish, whose binary structure of presence and absence, belief and disavowal, subtends the work of art, while it additionally underwrites its cultural valuation. Martínez Celaya's work alludes often to the metaphorics of castration via the substitutive mechanism of the fetish. In addition to the theme of decapitation so central in his production, work such as *The Tiger of Corners*, 1998, is in part composed of human hair, a substance conventionally associated with fetishism. Even more tellingly, there is the ubiquitous presence of disembodied arms and heads, amputation and decapitation, further bespeaking the artist's engagement with the theme. Images of impalation as in *Black*

12. "The fear of the feminine genital organ is in all cases so intense that prehistoric artists conjure its power by replacing it with a female skull or face." "Qui est Medusa?" in Kristeva, op. cit., 37.
13. "Against the fear of death, the horror of castration is, however, eroticizable, playable. It isn't the entire survival of the body which is threatened, as castration fantasy says, it's a question only of phallic power: what is missing in the woman and can be taken away from the man if he is punished by a father or by an all-powerful mother. However, against the terrifying risk of castration, the subject can, however, prevail upon the resources of his eroticism and upon the language he didn't have at the time of his infantile powerlessness. Seduction and representation come to the rescue of the fear of death and bereavement, and the catastrophic melancholy can be possibly combated by the pleasures of sadomaschochist perversity." Kristeva, "Decollations" in Kristeva, op. cit., 94.

Hummingbird, White Birch, 1999, depicting the bird's body pierced through by a sharpened birch twig; titles such as *The Size of a Wound*, 1998, works such as *The Account*, 1997, a red vaginal-like slit inscribed on a white rectangle on a field of red velvet all testify to the centrality of castration and fetishism as inseparably linked thematics. In this respect too, the presentation of the isolated sculptural head cushioned or pedestaled, stages the fetish as both memorial to a lost–if illusory–wholeness, and ultimately as a mournful and eminently fitting synonym for the identity of the art object as such.

That Martínez Celaya's is thus an art of melancholy, loss and nostalgia, is, as I have suggested, a condition rather than an effect of its production. His art's preoccupation with dismemberment, amputation, fragmentation, and decapitation bespeaks an acknowledgment of losses that are as much historical and cultural as they are psychical and subjective. The formal beauty of Martínez Celaya's surfaces, objects, images, be they roughly or finely wrought, be they connotatively violent or poetic, be they lapidary or heroic, collectively support Kristeva's diagnostics: "Seduction and representation come to the rescue of the fear of death and bereavement..." In this we may identify the ultimately compensatory function of the aesthetic.

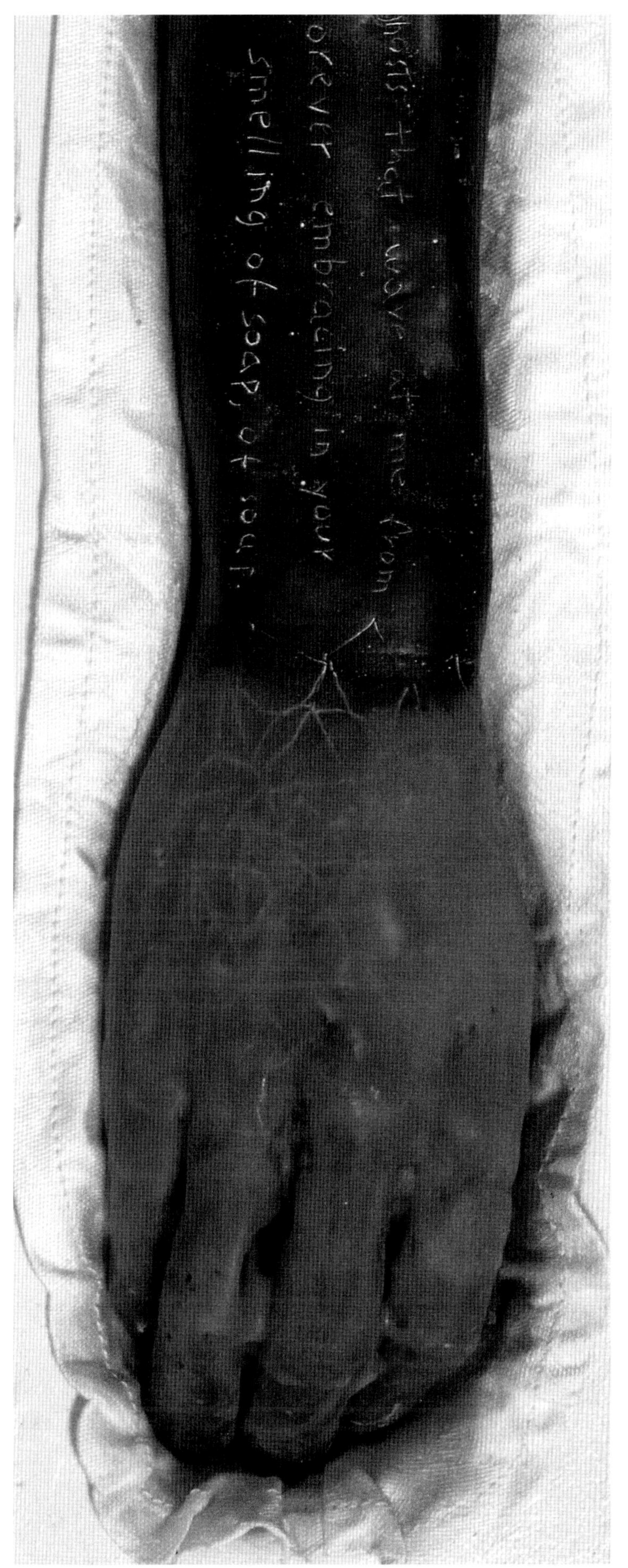

THE HOUSE OF ARMS, detail
/DAS HAUS DER ARME, Ausschnitt, 1998
Collection of Stephen Cohen, Los Angeles, California

FRAGMENTE EINER WIEDERHERSTELLUNG

Abigail Solomon-Godeau

> Sommes-nous fatalement de esclaves de l'image? Ce n'est pas sûr, répondent les philosophes, par métier incertains, l'image est potentiellement un espace de liberté: elle anéantit la contrainte de l'objet-modèle et lui substitue l'envol de pensée, le vagabondage de l'imagination. J'ajoute, et c'est mon parti pris, que l'image est peut-être le seul lien qui nous reste avec le sacré: avec l'épouvante que provoque le morte et le sacrifice, avec la sérénité qui découle du pacte d'identification entre sacrifié et sacrifiants, et avec la joie de la répresentation indissociable du sacrifice, sa seule traversée possible.[1]
>
> Julia Kristeva, *Visions Capitales*

gegenüberliegende Seite

QUIET NIGHT (DIRT)/STILLE NACHT (ERDE), 1999
Sammlung Ramis Barquet, New York, New York

Ein durchscheinender menschlicher Kopf, etwa lebensgroß und offenbar mit Blut an der Stelle, wo er abgetrennt ist, ruht auf einem reinen weißen Kissen wie eine seltsame Votivgabe. Er ruht auf einem schmucklosen eleganten Holzsockel, auf Hüfthöhe, so dass der Betrachter gezwungen ist auf ihn hinunterzuschauen. Der milchige Kunstharzabguss reflektiert das Licht, die Gesichtszüge wirken heiter, gefasst. Da Kopf und Gesicht eher auf die Gattung als auf eine bestimmte Person deuten, ist das Geschlecht nicht offensichtlich, aber der Titel macht es klar: *St. Catherine (Absolution)*/ *Die heilige Katharina (Absolution)*, 1997.

Was heißt es, in der zeitgenössischen Kunst eine religiöse Gestalt – insbesondere eine weibliche Heilige – in ikonographischem Sinne zu verwenden? Was soll man an der Schwelle zum 21. Jahrhundert von der Verwendung der heiligen Katharina als Bildgegenstand oder Motiv halten? Was könnte es für den Handel mit weiblichen Porträts bedeuten, die einst Devotionalien waren und sich nun weitgehend in religiösem Kitsch erschöpfen? Und was mag es für einen gebildeten, weltlichen und in seiner Profession ausgebildeten Künstler bedeuten, als eigene Heilige ausgerechnet eine zu wählen, die selbst der Vatikan mehr oder weniger fallen gelassen hat? (Der Festtag der heiligen Katharina wurde 1969 abgeschafft, was erhebliche Zweifel an ihrer historischen Existenz vermuten läßt.)

Aber Enrique Martínez Celayas Variationen zum Thema der enthaupteten Katharina von Alexandrien – Schutzpatronin der Gelehrten und Philosophen, aber auch der Wagner und Mechaniker –, die er 1997 in einer Werkgruppe vorstellte, sind ihrerseits bereits die Fortführung einer vorangegangenen Werkgruppe. In jener früheren Serie nahm Martínez Celaya Bezug auf eine andere Heilige – diesmal eine historisch verbürgte Gestalt – nämlich auf Jeanne d'Arc, die Jungfrau von Orléans. Auch sie war eine legendäre Heilige, die mystische Visionen hatte und einen gewaltsamen Märtyrertod starb. Da Jeanne d'Arc in ihren Visionen die heilige Katharina, zusammen mit dem heiligen Michael, erschien, mag Martínez Celayas Interesse für die zweite jungfräuliche Märtyrerin durch seine thematische Auseinandersetzung mit dem Martyrium der Jeanne d'Arc im Jahr 1996 bedingt sein. Keine der beiden Heiligen, ob apokryph oder real, scheint jedoch für einen Künstler wie Martínez Celaya eine naheliegende Wahl zu sein. Tatsächlich wurde Jeanne d'Arc in Frankreich von der nationalistischen, fremdenfeindlichen

1. „Sind wir unweigerlich Sklaven des Bildes? Das ist nicht sicher, antworten die von Berufs wegen nie sicheren Philosophen, das Bild ist potenziell ein Raum der Freiheit: Es löst die engen Schranken des gegenständlichen Modells auf und setzt an ihre Stelle den Gedankenflug, das freie Schweifen der Fantasie. Ich füge hinzu, und das ist meine feste Überzeugung, dass das Bild vielleicht die letzte uns verbleibende Verbindung zum Sakralen ist: mit dem ganzen Schrecken, den der Tod und das Opfer hervorrufen, mit der Heiterkeit, die aus dem Pakt der Identifikation zwischen Geopfertem und Opfernden fließt, und mit der Lust an der Repräsentation, die untrennbar mit dem Opfer verbunden, ja der einzig mögliche Weg seiner Durchführung ist." Julia Kristeva, *Visions capitales*, Ausstellungskatalog, Musée du Louvre, Paris 1998, S. 11 (alle Zitate aus diesem Buch wurden von der Übersetzerin des Essays aus dem Französischen übertragen).

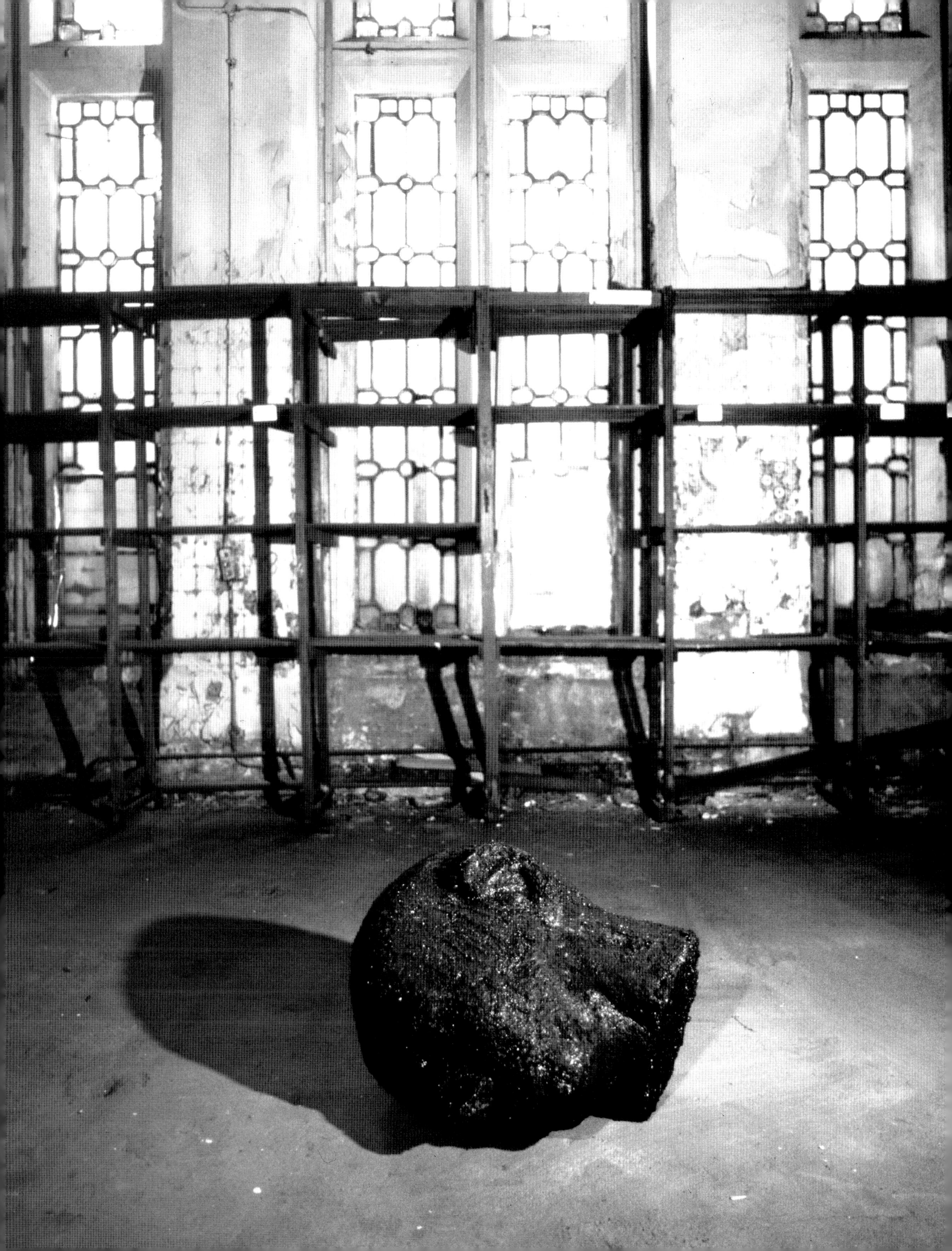

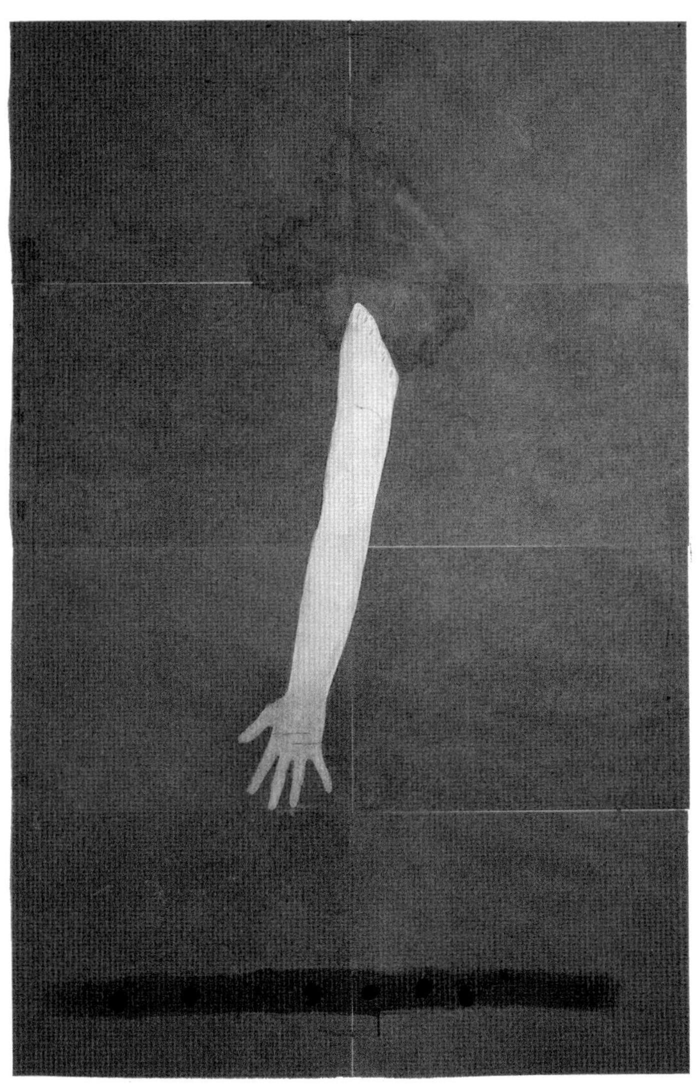

POWERS AND DOMINIONS
/MÄCHTE UND MACHTBEREICHE, 1997
Privatsammlung, Naples, Florida

politischen Rechten in Besitz genommen und dient dieser als reaktionäres Pendant zur republikanischen Marianne, der säkularen Gottheit der Französischen Revolution. Die heilige Katharina wacht laut Lexikon der katholischen Heiligen über die Jungfrauen im Kloster sowie die jungen Frauen überhaupt. Interessanterweise war einer der Gründe für Johannas Hinrichtung als Ketzerin ihr halsstarriges Bestehen auf ihrem direkten und unmittelbarem Kontakt zu Gott (im Widerspruch zur Notwendigkeit der Vermittlung und der Hierarchie der Kirche). Im (apokryphen) Fall war es die bestürzende geistige Überlegenheit, mit der Katharina ihre heidnischen Gesprächspartner widerlegte und (laut Legende) sogar die Gattin des Kaisers Maxentius bekehrte, die sie zu einer Bedrohung werden ließ. Ebendiese Qualitäten machten sie zur Schutzpatronin der Gelehrten, Rhetoriker und Philosophen. Aber aufgrund der Werke selbst scheint es Martínez Celaya in beiden Serien weniger um die biographischen Einzelheiten der Heiligenvita oder um die Legenden, die sich um sie ranken, zu gehen, sondern mehr um ökumenische, allgemeinere Begriffe von Opfer und Erlösung. Aber während die Arbeiten von 1996, die das Ensemble New Works for Jeanne d'Arc/Neue Arbeiten zu Jeanne d'Arc bildeten, den Gipsabguss eines intakten, auf dem Rücken liegenden weiblichen Körpers einschlossen, zeigen die Arbeiten der Werkreihe von 1998, Berlin, the Fragility of Nearness/Berlin: Die Zerbrechlichkeit der Nähe – mehr oder weniger abstrakt, mehr oder weniger figurativ, sowohl als Skulptur als auch in zweidimensionaler Form – immer nur Katharinas abgetrenntes Haupt. Selbst das Instrument ihres Martyriums, das nagelbewehrte Rad fehlt, das sie hätte umbringen sollen, aber auf wunderbare Weise zersprang und so zu ihrer Enthauptung führte. Wir bekommen nur dieses schwebende, körperlose Haupt zu sehen, ohne Haare, ohne Blut und fast ohne Gesichtszüge. Sozusagen ein Haupt ohne Eigenschaften.

Jedenfalls sollte es klar sein, dass die Verwendung von Gestalten aus der Geschichte des Christentums und seiner Hagiographie im Werk eines zeitgenössischen Künstlers wie Martínez Celaya nicht zum Nennwert genommen werden kann, selbst wenn Martínez Celaya, biographisch gesehen, aus einer katholischen kubanischen Familie stammt und auch in Spanien gelebt hat. Was immer man davon halten mag, ein zeitgenössischer Künstler, sei er gläubig oder nicht, kann heute gar nicht mehr dasselbe Verhältnis zur christlichen Ikonographie haben wie ein Bildkünstler der Vormoderne. Dagegen scheint es sehr viel plausibler, Martínez Celayas eigenartige Bildsprache auf einer allegorischen statt auf einer direkten Bezugsebene anzusiedeln. Darüber hinaus kann ein abgetrenntes Haupt auch kulturelle und psychoanalytische Bedeutungen haben, die überhaupt nichts mit dem Schicksal einer apokryphen Heiligen zu tun haben müssen. So hat das Bild des abgeschlagenen Kopfes, das in Martínez Celayas Werk seit 1995 immer wieder auftritt, mindestens noch einen weiteren ikonographisch-historischen Hintergrund, der im Surrealismus und im Begriff des Azephale, des kopflos geborenen Körpers, zu finden ist. Das will nicht etwa heißen, dass Martínez Celayas Bildsprache eine bewusste Hommage an den Surrealismus darstellt, sondern vielmehr, dass sein Vorgehen insgesamt – auch bei anderen wiederkehrenden Motiven in seinem Werk – eher synkretistisch als symbolisch ist. Bei Martínez Celaya ist es jedoch, anders als bei den Surrealisten, nicht der kopflose Körper, sondern immer wieder das abgetrennte Haupt, das beschworen wird. Das gilt für gemalte und graphische Werke wie *Soundless: Anywhere But In Between/ Tonlos: Überall, aber nicht dazwischen*, 1997, *The Secrets/Die Geheimnisse*, 1997, *Accumulation of Tiredness/Anhäufung der Müdigkeit*, 1998, wie auch für die modellierten oder gegossenen Arbeiten (etwa die verschiedenen Häupter von *St. Catherine (Artificer)/Die heilige Katharina (Schöpfer)*, 1997, *Quiet Night (Dirt)/Stille Nacht (Erde)*, 1999, u. a.). Die Implikationen sind dabei etwas anders als beim Azephale der Surrealisten. Für Letztere war es nicht nur emanzipatorisch, „den Kopf zu verlieren"; das Kopflose stand genauso für die Ablehnung des mörderischen, die Seele tötenden Rationalismus, Positivismus und Instrumentalismus der modernen Industriegesellschaft. Der Azephale war auch ein Gegenbild zur Vorstellung des zentrierten, sich seiner selbst bewussten und souveränen Subjekts und kam einer Feier des „Niederen", des Abscheulichen, des Irrationalen und des Unbewussten gleich. Während die Verwendung des isolierten Kopfes in gewissen Werken Martínez Celayas sofort an Enthauptung denken läßt (etwa der blutige Halsstumpf in *Soundless*) und auch die Bilder und Abgüsse auf Verstümmelung oder Amputation hindeuten, sind Haupt oder Glieder in anderen Werken stark schematisiert, wenn nicht gar abstrakt. In diesen Fällen (z. B. *A Boy in His Room/Ein Knabe in seinem Zimmer*, 1997, *Powers and Dominions/Mächte und Machtbereiche*, 1997) entsprechen die Darstellungen eher den Konventionen des Exvoto als der blutenden Reliquie oder einer naturgetreuen Abbildung eines bestimmten Körperteils. Angesichts der Bandbreite der ikonographischen Assoziationen und Vorläufer und ihrer klar zutage tretenden religiösen Bezüge, scheint es angebracht, Martínez Celayas Ikonographie eher vor dem Hintergrund einer postmodernen Appropriation oder Re-appropriation zu verstehen denn als rein subjektives und persönliches Lexikon. Aber anders als bei anderen Künstlern der Postmoderne haben wir es hier weder mit einer Kunst zu tun, die direkt zitiert, noch mit einer wiederherstellend „heilenden" Verwendung populärreligiöser Kultgegenstände wie etwa in den Altären von Amelia Mesa-Bains. Aber im gleichen Atemzug, in dem wir zugestehen, dass in Martínez Celayas hybridem Ensemble von Objekten, Bildern und Mixed-media-Assemblagen oft ein nominales Subjekt tonangebend ist – etwa das abgeschlagene Haupt der Katharina, der Kolibri, die Birke –, was wiederum eine Betrachtung der spezifischen Assoziationen zu jedem Motiv nach sich zieht, müssen wir auch den möglichen Bedeutungen von Martínez Celayas Formen und Materialien Beachtung schenken, denn diese sind ebenso zentral für die Bildbedeutung wie der Gegenstand selbst. Mit anderen Worten, wir müssen der Funktion des Zeichens ebenso viel Aufmerksamkeit schenken wie der Beschaffenheit des Bezeichneten. In dieser Hinsicht ist es wichtig, zu sehen, dass Martínez Celaya nicht einfach ein simpler „Maler" oder „Bildhauer" ist. Im Gegenteil, obwohl Martínez Celaya Bilder und Skulpturen hervorbringt, ist er eigentlich ein typischer Vertreter der so genannten Post-Atelier-Kunst, das heißt, er benutzt jeweils die Formensprache und das Material, welche seine Ideen gerade am besten zum Ausdruck bringen. Das können Skulpturen sein, Installationen, bemalte Objekte, Assemblagen oder Lyrik, aber genauso gut Materialien verschiedenster Art, von Rosenblättern über Teer zu industriell hergestellten Kunstharzen. In jüngster Zeit hat er eine Serie großformatige, auf mannigfaltige Weise bearbeitete Photographien gemacht, eine Technik, die als das postmoderne Medium schlechthin eingestuft wird.[2] Dieser neue Werkkorpus mit dem Titel

2. Vgl. dazu: Douglas Crimp, „Die fotografische Aktivität des Postmodernismus" in Crimp, *Über die Ruinen des Museums* (Dresden/Basel: Verlag der Kunst, 1996); Rosalind Krauss, „Die Originalität der Avantgarde" in *Die Originalität der Avantgarde und andere Mythen der Moderne* (Amsterdam/Dresden: Verlag der Kunst, 2000); Craig Owens, „The Allegorical Impulse: Toward a Theory of Postmodernism, Part 2" in Owens, *Beyond Recognition: Representation, Power and Culture* (Berkeley and Los Angeles: The University of California Press, 1992).

Elegias Series/Elegienserie, 2000/01, besteht aus sechs großformatigen, vielfältig bearbeiteten Photographien; in einigen Fällen wurde das Negativ mit Tusche handkoloriert, in einem anderen Fall umgibt eine vernähte Bandage den Kopf der Gestalt, in weiteren Arbeiten erscheint der Hintergrund wie ausgebleicht, in anderen wiederum ist das Bild selbst eingefärbt worden. Es ist dieser proteische und tatsächlich oft experimentelle Arbeitsprozess sowie die unerschöpfliche Vielfalt konzeptueller und formaler Untersuchungen, die seine Kunst komplex und immer wieder anders erscheinen lässt und oft jede Kategorisierung vereitelt.

Aber was hier von besonderem Interesse ist, gerade im Zusammenhang mit den Arbeiten, die unter dem Sammeltitel Berlin, the Fragility of Nearness/Berlin: Die Zerbrechlichkeit der Nähe, 1998, zusammengefasst sind, den Winter-Arbeiten auf Papier, 2000, oder in jüngster Zeit die Photoserien und der Gipsabguss einer stehenden Frau (*The River/ Der Fluss*, 1997), ist eine Art Oszillieren zwischen der Herstellung von Kunstwerken, die auf indexikalischer Ebene funktionieren – zum Beispiel die Werke, die aus dem Abguss eines lebenden Körpers entstehen, oder die Photoarbeiten –, und jenen anderen, meist graphischen Arbeiten, die auf ikonischer Ebene operieren, also Bilder, die nur einen konventionellen Bezug zum Bezeichneten haben. So erzeugen die modellierten Köpfe und Arme aus Kunstharz eine bestimmte Art der Wahrnehmung, die großformatigen Photographien eine andere, während das ikonische Werk – die großen Leinwände, auf denen die stark vereinfachten und oft geisterhaften Köpfe zu schweben scheinen, oder jene, auf denen der emblematische Kolibri vorkommt – wiederum eine ganz andere Reaktion hervorruft. Im ersten Fall ist das Objekt direkt mit dem Körperlichen verbunden und ruft eine beinahe körperlich spürbare Reaktion hervor; im letzten Fall ist die Wirkung weniger unvermittelt, nurmehr eine Anspielung, weil sie auf der Ebene des Bildes spielt.

Demnach sind die Formen, mit denen Martínez Celaya seine Untersuchungen verschiedenster Themen und Motive zum Ausdruck bringt, so wichtig wie die Bedeutungen, die die Motive selbst erzeugen. Und obwohl Martínez Celaya vielleicht ein sogenannter „literarischer" Künstler ist, einer, dessen Werk von einer persönlichen, ja autobiographischen und deshalb auch eigentümlichen Bildsprache geprägt ist, kommen in diesem Werk dennoch Themen zur Sprache, die über das rein Persönliche oder Subjektive hinausführen. Insbesondere die Erforschung der jüngsten Arbeiten scheint besonders interessant und ich möchte im Folgenden einige Aspekte von Martínez Celayas Arbeiten der letzten Jahre indirekt dahingehend untersuchen, wie und warum die vielseitige Produktion dieses Künstlers im Rahmen der geltenden Auffassung des Postmodernen begriffen werden kann. Es geht hier darum, wie selbst die ernsthaftesten und gründlichsten Versuche, eine Bildsprache des „authentischen" Ich zu entwickeln, durch das schiere Gewicht und die Fülle kultureller Bedeutungen, die mit jeder erkennbaren Ikonographie verbunden ist, ins Schlingern geraten, wenn nicht zum Untergang verurteilt sind. Wie das abgeschlagene Haupt, oder auch jeder Gegenstand und jede Geschichte in unseren Träumen, können Zeichen und Objekte gleichzeitig persönlich – an die Geschichte und Subjektivität einer Person gebunden – und konventionell, das heißt durch geschichtliche und kulturelle Bedeutungen vorgezeichnet sein. Es ist, wie ich vorschlagen möchte, die Spannung zwischen Martínez Celayas Verquickung von privaten Bedeutungen, Anspielungen und Symbolen mit dem bereits existierenden „Wald von Zeichen", der unser Bewusstsein und Unterbewusstsein formt und unweigerlich unsere Rezeption von Kunst bestimmt, die jenes charakteristische Gefühl von Melancholie, Verlust und Sehnsucht hervorruft, auf das Martínez Celayas Publikum so heftig reagiert.

Bis zu einem gewissen Grad ist diese melancholische Atmosphäre in der Kunst der Postmoderne allgegenwärtig, besonders in der Malerei. Viele Kritiker betrachten dies als ein Zeichen der „Unmöglichkeit" bzw. des Atavismus des malerischen Aktes, ja der traditionellen Ambitionen der Kunst in der neuen postmodernen Welt der Simulation und Simulakra, des Cyberspace, der globalen Konsumwelt und der Beherrschung des Bewusstseins durch den übermächtigen Götzen der Konsumgüterkultur.[3] Die melancholische Aura, die so vielen Werken Martínez Celayas zu eigen ist, muss in diesem Sinn als Bedingung ihrer Entstehung verstanden werden und nicht als Wirkung. Denn selbst wenn Martínez Celayas Werk sich dem Heiligen zuwendet, ist es dennoch an ein durch und durch weltliches Publikum und eine ebensolche Kultur gerichtet (die Kirchgänger bilden wohl eine verschwindende Minderheit innerhalb der Kunstszene); wo es die mit dem religiösen Opfer verwandten rituellen Ursprünge des Kunstobjekts zur Sprache bringt, spricht es dennoch zu einer Welt, deren Totems Konsumgüter sind; wo es sich darum bemüht, im Betrachter eine Ahnung des Transzendentalen oder Metaphysischen zu wecken, kann es dennoch nicht wiederbeleben, was unwiederbringlich verloren ist. Schon die Titel seiner Werke spielen auf diese Widersprüche und Aporien an – *The Acceptance of Longing/ Die Akzeptanz der Sehnsucht*, 1997, *The Undeniable and Unfortunate Truths/ Die unleugbaren und unglückseligen Wahrheiten*, 1998, *The End of Tragedy/ Das Ende des Tragödie*, 1998, um nur einige zu nennen. Ich möchte im Folgenden einige charakteristische Merkmale von Martínez Celayas Werk etwas näher betrachten, Merkmale, die seine Objekte und Bilder durchgehend auszeichnen, aber auch zu allgemeineren Themen und Strömungen der Gegenwartskunst in Beziehung stehen.

Der Körper in Stücken

„Kopfabschneiden = Kastrieren", schrieb Freud 1922 in seinem Essay „Das Medusenhaupt".[4] Angesichts der Häufigkeit, mit der der abgetrennte Kopf oder Arm in Martínez Celayas Werk auftaucht, und abgesehen von anderen möglichen Bedeutungen: Könnte dieses Motiv nicht auf eine spezifisch männliche Angst hinsichtlich körperlicher Unversehrtheit hinweisen? Könnte es nicht auch eine Beunruhigung in Bezug auf Rolle und Status des Künstlers andeuten, im Sinn dessen, was Roland Barthes in seinem berühmtem Text als „Tod des Autors" beschrieb? Im Allgemeinen (wenn auch mit wichtigen Ausnahmen) treten Figuren in Martínez Celayas Werk nur als Ganzes in Erscheinung, wenn es sich um Frauen handelt oder, in gewissen Ausnahmem, wenn der Körper des Künstlers selbst zum Thema wird (meist als Silhouette); auch in diesen Fällen bilden ganze Figuren eher die Ausnahme als die Regel. Charakteristischer ist da zum Beispiel das Bild *Pena(Sorrow)/ Pena(Schmerz)*, 1997–99, das ein blutendes amputiertes Handgelenk andeutet, ähnlich wie einige der anonymen Köpfe (etwa in *Soundless: Anywhere But In Between/ Tonlos: Überall, aber nicht dazwischen*, 1997) oder der Umriss eines Kopfes auf dem Ergänzungsbild zu *The Empty Garden/ Der leere Garten*, 1999, mit seinen blutähnlichen Farbströmen auf eine gewaltsame Enthauptung schließen lassen. Dass die rinnenden Linien und Tropfen, die von Kopf und Hand fließen, nicht die Farbe von Blut haben, sondern braun und schwarz sind – wie die gemalten Formen –, weist neben der Verstümmelung des Körpers darauf hin, dass das Bild selbst Schauplatz einer Verstümmelung ist: Malerei als Verletzung und Wunde. So betrachtet ist das Verhältnis zwischen Körper und Werk ein ehrwürdiges; es ist ein

3. Die Standardtexte zu dieser erkenntnistheoretischen Veränderung in Kultur und Bewusstsein sind Frederic Jamesons Essays „Postmodernism or the Cultural Logic of Postmodernism" in *The New Left Review* 146 (Juli/Aug. 1984) sowie „Postmodernism and Consumer Culture" in Hal Foster (Hrsg.), *The Anti-Aesthetic: Essays on Postmodernism* (Seattle: Bay Press, 1986). Eine Diskussion der melancholischen Züge postmoderner Kunst findet sich bei: Yve-Alain Bois, „Endgame" im gleichnamigen Ausstellungskatalog (Boston: ICA, 1984); Thomas Lawson, „Last Exit: Painting" in Brian Wallis, *Art After Modernism: Rethinking Representation* (Boston/New York: David Godine & The New Museum of Contemporary Art, 1986); Craig Owens, „The Allegorical Impulse, I–II" in Owens, *Beyond Recognition*, op. cit.

4. Sigmund Freud, „Das Medusenhaupt" in Freud, *Gesammelte Werke*, Bd. 17 (Frankfurt am Main: S. Fischer, 1960), S. 47.

Verhältnis, das in der Sprache zum Ausdruck kommt, wenn wir von einem Werkkörper oder -korpus sprechen. Diese Entsprechung zwischen Körper und Kunstwerk lässt an solche Vorgänger denken wie Joan Mirós biomorphe Bilder oder, in jüngerer Zeit, Fontanas aufgeschlitzte und durchbrochene Bildflächen, bei denen die Leinwand virtuell oder buchstäblich durchstochen, zerknittert oder aufgeschlitzt wird; die Leinwand als körperliche Membran von Öffnungen durchlöchert. Ähnlich könnte man auch Martínez Celayas *The Liar and the Thief/Der Lügner und der Dieb*, 1996, mit seinen Schnitten, Schlitzen und groben Stichen als „verletzte" Leinwand wahrnehmen. Eine solche Deutung verweist uns wiederum auf die Wirkungsweise des Zeichens – die materielle Beschaffenheit des Bildes selbst. Will heißen, wenn der (menschliche) Körper nicht länger als intaktes und vollkommenes Ganzes (wie in der klassischen Kunst) vorgestellt werden kann, so gilt vielleicht genauso, dass Malerei und Skulptur (die klassischen Medien schlechthin) ebenfalls als Schauplätze von Verlust, Verletzung und Zerfall betrachtet werden müssen. Diese Interpretation wird unterstützt, wenn man Freuds Kastrationsbegriff in Betracht zieht, vorausgesetzt man versteht ihn nicht ganz so strikt, sondern in einem erweiterten Sinn. So ließe sich die Kastration als Urbild des Verlustes auffassen. Und so gesellt sich zum unersetzlichen Verlust der klassischen Ideale der Harmonie, Ganzheit und Autonomie (ganz gleich, ob nur im Zusammenhang mit dem Körper als solchem oder im Kontext der Souveränität des Subjekts betrachtet) der Verlust der Autorität und Meisterschaft, welche der Künstler selbst einst verkörperte. Also stehen die Melancholie und Sehnsucht, auf die Martínez Celaya in seinen Interviews und Schriften immer wieder Bezug nimmt und die praktisch alle Kritiker in seinem Werk gesehen haben, in Verbindung mit dem Verlust der Meisterschaft, der die zeitgenössische männliche Subjektivität und einen großen Teil ihrer kulturellen Produktion prägt.[5] Jedenfalls ist es evident, dass unsere Epoche wenig Vertrauen in die Ganzheit, Unversehrtheit und Totalität des Körpers hat (tatsächlich spricht der Sportstudio- und Fitnesskult eher für akute Ängste als für eine unbekümmerte Akzeptanz des Körpers). Wenn also die Vorstellung eines intakten und unverletzten Körpers überhaupt noch vorhanden ist, so nur als unrealisierbares, ja verlorenes Ideal. Ganz folgerichtig und den psychischen und gesellschaftlichen Realitäten unseres unbehaglichen Fin-de-siècle-Lebensgefühls Rechnung tragend, orientieren sich auch die Darstellungen des Körpers in der zeitgenössischen Kunst am Fragment, das seinerseits Verstümmelung und versteckte Gewalt suggeriert (etwa im Werk von Robert Gober oder Kiki Smith), oder am Ungestalten (John Miller) oder Monströsen (Charles Ray, Cindy Sherman). Martínez Celayas Werk scheint häufig die ersten beiden Register zu ziehen. Offensichtlich halten die abgetrennten Arme und Köpfe, die in seinen zwei- und dreidimensionalen Werken gleichermaßen vertreten sind, jederzeit Schritt mit der Metaphorik des Traumas, der Verstümmelung, des Zerfalls und der körperlichen Entfremdung, die einen so bedeutenden Teil der zeitgenössischen Subjektivität und ihrer kulturellen Vorstellungswelt ausmacht. Das Formlose – ursprünglich vom französischen dissidenten Surrealisten Georges Bataille in den dreißiger Jahren theoretisch abgehandelt und kürzlich von Yve-Alain Bois und Rosalind Krauss erneut aufgegriffen[6] – tritt in den dicht gearbeiteten Bildflächen aus Teer, Schmutz- und Abfallmixturen in Erscheinung sowie in den auf verschiedenste Weisen strapazierten Flächen aus Leinwand, Papier, Textilien oder Wandverkleidungen. Etwa in Skulpturen wie *The Border of Night/Die Grenze der Nacht*, 1997, wo ein roh, beinahe brutal modellierter Kopf aus seiner klaffenden Wunde einen Schwall zusammengerollter Socken spuckt; sozusagen das „Niedere", das aus dem vermeintlich Hohen hervorbricht, dem Sitz der Vernunft – eine durch und durch

5. Vgl. dazu Craig Owens' Essay „Honor, Power and the Love of Women" in Owens, *Beyond Recognition*, op. cit.
6. Yve-Alain Bois und Rosalind Krauss, *Formless: A User's Guide* (Cambridge: Zone Books, 1997).

Bataillesche Anschauung. In vielen Bildern wird die Oberfläche selbst zum Nährboden der Gewalt oder des Abscheus und tritt in ein Spannungsverhältnis zu jenem Teil von Martínez Celayas ikonographischem Lexikon, der heilsamere, „poetischere" Assoziationen bereithält (Blumen, Blütenblätter, Vögel, fragile Vogelschwingen usw.). Diese Gegenüberstellung von Lyrischem und roher Gewalt, dem Lapidarem mit dem brutal-Gestischem ist an sich schon eine durch und durch postmoderne Strategie. Genauso wie das Nebeneinander von „hohen" und „niederen" Elementen in ein und demselben Werk das Zusammenbrechen der traditionellen Hierarchien der Repräsentation signalisiert, verweist auch die Vermischung von expressiver Geste und mimetischer Abbildung auf das Konventionelle aller Bezeichnungs- und Repräsentationssysteme.

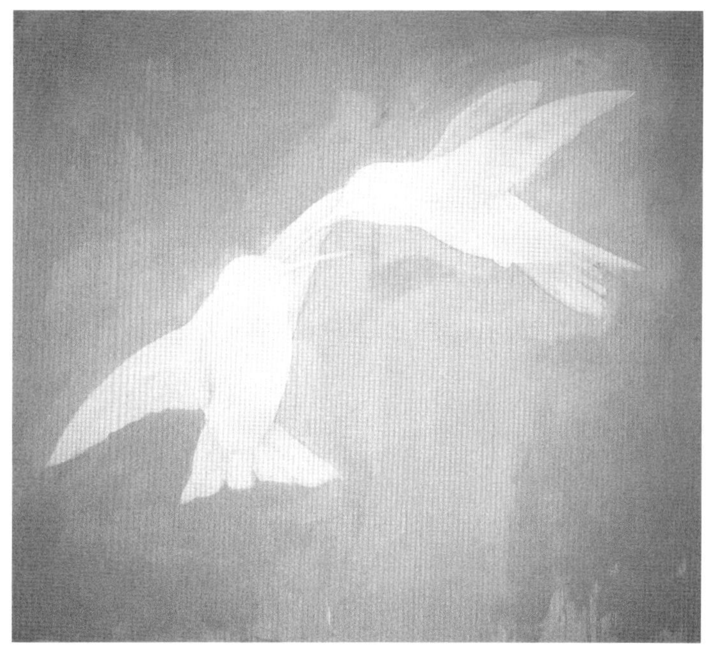

CIRCUMSTANCE/UMSTAND, 1997
Sammlung Marano Elena Bowes, London, Großbritannien

Kitsch

Auf ähnliche Art verweisen die Verwendung von Malgründen aus Brokat und schwarzem Samt, die der Künstler in seinen Drafts of a Landscape/Skizzen einer Landschaft ausgiebig einsetzt, und der Gebrauch so klischeehafter Motive wie Rosen, Herzen und Vögel auf etwas, was man als die Promiskuität postmodernen Kunstschaffens bezeichnen könnte. Dies kommt wiederum dem schweigenden Zugeständnis gleich, dass das Gravitätische der Klassischen Moderne einem anderen Zeitalter angehört. Wie können dann aber Blumen und Vögel, Heilige und Blütenblätter oder entwertete Materialien wie schwarzer Samt oder falsche Brokattapeten aus Velours dem Betrachter etwas vermitteln, was weder ironisch noch parodistisch gemeint ist? Hier stellt sich dasselbe Problem wie bei Martínez Celayas jungfräulichen Märtyrerinnen. In beiden Fällen könnte man denken, es gehe um einen Versuch, gefühlsbezogene Bedeutungen freizulegen, die gerade durch die historische Rolle der Motive in den Hintergrund und schließlich in die Banalität und Abscheulichkeit des Kitsches abgedrängt worden sind. Peter Schjeldahl bemerkte jüngst, es gebe im modernen Denken eine Tradition, die das Böse mit dem sogenannten Kitsch verbinde.[7] Vermutlich bezieht er sich dabei auf jenes Argument der modernistischen Ästhetik, welches man in erster Linie mit dem Kritiker Clement Greenberg verbindet und das den Kitsch als bösen Zwillingsbruder der hohen oder elitären Kultur der Moderne versteht.[8] Aber, so argumentiert Schjeldahl: Kitsch kann als „Massenprodukt-Variante des ‚guten Geschmacks' selbst aufgefasst werden, den wiederum ein geistreicher Bekannter von mir als Überrest des Privilegs von jemand anderem definiert. Ich kann keinen moralischen Notstand darin entdecken, dass jemand sich auf eine Ästhetik aus zweiter oder auch aus elfter Hand stützt."[9] An dieser Stelle geht es jedoch vielmehr darum, wie Kitsch trotz seiner ästhetischen Unglaubwürdigkeit als Vehikel authentischer Gefühle funktionieren kann. In einer von Martínez Celayas spektakulärsten Mixed-Media-Arbeiten, die mit Kitschelementen spielt, *The House of Arms/ Das Haus der Arme*, 1998, ruht der aus Wachs und Titanoxid hergestellte Abguss eines Arms und einer Hand auf einer sargähnlichen Wiege aus Samt und Gips. Auf einem mit gelben, rosa und roten Rosenblättern übersäten Boden photographiert, erinnert das Ganze ein bisschen an die Schaufensterdekoration eines billigen Geschenkladens, zugleich aber auch an einen Reliquienschrein und an ein Wachsfigurenkabinett. Auf der Oberseite des Arms sind

7. Peter Schjeldahl, „The Blooming Beast" in *The New Yorker*, July 3, 2000. „Notes on the Problem of Kitsch" in Gillo Dorfles (Hrsg.), *Kitsch: The World of Bad Taste* (New York: Universe books, 1969), S. 76.

8. Der 1939 erstmals publizierte Standardtext zu diesem Thema ist: Clement Greenberg, „Avantgarde und Kitsch" in Greenberg, *Die Essenz der Moderne: Ausgewählte Essays und Kritiken* (Amsterdam/Dresden: Verlag der Kunst, 1997).

9. Peter Schjeldahl, op. cit., S. 76. (Das Zitat wurde von der Übersetzerin des Essays ins Deutsche übertragen.)

SACRIFICE/OPFER, 1995
Privatsammlung, Virginia

einige Verse eines Gedichts (*Berlin*) von Martínez Celaya flüchtig wie ein Graffito eingeritzt. Sie lauten wie folgt:

> All die Schätze in den Fenstern,
> all die Geister, die mir von euren Balkonen zuwinken,
> lächelnd, all jene großen Liebenden,
> die sich auf ewig in euren Zimmern umarmen,
> all die Wasser kochenden Mütter,
> all die Jungen, die nach Seife, all die Mädchen, die nach Puder duften.

Auch hier setzt sich Martínez Celaya dem Risiko der Sentimentalität aus, die mit jedem Ersatzobjekt und so mit Kitsch verbunden ist, aber er spekuliert darauf, dass die Beschwörung von Verlust und Sehnsucht das konventionelle Gefühl überwiegen wird.

Natürlich gibt es einen Strang innerhalb der modernen und zeitgenössischen Kunst, der sich von Joseph Cornell über Mike Kelley bis zu Jeff Koons erstreckt (um nur einige zu nennen), in dem kitschige Gegenstände oder Materialien ein wesentliches Element des Werks, wenn nicht das Werk überhaupt ausmachen. In diesem Zusammenhang ist klar, dass Martínez Celayas Umgang mit Kitsch dem eines Cornell, dessen Werk ebenfalls von Melancholie und Nostalgie berührt ist, sehr viel näher steht als dem aggressiven Zynismus eines Jeff Koons. Martínez Celayas Verwendung von Materialien wie Seidenblumen (in: *Strawberry/Erdbeere*, *Watering Can/Gießkanne*, beide 1994), Velours (in: *Map/Landkarte*, 1998) oder synthetischen Kissen in schreienden Farben, auf die er seine Heiligenhäupter bettet und uns geradezu formell präsentiert, sowie seine graphische Wiedergabe von Herzen (in: *Destiny/Schicksal*, 1996) können insgesamt vielleicht als eine einzige Geste der Erlösung verstanden werden. Eine solche Geste könnte man als Erhöhung entwerteter Materialien oder einer entwerteten Ikonographie verstehen, die eine starke Bewegung auslösen soll und alles andere als ironisch gemeint ist. In der Tat sind diese Objekte, Bilder und Materialien traurige Zeugen einer primitiven Sehnsucht nach dem „Schönen", die als utopischer Impuls den Absatz (wenn nicht schon die Produktion) der niedrigsten und erbärmlichsten Formen des in Massen produzierten Kitsches garantiert. Manche Kritiker haben Martínez Celayas Verwendung von Kitschmaterialien und -symbolen direkt mit der lateinamerikanischen und spanischen Kultur seiner Jugend in Verbindung gebracht, aber es gibt vielversprechendere Herangehensweisen an diesen möglichen Aspekt ihres Ursprungs. Kitsch ist immerhin eine der vorherrschenden Erscheinungsformen eines Großteils des zeitgenössischen religiösen Brimboriums; das blutende Herz Jesu, Plastikmadonnen mit blinkenden Lichterkronen und Ähnliches. Als Objekt der Anbetung und Verehrung ist die Kitsch-Ikone dennoch von authentischem Gefühl umgeben – Frömmigkeit, Hoffnung, Sehnsucht, was auch immer transzendiert ihre erniedrigte Grundsubstanz. Auf ähnliche Weise versucht auch Martínez Celaya, sich seine Heiligen für poetische Zwecke anzueignen, und arbeitet ebenfalls daran, seinen kitschigen Stoff neu hervorzubringen und zu erlösen. Also sind die Werke – entsprechend der Wahl von Heiligen als Protagonisten – als eine Art Votiv- oder Bußgabe gefertigt und es ist der materielle Stoff, aus dem sie gemacht sind, aber auch die verschiedenen Elemente, aus denen sie sich zusammensetzen und die den Kategorien des Niederen (Erde), des ästhetisch Ausgezeichneten (die Rose) und des Industriellen (Kunstharze, chemische Farben) entstammen, die zusammen eine Art subtile Wiederherstellung leisten.

Wiederherstellung

Etymologisch stammt das Wort Restitution vom lateinischen Wort restituere ab und bezeichnet einen Akt oder Zustand der Wiederherstellung. Im Lateinischen handelt es sich um ein zusammengesetztes Wort mit der Vorsilbe re-, dessen Stamm das Wort statuere bildet. Nun heißt statuere (das auch den Stamm des Wortes Statue bildet) aufstellen, hinstellen. Während Restitution im zeitgenössischen Sprachgebrauch oft eine rechtliche oder praktische Bedeutung hat, ist es sprachgeschichtlich mit einer der ältesten kulturellen Tätigkeiten verknüpft, nämlich mit dem Aufstellen von Reliquien, Fetischen und Statuen als heiligen Weihegaben, einer Ersatzhandlung für das ursprüngliche Menschenopfer.

In diesem archaischen Sinn liegen die Wurzeln der Statue wie des Kunstwerks überhaupt nicht nur im religiösen Kult, sondern im Opferritual. So gesehen werden die ältesten kulturellen und religiösen Kunstgegenstände nicht für die Lebenden, sondern für die Toten angefertigt und aufgestellt. Diese werden also selbst zu Opfergaben und schließlich übernehmen sie die Rolle von Vermittlern wie im Devotionalienkult der christlichen Heiligenverehrung

> Tournées vers les morts, destinées aux morts, ces créations devaient leur être restituées: renvoyées à l'invisible, elles étaient en ce sens et littéralement „sacrifiées". Mais, en mettant en acte le sacrifice, elles s'imprégnaient de la puissance à laquelle on sacrifiait, puissance de vie et de mort. Et même lorsqu'elle était exposée, l'œuvre sacrée n'était pas destinée à être goûtée par les yeux des vivants, comme il est de mise dans la culture désormais muséiforme de notre modernité. Quand il leur arrivait de prendre place dans le monde du paraître, les artefacts inventés par les hommes continuaient à intercéder auprès des pouvoirs invisibles, pour transposer leurs vertus aux vivants. Telle était leur logique sacrée.[10]

Vieles in Martínez Celayas Werk spielt auf diese atavistische Funktion an oder weist sogar ausdrücklich darauf hin. Tatsächlich beschwören die einleitenden Zeilen zu Neue Arbeiten zu Jeanne d'Arc sowohl den Buß- wie auch den Wiederherstellungsaspekt der Opferhandlung: „One dress and one dove / for her marriage of fire / and four blankets to prevent / her from burning." (Ein Kleid und eine Taube / für ihre Feuerhochzeit / und vier Leintücher / damit sie nicht verbrennt.) Dann gibt es auch noch jene Werke, deren Titel unzweideutig auf religiöse Rituale Bezug nehmen wie *Sacrifice/Opfer*, 1995, *Ascension/Himmelfahrt*, 1998, u. a. m. Aber auch hier entstehen die Bedeutungen auf der Ebene des Zeichens und es dürfte in diesem Zusammenhang von Bedeutung sein, dass Martínez Celaya zwischen 1992 und 1995 eine Reihe von Werken geschaffen hat, bei denen die Bildfläche der Gemälde und Zeichnungen zerrissen, verstümmelt und auf unterschiedlichste Weisen verletzt wurde, um daraufhin wieder vernäht oder provisorisch mit Drahtschlingen, Stichen oder durch Kleben zusammengeflickt zu werden. Es ist, als würde hier das Werk selbst in der Rolle des zu opfernden Objekts präsentiert und würde zu einem zweiten Zeitpunkt seiner Formwerdung selbst zum Gegenstand der Wiederherstellung. In einer der Kunstharzversionen des Hauptes der heiligen Katharina sind am Hals die durchtrennten Venen und Arterien angedeutet, allerdings geschieht dies nur durch die Verdickungen, die sich um die in den abgetrennten Hals gesteckten Rosen gebildet hatten und durch den Erstarrungsprozess des Harzes ebenfalls verewigt wurden. In einem neueren Werk, *Auto retrato con dibujos (23 de abril)/Selbstporträt mit Zeichnungen (23. April)*, 2000, verwendet Martínez Celaya ein Bild seines eigenen Kopfes, bei dem eine Schnittwunde von Zeichnungen aus seiner Kindheit bedeckt ist. Mit Sicherheit handelt es sich dabei um eine Art bewusste Reinszenierung eines Rituals. Denn wenn, wie Walter Benjamin in seinem berühmten

10. „Den Toten zugewandt, für die Toten bestimmt, sollten diese Gebilde ihnen zurückgegeben werden: zurückgeschickt ins Unsichtbare wurden sie in diesem Sinn buchstäblich ‚geopfert'. Aber indem sie den Akt des Opfers durchliefen, wurden sie von der Macht erfüllt, der man opferte, einer Macht über Leben und Tod. Und selbst wenn es ausgestellt wurde, war das sakrale Kunstwerk nicht zur Augenweide der Lebenden bestimmt, wie das in der nunmehr museumsgerechten Kultur der Moderne der Fall ist. Wenn es geschah, dass sie einen Platz in der Welt des Sichtbaren einnahmen, so fuhren diese von Menschen geschaffenen Werke fort, bei den unsichtbaren Mächten zu plädieren, damit sie den Lebenden ihre Tugenden verliehen. Das entsprach ihrer heiligen Logik." Julia Kristeva, „Le crâne: culte et art" in Kristeva, op. cit., S. 19.

Aufsatz bemerkte, die künstlerische Produktion mit Gebilden begann, die im Dienste von Kult und Ritual standen, so zeichnet sich die spätere Kunst dadurch aus, dass sie den Kultwert allmählich zugunsten des Ausstellungswerts zurückdrängt.[11] Eines Tages knien wir nicht mehr vor dem Fresko oder Altarbild, wir geben das Heilige auf und auch die Opferhaltung und sitzen unentrinnbar fest in der Welt der Tauschwerte, der Konsumgüter und des Kunstwerks als Konsumfetisch. Für Künstler wie Martínez Celaya, die dem Kunstobjekt wieder eine Spur seiner ursprünglichen Magie zurückgeben wollen und für die traditionelle Medien wie Malerei und Skulptur nach wie vor einen gangbaren Weg darstellen, liegt die Herausforderung darin, überzeugend darzulegen, dass der „handgefertigten" Kunst jenseits des dichten Netzes alles längst Bekannten, längst Gelesenen und längst Gewussten immer noch eine unabhängige Kraft zu eigen ist. Wenn Martínez Celaya also einerseits den konventionellen Codes und Praktiken der Repräsentation Rechnung trägt („gestische" Malerei als Hinweis auf die Subjektivität des Künstlers; Symbolismus, der an der Biographie des Künstlers festgemacht werden kann usw.), so versucht er auf der anderen Seite, seine Werke mit einer Melancholie und einer elegischen Wirkung auszustatten, die sich dem Betrachter mitteilt und eine Wiederherstellung von Wert und Präsenz darstellt, deren schiere Unmöglichkeit den Werken ihre charakteristische Melancholie verleiht.

Kastration

„Kopfabschneiden = Kastrieren". Und wie Kristeva bemerkt: „La peur de l'organe génital féminine est dans tous les cas si intense que les artistes préhistorique conjurent son pouvoir en le remplaçant par le crâne ou le visage féminin ..."[12] Natürlich wollte Freud nicht sagen, dass diese Gleichung auf die tatsächliche Enthauptung historischer Gestalten zutrifft. Zudem gelten Frauen im Freudianischen Modell ohnehin schon immer als kastriert. (Lacan verweist allerdings auf den bei Freud implizit enthaltenen Gedanken, dass alle menschlichen Subjekte als kastriert gelten müssen.) Freud wählt als Beispiel jedoch den antiken Mythos eines weiblichen Ungeheuers, das bereits eine längere Geschichte der visuellen Darstellung durchlaufen hat (ist es notwendig auszuführen, dass es sich um die Darstellung durch männliche Künstler handelt?) als Beispiel, in welchem die Kastrationsangst, die – unausweichlich – zum Prozess der Subjektwerdung gehört, in ein und demselben Moment zur Figur der Kastration und ihrer gleichzeitigen Verleugnung wird. Figuration ist der entscheidende Begriff; das Bild der Medusa verkörpert die psychische Bedrohung, die der weibliche Körper darstellt (und hält sie zugleich in Schach). Deshalb einerseits der abgehauene Kopf, Figur der Kastration, und andererseits das Gewühl der phallischen Schlangen, die das Gorgonenhaupt krönen; daher auch folgerichtig die apotropäische Versteinerung des Hauptes, das durch Perseus' Schwert vom Rumpf getrennt wurde. In den wesentlichen Bestandteilen und der dialektischen Struktur des Mythos der Medusa scheint die Dynamik des Fetischismus auf. „Contre la peur de la mort", schreibt Kristeva, „l'épouvante de la castration est cependant érotisable, jouable." Und sie fährt fort:

> Ce n'est pas la survie entière du corps qui est menacée, dit le fantasme de castration, il s'agit seulement du pouvoir phallique: celui qui manque à la femme et qui peut être enlevé à l'homme, s'il est châtié par un père ou par une mère toute-puissante. Pourtant, contre le risque terrifiant de la castration, le sujet dispose désormais des ressources de son érotisme et de son langage qu'il n'avait pas au temps de son impotence infantile. Séduction et représentation viennent à la rescousse de la peur de la mort et du deuil, et la mélancholie catastrophique peut être combattue par les délices de la perversité sadomasochiste.[13]

11. Walter Benjamin, „Das Kunstwerk im Zeitalter seiner technischen Reproduzierbarkeit" in Benjamin, *Illuminationen* (Frankfurt am Main: Suhrkamp, 1961).
12. „Die Angst vor dem weiblichen Geschlechtsorgan sitzt in jedem Fall so tief, dass die prähistorischen Künstler seine Kraft zu bannen suchten, indem sie den weiblichen Schädel oder das weibliche Gesicht an seine Stelle setzten ..." Julia Kristeva, „Qui est Méduse?" in Kristeva, op. cit., S. 37.
13. „Im Vergleich zur Todesangst ist der Schrecken der Kastration immerhin erotisierbar, man kann damit spielen. Nicht das Überleben des ganzen Körpers ist bedroht, sagt die Kastrationsphantasie, es geht nur um die Macht des Phallus: eine Macht, die der Frau fehlt und die dem Mann genommen werden kann, wenn er von einem Vater oder einer allmächtigen Mutter gezüchtigt wird. Aber gegen die schreckliche Gefahr der Kastration verfügt das Subjekt mittlerweile über erotische und sprachliche Hilfsmittel, die ihm zur Zeit seiner kindlichen Impotenz nicht zur Verfügung standen. Verführung und Repräsentation erretten uns aus Todesangst und Trauer und die verheerende Melancholie kann mit den süßen Verlockungen der sadomasochistischen Perversion bekämpft werden." Julia Kristeva, „Décollations" in *Kristeva*, op. cit., S. 94.

Repräsentation an sich ist also laut Kristeva ein Mittel, mit dem das Subjekt psychische Bedrohungen abwehrt. Ähnliches leistet der Fetisch, dessen dualistische Struktur von Gegenwart und Abwesenheit, Glauben und Abschwören dem Kunstwerk Spannung verleiht, während sie zusätzlich seine kulturelle Wertschätzung garantiert. Martínez Celayas Werk spielt oft mit der Kastrationsmetaphorik mittels der Ersatzfunktion des Fetisch. Zusätzlich zu dem in seinem Schaffen so zentralen Thema der Enthauptung finden wir in einem Werk wie *The Tiger of Corners/Der Tiger der Ecken*, 1998, die Verwendung von menschlichem Haar, ein Material, das gewöhnlich mit Fetischismus in Verbindung gebracht wird. Verräterischer noch ist die Allgegenwart abgetrennter Arme und Köpfe, von Amputation und Enthauptung, die aufzeigt, wie besessen der Künstler von diesem Thema ist. Bilder von Pfählungen wie in *Black Hummingbird, White Birch/Schwarzer Kolibri, weiße Birke*, 1999, wo der Vogelkörper von einem zugespitzten Birkenzweig durchbohrt wird, Titel wie *The Size of a Wound/Die Größe einer Wunde*, 1998, oder Werke wie *The Account/Der Bericht*, 1997, ein roter, vagina-ähnlicher Schlitz in einem weißen Rechteck auf einer Fläche aus rotem Samt: Sie alle zeugen von der zentralen Bedeutung von Kastration und Fetischismus als untrennbar verbundenen Themen. Und so inszeniert auch die Präsentation des einsamen, modellierten Hauptes auf einem Kissen oder Sockel den Fetisch als Erinnerung an eine verlorene – wenn auch illusorische – Ganzheit und zugleich abschließend als ein trauriges und ausgesprochen passendes Synonym für die Identität des Kunstobjektes an sich.

Wie ich bereits sagte, ist die Tatsache, dass Martínez Celayas Kunst eine Kunst der Melancholie, des Verlusts und der Sehnsucht ist, eher eine Bedingung ihrer Produktion als eine ihrer Wirkungen. Die intensive Beschäftigung des Künstlers mit Verstümmelung, Amputation, Fragmentation und Enthauptung bezeugt die Anerkennung von Verlusten, die ebenso historischer und kultureller wie psychischer und subjektiver Art sind. Die formale Schönheit von Martínez Celayas Oberflächen, Objekten und Bildern, seien sie grob oder fein gewirkt, gewaltsam oder poetisch, schlicht oder heroisch, spricht insgesamt für Kristevas Diagnose: „Verführung und Repräsentation erretten uns aus Todesangst und Trauer ...“. Darin mögen wir die letztlich kompensatorische Funktion des Ästhetischen erkennen.

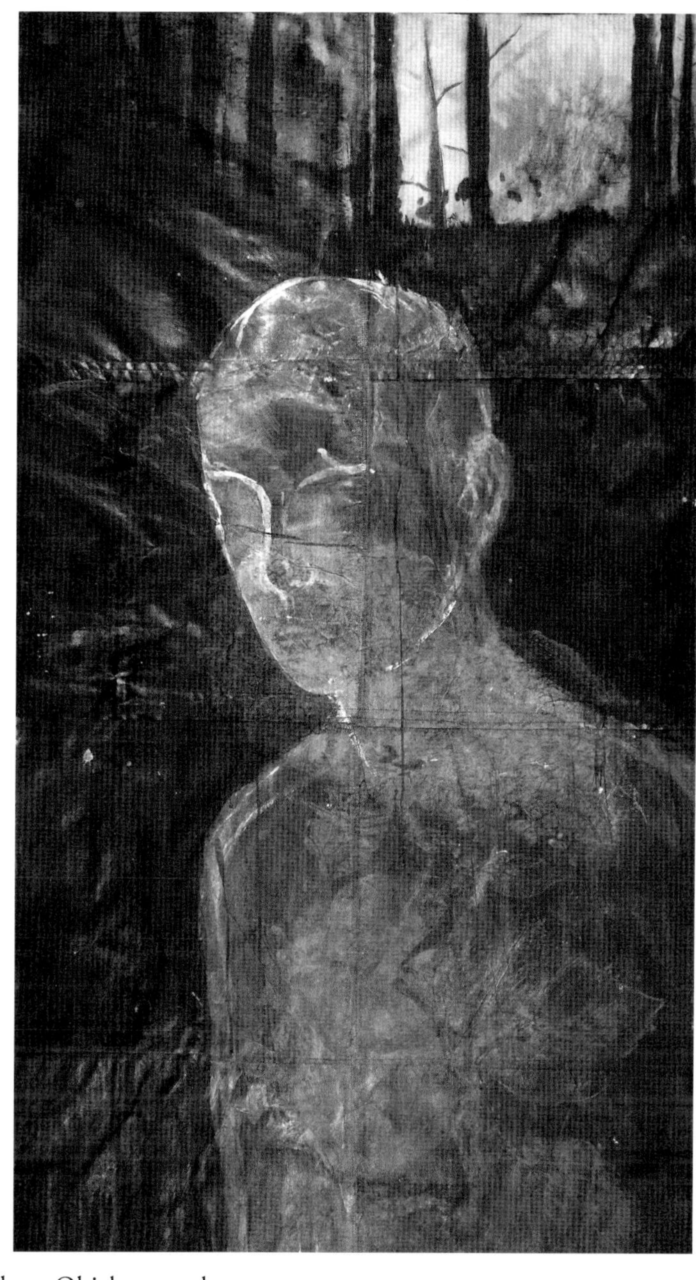

A VOICE TO SPEAK/EINE STIMME ZUM SPRECHEN, 2000
Microsoft Corporation, Seattle, Washington

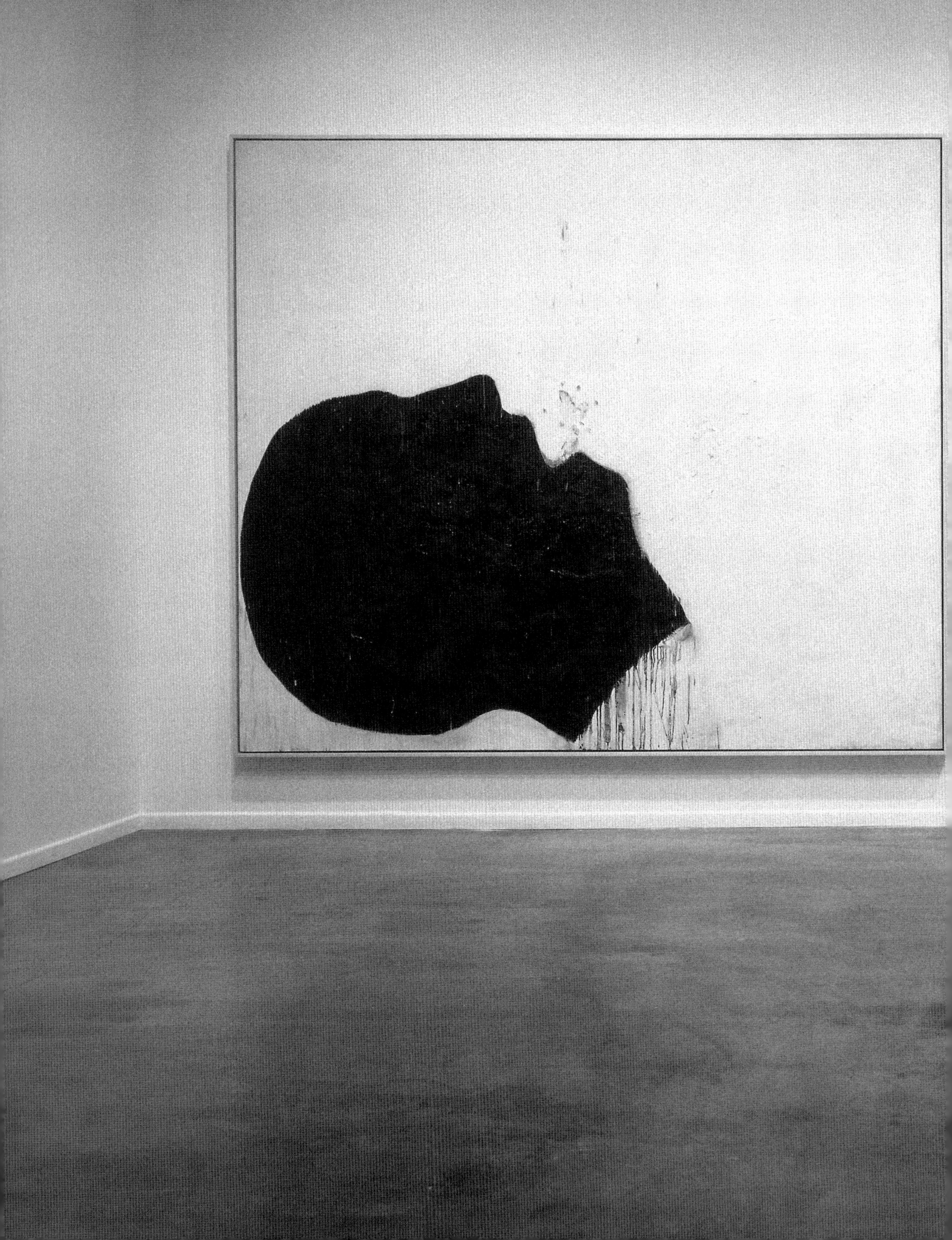

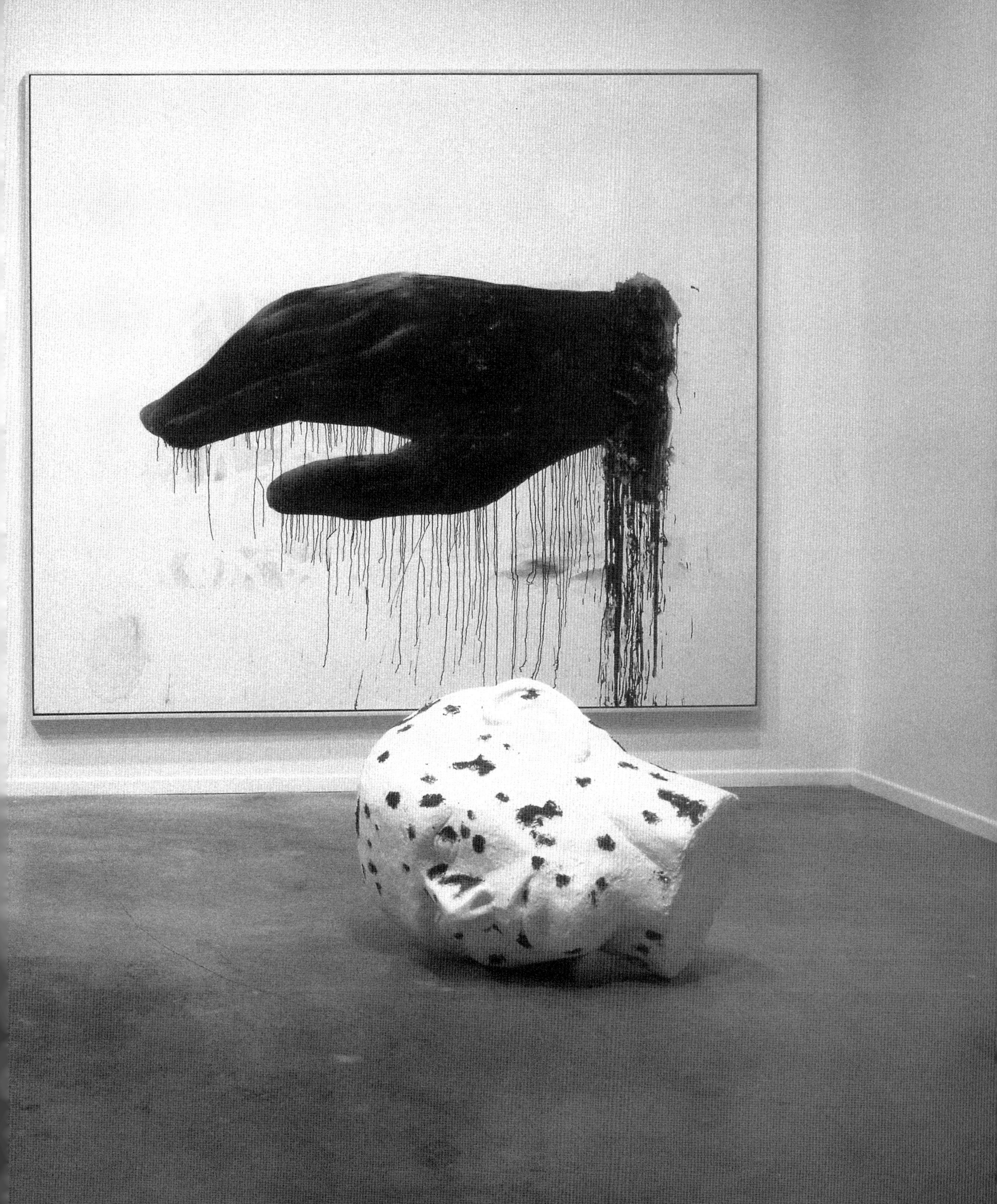

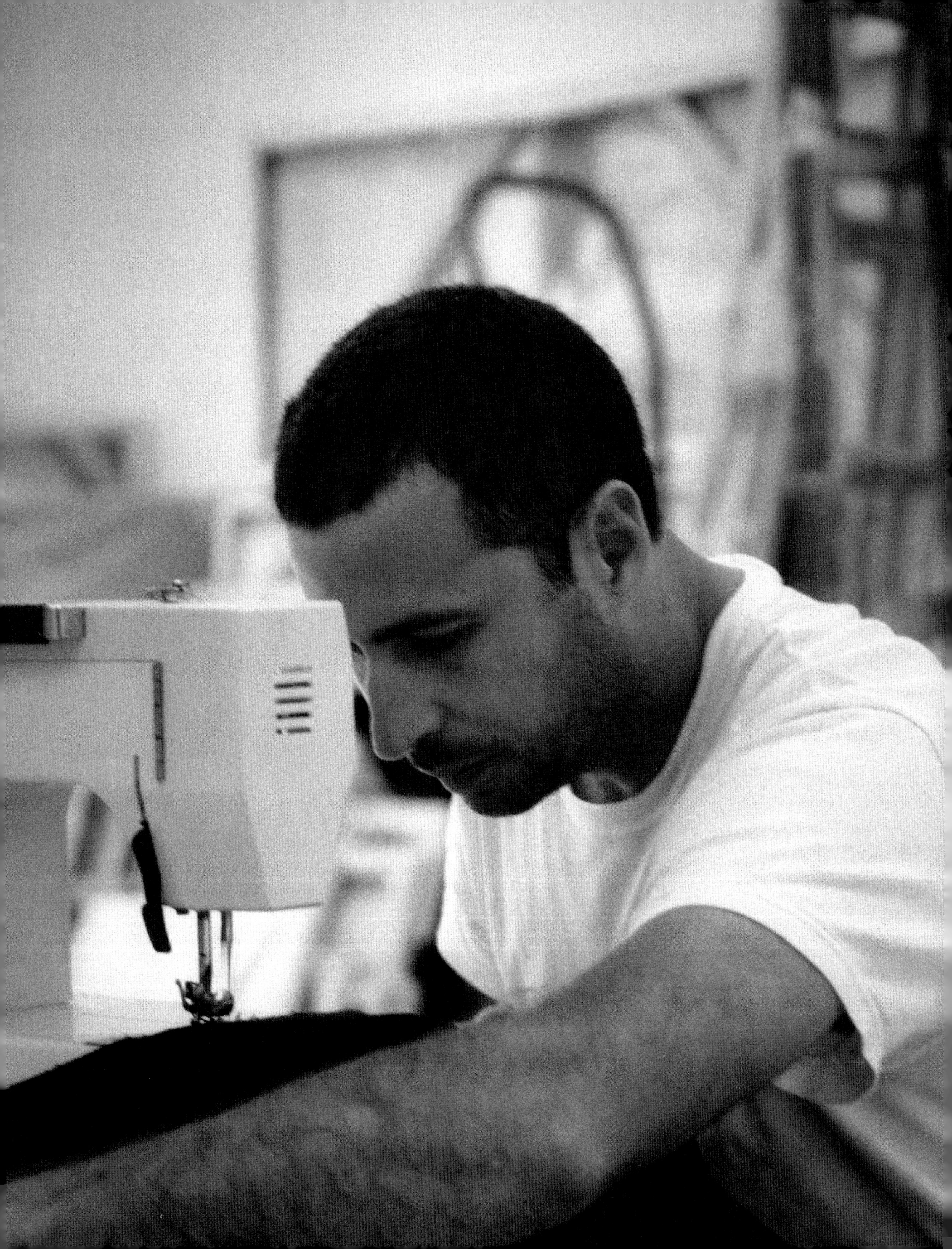

INTERVIEW WITH ENRIQUE MARTINEZ CELAYA†

Howard N. Fox

Howard Fox: This evening we are privileged to be in the company of truly an exceptional artist. Based here in Los Angeles, Enrique Martínez Celaya has produced a body of work that has commanded a great deal of respect internationally among critics and collectors alike. Last year LACMA elected to represent Martínez Celaya in the permanent collection with a remarkable painting, *Acceptance of Longing*, 1997–a poetically evocative work steeped in Surrealism, high Romanticism, and Modern painterly abstraction; a large painting that features the image of a dead hummingbird. Doubtless you've all seen it on exhibition at the museum, where it has a powerful presence in the galleries.

And yet, for all its visceral presence, that painting, with its palette of glinting whites and cool grays, feels very elusive, sliding in and out of our visual and mental perceptions. And that, I feel, is very typical of Enrique's distinctive, exquisite aesthetics of shifting and eliding–what could be called a 'quantum' aesthetics. I'll try to explain: Enrique Martínez Celaya's art is not only about ambiguity and mystery, although it certainly is steeped in those qualities; but it is also about simultaneity and duality, as his art mediates between art and philosophy, between visible and invisible truths. His paintings seem, like a quantum particle, to have the uncanny and incomprehensible nature of existing in two places and in different states simultaneously. As you look at Enrique Martínez Celaya's latest works surrounding us here tonight, I think you'll agree that they suggest something stridently present and palpable yet equally mysterious, even sublime. And maybe the analogy to quantum physics is not so far fetched.

Enrique Martínez Celaya was born in Cuba, studied in Europe and the United States, and made his way here to Los Angeles. Enrique, tell us a little bit about your biography, your migration here, and also your scholastic background. I know that you did not study originally to be a painter, but that you graduated with a degree in science.

Enrique Martínez Celaya: As a child, I was an apprentice for a painter who did mostly landscapes and portraits. But in high school, my attraction to physics and mathematics made science a more desirable pursuit as a career. I went to Cornell to study physics; specifically, quantum physics, and then did research at Brookhaven before going to graduate school. I always painted, but in my second year of graduate studies, I realized that I wanted to be an artist. So, for a while, I was pursuing two graduate degrees at the same time.

HF: Let's explore that just a little bit. How did you make this radical decision? What were you doing in your studio at the same time that you were doing physics research and writing your papers and everything? How did you reconcile this departure? Or, perhaps in your mind, it was not such a departure from what you were already doing?

facing page

THE ARTIST IN HIS STUDIO
/DER KÜNSTLER IN SEINEM ATELIER, 2000
Venice, California

† This text is transcribed and edited from a program at Griffin Contemporary Exhibitions, Venice, California, on December 14, 1999, for members of the Modern and Contemporary Art Council of the Los Angeles County Museum of Art.

EMC: At the time, I was working in an area of research that requires the same kind of extrapolations and leaps of faith that you may associate with the arts. I never thought of the duality of my graduate studies as strange; I never saw it as a duality at all. The real problem came from hearing too many opinions about what I should do...so I left the art and physics programs at UC Berkeley. I lived in Oakland, working on my own and selling my work in the parks of San Francisco with the Artists' Guild.

HF: I have a sense that 'science'–in the ancient sense of knowledge and human understanding, and the attempt to discern truth–in some way relates to your work. I was reading an article by a mathematician who was speculating on whether mathematics is an invention of man or whether it exists in nature, independent of humankind. In other words, a kind of ideal order, or natural law, if you will–very abstract concepts that seem to intercept physical reality. Does this, in any way, inflect or inform your art?

EMC: Nature is a building with an invisible exterior and we live on the inside. Science and mathematics are a scaffolding that facilitates investigations on the structure as well as one of the best things we have to make any inferences about its shape. The scaffolding is made by us but as it becomes finer and more flexible it resembles the building which is not constructed by us. It could become difficult to distinguish between what reveals the building and what inherently *is* the building. These questions profoundly affect my work and they are very relevant in contemporary art.

HF: So much of contemporary art often looks theoretical, as if it were an exercise in an idea about art that is carried out almost as a clinical pursuit, not unlike a scientific inquiry in a laboratory. Many artists position themselves to respond to something that other artists have said before to advance to the next phase in a critical dialectic. But this is not the kind of 'science' I'm describing in your work. For you there seems to be more of a search for some intuitively discerned higher or deeper truth that's not about some current discourse in the art world. So much contemporary art that is formulated as a specific response to critical discourse seems hermetic. And I think that to many viewers such art appears, rightly or wrongly, to have very little to do with the world at large or what they experience in their own lives.

EMC: Many people involved in contemporary art think that the construct of culture is not only the means, but also the end. Most scientists, on the other hand, think that the tools of science are a construct but the end is not.

HF: I think that your work mediates those realms–the very worldly and whatever is not worldly. Let's talk about some of your paintings. These pieces (*The Empty Garden*, 1998 and *Pena (Sorrow)*, 1998) suggest mortality, possibly violence, anger, the intrusion of some rude force into the way life is lived. Is there struggle in your work? Is there anguish?

EMC: Most of the time, pursuing a resonant and moving work is a struggle. And because of this, there is violence and anguish, not only in the images, but also in the process. I am trying to hold violence close enough to remain urgent but distant enough to see it and, in the process, make objective what is extremely subjective. Memory, for example, is one of those ideas that is violent, difficult and subjective. I want to know what memories do, how time erodes them and what or who is the 'me' that is doing the inventory of the past.

HF: You mean, not specific memories, but the activity of the imagination, just left alone to contemplate itself?

EMC: Yes, but I do not usually think of imagination as involved in this process. I am seeking a clearer vision and that leads me to objectify and separate the subjective from myself. This is neither about sentimentality nor about detachment, both of those positions are very easy to understand but not very revealing.

HF: The fact that your paintings resist very specific interpretation is exactly the response that you are eliciting from the viewer.

EMC: Yes, but this is because the works are an experience that is not readily available as a simple pointer. It is not about confusion.

HF: It's wonderment, not confusion.

EMC: Yes, but focused. This preoccupation started for me with religious paintings. In religious paintings, the entire human being was the destination for the work, not the mind or the heart. The religious work wants to suggest some experience that is extremely clear but unnamable.

HF: I think you intend something very similar to happen to the viewer. We have some questions from the audience.

AUDIENCE: I understand this as a sort of spirituality that you're seeking. Does any of this have to do with the Revolution in Cuba? I mean, in the view that this experience happened, is that part of this anguish and violence?

EMC: When I left Cuba, I understood what that meant to other people, and later, what that meant to myself. The exile facilitated the possibility of the world at certain costs. It is a persisting struggle to remain unexplained as a foreigner. Everyone seems to know better. I do not long for spirituality or reason as an answer to my condition of exile. Culture and politics are not directly the subject of my work. All the issues of culture and politics always have their struggles in the individual. I am interested in the person. If you wish, you can see all my works as an examination of the idea of self-portraiture separated from the autobiographical. In the process of working I disappear.

HF: As long as you're talking about disappearance, let's talk about your palette, the almost bleached faint feeling that your images often have, as if they're fading into a space or time or they're just coalescing out of it. You do have some use of bright and saturated colors in your canvases, mostly associated with blood-red. But most often you have a very grayish, ashy white or a dark, inky black. Sometimes the whites are ethereal and can almost 'snow-blind' you, while the blacks are often dense and unfathomable. Everything seems to fade in and out of vision. At least that's how your palette works for me.

EMC: In 1990, I was trying to reinvent painting for myself. The fastest way I found to dismantle the way I worked was to take out what people said was interesting about paintings. I took out drawing, I took out color…I took out what people had complimented in my paintings, to see what was left. I was left with black and white, and red, which seems like a form of black and white. So I have tried to keep the options in these paintings very rigid on purpose. I think that if you keep the structure of the paintings very rigid then you can take huge liberties within them.

HF: You've described 'reinventing' painting for yourself and working within a rigid structure. I get the impression, in looking at your work, that structure is like a visual language with its own vocabulary and syntax–a language that is personal to you yet rooted in Western art and iconography, so that it has resonance for viewers. Is this a fair impression, that your painting strives to the condition of language? Does language somehow edify your art?

EMC: Language exists in my work, in the books that are published and the poems that are included in the exhibitions. But, I do not think of my visual pieces as a language, or even as constructed in language. Instead, I see them as objects, concepts and images that exist as an experience. This experience is not a private language nor is it translatable to language. Images and gestures re-appear in the work but not as parts of a hieroglyph. They, perhaps like trees in a forest, are different and the same in each encounter. Some of the ideas in my work have interested many people before me and that is why my exploration seems to connect with the Western tradition of art and literature, and even folklore.

facing page

THE ARTIST IN HIS STUDIO
/DER KÜNSTLER IN SEINEM ATELIER, 1999
Venice, California

HF: Speaking of paintings in terms of language also underscores another impression that your art is very literary–'poetical' and 'lyrical' are words that many people have used to describe your art. And you are a poet and a great reader of books and a literary publisher in addition to being a visual artist. Is your painting and sculpture steeped in literature? Who are the writers or philosophers who've influenced your art?

EMC: I did not look at anyone's paintings other than Leonardo's until I was twelve. I was not interested in art. When I started painting I did it to understand myself. In contrast, I read everyone I could find. It was through literature that I began to understand the world. Literature became a much better model for my work than visual art and it was more or less free of the burden of commodity and 'look'. I sought physics and philosophy to better understand where I was but I always came back to art and literature as a way to internalize and to clarify experience. And about your question of influences, I am in debt to a very a long list of writers and philosophers but naming them often misleads more than reveals. I have not figure out a way to talk about these things in a way that is useful.

AUDIENCE: Your paintings, and also your drawings, are absolutely elegant in the way you painted them. It's just a formal thing, but you're very conscious of the kind of surface, are you not, that the paintings have?

EMC: Yes.

AUDIENCE: Very careful use of accidents.

EMC: I work with accidents in all the works. I create situations for them to occur. But once

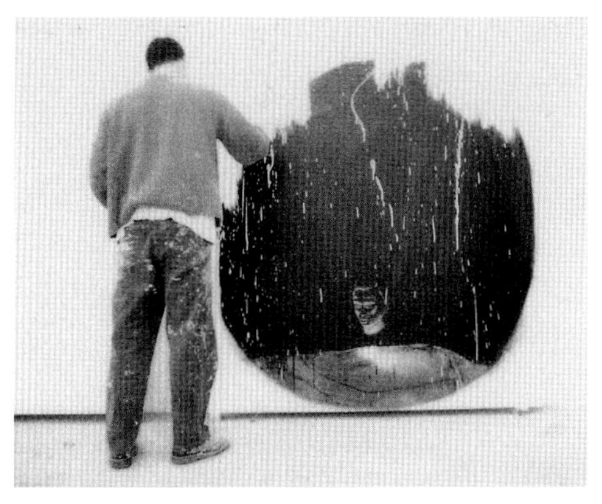
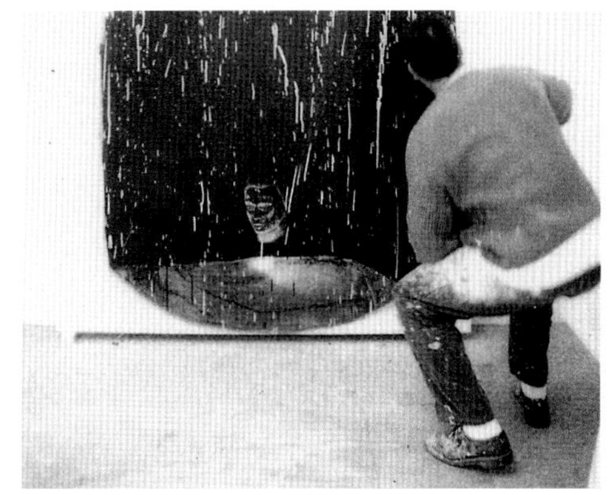
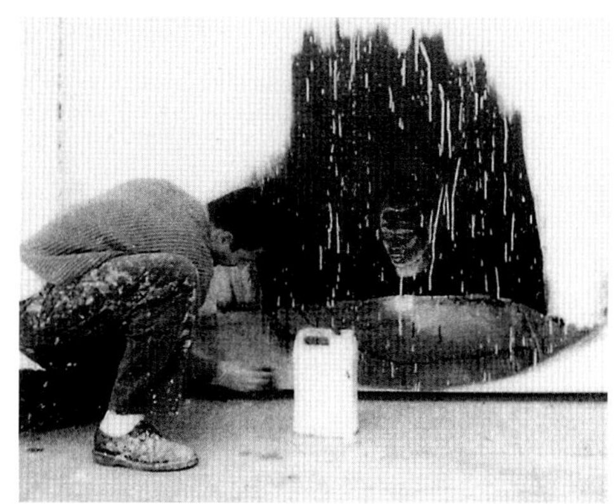
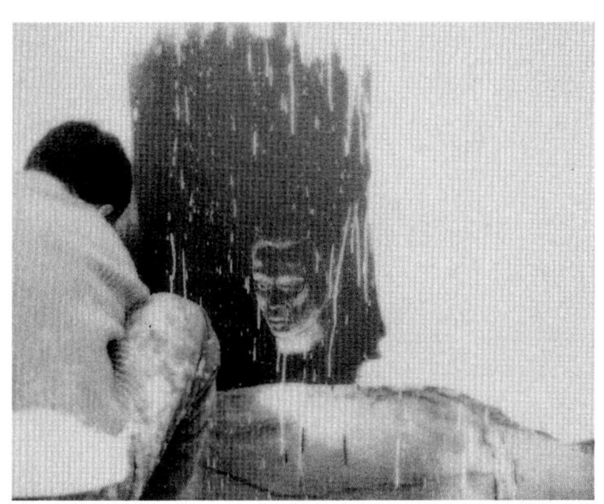
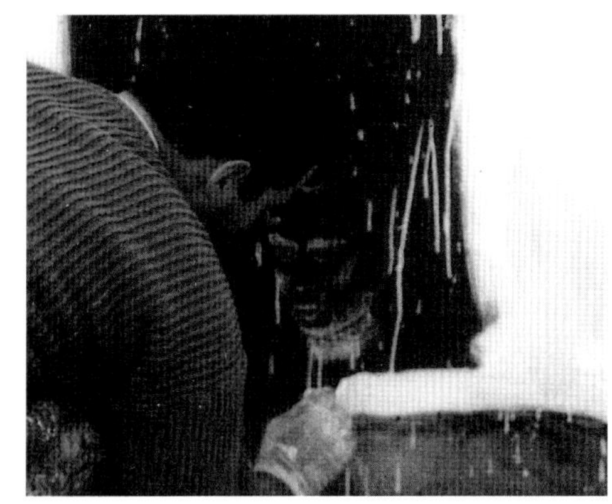
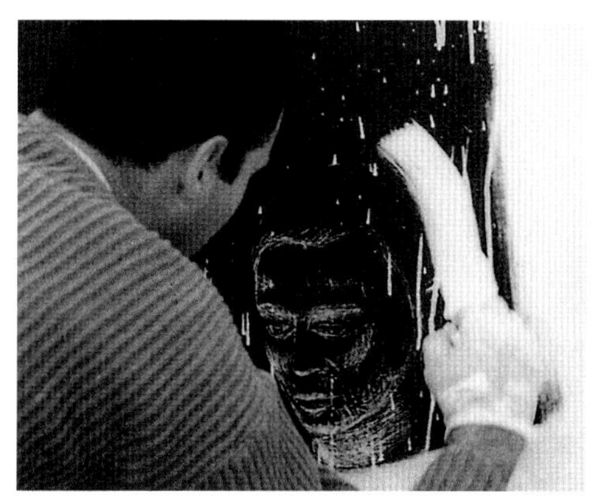
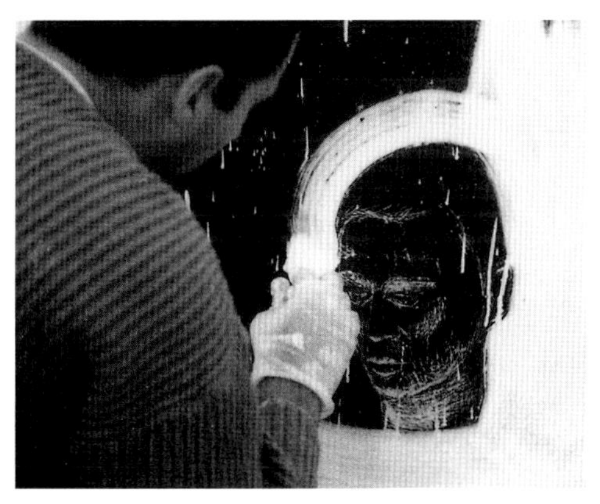
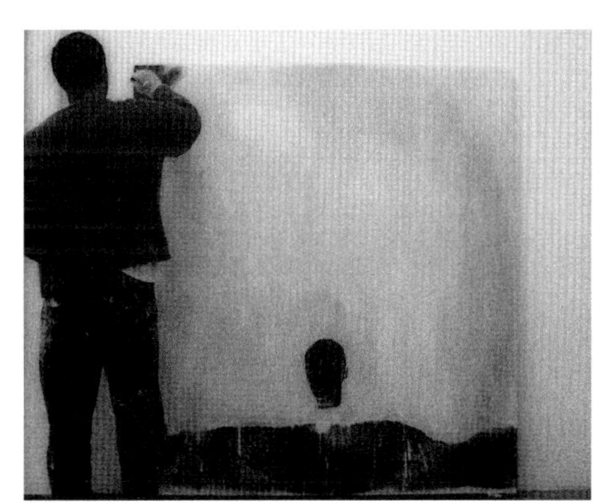
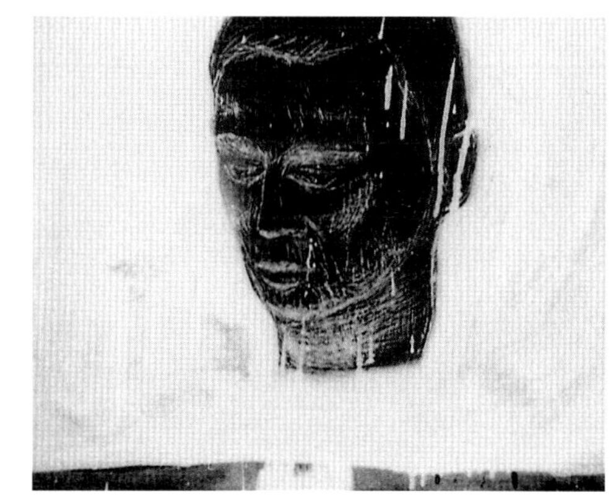
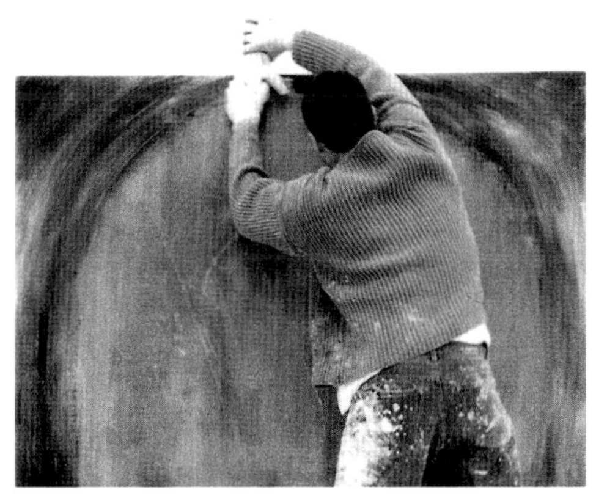
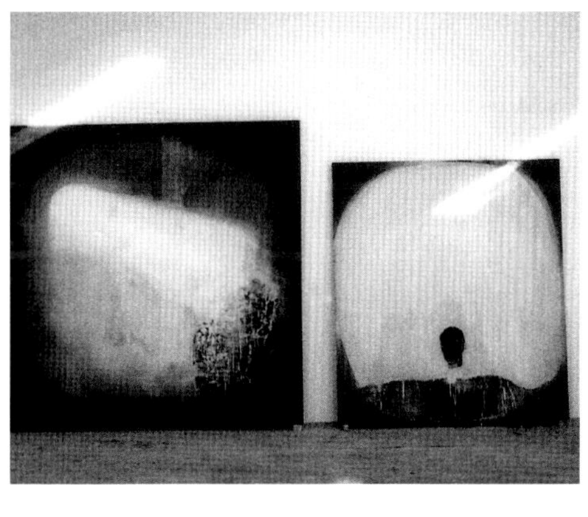
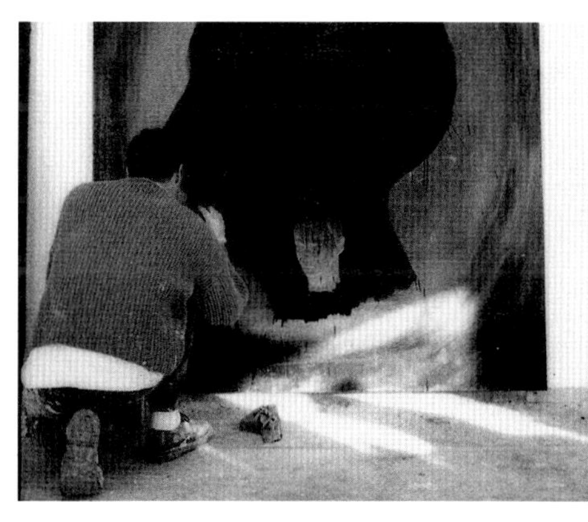

THE ARTIST IN HIS STUDIO
/DER KÜNSTLER IN SEINEM ATELIER, 1998
Venice, California

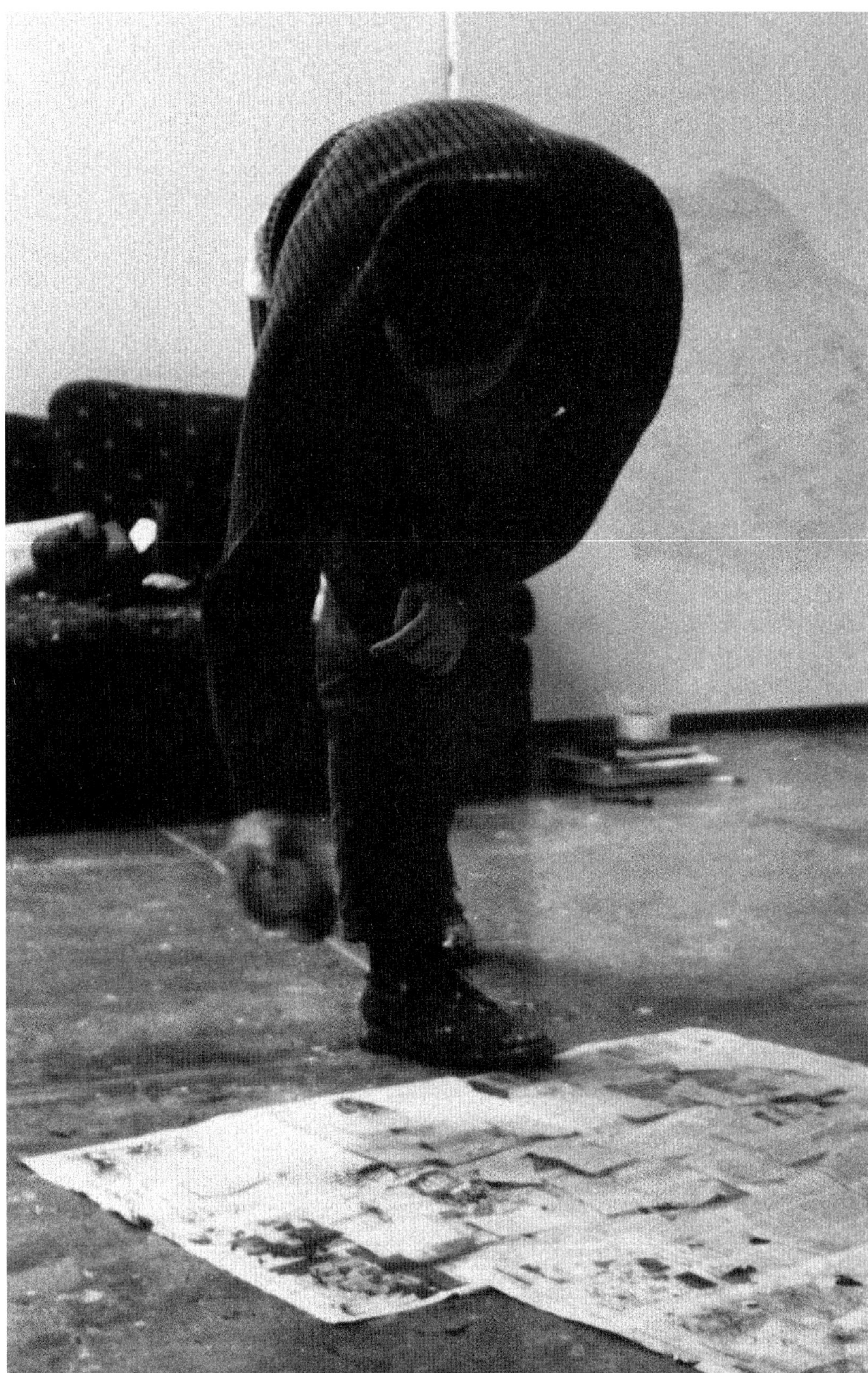

they occur, I spend a lot of time deciding whether I could live with them or not. I am very conscious of the surfaces and everything that ends up in these paintings. And often, they are much more superficially appealing before I finish.

HF: How so?

EMC: They have more of what people often seek in paintings. A moving work is sometimes encumbered by the issues of the visual, and paintings have the burden of being caught up in the decorative.

AUDIENCE: What is the relationship that you're looking for between the images of the head and the tree in *Quiet Night (Marks)*?

EMC: Well, in general, the objects in my works are elemental: trees, birds, heads, the sky, figures, arms, mirrors, water. They are fragments of the forest which I mentioned earlier. These are the fundamental building blocks of experience. So, in the juxtaposition between the birches and the head something new will emerge, something that was maybe hidden by appearances. So the relationships between these things are not really intended to be poetic, as in 'flowery', but as in essential to some truth.

AUDIENCE: I'm curious why you don't leave in the emotional side...you just leave the chronic, the violent. Could you comment?

EMC: I leave the emotional side. But the emotional side is not the same thing as the sentimental side. The sentimental is not specific. What's left in emotion once you remove affectation from it? I am after a state that breaks the barrier between intellect and feelings.

HF: I think you've succeeded in that, Enrique. Characteristically, your work has an almost monastic quality about it. It's disciplined in its austerity, in it's editing, as you've just described. What you decide to leave out–that is, the veneer, the allure of cheap sentiment–rather than allow to reside or preside in the painting, alludes by its absence to something vague and unknowable, but something perhaps absolute, or sublime. When we look at the powerful image of this head–and to me this is the essential Martínez Celaya painting, and I've seen quite a few of them–you set forth a visual symbol of intelligence, an icon of thought and every emotion and intellectual aspiration. Yet absent the rest of the body, the head appears severed, suggesting mortality. And then there's this reddish utterance coming from its mouth. I've heard you describe paint as something that has to be spilled. But in this image it's also what comes from being human: it's the utterance, the wonder that is expressed to possibly nobody or to no thing but the void beyond. Is it an absolute? Is it a construct? It's not answered in these paintings. It's the aching question perpetually asked in your art.

INTERVIEW MIT ENRIQUE MARTINEZ CELAYA†

Howard N. Fox

gegenüberliegende Seite

THE ARTIST IN HIS STUDIO
/DER KÜNSTLER IN SEINEM ATELIER, 2001
Venice, Kalifornien

Howard N. Fox: Wir haben heute Abend die Ehre, einen wirklich außergewöhnlichen Künstler begrüßen zu dürfen. Enrique Martínez Celaya lebt und arbeitet in Los Angeles und sein Werk findet heute weltweit bei Kritikern und Sammlern gleichermaßen große Anerkennung. Erst im vergangenen Jahr hat das Los Angeles County Museum of Art Martínez Celaya mit der bemerkenswerten Arbeit *Acceptance of Longing/Akzeptanz der Sehnsucht* aus dem Jahr 1997 in seine ständige Sammlung aufgenommen – einem poetisch-evokativen Werk, das von Surrealismus, Hochromantik und moderner Abstraktion durchdrungen ist. Das große, fast zwei Meter breite Gemälde zeigt die Gestalt eines toten Kolibris. Sicher haben Sie es alle bereits an seinem Platz in den Ausstellungsräumen des Museums bewundert, wo es seine ganze kraftvolle Wirkung entfalten kann.

Doch trotz der ihm innewohnenden Präsenz ist diese Arbeit mit ihrer Palette von glitzernden Weiß- und kühlen Grautönen nur schwer greifbar, scheint unserer visuellen und mentalen Wahrnehmung immer wieder zu entgleiten. Und das ist, denke ich, typisch für Enriques unverwechselbare, sensible Ästhetik der Veränderung und Auslassung – einer Art „Quantenästhetik". Ich will es zu erklären versuchen: Enriques Werk beschäftigt sich nicht nur mit Vieldeutigkeit und Geheimnisvollem – zweifellos zwei seiner wesentlichen Merkmale –, sondern auch mit Simultaneität und Dualität, denn es vermittelt zwischen Kunst und Philosophie, zwischen sichtbaren und unsichtbaren Wahrheiten. Jedes einzelne seiner Gemälde gleicht einem Quantenteilchen, das die unheimliche und unbegreifliche Eigenschaft besitzt, gleichzeitig an zwei Orten und in unterschiedlichen Zuständen zu existieren. Wenn Sie Enriques jüngste Arbeiten betrachten, die uns heute Abend umgeben, werden Sie mir sicher zustimmen, dass sie einerseits von einer durchdringenden Präsenz und Greifbarkeit sind, andererseits jedoch geheimnisvoll, ja erhaben erscheinen. Die Analogie zur Quantenphysik ist vielleicht gar nicht so weit hergeholt.

Enrique Martínez Celaya ist in Kuba geboren, hat in Europa und in den Vereinigten Staaten studiert und lebt und arbeitet heute in Los Angeles. Enrique, erzählen Sie uns ein wenig aus Ihrem Leben, wie es Sie hierher verschlagen hat, von Ihrem akademischen Werdegang. Meines Wissens haben Sie zunächst einen naturwissenschaftlichen Abschluss gemacht, bevor Sie sich der Malerei zuwandten.

Enrique Martínez Celaya: Als Jugendlicher bin ich bei einem Künstler in die Lehre gegangen, der überwiegend Landschaften und Porträts malte. In der High School entdeckte ich dann meine Leidenschaft für Physik und Mathematik und entschied mich für die Naturwissenschaften als wünschenswertere Laufbahn. Ich ging nach Cornell, um Physik zu studieren, mit Schwerpunkt Quantenphysik, und forschte in Brookhaven, bevor ich mich meinem Abschluß zuwandte. Ich habe immer gemalt, aber im zweiten Jahr meines Promotionsstudiengangs in Berkeley wurde mir klar, dass ich Künstler sein wollte. Eine gewisse Zeit lang habe ich dann parallel Kunst und Physik studiert.

† Dieser Text stammt von einer Veranstaltung, die von Griffin Contemporary Exhibitions, Venice, Kalifornien, am 14. Dezember 1999 für Mitglieder des Modern and Contemporary Art Council des Los Angeles County Museum of Art durchgeführt wurde. Er wurde für die vorliegende Publikation bearbeitet.

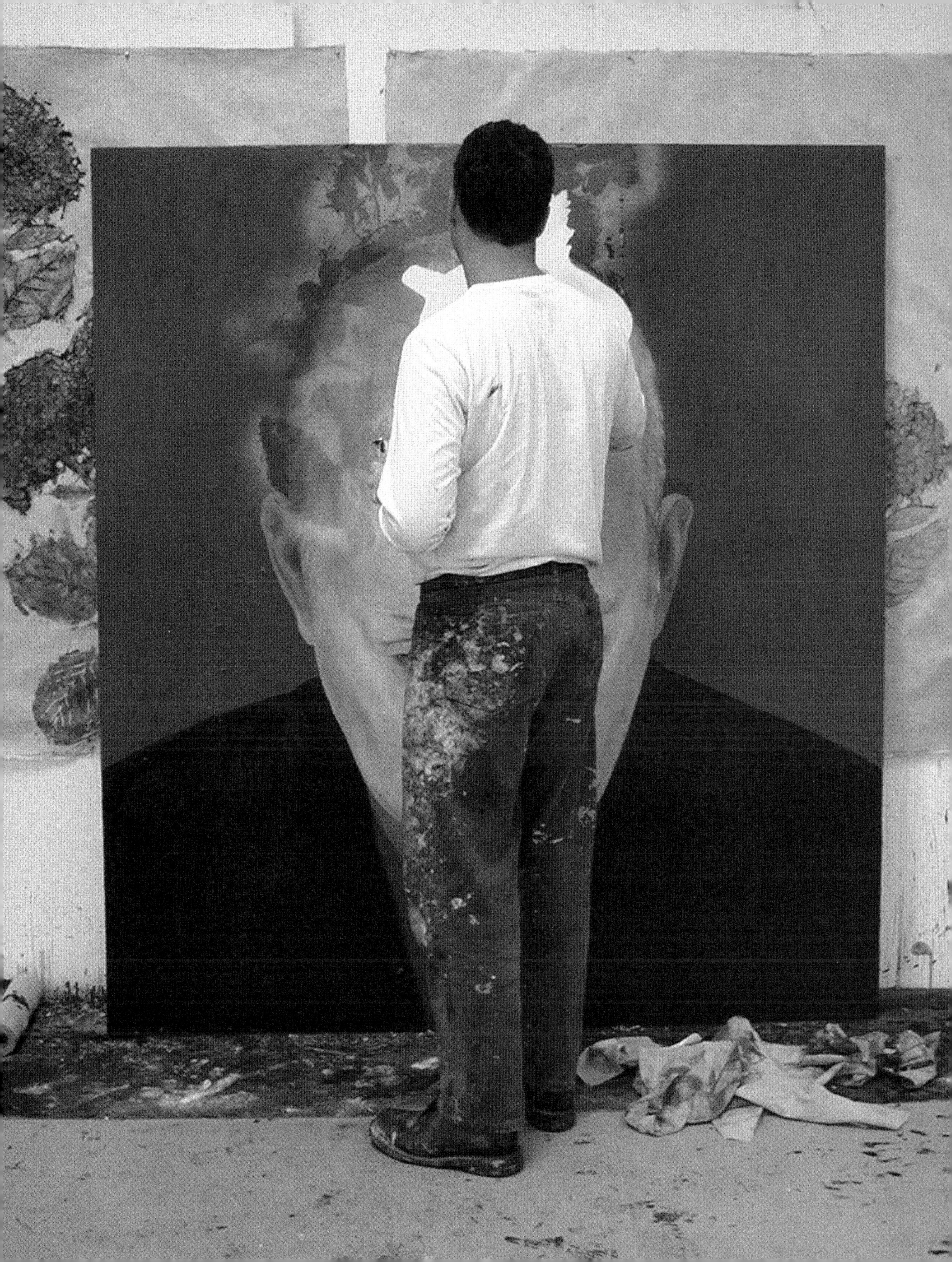

HF: Lassen Sie uns das noch ein wenig vertiefen. Wie ist es zu dieser radikalen Entscheidung gekommen? Was haben Sie im Atelier gemacht, während Sie am Experimentiertisch standen, Berichte schrieben und so weiter? Wie ist es Ihnen gelungen, diese beiden Welten unter einen Hut zu bringen? Oder war der Schritt zur Kunst vielleicht gar nicht so groß?

EMC: Zu der Zeit forschte ich auf einem Gebiet, das die gleiche Art von Extrapolationen und Glaubenssprüngen erforderte, die man auch mit der Kunst in Verbindung bringen könnte. Für mich war die Dualität der beiden Studiengänge nie befremdlich, ich habe sie nie als Dualität empfunden. Mein Problem waren eher die anderen, die alle genau wussten, was ich tun sollte ... Also zog ich einen Schlussstrich und ging nach Oakland, wo ich in Ruhe arbeiten konnte. Meine Bilder verkaufte ich über die Artists' Guild in den Parks von San Francisco.

HF: Ich erkenne in Ihrer Arbeit durchaus Anknüpfungspunkte an die Wissenschaft in ihrer klassischen Bedeutung von Wissen und Begreifbarkeit der Welt durch den Menschen, dem Versuch, die Wahrheit zu ergründen. Neulich habe ich einen Artikel gelesen, in dem sich ein Mathematiker fragt, ob die Mathematik eine Erfindung des Menschen ist oder ob sie unabhängig von der Menschheit in der Natur existiert. Als eine Art ideale Ordnung, ein Naturgesetz, wenn Sie so wollen, sehr abstrakte Konzepte, die Schnittpunkte zur physischen Realität aufzuweisen scheinen. Inwiefern hat die Naturwissenschaft Ihre Kunst verändert oder beeinflusst?

EMC: Die Natur ist ein Gebäude mit unsichtbarem Äußeren und wir leben im Inneren. Die Naturwissenschaft und die Mathematik sind ein Gerüst, das Untersuchungen über die Struktur des Gebäudes erleichtert, und auch das beste Mittel, Schlüsse über seine Gestalt zu ziehen. Das Gerüst ist von uns errichtet, doch indem es genauer und flexibler wird, ähnelt es dem Gebäude, das nicht von uns konstruiert wurde. Es könnte schwierig werden, zwischen dem, was das Gebäude enthüllt, und dem, was zu ihm gehört, zu unterscheiden. Diese Fragen beeinflussen meine Arbeit stark und sind sind von hoher Relevanz für die zeitgenössische Kunst.

HF: Oft erscheint die zeitgenössische Kunst theoretisch, wie eine klinische Übung zu einer Idee über Kunst, einer wissenschaftlichen Untersuchung im Labor nicht unähnlich. Viele Künstler reagieren auf das, was andere Künstler gesagt haben, um zur nächsten Phase einer kritischen Dialektik zu gelangen. Wenn ich Ihr Werk beschreibe, meine ich aber nicht diese Art „Wissenschaft". Ihre Arbeit gleicht vielmehr der Suche nach einer intuitiv erkannten, höheren oder tieferen Wahrheit, die mit aktuellen Diskursen in der Kunstszene wenig zu tun hat. Kunst, die ausschließlich als Antwort auf den kritischen Diskurs formuliert wird, hat oft etwas Hermetisches. Und ich bin davon überzeugt, viele Betrachter empfinden – ob zu Recht sei dahingestellt –, dass solche Arbeiten kaum etwas mit der Welt als Ganzes oder mit dem eigenen Leben zu tun haben.

EMC: Viele Kunstschaffende halten heute die Kultur nicht nur für das Mittel, sondern auch für das Ziel. Die meisten Naturwissenschaftler hingegen bedienen sich der Konstruktion als Werkzeug, das letztendlich zu etwas Realem führen wird.

HF: Ihr Werk schlägt eine Brücke zwischen diesen beiden Bereichen – dem eindeutig Weltlichen und dem wie auch immer gearteten Nicht-Weltlichen. Beschäftigen wir uns mit einigen Ihrer Bilder. Diese Arbeiten (*Empty Garden*/*Leerer Garten*, 1998, und *Pena (Sorrow)*/*Pena (Schmerz)*, 1998) erzählen von Vergänglichkeit, vielleicht auch von Gewalt, Wut, von einer rohen Kraft, die in unser Leben eindringt. Ist die Arbeit an Ihren Bildern manchmal ein Kampf, eine Qual?

EMC: Die kontinuierliche Arbeit an einem eindringlichen und bewegenden Werk ist fast immer ein Kampf. Und genau aus diesem Grund sind nicht nur die Bilder, sondern auch der Schaffensprozess von Gewalt und Schmerz erfüllt. Ich versuche, die Gewalt so nahe heranzulassen, dass sie brisant bleibt, und gleichzeitig so weit auf Distanz zu halten, dass sie noch erkennbar ist, und in diesem Prozess verwandele ich das extrem Subjektive ins Objektive. Nehmen wir die Erinnerung, ein gutes Beispiel für ein Thema, das brutal, schwierig und subjektiv ist. Ich interessiere mich dafür, wie Erinnerung funktioniert, wie die Zeit an ihr nagt und was oder wer hinter diesem „Ich" steckt, das dieses „Vergangenheitsinventar" zusammenstellt.

HF: Sie sprechen nicht von einer bestimmten Erinnerung, sondern von dem, was die Vorstellungskraft leistet, wenn sie sich selbst überlassen bleibt?

EMC: Ja, aber ich glaube nicht, dass die Vorstellungskraft an diesem Prozess beteiligt ist. Auf meiner Suche nach mehr Klarheit lerne ich, zu objektivieren und das Subjektive von mir selbst zu trennen. Das hat nichts mit Sentimentalität oder Loslösung zu tun, zwei Positionen, die sehr einfach zu begreifen, aber nicht sehr aussagekräftig sind.

HF: Die Unmöglichkeit, Ihre Bilder eindeutig zu interpretieren, entspricht der Reaktion, die Sie beim Betrachter hervorrufen.

EMC: Ja, doch der Grund für diese Reaktion ist eher, dass die Bilder eine Erfahrung bergen, die nicht so einfach zugänglich ist. Es geht nicht darum, zu verwirren.

HF: ... Sondern darum, Staunen hervorzurufen, nicht Verwirrung.

EMC: Ja, aber auf etwas fokussiert. Die religiöse Malerei hat meine starke Beschäftigung mit diesem Thema ausgelöst. Sakrale Gemälde befassen sich immer mit dem Menschen als Ganzes, nicht nur mit dem, was er denkt oder fühlt. Die religiöse Kunst will eine Erfahrung vermitteln, die völlig klar und doch unbenennbar ist.

HF: Mir scheint, Sie bezwecken mit Ihren Bildern etwas ganz Ähnliches. Ah, da gibt es eine Frage im Publikum.

Publikum: Ich habe den Eindruck, Sie suchen eine Art Spiritualität. Steht diese Suche in irgendeinem Zusammenhang mit der Revolution auf Kuba? Fließt diese Erfahrung von Gewalt und Schmerz in Ihre Arbeit ein?

EMC: Als ich Kuba verließ, wußte ich, was dies für andere Leute bedeutete, und später, was es für mich selbst bedeutete. Das Leben im Exil bietet zwar tausend neue Möglichkeiten, hat aber auch seinen Preis. Als Fremder in einem fremden Land kämpfe ich ständig darum, mich nicht erklären zu müssen. Alle scheinen es besser zu wissen. Ich brauche keine Spiritualität oder Vernunft, um mein Dasein im Exil zu begründen. Kultur und Politik sind nur mittelbar Thema meiner Arbeit. Ich bin vielmehr daran interessiert, wie sich der Einzelne mit kulturellen und politischen Fragen auseinander setzt. Wenn Sie möchten, können Sie alle meine Werke als Untersuchung der Idee des Selbstporträts im Unterschied zur Autobiographie sehen. Ich verschwinde im Schaffensprozess.

HF: Wo sie über Verschwinden reden, lassen Sie uns über ihre Farbpalette sprechen. Viele Ihrer Bilder wirken bleich und matt, als würden sie sich im Raum oder in der Zeit auflösen oder damit verschmelzen. Sie verwenden ja leuchtende, satte Farben, häufig in Verbindung mit

Blutrot. Aber meistens verwenden Sie ein sehr gräuliches, aschfarbiges Weiß oder ein dunkles Tintenschwarz. Einige der Weißtöne in Ihren Arbeiten sind so ätherisch, dass sie den Betrachter förmlich „schneeblind" machen. Das Schwarz hingegen ist oft undurchdringlich, unergründlich. Auf mich wirkt die Art, wie Sie Farbe einsetzen, wie ein kontinuierliches Ein- und Ausblenden.

EMC: 1990 versuchte ich, die Malerei für mich neu zu erfinden. Die schnellste Art, meine Arbeitsweise zu ändern, war, die Dinge wegzulassen, die an einem Gemälde gemeinhin als interessant gelten: das Gezeichnete, die Farbe, kurz das, was den Leuten an meinen Bildern bislang gefallen hatte. Mir blieben die Farben Schwarz, Weiß und Rot, wobei Letzteres eine Spielart der Ersteren zu sein schien. So habe ich versucht, die Optionen in diesen Gemälden stark einzuschränken. Ich denke, wenn man den Gemälden eine sehr starre Struktur verleiht, kann man sich innerhalb von ihr große Freiheiten erlauben.

HF: Sie haben beschrieben, dass Sie die Malerei für sich selbst „wiedererfunden" und innerhalb einer strengen Struktur gearbeitet haben. Wenn ich Ihre Bilder betrachte, habe ich den Eindruck, dass Struktur für Sie eine Art Bildersprache mit eigenem Vokabular und eigener Syntax ist, eine sehr persönliche Sprache, die jedoch in der westlichen Kunst und Ikonographie verwurzelt bleibt, damit sie bei den Betrachtern Resonanz findet. Würden Sie mir zustimmen, wenn ich Ihre Malerei in die Nähe von Sprache rücke? Ist Sprache der Baumeister Ihrer Kunst?

EMC: Sprache findet in meiner Kunst in den Büchern und den in die Ausstellungen einbezogenen Gedichten Verwendung. Die Arbeiten selbst aber betrachte ich nicht als Sprache oder als durch Sprache konstruiert, sondern als Objekte, Konzepte und Bilder, die als Erfahrung existieren. Und diese Erfahrung ist weder eine private Sprache noch kann sie in Sprache übersetzt werden. Bestimmte Bilder und Gesten kommen zwar immer wieder vor, doch nicht als Bestandteil einer Hieroglyphe. Sie sind, vielleicht wie Bäume in einem Wald, bei jeder Begegnung gleich und verschieden. Dass mein Werk in die Tradition der westlichen Kunst, Literatur und sogar Folklore eingeordnet wird, liegt daran, dass sich viele Menschen vor mir bereits für die Ideen interessiert haben, die ich in meiner Kunst behandele.

HF: Die Verwendung sprachlicher Termini für Gemälde unterstreicht den Eindruck, dass Ihre Kunst eine sehr literarische ist – „poetisch" und „lyrisch" sind zwei Begriffe, die in Texten zu Ihren Arbeiten häufig auftauchen. Und tatsächlich schreiben Sie ja Gedichte, sind sehr belesen, geben Bücher heraus. Gründet Ihre Kunst in der Literatur? Welche Schriftsteller und Philosophen haben Ihr Werk beeinflusst?

EMC: Bis ich zwölf war, kannte ich nur Leonardos Bilder. Kunst interessierte mich nicht. Später fing ich dann an zu malen, auf der Suche nach mir selbst. Mit der Literatur war es etwas anderes: ich las, was ich in die Finger bekam. Durch die Literatur begann ich, die Welt zu verstehen. Und die Literatur wurde zu einem sehr viel besseren Modell für meine Arbeit als optisch wahrzunehmende Kunstwerke, zumal sie mir in der gestalterischen Umsetzung praktisch freie Hand ließ. Die Physik und die Philosophie brauchte ich, um die Welt und mich selbst besser zu verstehen, doch ich kehrte stets zurück zur Kunst und zur Literatur, um Erfahrung zu verinnerlichen und zu klären. Und zu Ihrer Frage der Einflüsse: Ich bin einer ganzen Reihe von Schriftstellern, Philosophen und auch einem Komponisten zu großem Dank verpflichtet, doch sie zu nennen, führt oft eher in die Irre, als etwas auszusagen. Ich habe noch keinen Weg gefunden, sinnvoll über solche Dinge zu reden.

Publikum: Die Ausführung Ihrer Gemälde und auch Ihrer Zeichnungen ist sehr elegant. Es ist zwar nur eine formale Sache, aber sie sind sich der Art der Oberfläche, die die Bilder haben, sehr bewußt, nicht wahr?

EMC: Ja

Publikum: Zufälle, mit Bedacht eingesetzt.

EMC: Der Zufall spielt in meiner Kunst eine große Rolle. Ich schaffe Situationen, in denen Zufälle passieren können, und überlege dann lange, ob ich mit ihnen leben kann. Natürlich ist jeder Zentimeter meiner Arbeiten bewusst gestaltet. Und oft erscheinen sie sogar vordergründig reizvoller, während ich noch daran arbeite.

HF: Wie kommt das?

EMC: Sie entsprechen dann noch mehr den gängigen Erwartungen an ein Bild. Ein bewegendes Gemälde ist manchmal visuell überladen, und Bilder haben das Problem, dem Dekorativen verhaftet zu bleiben.

Publikum: In welchem Verhältnis stehen die Motive Kopf und Baum in *Quiet Night (Marks)/ Stille Nacht (Markierungen)*?

EMC: In der Regel verwende ich in meinen Arbeiten elementare Objekte: Bäume, Vögel, Köpfe, den Himmel, Figuren, Arme, Spiegel, Wasser. Sie sind Fragmente des eben erwähnten Waldes, fundamentale Bausteine von Erfahrung. Aus der Nebeneinanderstellung der Birken mit dem Kopf entsteht etwas Neues, etwas, das vielleicht durch den äußeren Schein verdeckt war. Das Verhältnis zwischen diesen Objekten ist also nicht poetisch im Sinne von „blumig", sondern im Sinne von einer Wahrheit verpflichtet.

Publikum: Ich würde gerne wissen, warum sie den emotionalen Aspekt aus Ihren Arbeiten herausnehmen. Übrig bleibt das Schlechte, die Gewalt. Könnten Sie dazu etwas sagen?

EMC: Ich beziehe den emotionalen Aspekt sehr wohl mit ein, was aber nicht mit Sentimentalität zu verwechseln ist. Sentimentalität ist unspezifische Affizierung. Und was bleibt, wenn man der Emotion die Affizierung nimmt? Ich bin auf der Suche nach dem Zustand, der die Mauer zwischen Intellekt und Gefühl einfallen lässt, nach der zielgerichteten Emotion.

HF: Eine Suche, die immer wieder zum Erfolg führt, Enrique. Im Kern ist Ihre Arbeit geradezu monastisch, von einer strengen Disziplin, die sich auch in der Reduzierung ausdrückt, von der Sie vorhin gesprochen haben. Indem Sie dem Beschönigenden, dem verlockenden, billigen Sentiment die Herrschaft über die Leinwand verwehren, es einfach auslassen, erzeugen Sie eine Abwesenheit, die auf etwas Vages, Unbekanntes, vielleicht Absolutes, Erhabenes verweist. In diesem kraftvollen Bildnis eines Kopfes – für mich eines Ihrer wichtigsten Gemälde, und ich habe eine ganze Anzahl davon gesehen – zeigen Sie ein Sinnbild für Intelligenz, eine Ikone des Denkens, Fühlens und intellektuellen Strebens. Da jedoch der Körper fehlt, erzählt der abgetrennte Kopf von Sterblichkeit, zumal aus dem Mund eine rötliche Substanz austritt. Sie haben einmal gesagt, Farbe muss „vergossen" werden. Doch in dieser Arbeit ist Farbe die Äußerung des Menschseins schlechthin, der Ausdruck des Erstaunens gegenüber nichts und niemand Anderem als dem leeren Raum. Ist diese Leere absolut? Eine Konstruktion? Die Bilder geben darauf keine Antwort. Es ist die dringliche Frage, die Ihre Kunst immer wieder stellt.

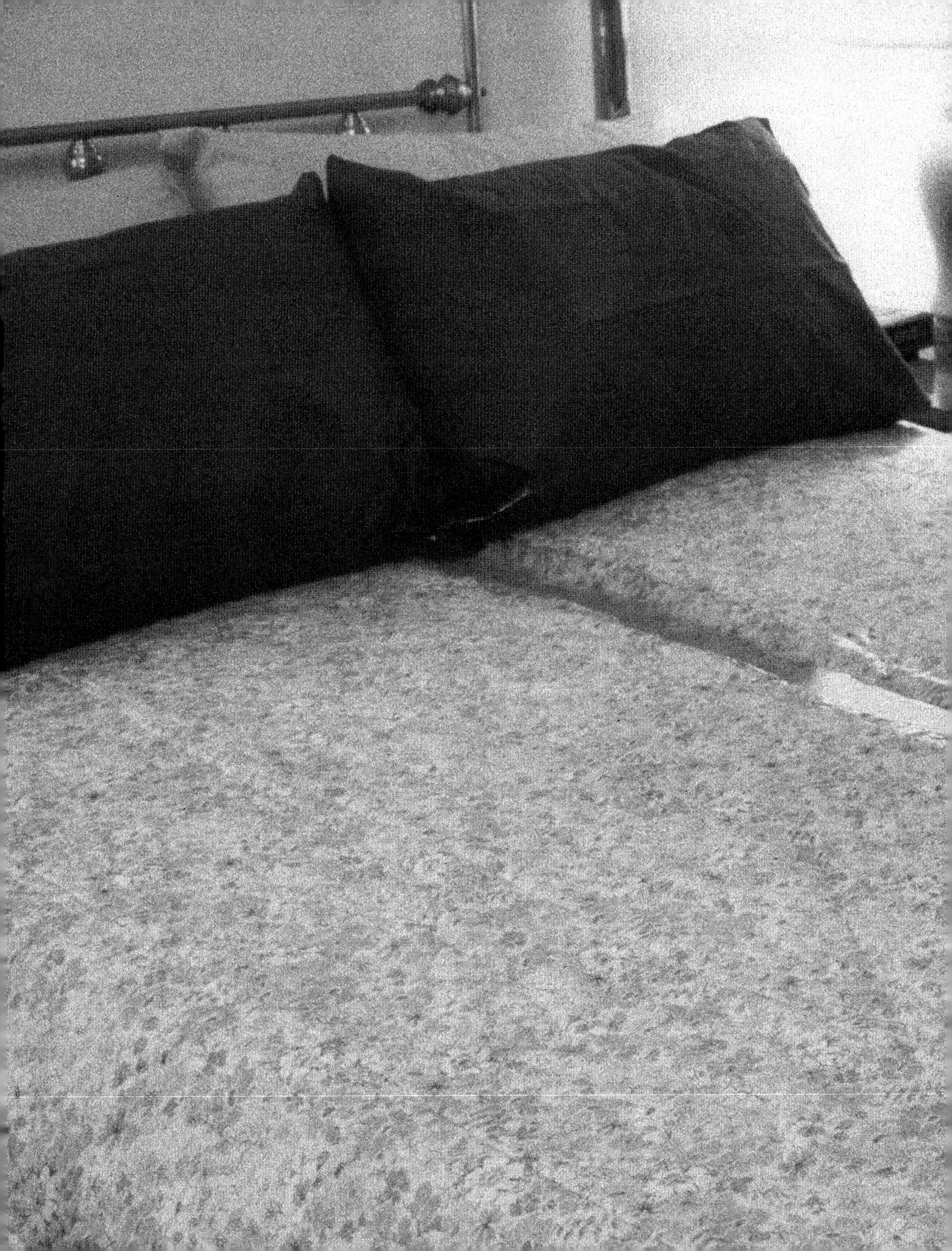

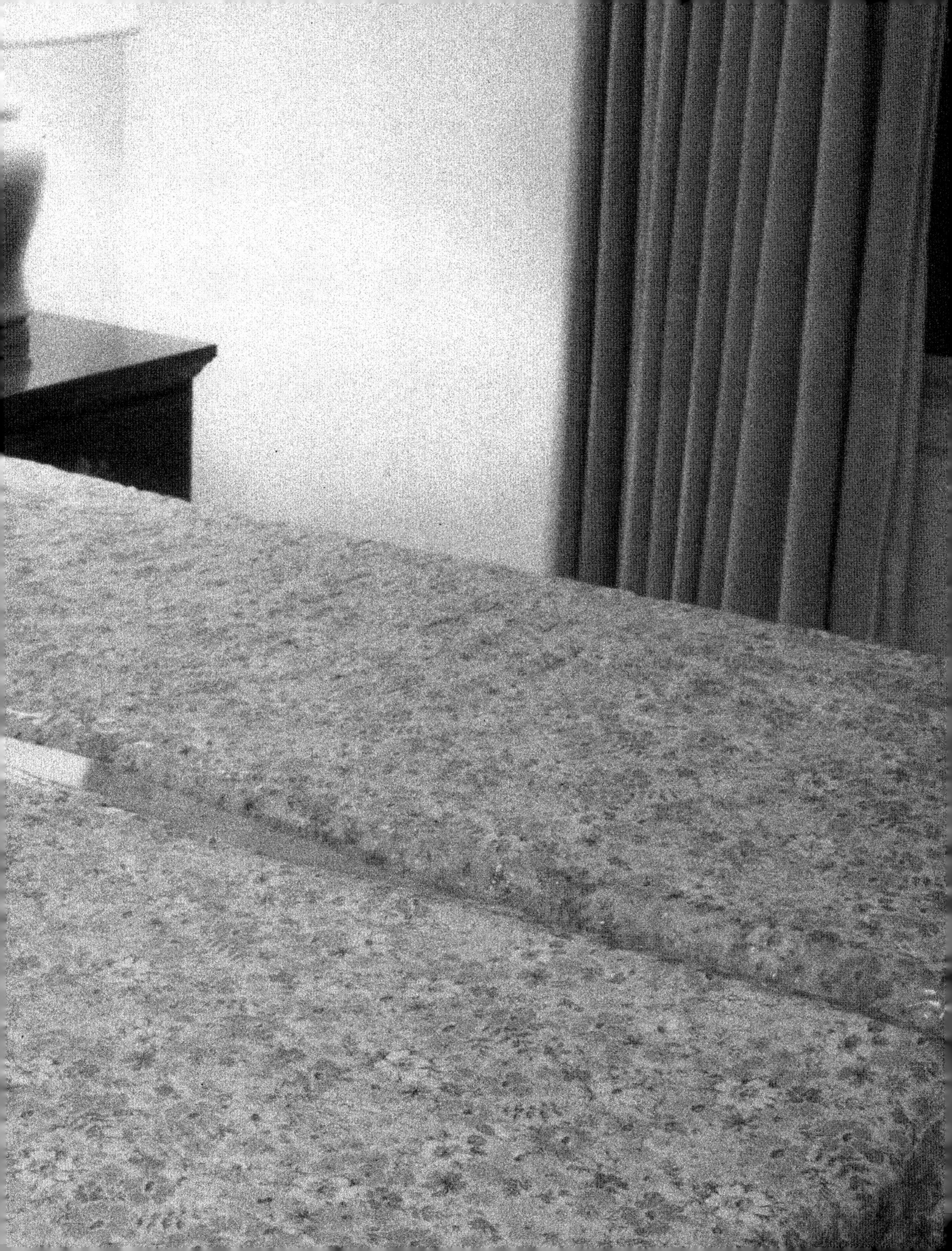

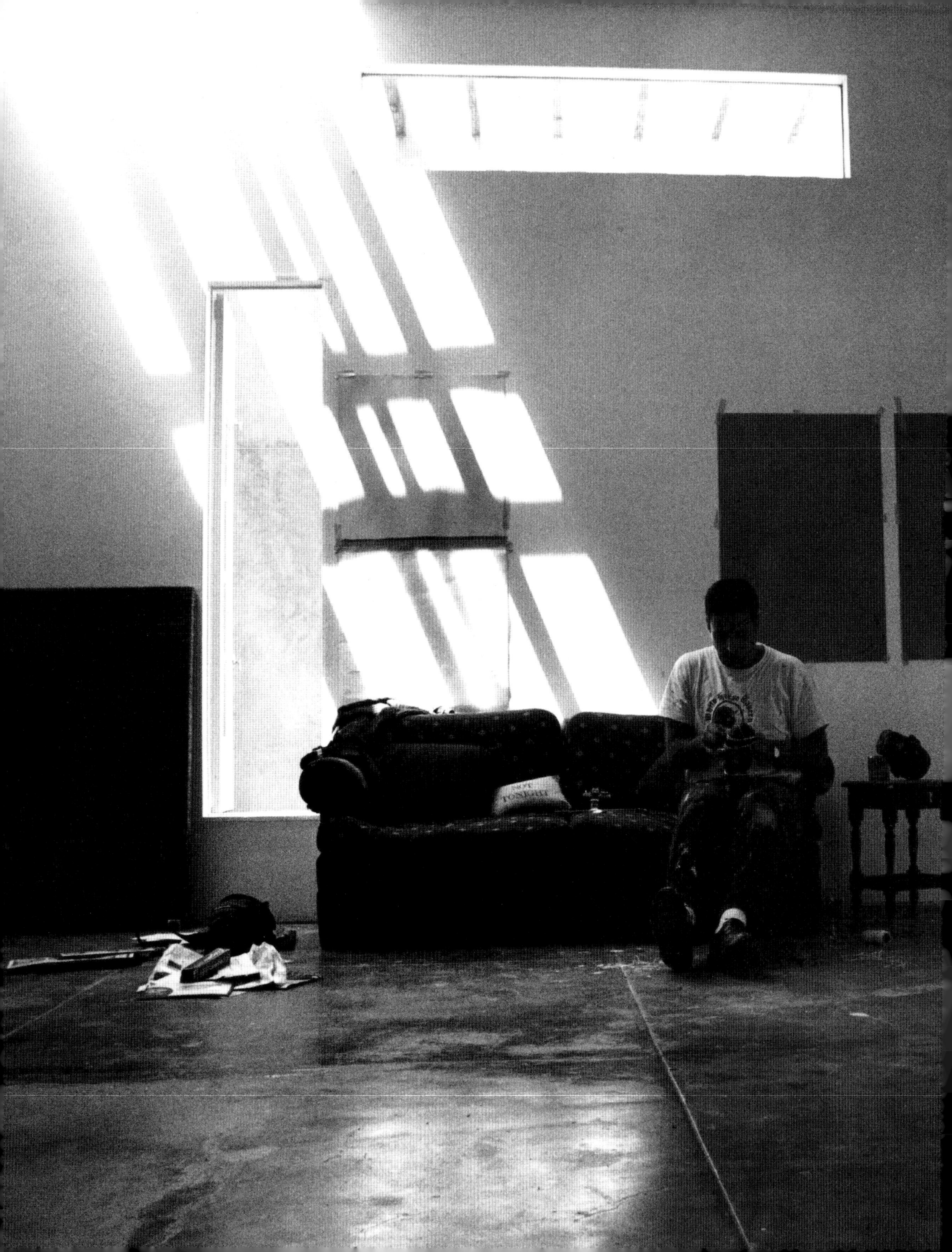

IN THE STILL OF LANGUAGE

Rosanna Albertini

> Each time we want words to really transgress boundaries, and we ask them to express something which is different from words, they usually line up making each other meaningless. This is, without any doubt, what gives all its charm to life.
>
> Samuel Beckett, *Le Monde et le Pantalon*, beginning of 1945

> And this is also what makes art a mesmerizing and opaque landscape, mainly resisting intellectual investigation. Yet our mind is a garden of thoughts, for the brain is wet.
>
> Rosanna Albertini, end of 2000

The studio that morning was a rush of sunshine and wind. An intense explosion of natural rays and shadows, of particles flickering in the air, almost raging against the large black paintings leaning against the walls. I still did not know, when I first stepped in, that the artist had been a physicist. I had only seen two of his paintings, one was a head set down carefully as if the empty space in which the head floats were a bed of invisible feathers, two small wings traveling on the face as alien clouds that have absorbed all the blue from the sky. The other painting was filled with two white humming birds pecking a human face around the nose and mouth, until a red mask of tiny wounds had been made, stroke by stroke. I wanted to meet the artist who had so harshly punished the doors of our breath and speech organs.

facing page

THE ARTIST IN HIS STUDIO
/DER KÜNSTLER IN SEINEM ATELIER, 1998
Venice, California

Enrique Martínez Celaya's painted or sculpted headless bodies, severed heads, arms without hands or hands cut at the wrist, are damaged presences, strikingly inactive. The legs are fused together like a single trunk, sexual organs are not visible: human bodies or trees? John Cage would say, "That's a painted world, a naked self-obscuring body of history." The artist in fact seems to be searching for a landscape that must be human. Wants he to reach the unshaped, almost theoretical particles, constituting one by one the single units of a human forest, the ones coming from a mythical time before genes and history had separated sexes, names, and behavior? We don't know, but his work does.

Each unit is a body, each body is naked. The heads are naked, and emptied. Naming them, we usually believe that, looking through the name, we can tell what they are. But by freezing those heads, or the hummingbirds, into a motionless literal word, we would be totally foiled. And in front of *Terrors and Remains*, 1998, one could not tell what the truth about the red bodies covering most of the canvas is. Are they petals or gigantic drops of blood? The heaviness, and impersonal pregnancy they give out are not to be compared to the quite resigned, transparent pensiveness of the other two painted presences, an arm and a head silently missing any reasonable conjunction. One can't tell whether they belong to the same body, unless the painting is their body, oil and embroidery on canvas. What remains of human features and limbs is a white shadow, as if life's colors and fluids had been released into an anonymous and repetitive pattern, the same body of history painted in *Map*, 1998, where a patterned tapestry soaked in blood-red paint grants separation, stillness, and mortality to a severed arm that hangs down vertically.

Meaning is inescapable; these paintings are portraits of feelings. And this essay can be, perhaps, easier to follow rowing your mind through the paragraphs, as if they were a river's bends.

When a glass fish glows like a flash of green, and opens his mouth flat in a forest with trees almost lost in a painted whiteness, the viewer's mind falters, wagging between the painting and its title: *Glass Fish in Dark Room (Grace)*, 1999. The same surprise happens while staring at a sculpted white head on the floor. Pupils dark with sadness saying, "I can remember seeing." An inside vision is at work in those eyes, and we can't know what it is. The title is *Quiet Night (Ocean)*, 1999. The same head in a photograph floating in the ocean in Marina del Rey, California, embraced by the artist. The photograph's title: *The Circumstances before Silence*, 1999.

Enrique Martínez Celaya's visions emerge from the unwritten layers of his pre- or unconscious mind, filled with stories that are neither matters of memory, nor matters of fact. The layers of paper and paint on canvas, often thickening his large paintings, could be called pages from the ghostly, hidden stories at the bottom of the artist's mind. Let the figures float, let them rise or rest, it's a bloody work for them to be born. They wear flowers and spines, never hiding the rupture that has generated them.

As images, symbols or descriptions, these figurative presences were born dead. Martínez Celaya celebrates their funeral with compassion, gently, either honoring the conventional space in which his visions are supposed to be born–the human head–or clearly cutting off the heads and putting them down on pillows to be what they really are, only heads that have been severed. *Objets d'affection*. Guillotine. Revolution or Resurrection? Flowers are put by the artist in their imaginary graveyard.

About fifty years ago the Italian artist Piero Manzoni tried to practice the implacable logic of revealing to the public the existence of primary images: images without form or composition, pure matter of pure energy. Implacable cleaner, Manzoni emptied his art of any limited dimension, perhaps didn't even believe that life had limits, and crossed the bridge at age 28.

"It is not by running that you can overcome the earth, you have to grow wings." Piero ravaging my mind when I saw Martínez Celaya's heads and arms growing wings. Why wings? Our age doesn't honor purity anymore. The fact that this artist gave up with conceptual purity, as practiced by scientists, doesn't directly imply the fundamental state of pain which is constantly suggested by his heads slightly bending to the earth. They are locked in their lack of expression like the yellow one, in *The Undeniable and Unfortunate Truths*, 1998.

Truths are blots of white floating in mental emptiness; a thread, thinner than a spider web, connects them in a random way. They look like intellectual illusions infected by uncertainty. Perhaps the artist's scientific experience–and giving it up, did not really cause such a deep, almost incurable uneasiness. Something more general and impersonal intervenes when the omnipresent head of his paintings vomits down from the mouth a cone of matter that reconnects mouth and earth (*Presos de Montaña*, 1999). The artist is actually throwing himself up, and makes the public aware of his private ritual, bringing up shadows that darken his own mirror. What we see is a man of today: a body pulled apart, expressing through the artist's work a ritual of re-conjunction.

In each painting a discontinuous, physical conversation goes on between waves of energy and particles in motion, that seems never to end. Images come into view as a matter of time, and birds, fish, hands, flowers, heads get lost in an undefined space.

In *Powers and Dominions*, 1997, for instance, an open hand appears. Did it drop the petals or not? As the arm goes through the paper, there is bleeding. Which one is virgin, the paper or the figure?–Feeling of intrusion, a conflict between two different fields of energy, discontinuity.

What happened to the hand of *Arm and Braille*, 1997? Was it already cut off or did it reenter the paper? Strong impression that the portion of that arm is still perfectly grafted on to a full body we cannot see; our hand is a blind tool.

Legs and feet in *Stonewall*, 1997, seem to pray, "Let me in, I'll give you a rose;" the paper, no less thick and impenetrable than a stone, is a fold which doesn't open up.

In the studio, a new piece gets along with resilience: a horizontal portion of an arm pulls wings, the human head stops resisting gravity and lies down. The green outline of a body in a watercolor is lying parallel to the ground–human leaf of a flat country, body of green letting its emptiness go. There is no head that blocks it. *The Forest V, Clearing*, 1999.

Many stories are suggested in the way some rarefied vestiges show up, as if paintings were a stage housing a mythological foreground.Vestiges shouldn't be confused with memories. They are not 'transparent things', as for Nabokov, "...through which the past shines!" Reading them by degrees, as if one by one they were morphemes of only one visual text, one can see that the time they give out is a present tense. Forms are petals floating on a tense surface–ultimately, a leaf on a mental flat-field. Who knows where the idea of flatness comes from... flatness spreads plainly, makes understandable the otherwise impenetrable volumes of life. Drawing and writing are nothing but threads to sort out the tangles.

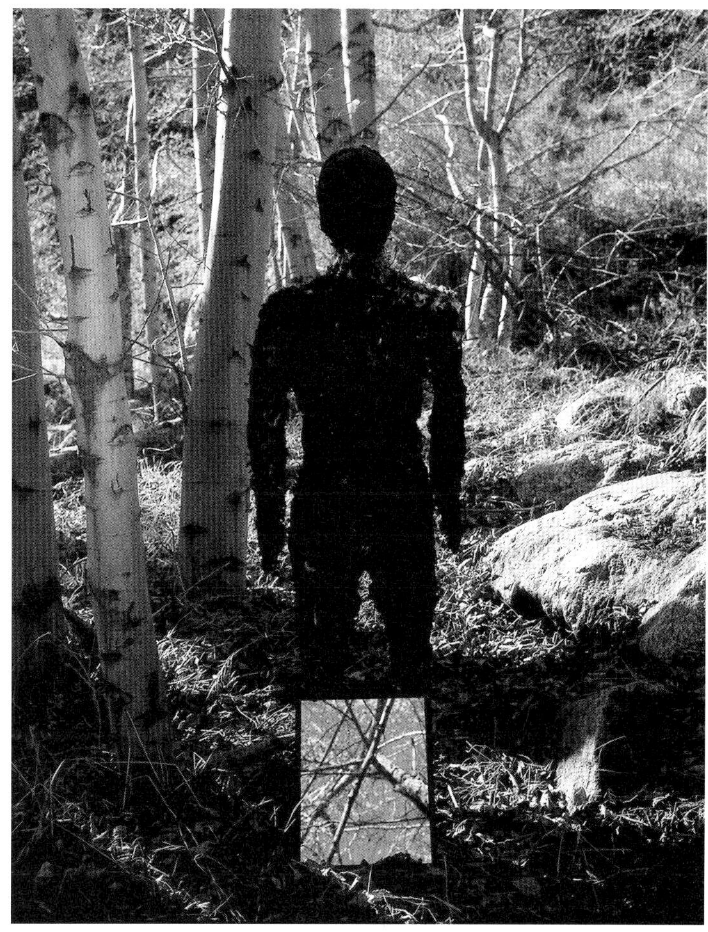

ARCHITECTURE/ARCHITEKTUR, 2001
Museum Ludwig, Cologne, Germany

Images by Martínez Celaya, always vanishing like dreams, produce the impression they are self-obscuring in a space/time without apparent coordinates. It is hard to call it background. As for Robert Ryman, whose undefined painted surfaces do not exist independently from space and light, for Martínez Celaya the limited space in between the four corners becomes a pulsing volume of particles suggesting that appearances fade quickly, they are not much more than optical illusions. What's stuck on paper or canvas is the attempt to scream, "This is life's primary substance, different in each painting as it is in each person. We spend our lifetime trying to erase its lack of form, and we fail. Air, light, sounds, temperature, time and history update the portrait of what we secretly keep in, so that our visible metamorphosis, and the different ways we feel at every instant, is reflected in other people's eyes." But, evidently, an artist fails if he doesn't find his own way of dealing with form, eventually stopping his mental wanderings in a physical outcome.

Martínez Celaya breaks such cohesive conjunction of space and time with a small number of figures: birds, trees, separate parts of the human body, flowers, leaves, fish, fragments of tapestry. Variations and repetitions are unlimited, like musical textures. Sometimes these mythological figures are brought completely out of flatland and become sculptures. Their silence doesn't cease. They are dead, born dead without despair like the dolls of my childhood. One mold for the trunk, one for each of the limbs, one for the head, no hair, no sex. Mute. Elastic cords used to keep the body together. If broken, the body is dismembered.

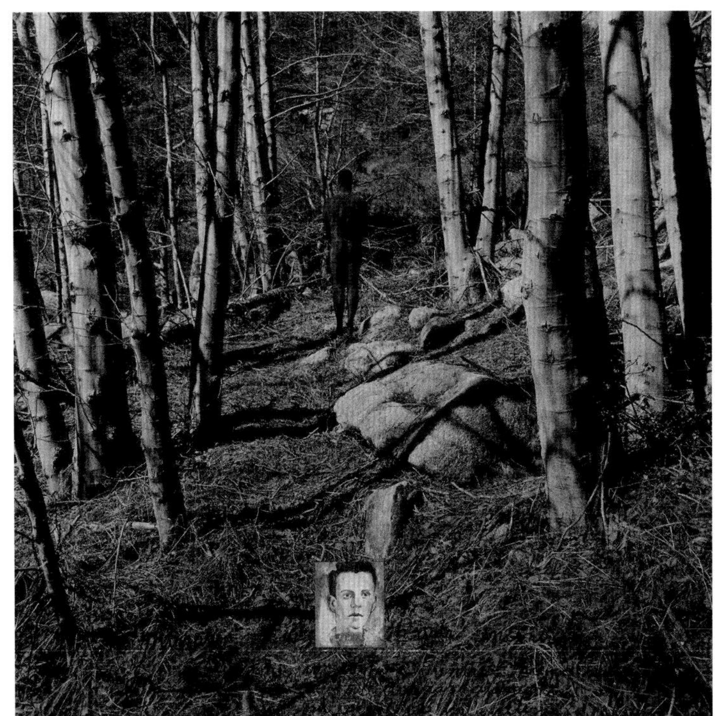

TU VOZ ENTRE LAS HOJAS (YOUR VOICE AMONG THE LEAVES) /TU VOZ ENTRE LAS HOJAS (DEINE STIMME UNTER DEN BLÄTTERN), 2000
Collection of Heidi Schneider, New York, New York

Near a small abstract piece made by Martínez Celaya a long time ago, a majestic presence fills vertically an entire wall of his house: a *Felt Suit* by Joseph Beuys. Minister of purity like Manzoni, and not less categorical than Immanuel Kant, Beuys found in this piece the perfect solution for a sculpture of human substance with no form. The wrapping cloth defines a space in which the human doll will never fall apart; identity is not required. Philosophically trapped by the *Felt Suit*, one could bring arguments on idealistic dreams, but it would only be a language game. If I think of an everyday use of the sentence "that's a felt suit missing the body," instead of a philosophical one, the meaning becomes clear and ordinary. In Martínez Celaya's house, the *Felt Suit* is a tree without roots, or a human body transformed into a soft, opaque, and stifling parody of any formalism: the more monumental, the emptier. It could also be the contemporary version of the *Bath Bâdgerd*, an ancient fairy tale. Later about that.

The physical translation of what is hidden in the mind is Enrique Martínez Celaya's principal subject–some heads carrying movable and fragile reflections, or galleries as if they had been excavated by worms, others blooming right there with primary colors, in a good season of life.

But, getting into the art's boat, Martínez Celaya's figures must pay a terrible toll: their appearing makes them an alienated presence, outlines of heads that clearly do not see where they are or why they are there. They fell perhaps from a lost paradise to become *simulacra*. If this wasn't enough, they also gave up their body's integrity and personal character. They could have been rescued, or saved.... The main elements of a story so much cherished by the artist that he repeats it endlessly.... A lost story is slowly coming back. It is not something to be explained. The artwork brings the artist's mind inside out in front of everybody, to show directly the lack of a way out, in which everyone is engaged[1]. There is a neck in ashes painted by Martínez Celaya, an uncertain shadow–either petal or wing–grows from the ashes.

> The artwork can be born when the human mind gives up the power of reasoning the physical matter. It's the triumph of carnal things. The lucid thinking, that starts the creative process, in the same process annihilates itself [2].

Let's start once more from the *Felt Suit*, pretend we are inside the suit. The felt is the way our consciousness physically hardens.

For the boy Enrique, the process toward self-awareness starts from a wound opened in one of his arms at age seven, when he left Cuba and never went back. Much later, he has remade the shape of that scar as a vertical cut on canvas. The small, three-dimensional piece, (*Fiber and Thread for a Seven Year Old*, 1993), has an empty volume of space behind the canvas and, in front, a silk transparent screen instead of the glass. The stitches that try to fasten the scar's edges leave the hole half open. Such carnal thinking. I'm not telling that the scar explains the art. For Enrique's lucid thinking, the scar, still visible on his arm, is the mark left by an event of crucial loss. For a viewer, it depends.... There I see the open lips of a vagina, an ark carrying the secret of all things that are being born. Maybe because the little piece is hung on the wall next to the *Felt Suit*, I see the edges, now clean from the blood, as a door through which neurons send out their conversation with the world. And the shape of a leaf looking like an island, very much like Cuba.

1. See Albert Camus, *Le Mythe de Sysyphe*, 1942.
2. *Ibid.*

By degrees, as if gently moving himself out of that primary wound, and lifting his ghosts (all alchemical-archetypal symbols) to the magnifying mirror of his paintings, the artist Martínez Celaya makes visible the hard process of taking shape, with images that do not want to reach a final form. To be shaped would be a hardening passage from freedom–lack of determination–to the finitude of being, as if every step towards a clear identification would imply the end of the creative process, and death.

So his figures seem to rest at the threshold of life, not really sure whether they want to cross the barrier of being. With Samuel Beckett, they could say, "We lived of flowers" (From an abandoned work, 1957). On canvas or paper they do have a life, almost flashes of existence from a plenitude which is dramatically lost during the making of consciousness, language, and formalized links between humans. To exist despite the prison of time, the fog of lies, and the pain of confession, waiting for an alchemical bird to bring back a hand, or a foot to the disoriented headless body, or to the head missing the body, is their transitory quality.

The artist fixes their *status nascendi*, reality will petrify them. So the heads, these incurable heads, are relics that the artist brings physically into the world. In the realm of ideas they had lost the ground. The artist doesn't change them, pretending they could come back to life; he doesn't replicate Orpheus. He carries them into the ocean, into a forest; and then, back to the studio. Some of the heads rest on pillows. Reality is something that human reason can grasp, but it won't change. No wonder Martínez Celaya feels attracted by Hegel's philosophy.

He visited Hegel's grave in 1998. Hegel's life, books, the immense architecture of his thoughts trying to make room for the incessant movement of life: waves that become barriers to themselves creating qualities, colors, and recognizable features or forms, and repeat over and over an involuntary swinging between being and becoming–all that had shrunk to a few letters and numbers engraved on a stone: *Georg Wilhelm Friedrich Hegel, 27 August 1770–14 November 1831.*

Martínez Celaya altered the outline of that stone in a photographic piece in black and white (*Last Flower*, 1998), in the same way that John Baldessari corrected with red crayon the outline of a mountain range (*Corrected Stonehenge*, 1984). A curve made with wooden sticks embraces the stone and suspends flowers over a head that pops up from the center of Hegel's funerary stone. Had the stone created it's own contradiction? It's Hegel's legacy, 'Words are stones'. Why not the heads? The bodies doing their best without them.

Wasn't art created to fight intellectual stiffness? While the collective unconscious of our present time is hardening more and more–as in many other times in the past–no utopias are proposed. The hummingbird flies over our face, menacing eyes and nostrils, pecking, (*A Dry Bed*, 1998) feeding, beating its wings frantically, "Wake up, wake up! Lost colors should be back, yes, even dripping blood. I flew into a savage rage, my body has been pierced by a birch. It was white, what then, statues of silence, how to know how I began? You don't know what you are not seeing." I can't dismiss the feeling, spread by these birds, that they are messengers of truth, as the white parrot of the *Tuti-Nameh* (*The Book of Parrot*, a collection of oriental stories) and the sacred dove in the Christian tradition. Hermes had been the first wearing wings on his feet. Over two thousand years the wings have become birds. Martínez Celaya could be considered a hermetic artist.

> Memory should not be called knowledge... Let us open our leaves like a flower and be passive and receptive... taking hints from every noble insect that favors us with a visit... I have not read any books–the Morning says I was right.[3]

3. John Keats, *Letter to his friend Reynolds*, February 19, 1818

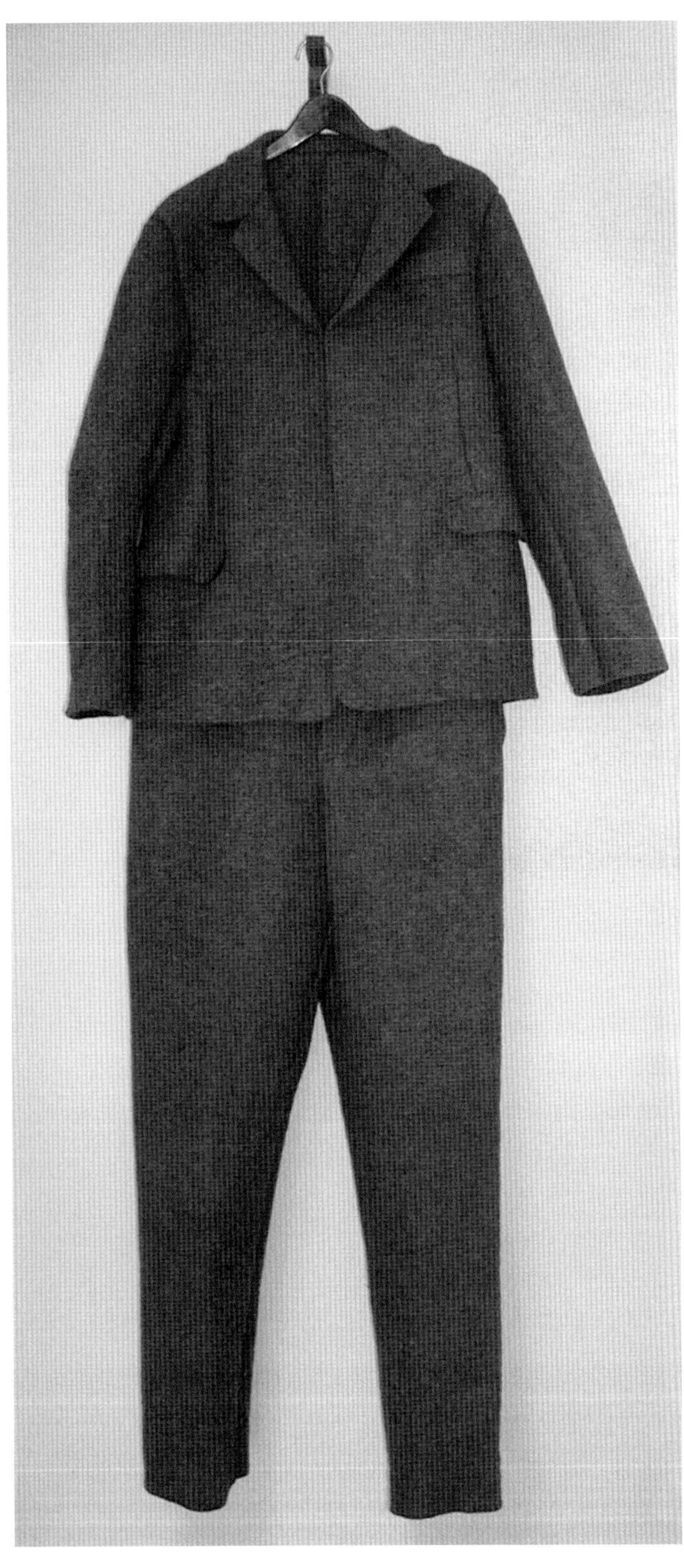

JOSEPH BEUYS
FELTSUIT/FILZANZUG, 1978
Collection of Enrique and Alexandra Martínez Celaya
(© VG Bild-Kunst, Bonn 2001)

Bringing vestiges out into the world, Enrique Martínez Celaya is exploring a place for visual stories. Drama rather than aesthetic. A rhapsody in black started to progress in his studio from September through December of the year 2000. First with a series of paintings; in one of them a boy was standing in the darkness–white rain and lightning around him. After a couple of weeks all the paintings had been sent to New York except one, a landscape in which the darkness had been pushed to the sides, and the mid space was a landscape as it appears sometimes at dawn (*The Blink*, 2000), when the light grows on a new born world, each day the very first.

New black paintings started to refill the studio, paintings covered with tar–the finest white threads emerging from underneath to outline profiles of human bodies and trees. In front of them, a boy's statue the size of an adolescent with identifiable sexual organs. His head is slightly bent down. Feet and hands are missing. Both the boy and the elk, covered with feathers and blackened with tar, look at each other's eyes as if they were magnetically tied (*Coming Home*, 2000). It was strange to feel the intensity of their eye-contact despite the absence of eyes, and to be fastened down there with them in the still of language. A few days after, a looking glass leans against the antlers of the elk. Because the glass surface doesn't absorb the images, the boy's head is reflected by the glass into a multiple life of conceptual reflections in paintings and photographic prints. A small white sculpted head lies on the floor. But the most surprising presence, on that same floor, is a broken bird, equally black.

If you can leaf through the *Bath Bâdgerd*, a fairy tale in which ancient stories are condensed in a sequence of dawning or decaying, mirrors or petrified bodies–the whole description is a confusing conquest of self awareness–you will find, literally, the same *prima materia* made by Enrique Martínez Celaya for his installation. Once the bird is killed, the treasure that had been lost reappears, the person is freed. Back to reality: in Enrique's studio the huge elk at rest makes me dream of a materialized feminine presence. Nobody can tell for sure what happened; if the artist, for instance, has sculpted his own feminine side as a mountain of flesh and bones that he can face without shame. But here, in the now, please don't break with reasonable associations the flexible threads of this rhapsody in black. One can walk through, they are still there. This is a place for thoughts in bloom, needing obstacles to be reflected.

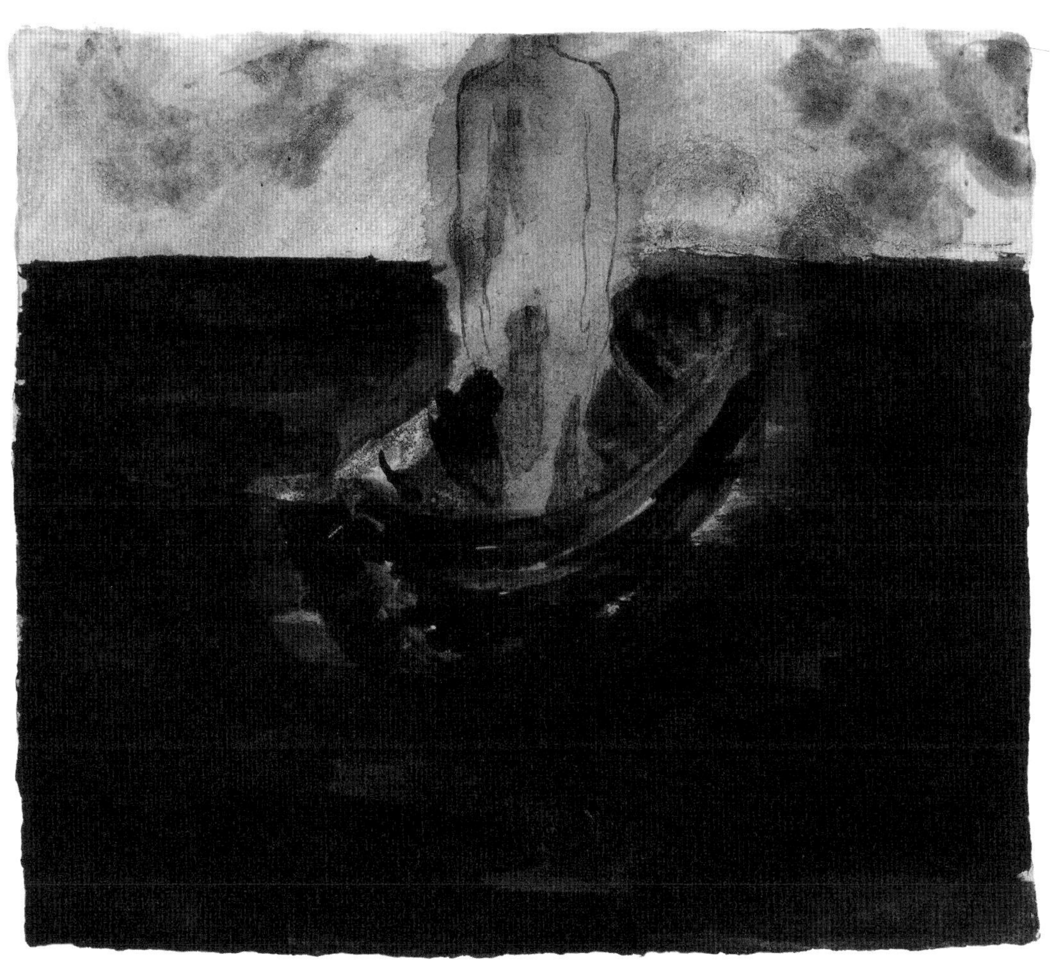

FIGURE IN BOAT (JUDGE)/FIGUR IN BOOT (RICHTER), 2001
Courtesy of Baldwin Gallery, Aspen, Colorado

IN DER STILLE DER SPRACHE

Rosanna Albertini

Jedesmal, wenn man die Wörter dazu bringen will, über ihre Grenzen hinaus zu wirken, jedesmal, wenn man erreichen will, dass sie etwas anderes ausdrücken als Wörter, reihen sie sich so aneinander, dass sie sich gegenseitig aufheben. Das verleiht dem Leben wohl gerade seinen Reiz.

Samuel Beckett, *Die Welt und die Hose* (Anfang 1945)

Und das ist ist es auch, was die Kunst zu einer faszinierenden und unergründlichen Landschaft macht, die dem intellektuellen Zugriff weitgehend widersteht. Dennoch ist unser Geist ein Gedankengarten, weil das Hirn feucht ist.

Rosanna Albertini, Ende des Jahres 2000

gegenüberliegende Seite

CONSTELLATION IV, detail/KONSTELLATION IV, Ausschnitt, 2001
Courtesy of Rena Bransten Gallery,
San Francisco, Kalifornien

An diesem Morgen war das Atelier ein einziger Sturm aus Sonne und Wind. Explosionsartig und beinahe wütend prallten die heftigen Lichtstrahlen, Schatten und in der Luft flimmernden Partikel auf die großen schwarzen Bilder, die an der Wand lehnten. Bei meinem Eintreten wusste ich noch immer nicht, dass der Künstler einst Physiker gewesen war. Ich hatte erst zwei seiner Bilder gesehen, eines war ein Kopf, so sorgfältig platziert, als wäre der leere Raum, in dem er schwebt, ein Bett aus unsichtbaren Federn, zwei kleine Flügel bewegen sich über das Gesicht wie Wolken aus einer anderen Welt, die alles Blau des Himmels aufgesogen haben. Das andere Bild bestand aus zwei weißen Kolibris, die auf ein menschliches Gesicht einpicken, bis um Nase und Mund herum, Hieb um Hieb, eine rote Maske aus winzigen Wunden entstanden ist. Den Künstler, der die Öffnungen unserer Atem- und Sprechorgane derart gezüchtigt hatte, wollte ich kennen lernen.

Enrique Martínez Celayas gemalte oder modellierte kopflose Körper, seine abgetrennten Köpfe, handlosen Arme oder an den Gelenken abgetrennten Hände vermitteln den Eindruck eines auffallend passiven Versehrtseins. Die Beine wirken wie zu einem einzigen Stamm verschmolzen, Geschlechtsorgane sind keine zu sehen: menschliche Körper oder Bäume? John Cage würde sagen: „Dies ist eine gemalte Welt, ein nackter, sich selbst verschleiernder Körper aus Geschichte.“ Tatsächlich scheint der Künstler auf der Suche nach einer Landschaft zu sein, die menschlich ist. Will er auf die ungestalten, beinahe theoretischen Teilchen zurückgreifen, die jedes einzeln für sich Einheiten eines menschlichen Waldes darstellen, Einheiten aus einer mythischen Zeit, in der Gene und Geschichte die Geschlechter, Namen und Verhaltensweisen noch nicht auseinander dividiert hatten? Wir wissen es nicht, aber sein Werk weiß es.

Jede Einheit ist ein Körper, jeder Körper ist nackt. Die Köpfe sind nackt und leer. Gewöhnlich glauben wir, weil wir sie benennen, durch die Brille des Namens hindurch sagen zu können, was sie sind. Ließen wir diese Köpfe oder Kolibris aber in bewegungsloser Sachlichkeit erstarren, wären wir vollkommen wehrlos. Und vor dem Bild *Terror and Remains/ Schrecken und Überreste*, 1998, könnte man nicht sagen, was es mit den roten Körpern, die die Leinwand fast ganz bedecken, in Wahrheit auf sich hat. Sind es Blütenblätter oder riesige

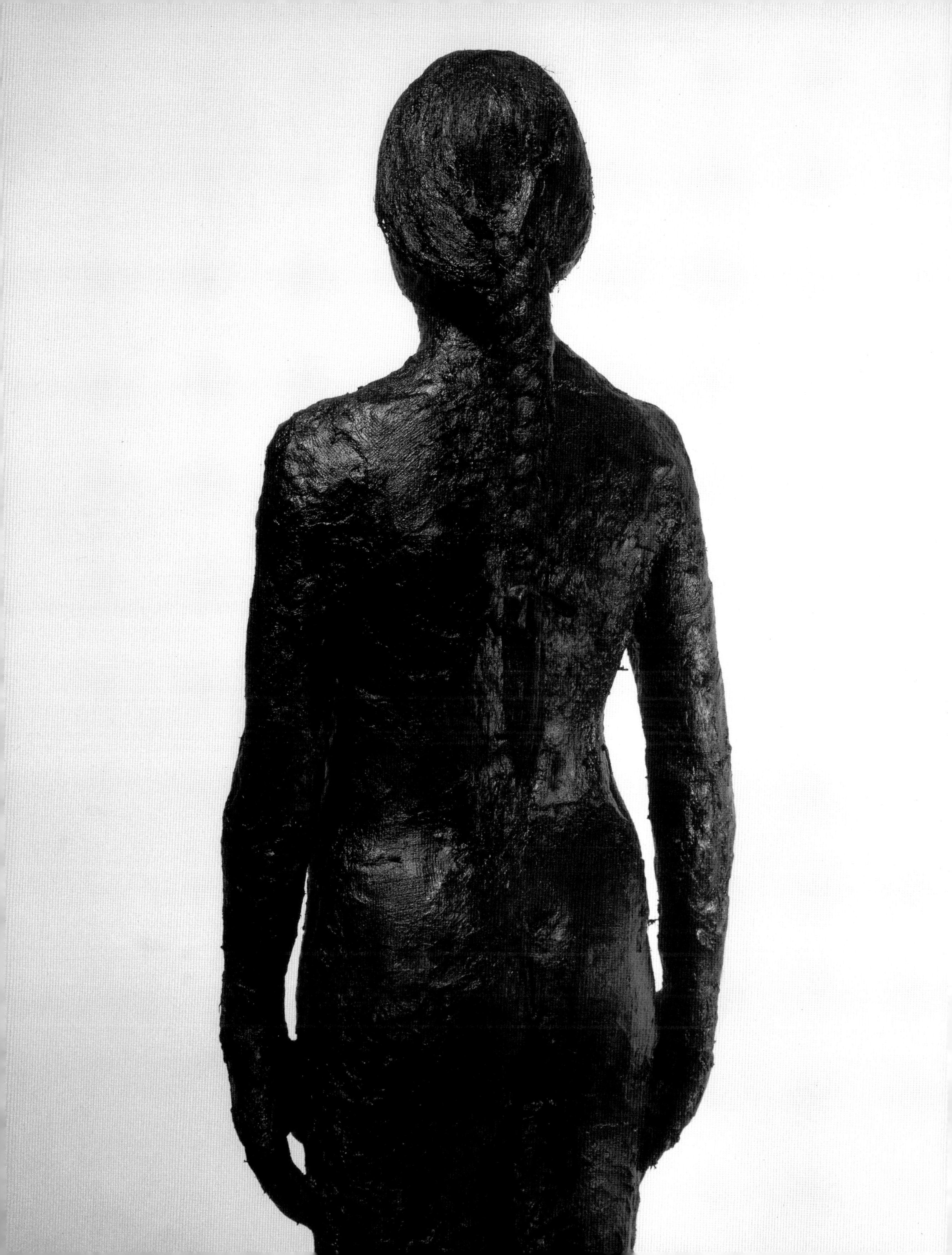

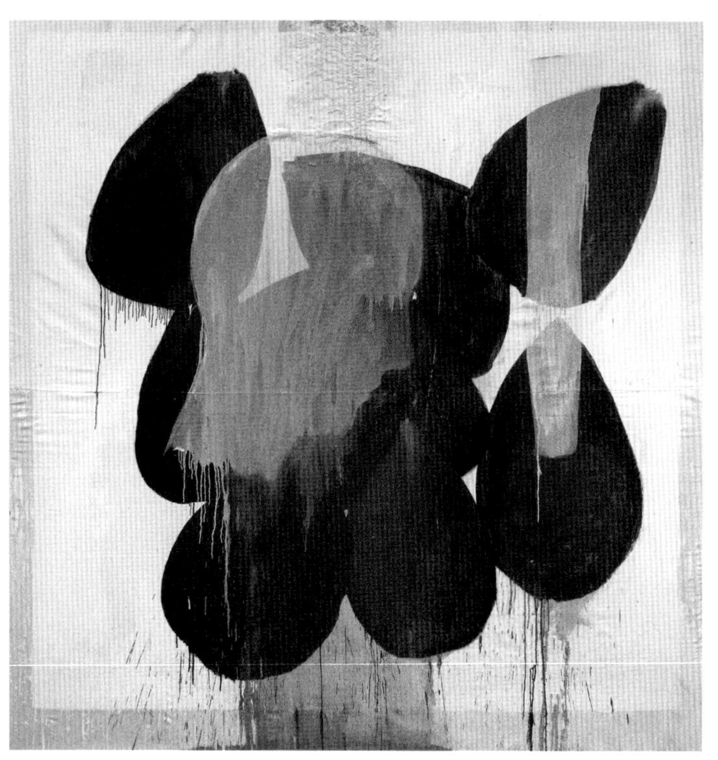

TERROR AND REMAINS
/SCHRECKEN UND ÜBERRESTE, 1998
Sammlung der Progressive Corporation, Cleveland, Ohio

Blutstropfen? Das Schwere und unpersönlich Bedeutungsschwangere, das sie ausstrahlen, steht in keinem Verhältnis zu der ergebenen, transparenten Nachdenklichkeit der anderen beiden gemalten Gegenstände, einem Arm und einem Kopf, denen stumm jede vernünftige Verbindung fehlt. Man weiß nicht, ob sie zum gleichen Körper gehören, es sei denn, das Bild ist ihr Körper, Öl und Stickerei auf Leinwand. Was von menschlichen Zügen und Gliedern bleibt, ist ein weißer Schatten, als wären die Farben und Flüssigkeiten des Lebens in einem anonymen, repetitiven Muster freigesetzt worden, derselbe geschichtliche Körper, den das Bild *Map/Landkarte*, 1998, zeigt, in welchem eine gemusterte, blutgetränkte Tapete einem abgetrennten, senkrecht herunterhängenden Arm Alleinsein, Ruhe und Sterblichkeit gewährt.

Der Sinn ist unausweichlich, diese Bilder zeichnen Gefühle auf. Und der vorliegende Essay läßt sich vielleicht leichter verstehen, wenn man sich geistig durch die Abschnitte treiben läßt wie durch die Mäander eines Flusslaufs.

Wenn ein Glasfisch zu einem grünen Blitz anschwillt und sein Maul weit aufreißt in einem Wald aus Bäumen, die sich beinahe im gemalten Weiß verlieren, mag der Betrachter unsicher werden und sich hin und her gerissen fühlen zwischen dem Bild und seinem Titel: *Glass Fish in Dark Room (Grace)/Glasfisch in dunkler Kammer (Anmut)*, 1999. Dieselbe Überraschung hält die Betrachtung eines weißen modellierten Kopfes auf dem Boden bereit. Die dunklen Pupillen scheinen wehmütig sagen zu wollen: „Einst konnte ich sehen." Ein nach innen gerichtetes Sehvermögen scheint in diesen Augen am Werk, wir wissen aber nicht, was es genau ist. Der Titel lautet *Quiet Night (Ocean)/Stille Nacht (Ozean)*, 1999. Denselben Kopf sehen wir auf einem Photo in den Armen des Künstlers im Meer bei Marina del Rey, Kalifornien, schwimmen. Der Titel der Photographie: *The Circumstances before Silence/Die Umstände vor der Stille*, 1999.

Enrique Martínez Celayas Visionen stammen aus den unartikulierten Tiefen seines Vor- oder Unterbewusstseins, das voller Geschichten ist, die weder der Erinnerung noch der Wirklichkeit angehören. Die Schichten aus Papier und Farbe, die seine großen Leinwände oft anschwellen lassen, könnte man als Seiten jener unheimlichen Geschichten auffassen, die sich auf dem Grund dieses Künstlergeistes verbergen. Lasst die Gestalten treiben, lasst sie aufsteigen oder ruhen; ihre Geburt bedeutet in jedem Fall ein verdammt blutiges Stück Arbeit. Sie tragen Blumen und Dornen und verleugnen niemals den Bruch, aus dem sie hervorgegangen sind.

Als Bilder, Symbole oder Beschreibungen sind diese figurativen Gestalten Totgeburten. Martínez Celaya zelebriert ihre Totenfeier voller Mitgefühl und Zartheit, indem er entweder dem konventionell vorgesehenen Geburtsort für seine Visionen – dem menschlichen Kopf – die Ehre erweist oder indem er die Köpfe geradewegs abschneidet und auf Kissen bettet, damit sie sein können, was sie in Wirklichkeit sind: bloß abgetrennte Köpfe. Gegenstände der Zuneigung. Die Guillotine. Revolution oder Auferstehung? Der Künstler legt Blumen auf ihr imaginäres Grab.

Vor rund fünfzig Jahren versuchte der italienische Künstler Piero Manzoni mit radikaler Folgerichtigkeit, dem Publikum die Existenz von Urbildern zu offenbaren: Bilder ohne Form und Komposition, reine Materie reiner Energie. Manzoni, dieser unbeirrbare Großreinemacher, befreite seine Kunst von jeder Beschränkung der Dimensionen, glaubte vielleicht sogar, dass das Leben selbst schrankenlos sei, und trat mit 28 Jahren seine letzte Reise an.

„Durch Laufen kann man die Erde nicht bezwingen, man muss sich schon Flügel wachsen lassen." Piero wollte mir nicht mehr aus dem Kopf, als ich sah, wie Martínez Celayas Köpfen und Armen Flügel wuchsen. Warum Flügel? Unser Zeitalter weiß mit Reinheit nichts mehr anzufangen. Die Tatsache, dass dieser Künstler mit einer begrifflichen Klarheit resigniert, die geradezu wissenschaftlich anmutet, erklärt noch nicht den fundamentalen Schmerz, der in seinen leicht der Erde zugewandten Köpfen unentwegt anklingt. Sie sind Gefangene ihres fehlenden Ausdrucks wie der gelbe Kopf in *The Undeniable and Unfortunate Truths/ Die unleugbaren und unglückseligen Wahrheiten*, 1998.

Wahrheiten sind weiße Flecken in der geistigen Leere; ein Faden, dünner als Spinnengewebe, verbindet sie lose untereinander. Sie sehen aus wie von Ungewissheit angekränkelte geistige Trugbilder. Vielleicht ist des Künstlers wissenschaftliche Erfahrung – und das Aufgeben dieser Laufbahn als nur eines unter vielen Ereignissen in seinem Leben – nicht wirklich die Ursache für diese tiefe, beinahe unheilbare Unruhe. Wenn der in seinen Bildern allgegenwärtige Kopf einen Kegel aus Materie erbricht, der Mund und Erde wieder miteinander verbindet (*Presos de Montaña*, 1999), kommt etwas Allgemeineres und Unpersönlicheres zum Ausdruck. Der Künstler kotzt sich hier wirklich selbst aus und führt dem Publikum sein privates Ritual vor, indem er Schatten ins Spiel bringt, die sein eigenes Spiegelbild verdunkeln. Was wir sehen, ist ein Mann von heute: ein zerrissener Körper, der im Kunstwerk ein Wiedervereinigungsritual vollzieht.

In jedem Bild findet eine anscheinend endlose, nicht kontinuierliche, physikalische Verständigung zwischen Energiewellen und bewegten Teilchen statt. Die zeitliche Dimension der Bilder wird sichtbar, und Vögel, Fische, Hände, Blumen, Köpfe verlieren sich im undefinierten Raum.

In *Powers and Dominions/ Mächte und Machtbereiche*, 1997, zum Beispiel, erscheint eine offene Hand. Hat sie die Blütenblätter verstreut oder nicht? Wo der Arm durchs Papier stößt, blutet es. Was ist hier jungfräulich, das Papier oder die Figur? – Ein Gefühl störenden Eindringens, ein Konflikt zwischen zwei verschiedenen Energiefeldern, Diskontinuität.

Was ist mit der Hand in *Arm and Braille/ Arm und Braille*, 1997, geschehen? War sie bereits abgeschnitten oder hat auch sie das Papier durchstoßen? – Der starke Eindruck, dass der sichtbare Teil dieses Arms immer noch vollständig mit einem Körper verbunden ist, den wir nicht sehen können; unsere Hand ist ein blindes Werkzeug.

Die Füße und Beine in *Stonewall/ Steinmauer*, 1997, scheinen zu betteln: „Lass mich ein, ich gebe dir eine Rose." Das Papier, nicht weniger dicht und undurchdringlich als ein Stein, ist eine Falte, die sich nicht öffnet.

Im Atelier zeigt sich ein neues Bild unverwüstlich: Der horizontale Teile eines Arms schwingt Flügel, der menschliche Kopf widersteht nicht länger der Schwerkraft und legt sich nieder. In einem Aquarell liegt der grüne Umriss eines Körpers parallel zum Boden – menschliches Laub eines flachen Landes, ein grüner Körper, der sich seiner Leere entledigt. Kein Kopf, der Einhalt geböte. *The Forest V, Clearing/ Der Wald V, Lichtung*, 1999.

In den wenigen kostbaren Spuren, die sichtbar werden, finden wir zahlreiche Geschichten angedeutet, als wären die Bilder eine Bühne mit mythologischer Kulisse. Aber Spuren dürfen nicht mit Erinnerungen verwechselt werden. Sie sind nicht „transparente Dinge, ... durch welche die Vergangenheit scheint!" wie bei Nabokov. Liest man sie Schritt für Schritt, als handelte es sich um verschiedene Morpheme eines einzigen visuellen Textes, sieht man, dass die Zeit, die sie zum Ausdruck bringen, das Präsens ist. Formen sind Blütenblätter, die auf einer gespannten Oberfläche schwimmen – letztlich ein Blatt auf geistigem Flachland. Wer weiß, woher die Vorstellung des Flachen kommt ... Das Flache dehnt sich nach allen Seiten aus und läßt uns die übrigen undurchdringlichen Dimensionen des Lebens verstehen. Zeichnen und Schreiben sind nichts als Garnenden, die vielleicht zur Entwirrung des Knotens führen.

Flüchtig wie Träume erzeugen die Bilder von Martínez Celaya den Eindruck der Selbstverschleierung in einer Raumzeit ohne erkennbare Koordinaten. Es fällt schwer, diesen Raum als Hintergrund zu sehen. Wie bei Robert Rymans undefinierten bemalten Flächen, die nicht unabhängig von Raum und Licht existieren, wird das begrenzte Raumviereck bei Martínez Celaya zu einer pulsierenden Vielzahl von Teilchen, was nahelegt, dass alle Erscheinungen kurzlebig sind, nicht viel mehr als optische Trugbilder . Was auf dem Papier oder der Leinwand zurückbleibt, ist der Versuch zu schreien: „Das ist die Grundsubstanz des Lebens und sie ist von Bild zu Bild so verschieden wie von Person zu Person. Wir versuchen ein Leben lang, ihre Formlosigkeit auszumerzen, und es gelingt uns nicht. Luft, Licht, Töne, Temperatur sowie Zeit und Geschichte verändern das Bild dessen, was wir heimlich in uns tragen, so dass unsere sichtbare Metamorphose und unsere unbeständigen, immerzu wechselnden Gefühle sich in den Augen anderer Leute widerspiegeln.“ Aber ein Künstler muss natürlich scheitern, wenn er nicht seinen eigenen Weg im Umgang mit der Form findet und seine Gedankengänge gelegentlich zugunsten eines sichtbaren Resultates abreissen lässt.

Martínez Celaya durchbricht diese Verbindung von Raum und Zeit durch eine Reihe kleiner Gestalten: Vögel, Bäume, einzelne Teile des menschlichen Körpers, Blumen, Blätter, Fische, Stücke von Tapisserie. Wie in der Musik sind die Variationen und Wiederholungen unbegrenzt. Manchmal werden diese mythologischen Gestalten aus der flachen Welt herausgehoben und zu Skulpturen. Ihr Schweigen ist damit nicht aufgehoben. Sie sind tot, ohne Verzweiflung tot geboren wie die Puppen meiner Kindheit. Eine Gussform für den Rumpf, je eine für jedes Glied, eine für den Kopf, kein Haar, kein Geschlecht. Stumm. Gummibänder, die den Körper zusammenhalten. Reißen sie, zerfällt der Körper in Stücke.

Neben einem kleinen abstrakten Werk von Martínez Celaya, das vor langer Zeit entstand, beherrscht eine majestätische Präsenz die ganze Höhe einer Wand seines Hauses: ein *Filzanzug* von Joseph Beuys. Ebenso puristisch wie Manzoni und nicht weniger kategorisch als Immanuel Kant, fand Beuys in diesem Werk die ideale Lösung für eine Skulptur der formlosen menschlichen Substanz. Das umhüllende Tuch definiert einen Raum, in dem die menschliche Puppe nie auseinander fallen wird; Identität ist nicht gefragt. In der philosophischen Falle des Filzanzugs könnte man Argumente für idealistische Träume ins Spiel bringen, aber es wäre nur ein Sprachspiel. Wenn ich mir anstelle der philosophischen eine alltägliche Verwendung des Satzes „Das ist ein Filzanzug, ohne Körper darin.“ vorstelle, so wird auch seine Bedeutung ganz klar und alltäglich. In Martínez Celayas Haus ist der *Filzanzug* ein Baum ohne Wurzeln oder ein menschlicher Körper, der zu einer weichen, undurchlässigen und erstickenden Parodie auf jeden Formalismus geworden ist: je monumentaler, desto leerer. Es könnte auch eine zeitgenössische Version von *Bath Bâdgerd* sein, jenem Palast des Nichtseins aus dem alten iranischen Märchen. Aber hierzu später.

Die physische Umsetzung verborgener Bewusstseinsinhalte ist Enrique Martínez Celayas Grundthema – einige Köpfe tragen bewegliche und fragile Spiegelbilder oder Galerien, die wie von Würmern ausgehöhlt wirken, andere erblühen unmotiviert in Grundfarben und strotzen vor Leben.

Aber um ins Boot der Kunst zu gelangen, müssen Martínez Celayas Gestalten einen schrecklichen Zoll entrichten: Ihre Erscheinung macht sie zu entfremdeten Wesen, zu Umrissen von Köpfen, die offensichtlich nicht sehen, wo sie sind und warum sie da sind. Vielleicht sind sie aus einem verlorenen Paradies vertrieben worden, um Simulakra zu werden. Und wenn das nicht genügte, gaben sie auch noch ihre körperliche Integrität und ihren persönlichen Charakter auf. Sie hätten gerettet oder erlöst werden können ... Die Grundelemente einer Geschichte, die der Künstler so sehr liebt, dass er sie endlos wiederholt ... Eine vergessene Geschichte taucht allmählich wieder auf. Das lässt sich nicht erklären. Das Kunstwerk kehrt das Innenleben dieses Künstlers für jedermann sichtbar nach außen und zeigt unverblümt die Ausweglosigkeit, in der wir alle gefangen sind.[1] Es gibt einen mit Asche bedeckten Nacken von Martínez Celaya, und ein unbestimmter Schatten – halb Blütenblatt, halb Flügel – erhebt sich aus der Asche.

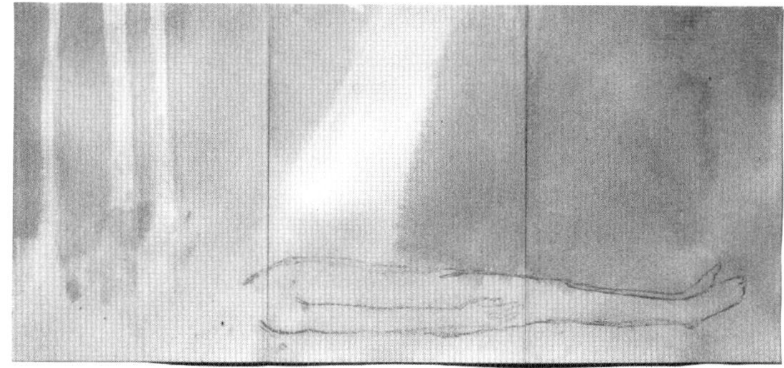

THE FOREST V, CLEARING/DER WALD V, LICHTUNG, 1999
Sammlung William Griffin, Venice, Kalifornien

> Das Kunstwerk kann in dem Augenblick entstehen, in dem der menschliche Geist die Macht aufgibt, über das Physische zu räsonnieren. Es ist der Triumph des Fleischlichen. Das klare Denken, das den kreativen Prozess einleitet, vernichtet sich selbst in demselben.[2]

Lassen Sie uns noch einmal vom *Filzanzug* ausgehen und so tun, als würden wir darin stecken. Der Filz entspricht der physischen Verhärtung unseres Bewusstseins.

Für den Knaben Enrique begann der Bewusstwerdungsprozess mit einer offenen Wunde an einem seiner Arme im Alter von sieben Jahren, als er Kuba für immer verließ. Viel später hat er die Form dieser Narbe als vertikalen Schnitt in einer Leinwand nachgebildet. In der kleinen dreidimensionalen Arbeit, *Fiber and Thread for a Seven Year Old*/*Gewebe und Faden für einen Siebenjährigen*, 1993, ist hinter der Leinwand ein leerer Raum und davor, anstelle des Glases, ein transparentes Seidengewebe. Die Stiche, welche die Enden der Wunde zusammenhalten sollen, lassen das Loch halb geöffnet. Eine Logik des Fleisches. Ich sage nicht, dass diese Narbe seine Kunst erklärt. Für Enriques klaren Geist ist die auf seinem Arm zurückgebliebene Narbe jedoch die Spur eines entscheidenden Verlusterlebnisses. Beim Betrachter kommt es ganz darauf an ... Ich sehe die offenen Schamlippen einer Vagina, eine Arche, die das Geheimnisse aller Dinge birgt, die noch geboren werden. Vielleicht weil das kleine Werk neben dem *Filzanzug* hängt, sehe ich seine nun von Blut befreiten Ränder als Tür, durch welche die Neuronen ihr Gespräch mit der Welt aufnehmen. Und als Form eines Blattes, das wie eine Insel aussieht, beinahe wie Kuba.

Schritt für Schritt, als bewege er sich vorsichtig aus dieser ersten Wunde heraus und halte seine Gespenster (alles alchemistisch-archetypische Symbole) vor den Vergrößerungsspiegel seiner Bilder, macht der Künstler Martínez Celaya den schwierigen Prozess der Gestaltwerdung in Bildern sichtbar, die keine endgültige Form anstreben. Geformtsein würde eine Verhärtung bedeuten, weg von der Freiheit – dem Mangel an Bestimmtheit – hin zur Endgültigkeit des Seins, als ob jeder Schritt in Richtung deutliche Identifikation das Ende des kreativen Prozesses und damit den Tod bedeuten würde.

So scheinen seine Gestalten auf der Schwelle zum Leben zu verharren, nicht ganz sicher, ob sie die Schranke zum Sein überwinden wollen. Mit Samuel Beckett könnten sie sagen: „Wir haben von Blumen gelebt." (Aus einem unvollendeten Werk, 1957). Auf Leinwand und Papier haben sie allerdings ein Leben, sozusagen Existenzblitze aus einer Fülle, die auf dramatische Weise verloren ging bei der Entstehung des Bewusstseins, der Sprache und der Regeln

1. Vgl. Albert Camus: *Le Mythe de Sysyphe*, 1942.
2. Ebenda.

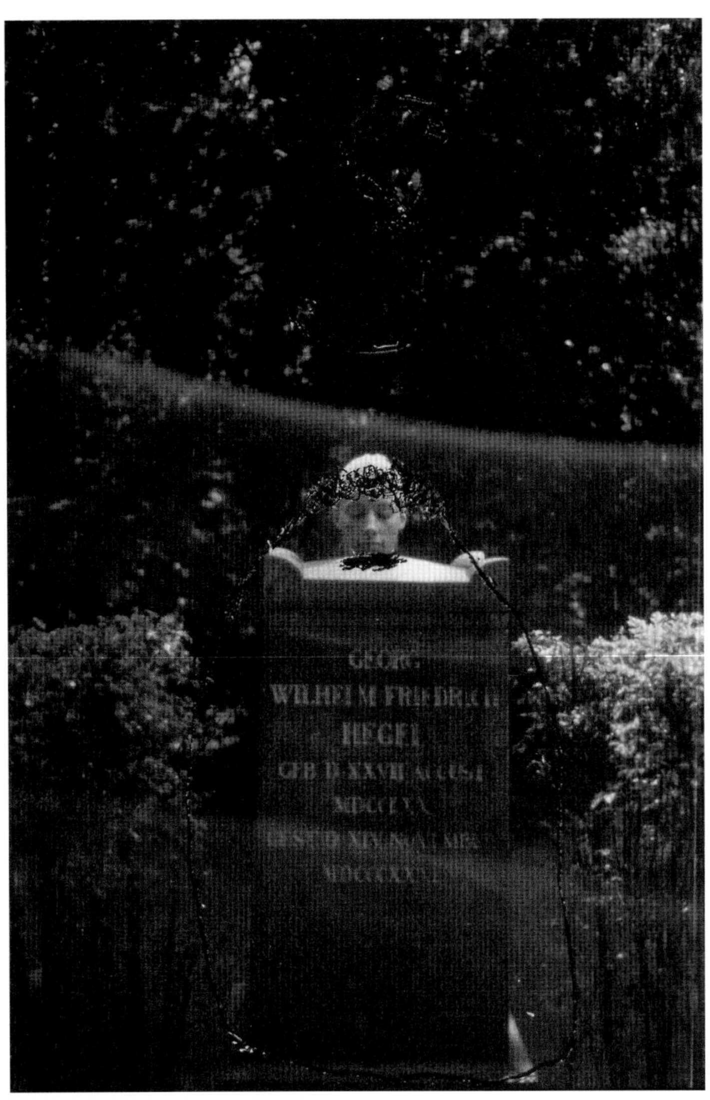

LAST FLOWER, detail/LETZTE BLUME, Ausschnitt, 1998
Sammlung Enrique and Alexandra Martínez Celaya

zwischenmenschlicher Beziehungen. Dem zeitlichen Gefängnis, dem Nebel der Lügen und dem Schmerz des Bekennens zu trotzen und in Erwartung des alchemistischen Wundervogels zu existieren, der womöglich eine Hand oder einen Fuß für den kopf- und orientierungslosen Körper oder aber den den Körper entbehrenden Kopf zurückbringen wird, darin besteht ihre transitorische Qualität.

Der Künstler belässt sie im Status nascendi, die Wirklichkeit wird sie versteinern lassen. So sind die Köpfe, diese nicht zu heilenden Köpfe, Reliquien, die der Künstler physisch zur Welt bringt. Im Reich der Ideen gab es für sie kein Halten mehr. Der Künstler verändert sie nicht und tut so, als könnten sie ins Leben zurückkehren; er verhält sich nicht wie Orpheus. Er trägt sie in den Ozean, in einen Wald und dann wieder zurück ins Atelier. Manche der Köpfe ruhen auf Kissen. Wirklichkeit ist etwas, was die menschliche Vernunft erfassen kann, aber sie verändert sich nicht. Kein Wunder, daß sich Martínez Celaya von Hegels Philosophie angezogen fühlt.

1998 besuchte er Hegels Grab. Hegels Leben, seine Bücher, sein ungeheures Gedankengebäude, das Raum zu schaffen suchte für die unablässige Bewegung des Lebens: Wellen, die sich selbst in die Quere kommen bei der Erzeugung von Eigenschaften, Farben und erkennbaren Zügen und Formen und die sich immer und immer wiederholen, in unwillkürlicher Schwingung zwischen Sein und Werden – all das war reduziert zu ein paar in Stein gehauenen Lettern und Ziffern: *Georg Wilhelm Friedrich Hegel, 27. August 1770–14. November 1831.*

Martínez Celaya hat den Umriss dieses Steins in einer Schwarzweiß-Photographie (*Last Flower/Letzte Blume*, 1998) auf dieselbe Weise verändert, in der John Baldessari einst eine landschaftliche Silhouette mit Rotstift korrigierte (*Corrected Stonehenge*, 1984). Ein Bogen aus Holzpflöcken umgibt den Stein und hält Blumen über einen Kopf, der in der Mitte von Hegels Grabmal erscheint. Hat der Stein seinen eigenen Widerspruch erzeugt? Es ist Hegels Vermächtnis: „Worte sind Steine." Warum nicht die Köpfe? Die Körper kommen so gut es geht ohne sie zurecht.

Wurde die Kunst nicht erfunden, um geistige Unbeweglichkeit zu bekämpfen? Während das kollektive Unbewusste unserer Gegenwart – wie schon so oft in der Vergangenheit – mehr und mehr erstarrt, werden keine neuen Utopien formuliert. Der Kolibri fliegt uns übers Gesicht und bedroht unsere Augen und Nasenflügel, pickend (*A Dry Bed/Ein trockenes Bett*, 1998), saugend, heftig mit den Flügeln schlagend: „Wach auf, wach auf! Die verlorenen Farben sollen zurückkommen, ja, selbst wenn Blut fließen muss. Ich geriet in eine rasende Wut, mein Körper wurde von einer Birke durchbohrt. Sie war weiß, was nun, ihr schweigenden Statuen, wie wollt ihr wissen, wie ich anfing? Ihr wisst nicht, was ihr nicht seht." Ich kann mich des Gefühls, das diese Vögel auslösen, nicht erwehren, nämlich, dass sie Wahrheitsboten sind wie der weiße Papagei des *Tuti-Nameh* (*Das Papageienbuch*, eine Sammlung von Geschichten aus dem Orient) und die heilige Taube in der christlichen Tradition. Hermes war der erste, der Flügel an den Füßen trug. Im Lauf von zweitausend Jahren sind die Flügel zu Vögeln geworden. Also könnte man Martínez Celaya als hermetischen Künstler betrachten.

Man sollte Erinnerung nicht als Wissen bezeichnen ... Öffnen wir unsere Blätter wie eine Blume und seien wir passiv und empfänglich ... nehmen wir die Anregungen jedes edlen Insekts auf, das uns mit seinem Besuch beehrt ... Ich habe keine Bücher gelesen – der Morgen gibt mir Recht.[3]

3. John Keats, Brief an seinen Freund Reynolds, 19. Februar 1818 (von der Übersetzerin des Essays ins Deutsche übertragen).

Indem er Spuren in der sichtbaren Welt legt, erforscht Martínez Celaya das Terrain für visuelle Geschichten, und zwar eher dramatischer als ästhetischer Art. Eine Rhapsodie in Schwarz nahm in seinem Atelier von September bis Dezember 2000 ihren Lauf. Sie begann mit einer Serie von Bildern; in einem stand ein Knabe im Dunkeln – umgeben von Regen und Blitzen. Nach einigen Wochen waren alle Bilder nach New York geschickt worden, außer einem, in der die Dunkelheit an die Ränder gedrängt war und der mittlere Raum eine Landschaft zeigte, wie man sie gelegentlich in der Morgendämmerung sieht *(The Blink/Der Augenblick,* 2000), wenn das Licht auf eine neugeborene Welt fällt, jeder Tag der allererste.

Erneut begannen schwarze Bilder das Atelier zu füllen, teerbedeckte Bilder – feinste weiße Fäden kamen daraus hervor und zeichneten die Umrisse von menschlichen Körpern und Bäumen. Davor stand die Statue eines Jugendlichen mit erkennbaren Geschlechtsorganen. Sein Kopf ist leicht geneigt. Füße und Hände fehlen. Beide, Knabe und Hirsch, mit Federn bedeckt und teergeschwärzt, schauen einander in die Augen, als würden sie magnetisch voneinander angezogen *(Coming Home/Heimkehr,* 2000*)*. Es war seltsam, die Intensität ihres Blickkontaktes zu spüren, obwohl sie keine Augen haben, und dort mit ihnen fest gebannt in der Stille der Sprache zu stehen. Einige Tage später lehnt ein Spiegel am Geweih des Hirschs. Weil die Glasfläche keine Bilder absorbiert, wird der Kopf des Knaben von ihr in einem vielfachen Leben gedanklicher Reflexionen in Gemälden und Photodrucken zurückgeworfen. Aber die erstaunlichste Erscheinung auf demselben Stockwerk ist ein zerbrochener Vogel, ebenfalls schwarz.

Wer Gelegenheit hat, *Bath Bâdgerd* durchzublättern, das iranische Märchen, in dem alte Legenden zu einer einzigen Sequenz von Düsternis und Verfall verdichtet sind und das nur so strotzt vor Spiegeln und versteinerten Körpern – das Ganze ist ein einziges verwirrendes Ringen um Selbsterkenntnis –, der wird das gleiche Ausgangsmaterial entdecken, das Enrique Martínez Celaya in seiner Installation einsetzte. Wenn der Vogel einmal tot ist, wird der verlorene Schatz wieder sichtbar und die Person ist erlöst. Aber zurück zur Realität: In Enriques Atelier gemahnt mich der riesige ruhende Hirsch an eine weibliche Präsenz. Niemand kann mit Sicherheit sagen, was wirklich geschehen ist, ob der Künstler vielleicht für seine eigene weibliche Seite eine Gestalt in Form dieses Fleisch- und Knochenberges gefunden hat, der er ohne Scham gegenübertreten kann. Aber bitte, schneiden Sie hier und jetzt nicht die schmiegsamen Fäden dieser Rhapsodie in Schwarz mit vernünftigen Assoziationen entzwei. Man kann hindurchgehen und sie sind immer noch da. Dies ist ein Ort für Gedankenblüten, die zu ihrer Reflexion der Hindernisse bedürfen.

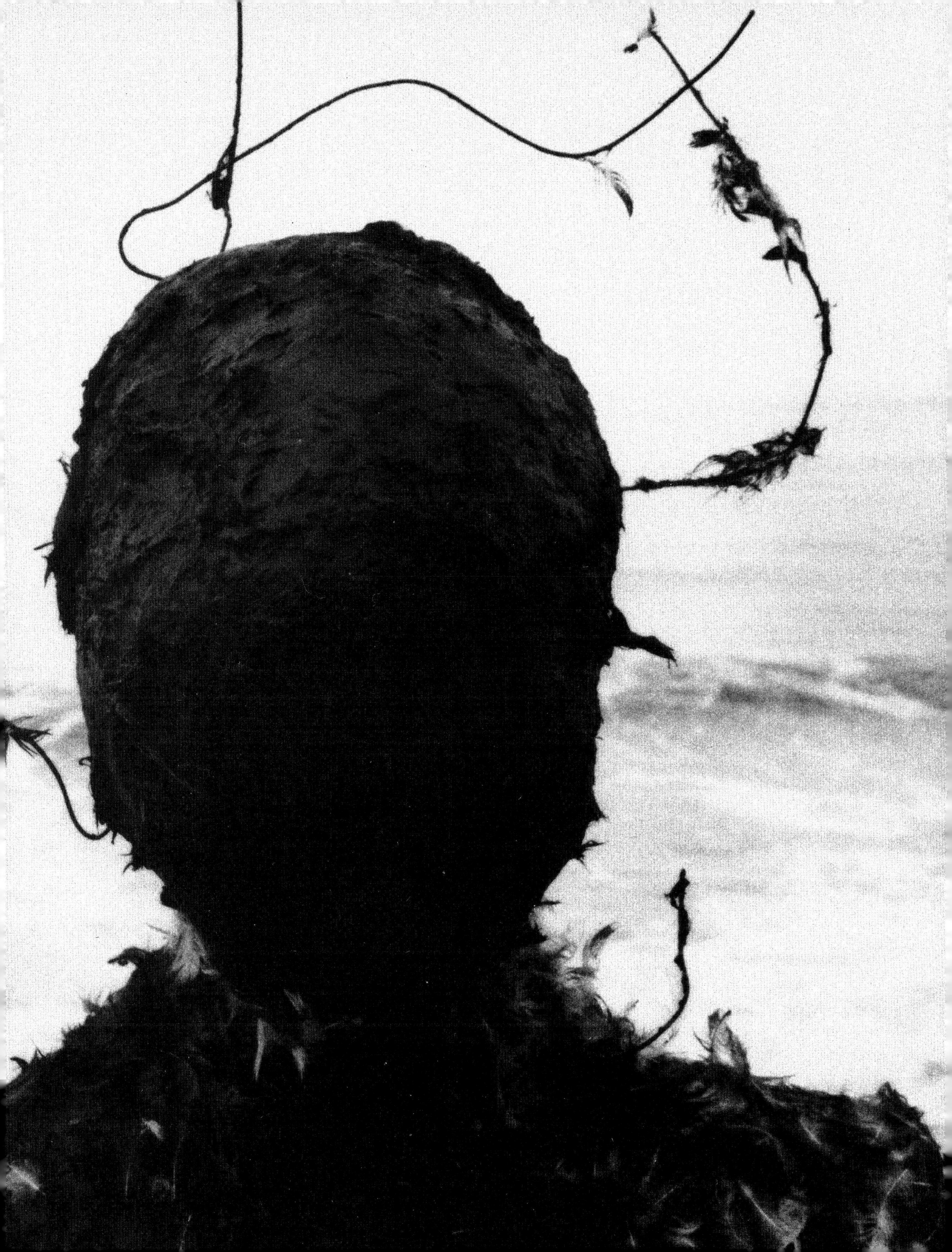

WORKS/WERKE 1992–2000

Commentary by/Kommentar von

Judson J. Emerick

Arden Reed

INTRODUCTION TO THE COMMENTARIES

Arden Reed

The following remarks are neither critical reviews nor interpretations, but commentaries. Therein lies a paradox, however, for writing commentary on Enrique Martínez Celaya is a deeply suspect undertaking. Because commentary by its character is positivistic: it pronounces, defines, clarifies, explains, classifies, compares. And commentary presupposes a stable object of inquiry, if it does not create that object. For many contemporary artists, explanation and classification are appropriate. One welcomes a commentary putting the object to rest, satisfying us that one has understood and appreciated. Not for Martínez Celaya. His work, not by design but simply by its character, resists any substantive remarks one might make about it. His work unsettles pronouncements, it remains stubbornly elsewhere.

What does it mean, today, for an artist to investigate truth? Martínez Celaya's background in physics exposed him to aspects of the world that we don't normally perceive, to a world having little to do with what is superficially apparent. To address that elusive world Martínez Celaya's art must be fugitive or nomadic, not present where it seems to be–even though it has a strong, often an uncomfortable physical presence. Maybe this is why he maintains that "the radical nature of art, while reached by means of its surface, is always about something else."

Martínez Celaya's work tends to address moments when things look like they're going to fit and they don't quite, moments just before collapse. "My work has always tried to undermine what is created, so there is a constant battle for the elimination of the work itself." On the other hand, this built-in failure frees him to treat, without irony, subjects that other contemporary artists would handle only with cool detachment if not cynicism. Against a scene where irony hedges every serious gesture, he stands out.

The physicality of Martínez Celaya's art is deceptive. He cultivates this quality of concreteness, of thingness, and at the same time wants to dematerialize his work. So he produces an object that suffers physical abuse–burns, tears, and mutilations–and patching, stitching, and grometting–but then treats this object as a trace. He persuades us that the work is at its best a glimpse of something else, and elsewhere. If by tradition illusionistic art carves out an imaginary space into the wall, Martínez Celaya's aim is not to recreate a three-dimensional world on canvas but to de-create the wall.

In the face of such resistance to commentary what is the commentator to do? First, write an introduction. Second, propose that my text be read under erasure, the way German existentialist philospher Martin Heidegger writes *Being* and then crosses out the word so that it is legible but qualified, as it were, out of existence. Third, invoke or imagine a mobility to our remarks, such that any position staked out or statement proffered is displaced if not evacuated by another. Fourth, translate the sequential nature of commentary into simultaneity.

VORBEMERKUNG ZU DEN KOMMENTAREN

Arden Reed

Die folgenden Anmerkungen sind weder Werkbesprechungen noch Interpretationen, sondern Kommentare. Darin liegt insofern ein Paradox, als Enrique Martínez Celaya zu kommentieren ein zutiefst suspektes Unterfangen ist. Denn der Kommentar ist seinem Wesen nach positivistisch: er verkündet, definiert, klärt, erklärt, klassifiziert, vergleicht. Er setzt ein beständiges Forschungsobjekt voraus, wenn er es nicht selbst erschafft. Und tatsächlich sind Erklärung und Klassifizierung häufig der geeignete Weg, sich dem Werk eines zeitgenössischen Künstlers zu nähern. Der Kommentar ist uns willkommen, bringt er doch das Untersuchte auf den Punkt und uns die Zufriedenheit, verstanden und richtig rezipiert zu haben. Nicht so bei Enrique Martínez Celaya. Weniger durch die äußere Form als vielmehr durch seinen Charakter entzieht sich sein Werk jeglicher Einordnung, widersteht jeder Festlegung, verharrt dickköpfig im Anderswo.

Was bedeutet es heute für einen Künstler, Wahrheit zu ergründen? In seinem Physikstudium hat Martínez Celaya eine Welt kennen gelernt, die uns normalerweise verborgen bleibt, eine Welt, in der nichts ist, wie es nach außen hin scheint. Um mit dieser ungewissen Welt in Kontakt zu treten, muss seine Kunst flüchtig oder nomadisch sein, darf nicht dort präsent sein, wo sie zu sein scheint – trotz ihrer starken, oft unbequemen physischen Präsenz. Vielleicht besteht Martínez Celaya deshalb darauf, dass „das radikale Wesen der Kunst sich zwar der Oberfläche als Mittel bedient, aber immer mit etwas anderem beschäftigt ist".

Martínez Celaya versucht mit seiner Kunst, Augenblicke einzufangen, in denen sich die Dinge ineinander zu fügen scheinen, um Sekunden später zu scheitern, den Moment kurz vor dem Zusammenbruch. „Ich habe in meiner Arbeit stets versucht, das bereits Geschaffene zu untergraben, so dass sie einem endlosen Kampf um die Eliminierung der Arbeit selbst gleichkommt." Dieses eingebaute Scheitern ermöglicht es ihm aber auch, bestimmte Themen ohne die leiseste Spur von Ironie anzugehen, Themen, die andere zeitgenössische Künstler nur mit kühler Distanziertheit oder gar Zynismus behandeln würden. Denn Martínez Celaya grenzt sich deutlich ab von einer Kunstszene, in der Ironie jede ernste Geste im Keim erstickt.

Die Materialität von Martínez Celayas Kunst ist trügerisch. Denn während er einerseits Konkretheit und Dinglichkeit kultiviert, ist er andererseits darum bemüht, seine Arbeit aufzulösen. So schafft er beispielsweise ein physisch geschundenes, zusammengeflicktes und -genähtes Objekt – Verbrennungen, Tränen, Verstümmelungen –, und betrachtet die fertige Arbeit nurmehr als Spur. Er überzeugt uns davon, dass das Objekt bestenfalls einen flüchtigen Eindruck von etwas anderem vermittelt, an einem anderen Ort existiert. Im Unterschied zur klassischen illusionistischen Kunst, die einen imaginären Raum in der Wand öffnet, will Celaya die Leinwand nicht mit einer dreidimensionalen Welt füllen; er versucht vielmehr, sie zu zersetzen.

Was also soll der Kommentator angesichts all dieser Stolpersteine tun? Zunächst eine Vorbemerkung schreiben. Zweitens, vorschlagen ebendiese zu lesen, als sei sie bereits gelöscht, frei nach Martin Heidegger, der das Wort *Sein* durchstrich, so dass es zwar lesbar, aber zur Nichtexistenz verurteilt war. Drittens, dem Kommentar eine Mobilität verleihen, die dafür sorgt, dass jeder Standpunkt potenziell durch einen anderen ersetzt oder entkräftet werden kann. Und viertens, das sequenzielle Wesen des Kommentars in Simultaneität übersetzen.

DIALECTIC OF RESISTANCE/DIALEKTIK DES WIDERSTANDES

silence, kitsch and the specific/Stille, Kitsch und das Spezifische

LA OTRA PRISIÓN (THE OTHER PRISON), 1992
Oil and wax on canvas with lights
70 x 45 inches (178 x 114 cm)
Collection of Enrique and Alexandra Martínez Celaya

We deal still with a picture here, with a panel painting in the long tradition that reaches back to ancient Greece where such framed window views first appeared around 400 B.C.E. You can tell because the rectangular canvas has a frame made of a string of electric lights; the framed expanse of the canvas thus becomes an imaginary window opening on some ideal space and time. The work drifts in and out of focus around the notion that it is somehow a religious icon, something carried in a religious procession, hung on an iconostasis, or propped on an altar. The picture has two 'figures': the hummingbird flying upward just above the center of the canvas, and the text, "la otra (prisión)," written in quick strokes near the bottom edge. These hover on the scumbled gray ground (space?) and almost turn metaphorical; I mean that we may be tempted to read the two together. We might make the bird a symbol. The text a gnomic utterance. Each might form some hermetic substitute for the holy man, the holy woman, or the sacred narrative that typically appears in altarpieces as the focus for prayer and worship. But the bird and the text defy linkage; they seem only remainders or traces of any number of gestures, both artistic and poetic, that we cannot see or read the leftovers of some pictures and poems. The textured surface of the painting resists illusion; no 'space' here! No 'figures' on a proper 'ground' after all. Indeed, the bird and text overlap other 'figures,' of which traces survive in the textured ground, huge ellipses or oval shapes. What was painted out? What painted in? An anti-picture that hides instead of reveals. The bird remains stubbornly 'what it is.' The text, a fragment.

JE

LA OTRA PRISIÓN (DAS ANDERE GEFÄNGNIS), 1992
Öl und Wachs auf Leinwand, Lichter
70 x 45 Zoll (178 x 114 cm)
Sammlung Enrique and Alexandra Martínez Celaya

Es handelt sich hier noch um ein Gemälde, eine Bildtafel nach einer Tradition, die bis ins alte Griechenland zurückreicht, wo ein solcher Blick durch ein Fenster um ca. 400 v. Chr. erstmals auftrat. Dies ist daran erkennbar, dass die rechteckige Leinwand einen Rahmen aus elektrischen Lichtern hat und die gerahmte Fläche so zu einem imaginären Fenster wird, das sich auf einen idealen Raum und eine ideale Zeit öffnet. Das Werk nähert und entfernt sich von der Vorstellung, dass es sich um ein wie auch immer geartetes religiöses Symbol handelt, dass es etwas ist, was in einer religiösen Prozession getragen, an eine Ikonostasis gehängt oder auf einen Altar gestellt wird. Das Bild zeigt zwei „Figuren": den Kolibri, der etwas über dem Zentrum der Leinwand nach oben fliegt, und den Text „La otra (prisión)", der mit schnellen Pinselstrichen nahe der unteren Kante geschrieben steht. Sie schweben über dem aus Farbschichten bestehenden grauen Boden (Raum?) und werden fast metaphorisch, womit ich sagen will, dass die Versuchung besteht, beide gemeinsam zu lesen. Wir könnten aus dem Vogel ein Symbol und aus dem Text eine gnomische Äußerung machen. Beides könnte ein hermetischer Ersatz für den heiligen Mann, die heilige Frau oder die heilige Geschichte sein, die üblicherweise auf Altären als Thema für Gebet und Verehrung erscheinen. Jedoch trotzen Vogel und Text jeder Verknüpfung; sie scheinen lediglich die Reste oder Spuren einer beliebigen Anzahl an Gesten künstlerischer und poetischer Art zu sein und wir können die Bilder- und Gedichtreste weder sehen noch lesen. Die strukturierte Oberfläche des Gemäldes widersetzt sich der Illusion; kein „Raum" hier! Keine „Gestalten" auf einem ordnungsgemäßen „Boden". Und wirklich überlappen Vogel und Text andere „Figuren", von denen Spuren im strukturierten Boden überleben, große Ellipsen oder ovale Formen. Was wurde herausgemalt? Was wurde hineingemalt? Ein Anti-Gemälde, das versteckt, anstatt zu offenbaren. Der Vogel bleibt starrsinnig „was er ist". Der Text ein Fragment.

JE

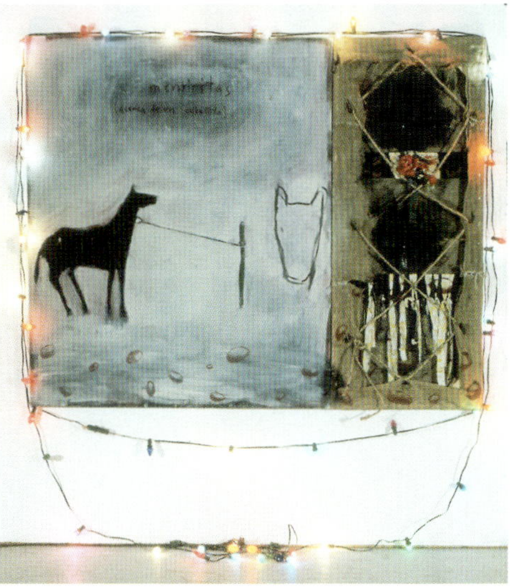

A LITTLE HORSE PAINTING
/GEMÄLDE EINES KLEINEN PFERDES, 1992
Collection of/Sammlung Brian Mountford,
New York, New York

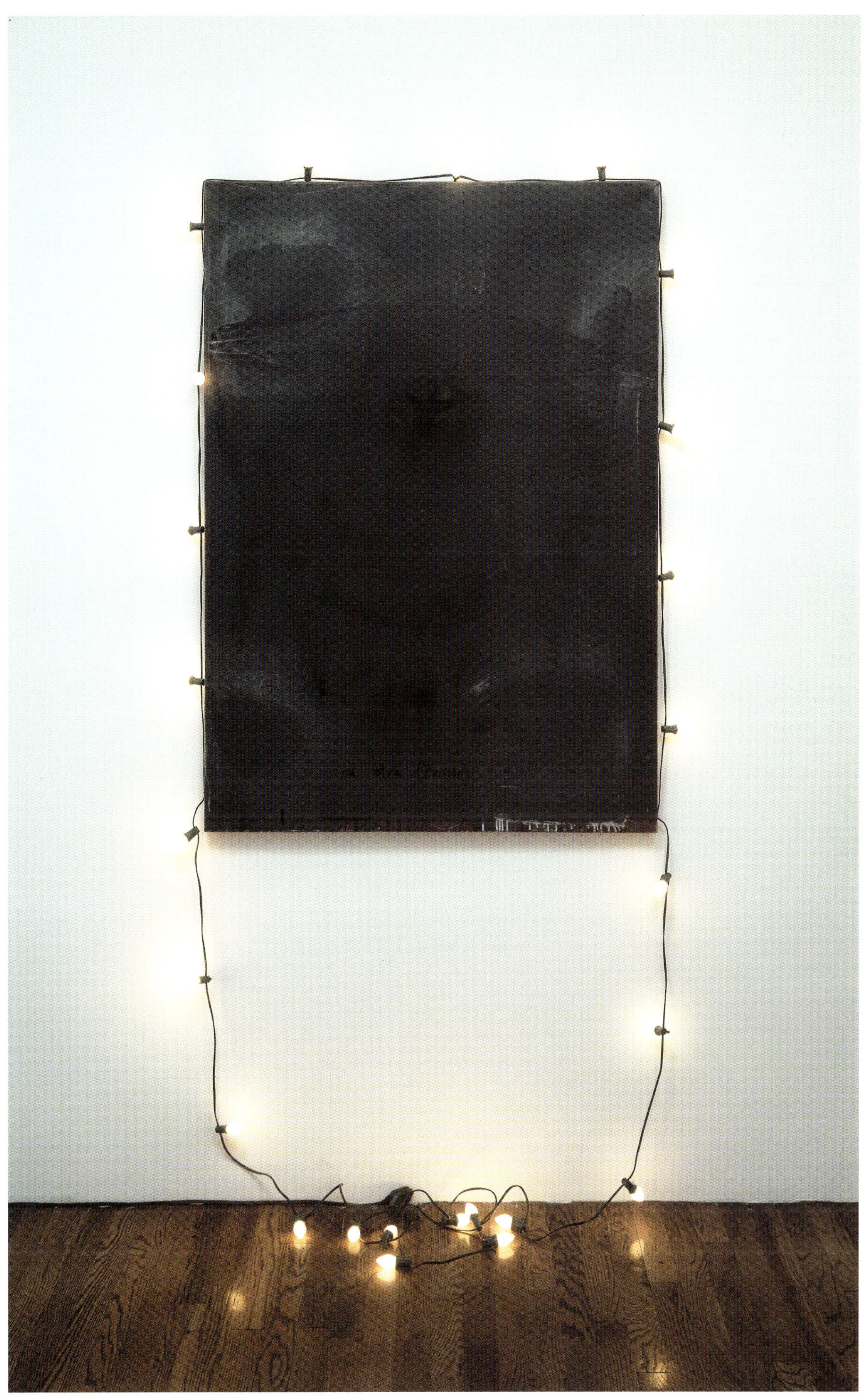

THE TROUBLE WITH MEMORY, 1993
Oil, wax, silk flowers and velvet on canvas
78 x 66 inches (198 x 168 cm)
Private Collection, London, United Kingdom

This canvas recalls the kind of pictorial relief, *rilievo schiacciato*, invented by Donatello (literally: squashed relief, a sculptor's answer to the painter of pictures). *The Trouble with Memory* works more or less in the traditional way and spreads out figures on planes parallel to the picture plane.

The dominance of black and gray in this work puts us in a somber mood (this comes from a series Martínez Celaya calls 'Black Paintings,' doubtless remembering Francisco Goya). The fake roses imprisoned in gesso, petrified, look, moreover, like symbols. We become wary. The picture's title, *The Trouble with Memory*, pushes us to interpret. We note the rose embroidered in white thread on the black, velvet hanging: perhaps a picture of a rose playing upon the three-dimensional roses hovering nearby. The image on the hanging could be the trace of them. We might deal with it as a meditation on Veronica's veil.[1] We might treat the works as some Modern icon exploring 'real presence,' if not of God's face, then of something else in a picture. Does the image on the hanging somehow supplement the image (the relief) that the hanging is part of? One illusion does seem to fold into another: fake silk flower/embroidered image of a flower; flower on a hanging, hanging along with flowers on a canvas hanging in a gallery. But just as soon as we get the imaginary machine up and running, an elegant thing indeed, (the small white embroidered rose electrifies us), it collapses into kitsch. An icon on black velvet? Oh, sure.

JE

DAS PROBLEM MIT DEM GEDÄCHTNIS, 1993
Öl, Wachs, Seidenblumen und Samt auf Leinwand
78 x 66 Zoll (198 x 168 cm)
Privatsammlung, London, Großbritannien

Diese Leinwand erinnert an die Art malerischen Reliefs, die von Donatello erfunden wurde (rilievo schiacciato: „zerquetschtes" Relief, die Antwort eines Bildhauers auf den Maler). *Das Problem mit dem Gedächtnis* arbeitet mehr oder weniger traditionell und breitet Gestalten auf Ebenen aus, die parallel zur Bildfläche verlaufen.

Die Dominanz von Schwarz und Weiß in diesem Werk versetzt uns in eine eher düstere Stimmung (es stammt aus der Serie, die Martínez Celaya „Schwarze Gemälde" nennt, wobei er sich zweifelsohne an Goya erinnerte). Die künstlichen Rosen, in Gips gefangen, sind wie erstarrt und sehen obendrein wie Symbole aus. Wir sind auf der Hut. Der Titel des Gemäldes, *Das Problem mit dem Gedächtnis*, verleitet uns zur Interpretation. Wir bemerken die mit weißem Faden gestickte Rose und den schwarzen Samtvorhang: vielleicht das Bild einer Rose, das auf die dreidimensionalen in der Nähe schwebenden Rosen anspielt. Das Bild auf dem Vorhang könnte eine Spur von ihnen sein. Wir könnten es als eine Meditation über den Schleier der Veronika sehen.[1] Wir könnten das Werk als ein modernes Symbol behandeln, das die „wahre Präsenz", wenn nicht von Gottes Gesicht so doch von etwas anderem, in einem Bild erforscht. Ergänzt das Bild auf dem Vorhang das Bild (das Relief), zu dem der Vorhang gehört, auf irgendeine Art? Eine Illusion scheint sich in die nächste zu mischen: künstliche Seidenblumen und gesticktes Bild einer Blume, Blume auf einem Vorhang, Vorhang zusammen mit Blumen auf einer Leinwand, die in einem Ausstellungsraum hängt. Aber sobald wir unserer Phantasie freien Lauf lassen, in der Tat eine sehr elegante Sache (die kleine weiße Rosenstickerei ist faszinierend), fällt es zusammen und wird zu Kitsch. Ein Symbol auf schwarzem Samt? Aber sicher.

JE

1. Veronica, present in legend at Christ's Crucifixion, mopped Christ's brow as he struggled to the place of execution, to discover afterward a miraculous image of his Holy Face upon the cloth (Saint Peter's at the Vatican preserves the relic).

1 Veronika, die der Legende nach bei der Kreuzigung Christi anwesend war, wusch sein Gesicht, als er sich zum Ort der Kreuzigung quälte, und entdeckte auf dem Tuch das wundersame Bild seines heiligen Antlitzes (der Petersdom in Rom bewahrt die Reliquie).

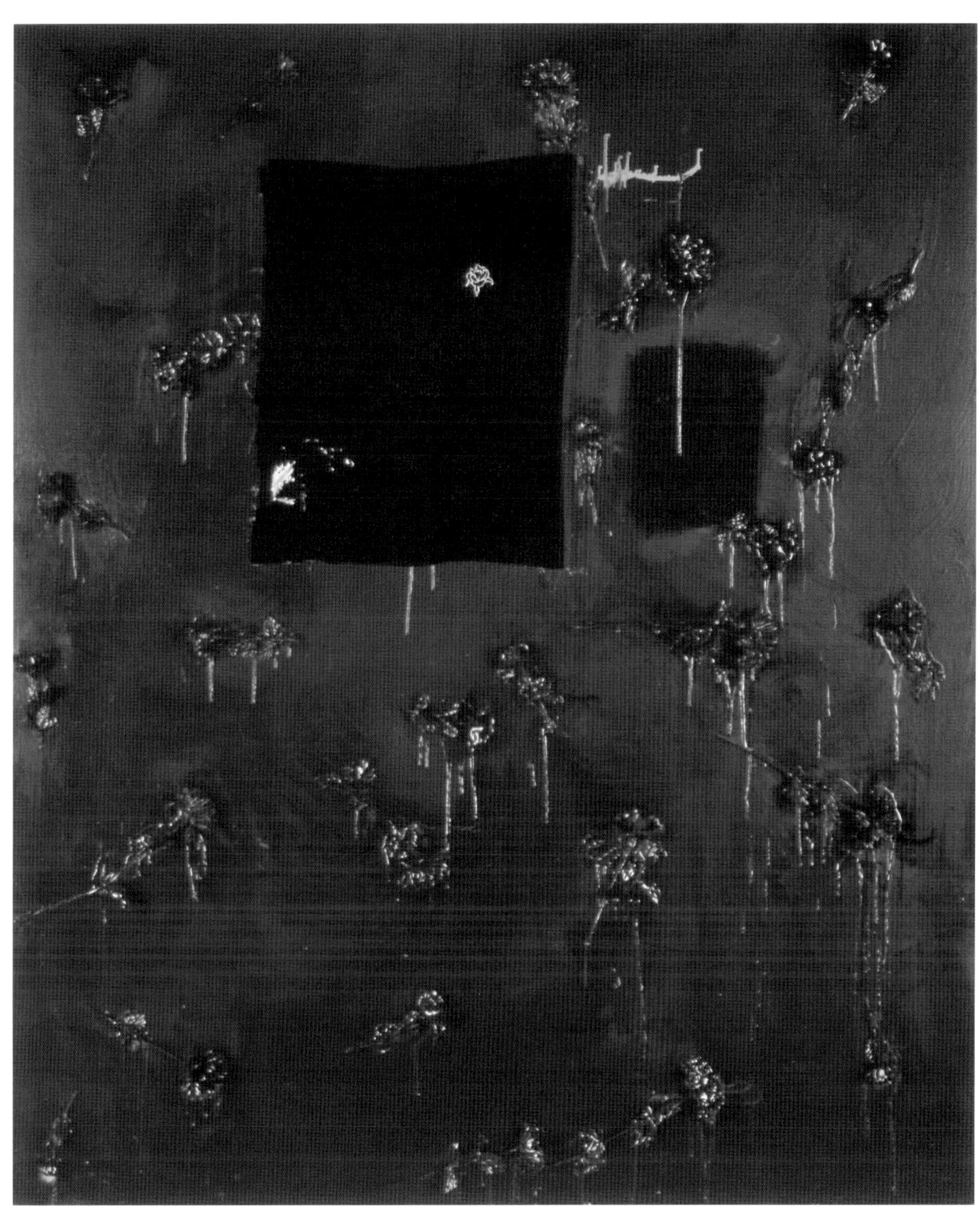

NO DOUBT GOOD WRITING, 1995
Charcoal and collage on paper
17 x 16 inches (43 x 41 cm)
Collection of Amy and Roger Faxon,
New York, New York

The title of the work might be a starting point: the artist penciled it across the center, lower portion of the graph paper. Everyone knows how machine-set type, as, say, in Linotype, makes handwriting over into even, straight lines stacked on pages in regular blocks. This piece could play upon such an image. The graph paper reminds one of the X and Y coordinates of pages in a book upon which the lines of type run. So Martínez Celaya's jet-black, matte, charcoal square could be an image of a block of type, of some writing. The piece might 'graph' a written page. "How graphic," we may say, smiling at the unfolding vistas, thinking how the ancient Greek word, *graphikos*, applied equally to both writing and painting. *No doubt, good writing.* A poem? *Ut pictura poesis*; a picture like a poem? Pictures once came in squares.

But the charcoal square has a texture: it's rough. The artist has applied layer after layer of the black here unrelentingly. To hide something? To hide some writing? A blank, unprinted endpaper from a book sits glued on top of the charcoal rectangle to clue us in, so to speak. Martínez Celaya wrote upon it, but then painted over his writing, leaving only traces of the words, now quite illegible. A line of text appears at the bottom of the graph paper, beneath the title of the work, but the artist cancelled it too, whiting it out sloppily. The piece presents words we can't read, and a window view we can't get inside of. A study in opacity energized by tantalizing possibility.

JE

ZWEIFELSOHNE ETWAS GUT GESCHRIEBENES, 1995
Kohle und Collage auf Papier
17 x 16 Zoll (43 x 41 cm)
Sammlung Amy und Roger Faxon,
New York, New York

Der Titel des Werks könnte ein Ausgangspunkt sein: Der Künstler malte ihn über die untere Mitte des Papiers. Wir wissen alle, wie elektronische Schrift wie zum Beispiel Linotypesätze aus Handschrift gleichmäßige gerade Linien erzeugt, die auf den Seiten zu regelmäßigen Blöcken gestapelt werden. Dieses Werk könnte mit einem solchen Motiv spielen. Das Graphikpapier erinnert uns an X- und Y-Koordinaten von Buchseiten, auf denen die Buchstabenlinien verlaufen. Martínez Celayas tiefschwarzes, mattes Kohlestift-Viereck könnte so das Bild einer Druckform oder einer Art Schrift sein. Das Werk könnte die schriftliche Darstellung einer geschriebenen Seite darstellen. „Wie graphisch!" möchten wir ausrufen, während uns die sich entfaltenden Deutungsmöglichkeiten ein Lächeln entlocken und wir an das altgriechische Wort *grafikos* denken, das Malen wie auch Schreiben bedeutet. Zweifelsohne etwas gut Geschriebenes. Ein Gedicht? Ut pictura poesis; ein Bild wie ein Gedicht? Bilder waren einst viereckig.

Jedoch hat das Kohlestift-Viereck eine Oberflächenstruktur: es ist uneben. Der Künstler hat hartnäckig eine Schicht Schwarz nach der anderen aufgetragen. Um etwas zu verstecken? Um etwas Geschriebenes zu verdecken? Das unbedruckte Vorsatzblatt eines Buches wurde oben auf das Kohlestift-Rechteck geklebt, um uns sozusagen einen Hinweis zu geben. Martínez Celaya schrieb darauf, malte aber dann über das von ihm Geschriebene und hinterließ nur Spuren von Wörtern, die jetzt mehr oder weniger unleserlich sind. Eine Zeile Text erscheint unten auf dem Papier, unterhalb des Werktitels, aber auch diese wurde vom Künstler ausgestrichen: nachlässig mit Weiß übermalt. Das Bild präsentiert Wörter, die wir nicht lesen können, und einen Fensterblick, in den wir nicht hineingelangen. Eine Undurchsichtigkeitsstudie, die durch verlockende Möglichkeiten ihre Energie erhält.

JE

INSTALLATION AT/IN GALLERY 144, 1993
Santa Barbara, California

no doubt, good writing

NONE OF IT REMINDS ME OF YOU, 1995
Oil, wax and silk flower on canvas
72 x 60 inches (183 x 152 cm)
The Bronx Museum of the Arts, Bronx, New York

A large white canvas with a single rose sewn into it, just a bit to the left of center. The desicated rose has been dipped partly in tar and attached to the canvas with great deliberation. The thread holding it forms a large X. Immediately alongside, and to the right of the rose, appear four black lines for 'balance'; together they take about as much area on the canvas as the flower. They look like strokes made with a Magic Marker to cancel some writing.

On second glance though, things get more complicated. We see faint traces of the broad, swinging patterns of some ornamental design that the white paint on the canvas' surface does not fully cover.

The ornamental pattern showing through the white paint is vivid enough. The writing? Vivid too? Very likely. And the rose? Once alive, its vividness here is incontestable, cancelled though it is, partly by the tar. Anyway, the rose sits in relief on the picture plane (casts a shadow on it). Slowly the machine whirs to life as each realm of the graphic, of the depicted, folds into, momentarily heightens, then cancels the one before.

JE

NICHTS DAVON ERINNERT MICH AN DICH, 1995
Öl, Wachs und Seidenblume auf Leinwand
72 x 60 Zoll (183 x 152 cm)
The Bronx Museum of the Arts, Bronx, New York

Eine große weiße Leinwand mit einer einzigen Rose, die etwas links der Mitte aufgenäht wurde. Die getrocknete Rose wurde teilweise in Teer getaucht und mit Überlegung auf der Leinwand angebracht. Der sie haltende Faden bildet ein großes X. Direkt daneben und auf der rechten Seite der Rose erscheinen, um das Gleichgewicht zu wahren, vier schwarze Linien; sie nehmen zusammen etwa so viel Raum auf der Leinwand wie die Rose ein und gleichen Strichen, die mit einem deckenden Stift gemacht wurden, um etwas Geschriebenes auszustreichen.

Auf den zweiten Blick werden die Dinge jedoch komplizierter. Wir sehen schwache Spuren der breiten, schwungvollen Muster eines Ornaments, die von der weißen Farbe auf der Oberfläche der Leinwand nicht ganz abgedeckt werden.

Das ornamentale Muster, das durch die weiße Farbe sichtbar ist, ist lebhaft genug. Die Schrift? Auch lebhaft? Höchstwahrscheinlich. Und die Rose? Sie lebte einst, ihre Lebendigkeit ist unbestreitbar, wurde jedoch teilweise durch den Teer ausgelöscht. Auf jeden Fall bildet die Rose ein Relief auf dem Gemälde (sie wirft einen Schatten). Die Maschine surrt und wird lebendig, da jeder Bereich des Graphischen, des Dargestellten, mit dem anderen in Beziehung gesetzt, für einen Augenblick hervorgehoben wird und dann das Vorige auslöscht.

JE

THE END OF TRAGEDY, 1995
Oil, graphite, varnish and collage on paper
37.75 x 31.75 inches (96 x 81 cm)
The Contemporary Museum, Honolulu, Hawaii
Purchased with funds derived from gifts of The Honolulu Advertiser Collection at Persis Corporation, Kenneth Kingrey, and John Kjargaard, by exchange, 1997.

This painting, treats many of the same issues as *No Doubt, Good Writing*. Or anyway, its varnished frame is square and can make one think of Leon-Battista Alberti and his scheme for making pictorial space compelling. Martínez Celaya first glued down an aquamarine hummingbird sticker on semi-transparent drafting paper. Then he glued a second piece of semi-transparent paper to the first (the hummingbird shows through) and on it painted the bright red lion and drew a toothpick. A carefully articulated animal striding out, he turns his head frontally to the picture plane.

Hummingbirds and lions are loaded with associations for all of us: they are genuine kitsch icons. Juxtaposed here, though, the associations we have with each cancel each other. The toothpick interrupting the picture plane, moreover, belongs to an entire other realm (it's not an image; it's not kitsch). It renders the animals unreadable. The images empty out and silence reigns. There is an 'afterward' here, a strangely vacant, but attractive (what?)...

JE

DAS ENDE DER TRAGÖDIE, 1995
Öl, Graphit, Lack und Collage auf Papier
37,75 x 31,75 Zoll (96 x 81 cm)
The Contemporary Museum, Honolulu, Hawaii
Erworben mit Mitteln aus Schenkungen der Honolulu Advertiser Collection at Persis Corporation, von Kenneth Kingrey und John Kjargaard, durch Austausch, 1997.

Dieses Gemälde behandelt viele der Fragen, die schon in *Zweifelsohne etwas gut Geschriebenes* auftraten. Auf jeden Fall ist sein lackierter Rahmen viereckig und könnte uns an Leon Battista Alberti und sein Schema, den Bildraum bezwingend zu gestalten, erinnern. Martínez Celaya befestigte zuerst einen Aufkleber auf halbtransparentem Konzeptpapier und malte einen Zahnstocher darauf. Dann klebte er ein zweites Stück halbtransparentes Papier auf das erste (der Kolibri scheint hindurch) und malte einen hellroten Löwen darauf. Ein überlegt dargestelltes Tier, das ausschreitet und seinen in Frontalansicht dargestellten Kopf in Richtung Bildebene dreht.

Kolibris und Löwen sind für uns mit Assoziationen beladen: Sie sind genuine Kitschsymbole. Obwohl sie hier nebeneinander gestellt sind, heben sich die Assoziationen, die wir mit ihnen verbinden, gegenseitig auf. Der Zahnstocher unterbricht die Bildebene und gehört obendrein zu einem ganz anderen Bereich (er ist kein Bild, er ist kein Kitsch). Die Tiere werden dadurch unleserlich. Die Bilder entleeren sich und es herrscht Stille. Es gibt hier ein „Danach", ein seltsam leeres, aber anziehendes (was?) ...

JE

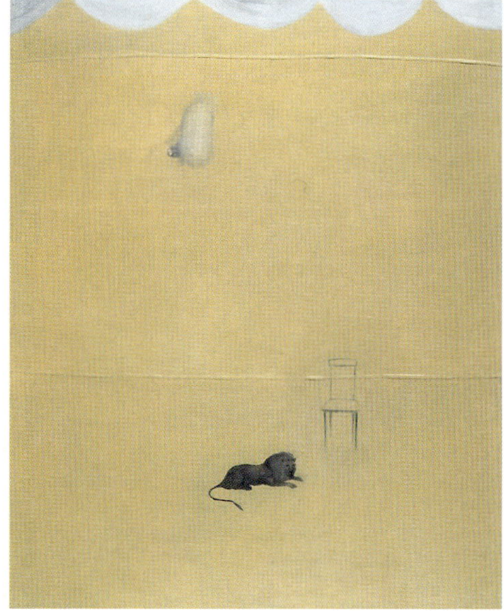

PAINTING WITH LION AND CHAIR
/GEMÄLDE MIT LÖWE UND STUHL, 1993
Private Collection/Privatsammlung,
Los Angeles, California

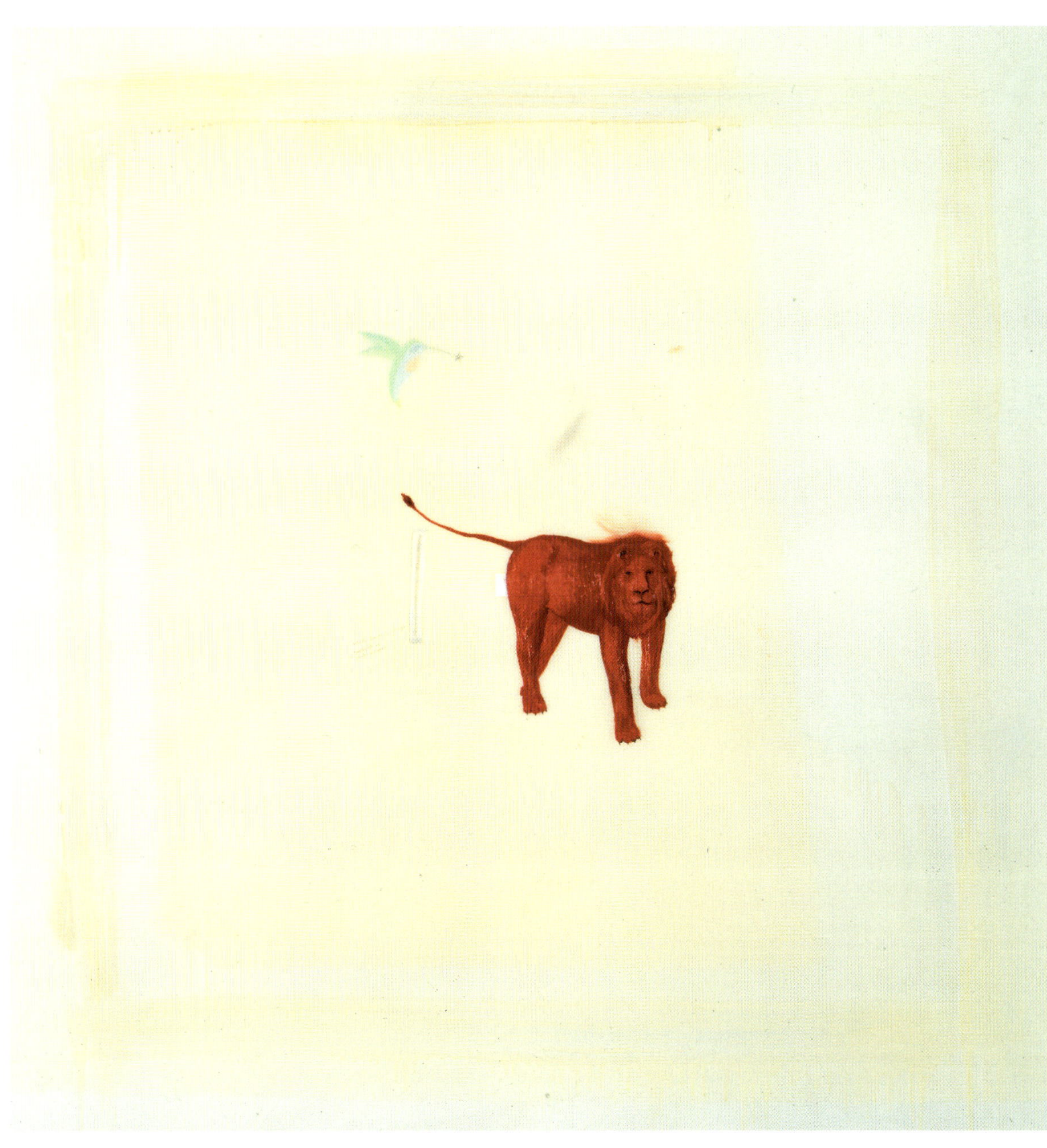

UNSAFE, 1996
Oil, wax and graphite on paper
65.5 x 41.5 inches (166 x 105 cm)
The Arkansas Art Center, Little Rock, Arkansas

The work is a large piece of paper hanging inside a shadow box. The single stroke of thick white paint covering the bouquet's stems has a strange integrity: it looks like some sort of short, stubby Band-Aid. So do all the other canceling brush strokes. They seem to cover over the picture like bandages cover so many minor scratches, cuts, and wounds in the skin. Far fetched? Think of it like this for a minute: the hyper-realistic flowers invite our eye to pierce the picture plane. The white brush strokes bring us back to that picture plane, and emphasize it; they do not just cancel the images, they 'heal' the ruptured membrane (the actual paper). We wince to see anything 'bleed through.'

Martínez Celaya here made the picture's surface what Hegel was talking about:[1] co-terminous with the viewers by suggesting, and none too subtly, it's likeness with our bodies. The shadow box presents the painting's support; the paper, as a metaphor of our skin.

Unsafe documents a major turn in the artist's thinking about the nature of a picture, and best shows where Martínez Celaya's visual inquiry during the mid 1990s was tending. In future, as Martínez Celaya works through the problem that the window view or picture presents, it will be possible for him to make it over into a 'figure' all by itself, that is, into a human body, one whole thing, a corpus. It's not that he'll leave space, and the illusion of space out of his calculus. It's that pictures will become bodies, human bodies. The idea seems to be that in this way painting might achieve a new kind of integrity or at least do so by implication and indirection.

JE

NICHT SICHER, 1996
Öl, Wachs und Graphit auf Papier
65,5 x 41,5 Zoll (166 x 105 cm)
The Arkansas Art Center, Little Rock, Arkansas

Das Werk ist ein großes Stück Papier, das in einem Schattenkasten hängt. Der eine Pinselstrich dicker weißer Farbe, der die Stengel des Blumenstraußes abdeckt, hat eine seltsame Beschaffenheit: Er sieht wie eine Art kurzes, stummeliges Pflaster aus. Dies ist auch der Fall bei allen anderen, etwas ausstreichenden Pinselstrichen. Sie scheinen das Bild abzudecken wie Pflaster kleine Kratzer, Schnitte und Wunden in der Haut abdecken. An den Haaren herbeigezogen? Denken Sie eine Minute lang wie folgt darüber nach: Die hyperrealen Blumen laden unser Auge ein, die Bildebene zu durchdringen. Die weißen Pinselstriche bringen uns zu dieser Bildebene zurück und betonen sie; sie löschen die Bilder nicht nur aus, sondern „heilen" die beschädigte Membran (das wirkliche Papier). Wir zucken zusammen, wenn wir etwas „durchbluten" sehen.

Martínez Celaya machte hier aus der Oberfläche des Papiers etwas, worüber Hegel spricht:[1] ein Medium der unmittelbaren Ansprache des Betrachters, dem auf nicht gerade subtile Weise die Ähnlichkeit des Kunstwerks zum eigenen Körper nahegelegt wird. Die Schattenbox trägt das Gemälde und das Papier ist die Metapher unserer Haut.

In dieser Ausstellung stellt *Nicht Sicher* eine wichtige Wende im Denken des Künstlers über das Wesen des Bildes dar und zeigt am besten die Richtung an, in die Martínez Celayas visuelle Untersuchungen Mitte der neunziger Jahre zielten. Da sich Martínez Celaya auch weiterhin mit dem Problem des Fensterblicks oder -bildes beschäftigte, sollte es ihm künftig möglich sein, es in eine für sich stehende „Gestalt", einen menschlichen Körper, eine ganze Sache, einen Korpus zu verwandeln. Nicht, dass er Raum und die Illusion von Raum außer Acht ließe. Es ist nur so, dass Bilder Körper, menschliche Körper werden. Es scheint darum zu gehen, dass die Malerei auf diese Art und Weise eine neue Art der Integrität erlangt oder dies zumindest durch Implikation und Umwege erreicht.

JE

1. G. W. F. Hegel (1770–1831) writes on painting (he was describing how the reduction of the three-dimensional world to the two-dimensional in painting was a sign of the triumph of subjectivity): "By displaying what is subjective, the picture, in its whole mode of presentation, reveals its purpose as existing for the subject, for the spectator and not on its own account. The spectator is, as it were, in it from the beginning, is counted in with it, and the picture exists only for this fixed point, that is, for the individual apprehending it." (*Aesthetics*, 1831).

1. G. W. F. Hegel (1770–1831) schreibt über das Malen (er beschrieb, wie eine Reduzierung der dreidimensionalen in eine zweidimensionale Welt in Gemälden ein Zeichen des Triumphs der Subjektivität sei): „Durch ein Anzeigen des Subjektiven bringt das Gemälde in seinem ganzen Präsentationsmodus seinen Zweck zum Vorschein, dass es für das Subjekt, für den Betrachter, existiert, und nicht für sich selbst. Der Betrachter ist sozusagen in ihm von Anfang an, wird mit eingeplant und das Gemälde existiert nur für diesen festgelegten Punkt, dass heißt, für die Person, die es versteht." (*Ästhetik*, 1831).

K, THE BATTLEFIELD, 1996
Oil on canvas
72 x 60 inches (183 x 152 cm)
Collection of Achille Murat-Guest, Virginia

If in *Unsafe*, the 'wound' was quite symbolic and small, a mere visual piercing of the picture plane, and easily remedied, covered over, or cancelled, here the painter declared the trauma from the outset (he represents a wound) and it spreads to encompass the entire painted surface. It's irremediable and uncoverable.

The image of the wound spreads scale-less on all four sides of the small shadow box near the center. The shadow-box sends up the notion of a window view or vista and it doesn't open out to an ideal space and time, but to our actual space and time. Nevertheless, this defective framing device inevitably puts the old discourse of the frame in play. Thus I read the narrow, vertical, black line that nearly bisects the canvas, and that gives the canvas' surface such great stress, as establishing a picture plane.

At the center of the ellipse in the lower right-hand corner of the canvas, however, we see a strange gap in the painting a series of three, very small, superimposed ellipses. The largest, painted a bluish gray, has four kitschy flowers in primary colors; the middle ellipse, painted gray-brown, has a prominent, but small white 'K,' and the smallest ellipse, painted white, has a diagonal red line. The nested ovals are doubtless the trace of some painting previous to that of the crimson. I find this tiny gap, this peephole in the vast expanse of a canvas six-feet tall, disturbing and quite unreadable in context. To me, it seems clear that the alizarin crimson figures the canvas' surface as the body. Viewers enter a realm of illusion (crimson stands for blood). But the gap Martínez Celaya also allows to appear there is jarring, even repellent. It partly dismantles the figure (as I am calling it) in that it calls attention to the crimson as plain paint. Willing to unleash emotion, the artist also tampers with it. Or do viewers of this work hover in quite another place beyond the dialectics of statement and denial?

JE

K, DAS SCHLACHTFELD, 1996
Öl auf Leinwand
72 x 60 Zoll (183 x 152 cm)
Sammlung Achille Murat-Guest, Virginia

Wenn in *Nicht Sicher* die „Wunde" eher symbolischer Art und klein, ein bloßes optisches Durchstechen der Bildebene war und leicht geheilt, überdeckt oder ausgestrichen werden konnte, thematisiert der Maler hier das grundliegende Trauma (er stellt die Wunde dar), das sich ausbreitet, um die gesamte bemalte Oberfläche zu überziehen. Es ist untilgbar und nicht zu verbergen.

Das Bild der Wunde verbreitet sich maßstabslos in alle vier Richtungen des kleinen Schattenkastens in der Nähe des Bildzentrums. Dieser ruft die Vorstellung eines Fensterblicks hervor und er öffnet sich weder auf einen idealen Raum noch auf eine ideale Zeit, sondern auf den tatsächlichen Raum und die tatsächliche Zeit. Dennoch kommt durch diese fehlerhafte Rahmenvorrichtung unvermeidbar der alte Diskurs über den Rahmen ins Spiel. Ich deute daher die schmale, vertikale, schwarze Linie, die die Leinwand fast in zwei Hälften teilt und der Leinwandoberfläche äußerste Spannung verleiht, als Mittel, eine Bildebene zu etablieren.

In der Mitte der Ellipse in der unteren rechten Ecke der Leinwand sehen wir jedoch eine seltsame Lücke im Gemälde, eine Serie von drei sehr kleinen übereinandergesetzten Ellipsen. Die größte, bläulich-graue Ellipse besitzt vier kitschige Blumen in Grundfarben, die mittlere , grau-braune hat ein auffälliges, aber kleines weißes K und die kleinste, weiße Ellipse eine diagonale rote Linie erhalten. Die ineinander gesetzten Ovale sind zweifelsohne die Spur eines Gemäldes, das vor dem karminroten existierte. Ich finde diese winzige Lücke, dieses Guckloch in der großen Fläche der etwa zwei Meter hohen Leinwand beunruhigend und in diesem Zusammenhang äußerst unleserlich. Mir scheint es klar zu sein, dass das krapprote Karmin die Leinwandoberfläche als Körper gestaltet. Der Betrachter tritt in eine Welt der Illusion (Karmin bedeutet Blut). Jedoch versetzt die Lücke, die Martínez Celaya dort erscheinen lässt, einen Schock und wirkt sogar abstoßend. Sie nimmt die Figur (so nenne ich sie zumindest) teilweise auseinander, da sie die Aufmerksamkeit auf das Karmin lenkt und es wie normale Farbe aussehen lässt. Obwohl der Künstler willens ist, Emotionen zu entfesseln, pfuscht er auch mit ihnen herum. Oder schweben die Betrachter dieses Werks an einem ganz anderen Ort, der über die Dialektik von Aussage und Gegenaussage erhaben ist?

JE

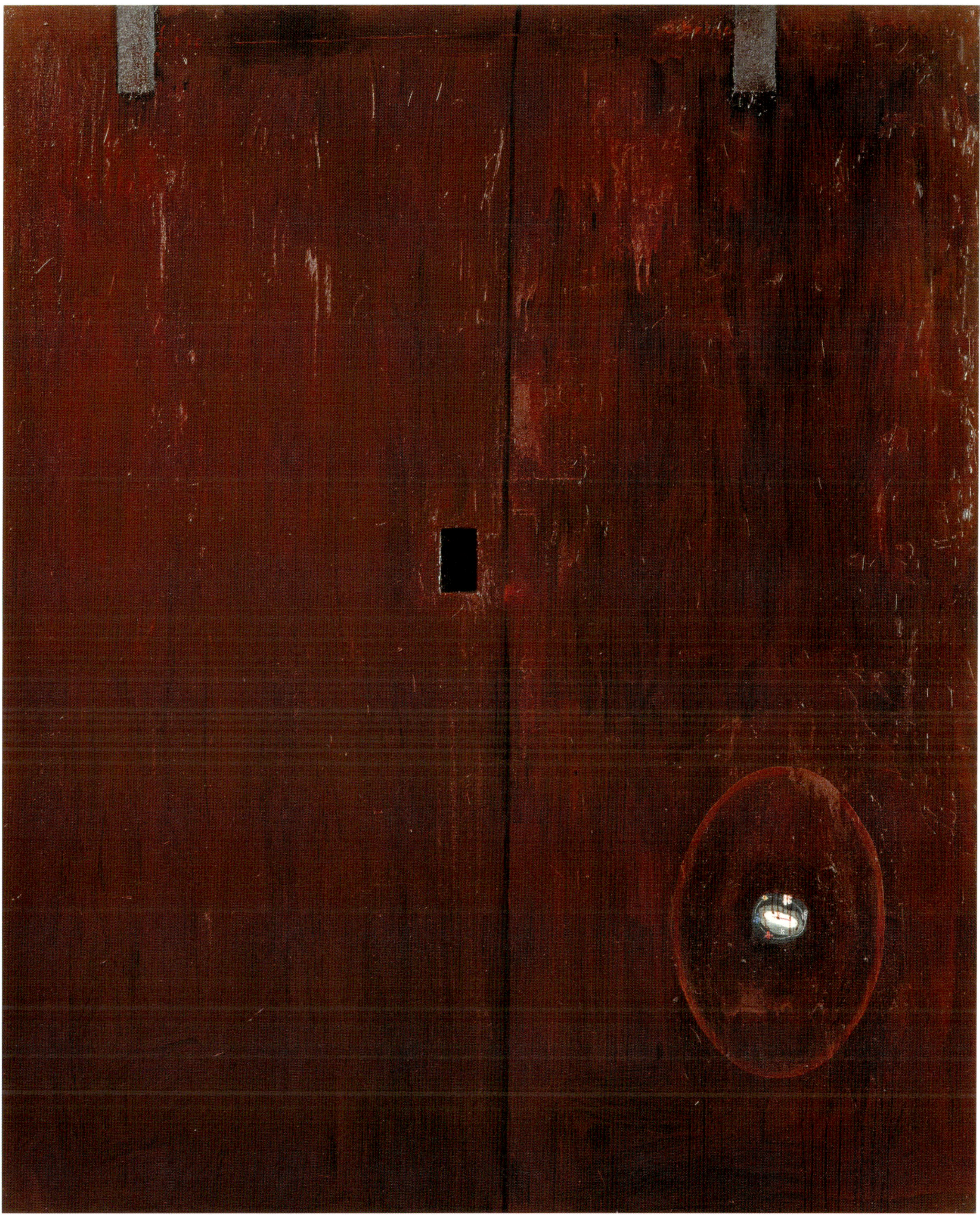

THE HABIT OF HUMMINGBIRDS, 1996
Oil, wax and fabric on canvas
72 x 60 inches (183 x 152 cm)
Courtesy of Enrique Martínez Celaya

At an early stage, the artist painted some sixty colorful hummingbirds on this large canvas: a mad gesture! Only fragments of three now survive, visible in three gaps left in the final painted surface (small traces of a fourth hummingbird appear in the upper right-hand corner of the work). That surface, composed of many layers of flat, opaque, waxy black paint, is far from formless. Once we tune into the painting's 'gray register,' we see complex patterns in the drips and scumblings, and visible brush strokes, one overlapping the other. The brush strokes run for the most part on vertical and horizontal axes, stressing the front plane of the work. There is no proper frame, but the 'four-square' properties of the paint's application certainly suggest one. I am reminded again of pictorial relief (see *The Trouble with Memory*, p. 118).

What is interesting here is the way the gaps in this picture, the vignettes with the three hummingbirds, do not dismantle the image, but are incorporated in it, even if crudely. The black ellipse connecting the gaps makes them part of the expansive and busy waxy-black image. But of course the colorful world of the kitschy hummingbirds still has nothing whatever to do with the austerities and abstractions of the gray-black world that encapsulates them. The hummingbird vignettes are 'wounds' in the picture plane, of another kind than those explored in *Unsafe*.

JE

DIE GEWOHNHEIT DER KOLIBRIS, 1996
Öl, Wachs und Stoff auf Leinwand
72 x 60 Zoll (183 x 152 cm)
Courtesy of Enrique Martínez Celaya

Der Künstler malte zu Anfang seiner Laufbahn etwa sechzig farbenprächtige Kolibris auf diese große Leinwand: eine verrückte Geste! Die Fragmente von nur dreien haben überlebt und sind in den drei Lücken auf der abschließend bemalten Oberfläche sichtbar (schwache Spuren eines vierten Kolibris erscheinen in der oberen rechten Ecke des Werks). Diese Oberfläche besteht aus vielen Schichten stumpfer, undurchsichtiger, wachsiger schwarzer Farbe und ist keineswegs formlos. Nachdem wir uns auf das „graue Register" des Gemäldes eingestellt haben, bemerken wir komplexe Muster in den Tropfen und den übereinander gespachtelten Farbschichten wie auch sichtbare Pinselstriche, die sich überlappen. Die Pinselstriche verlaufen größtenteils vertikal und horizontal, sie betonen die vordere Bildebene. Es gibt keinen Rahmen an sich, jedoch legt die Rechtecke erzeugende Anwendung der Farbe einen solchen nahe. Dies erinnert mich wieder an das malerische Relief (wie in *Das Problem mit dem Gedächtnis*, S. 118).

Interessant ist die Art und Weise, in der die Lücken in diesem Bild, die Vignetten mit drei Kolibris, das Bild nicht demontieren, sondern in es integriert sind, wenn auch etwas grob. Die schwarze Ellipse, welche die Lücken verbindet, macht sie zum Bestandteil des großen und belebten wachsartigen schwarzen Bildes. Natürlich hat die farbenfrohe Welt der kitschigen Kolibris noch immer nichts mit den Kargheiten und Abstraktionen der grauschwarzen Welt zu tun, die sie umgibt. Die Kolibri-Vignetten sind „Wunden" auf der Bildebene, aber einer anderen Art als die, die wir in *Nicht Sicher* ermittelten.

JE

SECOND ORNAMENT, 1996
Oil on canvas
72 x 60 inches (183 x 152 cm)
Bilbao/Mekis Collection, Coconut Grove, Florida

Once again the gap in the canvas' surface, here the tondo, is incorporated (see my comments on the previous entry on *The Habit of Hummingbirds*). Both the tondo and the drawing in this work pierce the canvas's surface, and both piercings, both 'wounds,' are left 'unhealed.' But here, more than in the other paintings in this series, the images 'need' each other. The one does not disable the other. We note with interest, moreover, that the line drawing floats freely on the canvas' surface without any frame. This dematerialization of the figure is a sign that the figure's status in the composition is 'other' than that of the figure in the tondo. With this experiment, I would hazard, Martínez Celaya came out at the end of the series of works on display in this first part of the exhibition with an effective strategy for figuring a canvas' surface without having to resort to the traditions of the window view (the 'second ornament' belongs to the canvas' flat surface, but remains palpable nevertheless). Given the various dismantlings and 'silences' in this series, I see the painter making a kind of affirmation here. The second ornament rises before our eyes quite intact (by contrast to the first ornament in the tondo). It has the status of an icon in another world than that of the cartoon, or of commerce. Thus the painter of Modern life, unburdened by painting's long history, reworks painting's subjectivity, so to speak. If formerly viewers saw themselves in an icon, saw themselves as the image of God there (no less!), now Martínez Celaya works to rescue what he can of such an image. By indirection to be sure. By refusing the heroics of the long tradition (not God's face; just a Christmas ornament). But by refusing irony also. I think that the kitsch icon in the *Second Ornament* is truly an icon.

JE

ZWEITE VERZIERUNG, 1996
Öl auf Leinwand
72 x 60 Zoll (183 x 152 cm)
Bilbao/Mekis Sammlung, Coconut Grove, Florida

Erneut ist die Lücke , hier der Tondo, auf der Oberfläche der Leinwand integriert (siehe meine Anmerkungen zu *Die Gewohnheit der Kolibris*). Der Tondo und die Zeichnung durchstechen in dieser Arbeit die Oberfläche der Leinwand und beide durchstochenen Stellen, beide „Wunden" werden nicht „geheilt". Jedoch „brauchen" die Motive einander hier mehr als in den anderen Gemälden der Serie. Das eine macht das andere nicht unwirksam. Mit Interesse bemerken wir obendrein, dass die Linienzeichnung frei auf der Oberfläche der Leinwand treibt, ohne jeglichen Rahmen. Die Entmaterialisierung dieser Figur ist ein Anzeichen dafür, dass ihr Status in der Komposition ein „anderer" als der der Figur im Tondo ist. Ich wage zu behaupten, dass Martínez Celaya in diesem Experiment zum Abschluss der Werkgruppe, die in diesem ersten Teil der Ausstellung gezeigt wird, eine effiziente Strategie der Darstellung auf der Leinwand gelang, ohne auf die Tradition des Fensterblicks zurückgreifen zu müssen (die zweite Verzierung gehört zur flachen Oberfläche der Leinwand, bleibt aber trotzdem greifbar). Angesichts der verschiedenen Demontageprozesse und Arten von „Stille" in dieser Serie sehe ich in diesem Bild eine Art Affirmation des Malers. Die zweite Verzierung erscheint fast völlig intakt vor unseren Augen (im Vergleich zur ersten Verzierung im Tondo). Sie hat den Status eines Symbols, in einer Welt, die nicht die der Cartoons oder des Kommerzes ist. Auf diese Weise erarbeitet der Maler des modernen Lebens erneut die Subjektivität des Bildes, unbelastet von der langen Geschichte der Malerei. Wenn Betrachter sich zuvor als Symbol oder als Bild von (keinem Geringeren als) Gott sahen, arbeitet Martínez Celaya nun daran, das zu retten, was er aus einem solchen Bild nur retten kann. Auf Umwegen, das steht fest. Durch das Ablehnen der Heldentaten der langen Tradition (nicht Gottes Gesicht, nur Weihnachtsschmuck). Aber auch durch das Ablehnen der Ironie. Ich denke, dass das Kitschsymbol der *Zweiten Verzierung* wirklich ein Symbol ist.

JE

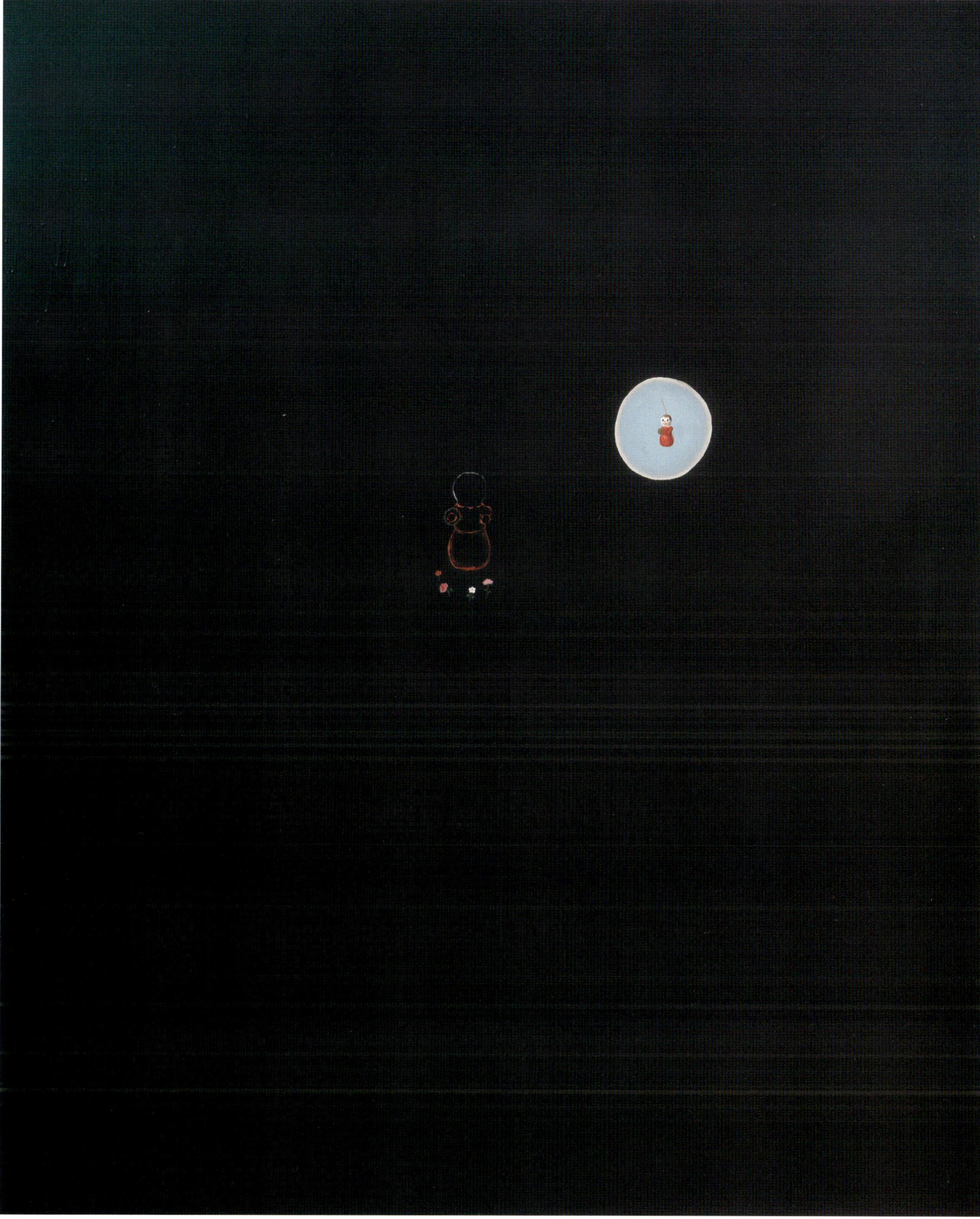

THE QUESTION OF THE OBJECT/DIE FRAGE DES OBJEKTS

presence, staging and authenticity/Präsenz, Inszenierung und Authentizität

THING AND DECEPTION, 1997
Oil on canvas
88 x 78 inches (224 x 198 cm)
Courtesy of Enrique Martínez Celaya

Scale is important in this painting and we are forced to deal with it (this is no picture depicting some ideal space; this rabbit is not of normal size and just seen 'close up' in this work). A gigantic Easter bunny? We deal with a kitsch icon again, just as in *Second Ornament* (p. 132), but in this work, the artist proceeded much more confidently to figure (as I am saying here) the canvas' surface. Images now appear straightforwardly upon that surface. Because it both emerges from the surface of the canvas, and yet forms part of that surface (as if it were some minor disturbance in the white paint there), the evanescent tulip signals Martínez Celaya's 'strategy.' Albertian spatial constructions and window views are refused here. Because we peer into no ideal space and time here, because this painting is not really a picture, we are forced to deal with the huge size of the rabbit. It is part of the space in the gallery and rises here before us as an object.

The cuteness of the 'bunny' is not complete, we note. As we saw in the previous series, here again Martínez Celaya avoids fashioning the kitsch icon in the manner of the cartoon, or as if it were some slick item of commerce. Irony does not look to be the theme. The size of this work recalls the heroic art of the museums; but, the subject, a rabbit, quite undermines that tradition. Disarmed, no longer sure what to expect, the viewer is forced to deal much more straightforwardly with the rabbit. I find it hard to escape seeing this object in a religious context as a remainder perhaps of the old-fashioned altarpiece in a sanctuary (it might be an 'Easter bunny.') Does it touch on an issue like resurrection, deal with the possibility of 'new life'? Such dangerous territory for an artist working today! Can it be explored visually in the new *sanctitas* of the Modern art gallery?

JE

DING UND TÄUSCHUNG, 1997
Öl auf Leinwand
88 x 78 Zoll (224 x 198 cm)
Courtesy of Enrique Martínez Celaya

In diesem Gemälde ist der Maßstab wichtig und wir müssen uns damit auseinandersetzen (hier handelt es sich nicht um ein Bild, das einen idealen Raum darstellt; dieses Kaninchen hat keine normale Größe und wird nicht einfach als „Nahaufnahme" gesehen). Ein Riesenosterhase? Auch hier haben wir wieder einmal mit einem Kitschsymbol zu tun, genau wie in *Zweite Verzierung* (S. 132), jedoch gestaltete (wie ich es hier sage) der Künstler die Leinwandoberfläche mit wesentlich mehr Vertrauen. Die Motive erscheinen jetzt direkt auf der Leinwand. Da sie aus der Leinwandoberfläche heraus auftaucht, jedoch zu dieser Oberfläche gehört (so als ob sie eine kleine Störung in der weißen Farbe ist) gibt Martínez Celayas dahinschwindende Tulpe seine „Strategie" zu erkennen. Räumliche Konstruktionen und Fensterblicke nach Alberti werden hier abgelehnt. Da wir in keinen idealen Raum und in keine ideale Zeit starren, da das Bild kein wirkliches Bild ist, sind wir gezwungen, uns mit der enormen Größe des Kaninchens auseinanderzusetzen. Er gehört zum Raum in der Galerie und erhebt sich hier vor uns als Objekt.

Wir bemerken, dass die Niedlichkeit des Kaninchens nicht ganz unbeeinträchtigt ist. Wie wir in den vorangehenden Serien sehen konnten, vermeidet Martínez Celaya auch hier, das Kitschsymbol cartoonmäßig oder als cleveren Handelsgegenstand zu gestalten. Die Ironie scheint hier kein Thema zu sein. Die Größe des Werks erinnert an die „heroische Kunst" des Museums; jedoch untergräbt das Thema, ein Kaninchen, diese Tradition! Entwaffnet und nicht mehr so ganz sicher, was wir erwarten sollen, sieht sich der Betrachter gezwungen, sich mit dem Kaninchen unmittelbar auseinanderzusetzen. Mir fällt es schwer, dieses Objekt nicht in einem religiösen Zusammenhang, vielleicht als Erinnerung an ein altmodisches Altarbild in einer heiligen Stätte, zu sehen (es könnte ja wirklich ein „Osterhase" sein). Berührt es Themen wie die Auferstehung, oder behandelt es die Möglichkeit eines „neuen Lebens"? Welch ein gefährliches Revier für einen heute tätigen Künstler! Kann es in der neuen Heiligkeit moderner Kunstgalerien visuell erforscht werden?

JE

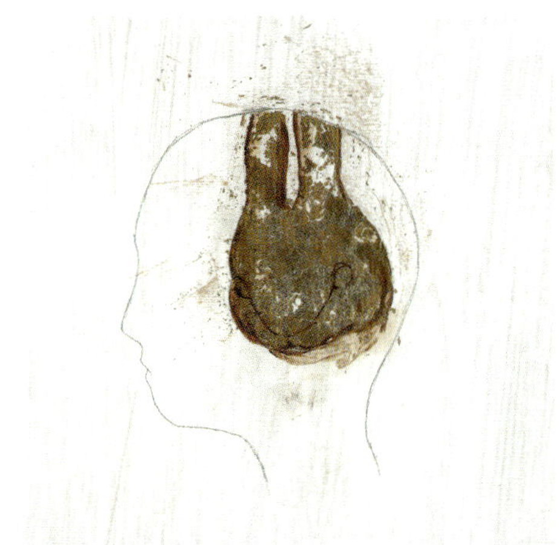

HEAD WITH RABBIT, detail
/KOPF MIT KANINCHEN, Ausschnit, 1997
Collection of/Sammlung Enrique and Alexandra Martínez Celaya

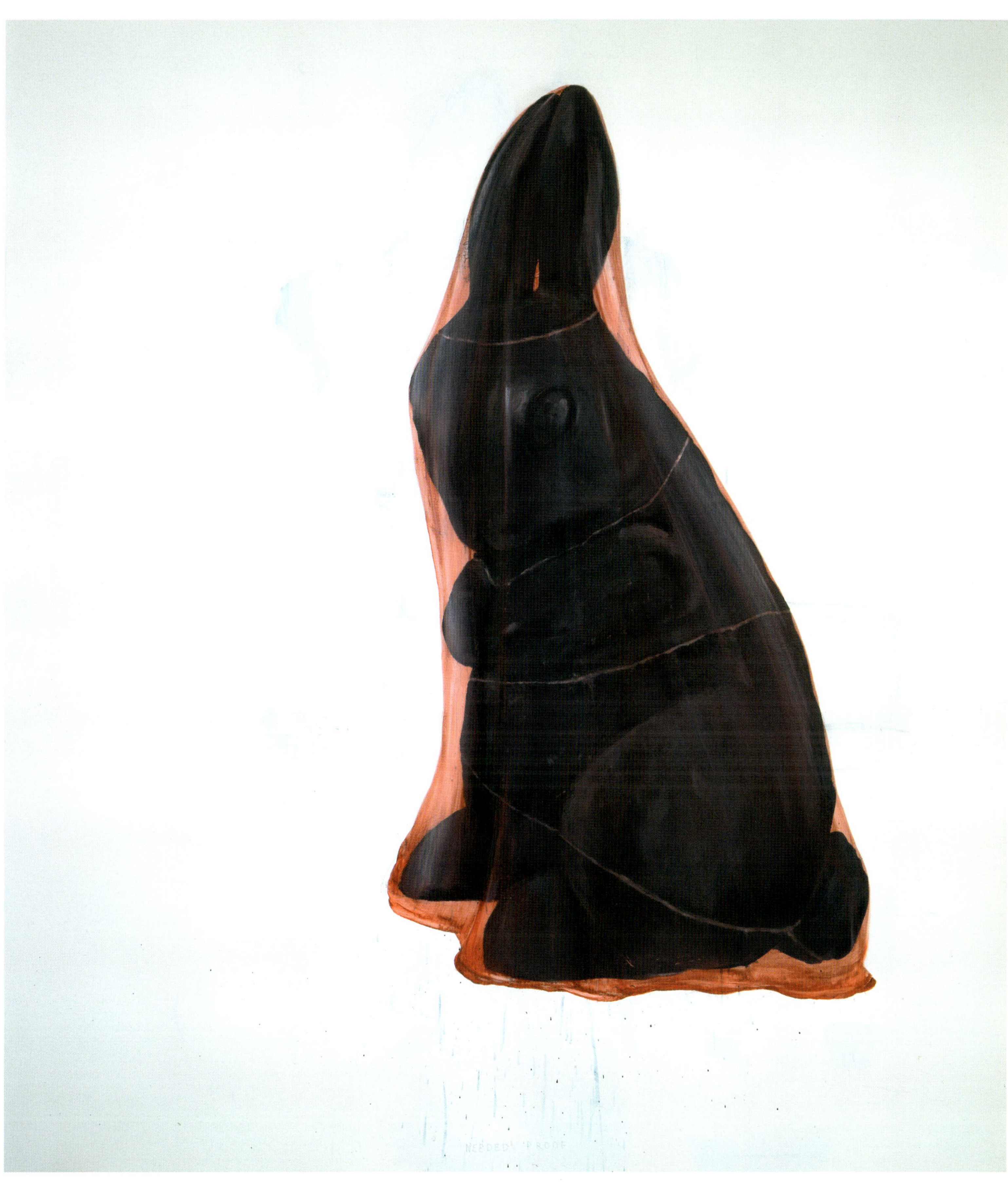
NEEDED PROOF

BED (THE CREEK), 1997
Bed, bedspread, pillows, resin and pots
60 x 85 x 22 inches (152 x 216 x 56 cm)
Destroyed in 1997 and re-made for this exhibition
Courtesy of Enrique Martínez Celaya

The conceit is loneliness, the loneliness of the users of a bed, of a couple whose presence the bed conjures. I imagine a gulf, a stream of water, a river dividing the hotel bed's two sections, opening a gap. We recognize many of the themes the artist's work dealt with through the mid 1990s. The hotel bed (this work was originally exibited at the Chateau Marmont, Gramercy Art Fair), usually covered when art is shown, and thus an absence in that exhibition space, gets figured here as a presence. The hotel bed is the analog of the artist's canvases during this period, the ones he sought to figure by indirection, by various processes of dismantling. Thus the tacky bedspread with its printed flowers could be a disarming image of felicity. We recognize Martínez Celaya's customary way to deal with the 'great themes' by indirection, slyly, and by creeping up on them from behind. Let me just say that the hotel bed here is an anti-picture that figures a landscape; that is, paradise with its sacred fountain. A paradise lost, too. Lost in a hotel room. The river pours into some dismally quotidian pottery . . . not much of a fountain of life after all.

JE

BETT (DER BACH), 1997
Bett, Tagesdecke, Kissen, Harz und Töpfe
60 x 85 x 22 Zoll (152 x 216 x 56 cm)
1997 zerstört und für diese Ausstellung wieder hergestellt
Courtesy of Enrique Martínez Celaya

Der zentrale Gedanke ist Einsamkeit, die Einsamkeit der Benutzer eines Betts, eines Paares, dessen Anwesenheit das Bett heraufbeschwört. Ich stelle mir einen Meerbusen, einen Wasserlauf, einen Fluss vor, der die beiden Teile des Hotelbetts trennt und eine Lücke entstehen lässt. Wir erkennen viele der Themen, mit denen sich der Künstler bis Mitte der neunziger Jahre beschäftigt hat. Das Hotelbett (das Werk wurde ursprünglich von Chateau Marmont, Gramercy Art Fair ausgestellt), das normalerweise bei Kunstausstellungen einbezogen wurde und daher in diesem Ausstellungsraum fehlt, wird hier als anwesend gestaltet. Es ist die Analogie zu den Leinwänden des Künstlers dieses Zeitraums, d. h. der Gemälde, die er durch Umwege und durch verschiedene Prozesse der Dekonstruktion zu gestalten suchte. Daher könnte die geschmacklose Tagesdecke mit den aufgedruckten Blümchen ein entwaffnendes Bild der Glückseligkeit sein. Wir erkennen Martínez Celayas übliche Verfahrensweise, „große Themen" durch Umwege, listig und durch ein Heranschleichen von hinten zu behandeln. Erlauben Sie mir hier kurz die Bemerkung, dass das Hotelbett hier ein Anti-Bild ist, das eine Landschaft verkörpert; d. h. das Paradies mit seinem heiligen Quell. Auch noch ein verlorenes Paradies. Es ging in einem Hotelzimmer verloren. Der Fluß ergießt sich in trübselig alltägliches Geschirr ... also nicht gerade ein Brunnen des Lebens.

JE

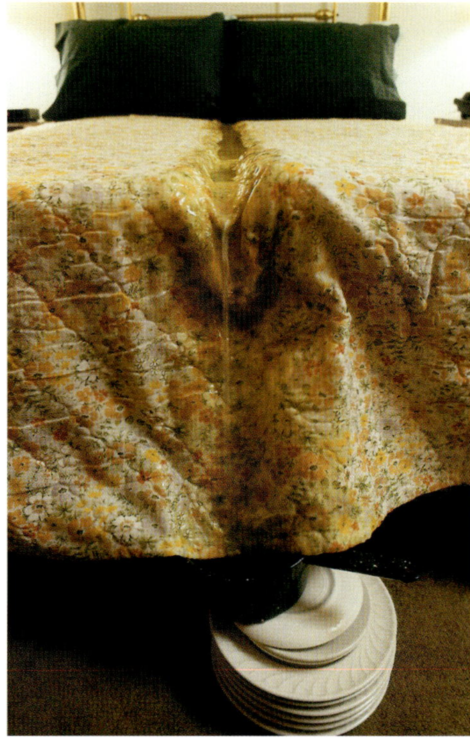

detail/Ausschnitt

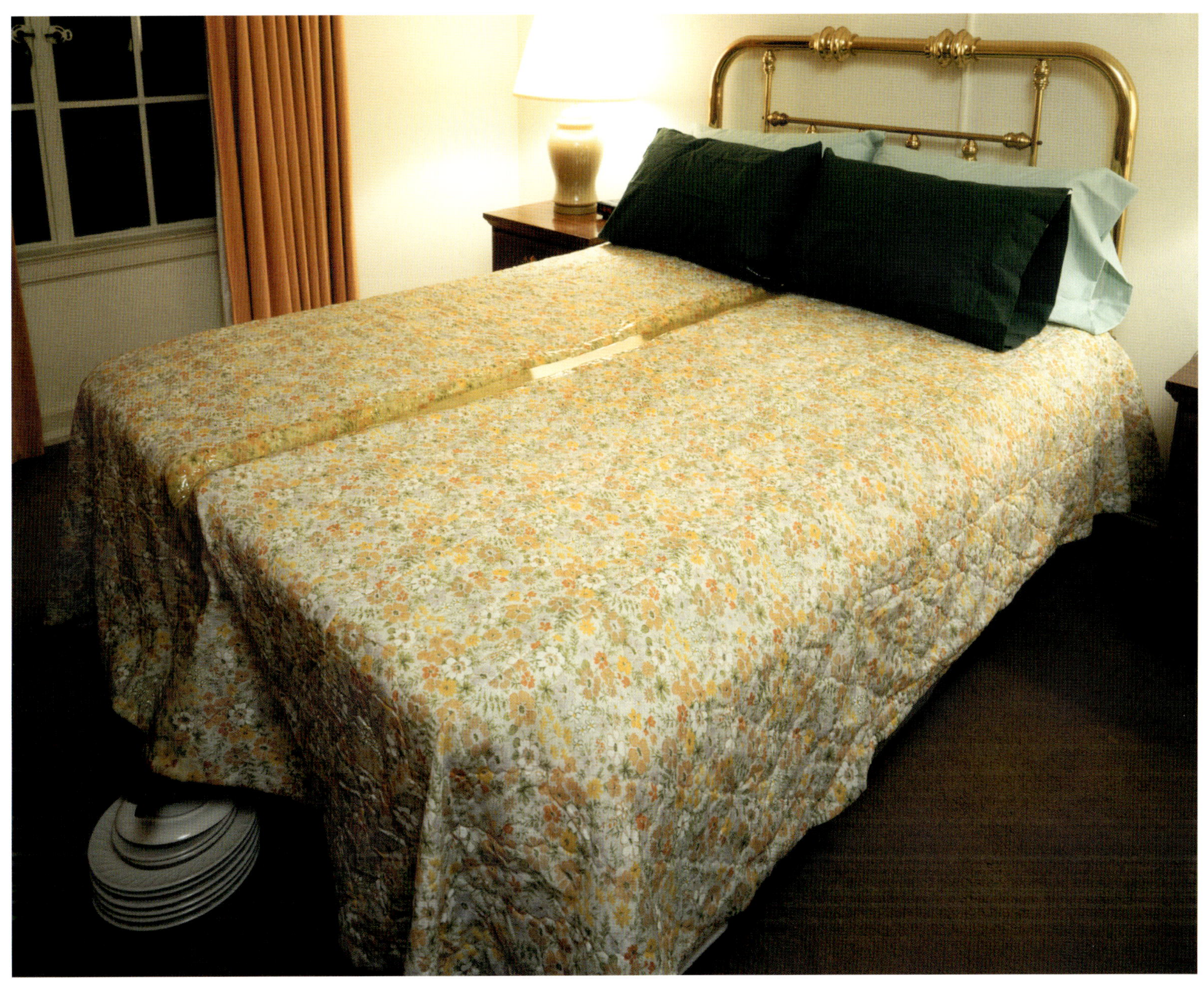

HOPSCOTCH, 1997
Oil on nylon parachute
72 x 60 inches (183 x 152 cm)
Collection of Michael and Christine McCullough, Newport Beach, California

We deal with another anti-painting.[1] The stretcher for the parachute cloth, quite visible beneath the almost transparent fabric, provides a robust, assertive frame that structures the image in this piece, which the complex system of curving seams in the parachute complete. They ray out over the wooden frame from left to right. One takes a distinct visual pleasure in seeing how these seams, the residue of the parachute's structure, contrast with the geometrical regularity of the various parts of the wooden stretcher, that is, with what's left of the structure of the old Albertian perspective projection. Together, I insist, they make a 'landscape.'

I judge so because the artist painted a child's hopscotch grid in white over the parachute's seams, and the two wooden cross pieces of the stretcher, smack-dab in the center of the work. A small torn paper with the name of the piece was attached at the bottom, probably to forestall our comparing this grid to all those other Modern ones from Mondrian to Agnes Martin. Given Martínez Celaya's previous visual experiments, I think we must be dealing here with an Albertian perspective construction slyly undone. The child's game of hopscotch receives an enshrining in art, and becomes a resonant visual icon. The act of jumping through space that the hopscotch grid subtends has an aesthetically satisfying correlate in the parachute, also used for such jumping. Here is a painting of a sort, not a window view to be sure, that opens on an ideal prospect, which is the trajectory of memory, the jump backward from now to childhood. It is a tender piece, quiet, even charming.

JE

HIMMEL UND HÖLLE, 1997
Öl auf Nylonfallschirm
72 x 60 Zoll (183 x 152 cm)
Sammlung Michael und Christine McCullough, Newport Beach, Kalifornien

Auch hier haben wir es mit einem Anti-Gemälde zu tun.[1] Das Gestell für den Fallschirmstoff, das unter dem fast durchsichtigen Stoff gut sichtbar ist, konstituiert einen robusten, definitiven Rahmen, der das Bildmotiv dieser Arbeit strukturiert, das von einem komplexen System gekrümmter Nähte vervollständigt wird. Sie strahlen über den Holzrahmen von links nach rechts aus. Es macht dem Betrachter wirklich Freude, wenn er sieht, wie diese Nähte, das Überbleibsel der Fallschirmstruktur, zu der geometrischen Regelmäßigkeit der verschiedenen Teile des Holzrahmens in Kontrast stehen, d. h. zu dem, was noch von der Struktur der alten Perspektivprojektion Albertis übrig bleibt. Ich bestehe darauf, dass sie gemeinsam eine „Landschaft" bilden.

Ich beurteile dies so, da der Künstler ein Himmel- und Höllegitter in weiß über die Nähte des Fallschirms und die beiden hölzernen Kreuzteile des Rahmens, genau in der Mitte des Werks malte. Ein kleines Stück zerrissenes Papier mit dem Werktitel wurde unten angebracht, wahrscheinlich, um unseren Vergleichen dieses Gitters mit allen anderen Gittern der Moderne von Mondrian bis Agnes Martin zuvorzukommen. Angesichts Martínez Celayas vorheriger visueller Experimente meine ich, dass wir es hier mit einer Perspektivkonstruktion nach Alberti zu tun haben, die auf listige Weise zunichte gemacht wird. Das Kinderspiel Himmel und Hölle wird künstlerisch bewahrt und zu einem klangvollen visuellen Symbol. Die Handlung des Springens durch den Raum, dem das Himmel- und Höllegitter entspricht, hat ein ästhetisch befriedigendes Korrelat im Fallschirm, der auch für eine Art von Sprüngen verwendet wird. Hier haben wir eine Art Gemälde (und auf jeden Fall keinen Fensterblick, der sich auf eine ideale Aussicht öffnet), das eine Flugbahn des Gedächtnisses ist, der Sprung zurück vom Jetzt zur Kindheit. Ein zartes Stück, ruhig und sogar charmant.

JE

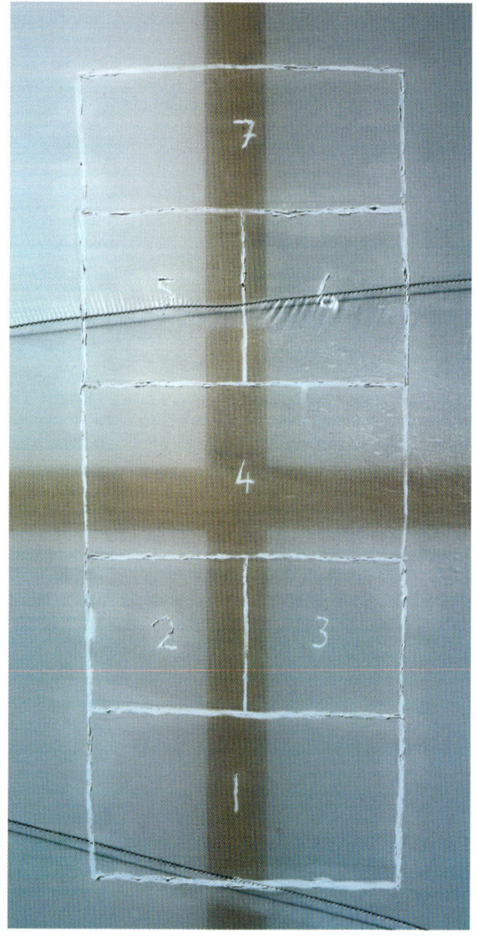

detail/Ausschnitt

1. In the preceding work a bedspread was figured as a landscape, here a parachute becomes a landscape. The opacity of Martínez Celaya's earlier paintings, their dense black cover, gives way to transparency. The complex strategies the artist played in earlier paintings as he negotiated picture planes and their various kinds of piercings underpin what happens here. Again the artist acknowledged the long tradition of the window view, but re-did it by putting the illusion of objects in space on the 'object in the gallery.'

1. Im vorangegangenen Werk wurde die Tagesdecke als Landschaft gestaltet; hier wird ein Fallschirm zu einer Landschaft. Die Undurchsichtigkeit von Martínez Celayas früheren Gemälden, ihre dichten schwarzen Decken, weichen der Transparenz. Die komplexen Strategien, die der Künstler in früheren Gemälden durchspielte, als er Bildebenen und die verschiedenen Arten ihres Durchstechens umkreiste, untermauern das, was hier geschieht. Der Künstler erkannte wieder die lange Tradition des Fensterblicks an, erneuerte diesen aber, indem er die Illusion des Gegenstands im Raum auf den „Gegenstand in der Galerie" übertrug.

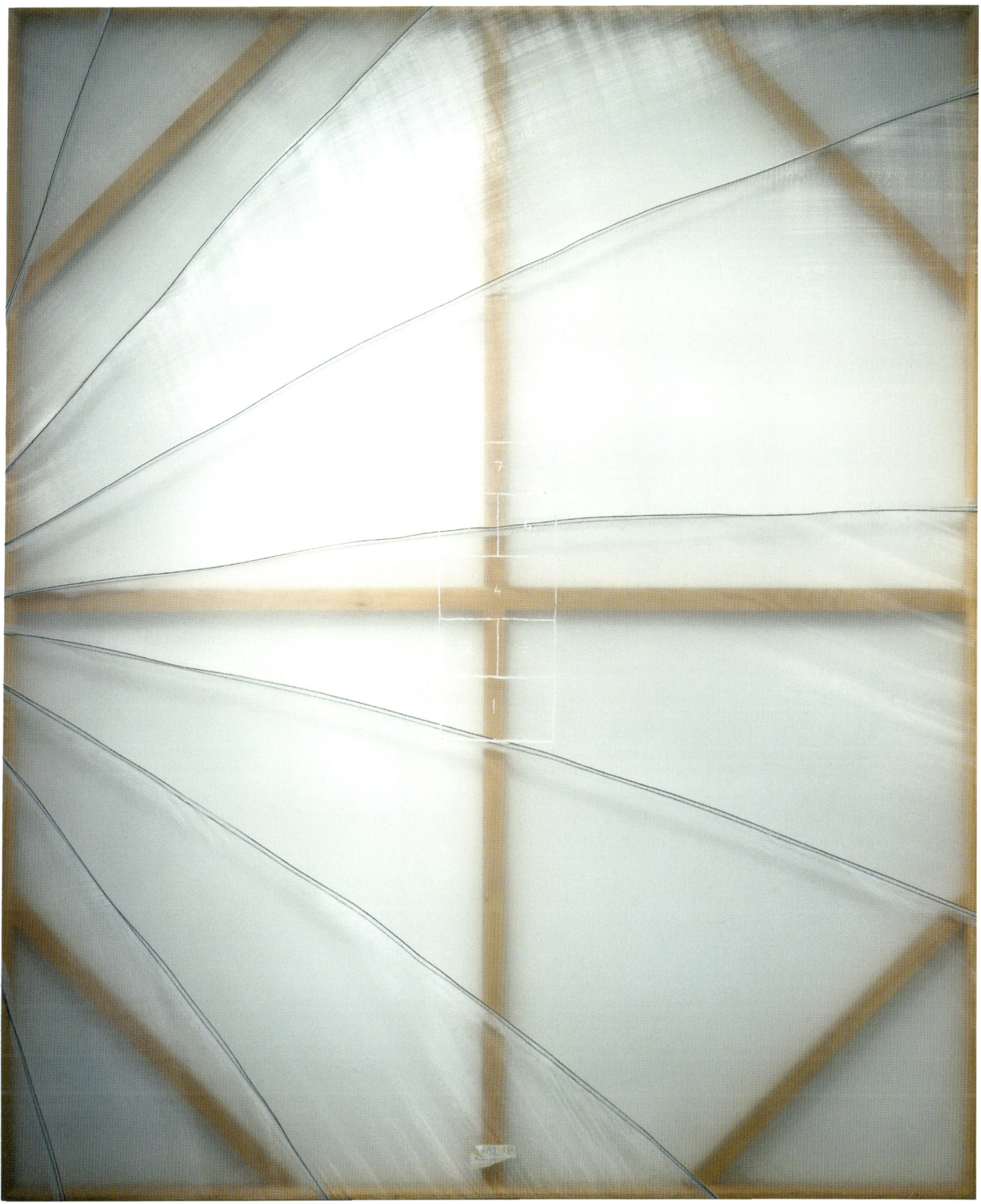

THE BURDEN OF YOUR HAND, 1997
Oil on nylon
80 x 66 inches (203 x 168 cm)
The Progressive Corporation, Cleveland, Ohio

I think we deal here with one of Martínez Celaya's figured surfaces, that is, with a painting whose integrity is like that of our own body (see the discussion for *Unsafe*, p. 128). Here's the 'strategy': to see the hand we must interpret the surface of the painting as a window that we look through; but here that 'hand' is an opaque patch of paint–casts a shadow on the gallery wall behind–that we cannot see through. It becomes an object in the space we occupy as viewers (not the ideal space and time of most pictures). About twice life-size (a little less than sixteen inches tall), the image of a hand takes on a 'special status.'

A severed hand? And hung by a piece of string from some invisible fixture? The bluish gray paint of which it is made has a suspicious impasto: it can suggest coagulated blood. So do the drips of blue-gray paint surrounding the hand. If *Hopscotch* seemed to tenderly explore memories of childhood games, this painting deals with much stronger emotion, with the violence of dismemberment. The title of the work comes from a poem that Martínez Celaya wrote: "I remove the burden of your hand." I cannot help but see this painting as iconic in all the serious senses of that term. It invokes, and here Martínez Celaya went into a dangerous territory indeed, the traditional role of the icon as that place where our images of ourselves become real during an act of worship. Specifically it presents, part for whole, a severed hand as the viewer's body. We cannot help but remember the ancient cult of relics, the worship of the remainders of the bodies of martyrs, witnesses in suffering to truth, people once believed. We glimpse, just for an instant, the body again as a locus of truth (or the truth in painting).

JE

DIE LAST DEINER HAND, 1997
Öl auf Nylon
80 x 66 Zoll (203 x 168 cm)
The Progressive Corporation, Cleveland, Ohio

Ich denke, dass wir es hier mit einer von Martínez Celayas zur Figur gemachten Oberflächen zu tun haben, d. h. mit einem Gemälde, dessen Integrität der unseres Körpers gleicht (siehe die Erörterung von *Nicht Sicher*, S. 128). So sieht die „Strategie" aus: Um die Hand zu sehen, müssen wir die Oberfläche des Gemäldes als ein Fenster betrachten, durch das wir blicken; doch ist die „Hand" hier ein undurchsichtiger Farbfleck – der einen Schatten auf die Galeriewand dahinter wirft –, durch den wir aber nicht hindurchsehen können. Er wird zu einem Gegenstand in dem Raum, in dem wir uns als Betrachter befinden (nicht der ideale Raum und die ideale Zeit der meisten Gemälde). Das Bild der Hand, das, fast 40 cm hoch, etwa doppelte Lebensgröße hat, nimmt einen „Sonderstatus" an.

Eine abgetrennte Hand? Die an einem Stück Schnur an einer nicht sichtbaren Vorrichtung hängt? Die bläulich-graue Farbe, aus der sie besteht, hat einen verdächtigen Impasto: Er könnte geronnenes Blut nahe legen. Das gleiche wäre der Fall für die blaugrauen Farbtropfen, die die Hand umgeben. Während *Himmel und Hölle* auf zarte Weise die Erinnerung an Kindheitsspiele zu erforschen schien, befasst sich dieses Gemälde mit wesentlich stärkeren Emotionen, und zwar mit der Gewalttätigkeit der Zergliederung. Der Titel des Werks stammt aus einem Gedicht von Martínez Celaya: „Ich beseitige die Last deiner Hand." Ich kann nicht umhin, das Bild als symbolisch im ernsten Sinne dieses Begriffs zu sehen. Es beschwört – und Martínez Celaya begibt sich hier in wirklich riskante Bereiche – die traditionelle Rolle des Symbols als einer Stätte herauf, wo unsere Bilder von uns selbst während einer Anbetung Wirklichkeit werden. Es zeigt insbesondere – ein Teil für das Ganze – eine abgetrennte Hand als den Körper des Betrachters. Wir können nicht umhin, uns an die alten Reliquienkulte zu erinnern, die Anbetung der Überreste der Körper der Märtyrer, die leidenden Zeugen der Wahrheit, an die Menschen einst glaubten. Wir sehen nur für einen Augenblick wieder den Körper als Ort der Wahrheit (oder der Wahrheit des Malens).

JE

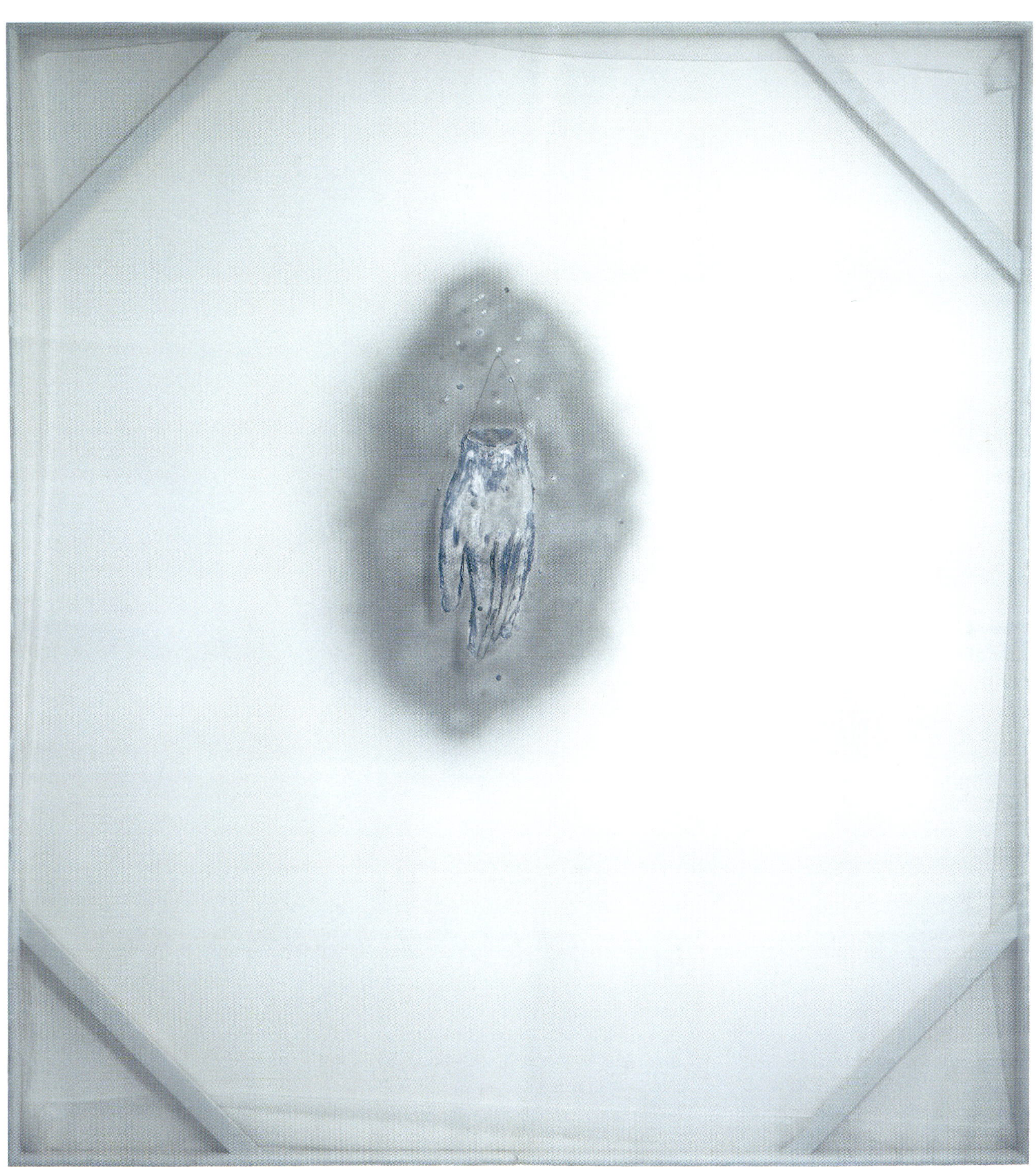

THE RIVER, 1997
Oil and wax on plaster
70 x 22 x 11 inches (178 x 56 x 28 cm)
Courtesy of Enrique Martínez Celaya

The 'statue' does not stand, but floats several feet above the gallery floor; the pose is quite unreadable.

Those who have read the commentary on the paintings so far will know what Martínez Celaya's 'strategy' is here (or at least what I think it must be): with this piece he most emphatically figures a painting's surface as our bodies. The 'picture plane' now actually takes on the shape of a body; it has no need of a frame because its 'shape' gives it all the integrity and coherence it needs. Martínez Celaya continued here, as he did formerly during the mid 1990s, to force a viewer to acknowledge the picture plane as a metaphor for our bodies by opening gaps in it, by 'wounding' it, then by covering the gaps up again, that is, by 'healing' them (see my commentary on *Unsafe*, p. 126). Both the slashed abdomen, and the cut-off hand in this piece read in this way. Part of the emotional impact of the piece is how we wince empathetically at the wounding of the picture plane.[1]

But that is not the main import of the landscape (it is not just a vision of paradise and its fountain of life, though of course it is that too). The landscape stands for the world outside us. This 'painting' tests our subject position with regard to that objective world. We note with interest the blue veins, blood vessels, painted by the artist on the statue's hands and feet: the body's internal rivers resonate with the pictured external one. We could see this piece as a high Modern philosopher would: as a study in subjectivity written large upon the world (Hegel's Idea). Or we could see it just as well as a late Modern philosopher might: the truth in painting may be the way one metaphor (our body) dissolves into another (the world outside) to make us wary of any and all claims to a subject position.

JE

DER FLUSS, 1997
Öl und Wachs auf Gips
70 x 22 x 11 Zoll (178 x 56 x 28 cm)
Courtesy of Enrique Martínez Celaya

Die „Statue" steht nicht, sondern schwebt mehrere Fuß über dem Boden des Ausstellungsraums; ihre Pose ist kaum zu deuten.

Diejenigen, die die Bemerkungen zu den Gemälden bis hierhin gelesen haben, wissen, wie Martínez Celayas „Strategie" hier aussieht (oder zumindest, was ich davon halte): In diesem Werk gestaltet er mit Nachdruck die Oberfläche eines Gemäldes als unsere Körper. Die „Bildfläche" nimmt nun tatsächlich die Gestalt eines Körpers an; es bedarf keines Rahmens, da seine „Form" ihm die erforderliche Integrität und Kohärenz verleiht. Martínez Celaya setzte hier fort, was er zuvor, Mitte der neunziger Jahre tat, d. h. er zwingt den Betrachter, die Bildebene als eine Metapher unserer Körper anzuerkennen, indem er Lücken im Körper öffnet, ihn „verwundet", und dann die Lücken zudeckt, d. h. sie wieder „heilt" (siehe meine Bemerkungen zu *Nicht Sicher*, S. 126). Der aufgeschlitzte Unterleib und die abgetrennte Hand in diesem Werk können so verstanden werden. Zu der emotionalen Wirkung dieses Werks gehört auch unser deutliches Zusammenzucken angesichts der Verwundung der Bildfläche.[1]

Dies ist jedoch nicht die Hauptbedeutung der Landschaft (sie ist nicht nur eine Vision des Paradieses und seines Lebensquells, obwohl sie das natürlich auch ist). Die Landschaft steht für die Welt, die sich außerhalb von uns befindet. Dieses „Gemälde" prüft unsere Subjektposition in Bezug auf diese objektive Welt. Wir bemerken mit Interesse die blauen Adern, Blutgefäße, die der Künstler auf die Hände und Füße der Statue gemalt hat: Die inneren Flüsse des Körpers klingen mit den abgebildeten, äußeren zusammen. Wir könnten dieses Werk so betrachten, wie es ein moderner Philosoph tun würde: als eine Studie der Subjektivität, die in Großbuchstaben auf die Welt geschrieben wurde (Hegels Gedanke). Oder wir könnten es genauso gut wie ein späterer moderner Philosoph ansehen: Die Wahrheit des Malens könnte die Art und Weise sein, in der eine Metapher (unser Körper) sich in einen anderen auflöst (der Außenwelt), damit wir sämtlichen Ansprüchen bezüglich einer Subjektposition misstrauen.

JE

1. Flowers play a constant role in Martínez Celaya's work, and here we begin to see that iconographically they never have just their 'face value.' Here they fill the gap left by the slash, and take the place of new life in a woman's womb.

1. Blumen spielen eine konstante Rolle in Martínez Celayas Arbeiten und hier beginnen wir zu sehen, dass man sie ikonographisch nie für bare Münze nehmen kann. Hier füllen sie die Lücke, die auf Grund des Schnitts hinterblieb und sie nehmen die Stelle eines neuen Lebens im Leib der Frau ein.

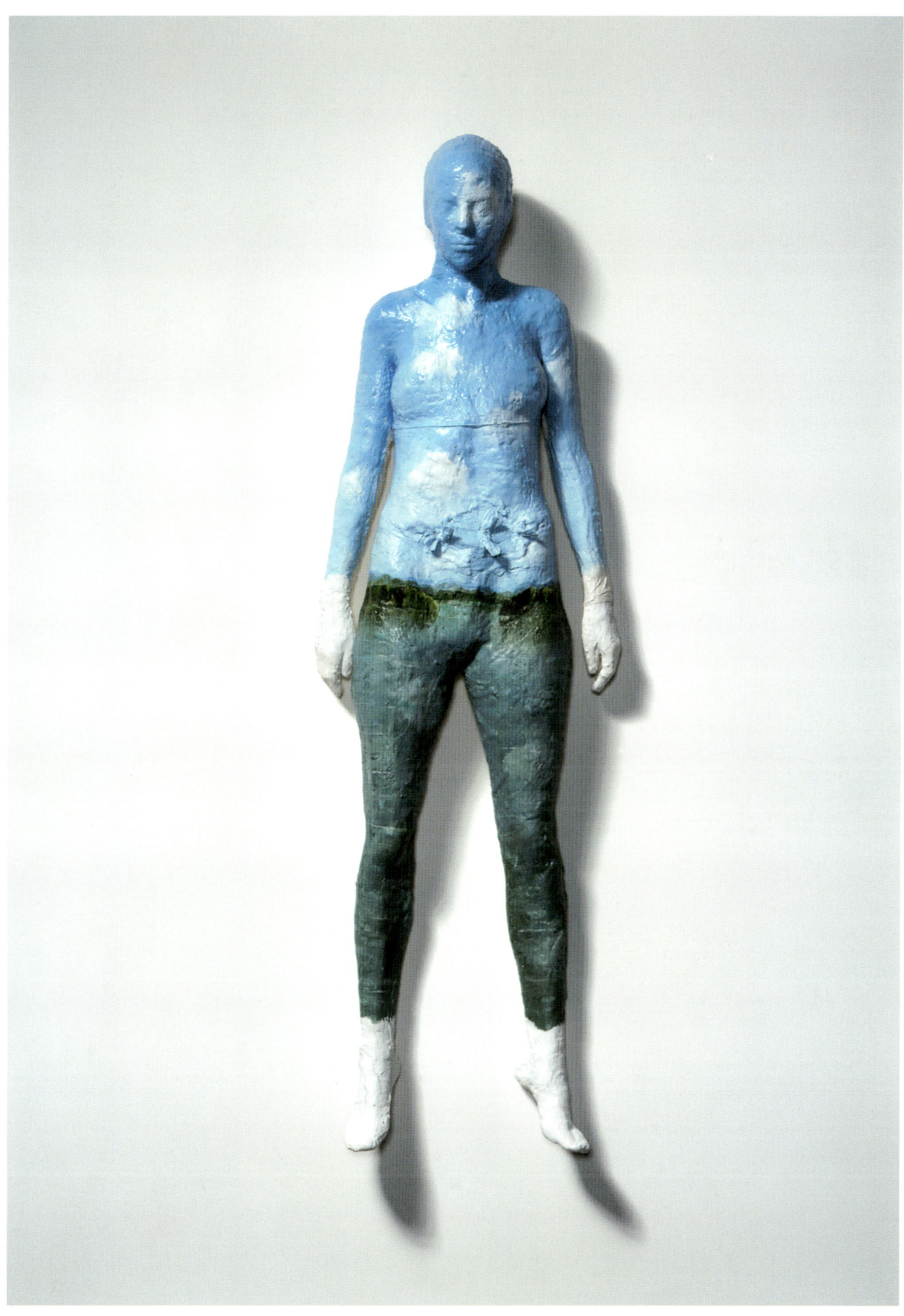

ACCEPTANCE OF LONGING, 1997
Oil on canvas
60 x 72 inches (152 x 183 cm)
Los Angeles County Museum of Art, Modern and Contemporary Art Council, Art Here and Now Purchase

The artist painted this piece in one session over two sleepless days. Again we encounter a giant monument, this time a strange bird, some amalgam of a penguin and a hummingbird, that reclines unmoving upon a cylindrical pedestal. The bird is white, the pedestal gray, both painted illusionistically in the long tradition of the imitation statue in *grisaille.* The conceit is coldness, an icy freeze, stasis. The bird is a shocking subject, absurd but not ironic; rather, poignant.

The artist called attention to the surface of the canvas by allowing the semi-transparent gray glaze to drip wetly, and by painting small 'wounds.' Closely akin to these 'cuts' are the gouges Martínez Celaya made in the image of the monument itself; he looks to have dragged a sharp point across its paint, combing or raking the surface of the canvas to reveal the white gesso beneath. The gouges certainly interrupt the illusion of solid form in space and make the image of the monument 'stick' to the surface. But the 'cuts' and gouges are more than some formal device. If one takes the canvases in this series as figured, that is, as standing in for our bodies, we might wince empathetically as we ponder the 'cuts' and gouges in this canvas. Flagellants inflict such wounds on themselves (and their bodies were depicted in art thus, especially in Trecento and Quattrocento Italian painting). The question is: as viewers could we take such a subject position with respect to this canvas?

The grisaille statue's icy coolness, its stasis, can make one think of the Christian notion of *refrigerium,* the state of the blessed after death, finally consoled. But if the painting produces such a reflection, viewers note also the passionate discourse of the 'cuts' and gouges, which is anything but icy, anything but a consolation.

JE

AKZEPTANZ DER SEHNSUCHT, 1997
Öl auf Leinwand
60 x 72 Zoll (152 x 183 cm)
Erworben duch das Los Angeles County Museum of Art, Modern and Contemporary Art Council, Art Here and Now

Der Künstler hat dieses Werk in nur einer Sitzung gemalt, die sich über zwei schlaflose Tage erstreckte. Auch hier treffen wir auf ein riesiges Monument, dieses Mal ein seltsamer Vogel, das Amalgam eines Pinguins und eines Kolibris, der unbewegt auf einem zylindrischen Sockel liegt. Der Vogel ist weiß, der Sockel grau, und beide wurden illusionistisch in der langen Tradition der Statuenimitation als Grisaille gemalt. Der zentrale Gedanke ist die Kälte, ein eisiger Frost, Stillstand. Der Vogel ist ein schockierender Bildgegenstand, absurd, aber nicht ironisch, eher ergreifend.

Der Künstler lenkte die Aufmerksamkeit auf die Oberfläche der Leinwand, indem er erlaubte, dass dort eine halbdurchsichtige graue Lasur nass tropft, und indem er kleine „Wunden“ malte. Eng verwandt mit diesen „Schnitten“ sind die Furchen, die Martínez Celaya im Bild des Monuments selbst zog; es sieht aus, als ob eine scharfe Spitze durch die Farbe gezogen wurde, die die Oberfläche der Leinwand kämmte oder harkte, um den weißen Kreidegrund zu enthüllen. Die Furchen stören auf jeden Fall die Illusion einer soliden Form im Raum und lassen das Bild des Monuments an der Oberfläche „kleben“. Jedoch sind diese Schnitte und Furchen mehr als ein formaler Kunstgriff. Wenn man die Leinwände in diesen Serien so nimmt, wie sie gestaltet sind, d. h. als für unsere Körper stehend, dürften wir deutlich zusammenzucken, wenn wir über die Schnitte und Furchen in diesem Gemälde nachdenken.

Flagellanten fügen sich selbst solche Wunden zu (und ihre Körper wurden in der Kunst auf diese Weise dargestellt, besonders in der italienischen Malerei des Trecento und Quattrocento). Die Frage ist: Können wir als Betrachter diese Subjektposition in Bezug auf dieses Gemälde einnehmen?

Die eisige Kälte der Grisaillestatue, ihr Stillstand, erinnern uns an die christliche Vorstellung des Refrigeriums, eines Zustands der Gesegneten nach dem Tod, endlich getröstet. Sollte das Bild aber eine solche Überlegung bewirken, kann der Betrachter auch den leidenschaftlichen Diskurs über die Schnitte und Furchen bemerken, der alles andere als eisig und alles andere als ein Trost ist.

JE

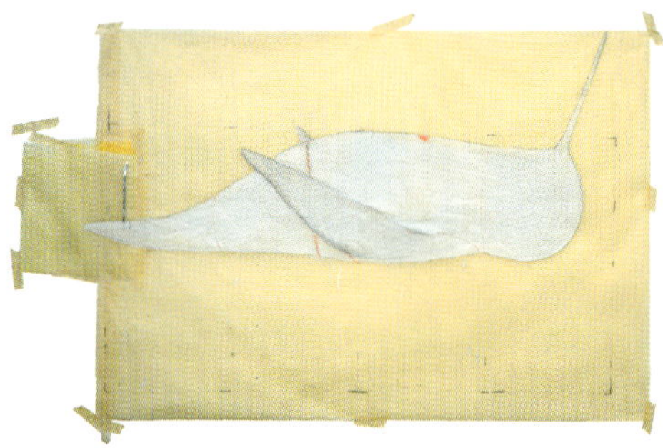

ACCEPTANCE OF LONGING (STUDY) /AKZEPTANZ DER SEHNSUCHT (STUDIE), 1997
Collection of/Sammlung Dr. and Mrs. Stephen Kulvin, Coral Gables, Florida

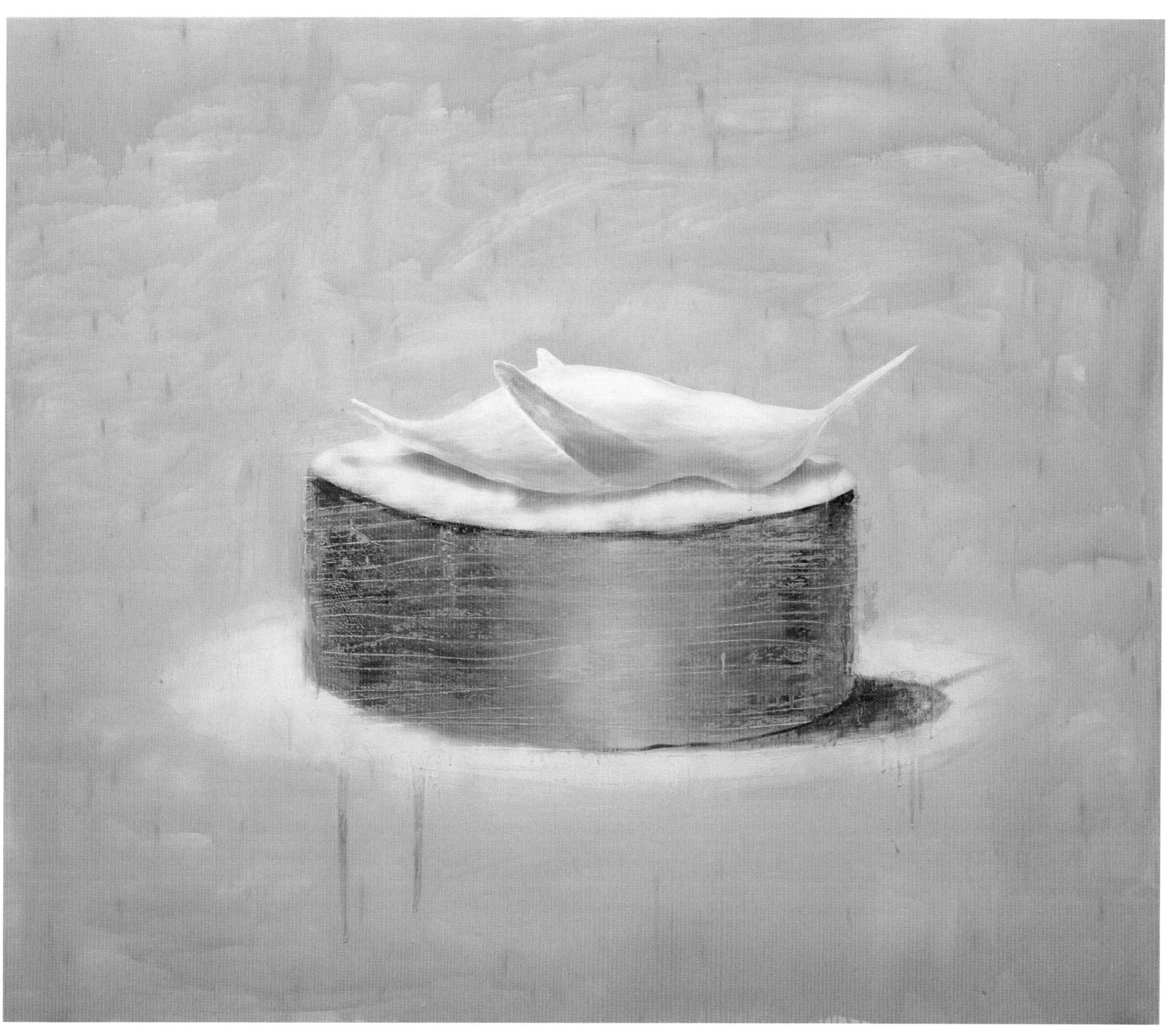

STONEWALL, 1997
Oil and graphite on paper
75 x 39 inches (190 x 99 cm)
Collection of Sara Nemeth Goodman,
Los Angeles, California

Could the spray of roses stand for genitalia? That's what the position of the flowers strongly suggests: it helps 'fill in' for those missing parts of the body, though it hardly reads in the spatial illusion as a substitute for them. Of course, roses are Venus' attribute: do we deal here with a kitsch icon of the erotic?

Again in Martínez Celaya's work we have two images that respond to each other, one painted in color, and one drawn in outline (or mostly). Compare, say, *Second Ornament* (p. 132). In that earlier painting, the 'strategie' was formal, a means by which the artist could explore the possibility of creating some sort of 'Modern Icon.' The artist insisted on the title of this piece, inscribing 'stone wall' in pencil near its bottom edge. The title suggests fences, barriers, and the stone walls that divide things up. We wonder how the painted and the penciled images go together here: there is a gap. Do the flower parts separate as well? Between the volumetric rose and the flat spray of rose buds? Is there a gap here too between male and female? The emptiness of the gulf between, the barrier between, that the title forces us to consider is figured here most elegantly and quietly. One reflects anew on the roses that the artist put in play in 1993 in *The Trouble with Memory.*

JE

STEINMAUER, 1997
Öl und Graphit auf Papier
75 x 39 Zoll (190 x 99 cm)
Sammlung Sara Nemeth Goodman,
Los Angeles, Kalifornien

Könnte der Rosenzweig für Genitalien stehen? Dies wird durch die Positionierung der Blumen sehr nahe gelegt: Sie hilft, die fehlenden Körperteile „auszufüllen", obwohl sie kaum als deren Ersatz in der räumlichen Illusion angesehen werden kann. Natürlich stellen Rosen ein Attribut der Venus dar: Haben wir es hier mit einem erotischen Kitschsymbol zu tun?

Wieder erblicken wir in einem Werk Martínez Celayas zwei Motive, die aufeinander antworten, wobei eines farbig und das andere (größtenteils) als Umriss dargestellt ist. Vergleichen Sie es beispielsweise mit der *Zweiten Verzierung* (S. 132). In dem früheren Gemälde war die „Strategie" formaler Art; ein Mittel, durch das der Künstler die Möglichkeit der Schaffung einer Art „modernen Symbols" erforschen konnte. Der Künstler bestand auf dem Titel dieser Arbeit und schrieb „Steinmauer" in Bleistift in die Nähe der unteren Kante. Der Titel suggeriert Zäune, Barrieren und die Steinmauern, die die Dinge trennen. Wir fragen uns, wie die gemalten und die mit Bleistift gezeichneten Motive zusammenpassen: Es gibt eine Lücke. Separieren sich auch die Teile der Blume? Die volumenhafte Rose und der flache Zweig mit Rosenknospen? Gibt es auch hier eine Lücke zwischen männlich und weiblich? Die Leere der dazwischen liegenden Kluft, der dazwischen liegenden Barriere, die der Titel uns zu bedenken zwingt, ist hier äußerst fein und ruhig dargestellt. Der Betrachter denkt erneut über die Rosen nach, die der Künstler 1993 in *Das Problem mit dem Gedächtnis* ins Spiel brachte.

JE

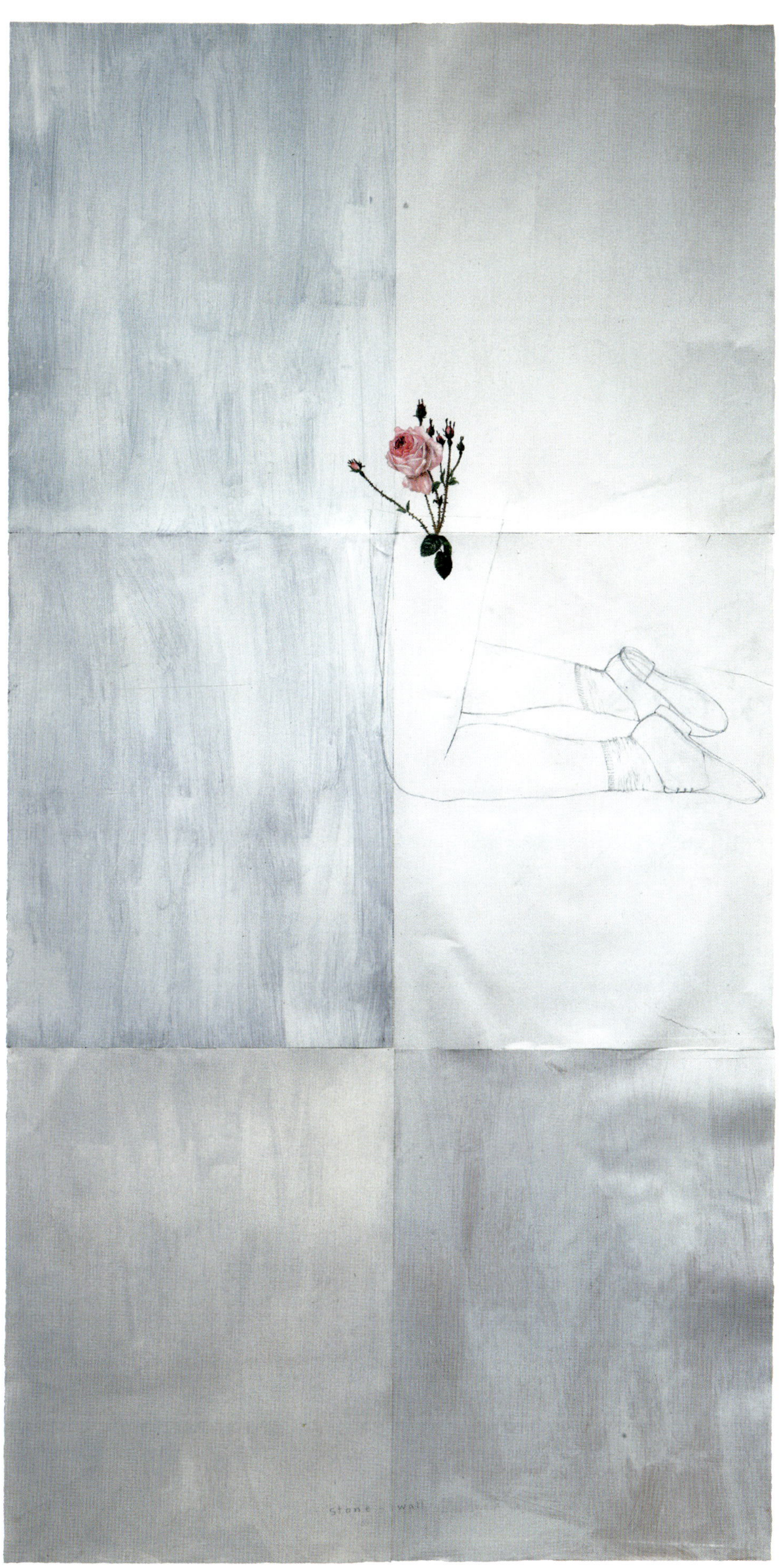
stone - wall

VANITY AND REDEMPTION, 1997
Oil on canvas
54 x 60 inches (137 x 152 cm)
Private Collection, Colorado

Vanity and Redemption introduces into this exhibition the motif of the poet's arm. It thereby embodies (or disembodies) the thematics of dismemberment, leading to the Saint Catherine heads, *Tu Brazo* (which also links the arm to tulips), *Map*, *The House of Arms*, and several of the Berlin photographs.

While Martínez Celaya more often depicts several tiny hummingbirds dwarfed by empty fields, here a single one fills and dominates the canvas. The painting is built on a play of gravity and weightlessness expressed in the hummingbird's body: head and chest heavy and corporeal (but significantly lacking a face) rising on wings that grow increasingly translucent, or expressed in the wings' motion and the arm's inertness.

Clearly this is a risky image: sweet colors, soft-focus, sentimental motif of an aerial/mythical creature bravely struggling against the weight of the world, and all too easy to read allegorically: the artistic life burdens awareness, vanity hampers redemption, alternatively, the redemption of the poet's arm ascends with an offering of flowers. But *Vanity and Redemption* works by oscillating between the invitation and denial of meaning; it relentlessly teases the beholder. The painting slips out of our interpretive nets by asserting a kind of resistance, a deadpan that makes such readings seem more or less beside the point.

AR

EITELKEIT UND ERLÖSUNG, 1997
Öl auf Leinwand
54 x 60 Zoll (137 x 152 cm)
Privatsammlung, Colorado

Eitelkeit und Erlösung führt in diese Ausstellung das Motiv des Arms des Dichters ein. Mit diesem verkörpert (oder „entkörpert") es die Thematik der Zerstückelung, die in den Häuptern der heiligen Katharina, *Tu Brazo* (das Werk, das auch eine Verbindung zwischen Arm und Tulpen herstellt), *Landkarte*, *Das Haus der Arme* und verschiedenen Berlin-Photographien fortgesetzt wurde.

Während Martínez Celaya meistens mehrere kleine Kolibris darstellt, die angesichts der leeren Bildfelder winzig erscheinen, füllt und beherrscht hier ein einziger Kolibri die Leinwand. Das Gemälde baut auf einem Spiel zwischen Schwerkraft und Schwerelosigkeit auf, denen der Körper des Kolibris Ausdruck verleiht – der Kopf und die Brust sind schwer und greifbar (wenn signifikanterweise auch ohne Gesicht) und erheben sich auf Flügeln, die immer durchsichtiger werden, – oder die sich in der Flügelbewegung und der Trägheit des Arms ausdrücken.

Dies ist eindeutig ein riskantes Bild: süße Farben, verschwommene Bilder, das sentimentale Motiv eines mythischen Luftgeschöpfs, das sich tapfer gegen das Gewicht der Welt zur Wehr setzt und dem nur allzu schnell allegorische Züge angedichtet werden können: Das künstlerische Leben wiegt schwer auf dem Bewusstsein, die Eitelkeit behindert die Erlösung und andererseits steigt der erlöste Dichterarm mit einem Blumenopfer in die Höhe. Aber *Eitelkeit und Erlösung* wirkt durch das Schwingen zwischen der Einladung, Verweigerung der Bedeutsamkeit und der Betrachter wird schonungslos aufgezogen. Das Gemälde entzieht sich unseren Interpretationsnetzen, indem es eine Art Widerstand, eine Ausdruckslosigkeit darstellt, die solche Deutungen mehr oder weniger sinnlos zu machen scheint.

AR

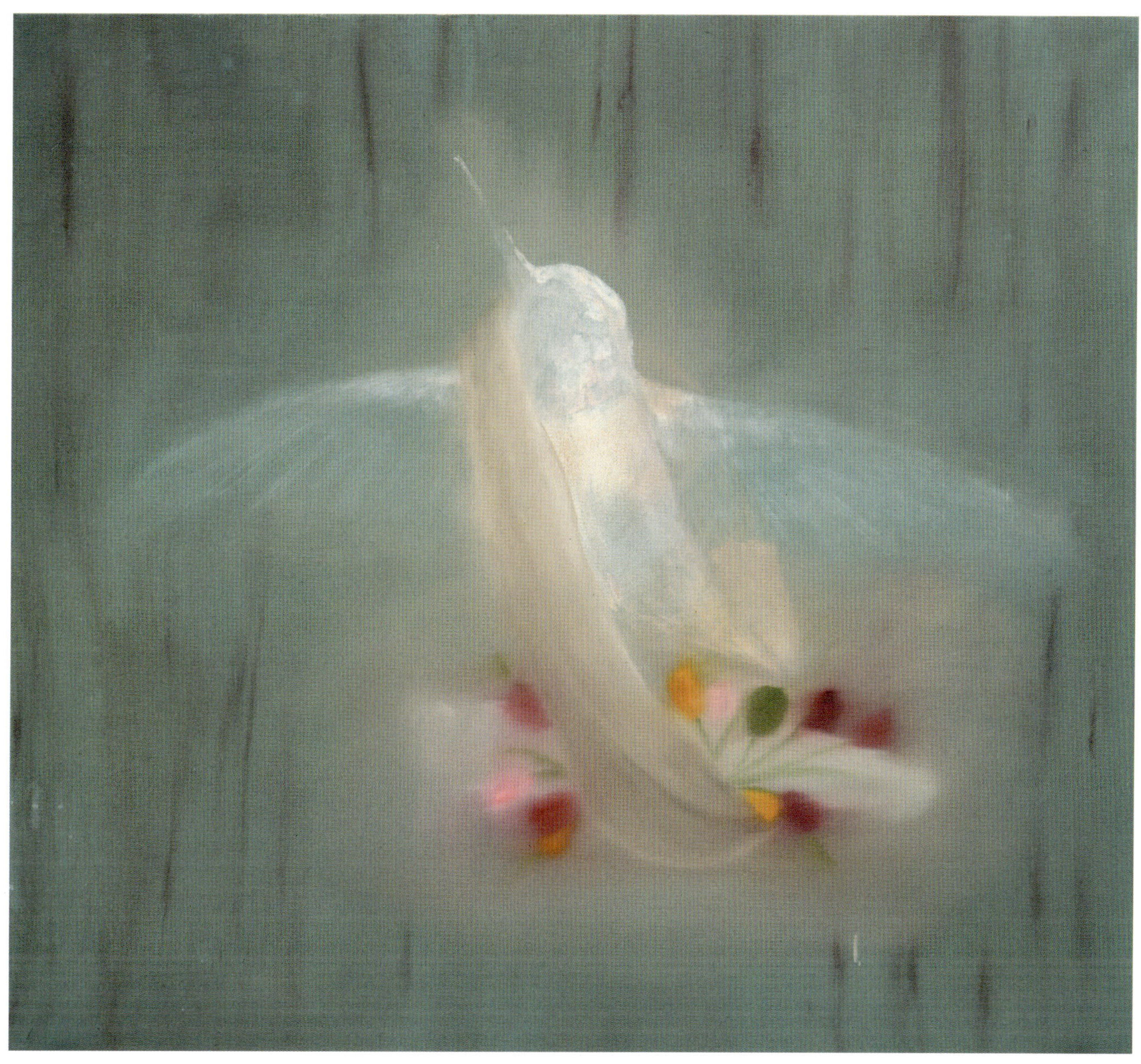

THE GARDEN OF FORGETFULNESS, 1997
Charcoal, rose petals and resin on paper
24 x 18 inches (61 x 46 cm)
Collection of Scott Dean Harrington,
Los Angeles, California

Together with *A Boy in his Room* and *The Secrets*, this painting forms a kind of triptych pointing to the experience of early adolescence and abuse.[1]

'Garden' might refer to rose petals, with which the paper was backed in resin. But 'Forgetfulness'? The title engages the paradox of cultivating forgetfulness, making negation palpable, something to harvest. (Think of Mallarmé's '*absence de tout bouquet.*') Ordinarily, the scent of roses might recall a memory, but these petals are doubly absent: sealed off in resin and blown away, scattered across the canvas. The rose has lost its character and integrity–while remaining a rose.

At first glance it is hard even to detect the outline of a head which, by contrast to the heads in *A Boy in his Room* and *The Secrets*, is dwarfed by its field. This head is intentionally awkward, and with its tears and its little collar, rather insistently dumb. Yet like certain works of Gustave Flaubert (Félicité, for instance, in *A Simple Heart*) it manages to achieve a kind of irony-proof claim on our attention. (To say that the head elicits sympathy would be going too far–we do not identify with the figure.) The more minimal or modest the means–no mouth to communicate emotion, no eye, except by implications since tears are falling from a certain spot–the greater the figure's expressiveness.

The Garden might take its strength from its willingness to risk sentimentality, nostalgia, kitsch, and then escaping such emotions at the last moment, displacing the painting into another realm. Sidestepping.

Like *The Garden* and unlike *Boy in his Room*, this head's gender and age are difficult to read. Yet compared to the masked *Boy*, *Secrets* is ironically the more exposed image: the head turned almost directly toward us to reveal bruises from a beating–the 'secrets' un-masked. A powerful image of abuse is rendered with the simplest of means: white oil on paper and blotches of red. All the blotches are related to the senses, situated near the eyes, above one ear, and directly on the nose. Of course the most dramatic blotch, which thanks to the added linseed oil 'bleeds' into the paper, occurs at the throat. This head is not simply isolated from its body by aesthetic convention, like a bust, for it bears the mark of violence.

DER GARTEN DER VERGESSLICHKEIT, 1997
Kohle, Rosenblütenblätter und Harz auf Papier
24 x 18 Zoll (61 x 46 cm)
Sammlung Scott Dean Harrington,
Los Angeles, Kalifornien

Zusammen mit den Bildnissen *Ein Knabe in seinem Zimmer* und *Die Geheimnisse* bildet dieses Gemälde eine Art Triptychon, Hinweis auf die Erfahrungen früher Jugend und Misshandlung.[1]

Der Begriff „Garten“ könnte sich auf die Rosenblütenblätter beziehen, mit denen die Rückseite des Papiers in Harz hinterlegt wurde. Aber „Vergesslichkeit“? Der Titel ruft das Paradox der Kultivierung der Vergesslichkeit auf die Tagesordnung und macht Verneinung zu etwas, das man schmecken, ernten kann. (Denken Sie nur an Mallarmés „absence de tout bouquet“.) Normalerweise ruft der Duft der Rosen eine Erinnerung wach; diese Blüten jedoch sind in zweierlei Hinsicht abwesend: Sie sind im Harz versiegelt und über die Leinwand verstreut. Die Rose hat ihren Charakter und ihre Integrität verloren – und bleibt doch eine Rose.

Auf den ersten Blick kann man sogar kaum den Umriss eines Kopfes erkennen, der im Gegensatz zu den Köpfen in *Ein Knabe in seinem Zimmer* und *Die Geheimnisse* im Vergleich zum Feld winzig erscheint. Dieser Kopf wirkt absichtlich linkisch und mit seinen Tränen und seinem kleinen Kragen beharrlich dumm. Ähnlich wie bestimmte Werken von Gustave Flaubert (zum Beispiel Félicité in *Ein einfaches Herz*) fesselt er ironiesicher unsere Aufmerksamkeit. (Man würde zu weit gehen zu behaupten, dass der Kopf Sympathie auslöst – wir identifizieren uns nicht mit der Figur.) Je minimalistischer oder bescheidener die Mittel – kein Mund, um Gefühle auszudrücken, kein Auge, das nur durch den Ursprungsort der Tränen impliziert wird, – desto ausdrucksstärker ist die Figur.

Der Garten schöpft seine Kraft aus seiner Bereitschaft, Sentimentalität, Nostalgie und Kitsch zu riskieren, um dann in letzter Sekunde solchen Gefühlen zu entkommen und das Gemälde in eine andere Sphäre zu versetzen. Ausweichen.

Wie *Der Garten* und im Gegensatz zu *Der Knabe in seinem Zimmer* verrät dieses Bild kaum das Geschlecht und das Alter des Kopfes. Allerdings ist *Geheimnisse* im Vergleich zum maskierten *Knaben* ironischerweise ein offeneres Bild: der Kopf ist uns fast zugewandt, um die Prügelwunden zu zeigen –

1. Martínez Celeya regarded the titles of these three works as particularly important, placing legends nearby at their first exhibition.
1. Für Martínez Celaya sind die Titel dieser drei Werke besonders wichtig und er sah bei ihrer ersten Ausstellung erläuternde Texte in ihrer Nähe vor.

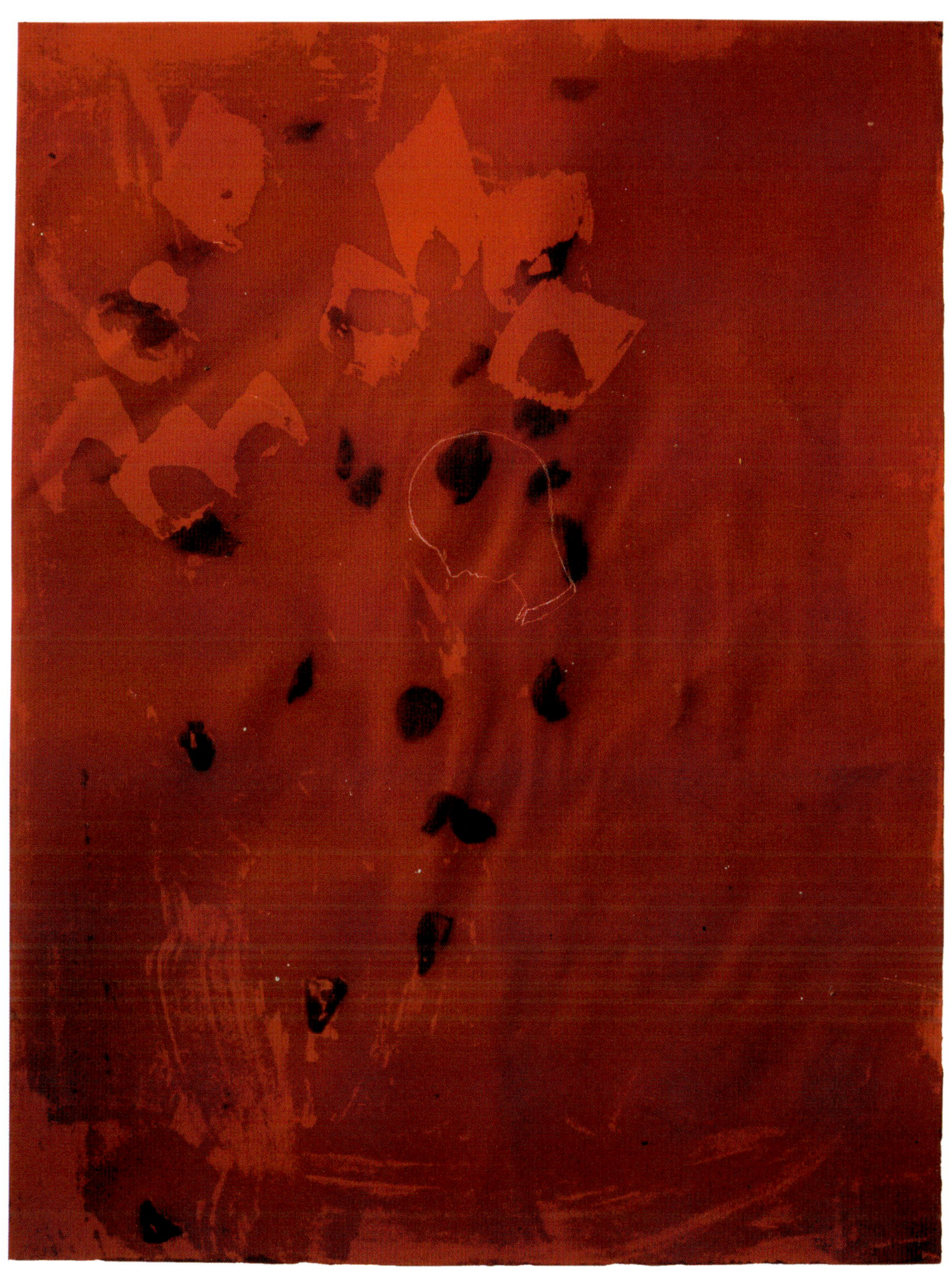

However unflinchingly violence is exposed, the expression remains illegible–closed mouth, closed eye. And so, this youth guards the secrets. Because it manages to be at once shocking and aloof–in an odd way almost meditative–*The Secrets* steers clear of the clichéd or manipulative territory one sees, for example, in public service advertisements for abused children.

This is one of Martínez Celaya's rare profiles, which like *The Garden of Forgetfulness* masks what it reveals.

A Boy in his Room signifies mental space and plays against the connotations of 'roominess'. Locked within the interiority, the boy can neither take in the world nor express himself. In fact he is triply enclosed, because the masked head is drawn on a tight piece of paper–which amounts to another 'room'–then collaged onto the larger paper and enclosed in that frame as well. The boy is at once constrained or imprisoned and also isolated and lost in the space of this last, large, empty 'room'.

The tie acts as a noose, cutting off the boy's access to the world of the living. However, tightening the constraint makes the face's features visible and gives them what definition we see, so that the act of representation is tied to acts of abuse or cruelty. What results is an illusionary interplay of flat and molded, leaving a haunting depth to eye sockets. One can see the wrinkles drawn on the white bag are echoed in the actual, material wrinkles on the brown paper caused by applying paint.

AR

die demaskierten „Geheimnisse". Ein eindrucksvolles Bild der Misshandlung wird mit einfachsten Mitteln erzielt: weiße Ölfarbe auf Papier und rote Flecken. Alle Flecken beziehen sich auf die Sinne und liegen nahe der Augen, über einem Ohr und direkt auf der Nase. Natürlich befindet sich der dramatischste Fleck, der dank dem hinzugefügten Leinöl in das Papier „blutet", an der Kehle. Dieser Kopf ist nicht nur gemäß ästhetischer Konvention von seinem Körper getrennt (wie zum Beispiel eine Büste), schließlich ist er von Gewalt gezeichnet.

Wenn auch die Gewalt ohne Zögern offenbart wird, verraten der geschlossene Mund, das geschlossene Auge nichts. Und so bewahrt dieser Jugendliche die Geheimnisse. Weil das Bild zugleich schockierend und zurückhaltend und auf merkwürdige Weise fast meditativ wirkt, entgeht *Die Geheimnisse* den Klischees und Manipulationen, die man beispielweise in Anzeigen öffentlicher Institutionen zum Thema Kindsmissbrauch sieht.

Dies ist eine der wenigen Profildarstellungen von Martínez Celaya, die wie der *Garten der Vergesslichkeit* maskieren was sie enthüllen.

Ein Knabe in seinem Zimmer verbildlicht mentalen Raum und nicht „Geräumigkeit" im räumlichen Sinne. Der Knabe ist im Innern gefangen und kann weder die Welt begreifen noch sich selbst ausdrücken. Tatsächlich ist er dreifach eingeschlossen, weil der maskierte Kopf auf einem kleinen Stück Papier, also einem weiteren Raum, gezeichnet, dann als Collage auf ein größeres Papier übertragen und dann auch von diesem Rahmen umschlossen wird. Der Knabe wird gehemmt oder gefangen und ist zugleich isoliert und verloren im Raum dieses letzten, großen, leeren „Zimmers".

Das Band ist wie eine Schlinge, die den Knaben von der Welt der Lebenden trennt. Allerdings macht das Engerziehen der Umhüllung die Gesichtszüge sichtbar und definiert sie erst für uns, so dass der Vorgang der Darstellung an Misshandlungen oder Grausamkeiten gebunden ist. Das Resultat ist ein täuschendes Wechselspiel von flach und geformt, das den Augenhöhlen eine quälerische Tiefe verleiht. Man kann sehen, wie die auf die weiße Tüte gezeichneten Falten sich auf die tatsächlichen, physischen Falten des braunen Papiers, ein Ergebnis des Farbauftrags übertragen.

AR

THE SECRETS, 1997
Oil on paper
24 x 18 inches (61 x 46 cm)
Collection of Scott Dean Harrington,
Los Angeles, California

DIE GEHEIMNISSE, 1997
Öl auf Papier
24 x 18 Zoll (61 x 46 cm)
Sammlung Scott Dean Harrington,
Los Angeles, Kalifornien

A BOY IN HIS ROOM, 1997
Oil on paper
24 x 18 inches (61 x 46 cm)
Collection of Scott Dean Harrington,
Los Angeles, California

EIN KNABE IN SEINEM ZIMMER, 1997
Öl auf Papier
24 x 18 Zoll (61 x 46 cm)
Sammlung Scott Dean Harrington,
Los Angeles, Kalifornien

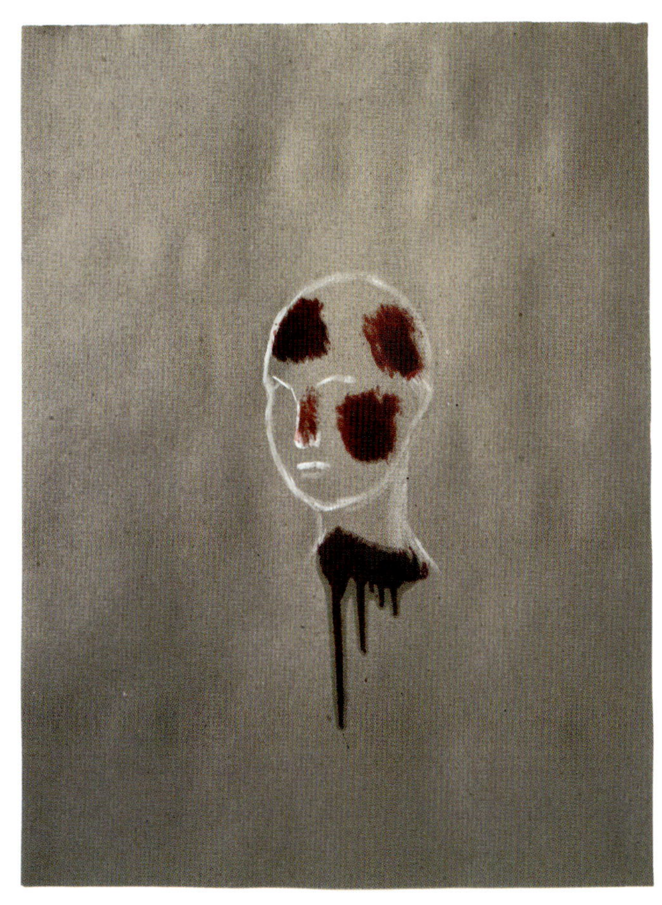

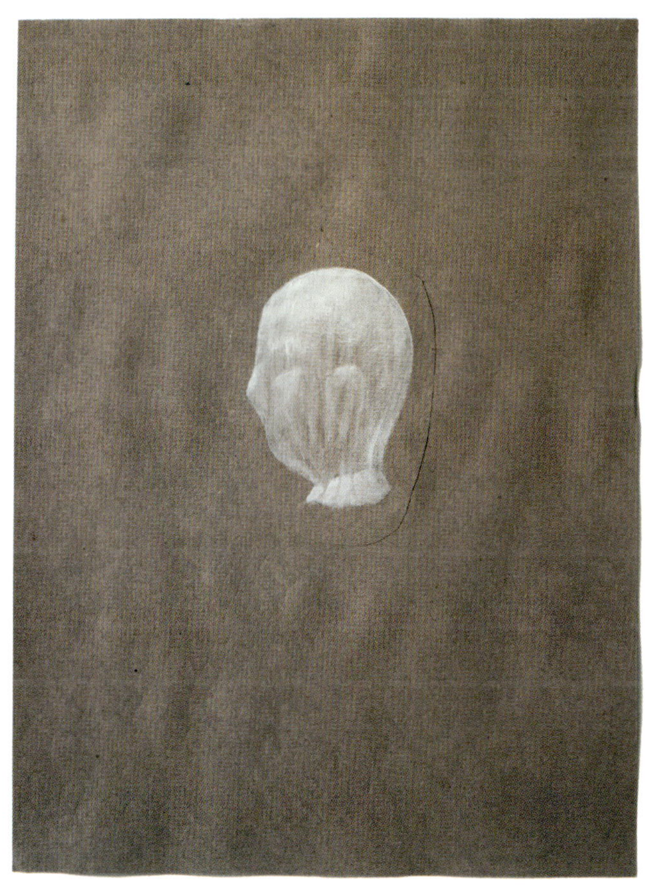

TU BRAZO (YOUR ARM), 1997
Oil and graphite on paper
18 x 48 inches (46 x 122 cm)
Collection of Willy J. Salet, Aspen, Colorado

Between illusion and disillusion: the white ground supporting the image is revealed as thin and artificial by the brown paper which forms a second ground, and whose own material character and thinness is signaled by the burn at bottom center. Materiality insists on itself, but at the same time invites interpretation: the charring suggests the double theme of transcendence or transmutation and destruction. The paper is burned just where the painter inscribed the title, thereby threatening both image and text. In turn, the fire is countered by the dripping paint, which threatens to extinguish the fire that would consume the image. The very stuff of the image saves the image in a moment of conflict, but also one of balance, or balance of terror.

Out of the arm of the poet the blooms of two tulips emerge. Perhaps they function as wings, taking the place of the hummingbird in *Vanity and Redemption* (p. 152). Transcendental tulips, counterpointing the drips, and whose white wash leaves only ghostly traces of original, terrestrial red? They might offer restitution to the arm. The very gesture reads in contradictory ways. The transcending arm becomes more capable–the inspired poet, freed of mundane concerns–but simultaneously less so: there is no hand to inscribe verse and no connection to the self to do the mind's will.

AR

TU BRAZO (DEIN ARM), 1997
Öl und Graphit auf Papier
18 x 48 Zoll (46 x 122 cm)
Sammlung Willy J. Salet, Aspen, Colorado

Zwischen Illusion und Desillusion: Der weiße Untergrund des Bildes wird durch das braune Papier, das einen zweiten Untergrund bildet, als dünn und künstlich enthüllt. Dessen Materialeigenschaften werden durch die Brandstelle unten in der Mitte verdeutlicht. Das Material besteht auf seinen Eigenschaften und lädt gleichzeitig zur Interpretation ein: Die verkohlte Stelle ist ein Hinweis auf das Doppelthema der Transzendenz oder Transmutation und Zerstörung. Das Papier ist genau an der Stelle verbrannt, auf die der Maler den Titel geschrieben hat, d. h. sowohl das Bild als auch der Text werden bedroht. Das Feuer wiederum ist der tropfenden Farbe entgegengesetzt, die das Feuer zu löschen droht, das sonst das Bild vernichten würde. Das bloße Material des Bildes rettet es in einem konfliktgeladenen Moment, der aber auch ein Moment des Schreckens oder ein Gleichgewicht des Schreckens ist.

Aus dem Arm des Dichters treten die Blüten zweier Tulpen hervor. Vielleicht haben sie die Funktion von Flügeln und übernehmen die Rolle des Kolibris in *Eitelkeit und Erlösung* (S. 152). Transzendente Tulpen, die den Tropfen entgegengesetzt sind und deren Blätter aus weißer Farbe nur geisterhafte Spuren des ursprünglichen Erdrots hinterlassen? Vielleicht bieten sie dem Arm Wiederherstellung. Diese Geste lässt sich auf widersprüchliche Weise deuten. Der im Zustand der Transzendenz befindliche Arm wird fähiger – der inspirierte Poet frei von weltlichen Sorgen – und gleichzeitig verliert er an Fähigkeiten: Er hat keine Hand zum Aufschreiben von Versen und keine Verbindung zum eigenen Ich, um den Willen des Geistes umzusetzen.

AR

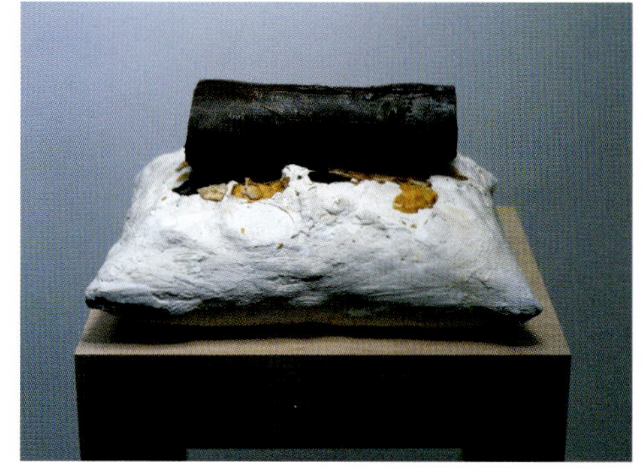

SNOW AND TIME/SCHNEE UND ZEIT, 1998
Courtesy of Griffin Contemporary, Venice, California

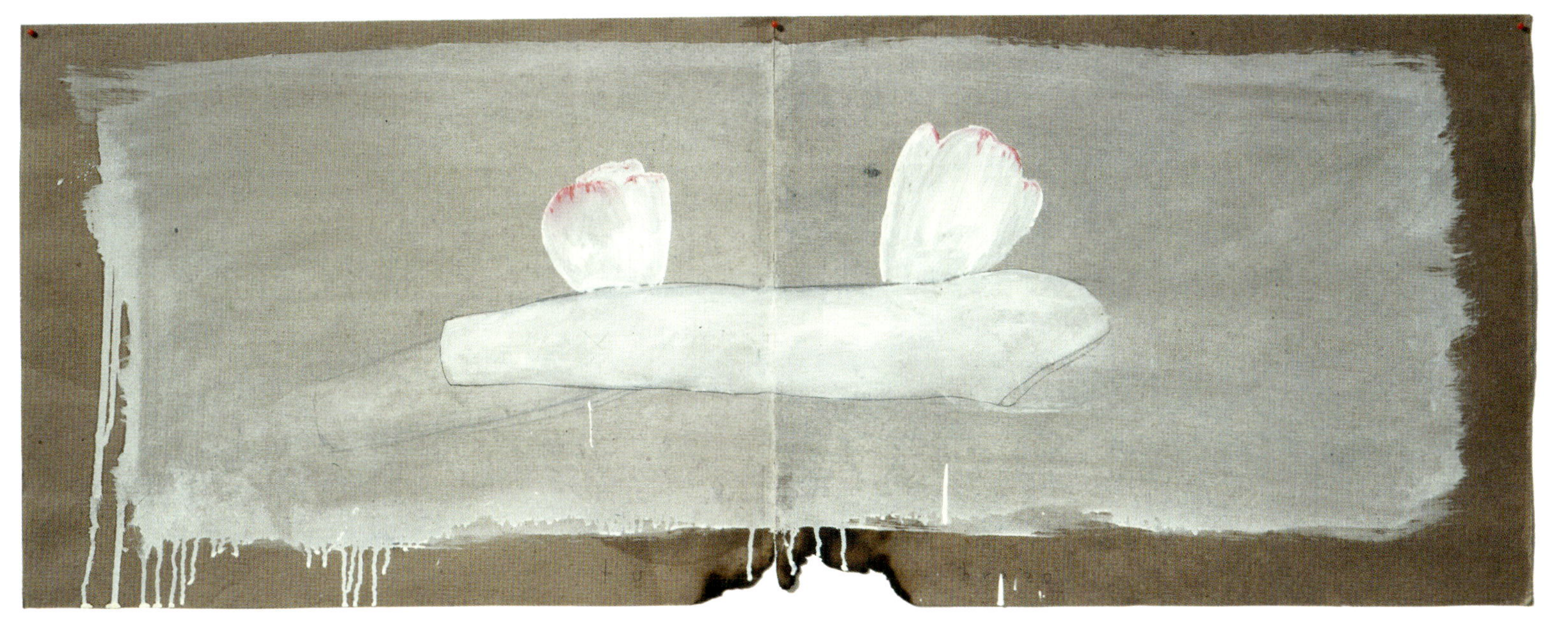

THE KING'S SHELTER, 1997
Leaves, dirt, roses and polyester resin
4 x 21 x 4 inches (10 x 53 x 10 cm)
Collection of Andrea King, Los Angeles, California

The dismembered arm in *Tu Brazo* (p. 158) or *Vanity and Redemption* (p. 152) [both from the same year as *The King's Shelter*] comes forward, like the Saint Catherine heads, to invade the beholder's space. In an expressive but indeterminate gesture, the hand turns up in supplication or to hold or maybe to protest. Cradled in plaster, resting on a piece of white fabric, the work hovers between kitsch and relic–but rather than insulated, relic-like, behind glass this arm is disturbingly exposed.

The title and the concept of shelter carries the double senses of activity and passivity. Coupled with the flesh's burnt and deadened quality–embedded in the resin the dirt and leaves signify passage, decay, transformation –the arm as shelter may also offer safety. Underpinning that ambiguity is ambivalence concerning time as maker and destroyer. So unsettling a work as this–the severing, the flowers, suffering internalized and constituent of this arm's identity–recalls conceptually Cézanne's early paintings, which similarly introduce cruelty into image making. *The King's Shelter's* twinning of creation and destruction is reinforced by the work's wedding of violence and beauty. The light-catching transparency of the fingers in direct contrast to the earthy raw beauty of the leaves, branches and dirt of the arm create a resonant embodiment of transfiguration.

AR

DER ZUFLUCHTSORT DES KÖNIGS, 1997
Blätter, Erde, Rosen und Polyesterharz
4 x 21 x 4 Zoll (10 x 53 x 10 cm)
Sammlung Andrea King, Los Angeles, Kalifornien

Der abgeschlagene Arm in *Tu Brazo* (S. 158) oder in *Eitelkeit und Erlösung* (S. 152) – beide aus dem gleichen Jahr wie *Der Zufluchtsort des Königs* – dringen wie die Häupter der heiligen Katharina in den Raum des Betrachters ein. Mit einer ausdrucksvollen und doch unbestimmten Geste öffnet sich die Hand flehend nach oben. Vielleicht soll sie auch etwas halten oder protestieren. Eingebettet in Gips auf einem Stück weißem Stoff bewegt sich die Arbeit zwischen Kitsch und Reliquie – allerdings wird dieser Arm nicht einer Reliquie gleich hinter Glas isoliert, sondern auf beunruhigende Weise entblößt.

Der Titel und der Begriff des Zufluchtsorts haben die Doppelbedeutng von Aktivität und Passivität. Gemeinsam mit dem verbrannten und toten Fleisch und eingebettet in Harz beschreiben die Erde und die Blätter Übergang, Zersetzung und Verwandlung – der Arm als Zufluchtsort bietet also vielleicht auch Schutz. Diese Zweideutigkeit wird durch die Ambivalenz der Zeit als schaffende und zerstörende Kraft unterstrichen. Eine so beunruhigende Arbeit – das Abtrennen, die Blumen, das verinnerlichte und für die Identität des Arms wesentliche Leiden – erinnert in ihrem Konzept an Cézannes frühe Gemälde, die auf ähnliche Weise Grausamkeit zum Teil des Schaffensvorgangs eines Bildes machten. In *Der Zufluchtsort des Königs* werden Erschaffung und Zerstörung zu Zwillingen, was durch die Vereinigung von Gewalt und Schönheit in dem Werk unterstrichen wird. Die lichteinfangende Transparenz der Finger im direkten Kontrast zur irdenen rohen Schönheit der Blätter, Zweige und Erde des Arms verkörpert die Verklärung sehr überzeugend.

AR

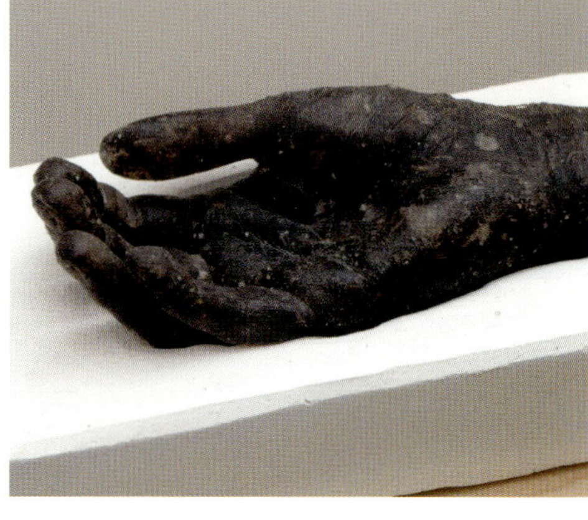

detail/Ausschnitt

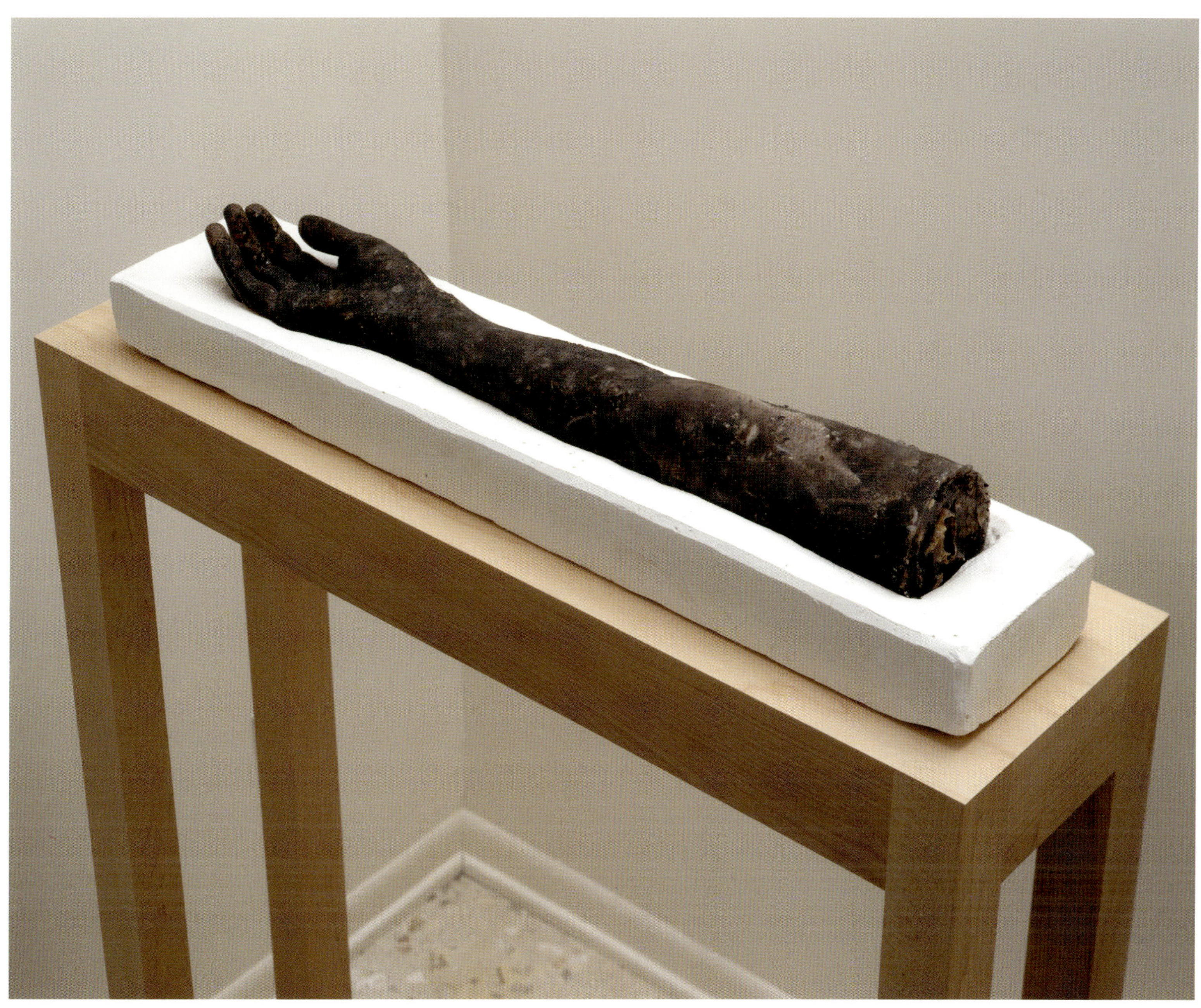

MAP, 1998
Oil on fabric
48 x 48 inches (122 x 122 cm)
Collection of Stephen Cohen,
Los Angeles, California

Violence spreads across the visual field as the figure of a dismembered arm answers the ground of blood-stained upholstery. While it hangs inert (recalling *The Burden of Your Hand*, p. 142), the digits are not quite limp.

Map's[1] organic and inorganic components do a dance of repetition and difference. The worn upholstery (it dates from the 1930s) has known many arms; and the diagonal lines running across the material are echoed in the red 'X' shape at mid-forearm. So too the red from the ground invades the space of the figure. But the manufactured, kitsch regularity of the diamonds is broken by the irregular red lines that resemble arteries (or the lifelines on *Counting Passage*). The illusion of modeling in the arm is repeated by the actual three-dimensionality of the fabric–even as that fabric fractures the arm's illusion of depth. Those all too prominent red veins (which also read simply as cracks in white paint that reveal the red underpainting) further fragment the already fractured body, and resemble a butcher's guide to carving meat–or a 'map' to cutting up the arm.

The painting meets violent domesticity: traces of an obscured childish drawing of a house can be made out to the right of the arm, balancing a large, dark red drip left of the arm.

AR

LANDKARTE, 1998
Öl auf Gewebe
48 x 48 Zoll (122 x 122 cm)
Sammlung Stephen Cohen,
Los Angeles, Kalifornien

Gewalt breitet sich im Gesichtsfeld aus, als sich ein abgetrennter Arm auf einem blutbeflecktem Polsterstoff findet. Während der Arm wirkungslos hängt (man denke an *Die Last deiner Hand*, S. 142), sind seine Finger nicht ganz erschlafft.

Die organischen und anorganischen Bestandteile der Arbeit *Landkarte*[1] tanzen einen Reigen aus Wiederholung und Unterschied. Der abgenutzte Polsterstoff (er stammt aus den dreißiger Jahren) hat Bekanntschaft mit vielen Armen gemacht und die diagonalen Linien, die über das Material laufen, finden sich im roten X in der Mitte des Unterarms wieder. So breitet sich das Rot des Untergrunds im Raum der dargestellten Figur aus. Allerdings wird die künstliche kitschige Regelmäßigkeit der Stoffrauten von unregelmäßigen roten Linien unterbrochen, die Arterien ähneln (oder den Lebenslinien in *Counting Passage*). Die Illusion des modellierten Arms wird durch die tatsächliche Dreidimensionalität des Gewebes wiederholt, selbst wenn das Gewebe die Illusion der Tiefe des Arms bricht. Die stark hervorstehenden roten Venen (die auch einfach als Risse in der weißen Farbe erscheinen, durch die die rote Untergrundfarbe enthüllt wird) führen zur weiteren Fragmentierung des bereits gebrochenen Körpers und ähneln einem Leitfaden für Schlachter zum Zerlegen von Fleisch oder einer „Landkarte" zum Zerschneiden des Arms.

Das Gemälde thematisiert auch die häusliche Gewalt: Spuren einer verborgenen kindlichen Zeichnung eines Hauses sind rechts vom Arm auszumachen, sie bilden ein Gegengewicht zu einem großen roten Tropfen links vom Arm.

AR

1. *Map* represented Martínez Celaya in the Los Angeles County Museum of Art's exhibition *Made in California: Art, Image, and Identity, 1900–2000.*

1. Martínez Celaya war mit *Landkarte* in der Ausstellung *Made in California: Art, Image, and Identity, 1900–2000* im Los Angeles County Museum of Art.

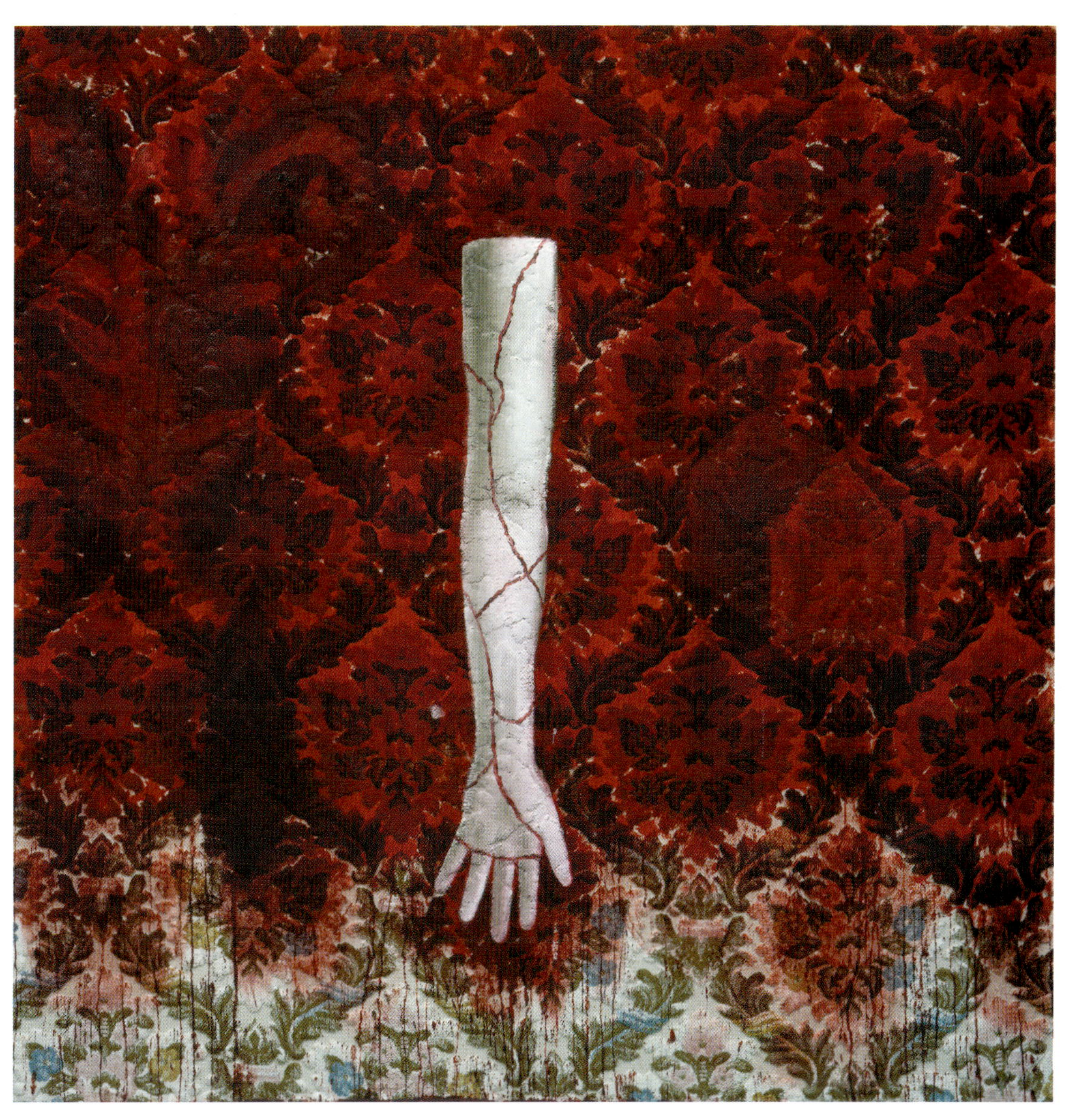

SAINT CATHERINE, 1997
7 x 9 x 9 inches (18 x 23 x 23 cm)

DIE HEILIGE KATHARINA, 1997
7 x 9 x 9 Zoll (18 x 23 x 23 cm)

All the Saint Catherine heads are the same size, just below human scale. In this way they underscore the objects' constructed character: they declare themselves cast from a piece of sculpture rather than from actual heads, in the manner of death masks.

In the series the titles are all drawn from different stages of Hegel's movement toward absolute knowledge. Simultaneously, however, the subject points to religious communion with some larger whole in a martyr's certainty that brooks no analysis. The Saint Catherine heads conflate revelation and philosophy to produce a kind of Enlightenment translation of the Stations of the Cross. Coupled with the heads' differing contents, these Hegelian titles suggest landmarks in a passage, each pillow marking a different 'station.'

But we need to resist (at least in part) the seduction of sequencing. The titles may arise from Martínez Celaya's intuitive sense of evolution that parallels Hegel's, but the artist uses them in a more or less arbitrary way. It is not self-evident why the series should begin with '*Absolution*,' for instance, or why '*Artificer*' should lead to '*Pleasure*,' whence to '*Culture*.' If we juxtapose the first throat and the last, we progress from the bloody fact of martyrdom in *Absolution* to the perfect rose in *Spirit*. Perhaps that flower signals the end of Dante's *Paradiso (XXX–XXXI)*, with its image of a celestial rose where are arranged the thrones of the saints, their robes making up the petals. Two details disrupt this progress, however: Dante's rose is white, and in Medieval texts red roses like *Spirit*'s symbolizes earthly love.

AR

Alle Häupter der heiligen Katharina sind gleich groß, etwas kleiner als ein menschlicher Kopf. So heben sie die Konstruiertheit der Objekte hervor: Sie erklären sich selbst zu Abgüssen einer Skulptur und nicht von echten Köpfen wie eine Totenmaske.

Alle Titel der Serie stammen aus verschiedenen Stadien des Wegs Hegels zum absoluten Wissen. Gleichzeitig deutet der dargestellte Gegenstand, mit der Sicherheit eines Märtyrers, die keine Analyse duldet, auf eine religiöse Kommunion mit einem größeren Ganzen hin. Die Häupter der heiligen Katharina vereinigen Offenbarung und Philosophie, um eine Art aufklärerische Übersetzung der Kreuzwegstationen zu schaffen. Zusammen mit den unterschiedlichen Inhalten der Häupter lassen diese Hegelschen Titel Orientierungspunkte auf einer Reise vermuten, wobei jedes Kissen eine andere „Station" markiert.

Allerdings müssen wir wenigstens teilweise der Versuchung der Einordnung widerstehen. Die Titel könnten sich aus Martínez Celayas intuitivem Sinn für die Evolution ergeben, die parallel zu der Hegels verläuft, aber der Künstler verwendet die Titel mehr oder weniger willkürlich. Es ist nicht ohne weiteres klar, warum die Serie zum Beispiel mit *Absolution* beginnen soll oder warum *Schöpfer* zu *Vergnügen* und von dort zu *Kultur* führen soll. Wenn wir die erste und die letzte Kehle nebeneinander betrachten, schreiten wir von der blutigen Tatsache des Märtyrertums in *Absolution* zur perfekten Rose in *Geist*. Vielleicht signalisiert die Blume das Ende von Dantes *Paradiso* (XXX/XXXI) mit seinem Bild einer himmlischen Rose, wo die Throne der Heiligen so gruppiert werden, dass ihre Roben die Blütenblätter bilden. Allerdings stören zwei Details dieses Fortschreiten: Dantes Rose ist weiß, und in mittelalterlichen Texten symbolisieren rote Rosen, wie die des *Geistes*, irdische Liebe.

AR

SAINT CATHERINE (SPIRIT), 1997
Polyester resin and silk flower
Collection of Heidi Schneider, New York, New York

DIE HEILIGE KATHARINA (GEIST), 1997
Polyesterharz und Seidenblume
Sammlung Heidi Schneider, New York, New York

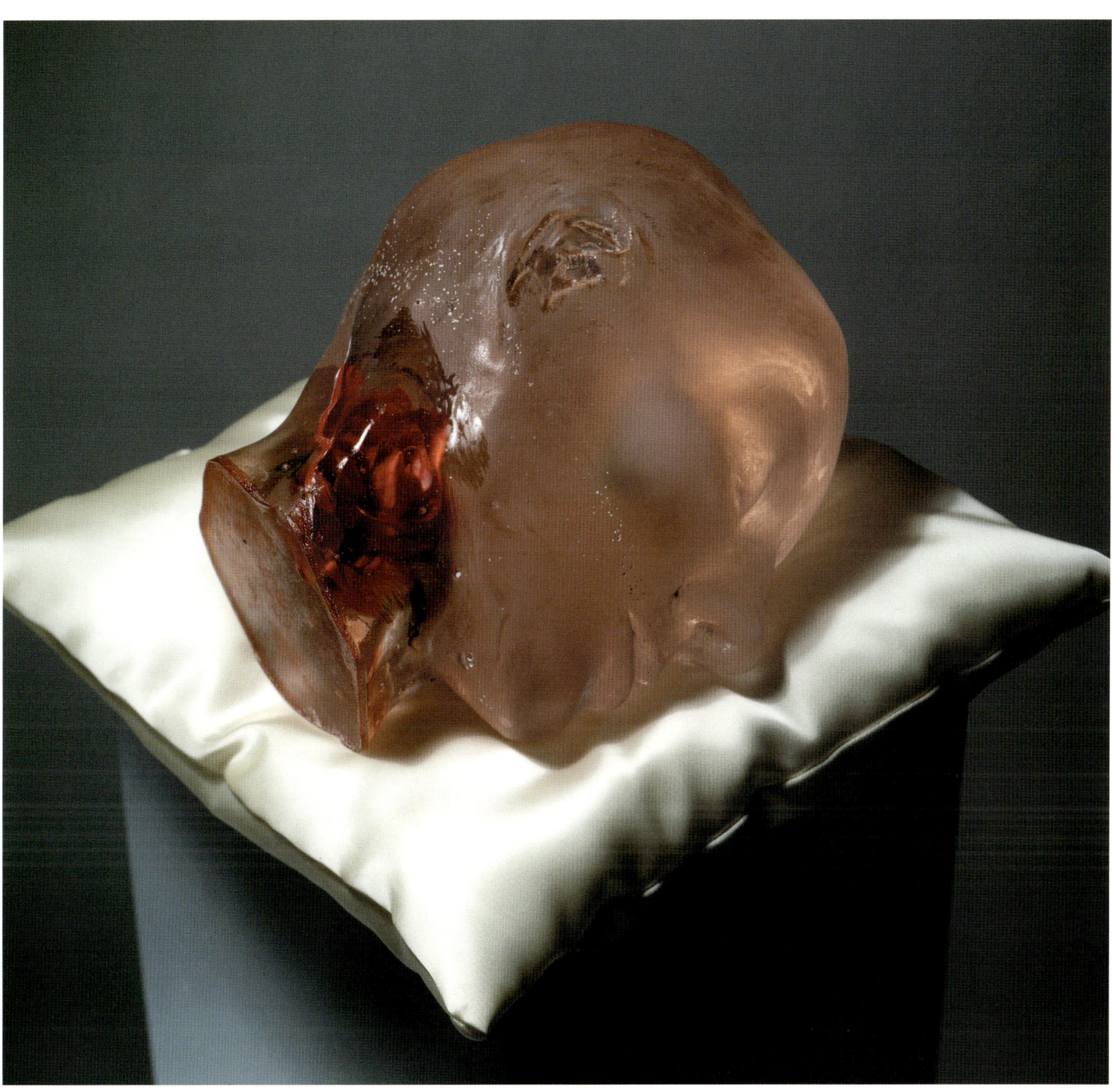

clockwise from upper left

SAINT CATHERINE (THE ETHICAL QUESTION), 1997
Polyester resin
Collection of Enrique and Alexandra Martínez Celaya

SAINT CATHERINE (ABSOLUTION), 1997
Polyester resin
Collection of Mary Paeng, San Francisco, California

SAINT CATHERINE (CULTURE), 1997
Polyester resin and hummingbird
Collection of Ross Bleckner, New York, New York

HALF AGAIN, FLOWER, 1997
Polyester resin, dirt and roses
Collection of Tom Peters, Los Angeles, California

SAINT CATHERINE (PLEASURE), 1997
Polyester resin and silk flowers
Collection of Marta Gutiérrez, Carolina, Puerto Rico

SAINT CATHERINE (BEAUTIFUL SOUL), 1997
Polyester resin
Collection of Patrick Aroff, Santa Monica, California

von oben links im Uhrzeigersinn

DIE HEILIGE KATHARINA (DIE ETHISCHE FRAGE), 1997
Polyesterharz
Sammlung Enrique and Alexandra Martínez Celaya

DIE HEILIGE KATHARINA (ABSOLUTION), 1997
Polyesterharz
Sammlung Mary Paeng, San Francisco, Kalifornien

DIE HEILIGE KATHARINA (KULTUR), 1997
Polyesterharz und Kolibri
Sammlung Ross Bleckner, New York, New York

WIEDER HALB, BLUME, 1997
Polyesterharz, Erde und Rosen
Sammlung Tom Peters, Los Angeles, Kalifornien

DIE HEILIGE KATHARINA (VERGNÜGEN), 1997
Polyesterharz und Seidenblumen
Sammlung Marta Gutiérrez, Carolina, Puerto Rico

DIE HEILIGE KATHARINA (SCHÖNE SEELE), 1997
Polyesterharz
Sammlung Patrick Aroff, Santa Monica, Kalifornien

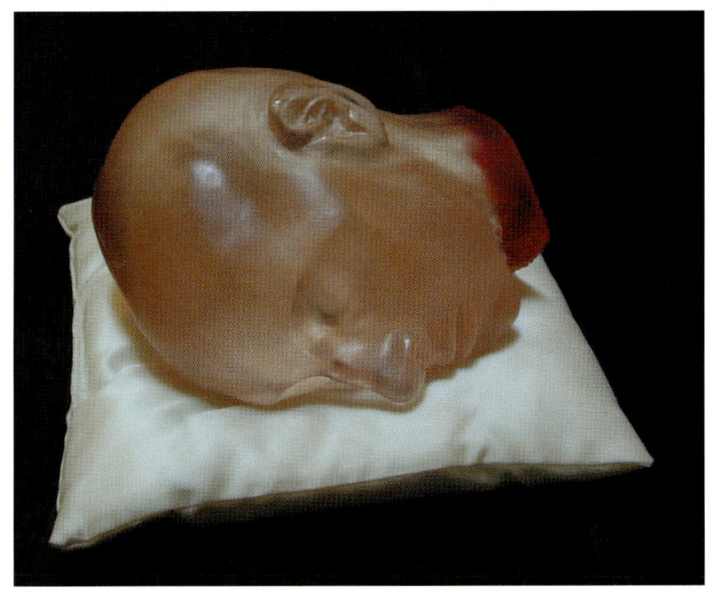
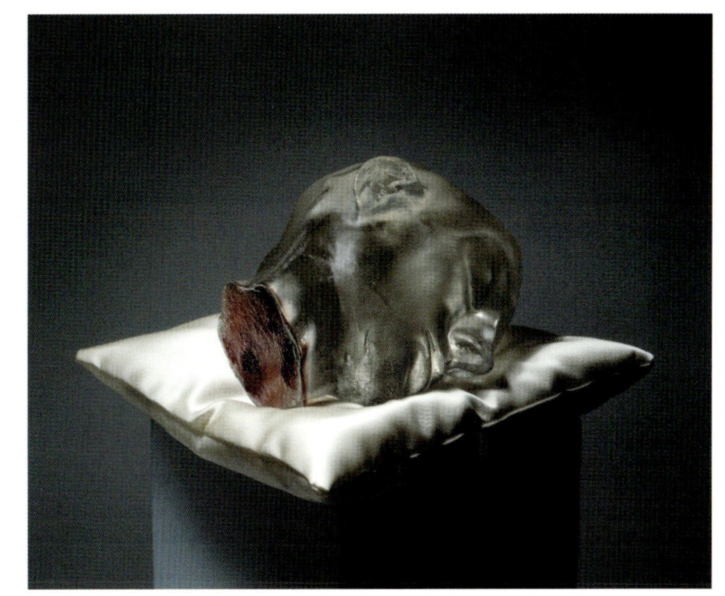
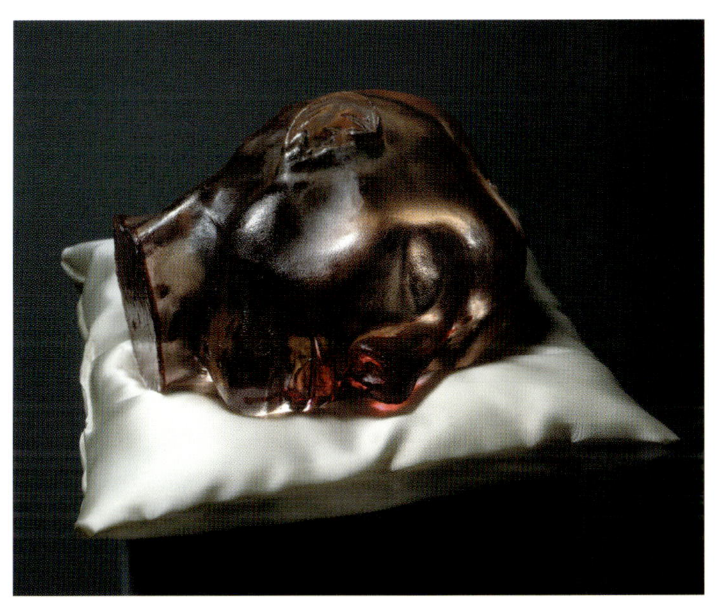
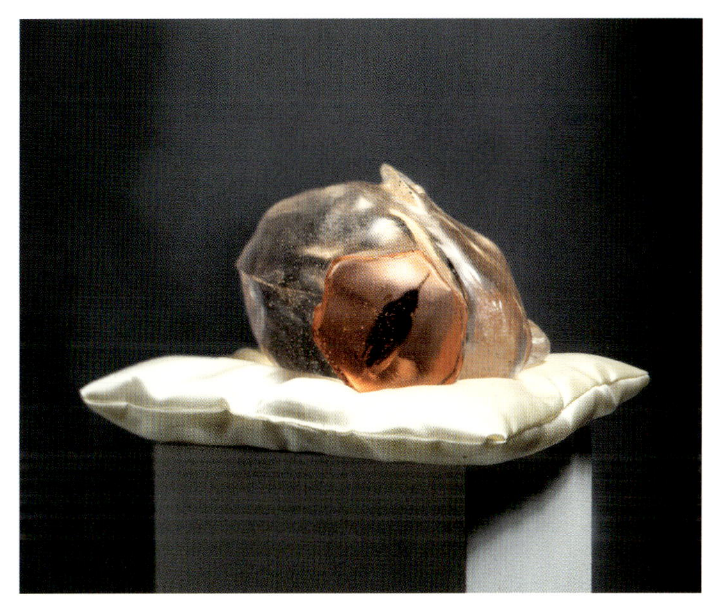
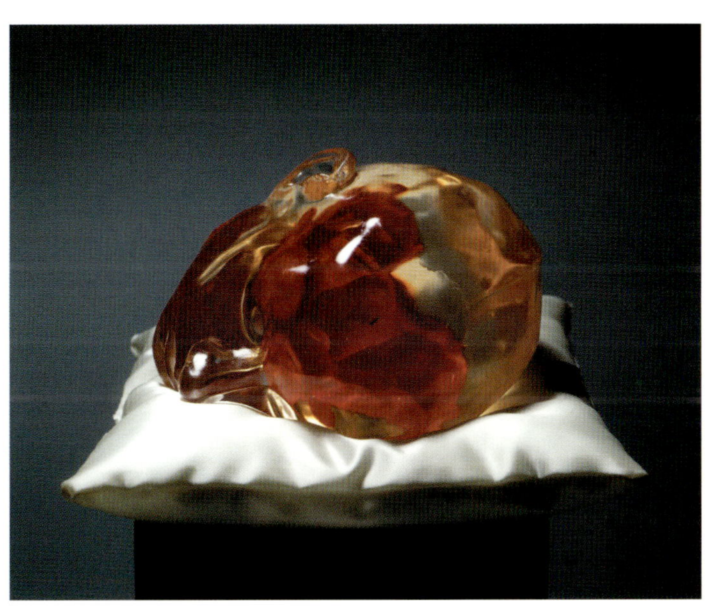
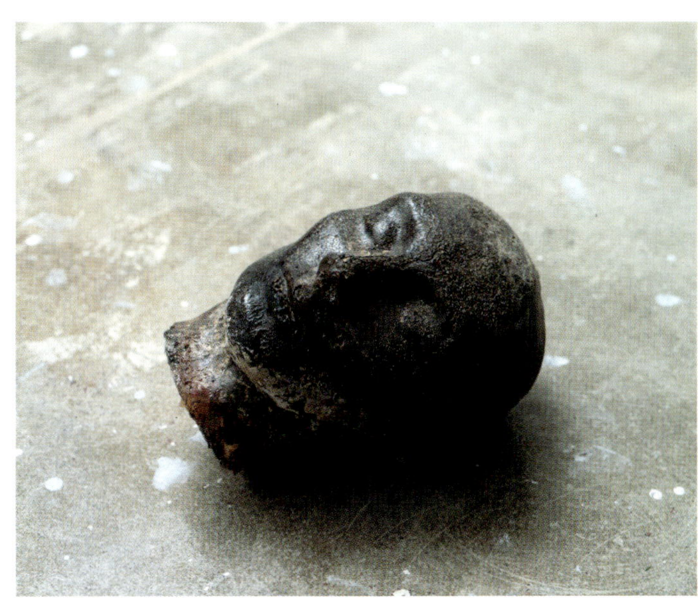

FIRST WAR, 1998
Oil and graphite on paper
61 x 51.5 inches (155 x 131 cm)
Collection of Steven Baigelman,
Los Angeles, California

Six pieces of heavy paper, each a different color, are painted flat gray that obscures the different shades, except around the edges. Martínez Celaya lays the ground for illusionistic painting and at the same time undermines illusion, particularly in the visible seam at lower right. Over this background he paints thick, crusted lines: a labyrinth, a thicket, a tangle–some sort of enmeshing, or the tracings of a journey.

Between the flat background and flat white markings appears a dark body of water–a small pool? an ocean?–an illusion that dissolves in the green drips at the paper's bottom edge. Out of the water, like a Duchamp infrathin, rise the legs and torso of a naked, pubescent girl, starkly modeled with Dürer-like precision. To this strange image the painter introduces four floating red balls. Colored traces are distributed rhythmically over the canvas, perhaps these balls shot down like comets. Two paintings superimposed and at war with each other, one representational, the other an abstraction of broad white lines that violate the illusion and the three-dimensional space. Yet each image complements or supplements the other and contributes to forming a puzzle we can't pass. *First War* invites us into the thicket only to perplex us. A dangerous spot?

AR

ERSTER KRIEG, 1998
Öl und Graphit auf Papier
61 x 51,5 Zoll (155 x 131 cm)
Sammlung Steven Baigelman,
Los Angeles, Kalifornien

Sechs Blatt schweres Papier in jeweils einer anderen Farbe werden grau gestrichen und verdecken die verschiedenen Farbtöne. Nur die Kanten werden nicht übermalt. Martínez Celaya legt den Grundstein für illusionistische Malerei und unterminiert gleichzeitig die Illusion, insbesondere unten rechts in der sichtbaren Naht. Auf diesem Hintergrund malt er dicke, krustige Linien: ein Labyrinth, ein Dickicht, ein Gewirr – eine Art der Verstrickung oder die Nachverfolgung einer Reise.

Zwischen dem flachen Hintergrund und den flachen weißen Markierungen erscheint eine dunkle Wasserfläche – ein kleines Schwimmbecken? ein Ozean? – eine Illusion, die sich in grüne Tropfen am unteren Rand des Papiers auflöst. Aus dem Wasser erheben sich wie ein Infra-Thin von Duchamp die Beine und der Torso eines nackten, jungen, sachlich wie mit Dürer-Präzision gezeichneten Mädchens. Der Maler ergänzt dieses eigenartige Bild durch vier schwimmende rote Bälle. Auf der Leinwand verteilen sich rhythmisch Farbspuren – vielleicht schossen diese Bälle wie Kometen in die Tiefe. Zwei übereinander gelagerte, sich bekämpfende Gemälde, eines darstellend und das andere eine Abstraktion breiter weißer Linien, die die Illusion und den dreidimensionalen Raum verletzen. Und trotzdem ist ein Gemälde die komplementäre Ergänzung des anderen und trägt zur Bildung eines Rätsels bei, das wir einfach lösen müssen. *Erster Krieg* lädt uns nur in das Dickicht ein, um uns zu verblüffen. Ein gefährlicher Ort?

AR

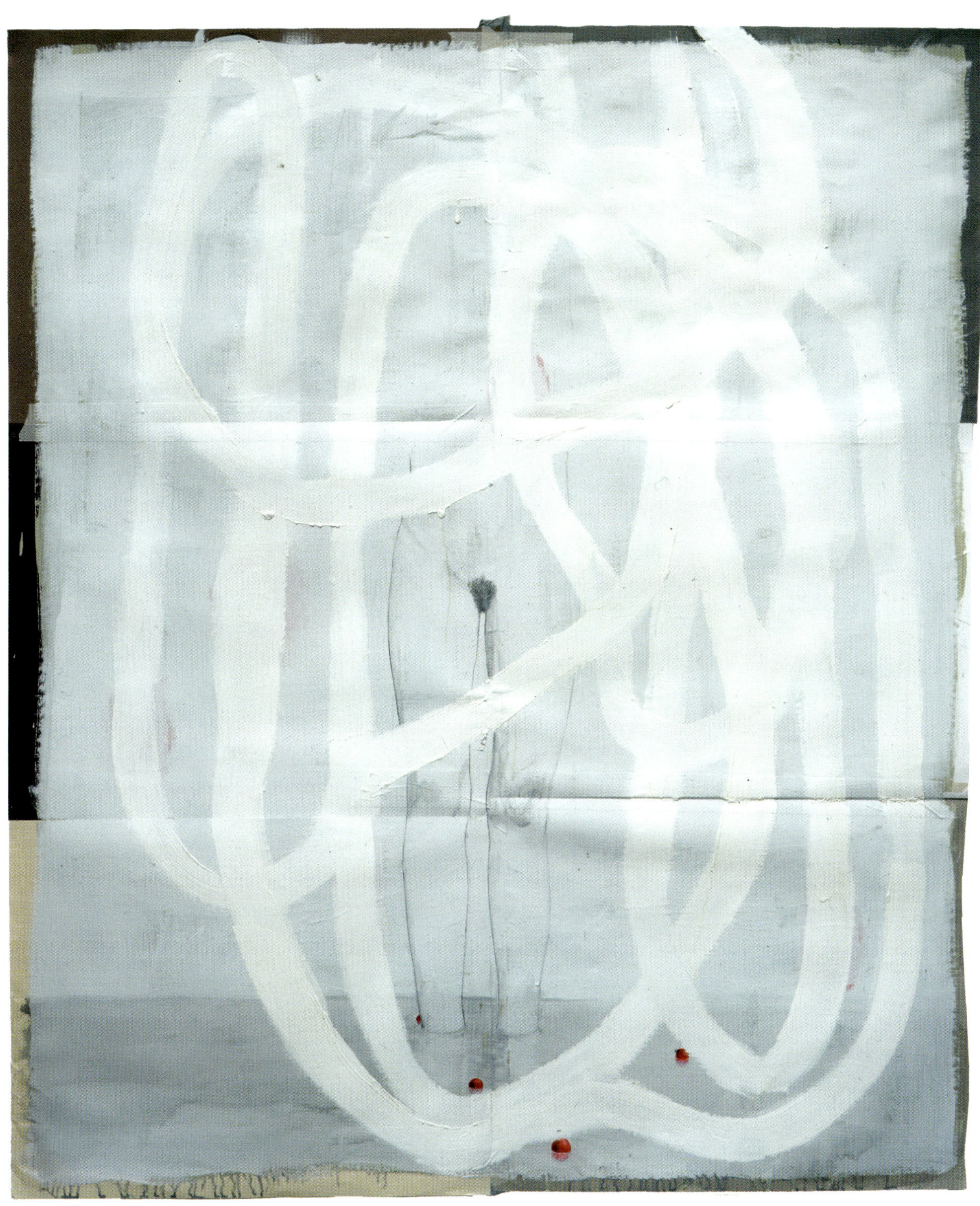

SECOND WAR, 1998
Oil and rose petals on paper
38.5 x 26.5 inches (98 x 67 cm)
Private Collection, New York, New York

Taken together, the titles *First War* and *Second War* might form the linguistic equivalent of Martínez Celaya's installations that group dissimilar objects. While the titles lead us to expect resemblance, the images strike us by their difference: a girl's body without a head vs. an androgonous head lacking a body; a three-dimensional setting vs. a flat one, a small body on large field vs. a large head on a small field. The academic sensibility of the drawing in *First War* is replaced with the less giving silhouette. But difference itself implies two faces of struggle.

The severe lack of articulation and absence of features suggest a wrapped, even a mummified, head and connects this image to *A Boy in his Room* (p. 154). What both forms and flattens the head are thick, chord-like lines that wrap or rope the shape and recall the interlacing, floating lines in *First War*. These lines at once constrain and create identity.

The images invoke the struggles of adolescence or imprisonment in the past and recontextualize loss as war.

AR

ZWEITER KRIEG, 1998
Öl und Rosenblütenblätter auf Papier
38,5 x 26,5 Zoll (98 x 67 cm)
Privatsammlung, New York, New York

Zusammengenommen könnten die Titel *Erster Krieg* und *Zweiter Krieg* ein linguistisches Äquivalent zu Martínez Celayas Installationen bilden, in denen unähnliche Objekte gruppiert werden. Während die Titel uns Ähnlichkeiten erwarten lassen, fallen uns die Bilder auf Grund ihrer Unterschiede auf: ein Mädchenkörper ohne Kopf im Vergleich zu einem androgynen Kopf ohne Körper; eine dreidimensionale Szene im Vergleich zu einer flachen, ein kleiner Körper in einem großen Bildfeld im Vergleich zu einem großen Kopf in einem kleinen. Die akademische Genauigkeit der Zeichnung in *Erster Krieg* wird durch eine wenig preisgebende Silhouette ersetzt. Dabei lässt selbst der Unterschied auf zwei Gesichter des Kampfes schließen.

Das gänzliche Fehlen von Artikulation und von Gesichtszügen lassen einen umwickelten, ja mumifizierten Kopf erahnen und stellt eine Verbindung zwischen diesem Bild und *Ein Knabe in seinem Zimmer* (S. 154) her. Dicke, tauartige Linien, die die Form umwickeln oder umschlingen und an die verflochtenen, fließenden Linien in *Erster Krieg* erinnern, formen und verflachen den Kopf. Diese Linien begrenzen und schaffen zugleich Identität.

Die Bilder beschwören die Kämpfe des Erwachsenwerdens oder die Gefangenschaft in der Vergangenheit und stellen den Verlust als Krieg in einem neuen Kontext dar.

AR

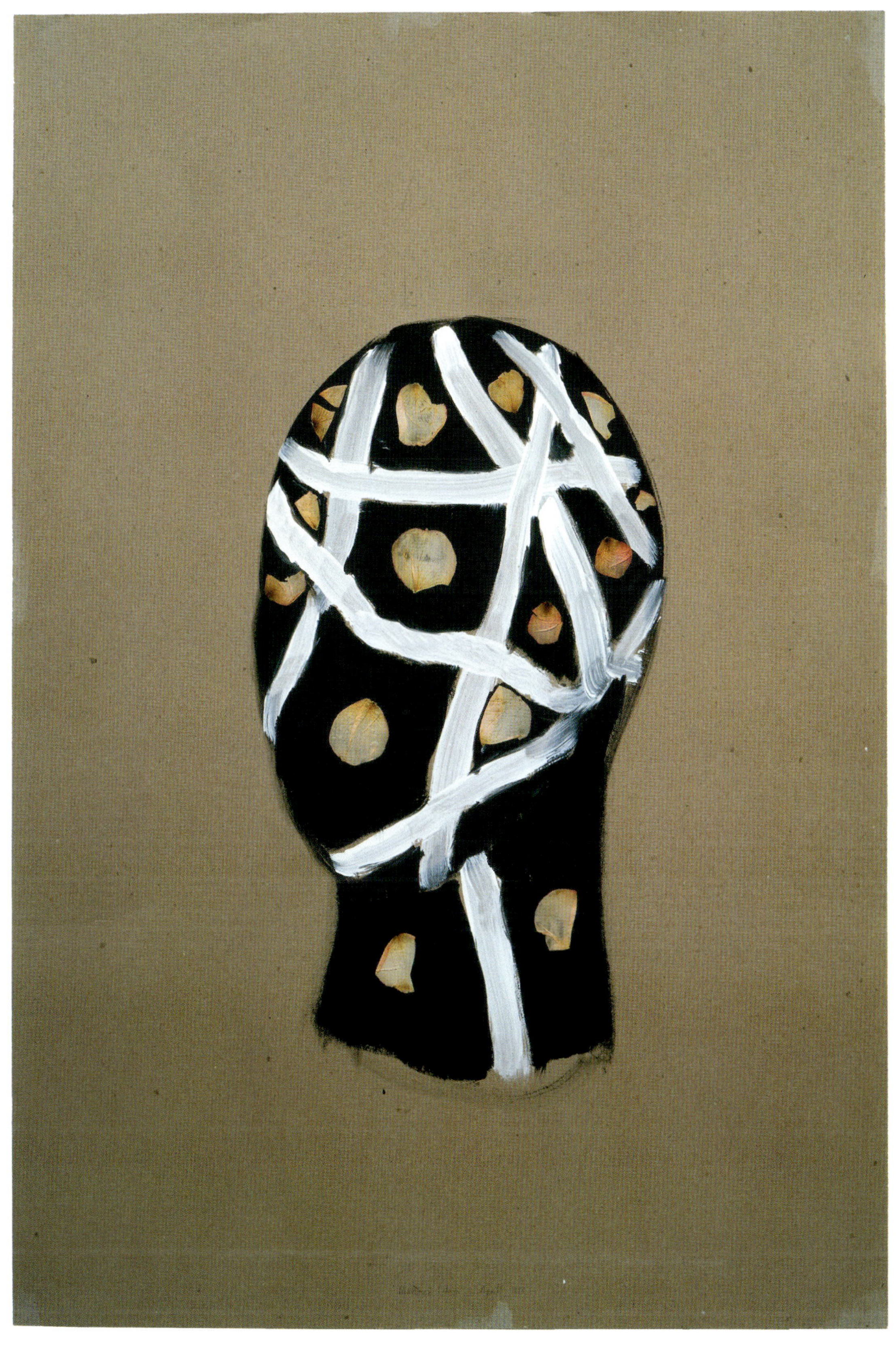

ACCUMULATION OF TIREDNESS, 1998
Oil on canvas
66 x 72 inches (168 x 183 cm)
RBC Dain Rauscher, Minneapolis, Minnesota

Another image at odds with itself: a still life that is 'about' being a still life, and at the same time 'about' movement in time.

The five candycane colored shapes (tears?) feel both hard and soft, sculpted and liquid. The head is a painted version of a dirt sculpture Martínez Celaya made, *Half Again, Flower* (p. 167) and it retains a strong sense of the former object. At the top a green hummingbird pecks at the skull and troubles the death-mask stillness of the head inside.

Charles Baudelaire might have read this painting as an allegory of time: what 'accumulates' in drips and drops are seconds, piled finally so high that they come to burden us. In Baudelaire's eyes the only form of heroism is to bear the weight, but for Martínez Celaya the one forced to record the weight bearing is the true Atlas.

The title suggests the accumulation of those moments that have shaped us into what we are–but that are also the accumulation that ages or tires you. Can an artwork make a solid object of that moment of accumulation?

AR

ANHÄUFUNG DER MÜDIGKEIT, 1998
Öl auf Leinwand
66 x 72 Zoll (168 x 183 cm)
RBC Dain Rauscher, Minneapolis, Minnesota

Ein weiteres Bild, das mit sich selbst nicht ins Reine kommt: ein Stillleben, das davon handelt, ein Stillleben zu sein, und gleichzeitig von der Bewegung in der Zeit handelt.

Die fünf lutscherfarbigen Formen (Tränen?) fühlen sich sowohl hart als auch weich, sowohl geformt als auch flüssig an. Der Kopf ist eine gemalte Version einer Erdskulptur von Martínez Celaya, *Wieder halb, Blume* (S. 167), und hat noch immer die starke Ausdruckskraft dieses zuvor geschaffenen Objekts. Oben pickt ein grüner Kolibri am Schädel und stört die totenmaskenähnliche Stille im Kopf.

Charles Baudelaire hätte dieses Gemälde vielleicht als eine Allegorie auf die Zeit gedeutet: Das, was sich in Tropfen „ansammelt" sind die Sekunden, die sich schließlich so hoch auftürmen, dass sie uns belasten. Baudelaire sieht nur im Tragen des Gewichts einen heroischen Akt. Für Martínez Celaya jedoch ist der wahre Atlas derjenige, der das Tragen des Gewichts darstellen muss.

Der Titel lässt die Ansammlung solcher Momente erahnen, die uns zu dem gemacht haben, was wir sind – aber diese sind auch die Anhäufung, die einen älter werden lässt oder ermüdet. Kann ein Kunstwerk ein solides Objekt dieses Moments der Anhäufung darstellen?

AR

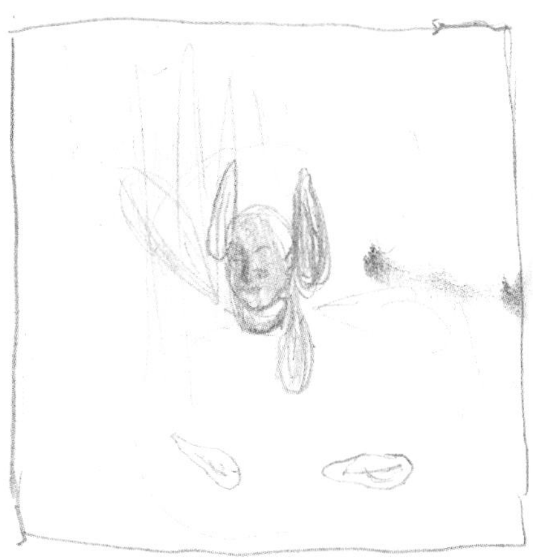

Sketchbook/Skizzenbuch, 1998

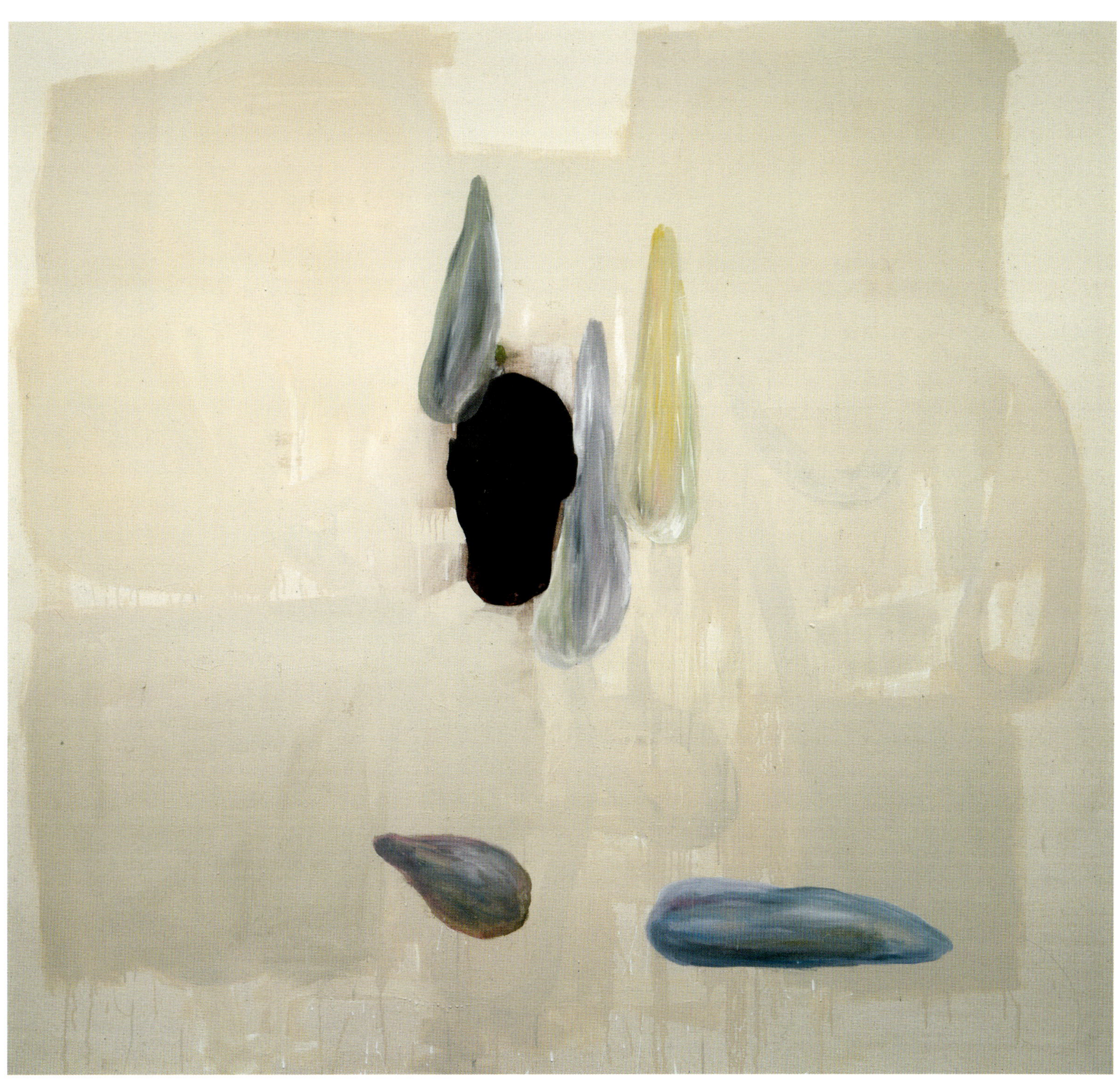

ESSENTIAL EQUATION, 1998
Oil, graphite and fabric on paper
43 x 33 inches (109 x 84 cm)
Collection of William Griffin, Venice, California

A haunting, androgynous face dominates the image, a face neither quite of this world, nor fully formed. But also a 'knowing' face, and so the expression pivots between innocence and experience. The severed head is related to the myriad forms that dismemberment takes across Martínez Celaya's work, but unlike the Saint Catherine heads, this one is strangely insubstantial.

As if falling to the left, the face seems literally to tilt, so that out of the head pours a translucent darker substance. The essence of that face empties itself, spilling out of the image, over a curious notch and off the paper. It subverts illusionistic qualities where they are most present, in the highly modeled mouth and bow. Emptying is reiterated in the translucent silouette below, which vomits in the same direction onto a spectacular bit of *trompe l'oeil* painted to look like fabric.[1] Why vomit? To purge sorrow? To toy with the Modernist tradition of collage? Perhaps, but vomit also literalizes the distasteful and so deflates ideas of art as expression of 'good taste,' or art as what can transform the distasteful into the beautiful.[2]

AR

WESENTLICHE GLEICHUNG, 1998
Öl, Graphit und Gewebe auf Papier
43 x 33 Zoll (109 x 84 cm)
Sammlung William Griffin, Venice, Kalifornien

Ein uns verfolgendes androgynes Gesicht dominiert das Bild – ein Gesicht, das weder ganz von dieser Welt noch ganz ausgeformt ist. Aber auch ein „wissendes" Gesicht mit einem Ausdruck, der zwischen Unschuld und Erfahrung schwankt. Der abgetrennte Kopf ist den unzähligen Formen der Zerstückelung in Martínez Celayas Werken verwandt. Aber im Gegensatz zu den Häuptern der heiligen Katharina wirkt dieser Kopf auf merkwürdige Weise unkörperlich.

Das Gesicht scheint sich zu neigen, als ob es nach links fällt, so dass aus dem Kopf eine durchsichtige dunklere Masse fließt. Das Wesen dieses Gesichts entleert sich selbst, fließt über eine eigenartige Kerbe aus dem Bild und vom Papier. Es untergräbt illusionistische Eigenschaften im stark modellierten Mund, dort wo sie am gegenwärtigsten sind. Das Motiv der Entleerung wird in der unteren durchscheinenden Silhouette wiederholt, die sich in die gleiche Richtung auf eine spektakuläres Stück *Trompe l'oeil* erbricht, das wie ein Gewebe aussieht.[1] Warum erbrechen? Um Trauer loszuwerden? Um mit der modernistischen Tradition der Collage zu spielen? Vielleicht. Aber Erbrechen ist auch ein Symbol des Ekelhaften und nimmt somit den Gedanken über Kunst als Ausdruck des „guten Geschmacks" oder als etwas, was Ekelhaftes in Schönes verwandeln kann, ihren Sinn.[2]

AR

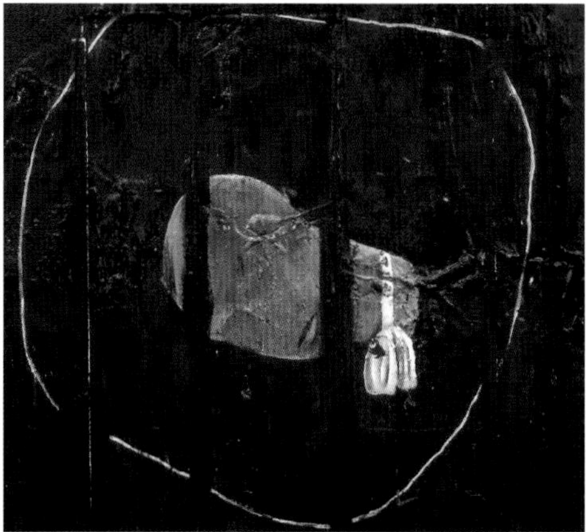

FRAGILITY OF MERIT, detail/DIE ZERBRECHLICHKEIT DES VERDIENSTES, Ausschnitt, 1998
Collection of Bob and Sheryl Anderson, Newport Beach, California

1. From a poem of Martínez Celaya's: "... let me find / a deserving rusted purging bucket / to dig the spilled remnants, / the ruins, / that an impartial vomit uncovers... / Show me your kindness now, / pretend that this bucket of vomits [sic] / is a rapture of lips and that the broken / marble clinking inside / a promise well kept." *Worksonpaperandsculpture*, exh. cat., 1997.
2. See Jacques Derrida's remarks on *Ekel*, the desire to vomit, in Kant's Critique of Judgment. "Economimesis," in *Mimesis des articulations* (Paris: Flammarion, 1975), 87–93.
1. Aus einem Gedicht von Martínez Celaya: „ ... lass mich finden / einen verdienten verrosteten Eimer zum Entleeren / zum Ausheben der verschütteten Reste, / der Ruinen, / die ein unbefangenes Erbrochenes sichtbar macht ... / Zeige mir jetzt deine Güte, / täusche vor, dass dieser Eimer mit Erbrochenem / eine Verzückung der Lippen ist und dass der zerbrochene / klirrende Marmor darin / ein gut gehütetes Geheimnis ist." *Worksonpaperandsculpture*, Ausstellungskatalog, 1997.
2. Siehe Jacques Derridas Bemerkungen über den Ekel, den Wunsch sich zu erbrechen, in Kants *Kritik der praktischen Vernunft*. „Economimesis", in *Mimesis des articulations* (Paris: Flammarion, 1975), S. 87–93.

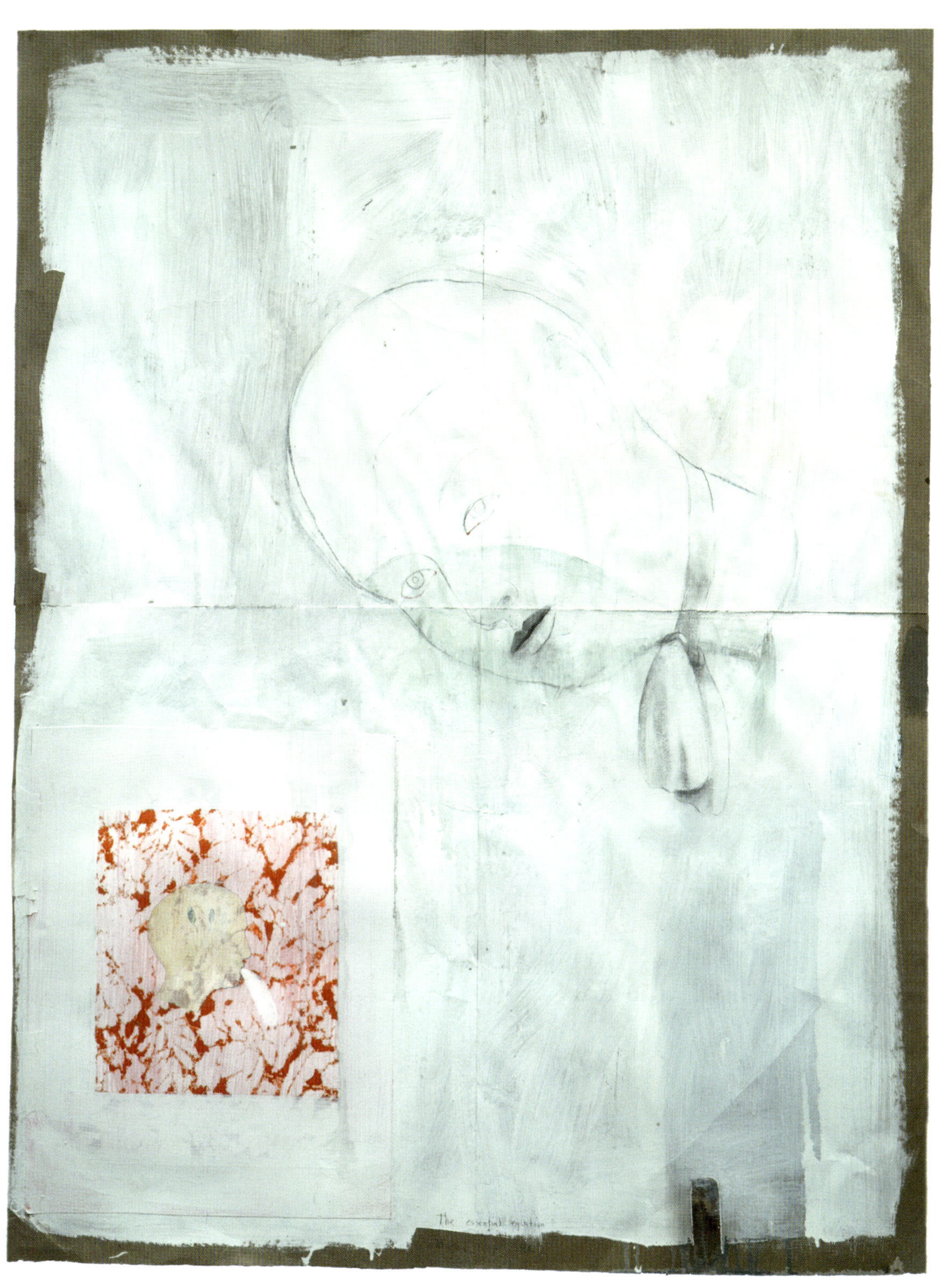

BERLIN, 1998
Silver gelatin prints

The Berlin photographs reverse the usual order of things, for they evolved from painting and they retain painterly traces. Martínez Celaya manipulates photographs the way he sometimes distresses canvases: juxtaposing images in one frame, incising words, letters, or other marks onto negatives; rephotographing to show Scotch tape borders that introduce a hard grid onto painterly surfaces. These manipulations separate the beholder from the subject and lend the photographs the character of objects, betraying aspects of their construction.

The Berlin photographs all accent memory and memorials. But why represent Berlin through graveyards? As 'monuments to belief,' tombs and cemeteries are poignantly divided against themselves: they "are constructed in defiance of time and, as such, they are profoundly tender in their futility. It is this futility that I find moving; it is insistent beyond the reasonable but carried out in a systematic and insightful way."[1] We find that insistence in *The Listener*, for example, where Martínez Celaya's wife places her ear at a grave as if to catch 'ancestral voices.' This is the tomb of nobody in particular–the 'Familie Vogl'–except that 'Vogl'='Bird,' which quietly points to Martínez Celaya's iconographic use of birds. But the grave of a world historical figure like Hegel is no less futile and fragile.

The subjects of these photographs include saints, a poet, a philosopher–every one reduced to a fragment. Fragments of nature and culture appear as flowers: real flowers, silk flowers, a photo of a gardenia next to a gardenia drawn on Paul Celan's head.[2] In *Last Flower*, transcendence is questioned by a ghostly/fleshy head, the repository of consciousness poised on the tomb. Even 'spirit' itself becomes a material thing, a letter scratched onto a photographic negative. The insistent materiality of these photographs stages a struggle between effacement and imprinting, even if it be the imprinting of effacement.

AR

BERLIN, 1998
Silbergelatineabzüge

Die Berlin-Photographien kehren die übliche Ordnung der Dinge um, da sie aus Malerei entstanden und noch immer deren Spuren tragen. Martínez Celaya manipuliert Photographien, wie er manchmal auch Leinwände peinigt: Er stellt Bilder in einem Rahmen nebeneinander, schneidet Wörter, Buchstaben oder andere Markierungen auf Negative ein, photographiert erneut, um die Ränder von Klebeband zu zeigen, die die wie gemalt wirkenden Oberflächen mit einem harten Raster versehen. Diese Manipulationen trennen den Betrachter vom Motiv und verleihen den Photographien den Charakter von Objekten, die Einzelheiten ihrer Konstruktion verraten.

Alle Berlin-Photographien akzentuieren die Themen Gedächtnis und Gedenken. Warum aber stehen für Berlin Friedhöfe? Als „Monumente des Glaubens" werden Gräber und Friedhöfe etnschieden gegen sich selbst abgegrenzt: sie „werden als der Zeit trotzend erbaut und sind als solche in ihrer Sinnlosigkeit in der Tiefe ihres Wesens äußerst verletzlich. Mich bewegt diese Sinnlosigkeit; sie ist über das Vernünftige hinaus eindringlich, wird jedoch auf systematische, verständliche Weise dargestellt."[1] Wir sehen diese Eindringlichkeit z. B. in *Der Zuhörer*, wo Martínez Celayas Frau ihr Ohr an ein Grab legt, wie um „Stimmen der Vorfahren" zu hören. Dies ist kein bestimmtes Grab – das Grab der „Familie Vogl". Allerdings bedeutet „Vogl" Vogel – ein Hinweis auf den ikonographischen Gebrauch von Vögeln in Martínez Celayas Werk. Aber das Grab einer Figur der Weltgeschichte wie Hegel ist nicht weniger sinnlos und zerbrechlich.

Die Motive der Photographien sind u. a. Heilige, ein Dichter, ein Philosoph – alle auf ein Fragment reduziert. Fragmente der Natur und Kultur erscheinen als Blumen: echte Blumen, Seidenblumen, das Photo einer Gardenie neben einer auf Paul Celans Kopf gezeichneten Gardenie.[2] In *Die letzte Blume* wird die Transzendenz durch einen auf dem Grab aufgestellten, geisterhaften, fleischigen Kopf hinterfragt, der Bewahrungsort des Bewusstseins. Sogar der „Geist" selbst wird zum materiellen Ding, ein auf das Negativ gekratzter Buchstabe. Die eindringliche Materialität der Photographien inszeniert einen Kampf zwischen Löschen und Aufdrucken, selbst wenn es das Aufdrucken des Löschens ist.

AR

LAST FLOWER
16 x 16 inches (41 x 41 cm)
Collection of Enrique and Alexandra Martínez Celaya

DIE LETZTE BLUME
16 x 16 Zoll (41 x 41 cm)
Sammlung Enrique and Alexandra Martínez Celaya

p. 178/S. 178

THE SIZE OF A WOUND
16 x 16 inches (41 x 41 cm)
The Manfred Heiting Collection, Amsterdam

DIE GRÖSSE EINER WUNDE
16 x 16 Zoll (41 x 41 cm)
The Manfred Heiting Collection, Amsterdam

p. 179/S. 179

THE LISTENER
16 x 16 inches (41 x 41 cm)
Courtesy of Stephen Cohen Gallery,
Los Angeles, California

DER ZUHÖRER
16 x 16 Zoll (41 x 41 cm)
Courtesy of Stephen Cohen Gallery,
Los Angeles, Kalifornien

1. *Berlin*, op. cit.,12.
2. "...when you go to your parents' yard and you see the gardenias that your mother liked. In the moment that you smell them memory does a strange thing." *Berlin, the Fragility of Nearness*, 79.

1. *Berlin*, op. cit., S. 12.
2. „...wenn du in den Garten deiner Eltern gehst und die Gardenien siehst, die deine Mutter liebte. Sobald du sie riechst, vollbringt die Erinnerung etwas Seltsames." *Berlin, the Fragility of Nearness*, S. 79.

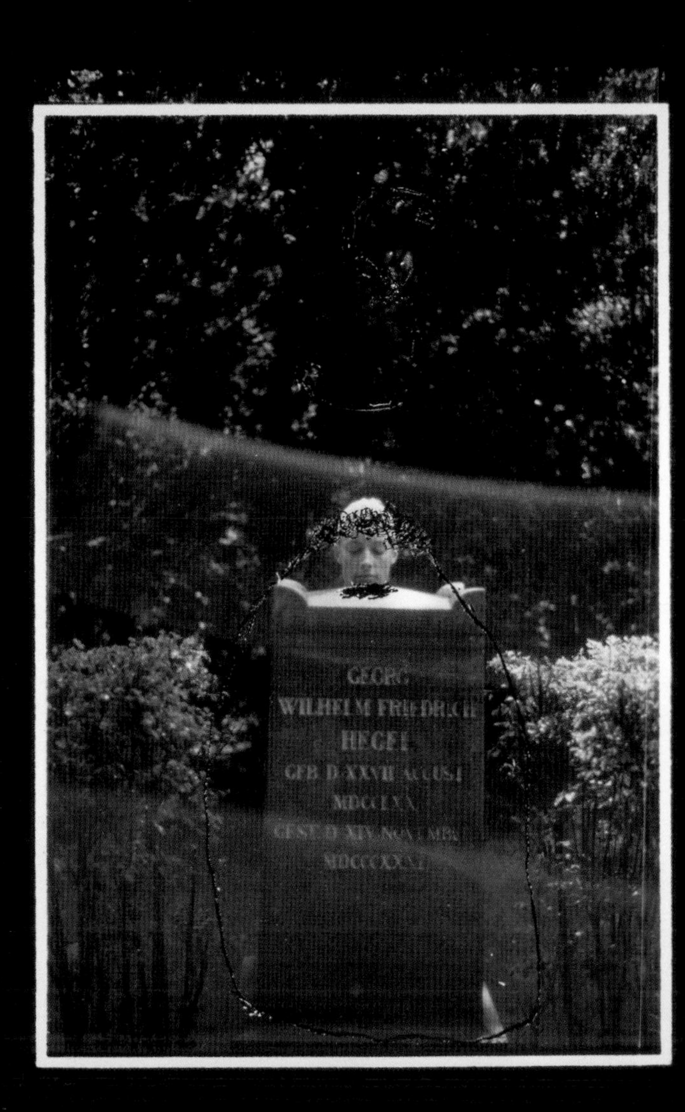
GEORG
WILHELM FRIEDRICH
HEGEL

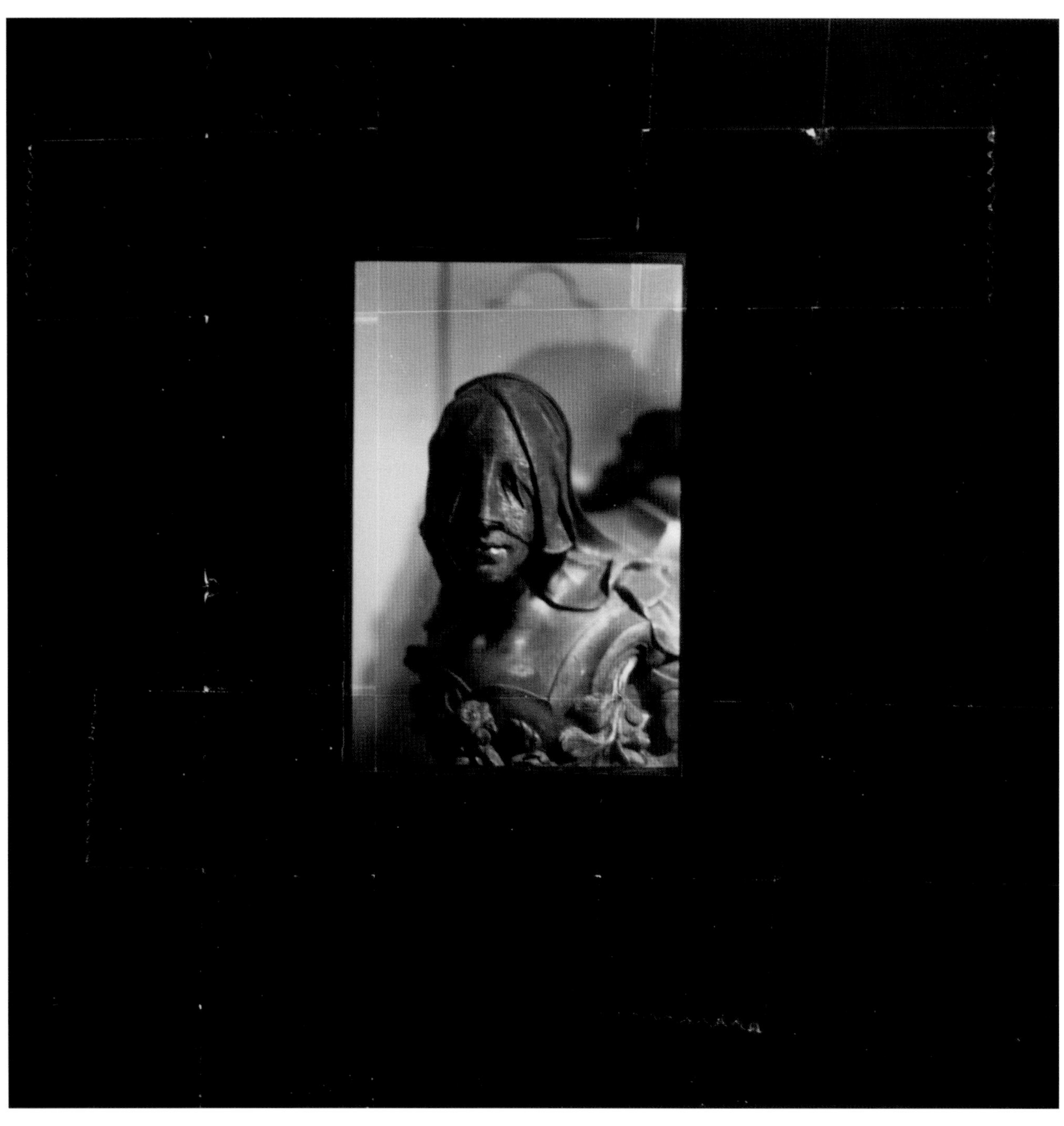

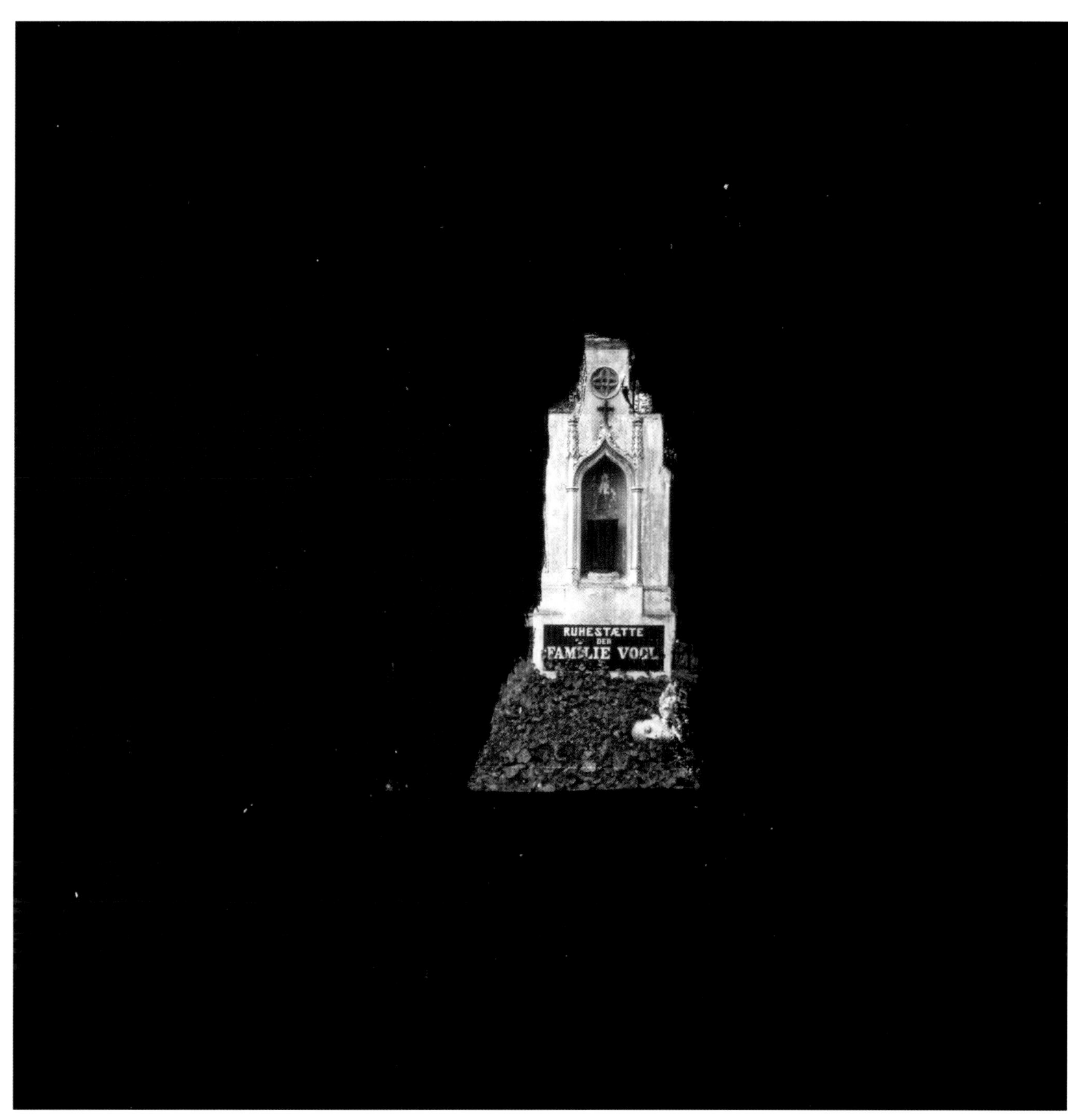
RUHESTÆTTE
DER

clockwise from upper left

FOURTH FLOWER FOR PAUL CELAN
7 x 7 inches (18 x 18 cm)
Collection of Joyce and Ted Strauss,
Solana Beach, California

CAPAZ DE LO MAS LEVE (CAPABLE OF THE MOST SUBTLE)
16 x 16 inches (41 x 41 cm)
The Davenport Museum of Art, Iowa,
Museum Purchase

WINTER AND SILK FLOWERS
16 x 16 inches (41 x 41 cm)
The Sheldon Memorial Art Gallery and Sculpture Garden,
University of Nebraska-Lincoln,
UNL-Olga N. Sheldon Acquisition Trust Purchase, 1999

THE WARDEN
16 x 16 inches (41 x 41 cm)
The Museum of Fine Arts, Houston, Texas
Gift of Jack V. Hoffmann

HEART AND BIRD
16 x 16 inches (41 x 41 cm)
The Frederick R. Weisman Art Museum,
University of Minnesota, Minneapolis,
Frances M. Norbeck Fund

von oben links im Uhrzeigersinn

DIE VIERTE BLUME FÜR PAUL CELAN
7 x 7 Zoll (18 x 18 cm)
Sammlung Joyce und Ted Strauss,
Solana Beach, Kalifornien

CAPAZ DE LO MAS LEVE (DES SUBTILSTEN FÄHIG)
16 x 16 Zoll (41 x 41 cm)
The Davenport Museum of Art, Iowa,
vom Museum erworben

WINTER UND SEIDENBLUMEN
16 x 16 Zoll (41 x 41 cm)
The Sheldon Memorial Art Gallery and Sculpture Garden,
University of Nebraska-Lincoln,
Erworben 1999 durch den UNL-Olga N. Sheldon Acquisition Trust

DER WÄCHTER
16 x 16 Zoll (41 x 41 cm)
The Museum of Fine Arts, Houston, Texas
Geschenk von Jack V. Hoffmann

HERZ UND VOGEL
16 x 16 Zoll (41 x 41 cm)
The Frederick R. Weisman Art Museum,
University of Minnesota, Minneapolis,
Frances M. Norbeck Fund

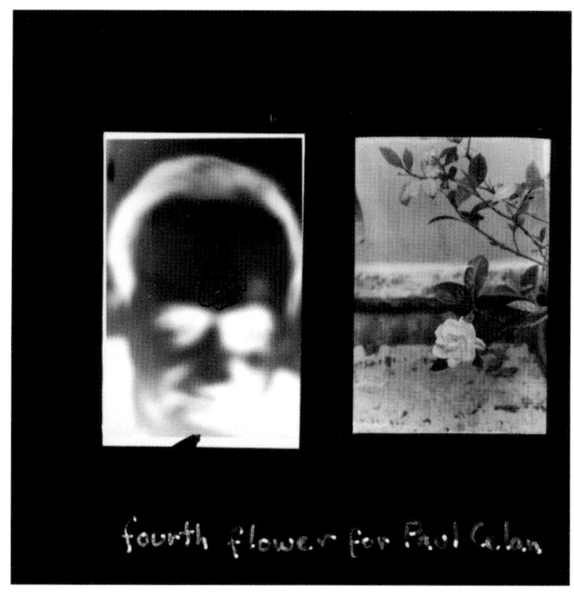
fourth flower for Paul Celan

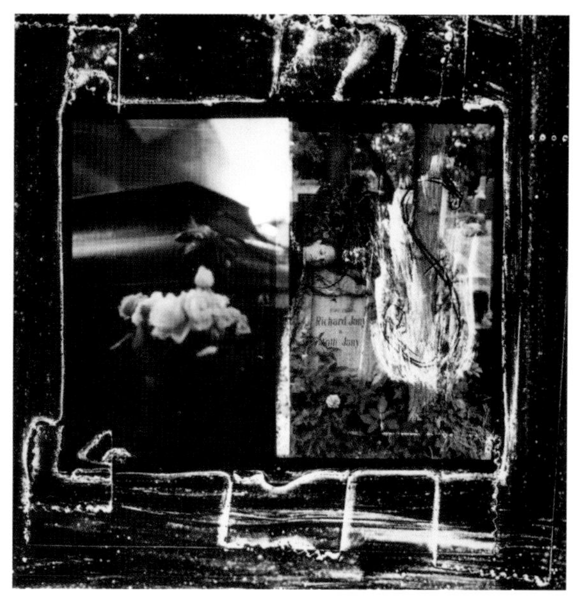

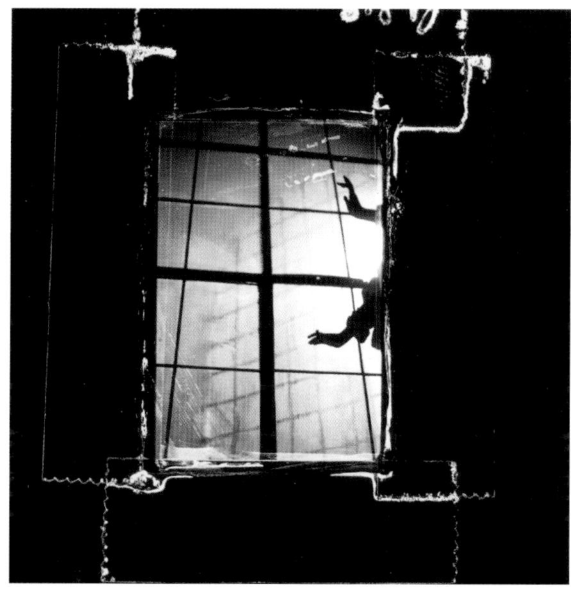

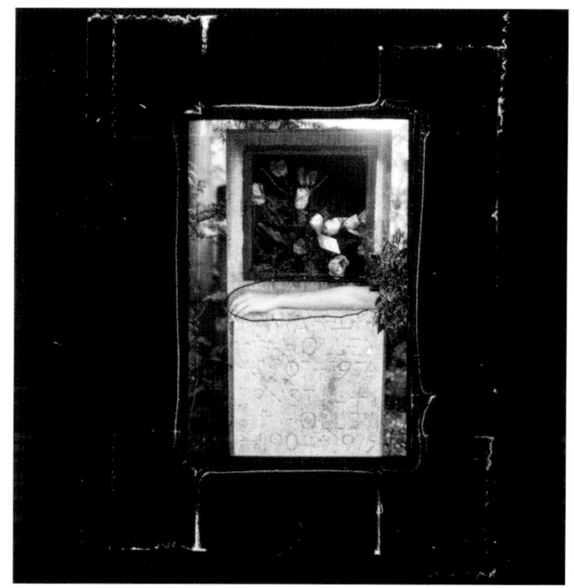

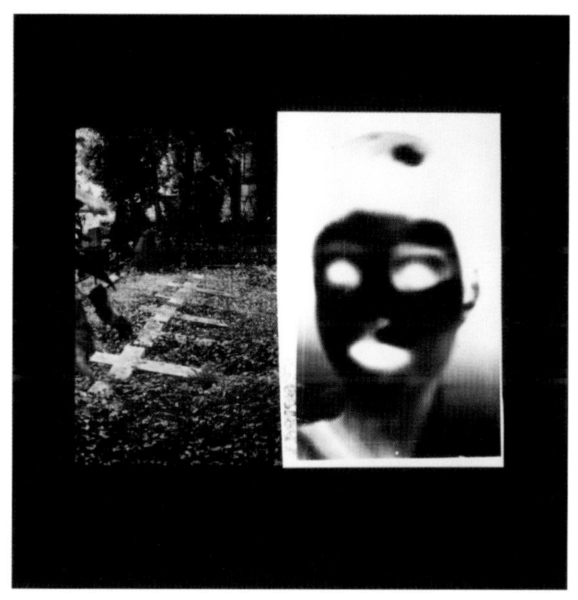

A LANGUAGE OF TRACES/EINE SPRACHE DER SPUREN

time, memory and mortality/Zeit, Erinnerung und Sterblichkeit

A NECK IN ASHES, 1999
Oil and graphite on two sheets of paper
35 x 90 inches (90 x 229 cm)
Collection of Jocelyn Grayson, Woodstock, Vermont

The exhibition's sole diptych—or not, since we can also treat it as a single work that *performs* dismemberment. (Note how Martínez Celaya uses one name for two images, neither of which depicts the things named in the title.) The felled, bodiless head appears to have been detached from the headless, crouching body to its right. And the impression is reinforced by the identical size and type of paper and medium. The title supplements, in words, the body part lacking in the image, connects the two sheets, that is, with the very organ of connection, which otherwise vanishes in the space or nonspace between the frames.

From *Tu Brazo* (earlier the same year) the tulip/wing returns, and with ambiguous purpose: to lift and redeem the head? To return it to its body? The head itself, as enigmatic as the one in *The Secrets*, offers no resolution, only tension between the abject and the erect.

In the right-hand drawing the flower morphs into a minimal forest–whether trees or branches–two in front of the body, two behind, with the pentimento of a fifth to the left. This miniature wood masks the meeting point between the body and pink scumbling. In a state of submission, supplication, prayer, or abjection, the red-haloed body folds in on itself.

AR

EIN HALS IN ASCHE, 1999
Öl und Graphit auf zwei Blatt Papier
35 x 90 Zoll (90 x 229 cm)
Sammlung Jocelyn Grayson, Woodstock, Vermont

Das einzige Diptychon der Ausstellung – oder nicht, da wir beide Blätter auch als zusammengehöriges Kunstwerk, das Zerstückelung durchführt, sehen können. (Beachten Sie, wie Martínez Celaya einen Namen für zwei Bilder verwendet, wobei keines die im Titel genannten Dinge zeigt.) Der körperlose Kopf wurde anscheinend von dem kopflosen, zusammengekauerten Körper zu seiner Rechten getrennt. Und der Eindruck wird durch die identische Größe und Art des Papiers und des Mediums verstärkt. Die ergänzenden Worte im Titel, d. h. das im Bild fehlende Körperteil, verbinden die beiden Blätter mit dem eigentlichen Verbindungsorgan, das ansonsten im Raum bzw. Nichtraum zwischen den Rahmen verschwindet.

Von *Tu Brazo* (ein früheres Werk aus dem gleichen Jahr) kehrt die Tulpe oder der Flügel zurück, und zwar voller Doppelsinnigkeit: Um den Kopf zu heben und zu erlösen? Um ihn wieder seinem Körper zurückzugeben? Der Kopf selbst, so rätselhaft wie der Kopf in *Die Geheimnisse*, bietet keine Lösung, sondern nur Spannung zwischen dem Verächtlichen und dem Erhabenen.

In der rechten Zeichnung verwandelt sich die Blume in einen winzigen Wald aus Bäumen oder Blättern, zwei vor dem Körper, zwei dahinter und die Unterzeichnung eines fünften auf der linken Seite. Dieser Miniaturwald verdeckt den Berührungspunkt zwischen dem Körper und dem geschichteten Rosa. In Unterwerfung, flehend, betend oder erniedrigt faltet sich der Körper im roten Schein in sich zusammen.

AR

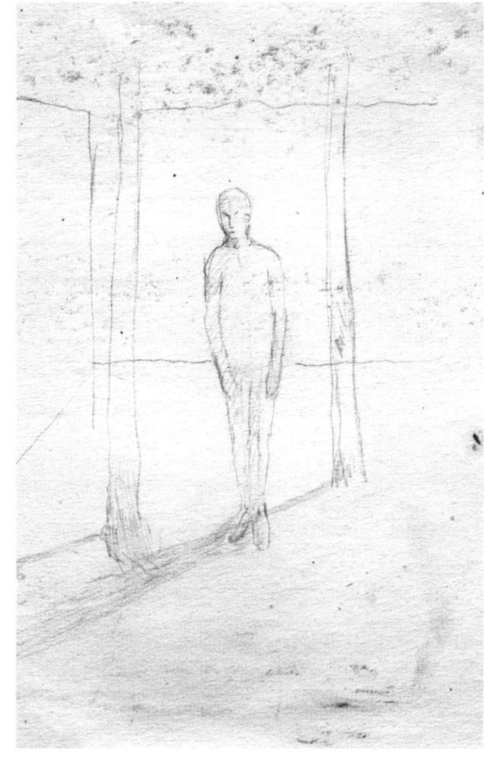

UNTITLED (MAN AND FOREST), Study for *Coming Home*/OHNE TITEL (MANN UND WALD), Studie für *Heimkehr*, 2000

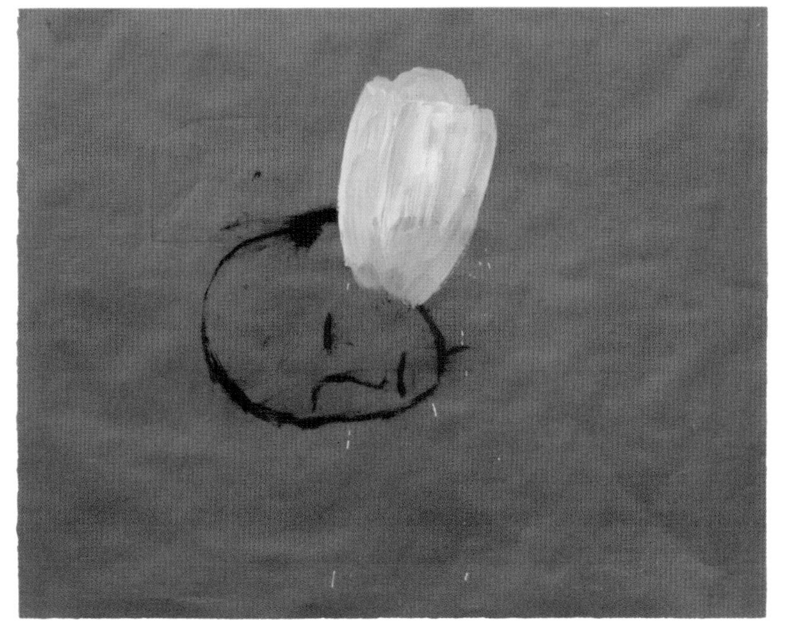

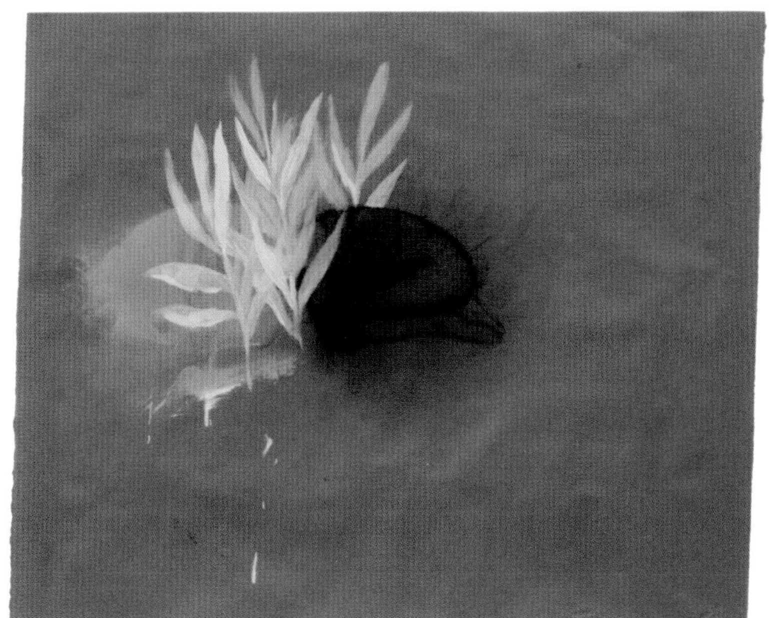

PENA (SORROW), 1997–1999
Oil, tar and objects on canvas
84 x 100 inches (213 x 254 cm)
Collection of Andrea King, Los Angeles, California

Monumental and startlingly graphic, a severed hand–delicate and archaic, precisely rendered, drippy and feathered, behind which a maze-like-space half opens. Uncanny, this painting; also straightforward and strange, brutal, calm, horrifying, insistent, expressing *pena*. At top and center inscribed 'Pena for Miguel Hernandez,' whose poem Martínez Celaya invokes with his reference to 'pena'–a Spanish word for a form of sadness or regret.

At the point of connection to the world Martínez Celaya situated the break, so strongly marked as to preclude any return to wholeness. Here he inserted actual objects, all coated with tar: baby shoes, feathers, ribbons, and flowers (real and plastic). Corporeal discontinuity stands for temporal discontinuity. Does this break suggest our disconnection from the past? Does the past cut us off from ourselves, dismember our integrity, leave us alienated from our being? But grimness is countered (and redoubled) in a different reading, for these objects around the wrist also suggest a child's charm bracelet.

Perhaps, *Pena* proposes a strange, silent connection between painting and violence– as the drips do violence simultaneously to the hand and to the legerdemain of painting as representation. In this way *Pena* reinforces the pattern seen in *Marker*, *Tu Brazo* (p. 158), and *House of Arms*. *Pena* also glosses *Artificer* from the Saint Catherine series: to call one head 'Artificer' is to claim identity with both martyr and executioner, thereby linking the marks of art to soiling and blood.

The punctuality or singularity of the cut with its vertical drips contrasts the endless loops of the labyrinthine background. Those lines or ropes (compare *First War*, p. 168) look like part of a larger maze, symptomatic perhaps of life lived now, 'in the midst,' having lost sight of beginning and end.

AR

PENA (SCHMERZ), 1997–1999
Öl, Teer und Objekte auf Leinwand
84 x 100 Zoll (213 x 254 cm)
Sammlung Andrea King, Los Angeles, Kalifornien

Monumental und überraschend graphisch, eine abgetrennte Hand – zart und archaisch, genau wiedergegeben, tropfend und gefiedert, hinter der sich ein labyrinthartiger Raum halb öffnet. Dieses Gemälde drückt den Schmerz, Pena, auf unheimliche, aber auch direkte und fremdartige, brutale, ruhige, erschreckende, eindringliche Weise aus. Oben und in der Mitte steht „Pena für Miguel Hernandez" geschrieben, auf dessen Gedicht sich Martínez Celaya mit dem Begriff „pena" – ein spanisches Wort für eine Art der Traurigkeit oder des Bedauerns – bezieht.

Am Verbindungspunkt zur Welt hat Martínez Celaya den Bruch angesiedelt und ihn so deutlich markiert, dass jede Rückkehr zur Ganzheit unmöglich wird. Hier hat er mit Teer bedeckte Objekte eingefügt: Babyschuhe, Federn, Bänder und Blumen (wirkliche und aus Plastik). Körperliche Unterbrechung ist ein Symbol für zeitliche Unterbrechung. Unterstellt dieser Bruch unsere Trennung von der Vergangenheit? Trennt uns die Vergangenheit von uns selbst, zerstückelt sie unsere Ganzheit, sorgt sie für die Entfremdung von unserem Wesen? Allerdings tritt der Grausamkeit eine andere Bedeutung entgegen, die ihr zugleich doppeltes Gewicht verleiht: Diese Objekte könnten auch ein Kinderarmband mit Glücksbringern darstellen.

Vielleicht ist *Pena* ein Hinweis auf eine seltsame, stille Verbindung zwischen Gemälde und Gewalt, da die Tropfen gleichzeitig der Hand und der im Gemälde zu findenden Schummelei Gewalt antun. So verstärkt *Pena* die Muster in *Markierung*, *Tu Brazo* (S. 158) und *Das Haus der Arme*. *Pena* deutet auch den *Schöpfer* aus dem Katharina-Zyklus: Durch die Benennung eines Kopfes als „Schöpfer" wird Anspruch auf die Identität mit dem Märtyrer und dem Scharfrichter erhoben und die Zeichen der Kunst werden mit Besudelung und Blut in Beziehung gesetzt.

Die Promptheit und Seltsamkeit des Schnitts mit seinen senkrechten Tropfen stehen im Gegensatz zu den endlosen Schleifen des labyrinthischen Hintergrunds. Diese Linien oder Seile (vergleiche *Erster Krieg*, S. 168) sehen wie Teile eines größeren Labyrinths aus, vielleicht symptomatisch für das jetzt gelebte Leben, des „Seins in der Mitte", das Anfang und Ende aus den Augen verloren hat.

AR

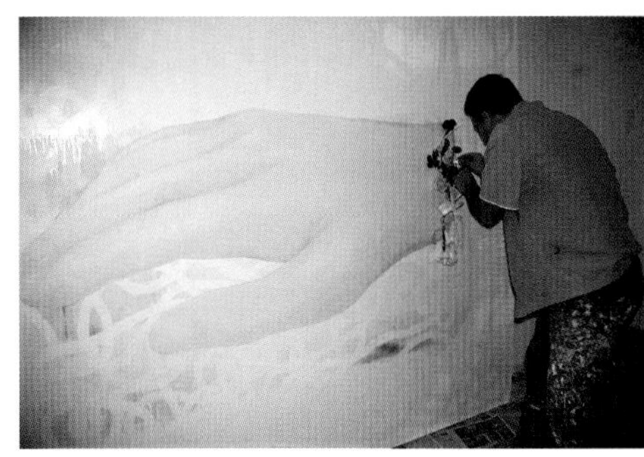
Work in progress/Bei der Arbeit, 1999

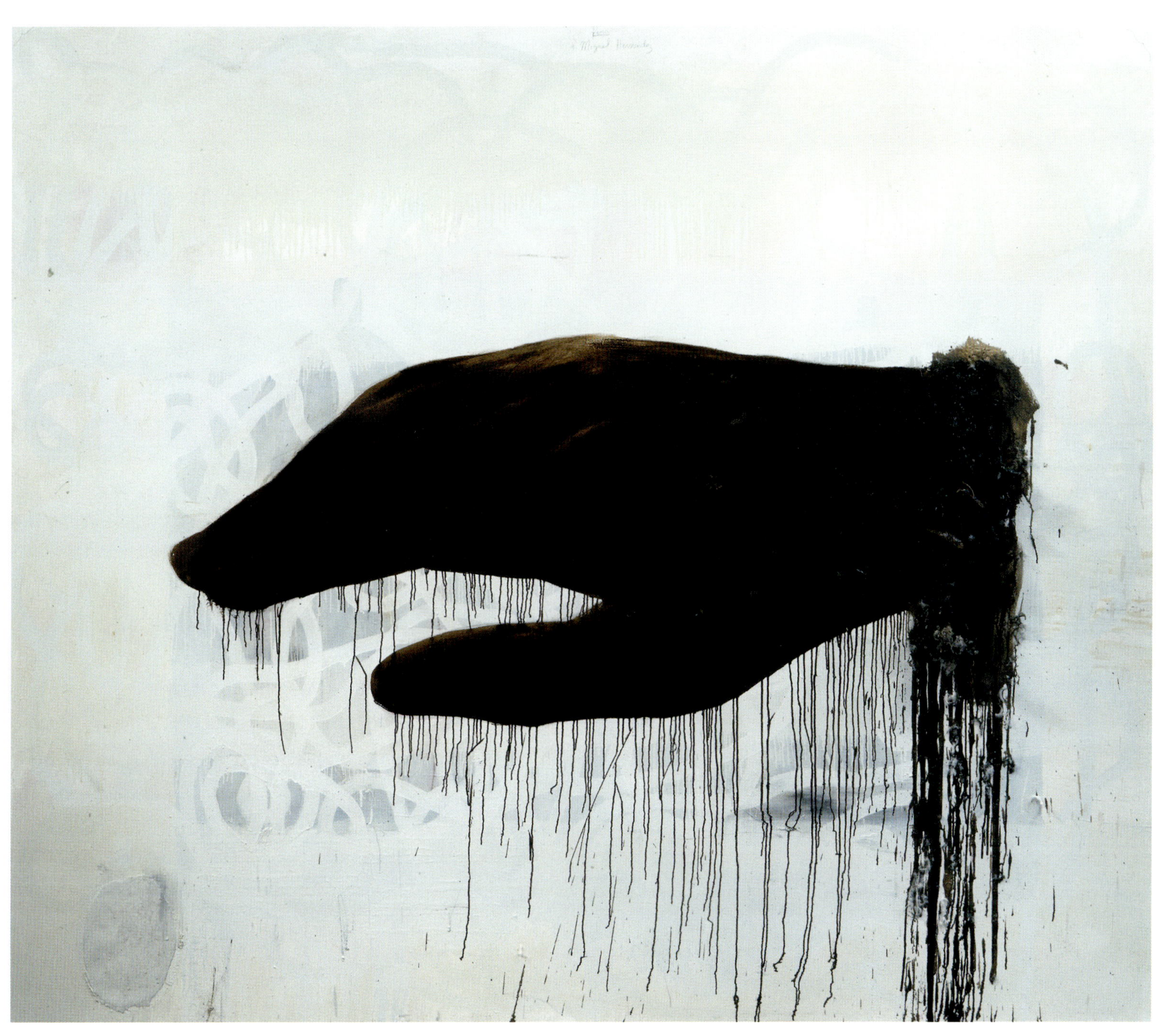

THE EMPTY GARDEN, 1997–1999
Oil, tar and objects on canvas
84 x 100 inches (213 x 254 cm)
Collection of Christopher and Tracy Keys,
Laguna Beach, California

The Empty Garden is distressed in every way: both the canvas as material fact and the image upon it–tears, stitches, dripping tar, feathers, traces of scars, objects embedded in tar, bloody marks and scumbles–a vast, crowded emptiness, a garden of emptiness.

The androgynous head is overpowering and restless, its weight hefted by anguish or despair. Is it exhaling, inhaling or crying? Is it crying for isolation, for inescapably having to bear witness, for the humiliation of tar and feathers, for the burden of exile or the past, or sheer nothingness? The gaping mouth suggests exhaling, but exhaling the last breath–which, *The Empty Garden* implies, every breath is. In any case, a suffering that is painfully intimate to us.

AR

DER LEERE GARTEN, 1997–1999
Öl, Teer und Objekte auf Leinwand
84 x 100 Zoll (213 x 254 cm)
Sammlung Christopher und Tracy Keys,
Laguna Beach, Kalifornien

Der Leere Garten ist in jeder Hinsicht ein Trauerspiel: im Hinblick auf den materiellen Zustand der Leinwand und auch auf das Bild auf ihr – Tränen, Stiche, tropfender Teer, Federn, Spuren von Narben, in Teer gebettete Objekte, blutige Markierungen und übereinanderliegende Farbschichten – eine große, beengte Leere, ein Garten der Leere.

Ein Zwitterkopf überwältigt und verbreitet Unruhe, er ist schwer von Qual oder Verzweiflung. Atmet er ein oder aus, oder weint er? Weint er, weil er einsam ist, weil er Zeuge sein muss, weil er auf demütigende Weise geteert und gefedert wurde, weil er im Exil oder in der Vergangenheit oder im schieren Nichts existieren muss? Der aufgesperrte Mund lässt Ausatmen, allerdings des letzten Atems vermuten – und im *Leeren Garten* ist jeder Atemzug der letzte. Wie dem auch sei, dies ist ein Leiden, mit dem wir schmerzlich vertraut sind.

AR

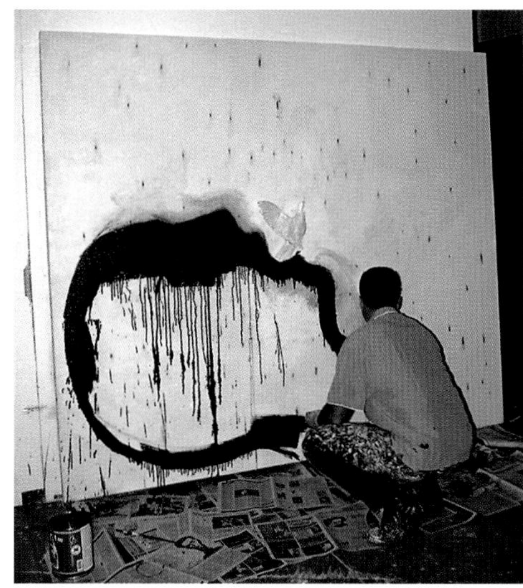

Work in progress/Bei der Arbeit, 1999

UNBROKEN POETRY (HERMAN MELVILLE), 1999
Oil, tar and fabric on linen
96 x 96 inches (244 x 244cm)
Private Collection, New York, New York

Unbroken Poetry is built on a series of contradictions: violence and tenderness, aggression and vulnerability, aggressor and victim, delicacy and dirt.

Subject matter and material are likewise at odds: the viscous, heavy quality of tar articulates the aerial impression of a bird in motion, and the fixity of the painted image opposes the instant that is caught: a 'blink' in time, arresting the hummingbird's wings. In other words, the mobile bird is fixed on canvas–literally tarred and feathered. And its gleaming, realistic eye, emerging from a flat black field, fixes the viewer. Do we see the present moment, the memory of a moment, the anticipation or conceputalizing of such a moment?

In fact, the material is at odds with itself, because the tar fights the intricate, diaphanous handwork of lace, which frames and cages the hummingbird. The hidden, decorative quality of a hummingbird's iridescent wings is displaced onto the lace.

If the hummingbird figures awareness, then all of these visual and conceptual tensions inscribed here figure the paradoxes of consciousness itself, as well as the yoking of art and aggression.

This hummingbird's enormous scale, so foreign to our experience of them, makes it Martínez Celaya's whale–Melville's white turned black. The association demonstrates how the painter's work will not be contained within a single medium. For *Unbroken Poetry*, *Moby Dick* plays a role analogous to the role Martínez Celaya's own poems play to his paintings and drawings: source? But of course 'unbroken' is an ideal never to be obtained; it could be thought of dialectically as the conjunction of violence and tenderness on a canvas that retains their individual, or broken characters.

Contrast the delicacy and lushness of *Vanity and Redemption* (p. 152)–to which *Unbroken Poetry* responds, understanding that conceptual differences underpin stylistic ones.

AR

UNGEBROCHENE DICHTUNG (HERMAN MELVILLE), 1999
Öl, Teer und Gewebe auf Leinen
96 x 96 Zoll (244 x 244cm)
Privatsammlung, New York, New York

Ungebrochene Dichtung baut auf einer Reihe Widersprüche auf: Gewalt und Sanftheit, Aggression und Verletzlichkeit, Angreifer und Opfer, Feinheit und Erde.

Auch das Motiv und das Material kommen nicht miteinander überein: der dickflüssige, schwere Teer macht das Bild eines Vogels im Flug deutlich und die Fixiertheit des gemalten Bildes widerspricht dem Moment, der eingefangen worden ist: ein „Augenblick" in der Zeit, der die Flügel des Kolibris stillstehen lässt. Der fliegende Vogel wird also auf der Landwand fixiert und buchstäblich geteert und gefedert. Und sein leuchtendes realistisches Auge tritt aus einem flachen schwarzen Feld hervor und fixiert den Betrachter. Sehen wir den gegenwärtigen Augenblick, die Erinnerung an einen Augenblick, die Erwartung oder Konzeptionalisierung eines solchen Augenblicks?

Das Material kann keine Einigkeit erzielen, weil der Teer einen Gegensatz zur feinen, durchsichtigen Handarbeit aus Spitze bildet, die den Kolibri rahmt und einsperrt. Die den Blicken entzogene, dekorative Qualität der farbenfrohen Kolibriflügel wird auf die Spitze übertragen.

Wenn der Kolibri Bewusstsein darstellt, stellen alle sichtbaren und konzeptionellen Spannungen in diesem Bild die Paradoxe des Bewusstseins und die Verbindung von Kunst und Aggression dar.

Die enorme Größe des Kolibris, die uns fremdartig anmutet, macht ihn zum Wal Martínez Celayas – Melvilles weißer Wal färbt sich schwarz. Diese Assoziation zeigt, dass die Arbeit des Malers nicht auf ein Medium beschränkt bleibt. Für *Ungebrochene Dichtung* spielt *Moby Dick* eine Rolle analog zur Rolle der Gedichte von Martínez Celaya in seinen Gemälden und Zeichnungen: Quelle? Natürlich ist „ungebrochen" ein Ideal, das nie erreicht werden kann; es könnte dialektisch als Verbindung zwischen Gewalt und Zartheit auf einer Leinwand gesehen werden, die deren individuelle oder gebrochene Charaktere beibehält.

Die Zartheit und Üppigkeit von *Eitelkeit und Erlösung* (S. 152) kontrastiert hierzu, das Werk, auf das *Ungebrochene Dichtung* mit der Einsicht, dass konzeptionelle Unterschiede stilistische untermauern, antwortet.

AR

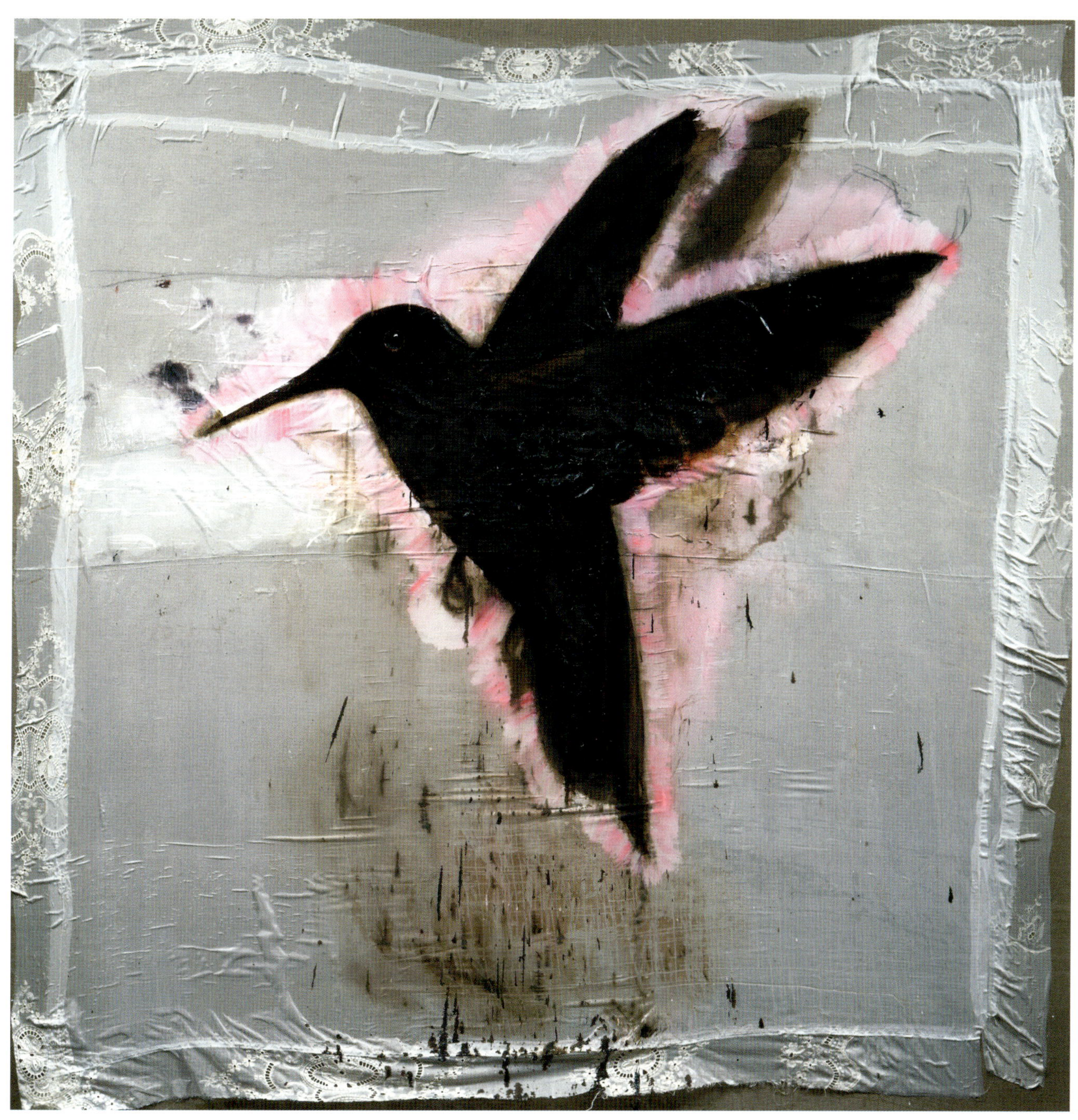

THE FIELD, 1999
Oil and petals on canvas
84 x 100 inches (213 x 254 cm)
Collection of Enrique and Alexandra Martínez Celaya

To call this painting *The Field* suggests naturalizing the canvas, a suggestion reinforced by the camellia petals spread over the surface, morphing color field painting into a field of flowers. (Thanks to its size, the flowers also comment on heroic painting from the Abstract Expressionists to Kiefer and Schnabel.) In the hands of most contemporary artists this profusion of petals would signal kitschy, sentimental, low brow taste, or an ironic riff on folk art. But here the petals assert themselves as visceral, physical presences, though their reading is unstable, hinged between nature and *nature morte*. That is, this painting stages a conflict between organic decay and life fixed in art's suspended animation.

But *The Field* also plays on object and illusion. The objecthood of the camellias, their representing nothing but themselves, is posed against simple traces that evoke a swan, so that the eye shifts between presentation and representation. Martínez Celaya began by arranging flowers on the canvas, and it was only the accident of a slight thinning in certain areas that suggested to him the bird's head and upper neck. The outline turns bare canvas into swan skin, and where petals do appear inside the outline one tends to discount their presence.

Classically overdetermined, the swan evokes a traditional image of beauty, a banalized beauty–a glass menagerie figurine blown up to absurd proportions, a mythological form of beauty, the romantic/symbolist interest in animism, and thanks to Leda, masculine aggression. By reading beauty together with that aggression, the painting insinuates the horror of beauty. In the striving of a monumental image so seemingly empty, subject matter matters.

AR

DAS FELD, 1999
Öl und Blütenblätter auf Leinwand
84 x 100 Zoll (213 x 254 cm)
Sammlung Enrique and Alexandra Martínez Celaya

Der Name des Gemäldes, *Das Feld*, lässt eine Naturalisierung der Leinwand vermuten, was durch die Kamelienblütenblätter auf der Oberfläche unterstrichen wird, die das mit Farbfeldern übersäte Gemälde in ein Blumenfeld verwandeln. (Dank seiner Größe kommentieren die Blumen auch die „heroische Malerei" von den Abstrakten Expressionisten bis hin zu Kiefer und Schnabel.) In den Händen der meisten zeitgenössischen Künstler wäre dieses Übermaß an Blütenblättern als Hinweis auf einen kitschigen, sentimentalen, ordinären Geschmack oder als eine Ironisierung der Volkskunst zu deuten. Hier allerdings treten die Blütenblätter mit physischer Präsenz auf, obwohl ihre Deutung labil und zwischen Natur und „nature morte" anzusiedeln ist. Das Gemälde stellt also den Konflikt zwischen organischem Verfall und dem in der Kunst im Status vorübergehender Leblosigkeit fixierten Leben dar.

Das Feld spielt aber auch mit dem Verhältnis zwischen Objekt und Illusion. Die Objekthaftigkeit der Kamelien, die sich nur selbst darstellen, wird den einfachen Strichen, die einen Schwan andeuten, kontrastiert, so dass das Auge zwischen Präsentation und Repräsentation hin- und herspringt. Martínez Celaya begann mit der Anordnung von Blumen auf der Leinwand und es war nur Zufall, dass sich ihm durch das Ausdünnen der Farbe in bestimmten Bereichen Kopf und Hals eines Vogels anboten. Der Umriss verwandelt die kahle Leinwand in Schwanenhaut und wo die Blütenblätter innerhalb des Umrisses erscheinen, ist man sich ihrer Gegenwart kaum bewusst.

Mit klassischen Bedeutungen überfrachtet, evoziert der Schwan ein traditionelles Bild der Schönheit, einer banalisierten Schönheit – einer Figurine aus der Glasmenagerie in absurden Proportionen, einer mythologischen Form der Schönheit, des romantisch-symbolistischen Interesses am Animismus und dank Leda der männlichen Aggression. Durch die Zusammendeutung der Schönheit und dieser Aggression spielt das Gemälde auf die Schrecken der Schönheit an. Im Bemühen eines monumentalen Bildes, das scheinbar so leer ist, gewinnt das Bildthema an Bedeutung.

AR

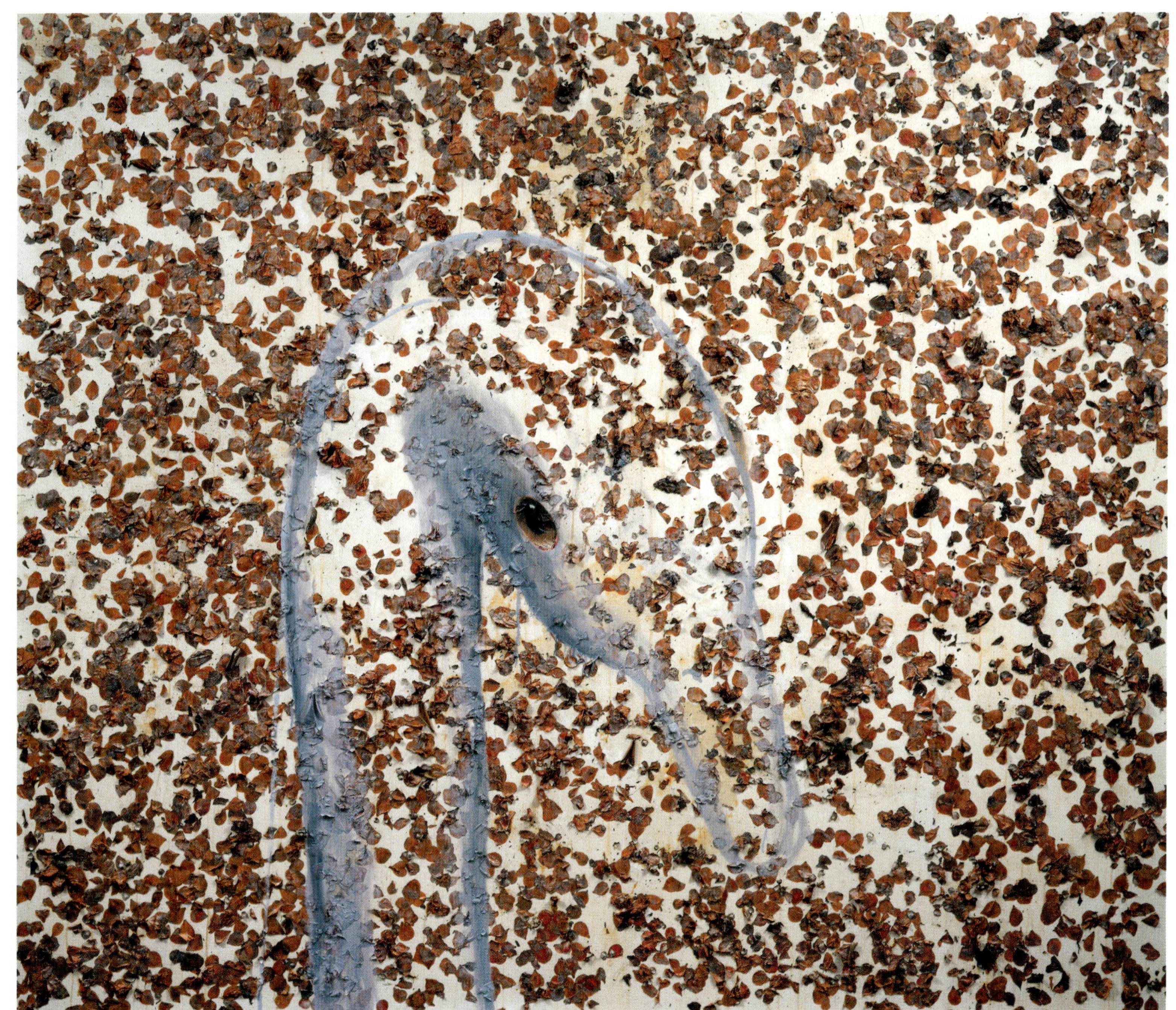

QUIET NIGHT (RECOLLECTION) I, 1999
Oil on canvas
103 x 113 inches (262 x 287 cm)
Collection of William Griffin, Venice, California

This, the largest painting Martínez Celaya has made to date, initiates the Quiet Night works, which include watercolors and sculptures from the same year, as well as recalling or anticipating other 'quiet nights' like The Forest and Winter series, *The Blink*, and so on. The title refers to the central image from one of the artist's short poems: "The key to the night / is kept in a safe of / quiet children dreams."[1] The title suggests zen explorations of quiet and intimations of mortality.

The parts of the face that are most legible or articulated are the parts soaked in blood–as if only violence could make them appear. The blood reinforces the hawkish or combative aspect of hummingbirds, as if blood were nectar. (Are three birds attacking here, or one at different moments?) Their whiteness recalls the Melvillian *Unbroken Poetry* and suggests something ghostly, something ominous. By contrast, the harder-to-read passages (like the outlined flowers behind the head) look peaceful. Neither are these flowers necessarily innocent. Melding them with the head invites the birds to feed on the blossom-face. The importance of flowers is literally underscored by the scumbled word 'flor' at the bottom of the canvas.

Quiet Night may be 'about' the troubled relationship among memory, time and consciousness. The canvas itself registers violence in the horizontal split, the drips and splatters, and the distressed oval where paint wrinkles the canvas–an oval that imprisons the head and recalls *A Boy in his Room.* To the head's right there half emerges a second head, spectral double to the first, enclosed by the oval as well. Reading left to right we might imagine two temporal states of the same head–the present of violence and its aftermath.[2] The painting exists in the difference between sequential explanation and the simultaneous experience of multiple emotions.

AR

STILLE NACHT (ERINNERUNG) I, 1999
Öl auf Leinwand
103 x 113 Zoll (262 x 287 cm)
Sammlung William Griffin, Venice, Kalifornien

Das bis heute größte Gemälde von Martínez Celaya ist die erste der Stille Nacht-Arbeiten, zu denen im selben Jahr entstandene Aquarelle und Skulpturen gehören und der darüber hinaus andere stille Nächte wie den Wald- und Winterzyklus, *Der Augenblick* und andere Werke erinnert oder antizipiert. Der Titel bezieht sich auf das zentrale Motiv eines der kurzen Gedichte des Künstlers: „Der Schlüssel zur Nacht / liegt in einem Safe / stiller Kinderträume."[1] Der Titel lässt an Zen-Erkundungen der Stille und an Andeutungen der Sterblichkeit denken.

Die am besten lesbaren oder deutlichsten Teile des Gesichts sind mit Blut getränkt, als ob sie nur mit Hilfe der Gewalt sichtbar würden. Das Blut betont den raubvogelartigen oder kämpferischen Zug der Kolibris, als ob Blut Nektar wäre. (Greifen hier drei Vögel an oder nur einer in verschiedenen Momenten?) Ihre Weiße erinnert an die mit Melville assoziierte *Ungebrochene Dichtung* und lässt etwas Geisterhaftes, Bedrohliches vermuten. Im Gegensatz dazu sehen die schwerer zu lesenden Passagen (wie die hinter dem Kopf umrissenen Blumen) friedlich aus. Aber auch diese Blumen sind nicht notwendigerweise unschuldig. Ihre Verschmelzung mit dem Kopf lädt die Vögel ein, sich am Blütengesicht zu laben. Die Bedeutung der Blumen wird buchstäblich durch das verwischte Wort „flor" unten auf der Leinwand unterstrichen.

Vielleicht handelt *Stille Nacht* von der gestörten Beziehung zwischen Erinnerung, Zeit und Bewusstsein. Der Leinwand wird Gewalt angetan, durch den waagerechten Spalt, durch die Tropfen und Spritzer und durch das Oval, in dem die Farbe die Leinwand in Falten wirft – ein Oval, das den Kopf gefangenhält und an *Ein Knabe in seinem Zimmer* erinnert. Rechts vom Kopf kommt ein zweiter Kopf als geisterhafte Kopie des ersten halb zum Vorschein, der ebenfalls von dem Oval umgeben ist. Von links nach rechts können wir uns zwei temporäre Zustände desselben Kopfes vorstellen – die Gegenwart der Gewalt und ihre Folgen.[2] Das Gemälde existiert im Unterschied von sequenzieller Erklärung und gleichzeitiger Erfahrung mehrerer Gefühle.

AR

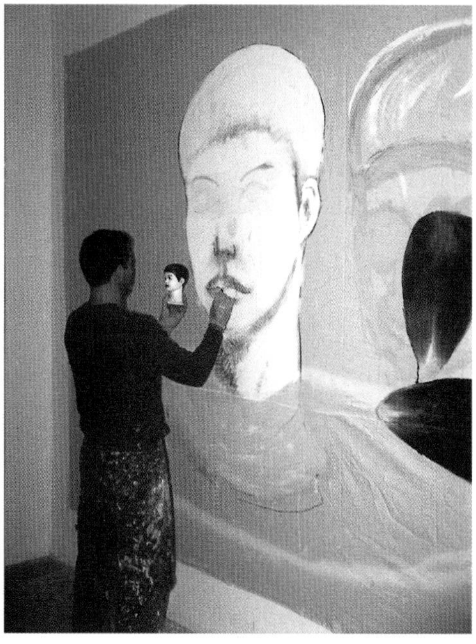

Work in progress/Bei der Arbeit, 1999

1. "Skinny Legs," in *Worksonpaperandsculpture*, op. cit.
2. *Quiet Night (Recollection) II*, from the same year and measuring the same size, repeats the two heads, the modeled one now supine while the right-side head is reduced to a mere outline.

1 „Dünne Beine" („Skinny Legs") in *Worksonpaperandsculpture*, op. cit.
2 *Stille Nacht (Erinnerung) II*, aus dem gleichen Jahr und mit den gleichen Maßen, wiederholt die beiden Köpfe, der modellierte Kopf liegt nun auf dem Hinterkopf, während der rechte Kopf zu einem bloßen Umriss reduziert ist.

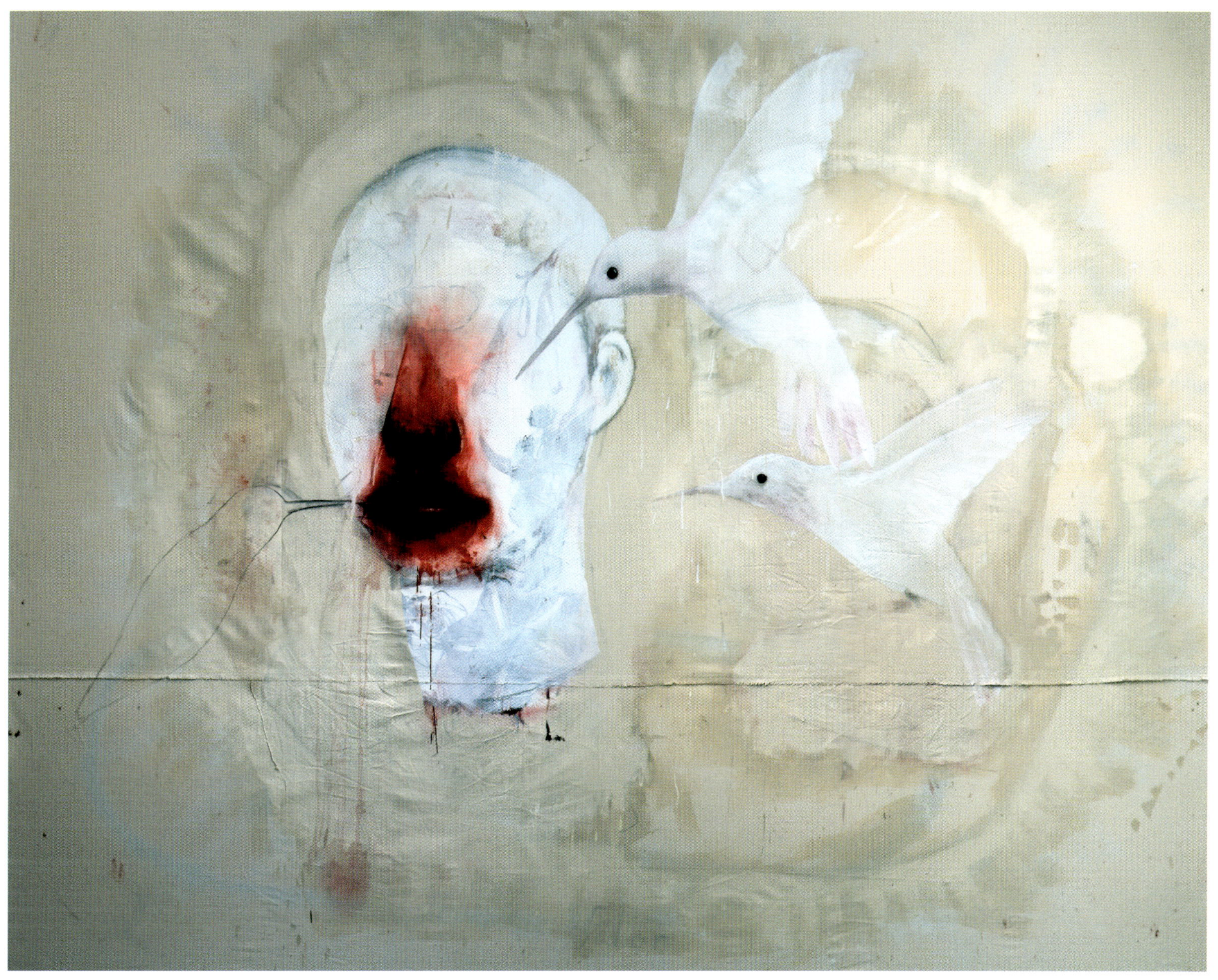

QUIET NIGHT, 1999
Dirt, oil, fiberglass and resin
each 25 x 34 x 30 inches (64 x 86 x 76 cm)

Constructed of fiberglass with polyester resin shells, the heads are strong but light–light enough that Martínez Celaya floated *Ocean* in the water in the Santa Monica Bay. Rather than establish an I/thou relationship with the viewer, Martínez Celaya's heads conjure the sublime, for their scale gravitates toward the monumental, and prompts associations with Shelley's famous sonnet *Ozymandias.*

> I met a traveler from an antique land
> Who said: Two vast and trunkless legs of stone
> Stand in the desert … Near them, on the sand,
> Half sunk, a shattered visage lies, whose frown,
> And wrinkled lip, and sneer of cold command,
> Tell that its sculptor well those passions read
> Which yet survive, stamped on these lifeless things,
> The hand that mocked them, and the heart that fed:
> And on the pedestal these words appear:
> 'My name is Ozymandias, king of kings:
> Look on my works, ye Mighty, and despair!'
> Nothing beside remains. Round the decay
> Of that colossal wreck, boundless and bare
> The lone and level sands stretch far away.

To place these heads into a narrative sequence would violate their detachment and sealed off presence, and at the same time, the sequence *Ocean, Marks, Dirt* inscribes an arc from birth to death. The fish on *Ocean's* forehead, we know, recalls memories of childhood;[1] *Marks* records the accumulating encounters with the world that both bruise and over time create the shape we call character; *Dirt* conveys the charred look of Hiroshima or Auschwitz–the fire next time–and so the opposite of *Ocean.* It's surface is related to the earth and cemetery themes of the Berlin photographs. *Dirt* is a face that has moved beyond human expression.

AR

STILLE NACHT, 1999
Erde, Öl, Glasfaser und Harz
jeweils 25 x 34 x 30 Zoll (64 x 86 x 76 cm)

Die Köpfe aus Glasfaser mit einer Hülle aus Polyesterharz sind solide und dabei leicht – so leicht, dass Martínez Celaya *Ozean* in der Bucht von Santa Monica im Wasser schwimmen ließ. Martínez Celayas Köpfe stellen keine Ich-Du-Beziehung zum Betrachter her, vielmehr beschwören sie das Erhabene, da ihre Größe an das Monumentale grenzt und Assoziationen mit Shelleys berühmtem Sonett *Ozymandias* hervorruft.

> Ein Mann berichtete aus mythischem Land:
> Zwei Riesenbeine, rumpflos, steingehauen
> Stehn in der Wüste. Nahebei im Sand
> Zertrümmert, halbversunken, liegt mit rauhen
> Lippen voll Hohn ein Antlitz macht-gewöhnt,
> voll Leidenschaften, die bestehn; es sagt:
> Der Bildner, der es prägte, wusste dies,
> Wess Herz und Hand sie speiste und verhöhnt.
> Und auf dem Sockel eingemeißelt lies:
> „Ich bin Ozymandias, Herr der Herrn.
> Schaut, was ich schuf, ihr Mächtigen, und verzagt!"
> Nicht bleibt. Um den Verfall her riesengroß
> Des mächtigen Steinwracks öd und grenzenlos
> Dehnt sich die Wüste nah und fern.

Diese Köpfe in einen erzählerischen Zusammenhang zu stellen würde ihre Distanz und Isolation verletzen. Gleichzeitig beschreibt die Reihenfolge *Ozean, Markierungen, Erde* einen Bogen von der Geburt bis zum Tod. Der Fisch auf *Ozeans* Stirn ruft, wie wir wissen, Erinnerungen an die Kindheit hervor;[1] *Markierungen* zeichnet die sich ansammelnden Begegnungen mit der Welt auf, die uns verletzen und im Laufe der Zeit das formen, was wir als Charakter bezeichnen; *Erde* vermittelt das verkohlte Aussehen von Hiroshima oder Auschwitz – das nächste Feuer – und stellt somit das Gegenteil von *Ozean* dar. Seine Oberfläche hängt mit den Erd- und Friedhofsthemen der Berlin-Photographien zusammen. *Erde* ist ein Gesicht, das über den menschlichen Ausdruck hinausgegangen ist.

AR

QUIET NIGHT (DIRT), 1999
Collection of Ramis Barquet, New York, New York

STILLE NACHT (ERDE), 1999
Sammlung Ramis Barquet, New York, New York

p. 198/S. 198
QUIET NIGHT (MARKS), 1999
Collection of Julien J. Studley, Inc.,
Los Angeles, California

STILLE NACHT (MARKIERUNGEN), 1999
Sammlung Julien J. Studley, Inc.,
Los Angeles, Kalifornien

p. 199/S. 199
QUIET NIGHT (OCEAN), 1999
Collection of Enrique and Alexandra Martínez Celaya

STILLE NACHT (OZEAN), 1999
Sammlung Enrique and Alexandra Martínez Celaya

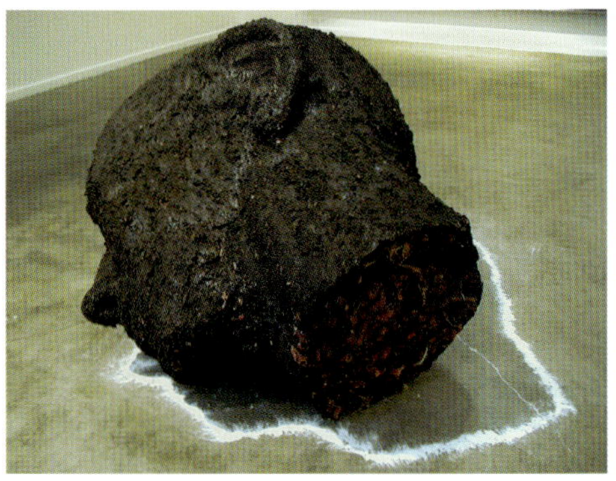

Installation at/bei Griffin Contemporary,
Venice, California, 1999

1. "The fish anchors, then pulls the whole ship of childhood", Anne Brodzky, *Unbroken Poetry*, op. cit., 30.
1. „Der Fisch ankert und zieht dann das ganze Schiff der Kindheit." Anne Brodzky, *Unbroken Poetry*, op. cit., S. 30.

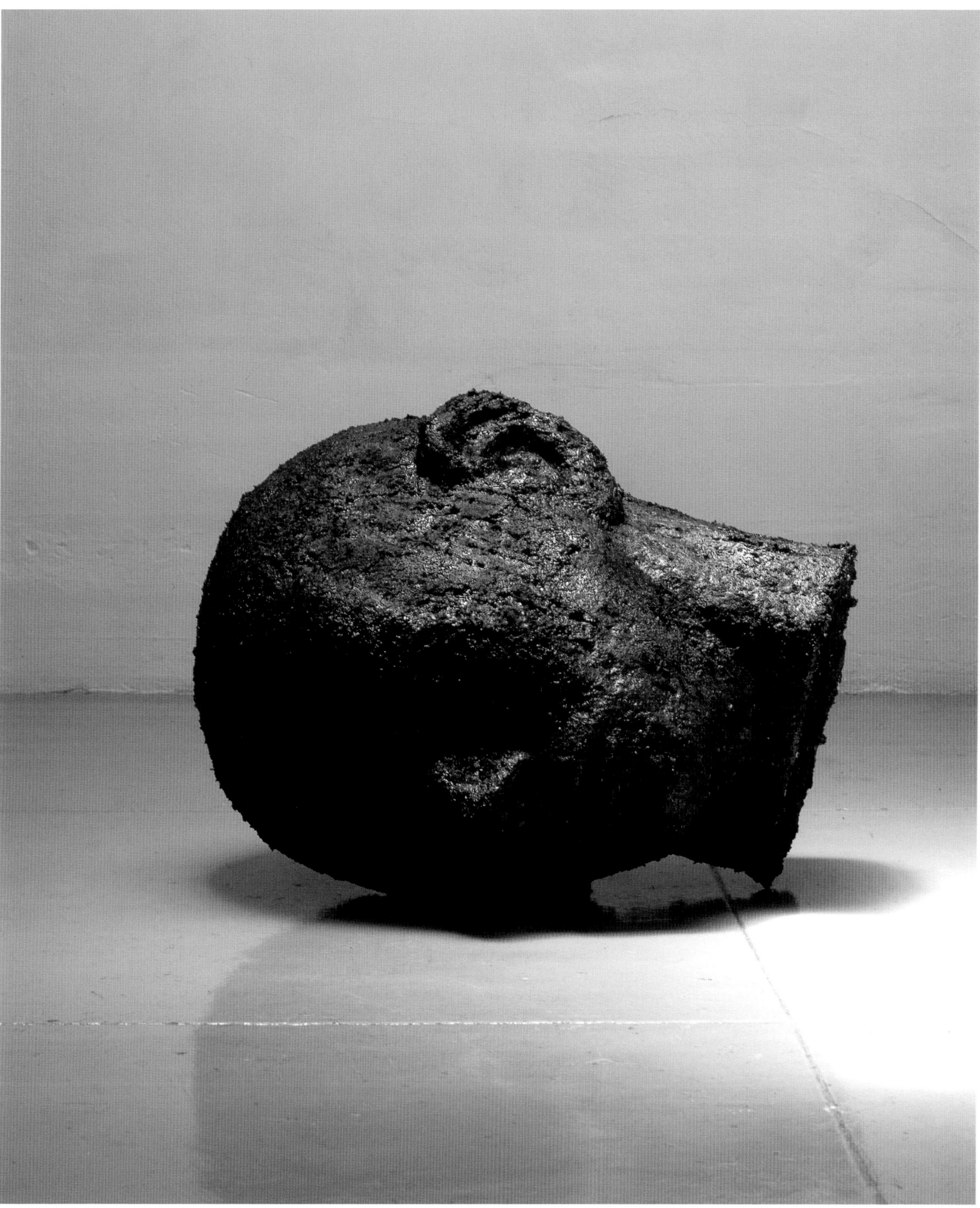

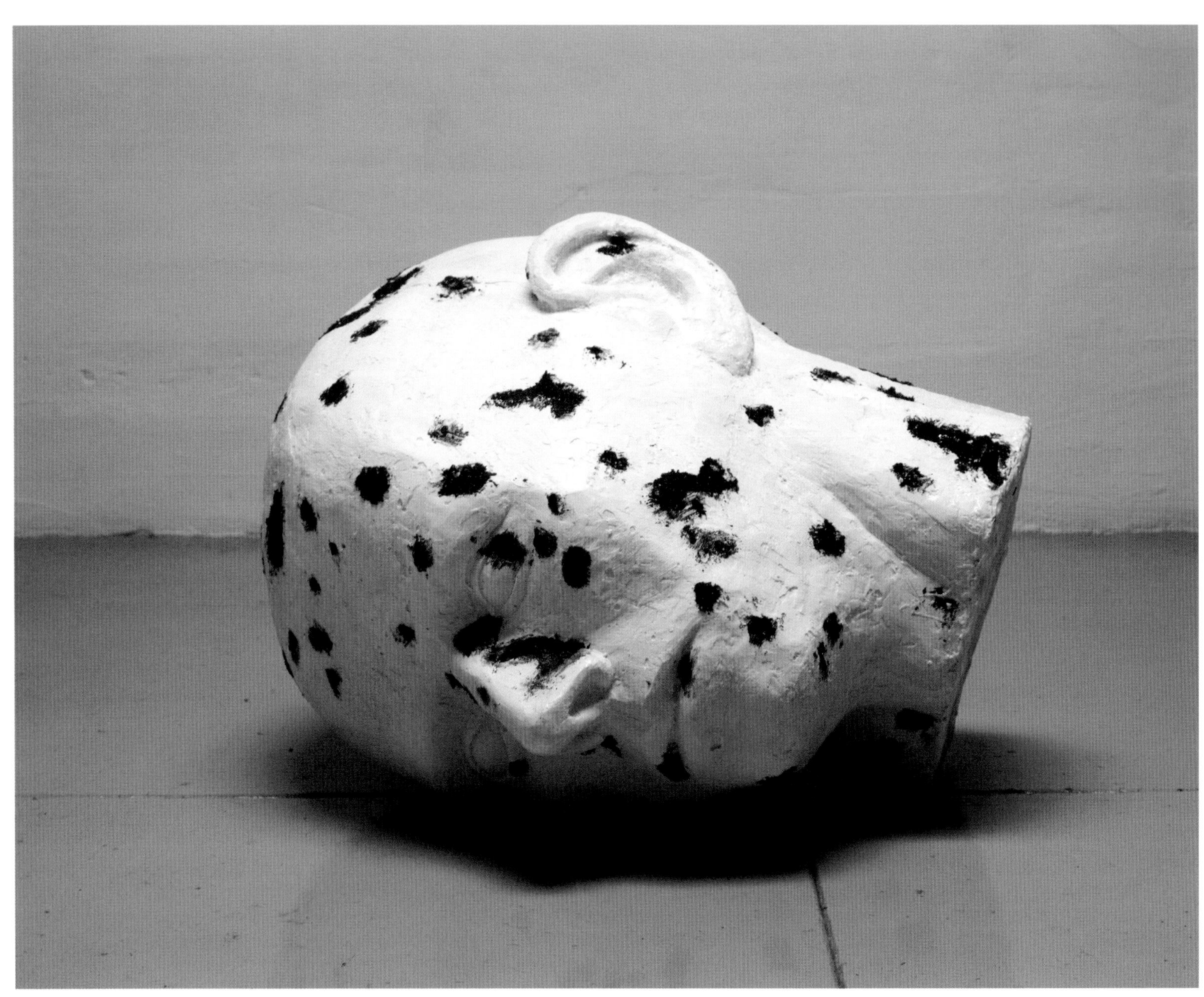

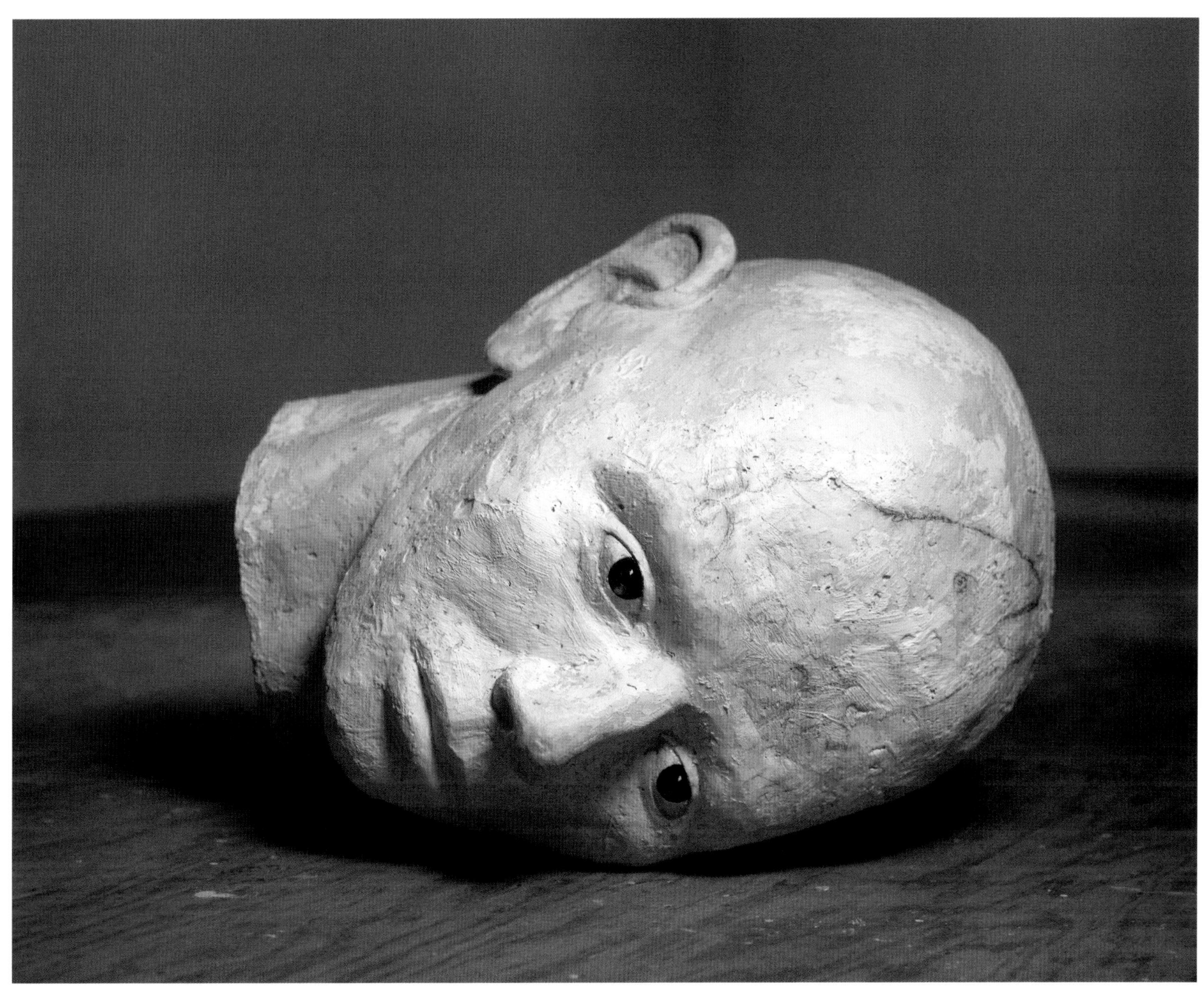

THE MOST FRAGILE, 1999
Oil and graphite on five sheets of paper
each 24 x 24 inches (61 x 61 cm)
Collection of J. H. Theodoracopulos,
New York, New York

As with Quiet Night, this series groups and juxtaposes severed heads. These drawings also constitute five meditations on fragility.

The mobius-strip middle panel recalls the labyrinthine paths in the background of *First War* (p. 168), *Pena* (p. 186) or *Empty Garden* (p. 189), as if their paths were brought forward and their body parts displaced to the flanking images in *The Most Fragile.* A pencilled text at bottom center reads 'To record your pass.'

Arm in arm: the series opens with a photograph of *The House of Arms,* mounted crudely on paper with tape showing (like the Berlin photos). The framing paper itself is then collaged to a larger sheet on which flower petals are also mounted. These two sheets are connected by a Spanish citation that begins on the top one and continues below. Recursively, that citation in turn recalls the lines from the poem *Berlin* inscribed on the photographed arm, as the real flowers echo the flowers in the photo above them.

And so a rhythm of detachment is established. Left to right: from arm with flowers, to head, to abstraction or withdrawal from imagery, to head and birch, to head and flowers. Falling and violence, for the red and crisply drawn nose and mouth echoes *Quiet Night (recollection) I.* An unmotivated and wonderful detail: the small, open-lided box in a triangle to which the figure may be directing its attention, as if contemplating order and beauty.

AR

DAS VERLETZLICHSTE, 1999
Öl und Graphit auf fünf Blatt Papier
jeweils 24 x 24 Zoll (61 x 61 cm)
Sammlung J. H. Theodoracopulos,
New York, New York

Wie in *Stille Nacht* gruppiert diese Serie mehrere Köpfe und stellt sie nebeneinander. Außerdem stellen diese Zeichnungen fünf Meditationen über die Zerbrechlichkeit dar.

Das Möbiusband der mittleren Tafel erinnert an die Labyrinthpfade im Hintergrund von *Erster Krieg* (S. 168), *Pena* (S. 186) oder *Der Leere Garten* (S. 189), als ob ihre Pfade in den Vordergrund gestellt und ihre Körperteile auf die flankierenden Bilder in *Das Verletzlichste* versetzt wurden. Ein mit Bleistift geschriebener Text unten in der Mitte lautet „To record your pass" („Um deinen Fortschritt zu dokumentieren").

Arm in Arm: Der Zyklus beginnt mit einem Photo von *Das Haus der Arme,* das unbeholfen, mit sichtbarem Klebeband aufs Papier geklebt wurde (wie die Berlin-Photos). Das rahmende Papier ist selbst mit Blütenblättern Teil einer Collage auf einem größeren Blatt. Diese beiden Blätter werden mit einem spanischen Zitat verbunden, das auf dem oberen beginnt und sich unten fortsetzt. Wiederum erinnert dieses Zitat an die Zeilen des Gedichts *Berlin* auf dem photographierten Arm, während die echten Blumen ein Nachhall der Blumen im darüber liegenden Photo sind.

Und so wird ein Rhythmus der Loslösung geschaffen. Von rechts nach links: vom Arm mit Blumen zum Kopf, zur Abstraktion oder zum Rückzug vom Bildhaften, zum Kopf und zur Birke, zum Kopf und zu den Blumen. Fallen und Gewalt, da die rot und scharf gezeichneten Nase und Mund *Stille Nacht (Erinnerung) I* zurückrufen. Ein unmotiviertes und wunderschönes Detail: der kleine geöffnete Kasten in einem Dreieck, auf das die Figur ihre Aufmerksamkeit richten könnte, als ob sie über Ordnung und Schönheit nachdenkt.

AR

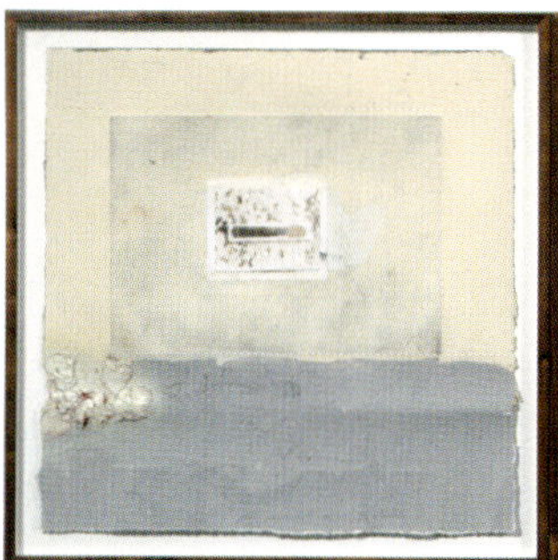
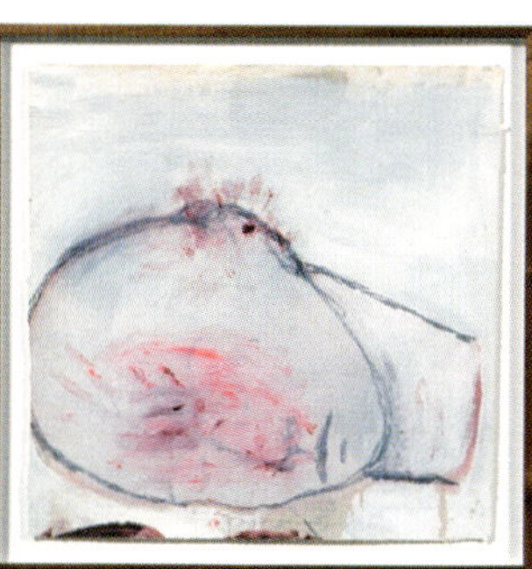
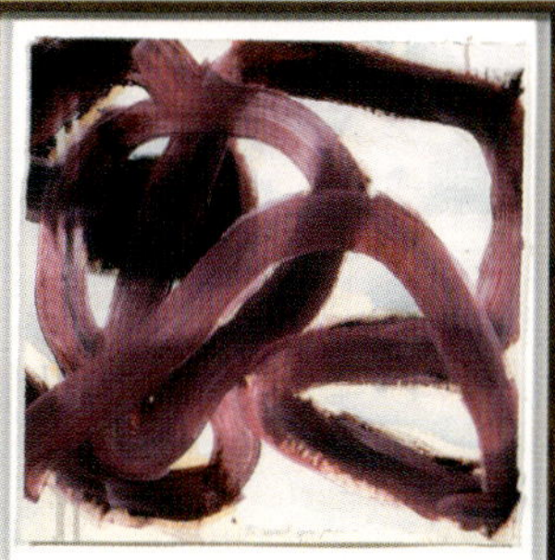
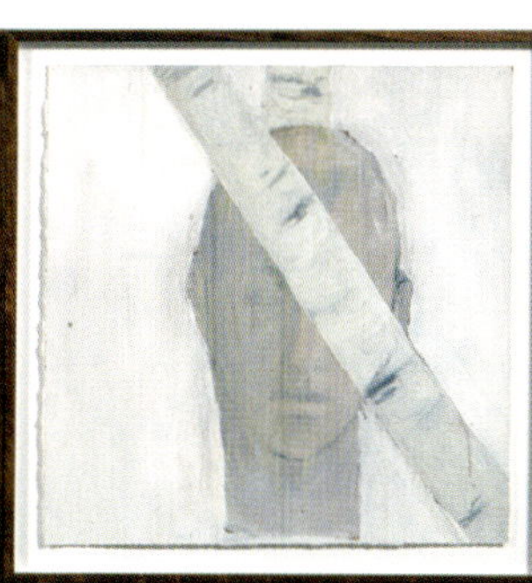
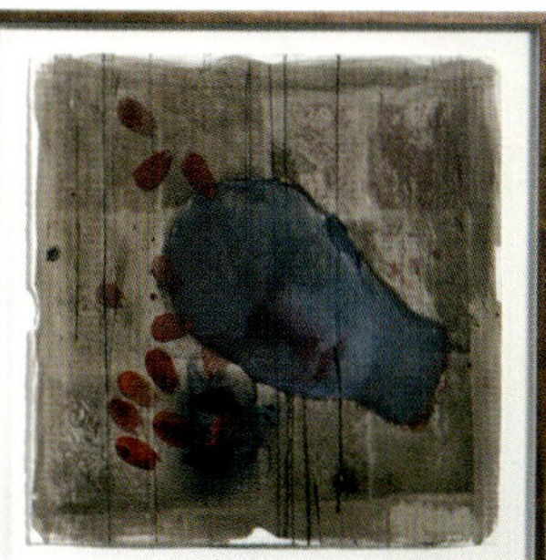

A DRY BED, 1999
Watercolor and graphite on paper
each 13 x 11 inches (33 x 28 cm)
Collection of Dieter and Si Rosenkranz,
Berlin, Germany

To date, nothing like a straight narrative has ever appeared in the work, but this suite draws more on narrative conventions than most of his other work. At the bottom of drawings 1–10 are inscribed phrases that taken together form a grammatically coherent sentence. If (as Martínez Celaya maintains) this legend is not a poem, at least it succinctly expresses the artist's central preoccupation with loss and futile efforts to recapture the past: Matters are not quite so simple, the image/text relationship is neither casual nor causal.

Although we cannot establish even whether the same face or different ones appear from image to image, the impulse to narrate is encouraged by the consecutive numbering, the connecting phrases, and the presence of a head in each drawing. Similarly, the suite's beginning and ending offer grounds for comparison, but does the first image express the speaker's initial state of mind and the last image his final condition? Do the heads speak the words beneath them? Highly doubtful. The series-likenesses offer a platform for difference, just as difference itself enfolds commonality: every drawing is the site of unimagined juxtapositions (whether accidentally overlaid or enacting Ovidian metamorphoses) that take on a feeling of inevitability.

1. A right hand emerges, from the right side of the head, with traces of violence at the wrist (see *Pena*, p. 186). There emerges out of that hand, among other objects, another right arm with a hand of its own. Is the first hand holding or releasing its contents?

2. Eyes and nose are replaced by the outline of a strange mechanical device, a cylinder or drum on which a bell shape is superimposed. The legend, 'must find me extinguished,' may resonate with this head, whose senses are all missing or obscured.

3. The head with twin tulips recalls *Tu Brazo* (p. 158), and displays a similar tension between an inert body and the upward-reaching flowers. At the neck, a trace of bloody dismemberment, a motif repeated elsewhere in this sheet.

4. This hummingbird emerges from the left eye's cavity, or flies across the head. Does the bird figure consciousness, an attack on consciousness, consciousness of attack? Does the mobile creature embody

EIN TROCKENES BETT, 1999
Aquarellfarbe und Graphit auf Papier
jeweils 13 x 11 Zoll (33 x 28 cm)
Sammlung Dieter und Si Rosenkranz,
Berlin, Deutschland

Bis zum heutigen Tage trat nichts, das einer geradlinigen Erzählung glich, in Martínez Celayas Arbeiten auf, aber diese Reihe nutzt narrative Konventionen mehr als die meisten seiner anderen Werke. Unten auf den Zeichnungen 1 bis 10 finden sich Sätze, die zusammen einen grammatisch kohärenten Satz bilden. Wenn (wie Martínez Celaya behauptet) dieser erläuternde Text kein Gedicht ist, drückt er doch zumindest auf knappe und treffende Weise die Besessenheit des Künstlers mit dem Verlust und den zwecklosen Anstrengungen aus, die Vergangenheit wieder zu erlangen: Jedoch ist alles nicht ganz so einfach, die Beziehung zwischen Bild und Text ist weder zufällig noch ursächlich.

Obwohl wir nicht einmal feststellen können, ob das gleiche Gesicht oder verschiedene Gesichter auf den Bildern erscheinen, wird der Impuls zur Erzählung durch die fortlaufende Nummerierung, die verbindenden Satzteile und die Gegenwart eines Kopfes in jeder Zeichnung unterstützt. Gleichermaßen bieten der Anfang und das Ende der Reihe Grundlagen für Vergleiche. Drückt aber das erste Bild den anfänglichen Gemütszustand des Sprechers aus, das letzte Bild seinen endgültigen Zustand? Sprechen die Köpfe die unter ihnen stehenden Worte? Dies ist sehr anzuzweifeln. Die der Reihe innewohnenden Ähnlichkeiten bieten eine Grundlage für Unterschiede, denn Unterschiede umfassen auch Gemeinsamkeiten: Auf jeder Zeichnung finden sich unvorgestellte Nebeneinanderstellungen (zufällig überlagert oder Ovidische Metamorphosen darstellend), denen ein Gefühl der Unvermeidbarkeit eigen ist.

1. Eine rechte Hand taucht an der rechten Seite des Kopfes auf. Sie trägt am Handgelenk Spuren der Gewalt (siehe *Pena,* S. 186). Dieser Hand entwächst unter anderem ein weiterer rechter Arm mit einer eigenen Hand. Hält die erste Hand ihren Inhalt oder lässt sie ihn los?

2. Augen und Nase werden durch den Umriss einer seltsamen mechanischen Vorrichtung ersetzt, einem Zylinder oder einer Trommel, die von einer Glockenform überlagert wird. Der erläuternde Text „must find me extinguished" („muss mich erloschen finden") könnte mit diesem Kopf zusammenklingen, dessen Sinnesorgane fehlen oder verdeckt sind.

clockwise from upper left
/von oben links im Uhrzeigersinn

1. THE IMPERFECT FUTURE
/DIE UNVOLLKOMMENE ZUKUNFT

2. MUST FIND ME EXTINGUISHED
/MUSS MICH ERLOSCHEN FINDEN

3. TRYING TO MAKE SENSE
/WENN ICH VERSUCHE, DEN SINN ZU FINDEN

4. OF FAULTS AND LACK OF MEANING
/VON FEHLERN UND BEDEUTUNGSLOSIGKEIT

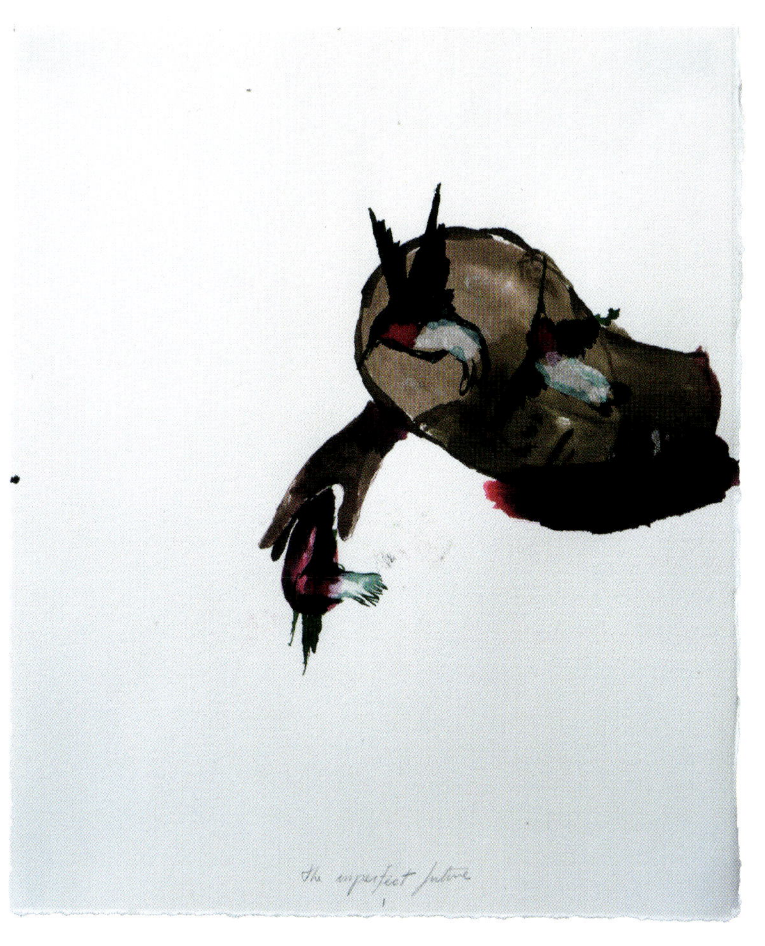
the imperfect future
1

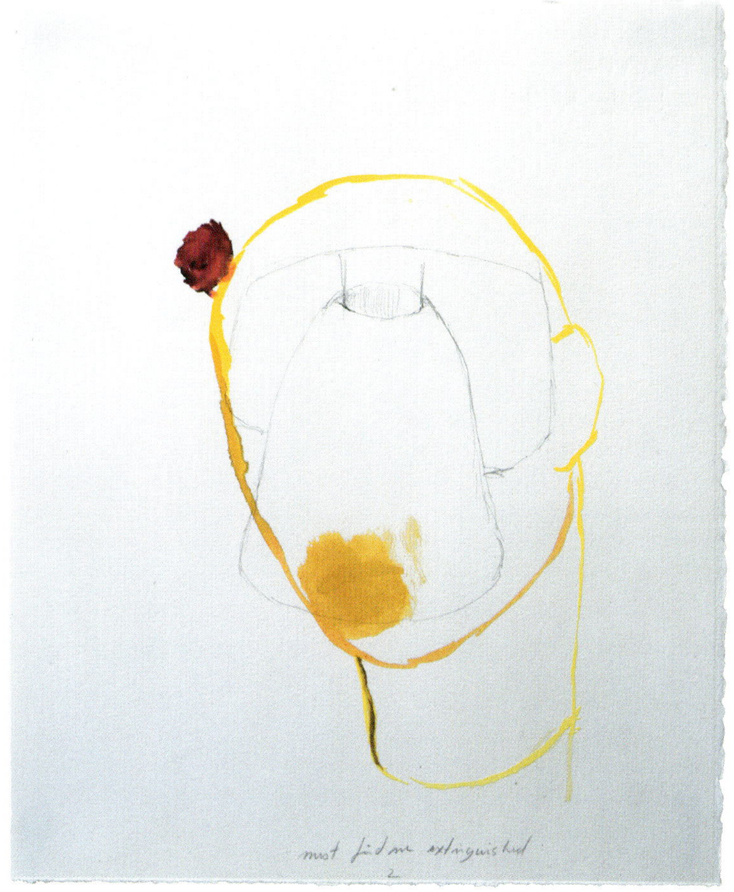
must find me extinguished
2

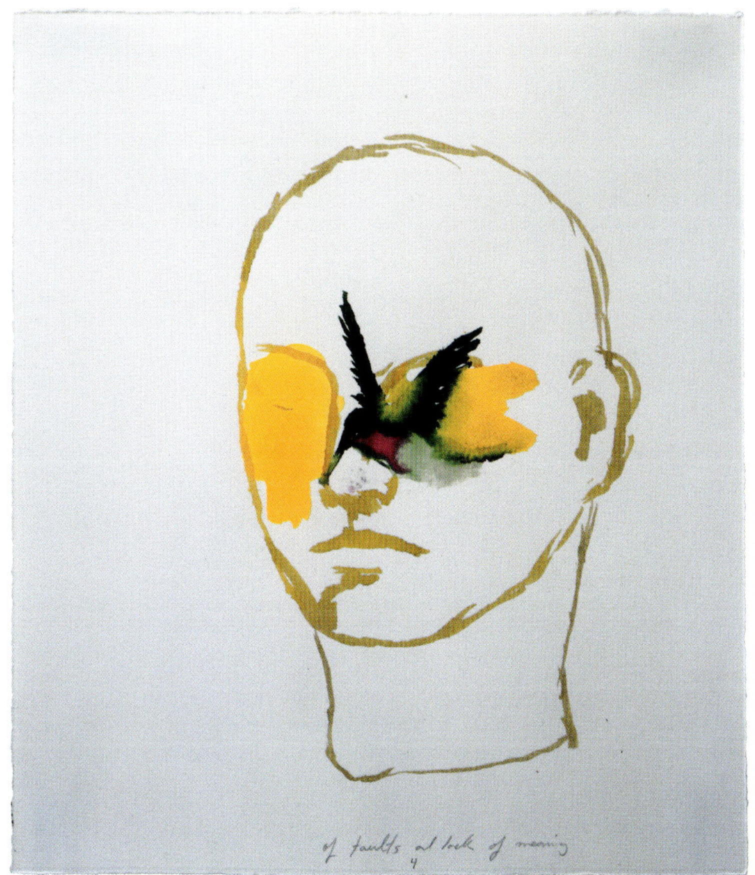
of faults and lack of meaning
4

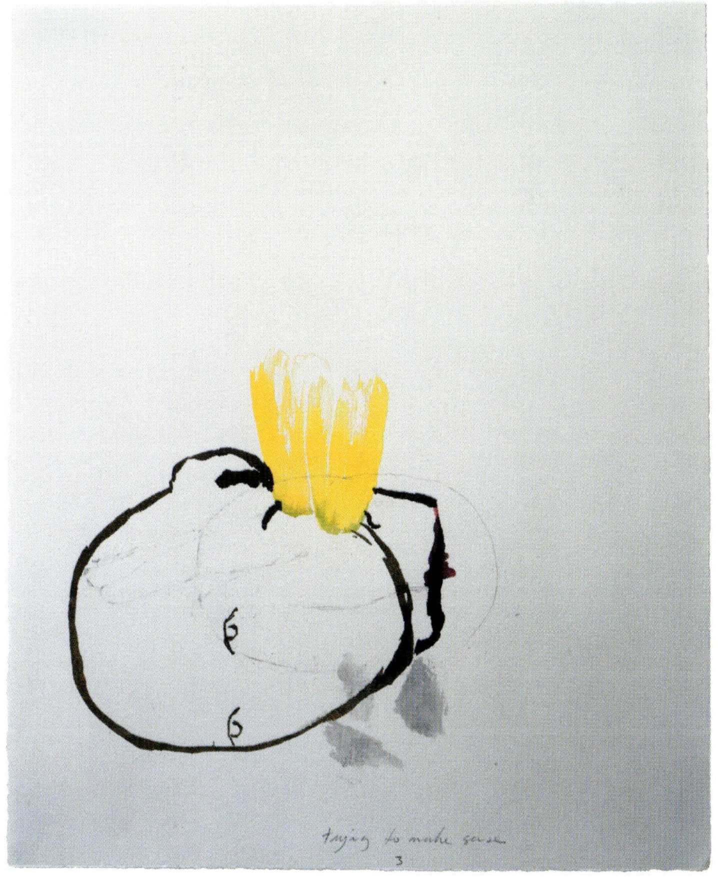
trying to make sense
3

time eroding memory?

5. If this dismembered head (the only one in the series to retain all five senses: 'trying to make sense') is planted or grounded in a tree, the foundational trunk is itself uprooted. This image extends Martínez Celaya's articulating head with trunk, and perhaps the impailed hummingbird as well.

6. Metamorphoses: part of the lip doubles as or merges with the curve of the lower bird's head; the upper bird's breast fills out the nose; and its wings form a mask over the figure's eyes.

7. Elements from earlier in the series reappear and collapse upon each other: the head, the tulip and the rose, and hummingbirds with fluttering wings, all obscured by a gray smear across the center.

8. Is this rose on the surface of the face, in front, or emerging from behind? Does it relate to its legend 'this is then past'? Does this intact rose suggest memory preserved? Or on the contrary, vulnerability, since the face/flower invites hummmingbirds to feed?

9. The two large red shapes might be tears or petals; the right-hand one also resembles the shell from which the hummingbird emerges. And why has the head turned away from us?

10. The poet's arm becomes a stake driven down and attacking sight, smell, and speech. Double dismemberment: the severed arm of *Tu Brazo* (p. 158) is superimposed on a severed head, a martyred head.

AR

3. Der Kopf mit den Zwillingstulpen erinnert an *Tu Brazo* (S. 158) und zeigt eine ähnliche Spannung zwischen einem schlaffen Körper und sich nach oben streckenden Blumen. Am Hals findet sich eine Spur der blutigen Zerstückelung, ein an anderer Stelle des Blattes wiederholtes Motiv.

4. Dieser Kolibri kommt aus der linken Augenhöhle oder fliegt über den Kopf. Stellt der Vogel Bewusstsein, einen Angriff auf das Bewusstsein oder das Bewusstsein eines Angriffs dar? Verkörpert dieses fliegende Lebewesen die Zeit, die die Erinnerung nach und nach auslöscht?

5. Wenn dieser abgeschlagene Kopf (der einzige Kopf im Zyklus mit allen fünf Sinnen: „ich versuche, den Sinn zu finden") in einem Baum wurzelt oder auf diesen gepflanzt wurde, ist der die Grundlage bildende Stamm selbst entwurzelt. Dieses Bild erweitert Martínez Celayas Thema des sich artikulierenden Kopfes mit Torso und vielleicht auch das des gepfählten Kolibris.

6. Metamorphosen: Ein Teil der Lippe stellt zugleich die Wölbung des Kopfes des unteren Vogels dar oder verschmilzt mit ihr. Die Brust des oberen Vogels füllt die Nase aus und seine Flügel bilden eine Maske über den Augen der Figur.

7. Elemente aus früheren Arbeiten der Serie erscheinen und fallen übereinander zusammen: der Kopf, die Tulpe, die Rose und Kolibris mit schlagenden Flügeln, die alle durch einen grauen Schmierfleck in der Mitte undeutlich gemacht werden.

8. Befindet sich diese Rose auf der Gesichtsoberfläche, vor dem Gesicht oder kommt sie von hinten? Hat sie etwas mit dem erläuternden Text „das ist dann die Vergangenheit" zu tun? Bezieht sich diese intakte Rose auf die bewahrte Erinnerung? Oder bezieht sie sich ganz im Gegenteil auf Verletzlichkeit, da das Gesicht bzw. die Blume die Kolibris zur Nahrungsaufnahme einladen?

9. Die beiden großen roten Formen sind vielleicht Tränen oder Blütenblätter; die rechte Form ähnelt auch der Muschel, aus der der Kolibri aufsteigt. Und warum wendet sich der Kopf von uns ab?

10. Der Arm des Dichters wird zum nach unten getriebenen Stab, der Sehvermögen, Geruchssinn und Sprache angreift. Doppelte Zerstückelung: Der abgetrennte Arm in *Tu Brazo* (S. 158) wird von einem abgetrennten Kopf, einem Märtyrerkopf, überlagert.

AR

clockwise from upper left
/von oben links im Uhrzeigersinn

5. OF REGRETS
/DES BEDAUERNS

6. AND PEOPLE INEVITABLY LEFT BEHIND
/UND UNVERMEIDLICHERWEISE ZURÜCKGELASSENE MENSCHEN

7. AND IRRETRIEVABLE MOMENTS WITH THEM
/UND UNWIEDERBRINGLICHE MOMENTE MIT IHNEN

8. THIS IS THEN THE PAST,
/DAS IST DANN DIE VERGANGENHEIT

9. AND I, THE COUNTER.
/UND ICH, DER ZÄHLER

10. (NO TEXT)
/(KEIN TEXT)

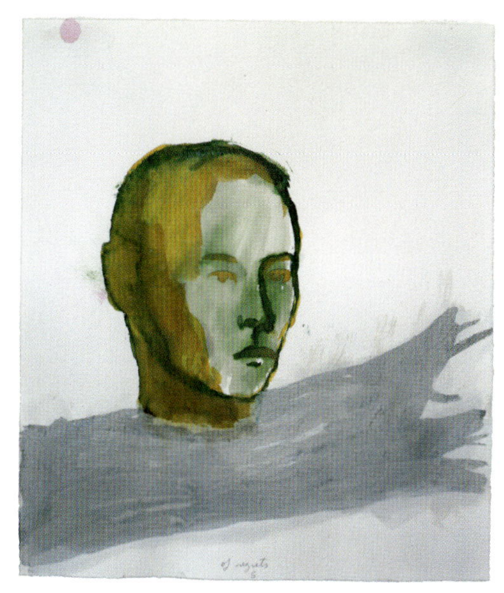

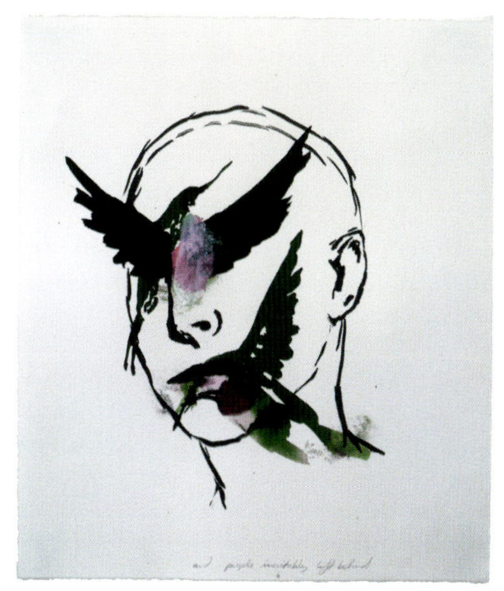

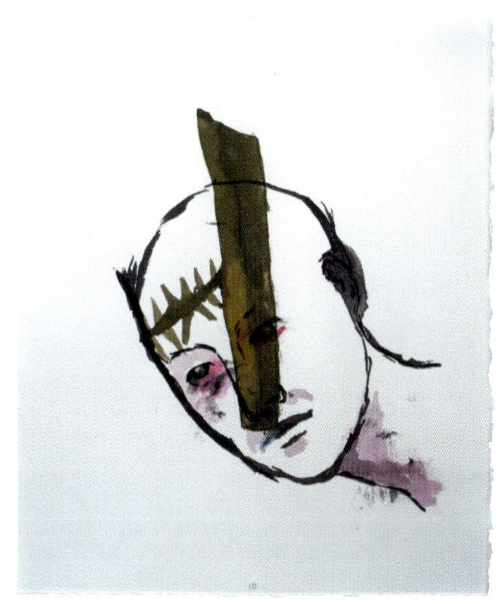

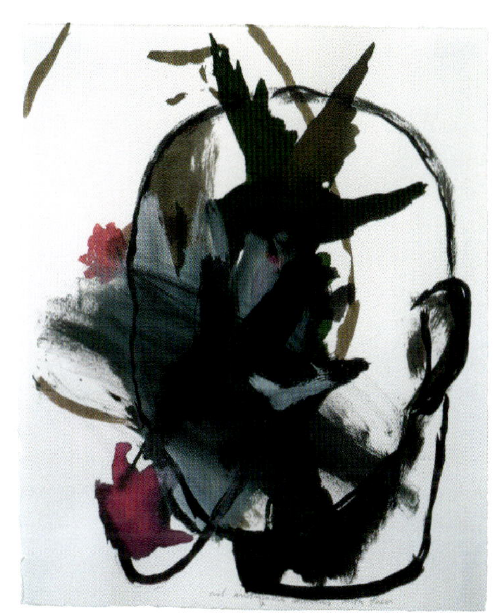

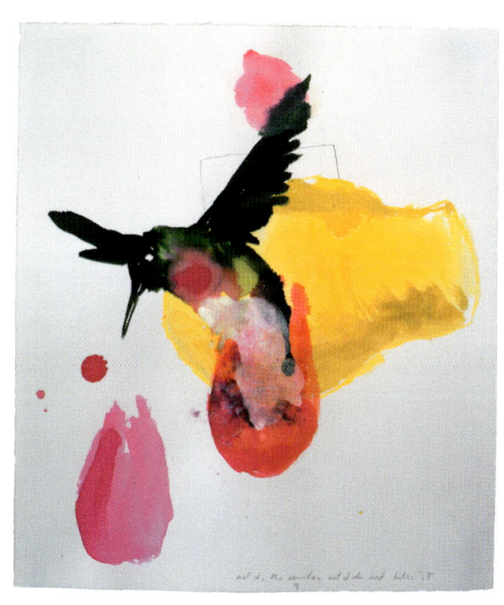

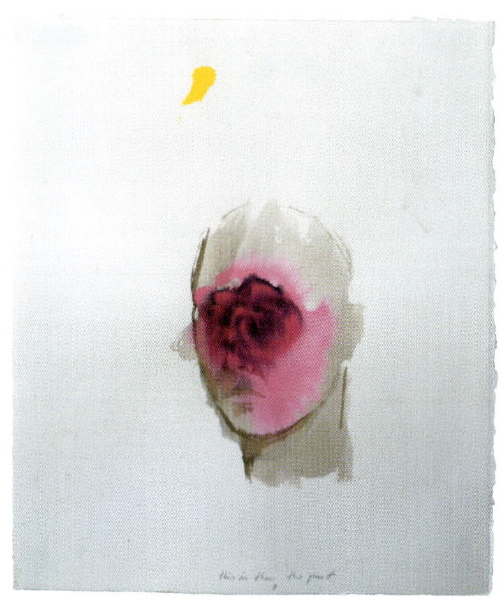

THE FOREST, 1999
Watercolor and india ink on paper

DER WALD, 1999
Aquarellfarbe und chinesische Tusche auf Papier

This suite of watercolors crosses the haunting aspect of Odilon Redon with Martin Heidegger's *Holzwege*, or labyrinthine, sylvan paths. With economical means Martínez Celaya evokes a forest barely there, of openness and enclosure, of luminosity and recession into darkness. The figure's gender is ambiguous but, as in the Winter series, looks to be adolescent. A certain development occurs here, for Martínez Celaya begins to work a body (more or less whole) into a distinct setting.

If *The Forest I* depicts a solitary, upright, haloed figure without feet on a dark ground, then *The Forest V*, conjures another solitary figure, supine on a light, olive ground, with a numinous ray of light shining on torso of a headless body.

In *The Forest II*, as in *The Forest I*, the figure either emerges from or disappears into the inky black ground, or both. Hovering over the body, the hummingbird recalls the 'S' over Hegel's tomb or the sunflowers from *Body at Rest*. The bird suggests both a protective tutelary spirit and the threatening aspect of time.

In *The Forest III*, a gigantic head, 'formed' of negative space, looms up behind and dwarfs the insubstantial tree trunks that enclose it. But the face is obscured by the impression of a tulip, whose internal organs are marked by stains of blue, green, and brown(Compare the faces juxtaposed with flowers in the previous year's *A Dry Bed*, VII and VIII.) Out of the throat are growing the outlines of three other flowers–are they lilies? Certainly a lily appears as a resist in *Forest IV*, which complements *Forest III* (head sans body/body sans head), in the very pose the artist would take in the photographs *Frankness(Work of Mercy)* [p. 224] and *Water and Figure* the following year.

The Forest V, Clearing stretches its supine figure in the clearing across three pieces of paper; it is almost three times as wide as the previous images. Green is stripped from the forest (whose spectral trees are manifest as absences, places where the olive wash was not applied) and displaced to outline the body (lying? floating?), whose feet bespeak vulnerability.

AR

In dieser Aquarellfolge überschneiden sich das Quälerische von Odilon Redon mit Martin Heideggers *Holzwegen* oder labyrinthischen Waldwegen. Mit sparsamen Mitteln ruft Martínez Celaya einen kaum vorhandenen Wald hervor, Offenheit und Geschlossenheit, Leuchten und Rückzug in die Dunkelheit. Das Geschlecht der Figur ist zweideutig. Doch scheint es sich, wie im Winterzyklus, um einen Jugendlichen zu handeln. Hier findet eine gewisse Entwicklung statt, da Martínez Celaya beginnt, einen mehr oder weniger ganzen Körper in eine deutliche Umgebung einzuarbeiten.

Wenn *Der Wald I* eine einsame, aufrechte Figur mit Heiligenschein und ohne Füße auf dunklem Grund zeigt, beschwört *Der Wald V* eine weitere, die auf hellem, olivfarbenem Untergrund auf dem Rücken liegt, wobei ein Lichtstrahl auf den Torso eines kopflosen Körpers scheint.

In *Der Wald II* wie in *Der Wald I* tritt die Figur entweder aus dem getuschten schwarzen Hintergrund hervor, verschwindet in diesem oder tut beides. Der über dem Körper schwebende Kolibri erinnert an das S über Hegels Grab oder die Sonnenblumen in *Ruhender Körper*. Der Vogel steht für einen Schutzgeist und die bedrohliche Seite der Zeit.

In *Der Wald III* türmt sich hinten ein riesiger Kopf aus „negativem Raum" und lässt die unkörperlichen, ihn umschließenden Baumstämme winzig erscheinen. Das Gesicht aber wird vom Abdruck einer Tulpe undeutlich gemacht, deren innere Organe durch blaue, grüne und braune Flecken gekennzeichnet sind (vgl. die Gesichter in *Ein trockenes Bett, VII* und *VIII* aus dem vorangegangenen Jahr, neben denen sich Blumen befinden). Der Kehle entwachsen die Umrisse von drei anderen Blumen. Sind es Lilien? Ganz gewiss erscheint eine Lilie als Widerstand in *Wald IV*, der *Wald III* (Kopf ohne Körper bzw. Körper ohne Kopf) in der gleichen Pose vervollständigt, die der Künstler in den Photographien *Offenheit (Werk der Gnade*, S. 224*)* und *Wasser und Figur* im folgenden Jahr einnehmen wird.

In *Der Wald V* erstreckt sich eine Figur in Rückenlage auf einer Lichtung über drei Blatt Papier. Sie ist fast dreimal so breit wie die vorherigen Abbildungen. Der Wald ist nicht mehr grün (dessen geisterhafte Bäume sich als Abwesenheit manifestieren, als Stellen, wo die Olivtönung nicht aufgetragen wurde) und das Grün wurde versetzt, um den Körper zu umreißen (liegend? schwebend?), dessen Füße von Verletzlichkeit zeugen.

AR

clockwise from upper left
/von oben links im Uhrzeigersinn

THE FOREST I, LIGHT
11.5 x 11.5 inches (29 x 29 cm)
Private Collection, Menlo Park, California

DER WALD I, LICHT
11,5 x 11,5 Zoll (29 x 29 cm)
Privatsammlung, Menlo Park, Kalifornien

THE FOREST II, BIRD
11.5 x 11.5 inches (29 x 29 cm)
Private Collection, Menlo Park, California

DER WALD II, VOGEL
11,5 x 11,5 Zoll (29 x 29 cm)
Privatsammlung, Menlo Park, Kalifornien

THE FOREST IV, LILY
11.5 x 11.5 inches (29 x 29 cm)
Private Collection, Menlo Park, California

DER WALD IV, LILIE
11,5 x 11,5 Zoll (29 x 29 cm)
Privatsammlung, Menlo Park, Kalifornien

THE FOREST V, CLEARING
15 x 32 inches (38 x 81 cm)
William Griffin, Venice, California

DER WALD V, LICHTUNG
15 x 32 Zoll (38 x 81 cm)
Sammlung William Griffin, Venice, Kalifornien

THE FOREST III, TULIP
11.5 x 11.5 inches (29 x 29 cm)
Private Collection, Menlo Park, California

DER WALD III, TULPE
11,5 x 11,5 Zoll (29 x 29 cm)
Privatsammlung, Menlo Park, Kalifornien

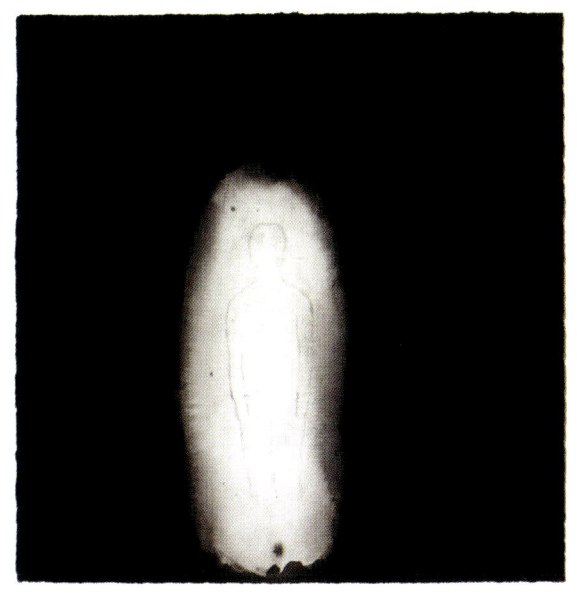
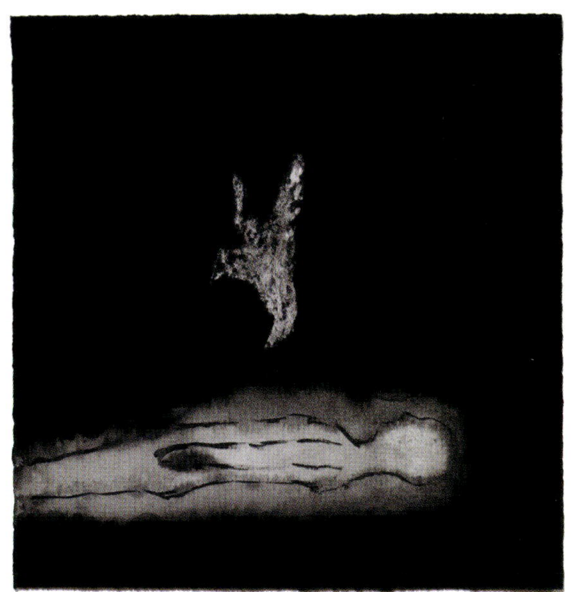
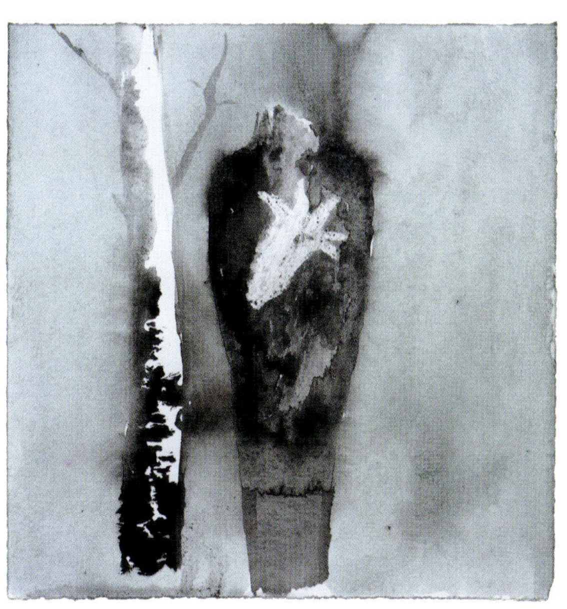
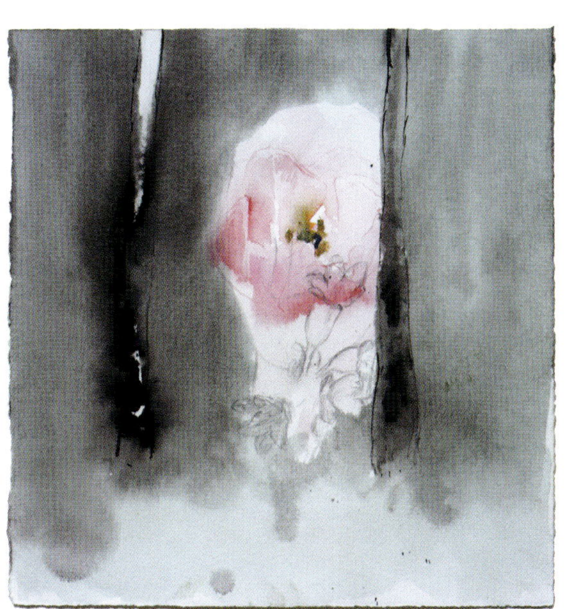
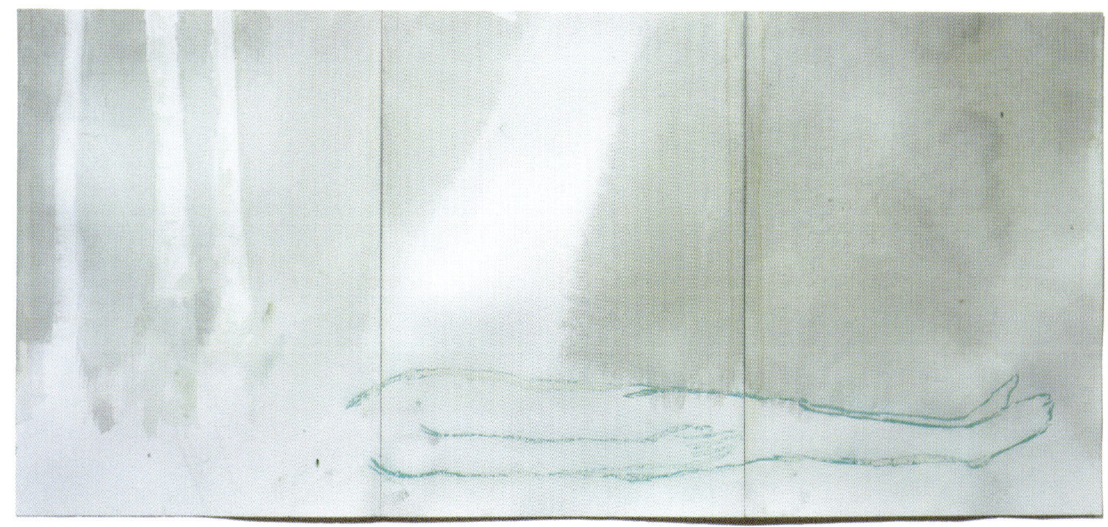

BODY IN A LARGE ROOM (BEAUTIFUL WORDS), 1999
Oil, graphite and tar on canvas
84 x 78 inches (213 x 198 cm)
RBC Dain Rauscher, Minneapolis, Minnesota

Is the water separated from the body by an indeterminate space, a distance we can never measure? Out of these stylized waves a fish head might emerge to take the place of the missing human head. A fish does just that in *Body in Obscurity (necessity)*, *Weight and Light* and *Glass fish in dark room (grace)*, all the same year, while a fish's head is drawn on a forehead in the sculptured head *Ocean* (p. 196). The body's proportions are related to the artist's body as a child. Is this body drowning in waves of memories? How can the 'large' room, the room of the mind, at once contain the past and constrain the body?

'Beautiful words' expresses judgment even though the image offers insufficient knowledge of the circumstances necessary to form a judgment. To this moment of evaluation we have no access because the face is missing, and the hands fold in on the body rather than express emotion. The pressure to judge coupled with insufficient grounds is a key source of the work's enigmas.

AR

KÖRPER IN GROSSEM ZIMMER (SCHÖNE WORTE), 1999
Öl, Graphit und Teer auf Leinwand
84 x 78 Zoll (213 x 198 cm)
RBC Dain Rauscher, Minneapolis, Minnesota

Wird das Wasser durch einen unbestimmbaren Raum vom Körper getrennt, eine Entfernung, die wir niemals messen können? Aus diesen stilisierten Wellen könnte ein Fischkopf auftauchen, um den Platz des fehlenden menschlichen Kopfes einzunehmen. In *Körper im Dunkeln (Notwendigkeit)*, *Gewicht und Licht* und *Glasfisch in dunkler Kammer (Anmut)*, die alle aus dem gleichen Jahr stammen, tut ein Fisch genau das, während sich auf der Stirn des Skulpturkopfes *Ozean* (S. 196) ein gezeichneter Fischkopf befindet. Die Körperproportionen beziehen sich auf den Körper des Künstlers als Kind. Ertrinkt dieser Körper in einem Meer der Erinnerungen? Wie kann das „große Zimmer", der Raum des Geistes, gleichzeitig die Vergangenheit enthalten und den Körper einzwängen?

„Schöne Worte" sprechen Urteile, obwohl das Bild ungenügendes Wissen über die Umstände bietet, die für eine Urteilsbildung erforderlich sind. Zu diesem Moment der Bewertung haben wir keinen Zugang, weil das Gesicht fehlt und die auf dem Körper gefalteten Hände keine Gefühle verraten. Der Zwang, ein Urteil ohne ausreichende Informationen zu fällen, ist ein wichtiger Schlüssel zu den Rätseln des Werks.

AR

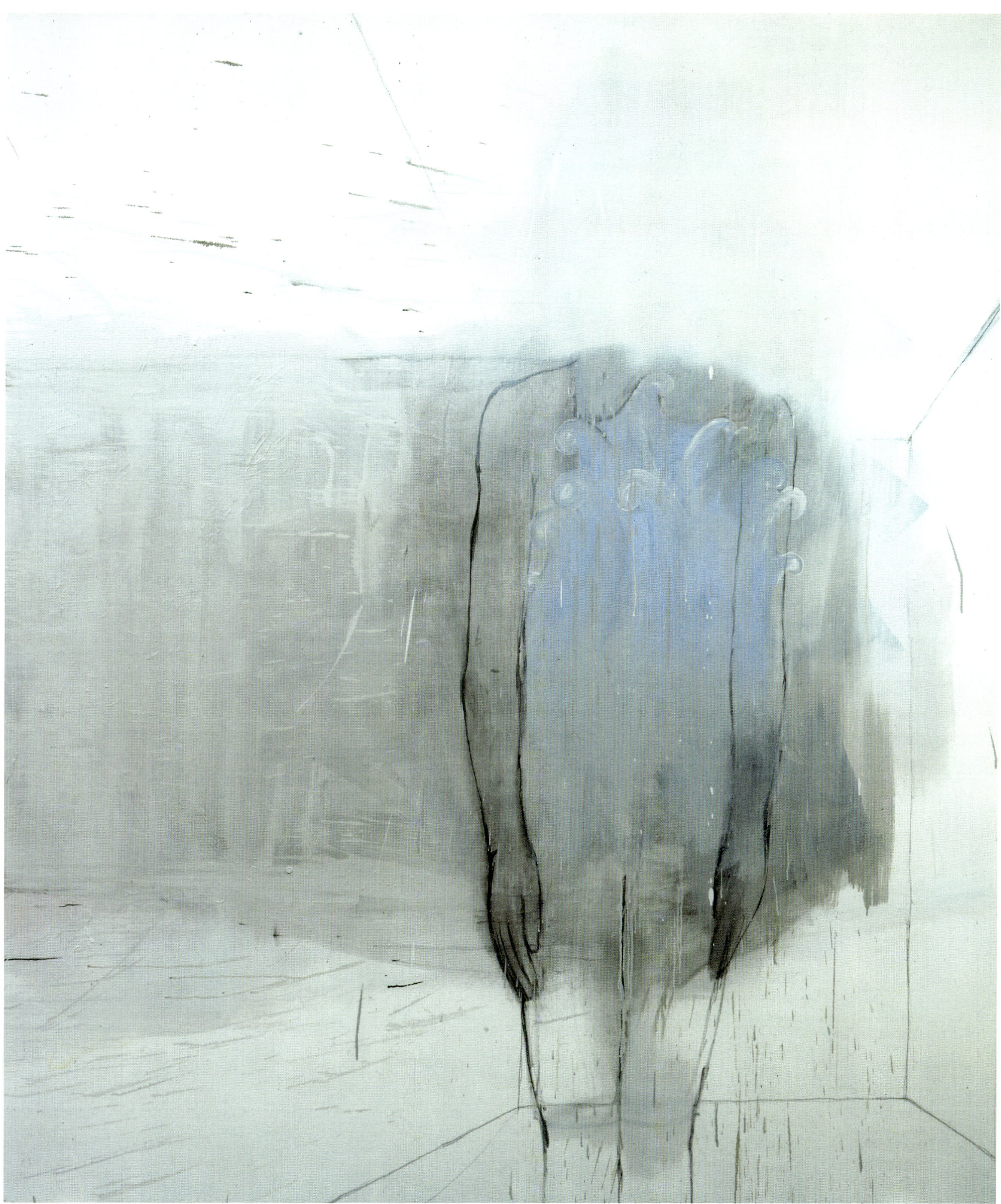

BODY AT REST (RENUNCIATION), 1999
Oil, and tar on canvas
66 x 72 inches (168 x 183 cm)
Collection of William Griffin, Venice, California

The figure from *Body in a Large Room* (p. 208) returns, now supine. And now flowers rise out of the body, just as the waves rise out of the *Body in a Large Room.* Those sunflowers are rendered with almost photographic realism, but so faint that they lose the substance the drawing conveys.

Is the present body asleep or dead? Which variety of 'rest'? And if dead, do the sunflowers then suggest the raising of the soul, or a version of the 'S' for Spirit, hovering over Hegel's tombstone in the Berlin photograph? Or is this image so deadpan, dumb, or lacking nuance as to cast doubt on such a reading? Maybe it is simply a figure at rest with flowers, a figure in nature. Or maybe we rest content with the bare fact of juxtaposition. The title's 'Renunciation' remains an irritant, however, for it seems in an undetermined way, to describe the juxtaposition.

By tradition, sunflowers signify temporality, as in William Blake's poem that marries uncannily with *Body at Rest.*

> Ah! Sun-flower! weary of time,
> Who countest the steps of the Sun:
> Seeking after that sweet golden clime
> Where the travellers journey is done.
>
> Where the Youth pined away with desire,
> And the pale Virgin shrouded in snow;
> Arise from their graves and aspire,
> Where my Sun-flower wishes to go.

Does the painting depict two blossoms or only one on the course of its diurnal journey? Turning toward the beholder or turning away? So that time itself moves across this still canvas?

Because this body extends beneath the bottom and off the right edge–the image posits an existence outside itself. The painting becomes less iconic, no longer the thing itself. 'Renunciation' or denial marks out a path of beauty.

AR

RUHENDER KÖRPER (VERZICHT), 1999
Öl und Teer auf Leinwand
66 x 72 Zoll (168 x 183 cm)
Sammlung William Griffin, Venice, Kalifornien

Die Figur aus *Körper in großem Zimmer* (S. 208) wird nunmehr in Rückenlage dargestellt. Und jetzt wachsen Blumen aus dem Körper, so wie dem *Körper in großem Zimmer* Wellen entspringen. Diese Sonnenblumen werden mit einem fast photographischen Realismus wiedergegeben, allerdings so zart, dass sie die von der Zeichnung vermittelte Substanz verlieren.

Schläft der dargestellte Körper oder ist er tot? Welche Art des „Ruhens" wird gezeigt? Wenn der Körper tot ist, bedeuten die Sonnenblumen das Aufsteigen der Seele oder eine Version des S für Spirit (Geist), das über Hegels Grabstein im Berlin-Photo schwebt? Oder ist dieses Bild so ausdrucksleer, dumm oder nuancenlos, dass Zweifel an einer solchen Auslegung angebracht sind? Vielleicht ist es nur eine Figur, die mit Blumen ruht, eine Figur in der Natur. Oder vielleicht geben wir uns mit der bloßen Tatsache der Nebeneinanderstellung zufrieden. Der Titel „Verzicht" bleibt aber irritierend, denn er scheint auf unbestimmte Weise die Nebeneinanderstellung zu beschreiben.

Traditionellerweise verkörpern Sonnenblumen die Zeitlichkeit, wie in William Blakes Gedicht, das sich auf unheimliche Weise mit *Ruhender Körper* verbindet.

> Ach Sonnenblume, müde der Zeit,
> in der du zähltest die Schritte der Sonne,
> Suchst jetzt nach dem süßgoldenen Grund
> Wo des Reisenden Weg ist zu End:
>
> Wohin auch der Jüngling, vor Sehnsucht verdorrt,
> Und die bleiche Jungfrau, bedeckt vom
> Leichentuch aus Schnee,
> sich erheben aus ihren Gräbern, um dorthin zu gehn,
> Wohin meine Sonnenblume sich sehnt.

Zeigt das Gemälde zwei Blüten oder nur eine auf ihrer täglichen Reise? Wendet sie sich dem Betrachter zu oder von ihm ab? So dass die Zeit selbst über diese reglose Leinwand streicht?

Da dieser Körper über den unteren Rand und die rechte Kante hinausreicht, postuliert das Bild eine Existenz außerhalb seines Selbst. Das Bild wird weniger ikonenhaft und ist nicht mehr die Sache selbst. „Verzicht" oder Verweigerung zeichnet einen Pfad der Schönheit.

AR

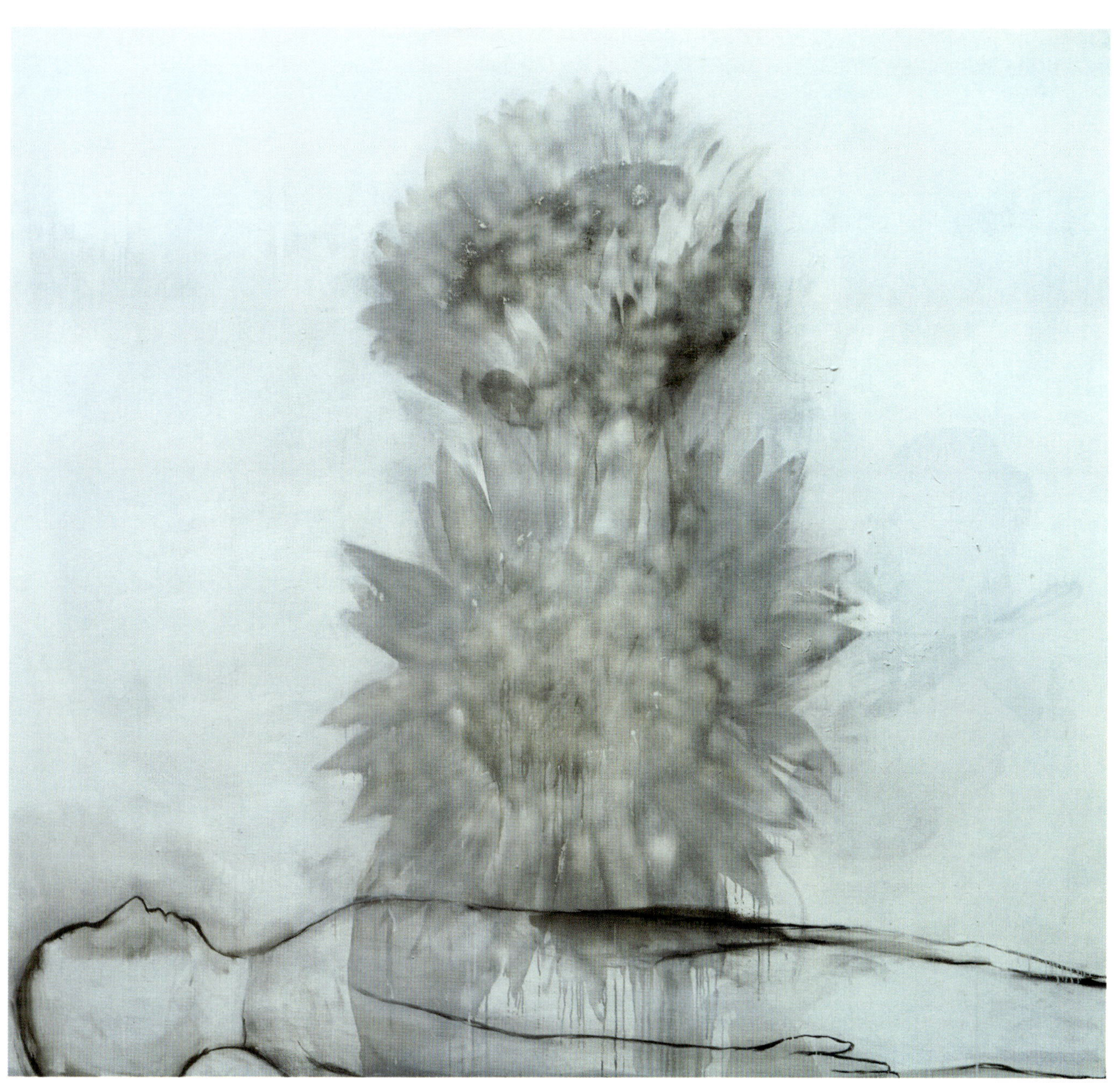

WINTER, 2000
each 18 x 18 inches (46 x 46 cm)

The notion of a winter journey is an old preoccupation of Martínez Celaya's as an unfamiliar landscape. Secondarily, the title points to the Schubert songs, with muted implications of a cycle, in this case of youth, thresholds, and wandering.

'Prohibidos,' or 'forbidden,' in the title of the first watercolor, suggests transgression of boundaries, here taking the form of the monstrous understood as the name for what cannot be classified. A human head turns egg, from which breaks forth a fully grown bird, wings already spread for flight. Is this youth imagining the bird, or the bird conjuring the youth? Both forms barely emerge from the watercolor–another sense of birth–as the application of watercolor wrinkles the craft paper and forms a kind of mandorla.

The series is bookended by two isolated figures done in white. The images could move from day to night and, if we like, through a life cycle; the weighted, oversized head suggesting old age. In any case, the flowers that ring the neck, rendered in blood-like tones, articulate decoration and violation, innocence and experience.

AR

WINTER, 2000
jeweils 18 x 18 Zoll (46 x 46 cm)

Die Vorstellung einer Winterreise als unbekannter Landschaft hat Martínez Celaya schon lange fasziniert. Weiterhin ist der Titel ein Hinweis auf die Schubert-Lieder mit den leisen Implikationen eines Zyklus, in diesem Fall von Jugend, Schwellen und Wanderung.

„Prohibidos" oder „Verboten", der Titel des ersten Aquarells, lässt die Überschreitung von Grenzen vermuten, die hier die Form des Monströsen annimmt, als Name für das verstanden, was nicht eingeordnet werden kann. Ein menschlicher Kopf verwandelt sich in ein Ei, aus dem ein ausgewachsener Vogel hervorbricht, dessen Flügel sich bereits zum Flug spreizen. Stellt sich dieser Junge den Vogel vor oder beschwört der Vogel den Jungen? Beide Formen treten kaum aus dem Aquarell hervor – ein weiteres Bild der Geburt –, wobei das Auftragen von Aquarellfarbe das Papier in Falten wirft und eine Art Mandorla bildet.

Der Zyklus wird von zwei isolierten Figuren in Weiß gerahmt. Die Bilder könnten sich vom Tag in die Nacht verschieben und, wenn wir so möchten, einen Lebenszyklus durchlaufen, wobei der gewichtige, übergroße Kopf hohes Alter vermuten lässt. Auf jeden Fall sprechen die blutfarbenen Blumen um den Hals von Verzierung und Gewalt, von Unschuld und Erfahrung.

AR

JUEGOS PROHIBIDOS (FORBIDDEN GAMES)
Watercolor on paper
Courtesy of Griffin Contemporary, Venice, California

JUEGOS PROHIBIDOS (VERBOTENE SPIELE)
Aquarellfarbe auf Papier
Courtesy of Griffin Contemporary, Venice, Kalifornien

p. 214/S. 214

THE PLAINS
Watercolor and india ink on paper
Collection of Ike and Marsha Coron,
Malibu, California

DIE EBENE
Aquarellfarbe und chinesische Tusche auf Papier
Sammlung Ike und Marsha Coron,
Malibu, Kalifornien

WANDERER (NIGHT)
Watercolor on paper
Collection of Michael Rank, North Carolina

WANDERER (NACHT)
Aquarellfarbe auf Papier
Sammlung Michael Rank, North Carolina

p. 215/S. 215

BIRCH AND MOUNTAINS
Watercolor and india ink on paper
Collection of Ike and Marsha Coron,
Malibu, California

BIRKE UND BERGE
Aquarellfarbe und chinesische Tusche auf Papier
Sammlung Ike und Marsha Coron,
Malibu, Kalifornien

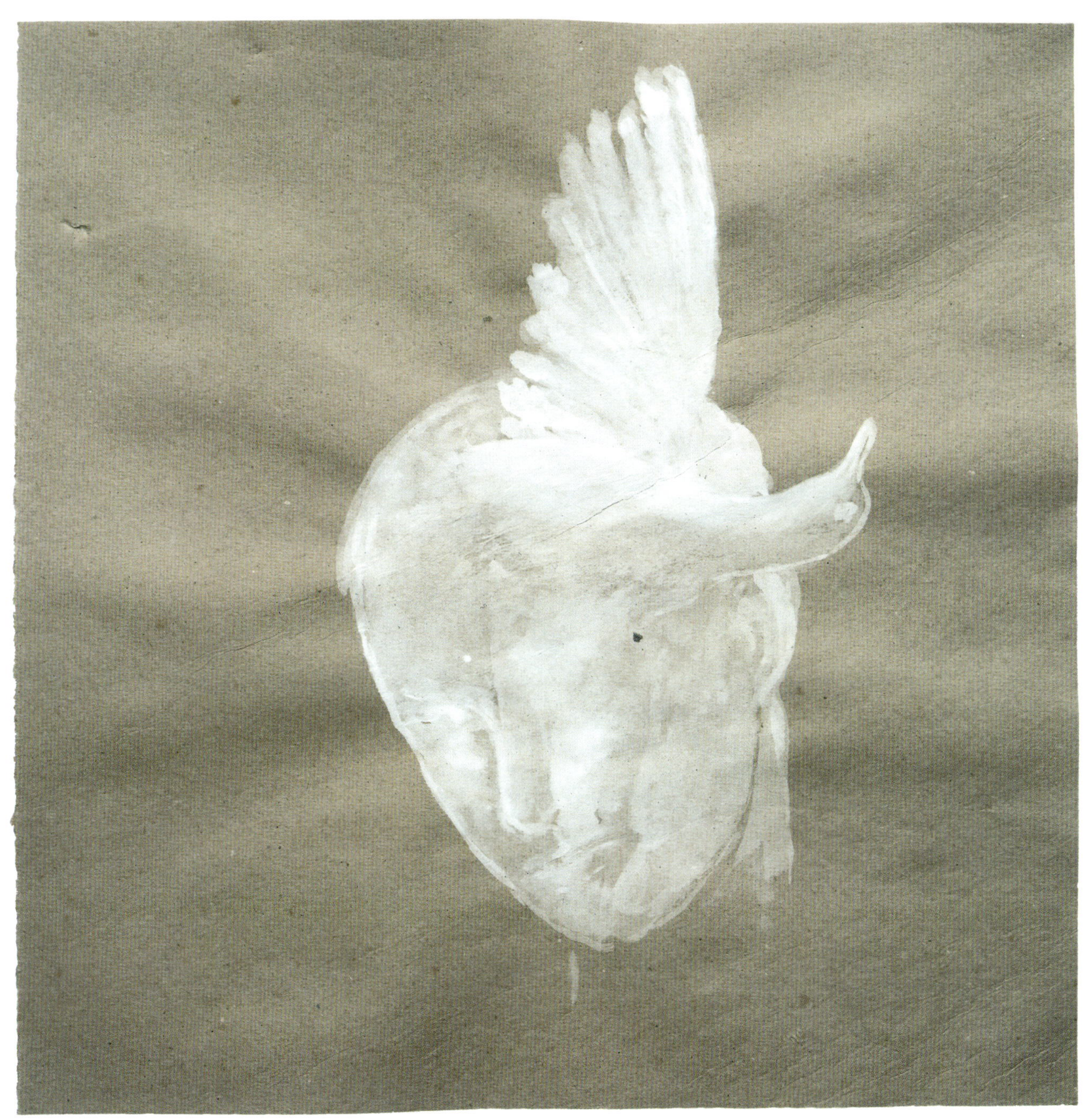

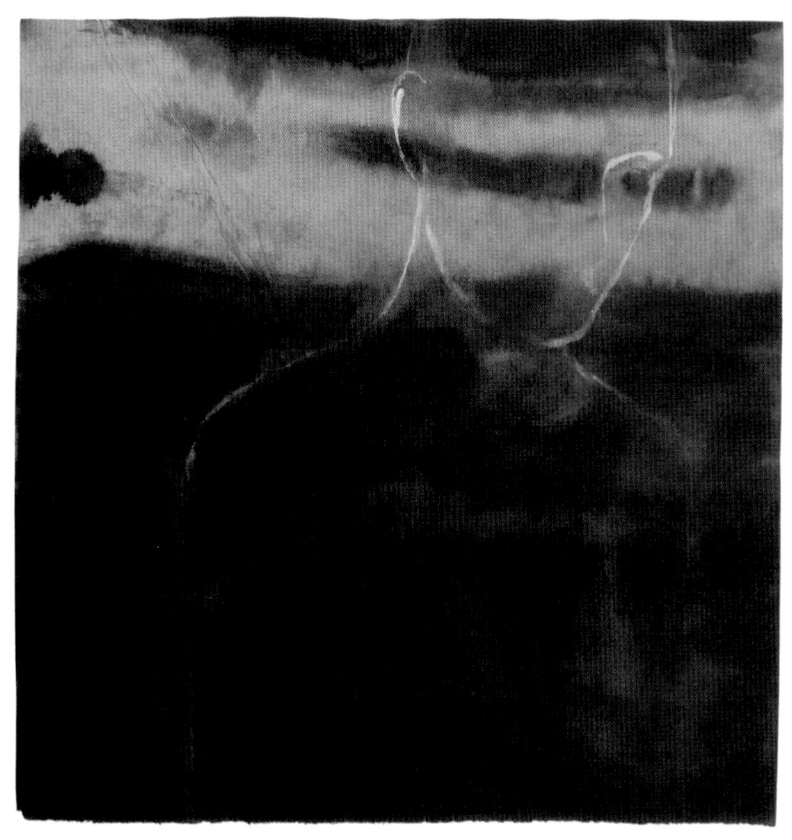

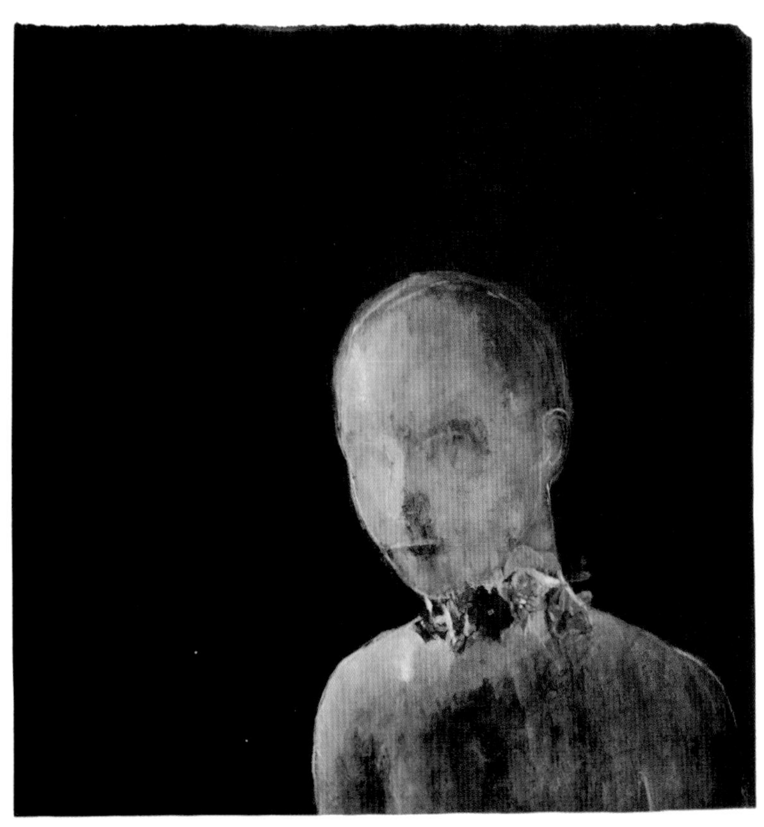

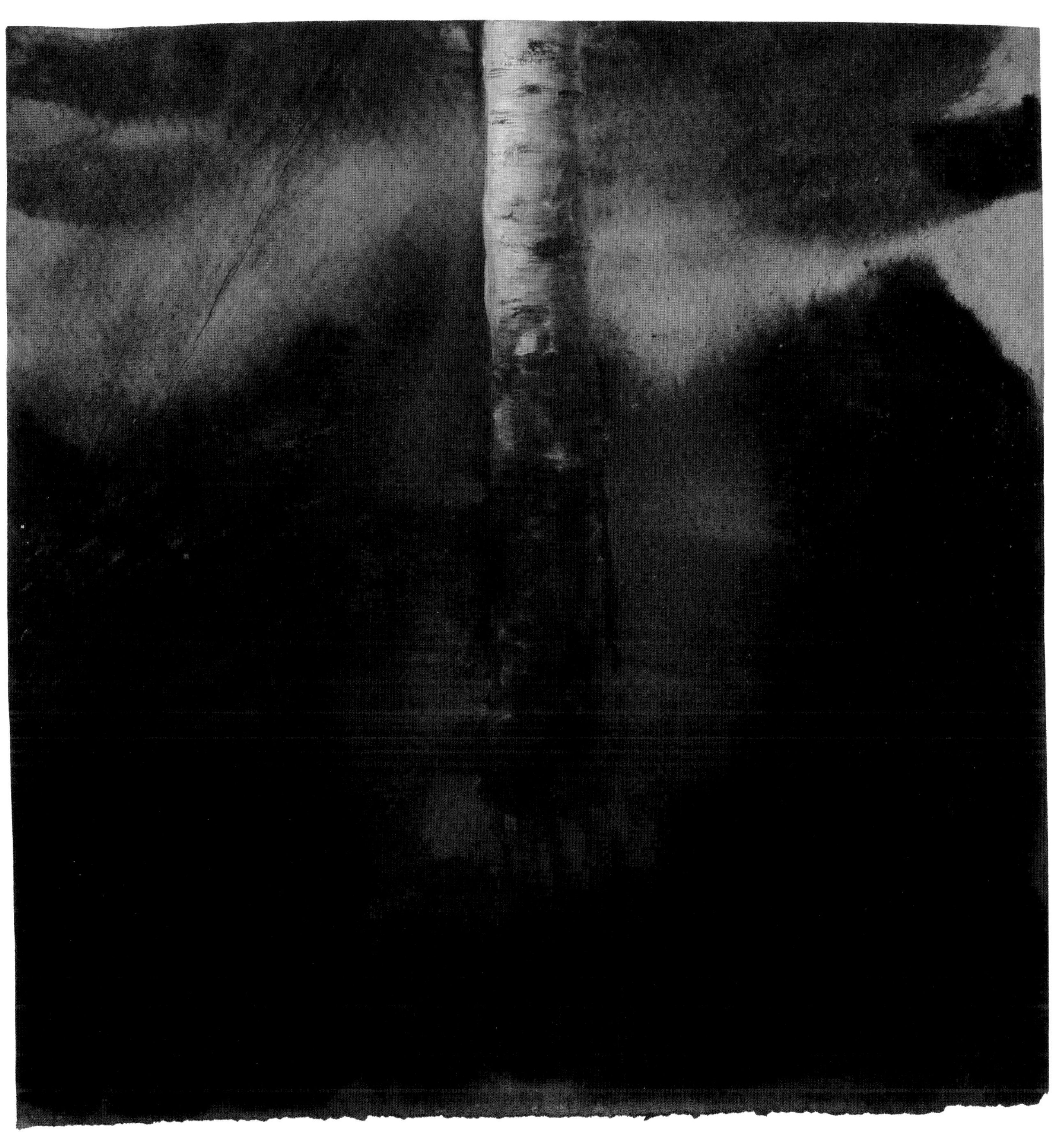

SELF AND OTHER/DAS SELBST UND ANDERES

the algebra of identity/die Algebra der Identität

ELEGIAS, 2000–2001
Chromogenic prints

A color photograph at a huge scale showing the frontal bust of the artist's wife at life size, or slightly larger. The model stares at the viewer–her eyes are red, bloodshot–her gaze made more potent by the way the paint that covers and whitens her skin outlines her eye sockets and eyebrows. The birch grove, the piece of the mountain, and the sky behind are out of focus, they appear in deep space behind the sharply focused bust; they provide a setting for the model. Because we cannot see just where the model stands, the landscape also reads on the picture plane as a flat pattern, and as such 'captures' or anchors the model in the composition. Consider how the movemented tree trunks in the grove criss-cross behind the woman's head. In an important compositional way these trees are more vivid and alive than the model, whose impassive, dead-pan aspect, whose frontality removes her from the world we know.

This photo and the next in this exhibition, which depicts the artist, are pendants, portraits of an odd sort, husband and wife. Let me begin with *Winter the Most Truthful, Release.*

Martínez Celaya works with/plays with a whole genre not unlike that of the kitsch objects he dealt with in the early and mid 1990s. And like those earlier explorations, his photo in this instance avoids any sort of slickness; it has a rawness that stops us and makes us attend to it as something special. Of course, kitsch objects (rabbits, Christmas tree ornaments) are one thing, representations of human beings quite another. Does Martínez Celaya try to turn the latter into objects too? What about the dead-pan tone of the image in this photograph?

No, not objects. We deal with another kind of figure in art, formal and still, but palpably human and present all the same. We deal with a portrait, to be sure, but the subject does not act. (One cannot help but think of the remoteness and austerity of Ancient Egyptian sculpture.)

Here Martínez Celaya exploits the transparency of the photo as medium in our culture to present an image within an image. I mean that he has used his wife's body as a support for a 'painting' that he then puts inside another 'painting,' that is, inside a landscape (a photo of a landscape can take the place of a painting of one). The artist neatly reverses his

ELEGIEN, 2000–2001
Chromogenic prints

Ein großes Farbphoto mit einer Frontalansicht des Oberkörpers der Frau des Künstlers, lebensgroß oder etwas größer. Das Modell starrt den Betrachter an – ihre Augen sind rot, blutunterlaufen, ihr Blick ist noch eindringlicher durch die Art, in der der Künstler ihre Haut bedeckt und weiß färbt, ihre Augenhöhlen und -brauen umreißt. Der Birkenhain, ein Stück des Berges und der Himmel im Hintergrund sind unscharf. Sie erscheinen im tiefen Raum hinter dem deutlich dargestellten Oberkörpet, bieten einen Schauplatz für das Modell. Da wir nicht sehen können, wo das Modell steht, erscheint auch die Landschaft als flaches Muster und fängt als solches das Modell ein oder verankert es in der Komposition. Beachten Sie, wie die Baumstämme im Hain sich hinter dem Kopf der Frau kreuz und quer bewegen. Bedeutsam an der Komposition ist, dass die Bäume lebendiger sind als das Modell, dessen Teilnahmslosigkeit, Ausdruckslosigkeit und Frontalität es von der uns bekannten Welt entfernt.

Dieses Photo und das nächste der Ausstellung, das den Künstler zeigt, sind Pendants, seltsame Porträts, Ehemann und Ehefrau. Lassen Sie mich mit *Winter der Wahrhaftigste, Befreiung* beginnen.

Martínez Celaya arbeitet und spielt mit einem ganzen Genre, das den Kitschobjekten ähnelt, mit denen er sich Anfang und Mitte der neunziger Jahre befasste. Wie die früheren Erkundungen vermeidet das Photo jede Glattheit; es hat eine Rohheit, die uns zwingt innezuhalten und es als etwas Besonders zu betrachten. Natürlich sind Kitschobjekte (Kaninchen, Weihnachtsbaumschmuck) und Menschendarstellungen nicht das Gleiche. Versucht Martínez Celaya, die Letzten auch in Objekte zu verwandeln? Und was heißt die Ausdruckslosigkeit in diesem Photo?

Nein, doch keine Objekte. Eine andere Art der Kunstfigur, formal und still, aber trotzdem greifbar menschlich und gegenwärtig. Sicherlich, ein Porträt, aber das Modell handelt nicht. (Man kann nicht umhin, an die Entrücktheit und Strenge altägyptischer Skulptur zu denken.)

Martínez Celaya bedient sich hier der Durchschaubarkeit des Photos als Medium in unserer Kultur, um ein Bild im Bild zu präsentieren. Damit meine ich, dass er den Körper seiner Frau als Unterlage für ein „Gemälde" benutzt, das er dann in einem anderen „Gemälde" unterbringt, in einer Landschaft (ein Landschaftsphoto kann den Platz eines Landschaftsgemäldes einnehmen). Der Künstler kehrt seine Experimente der ersten beiden Ausstellungssektionen raffiniert um, wo er

WINTER THE MOST TRUTHFUL, RELEASE, 2000
42 x 57.5 inches (107 x 146 cm)
Courtesy of Enrique Martínez Celaya

WINTER DER WAHRHAFTIGSTE, BEFREIUNG, 2000
42 x 57,5 Zoll (107 x 146 cm)
Courtesy of Enrique Martínez Celaya

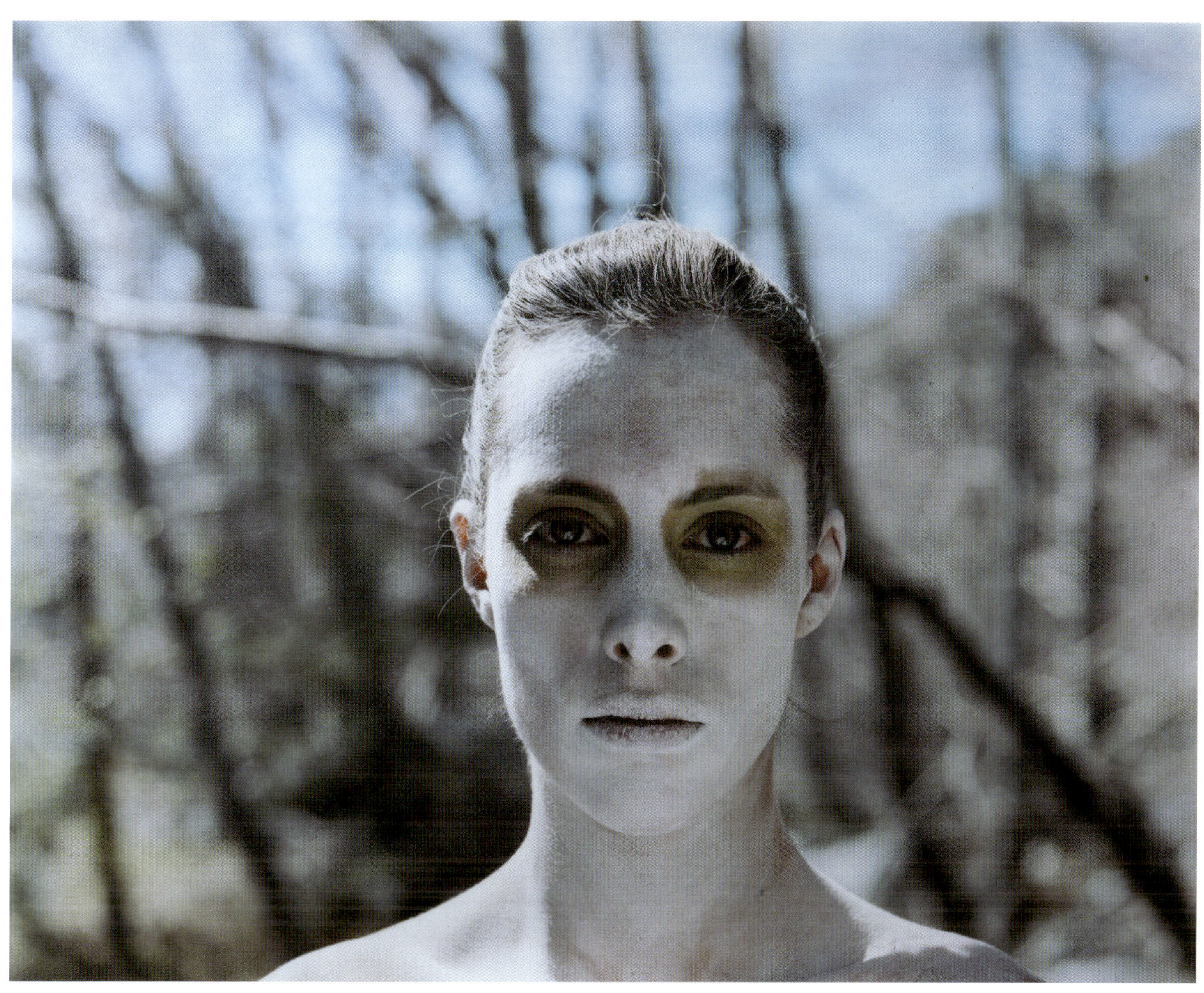

experiments in the first two sections of this exhibition where he presented canvas, paper, and plaster figured as our bodies (see my comments above). Here the presentation is a landscape, made vivid by the landscape (the criss-crossing tree trunks), a head which functions to enshrine awareness as eyesight, as the gaze. Those reddish eyes: red with trying to see?

We deal with one of Modernity's oldest icons: with the landscape ordered by the human gaze, by human perception, by sight. One thinks immediately of the British pre-Romantic and Romantic theorists of landscape gardening, who invented the discourse of the Picturesque. They theorized about the viewer and his/her subject position, about his/her role as the orderer, indeed the creator of vistas by means of taking a position and looking, by framing the landscape as if it were a painted picture. In this way the Romantic subject wrote himself and herself into Nature. By indirection, by creeping up on the issue slyly, by distilling our everyday awarenesses (of fashion photos, say), Martínez Celaya again creates a new icon of awareness. So, not just the canvas, paper, or plaster figured, but the picture figured.

The title in parentheses here, 'The River,' refers to the plaster sculpture of a woman in this exhibition (p. 144) that the artist used as a 'canvas'; that he transformed into a painting (into a riverine landscape). In my commentary on *The River*, I said that Martínez Celaya had most emphatically figured a painted surface as our bodies. In the huge photograph now before us the artist's body becomes the support for a painting, photograph as painting. The upper half of his body, his back, rises at the center of, and parallel to the picture plane, over life-size. The photo's frame cuts off the top third of the artist's head. The artist stands in a birch grove to gaze out into the mountain landscape. As in the previous work, the out-of-focus tree trunks and limbs anchor the body, both in space (the birch grove can appear to be the setting) and in the composition's flat design (the vivid, movemented trees criss-cross behind the artist's body and 'capture' it). And here the artist's wife, Alexandra, became the painter, covering her husband's skin with red paint, then drawing a diagram on his back, a 'life line.' Our eye follows the life line to various 'stations,' each labeled. At the top is the station called 'estrella' or star. Halfway down the artist's back is 'cicatriz' or scar; at the bottom is '10 años' or ten years.

This photo presents a figured landscape just as the previous work does. Again we have a 'painting' inside a 'painting.' Again we have

Leinwand, Papier und Gips als unsere Körper verwendete (s. meine obigen Kommentare). Hier ist die Darstellung eine Landschaft, die durch die Landschaft belebt wird (die kreuz und quer stehenden Baumstämme), die Funktion des Kopfes ist es, Bewusstsein als Sehvermögen, als Blick zu bewahren. Diese geröteten Augen: rot vom Versuch zu Sehen?

Sie ist eines der ältesten Sinnbilder der Moderne: die Landschaft, die der menschliche Blick, die menschliche Wahrnehmung, das Sehvermögen ordnet. Man denkt sofort an die britische Vorromantik und die romantischen Theoretiker des Landschaftsgartens, die den Diskurs über das Malerische begannen. Sie theoretisierten über den Betrachter und seine Position, seine Rolle als Ordnender, sogar als Schöpfer von Sichtachsen durch die Einnahme einer Position und das Schauen, durch das Rahmen der Landschaft, als wäre sie ein Gemälde. So drückte das romantische Ich der Natur seinen Stempel auf. Durch indirektes Vorgehen, Heranschleichen an die Thematik und Destillieren unseres alltäglichen Bewusstseins (wie von Modephotos) schafft Martínez Celaya wieder ein neues Symbol des Bewusstseins. Und nicht nur Leinwand, Papier oder Gipsfigur, auch das Bild wird zum Gegenstand.

Der Titel in Klammern, „Der Fluss", bezieht sich auf die Gipsfigur einer Frau in Abteilung II dieser Ausstellung (S. 144), die der Künstler als „Leinwand" benutzte und in ein Gemälde, eine flussartige Landschaft verwandelte. In meinem Kommentar zu *Der Fluss* sagte ich, dass Martínez Celaya eine gemalte Oberfläche mit Nachdruck als unsere Körper gestaltete. Auf dem riesigen Photo vor uns wird der Körper des Künstlers Fundament für ein Gemälde, für ein Photo als Gemälde. Sein Oberkörper und sein Rücken erheben sich überlebensgroß aus der Mitte, parallel zur Bildfläche. Der Rahmen des Photos schneidet das obere Kopfdrittel ab. Der Künstler steht in einem Birkenhain und blickt auf die Berglandschaft. Wie im vorausgehenden Werk verankern die unscharfen Baumstämme und -äste den Körper im Raum (der Birkenhain ist wohl die Umgebung) und in der flachen Komposition (die lebendigen Bäume bewegen sich kreuz und quer hinter dem Körper des Künstlers und „fangen diesen ein"). Und hier wird Alexandra, die Frau des Künstlers, zur Malerin, die die Haut ihres Mannes mit roter Farbe bestreicht und dann ein Diagramm, „eine Lebenslinie", auf seinen Rücken zeichnet. Unser Auge folgt dieser zu verschiedenen beschilderten „Stationen". Oben findet sich „estrella" (Stern), auf halbem Weg „cicatriz" (Narbe), unten „10 años" (zehn Jahre).

Wie bei der vorangehenden Arbeit ist dieses Photo eine gestaltete Landschaft. Wieder haben wir ein „Gemälde" in einem „Gemälde", wieder

TRACES AND MARKS (THE RIVER), 2000
42 x 64 inches (107 x 163 cm)
Courtesy of Enrique Martínez Celaya

SPUREN UND MARKIERUNGEN (DER FLUSS), 2000
42 x 64 Zoll (107 x 163 cm)
Courtesy of Enrique Martínez Celaya

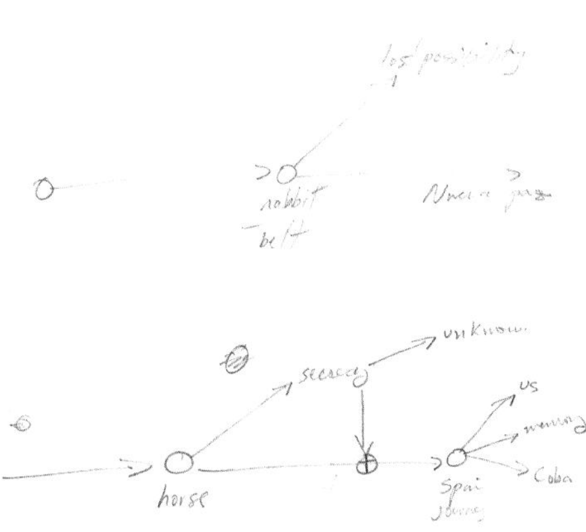

Sketchbook/Skizzenbuch, 2000

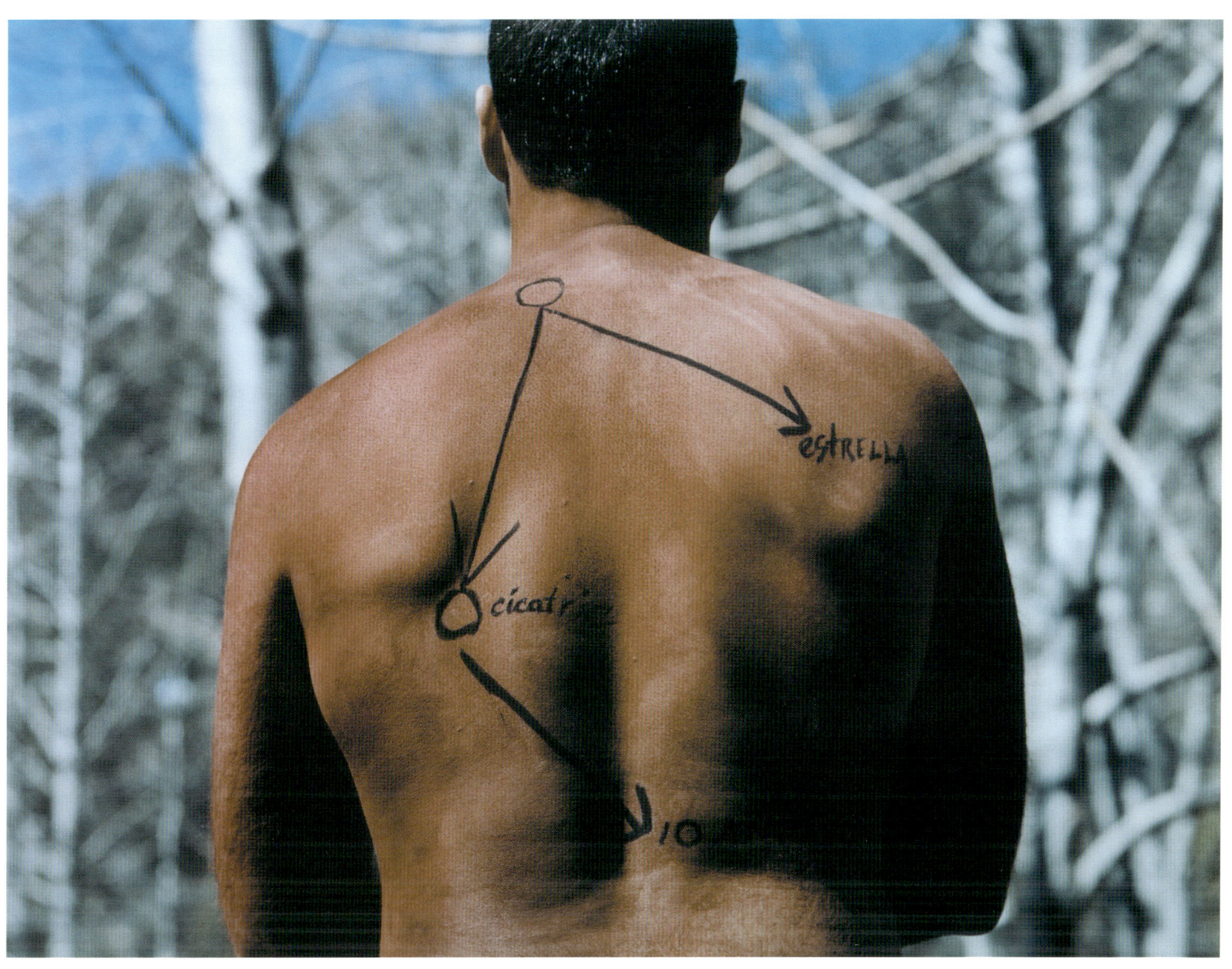
ESTRELLA

the contrast of wintry grays and whites with the color red. Again the stillness and the quiet of the frontal bust and winter landscape, but the vividness of the movemented trees and the urgency of the red; here the body presented as a wound.

The reciprocity of these 'portraits' can fascinate: I mean that in *Winter the Most Truthful, Release* the husband 'paints' his wife, and in *Traces and Marks*, the wife 'paints' her husband. Notions of depiction, of representation, come newly under scrutiny. The artist and his model? Who does the 'painting' here? Who the modeling? This pair of 'portraits' mixes up notions of artists gazing at their subjects, to put before the viewer a visual metaphor of human beings joined.

A large color photograph of a young woman, nude, standing in a birch grove early on a winter afternoon, much as the artist stood at the seaside in *Frankness*. Again a 'painting' inside a 'painting.' The photo, I insist, counts as a kind of painting. And the model's body counts as another. White paint covers most of her skin, she becomes the color of the birches and dull brown tints her hair the color of wintry leaves. The artist's wife drew a life-line upon her torso. The model, centered, frontal, and all but unmovemented, dominates the picture plane. All but unmovemented? Her head tips from vertical ever so slightly. A photo allows us to read any figure's slightest movement, she shocks us with her presence as a human being, her vulnerability in this setting, and her nakedness which the white body paint and the life line hardly dissemble. Moreover, we can see how she stands on the forest floor. The spatial stage is deep and convincing, one which we know in our bones how to read (we are that familiar with what camera lenses can do).

As in the other photos in this series, we deal with a figured landscape. The artist writes the human body upon the world (here the model takes on aspects of birch trees). But by putting the female nude in the birch grove, Martínez Celaya does not simply tap into some old Romantic project (Picturesque landscape, say), but a great Humanist one. Painters have explored the nude in a landscape from the time of Giorgione and Titian on down to Cézanne (and beyond). This long Western story adds resonances, and not just to this piece, but to the series to which this photo belongs.

JE

den Kontrast zwischen winterlichen Grau- und Weißtönen und Rot. Wieder die Stille der Frontalbüste und der Winterlandschaft und zugleich die Lebendigkeit der bewegten Bäume und die Dringlichkeit des Rots; hier ist der Körper als Wunde dargestellt.

Die Gegenseitigkeit dieser „Porträts" kann faszinieren: Ich meine, dass in *Winter der Wahrhaftigste, Befreiung* der Mann seine Frau „malt" und dass in *Spuren und Markierungen* die Frau ihren Mann „malt". Die Vorstellungen von Schilderung und von Darstellung werden erneut durchleuchtet. Der Künstler und sein Modell? Wer „malt" hier? Wer ist das Modell? Dieses Paar „Porträts" vermischt Vorstellungen von Künstlern, die auf ihr Modell blicken, um dem Betrachter eine visuelle Metapher verbundener menschlicher Wesen zu bieten.

Eine große Farbphotographie einer jungen nackten Frau, an einem frühen Winternachmittag in einem Birkenhain, wie der Künstler in *Offenheit* an der Küste steht. Wieder ein „Gemälde" in einem „Gemälde". Ich bestehe darauf, dass das Photo als eine Art Gemälde gelten kann. Und der Körper des Modells zählt als ein weiteres. Ein Großteil ihrer Haut ist mit weißer Farbe bedeckt. Sie nimmt die Farbe der Birken an und ein stumpfes Braun verleiht ihrem Haar die Farbe von Blättern im Winter. Die Frau des Künstlers zog auf ihrem Körper eine Lebenslinie. Das Modell steht zentriert und frontal und fast bewegungslos, es beherrscht die Bildfläche. Fast unbeweglich? Ihr Kopf neigt sich ganz leicht aus der Senkrechten. Ein Photo ermöglicht uns, die winzigste Bewegung einer jeden Figur zu sehen. Sie schockiert uns mit ihrer Präsenz als menschliches Wesen, ihrer Verletzlichkeit in dieser Umgebung, und ihre Nacktheit mit der weißen Körperfarbe und die kaum verborgene Lebenslinie können sich kaum verstellen. Auch können wir sehen, wie sie auf dem Waldboden steht. Die räumliche Bühne ist tief und überzeugend, und wir wissen sie mit jeder Faser unseres Körpers zu deuten (wir wissen, was Kameraobjektive erreichen können).

Wie bei den anderen Photos der Serie handelt es sich um eine gestaltete Landschaft. Der Künstler schreibt den menschlichen Körper auf die Welt (hier erhält das Modell Merkmale der Birken). Allerdings setzt Martínez Celaya mit der Platzierung einer nackten weiblichen Figur in einen Birkenhain nicht nur ein altes romantisches (wie die malerische Landschaft), sondern auch ein großes humanistisches Projekt fort. Maler haben seit der Zeit Giorgiones und Tizians bis zu Cézanne (und darüber hinaus) nackte Figuren in einer Landschaft erkundet. Diese lange abendländische Tradition verleiht nicht nur diesem Werk, sondern auch der Serie, zu der dieses Photo gehört, Nachhaltigkeit.

JE

WITNESS AND RECORD, 2000
42 x 43 inches (107 x 109 cm)
Courtesy of Enrique Martínez Celaya

ZEUGE UND PROTOKOLL, 2000
42 x 43 Zoll (107 x 109 cm)
Courtesy of Enrique Martínez Celaya

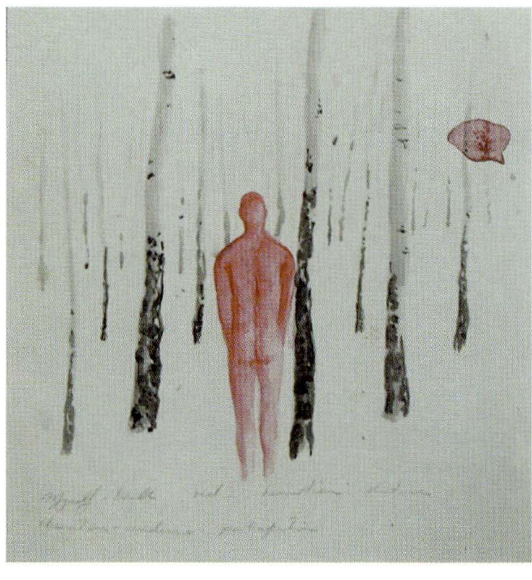

STUDY FOR TRACES AND MARKS
/STUDIE FÜR SPUREN UND MARKIERUNGEN, 2000
Courtesy of Enrique Martínez Celaya

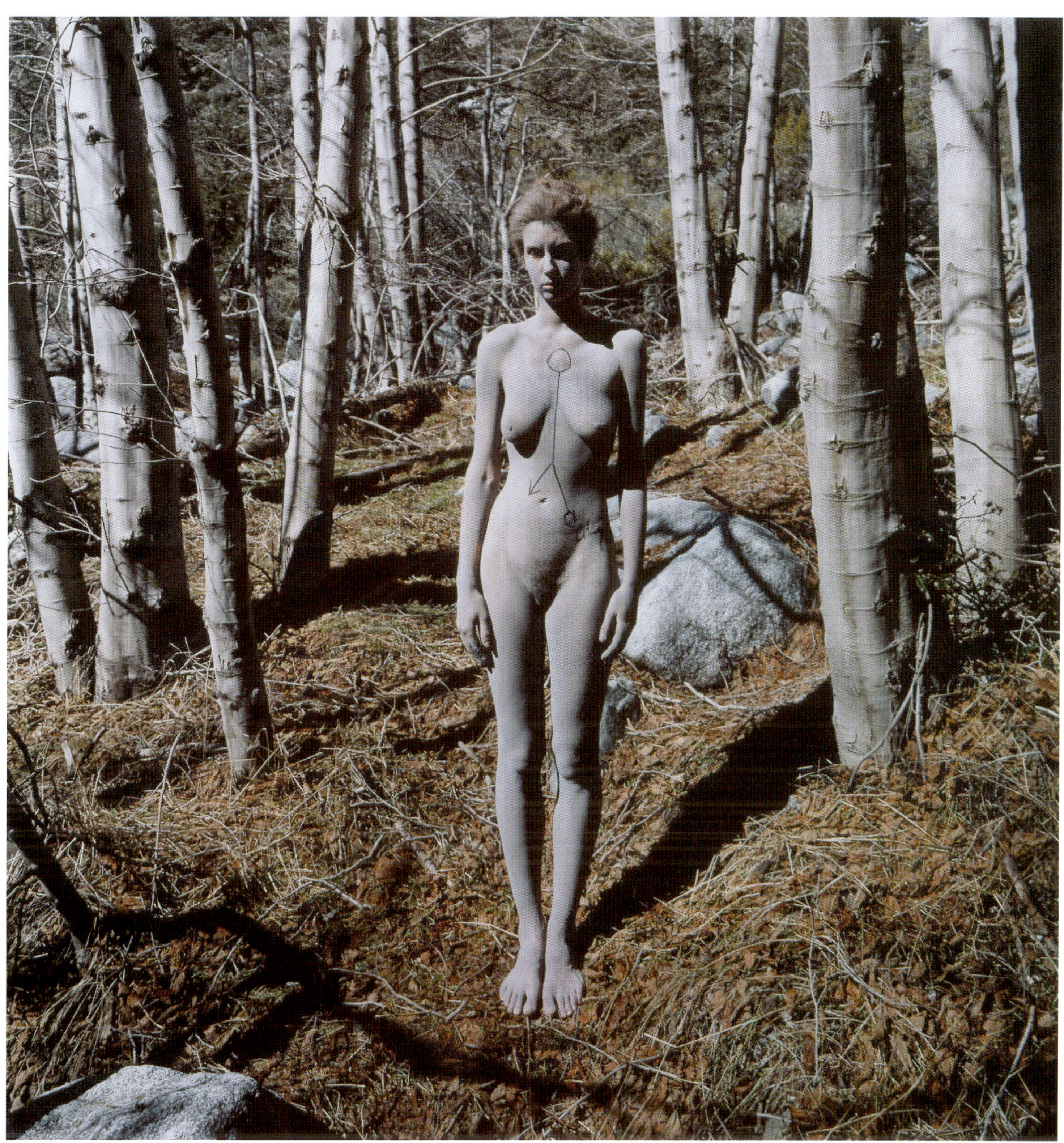

FRANKNESS (WORK OF MERCY), 2000
Acrylic on silver gelatin print
60 x 30 inches (152 x 76 cm)
Neuberger Berman Collection

Another figured landscape. This five-foot-high, black-and-white photograph shows a silhouetted image of the artist, naked, at beachside, only slightly less than life-size. He stands centered at the picture plane, parallel to it, and gazes either outward toward the ocean, or toward the viewer, one cannot tell which. The silhouette is heightened by an aureole, and by the fact that the body is seen from slightly below looking up (the horizon cuts across the figure's chest). A self-portrait. Again we have a 'painting' inside a 'painting.' The artist's body, non-movemented, standing utterly still, becomes a kind of canvas which the artist painted with blotchy polka dots and with a hummingbird in grisaille (both the polka dots and hummingbird were painted in acrylic directly on the photographic print; the aureole was created in the photographic printing process). Martínez Celaya treats his silhouette in this photo as he might treat stretched canvas: both as a flat surface (note the pattern of polka dots) and as a window (note the hummingbird hovering in space).

The bird flies at the level of the voice box, at the larynx of the silhouetted figure, and thus at the place of breathing (of life) and of language. As in previous works in this exhibition, Martínez Celaya activates imagery conjured by the poet Paul Celan (see, for example, the commentary for *Berlin*, p. 176). The bird dissembles the poet's violent imagery of life cut off, of breathing and words stopped, and alarmingly, telescopes signs of liberation (the bird's flight) with the memory of the poet's death by drowning. The life-giving sea? Life taking?

The aureole puts a stress on the old Romantic theme of human awareness being coextensive with the world (with the seascape). But the way the body disappears, in the surface of the photo (it becomes a polka dotted silhouette), in being treated as a window by itself, reinvigorates the old theme.

JE

OFFENHEIT (WERK DER GNADE), 2000
Acryl auf Silbergelatineabzug
60 x 30 Zoll (152 x 76 cm)
Sammlung Neuberger Berman

Eine weitere gestaltete Landschaft Diese 1,50 m hohe Schwarzweißphotographie zeigt die Silhouette des Künstlers, nackt am Strand, etwas unter Lebensgröße. Er steht mitten auf der Bildfläche und parallel zu ihr. Man kann nicht feststellen, ob er entweder nach außen in Richtung Meer oder in Richtung Betrachter blickt. Die Silhouette wird durch eine Aureole und durch die schwache Untersicht (der Horizont liegt in Höhe ihrer Brust) „erhöht". Ein Selbstporträt. Wieder haben wir ein „Gemälde" in einem „Gemälde". Der völlig stille Körper des Künstlers wird zu einer Art Leinwand, die der Künstler mit einem fleckigen Punktmuster und mit einer Kolibri-Grisaille bemalte (das Punktmuster und auch der Kolibri wurden mit Acrylfarben direkt auf den Photoabzug gemalt; die Aureole wurde im Entwicklungsprozess geschaffen). Martínez Celaya behandelt seine Silhouette in diesem Photo, wie er eine Leinwand behandeln könnte: zugleich wie eine flache Oberfläche (beachten Sie das Punktmuster) und als Fenster (beachten Sie den im Raum schwebenden Kolibri).

Der Vogel fliegt auf Höhe des Kehlkopfes der als Silhouette dargestellten Figur, also dem Ort des Atmens (des Lebens) und der Sprache. Wie in vorangegangenen Werken der Ausstellung erweckt Martínez Celaya Bilder zum Leben, die vom Dichter Paul Celan heraufbeschworen wurden (siehe zum Beispiel den Kommentar zu *Berlin*, S. 176). Der Vogel verbirgt die gewalttätigen Bilder des Dichters über das jäh beendete Leben, den angehaltenen Atem und die nicht ausgesprochenen Worte und schiebt alarmierenderweise Zeichen der Befreiung (der Flug des Vogels) mit der Erinnerung an den Tod des Dichters durch Ertrinken ineinander. Das Leben spendende Meer? Das Leben nehmend?

Die Aureole betont das alte romantische Thema der Identität von menschlichem Bewusstsein und der Außenwelt (mit der Meereslandschaft). Aber die Art und Weise, wie der Körper in der Oberfläche des Photos verschwindet und zur Punktmustersilhouette wird, weil er sich selbst wie ein Fenster behandelt, erweckt das alte Thema wieder zum Leben.

JE

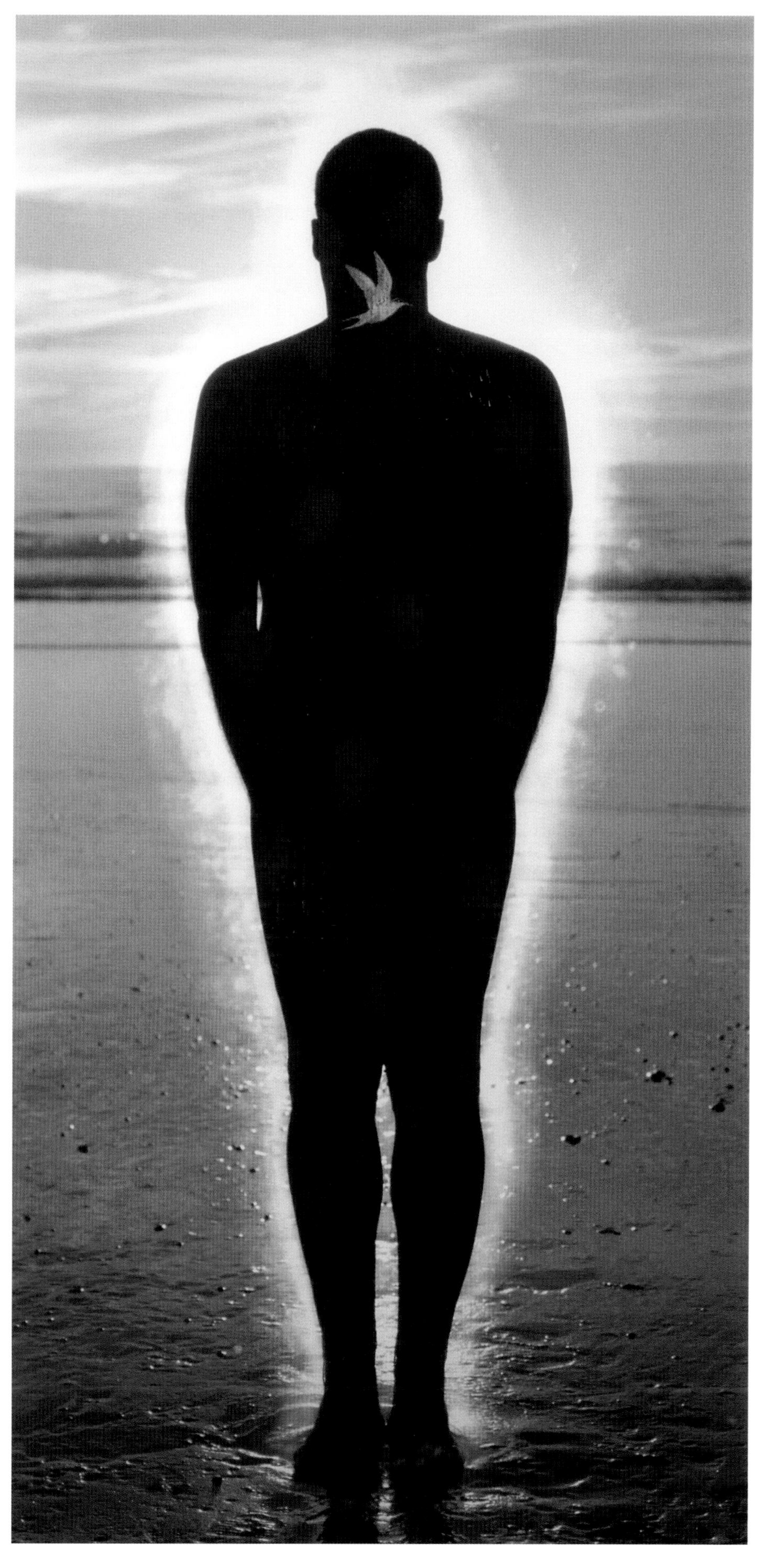

REDEMPTION, 2000
Oil, wax and gesso on black velvet
96 x 108 inches (244 x 274 cm)
Courtesy of Galeria Ramis Barquet, New York

A monumental eight-by-nine-foot painting of a giant conch shell on black velvet, a kind of 'icon' much like the chocolate rabbit in *Thing and Deception* of 1997 (p. 136). We do not deal with a picture *per se*, we are forced to accept the image of the shell as occupying the same space in the gallery that we viewers do. Like the chocolate rabbit, the shell hovers between kitsch and seriousness in a way that rivets our attention. Its aureole of light makes us understand that, given the play of signs in this show, the shell stands in for a human being (compare with *Frankness*).

A mirror held to our own faces? Isn't that what black velvet means in the context of this show? The shell, an image of who we are? A living being's home, a mollusk's house, now empty, quite hollow and unoccupied? But a shrine to life's ebb and flow; Martínez Celaya again plays dangerously with items of kitsch in our culture, of which the shell is a trace. Despite the elaborate, diagonal, twisting motion of the unfolding of the conch, we cannot read the image. Cannot personify it. In this, the painting breaks sharply with the rest of the pictures in this section, the ones I call figured landscapes.

JE

ERLÖSUNG, 2000
Öl, Wachs und Gesso auf schwarzem Samt
96 x 108 Zoll (244 x 274 cm)
Courtesy of Galeria Ramis Barquet, New York

Ein monumentales, 2,44 x 2,74 m großes Gemälde einer riesigen Schneckenmuschel auf schwarzem Samt, eine Art Symbol wie das Schokoladenkaninchen in *Ding und Täuschung* von 1997 (S. 136). Wir befassen uns nicht mit einem eigentlichen Bild. Wir werden gezwungen, das Bild der Muschel im gleichen Raum zu akzeptieren, in dem wir uns als Betrachter in der Galerie befinden. Wie das Schokoladenkaninchen bewegt sich die Muschel zwischen Kitsch und Ernsthaftigkeit und nimmt so unsere Aufmerksamkeit gefangen. Ihr Lichtstrahlenkranz gibt uns zu verstehen, dass die Muschel, unter Berücksichtigung des Spiels der Zeichen dieser Ausstellung, das menschliche Wesen repräsentiert (vergleiche mit *Offenheit*).

Wird uns eine Spiegel vorgehalten? Ist dies nicht das, was schwarzer Samt in dieser Ausstellung bedeutet? Die Muschel als Abbild unseres Wesens? Das Heim eines Lebewesens, das Haus eines Weichtiers, jetzt leerstehend, hohl und unbewohnt? Aber ein Schrein der Ebbe und des Flusses des Lebens; Martínez Celaya spielt wieder auf gefährliche Weise mit kitschigen Objekten unserer Kultur und die Muschel stellt ihre Spur dar. Trotz der sorgfältig ausgearbeiteten, diagonalen, sich windenden Bewegung der Schneckenmuschel können wir das Bild nicht deuten. Wir können es nicht personifizieren. In diesem Punkt vollzieht das Gemälde einen scharfen Bruch mit den anderen Bildern in dieser Abteilung, die ich als gestaltete Landschaften bezeichne.

JE

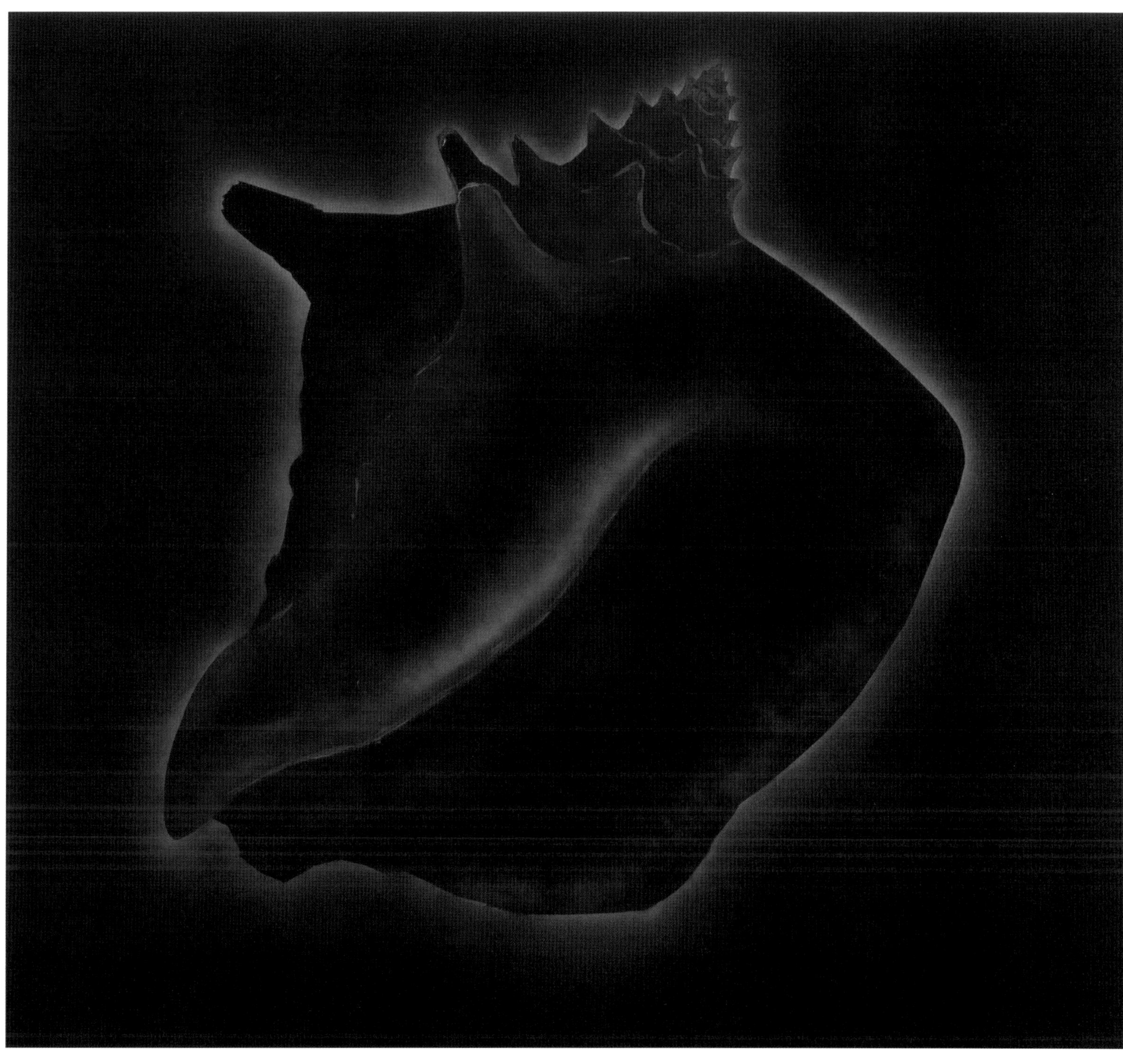

RECENT WATERCOLORS, 1999–2000
Watercolor on paper

NEUE AQUARELLE, 1999–2000
Aquarellfarbe auf Papier

The artist further explores themes from the poetry of Paul Celan: telescoping breathing and suffocation (speech and silence), thus not only translating Celan's search for poetic meaning into a similar search in painting, but also raising all the issues of statement and denial that energize Martínez Celaya's work throughout the exhibition. In *The Remembered,* this experiment, nested in the artist's memory of violence, puts the artist himself on view as some kind of martyr or witness to the truth ('martyr,' from the Greek word for 'witness'). All these pieces work against painting's long tradition, and here especially, the vivid images of martyrdom that the Counter-Reformation church demanded. The 'truth' in this small watercolor, however, is awareness, consciousness, memory, rather a different kind of witness than that imagined by the church.

Reading the paper's surface in *Signal,* we recognize the artist's usual flat layering of color–in patches, some almost rectangular and aligned with the paper's edges. The pink resonates with the bright red of *The Remembered,* just discussed: again a wound? We recognize themes explored previously in the series of watercolors entitled, The Forest: dismemberment by extension, martyrdom, with its echoes of the images in churches.

In *Birches and Scabs,* Martínez Celaya remembers The Forest series, but also his large photographs at the beginning of this section of the exhibition. The theme of martyrdom continues. A silhouetted male figure rises at center above a section of the trunk of a birch tree that stretches horizontally across the bottom quarter of the picture. Since the tree trunk overlaps the figure, we still have pictorial space here; but everything is quite flat, as if tree and figure were mere veils spread upon the surface of the paper, which is exactly how the painting was actually made (in veils or washes of gray paint). Viewers enjoy the bravura way in which images appear in the washes, as paint applied to the dry parts of the paper bled into the wetted. Birch bark painted in this way can suggest wounds, scabs. Birch bark flays like skin. The one bit of color in this painting, the red at the silhouetted figure's neck, suggests blood and/or a wound.

In the fourth and final watercolor from

Der Künstler erkundet weitere Themen aus den Gedichten Paul Celans: Er lässt Atmen und Ersticken (Sprache und Stille) zusammenfließen und übersetzt so nicht nur Celans Suche nach dichterischer Bedeutung in eine ähnliche Suche der Malerei, sondern bringt gleichzeitig alle Themen der Darstellung und der Verweigerung zur Sprache, die den gesamten Arbeiten Martínez Celayas in dieser Ausstellung Energie verleihen. In *Der Erinnerte* macht dieses Experiment, aus der Erinnerung des Künstlers an die Gewalt, den Künstler selbst zu einer Art Märtyrer oder Zeugen der Wahrheit („Märtyrer" stammt vom griechischen Wort für „Zeuge"). Alle diese Werke arbeiten gegen die lange Tradition der Malerei und hier insbesondere gegen die lebendigen Bilder des Märtyrertums, die die Kirche der Gegenreformation verlangte. Die „Wahrheit" in diesem kleinen Aquarell ist allerdings das Bewusstsein, die Kenntnis, die Erinnerung, eine andere Art Zeuge als der, den sich die Kirche vorstellte.

Beim Deuten der Papieroberfläche von *Signal* erkennen wir die übliche flache Schichtung der Farbe, in Flecken, wobei einige fast rechteckig und am Papierrand ausgerichtet sind. Im Rosa klingt das leuchtende Rot des gerade besprochenen *Der Erinnerte* nach: Wieder eine Wunde? Wir erkennen Themen, die zuvor in der Aquarellserie Der Wald erkundet wurden: Zerstückelung durch Erweiterung, Märtyrertum mit seinen Anklängen an Kirchenbilder.

In *Birken und Schorf,* erinnert Martínez Celaya an die Serie Der Wald, aber auch an seine großen Photographien am Anfang dieser Ausstellungssektion. Das Thema Märtyrertum wird fortgeführt. Eine männliche Silhouette erhebt sich in der Mitte über einen Teil eines Birkenstamms, der sich waagerecht über das untere Viertel des Bildes erstreckt. Da der Baumstamm mit der Figur überlappt, ist noch Bildraum vorhanden; allerdings ist alles ziemlich flach, als ob sich der Baum und die Figur nur wie Schleier über die Papieroberfläche erstrecken. Und genauso wurde das Gemälde gemalt: mit Schleiern oder Lavierungen grauer Farbe. Betrachter erfreuen sich an der Meisterschaft, mit der Motive dort erscheinen, wo die auf dem trockenen Papier aufgetragene Farbe in das feuchte Papier blutet. Die so gemalte Birkenborke kann man als Wunden, Schorf deuten.

THE REMEMBERED, 2000
11 x 11 inches (28 x 28 cm)
Collection of Scott Dean Harrington,
Los Angeles, California

DER ERINNERTE, 2000
11 x 11 Zoll (28 x 28 cm)
Sammlung Scott Dean Harrington,
Los Angeles, Kalifornien

BIRCHES AND SCABS, 1999
11 x 11 inches (28 x 28 cm)
Courtesy of Griffin Contemporary, Venice, California

BIRKEN UND SCHORF, 1999
11 x 11 Zoll (28 x 28 cm)
Courtesy of Griffin Contemporary, Venice, Kalifornien

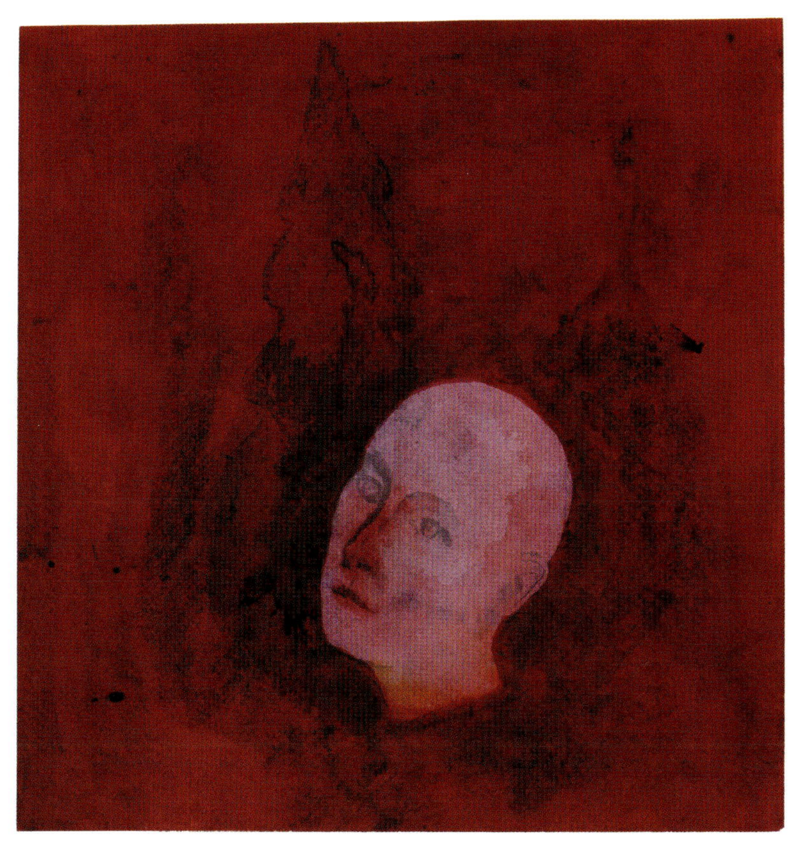

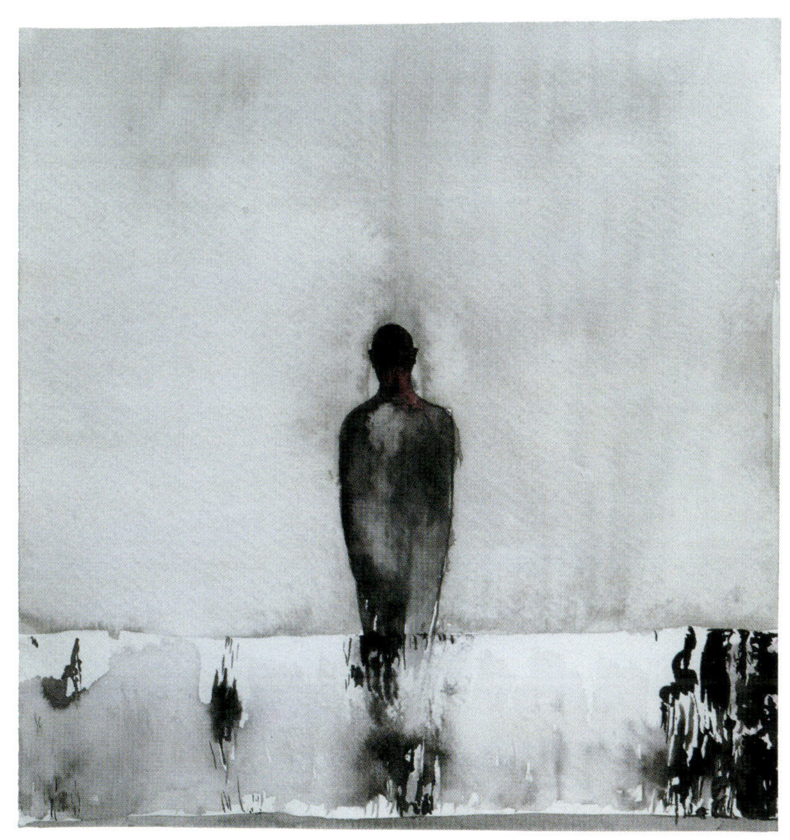

this series, *Figure at Rest with Head*, Martínez Celaya remembers the image of a head paired with a tree trunk from the work, *A Dry Bed*, seen previously. The red aureole surrounding the decapitated male body pictured here cannot help but make us recall the golden mandorlas that enshrined images of God in the Medieval and Modern church; its red color suggests (in this series anyway) blood, and hints at the violence of martyrdom. But in this small watercolor, whose imagery seems so casually and quickly sketched, where the brush touched the paper so briefly, Martínez Celaya refused the customary vividness with which martyrdoms were traditionally depicted in churches. By so doing, of course, he puts 'vividness' in play against this image's reticence and mysteriousness. The 'Modern mandorla' enshrines what kind of human awareness?

JE

Birkenborke lässt sich wie Haut abziehen. Der einzige Farbfleck in diesem Gemälde, das Rot am Hals der silhouettenhaften Figur lässt Blut oder eine Wunde, oder auch beides, vermuten.

Im vierten und letzten Aquarell der Serie, *Ruhende Figur mit Kopf* erinnert Martínez Celaya an das Bild eines mit einem Baumstamm gepaarten Kopfes, *Ein trockenes Bett*, aus derselben Serie, das bereits vorgestellt wurde. Die rote Aureole um den hier abgebildeten, enthaupteten Körper eines Mannes erinnert uns zwangsläufig an die goldenen Mandorlas, die die Gottesabbildungen in mittelalterlichen und modernen Kirchen fassen; die rote Farbe lässt (zumindest in dieser Serie) Blut als Hinweis auf die Gewalt des Märtyrertums vermuten. Aber in diesem kleinen Aquarell, dessen Motive so zufällig und schnell gezeichnet scheinen, wo der Pinsel das Papier so flüchtig berührte, verweigert sich Martínez Celaya der üblichen Lebendigkeit, mit der Märtyrertode traditionellerweise in Kirchen dargestellt wurden. Dadurch natürlich stellt er spielerisch die „Lebendigkeit" der Reserviertheit und Rätselhaftigkeit dieses Bildes gegenüber. Die „moderne Mandorla" bewahrt welche Art des menschlichen Bewusstseins?

JE

SIGNAL, 2000
11 x 11 inches (28 x 28 cm)
Courtesy of Griffin Contemporary, Venice, California

SIGNAL, 2000
11 x 11 Zoll (28 x 28 cm)
Courtesy of Griffin Contemporary, Venice, Kalifornien

FIGURE AT REST WITH HEAD, 2000
11 x 11 inches (28 x 28 cm)
Collection of Scott Dean Harrington, Los Angeles, California

RUHENDE FIGUR MIT KOPF, 2000
11 x 11 Zoll (28 x 28 cm)
Sammlung Scott Dean Harrington, Los Angeles, Kalifornien

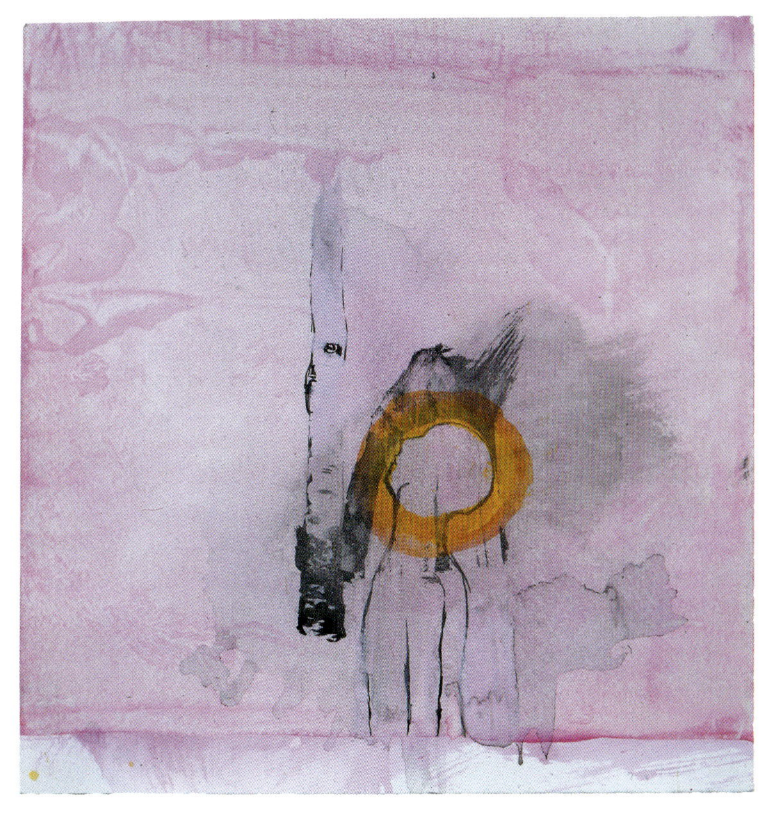

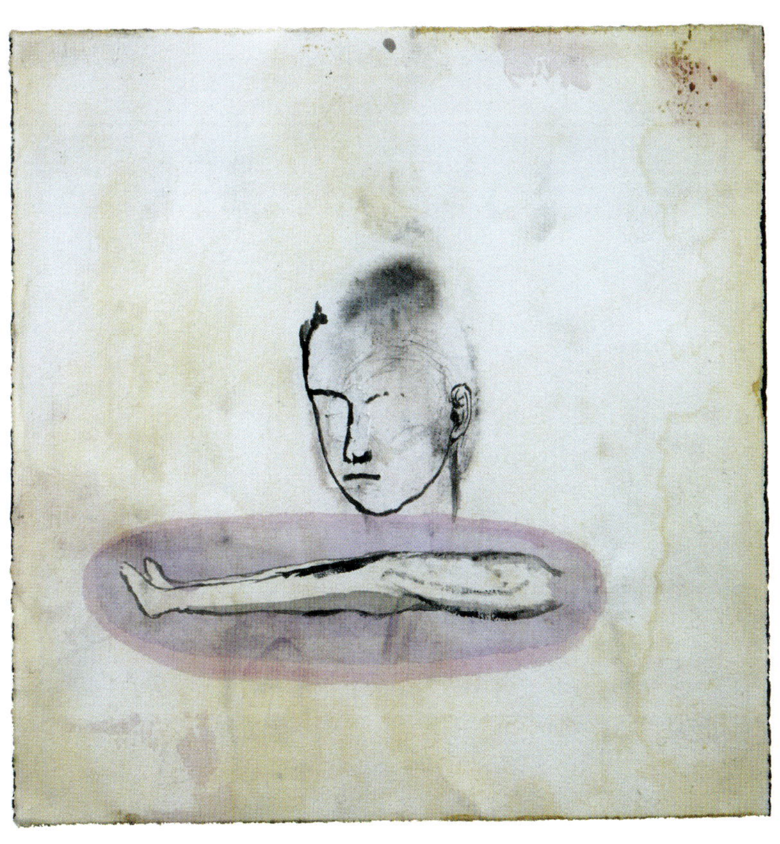

TRANSIENT (OAK FOREST), 2000
Watercolor and india ink on paper
57.5 x 59 inches (146 x 150 cm)
Collection of Danny First, Los Angeles, California

A huge five-foot-square piece of thick, handmade paper with a watercolor painting of the bust of a boy; worked both wet and dry, the artist brushed on a layer of white before starting. Veils of watercolor washes build up an image, with a leafy branch in gray-black, and the bust of the boy in dark black, over gray and yellow-ochre washes. Blotchy traces of tree trunks in black paint (that bled into the paper's wet surface) accompany the figure on the left. They double for scabs and wounds. Hovering over all is the artist's theme of martyrdom (see preceding commentary on Recent Watercolors).

JE

FLÜCHTIGE ERSCHEINUNG (EICHENWALD), 2000
Aquarellfarbe und chinesische Tusche auf Papier
57,5 x 59 Zoll (146 x 150 cm)
Sammlung Danny First, Los Angeles, Kalifornien

Ein riesiges Blatt dickes, handgeschöpftes Papier mit dem Aquarell einer Knabenbüste: Der Künstler bearbeitete das Papier nass und trocken und bestrich es vor dem Arbeitsbeginn mit einer Schicht weißer Farbe. Schleier von Aquarelllavierung ergeben das Bild eines Zweiges mit Blättern in Grauschwarz und der Knabenbüste in Tiefschwarz über grau und ockergelb getuschten Flächen. Fleckige Spuren von Baumstämmen in schwarzer Farbe, die in die nasse Papieroberfläche blutete, begleiten die linke Figur. Sie stehen auch für Schorf und Wunden. Alles wird vom Thema des Märtyrertums bestimmt (siehe den vorausgegangenen Kommentar zu Neue Aquarelle).

JE

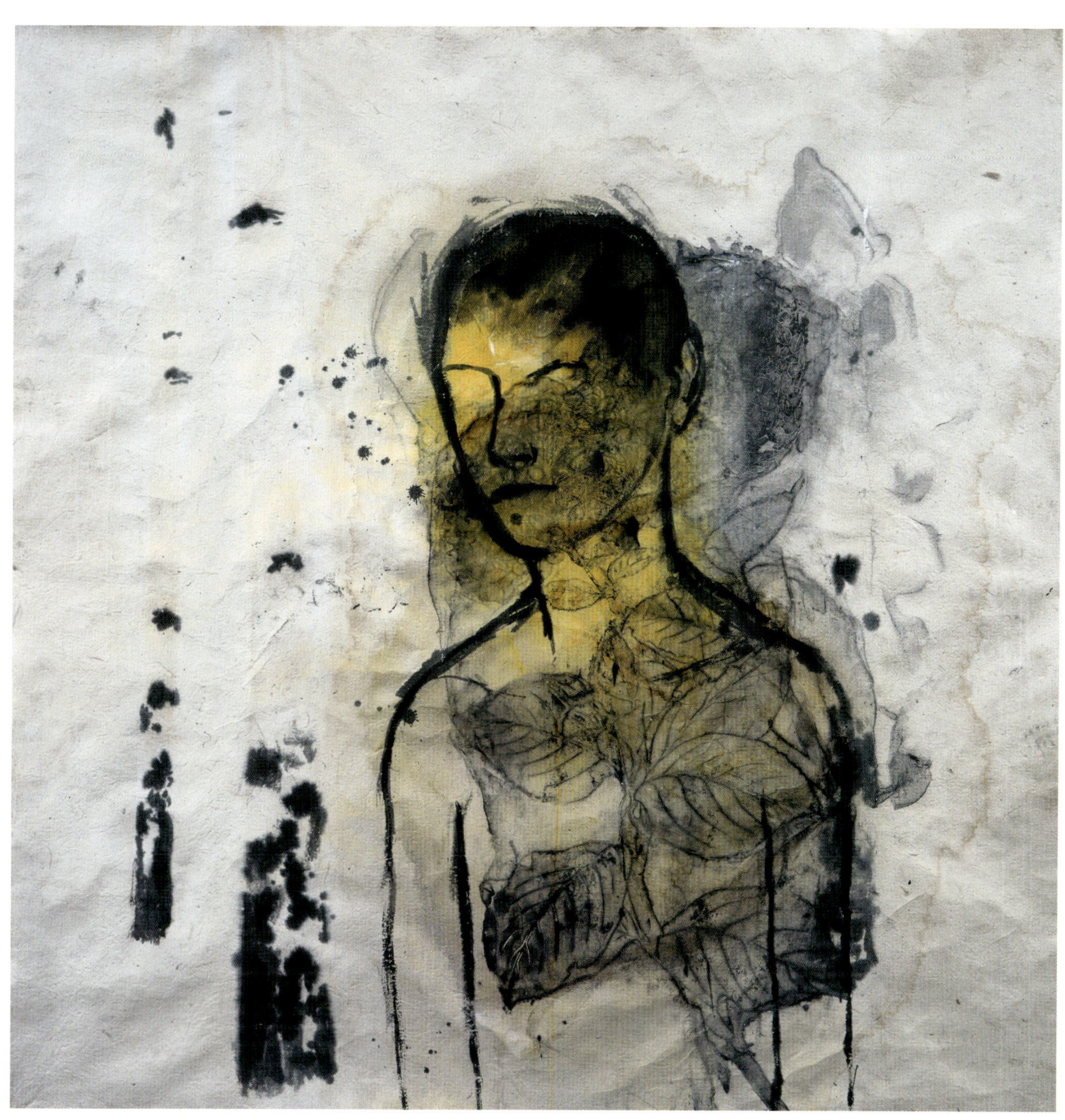

SPECIAL ISLAND (THE KISS), 2000
Tar and pencil on paper
37 x 35.5 inches (94 x 90 cm)
Collection of Dieter and Si Rosenkranz,
Berlin, Germany

A large painting on paper, in tar, with a conté-crayon line-drawing in white of two, apparently youthful, male busts. The artist describes it as "an image of a boy and himself," telling how the title was taken from a Billy Joel song, *Special Island.* This text in lower-case cursive appears at the center of the composition, written across the neck of the boy, at the level of the larynx, a poignant 'place of meaning' in the artist's works generally. The drawing seems mainly to silhouette the two figures, but lines are not just outlines; some indicate interior features; mouths, arms, and the male breast. The reticence of the drawing saves it from kitchy-ness. The doubling and tripling of white lines at the neck of the boy, at just the site of the text, 'special island,' heightens the 'poignant place of meaning.' A study of loneliness and isolation, but also an appreciation of this state–it's 'special,' the self kisses the boy.

JE

DIE BESONDERE INSEL (DER KUSS), 2000
Teer und Bleistift auf Papier
37 x 35,5 Zoll (94 x 90 cm)
Sammlung Dieter und Si Rosenkranz,
Berlin, Deutschland

Ein großes Teergemälde auf Papier mit einer Conté Crayon-Linienzeichnung in Weiß, die zwei anscheinend jugendliche männliche Oberkörper zeigt. Der Künstler beschreibt es als „Bild eines Knaben und ihm selbst" und erzählt, dass der Titel aus „Special Island", einem Song von Billy Joel, stammt. Dieser Text erscheint in kursiven Kleinbuchstaben in der Mitte der Komposition, am Hals auf der Kehle des Knaben, in den Arbeiten des Künstlers generell eine bedeutungsvolle Stelle. Die Zeichnung scheint hauptsächlich aus den Silhouetten dieser beiden Figuren zu bestehen, allerdings sind die Linien nicht nur Umrisse. Einige beschreiben innere Körperteile, Münder, Arme und die männliche Brust. Die Reserviertheit der Zeichnung lässt sie nicht kitschig erscheinen. Die Verdoppelung und Verdreifachung der weißen Linien am Hals des Knaben, genau dort wo sich der Text „Special Island" befindet, erhöht die Bedeutung dieser Stelle. Eine Studie der Einsamkeit und Isolation, aber auch eine Wertschätzung dieses Zustands – er ist „besonders", das Selbst küsst den Knaben.

JE

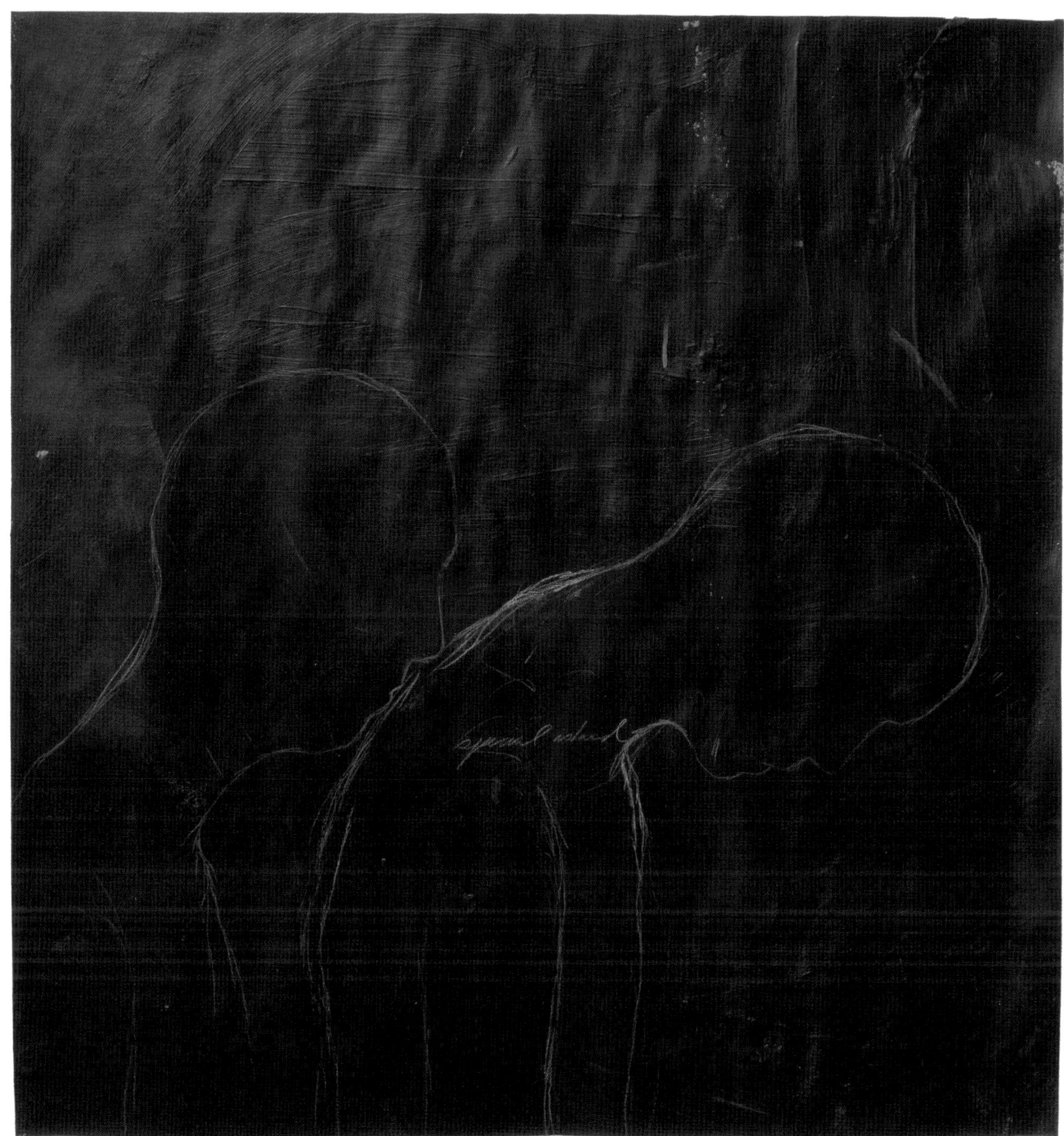

THE BLINK, 2000
Watercolor, india ink and pencil on paper
72 x 108 inches (183 x 274 cm)
Collection of Dieter and Si Rosenkranz,
Berlin, Germany

In the large oil painting on canvas, *Body at Rest (Renunciation)* [p. 210], seen earlier in the exhibition, Martínez Celaya superimposed a youthful male figure lying horizontally who extends across the bottom of the picture upon some huge, ghostly, gray sunflowers in a kind of montage.

In *The Blink*, an even larger painting on paper, the artist remakes this earlier piece. He reinvokes the same male figure, lying in the same position in the composition, and superimposes him upon a partly wilting garden of flowers, daisies, hydrangeas, and leggy clover blossoms among them. We deal with a iconographical motif, with an image of stasis (the boy at rest) paired with one incessant, but cyclical birth, flowering, and decay (the vegetation).

Martínez Celaya takes the idea further in this work. Starting out, he said, to produce a triptych showing morning, end of the day, and night, each on a separate piece of paper, he ends by creating one, single composition in which 'daytime' shrunk in size. The black ink of 'night' takes over; 'day' becomes a mere blink of the eye. And in the inky darkness, almost hiding there, drawn in thin pencil lines and modeled by scumbling in the black ink staining the paper's surface, we are astounded to see depicted a huge elk, whose neck and head rise to an impressive, carefully delineated rack of antlers. The elk confronts the boy, kneeling before him. The boy and elk, all in blackness, belong to 'night,' to the unseen and unchanging realm beyond awareness.

It helps me to think about this work to remember Francisco Goya's famous print entitled, *The Sleep of Reason Produces Monsters*. Martínez Celaya attempts here to imagine the world beyond that of waking awareness. But unlike the Romantic Enlightener, Goya, who warned of the monstrous, Martínez Celaya looks to be seeing the world as a source of some kind of mysterious energy. Awe replaces the monstrous.

JE

DER AUGENBLICK, 2000
Aquarellfarbe, chinesische Tusche und Bleistift auf Papier
72 x 108 Zoll (183 x 274 cm)
Sammlung Dieter und Si Rosenkranz,
Berlin, Deutschland

Auf dem großen Ölgemälde auf Leinwand, *Ruhender Körper (Verzicht,* S. 210*)*, das schon in dieser Ausstellung zu sehen war, überlagerte Martínez Celaya eine waagerecht liegende, jugendliche männliche Figur, die sich in einer Art Montage über das untere Ende des Bildes hinaus auf einigen riesigen, geisterhaften, grauen Sonnenblumen erstreckt.

Mit *Der Augenblick*, einem noch größeren Gemälde auf Papier, schafft der Künstler diese frühere Arbeit neu. Er verwendet die gleiche männliche Figur, die in der Komposition die gleiche Position einnimmt, und setzt sie auf einen teilweise welkenden Blumengarten, Gänseblümchen, Hortensien und langstieliger Klee unter den Blumen. Wir haben es mit einem ikonographischen Motiv zu tun, mit einem Abbild der Stasis (der ruhende Knabe), gepaart mit unaufhörlicher, aber zyklischer Geburt, Blüte und Verfall (der Vegetation).

Martínez Celaya hat die Idee in dieser Arbeit weiterentwickelt. Zuerst, sagte er, wollte er ein Triptychon mit Morgen, Tagesende und Nacht auf jeweils einem Blatt Papier schaffen. Er endete mit einer einzigen Komposition, in der die Größe des „Tages" geschrumpft war. Die schwarze Tinte der „Nacht" gewinnt, der „Tag" wird zu einem bloßen Augenblick. Und in der tintenschwarzen Dunkelheit steht fast versteckt, gezeichnet mit dünnen Bleistiftlinien und durch die Flecken der schwarzen Tusche modelliert, zu unserem Erstaunen ein riesiger Hirsch, auf dessen Hals und Kopf sich ein beeindruckendes, sorgfältig gezeichnetes Geweih erhebt. Er konfrontiert den vor ihm knienden Knaben. Ganz in Schwarz, gehören Knabe und Hirsch der „Nacht" an, dem ungesehenen und unveränderlichen Reich jenseits des Bewusstseins.

Ich kann besser über dieses Werk nachdenken, wenn ich mich an Francisco Goyas berühmten Druck *Der Schlaf der Vernunft gebiert Ungeheuer* erinnere. Martínez Celaya versucht, sich eine Welt jenseits des wachen Bewusstseins vorzustellen. Aber im Gegensatz zum romantischen Aufklärer Goya, der vor dem Monströsen warnte, möchte Martínez Celaya die Welt als Quelle einer Art mysteriösen Energie sehen. Ehrfurcht ersetzt das Monströse.

JE

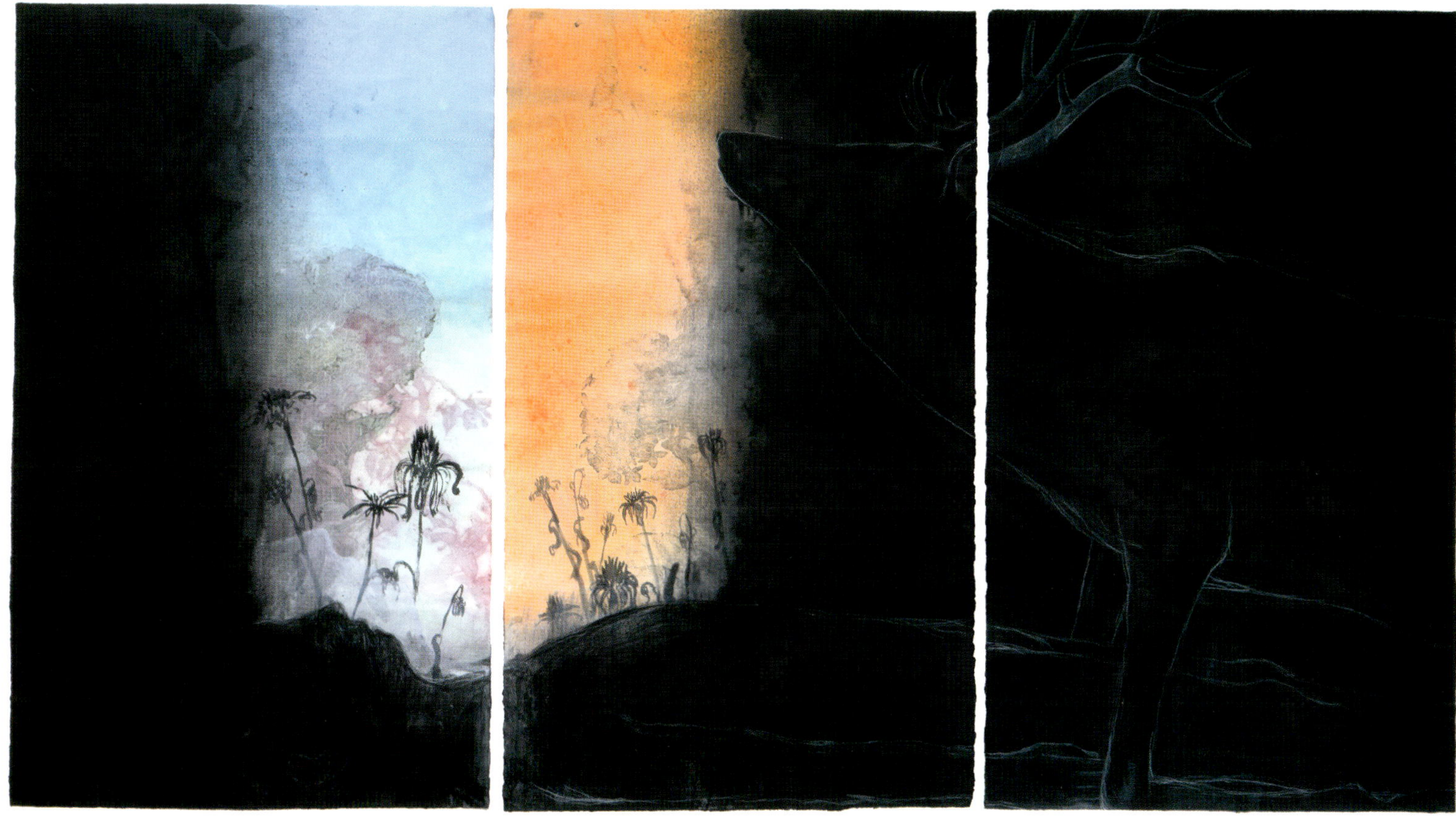

OCTOBER, 2000
Oil and wax on black velvet
66 x 66 inches (168 x 168 cm)
Courtesy of Enrique Martínez Celaya and Galeria Ramis Barquet, New York

This painting accompanies a poem of the same title published by the artist in a small book (Amsterdam [Cinubia], 2001). The poet conjures the coming of winter and first snow in a clearing in a birch grove, then personifies the grove.

Far from recondite and hermetic, the poem (p. 266) plays directly upon the age-old Christian imagery of salvation. The 'living wood' or the 'tree of life' in the garden of paradise is one of Christendom's most poignant and most ancient images; that wood, indeed, was the wood of the cross upon which Christ suffered to redeem humankind. The dove of the Holy Spirit appears constantly in Christian art. Moreover, in the legends of the saints, rehearsed incessantly in Medieval and Modern times, God spoke to the proto-martyr, Eustace, from an image which Eustace was astonished to see, poised miraculously between the antlers of the stag he was hunting.

Throughout the nine years of work on view in this retrospective, Martínez Celaya has wrestled with the art of the church, especially that of the Counter-Reformation church with its insistence (since the mid 1500s) on the vivid portrayal of martyrdom. The struggle, we have seen, was with painting's past, one in which Modern artists have been engaged generally since the Romantic revolution in the early 1800s. In *October*, the painting on velvet, we cannot help but recall Martínez Celaya's experiment at the beginning of this exhibition, in the painting called *The Trouble with Memory* (1993), which featured velvet hanging so provocatively (the one with the sewn-on roses). With that elaborate machine, the artist negotiated intriguingly the demands and complexities of picture planes to put the pictorial (the iconic?) into play as an image of awareness or subjectivity. Now the conceit has matured considerably: a body of work has established a coherent iconography of awareness (the figured landscape). The birch grove in *October* that almost cancelled the picture of the boy beneath, a grove in winter signaling human death confronts us with our condition, confronts us with memory's tomb. "The remembered . . . collapses unheard on icy leaves," Martínez Celaya writes in the poem, *October*. The wood in this garden, both life-giving and life-taking, cancels who we claim to be. The artist presents us with a mirror in a shrine, but it does not reflect who we think we are.

JE

OKTOBER, 2000
Öl und Wachs auf schwarzem Samt
66 x 66 Zoll (168 x 168 cm)
Courtesy of Enrique Martínez Celaya and Galeria Ramis Barquet, New York

Das Gemälde begleitet ein gleichnamiges Gedicht, das der Künstler in einem kleinen Buch (Amsterdam: Cinubia, 2001) veröffentlichte. Der Dichter beschwört die Ankunft des Winters und des ersten Schnees in der Lichtung eines Birkenhains und er personifiziert den Hain.

Das Gedicht (S. 267) ist weder dunkel noch verschlossen und befasst sich mit den uralten Bildern christlicher Erlösung. Das „lebende Holz" oder der „Lebensbaum" im Garten Eden ist eines der eindrücklichsten und ältesten Bilder des Christentums. Dieses Holz war das Holz des Kreuzes, an dem Christus litt, um die Menschheit zu erlösen. Die Taube des Heiligen Geistes erscheint ständig in der christlichen Kunst. Auch sprach Gott in den Heiligenlegenden, die in Mittelalter und Moderne unaufhörlich herangezogen wurde, mit einem Bild zum Erzmärtyrer Eustachius, das sich wundersamerweise im Geweih des vom Heiligen gejagten Hirsches befand.

In den neun Jahren der Arbeit an den Werken dieser Retrospektive hat Martínez Celaya mit der sakralen Kunst gerungen, insbesondere mit der der Gegenreformation, die seit Mitte des 16. Jahrhunderts auf der lebendigen Darstellung des Märtyrertums bestand. Der Kampf fand mit der Vergangenheit der Malerei statt, in den Künstler der Moderne seit der romantischen Revolution im frühen 19. Jahrhundert verwickelt waren. Bei *Oktober*, dem Gemälde auf Samt, können wir nicht umhin, uns an Martínez Celayas Experiment am Anfang dieser Ausstellung zu erinnern, an das Bild *Das Problem mit dem Gedächtnis*, 1993, in dem Samt so provokativ gehängt wurde (mit den aufgenähten Rosen). Mit dieser sorgfältig ausgearbeiteten Maschinerie erwog der Künstler fesselnd die Forderungen und Komplexitäten von Bildebenen, um das Bildhafte (Ikonenhafte?) als ein Symbol des Bewusstseins oder der Subjektivität in Szene zu setzen. Jetzt ist dieser Gedanke sehr gereift: Eine Werkgruppe hat eine einheitliche Ikonographie des Bewusstseins geschaffen (die gestaltete Landschaft). Der Birkenhain in *Oktober* hat das darunter liegende Bild des Knaben fast aufgehoben. Ein Hain im Winter als Zeichen des Todes des Menschen konfrontiert uns mit unserem Zustand, dem Grab der Erinnerung. „Der Erinnerte ... bricht ungehört auf eisigen Blättern zusammen", schreibt Martínez Celaya im Gedicht *Oktober*. Das Leben spendende aber auch tötende Holz im Garten hebt auf, was wir zu sein behaupten. Der Künstler zeigt uns einen Spiegel in einem Schrein, aber dieser reflektiert nicht die Person, die wir zu sein glauben.

JE

COMING HOME, 2000
Tar, feathers, metal, wood and mirror
96 x 96 x 160 inches (244 x 244 x 406 cm)
Collection of Dieter and Si Rosenkranz,
Berlin, Germany

A huge sculpture in tarred burlap, feathers, and wood, an installation with two great figures, of a huge elk rising to confront a boy. Between the elk's antlers, the artist suspends a mirror with a thin, molded, black frame. This is a version of the garden pictured in *October*, and makes the imagery in that landscape and in the poem of the same name 'come to life,' so to speak. Or at least take on three dimensions. The feathers suggest both life ("a dove of lightest wood") and death ("A morning of feathers, of the frail water of snow," as the artist writes in the poem, *October*). The mirror is a substitute for the speaking crucifix which the second-century C.E., proto-martyr Eustace saw in legend between the horns of a great stag he was hunting. In a manner uncharacteristic of the artist, the boy is presented in this work in movemented form. His pose is readable: he bows toward the beast in humility. The image of the boy that we have encountered in so many of the previous works in this exhibition, now takes the "place of humiliation" (Martínez Celaya's own words), that is, he quite clearly takes the place of a Christian martyr. Let me state the obvious: this confrontation of a human being with mystery happens here in an art gallery, not a church.

JE

HEIMKEHR, 2000
Teer, Federn, Metall, Holz und Spiegel
96 x 96 x 160 Zoll (244 x 244 x 406 cm)
Sammlung Dieter und Si Rosenkranz,
Berlin, Deutschland

Eine riesige Skulptur aus geteertem Sackleinen, Federn und Holz, eine Installation mit zwei großen Figuren, ein Hirsch, der sich erhebt, um einen Knaben zu konfrontieren. Zwischen den Geweihschaufeln des Hirschs hat der Künstler einen Spiegel mit einem dünnen, schwarzen Rahmen aufgehängt. Dies ist eine Version des Gartens in *Oktober* und erweckt die Bilder in dieser Landschaft und im gleichnamigen Gedicht sozusagen „zum Leben". Zumindest nehmen sie eine dreidimensionale Form an. Die Federn sind sowohl ein Hinweis auf Leben („eine Taube aus leichtestem Holz") als auch auf Tod („Ein Morgen der Federn, des zarten Schneewassers", wie der Künstler im Gedicht *Oktober* schreibt). Der Spiegel ersetzt das sprechende Kreuz, das Eustachius, der Erzmärtyrer des 2. Jahrhunderts, in der Legende im Geweih eines riesigen, von ihm gejagten Hirsches sah. Auf eine für den Künstler uncharakteristische Weise wird in diesem Werk ein sich bewegender Knabe dargestellt. Seine Pose ist deutbar: Er verneigt sich voller Demut vor dem Tier. Der Knabe, auf den wir in so vielen Werken in dieser Ausstellung gestoßen sind, nimmt jetzt in Martínez Celayas eigenen Worten den „Platz der Demütigung" ein, d. h. der Knabe tritt eindeutig an die Stelle eines christlichen Märtyrers. Lassen Sie mich das Offensichtliche aussprechen: diese Konfrontation eines menschlichen Wesens mit einem Mysterium geschieht in einer Kunstgalerie und nicht in einer Kirche.

JE

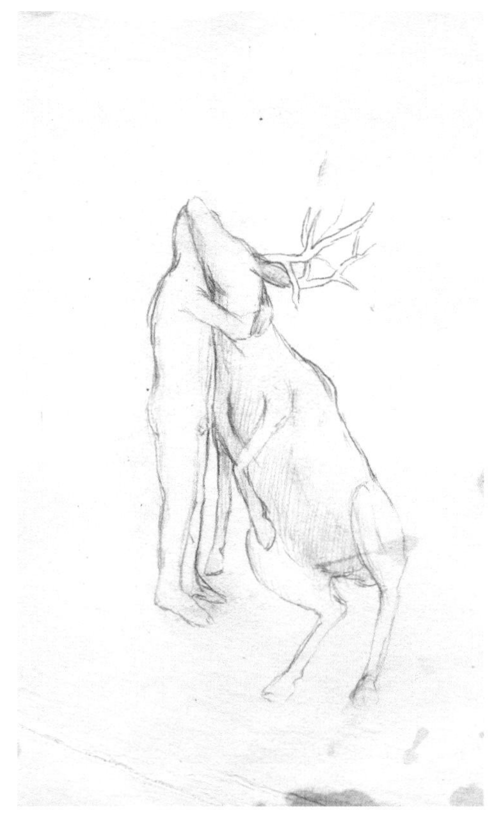

UNTITLED (BOY AND ELK), detail/OHNE TITEL (KNABE UND HIRSCH), Ausschnitt, 2000

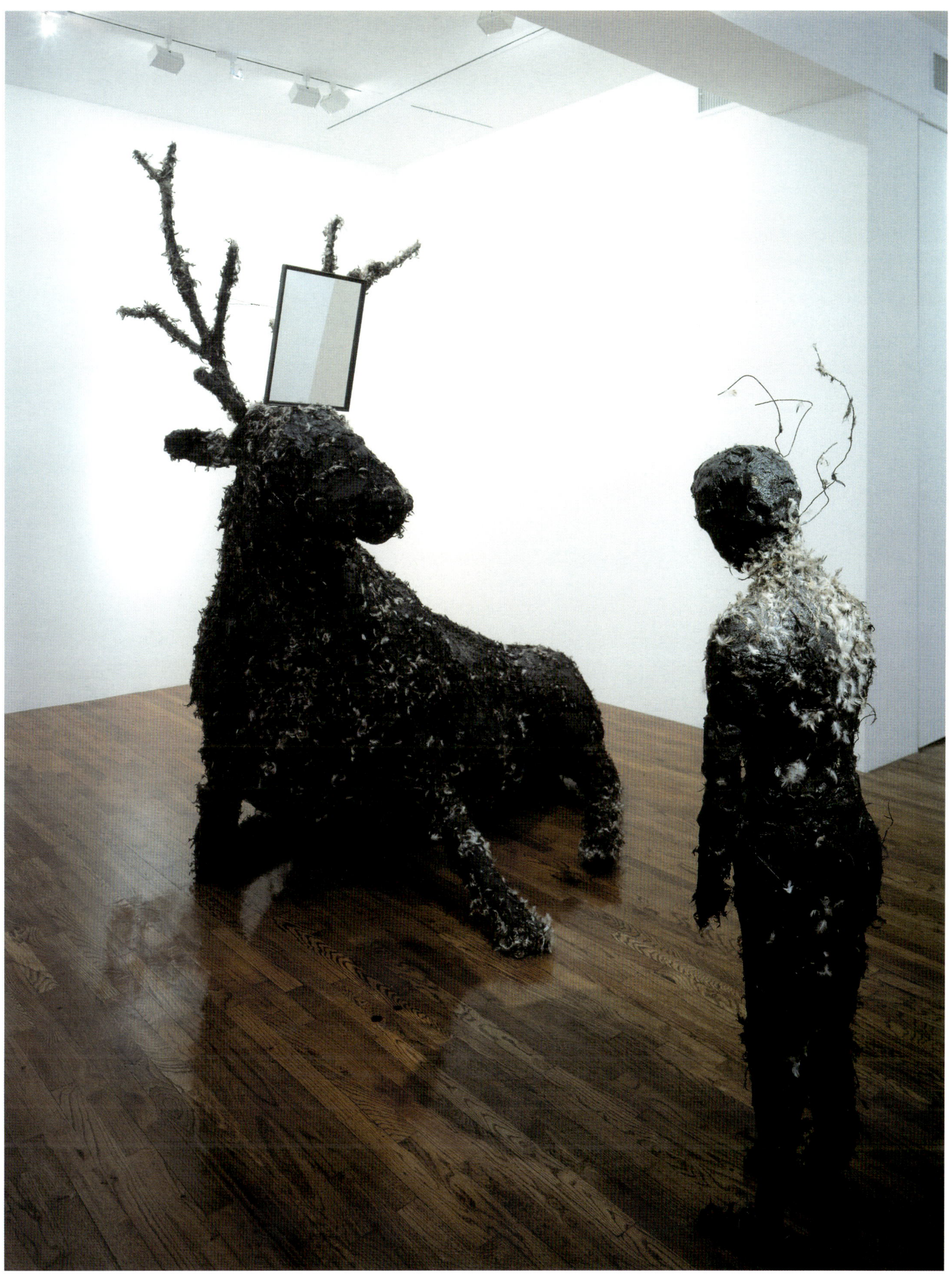

DOVE AND THE LIGHTEST WOOD, 2000
Watercolor, pastel and ink on paper
68 x 53 inches (173 x 135 cm)
Courtesy of Galeria Ramis Barquet, New York

A very large painting in watercolor, ink, and pastel on twelve square pieces of paper carefully stitched together, three squares wide by four high. All the issues in *October* return as the title shows. The illusion of space is strong and the relief conception governs. By making the boy stand in three-quarter view next to the picture plane, the artist identifies him with the white birch tree trunks that rise thickly alongside, likewise standing close to the picture plane. Vigorously blooming flowers, drawn hastily in thin, rapid strokes of bright red pastel, partially cancel this picture. They cover the picture plane, looming without scale, as ghostly presences in the viewer's space in the gallery. A line drawing in one artistic realm plays off against a painting in another.

JE

TAUBE UND DAS LEICHTESTE HOLZ, 2000
Aquarellfarbe, Pastellkreide und Tusche auf Papier
68 x 53 Zoll (173 x 135 cm)
Courtesy of Galeria Ramis Barquet, New York

Ein sehr großes Gemälde auf zwölf quadratischen, sorgfältig vernähten Papierstücken, drei Quadrate breit und vier Quadrate hoch. Wie der Titel besagt, werden die Themen aus *Oktober* wieder aufgegriffen. Die Raumillusion ist stark und das Relief dominiert. Der Künstler hat den stehenden Knaben in Dreiviertelansicht neben die Bildebene gestellt und identifiziert ihn somit mit den weißen Birkenstämmen, die dicht neben ihm wachsen und sich ebenfalls nahe der Bildebene befinden. Üppig blühende Blumen, die hastig mit dünnen, schnellen Strichen in hellroter Pastellkreide gezeichnet wurden, heben das Bild teilweise auf. Sie bedecken die Bildfläche und drohen maßstabslos als geisterhafte Erscheinungen im Raum des Betrachters in der Galerie. Eine Linienzeichnung in einem künstlerischen Reich wird gegen ein Gemälde in einem anderen ausgespielt.

JE

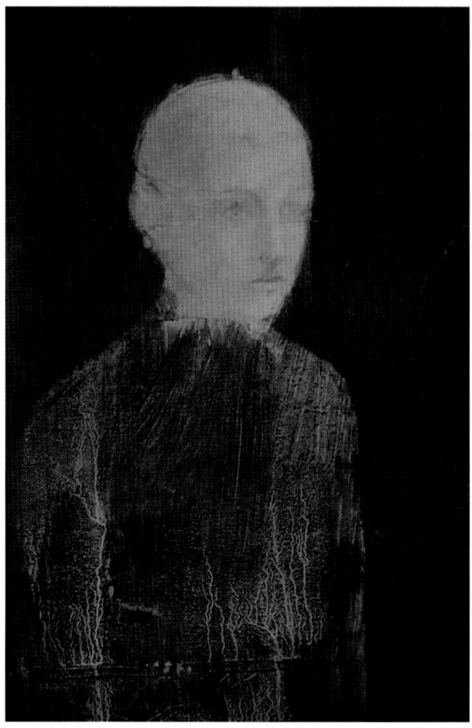

Work in progress/Unvollendete Arbeit, 2000

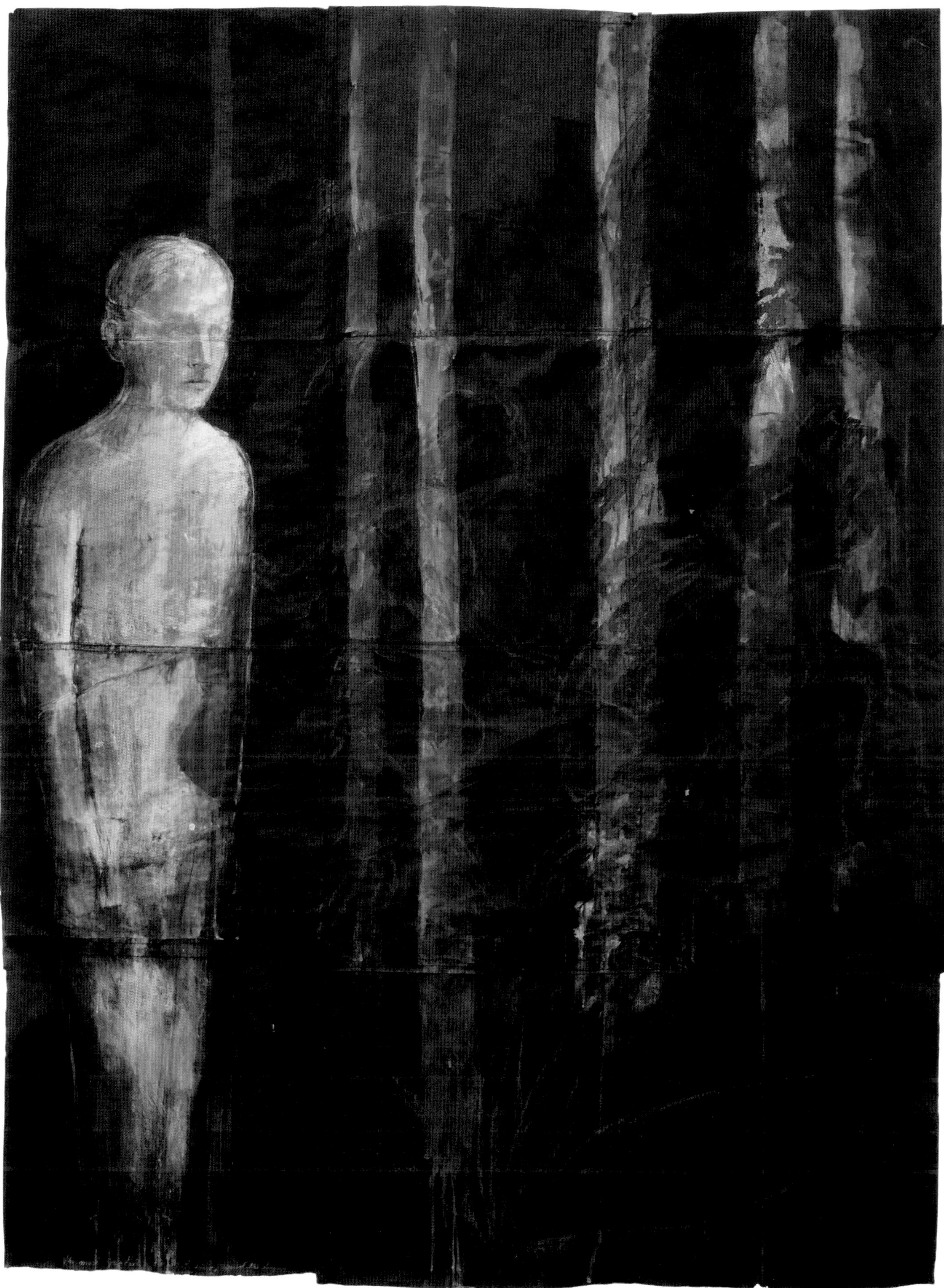

THE OPENING, 2000
Oil, tar, pencil and spray paint on paper
37 x 35.5 inches (94 x 90 cm)
Collection of Dieter and Si Rosenkranz,
Berlin, Germany

The first line in the artist's poem, *October*, reads: black and white birches / open / and then dissolve / in the light of morning. Readers quickly recognize the reference made here to Biblical imagery of the Last Judgment (when Christ will reappear at the end of time in the last morning's sunrise). In this work the artist translates the poem's first sentence into a painting in tar, pencil, oil, and copper spray-paint on a piece of paper about three feet square. Its kitschy aspects (a copper spray-painted aureole of light?) must be acknowledged. The artist presents us with a mirror in a shrine (the paradise garden, the birch grove, which transform themselves into antlers in the poem, *October*, and the antlers were placed there to frame a mirror). We might find ourselves reflected here, nested deep in the wood. We might empathize as viewers with the boy who appears in so many of the paintings in this exhibition, empathize by taking his 'place of humiliation' before a mystery. In this case the mirror in the shrine casts back no recognizable image.

JE

DIE ÖFFNUNG, 2000
Öl, Teer, Bleistift und Spritzlackierung auf Papier
37 x 35,5 Zoll (94 x 90 cm)
Sammlung Dieter und Si Rosenkranz,
Berlin, Deutschland

In der ersten Zeile von Martínez Celayas Gedicht *Oktober* heißt es: „Schwarzweiße Birken öffnen sich und lösen sich dann auf im Morgenlicht." Leser erkennen schnell den Bezug auf die biblische Symbolik des Jüngsten Gerichts (in dem Christus am Ende der Zeit, bei Sonnenaufgang des letzten Tages erscheint). Mit dieser Arbeit übersetzt der Künstler den ersten Satz des Gedichts in ein Gemälde aus Teer, Bleistift, Öl und Kupferspritzlackierung auf einem etwa 1 qm großen Blatt Papier. Die kitschige Seite (eine Aureole aus Kupferspritzlackierung?) ist unübersehbar. Der Künstler präsentiert uns einen Spiegel in einem Schrein (der Garten Eden, der Birkenhain, der sich im Gedicht *Oktober* in ein Geweih verwandelt, und das Geweih dienen als Rahmen für einen Spiegel). Wir finden uns hier vielleicht selbst als Abbild, tief im Wald. Vielleicht fühlen wir uns in den Knaben ein, der in so vielen Bilder dieser Ausstellung zu sehen ist, versetzen uns in seine Lage, in dem wir seinen „Platz der Demütigung" vor einem Mysterium einnehmen. In diesem Fall wirft der Spiegel im Schrein kein erkennbares Bild zurück.

JE

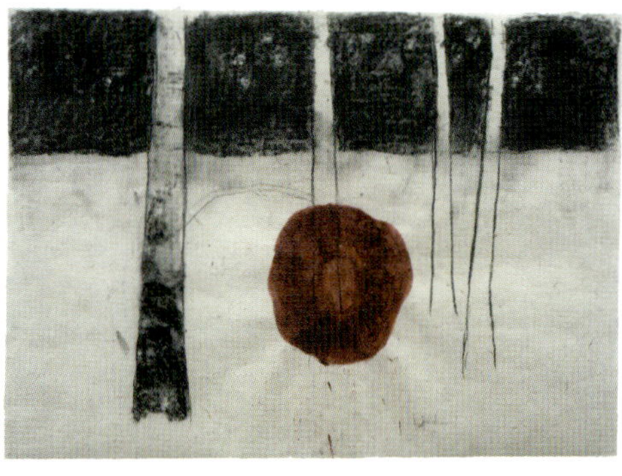

DRAWING WITH BIRCHES AND RED
/ZEICHNUNG MIT BIRKEN UND ROT, 2000
Collection of/Sammlung Dieter and Si Rosenkranz,
Berlin, Germany

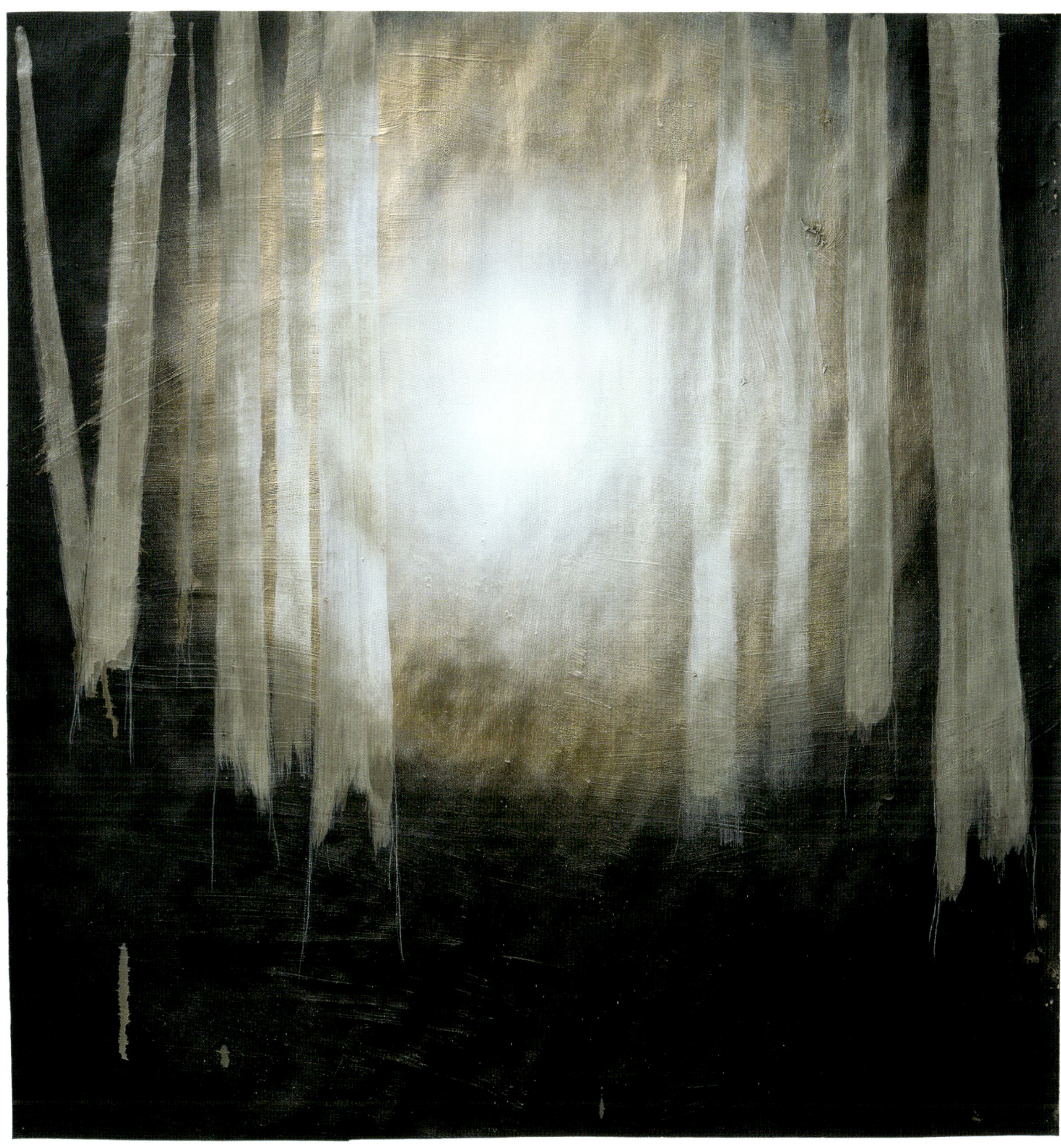

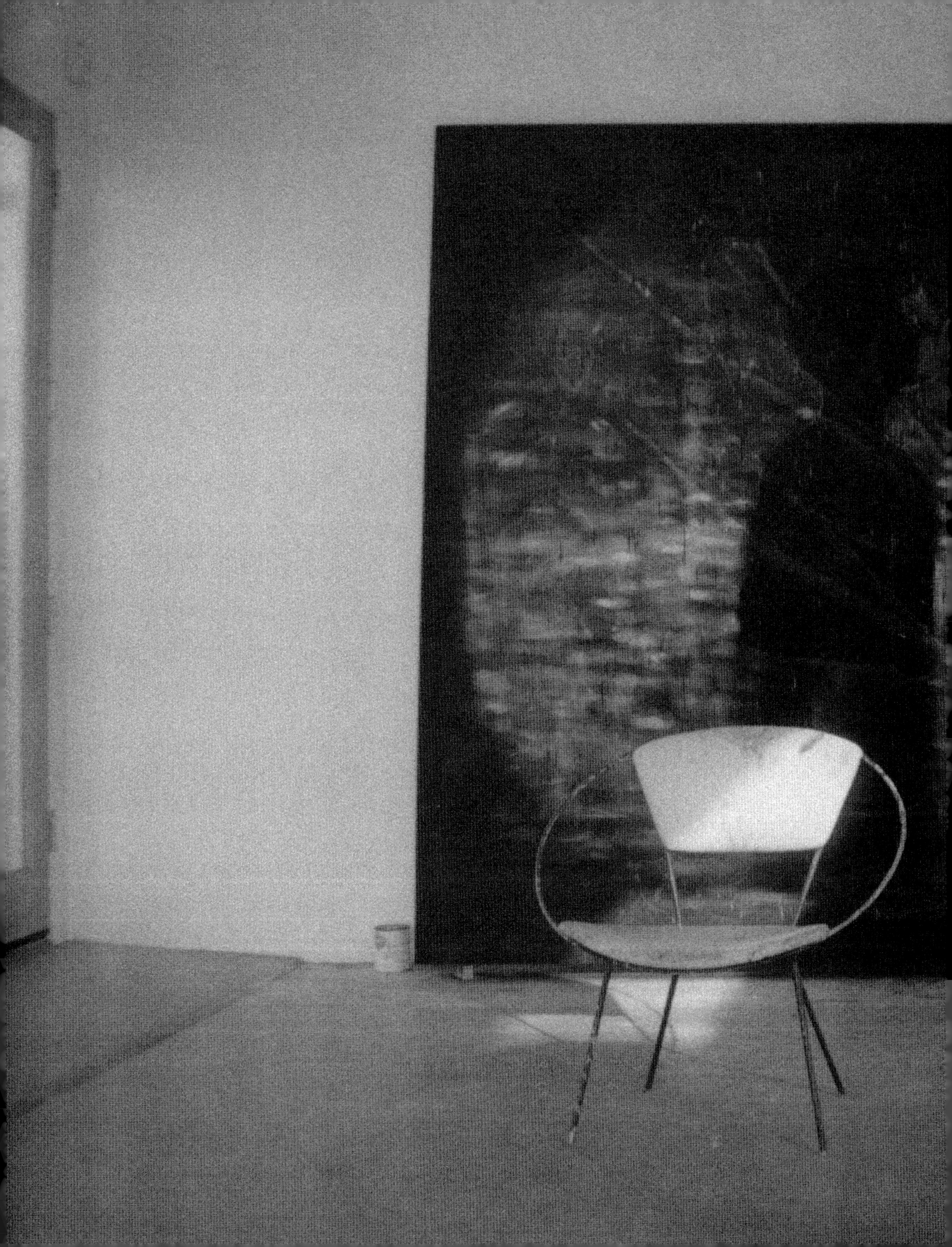

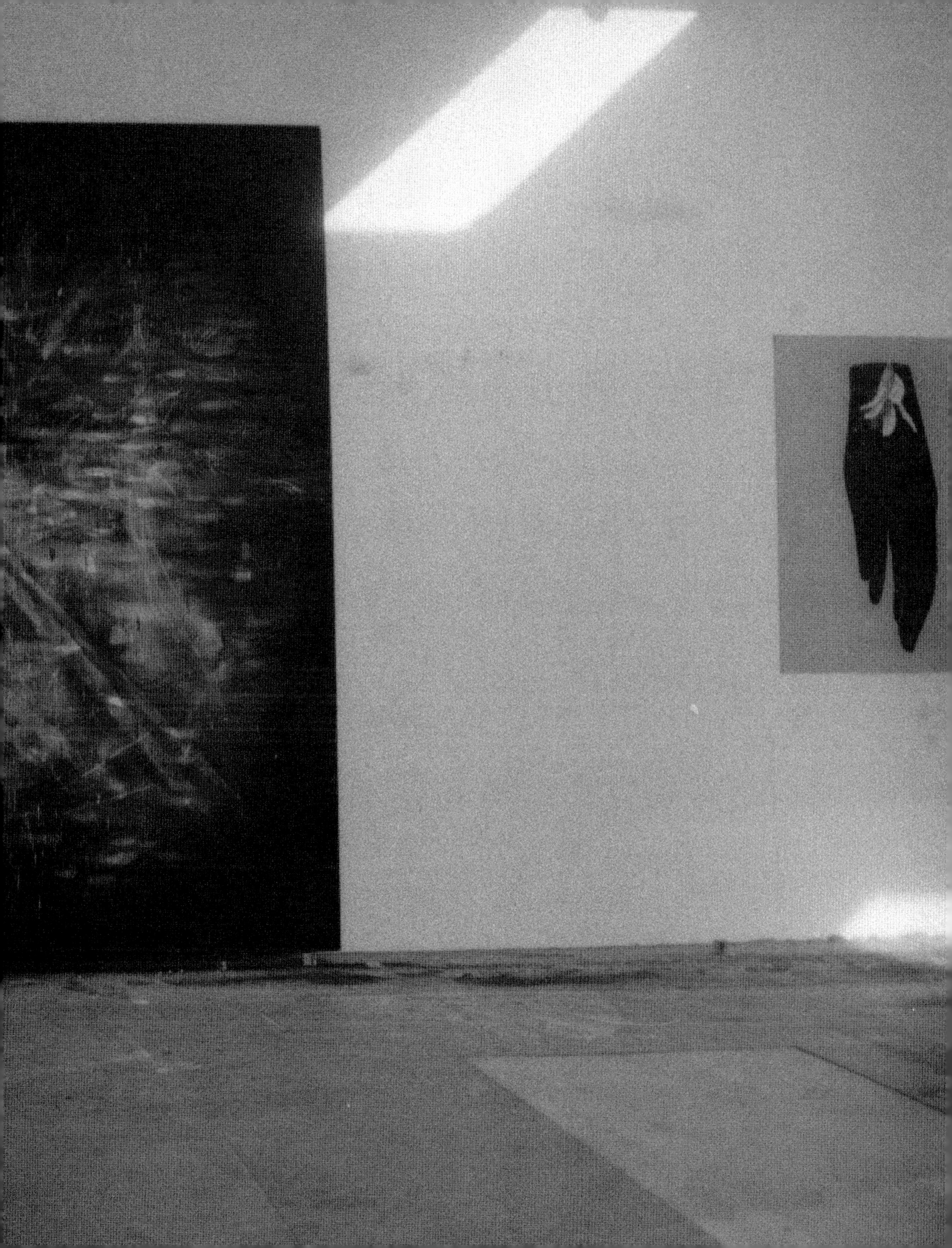

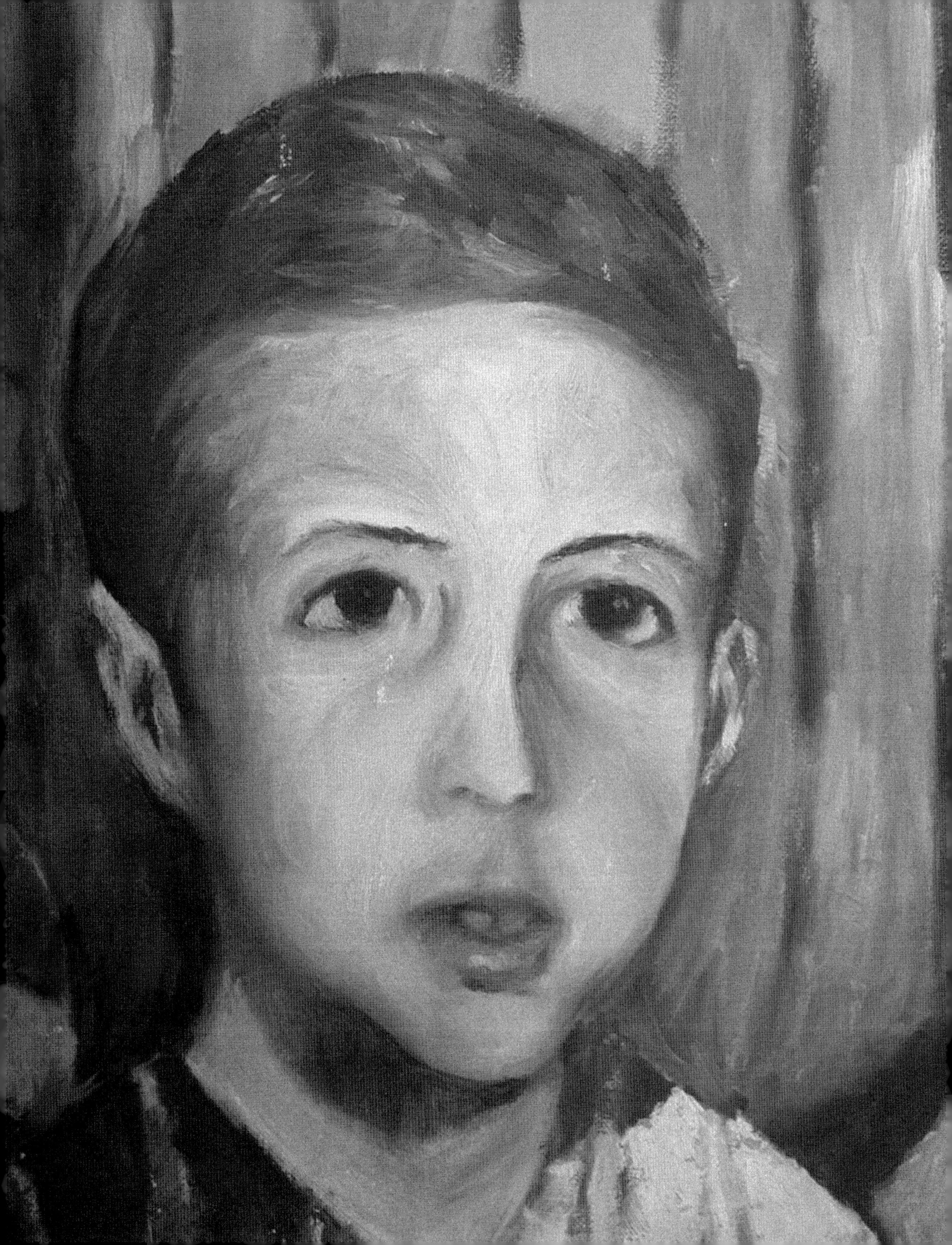

BIOGRAPHY

Colette Dartnall

1964
Born in Palos, Cuba to Edilia Maximina Celaya Venereo and Marcos Enrique Fernando Martínez Rodriquez on June 9, 1964, six years after the Cuban Revolution.

1970
Father leaves for Madrid, Spain.

1972
Emigrates with his mother and younger brother, Carlos (b. 1967), to join his father in Madrid where they experience financial difficulties. Their economic struggles and the need to change schools several times within the span of two years, mark the beginning of his search for identity and his place in the world through drawing.

1973
Youngest brother, Fernando, is born. Collects papers for a recycling company. Begins to experiment with paint.

1975
Moves to Puerto Rico with his family. Takes on an apprenticeship with painter Bartoldo Mayol which he describes in a 1999 interview with Anne Trueblood Brodzky. "When he [Bartoldo Mayol] was drawing he would surrender to it, he was still enamored with making something appear out of nothing, like somebody who learns to draw for the first time. There was a lot of tenderness in him, and tenderness toward his work. To see his love for the work was the greatest lesson I learned during my time with him."

1976
Attends the University of Puerto Rico High School where he meets his mentor, Manuel Alonso, a trained socio-psychologist and the school's principal.

1978
Begins his studies in the arts at the Liga de Arte de San Juan. Publishes two of four essays on Nietzsche, wins numerous science competitions and begins research on laser physics at the early age of 13.

1982
Graduates valedictorian of his high school class. Studies physics at Cornell University. Paints primarily with oils and acrylics. Begins

BIOGRAPHIE

Colette Dartnall

1964
Am 9. Juni 1964, sechs Jahre nach der Kubanischen Revolution, in Palos, Kuba, als Sohn von Edilia Maximina Celaya Venereo und Marcos Enrique Fernando Martínez Rodriquez geboren.

1970
Der Vater zieht nach Madrid, Spanien.

1972
Um mit dem Vater zusammenzuleben, emigriert er mit der Mutter und dem jüngeren Bruder Carlos (geb. 1967) nach Madrid. Ihre finanziellen Schwierigkeiten in Spanien und der Zwang, die Schule innerhalb von zwei Jahren mehrmals zu wechseln, bestimmen den Anfang seiner Suche nach Identität und seiner Stellung in der Welt durch das Zeichnen.

1973
Geburt des jüngsten Bruders Fernando. Sammelt Altpapier für eine Recyclingfirma. Erste Experimente mit Farbe.

1975
Zieht mit seiner Familie nach Puerto Rico. Beginnt eine Lehre bei dem Maler Bartoldo Mayol, den er 1999 in einem Interview mit Anne Trueblood Brodzky beschreibt: „Wenn er malte, war er der Sache völlig hingegeben, er war immer noch darin verliebt, aus dem Nichts etwas erscheinen zu lassen, wie jemand, der mit dem Zeichnenlernen gerade erst beginnt. Es war viel Zärtlichkeit in ihm, Zärtlichkeit für seine Arbeit. Seine Liebe zur Arbeit zu sehen, war das Bedeutendste, was ich in meiner Zeit mit ihm gelernt habe."

1976
Besucht die University of Puerto Rico High School, wo er seinen Mentor Manuel Alonso, Soziopsychologe und Rektor der Schule, trifft.

1978
Beginnt seine Kunstausbildung an der Liga de Arte de San Juan. Veröffentlicht zwei von vier Artikeln über Nietzsche, gewinnt zahlreiche wissenschaftliche Wettbewerbe und beginnt im Alter von nur 13 Jahren, auf dem Gebiet der Laserphysik zu forschen.

1982
Besteht die High School-Abschlussprüfung mit Auszeichnung. Studiert Physik an der Cornell University. Malt hauptsächlich mit

facing page/gegenüberliegende Seite

ME AND MY BROTHERS, detail /ICH UND MEINE BRÜDER, Ausschnitt, 1987

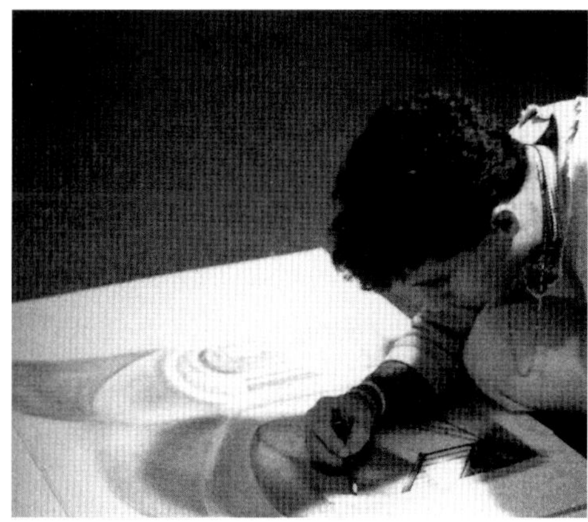

NEW YORK/NEW YORK, 1982

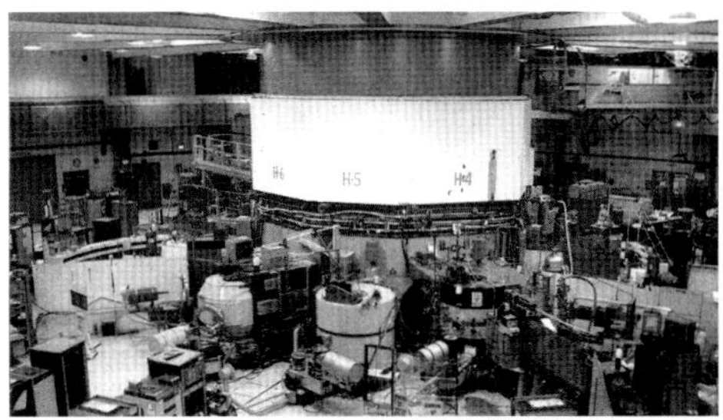

BROOKHAVEN NATIONAL LABORATORY, UPTON, NEW YORK, 1987

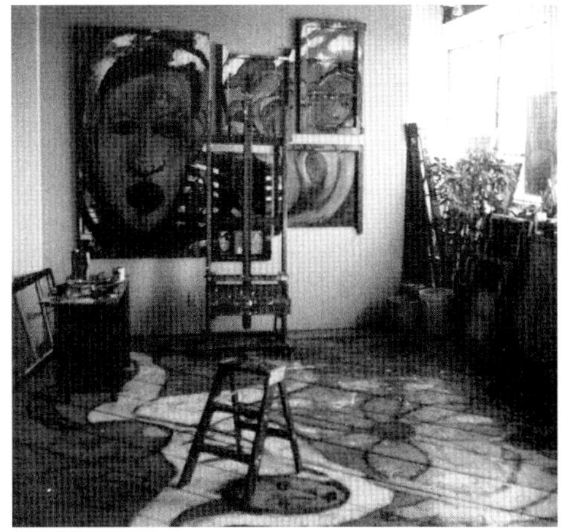

THE ARTIST'S STUDIO/DAS ATELIER DES KÜNSTLERS, OAKLAND, CALIFORNIA, 1991

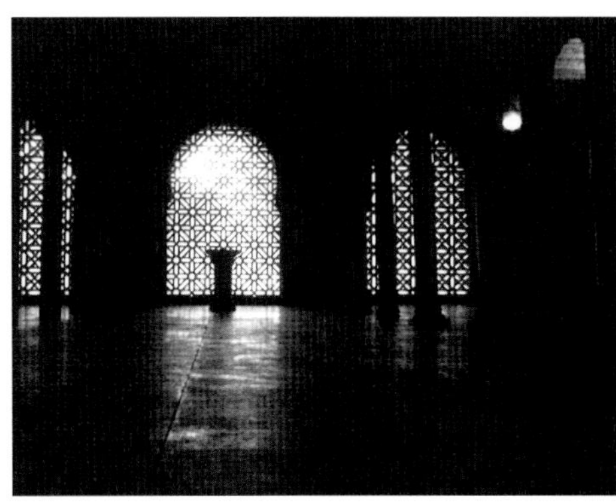

MEZQUITA, CORDOBA, SPAIN/SPANIEN, 1991

1. Anne Brodzky, *Unbroken Poetry, the work of Enrique Martínez Celaya* (Venice: Whale and Star Press, 1999).
2. Enrique Martínez Celaya, "About the Works" in *Presents & Proofs*, exhibition catalog/Ausstellungskatalog (San Francisco: Meridian Gallery and Santa Barbara: Ro Snell Gallery, 1994).

his first artist's sketchbook, two of which he fills each year, with notes about his work, his poetry, and his inspirations.

1986
Graduates from Cornell University and enrolls in a PhD program in Quantum Electronics at the University of California at Berkeley. Father begins to paint. Describes his father's passion for painting as follows: "He paints with great belief in the power of painting and with love for the objects and subjects that he renders."[1]

1987
Works at Brookhaven National Laboratory in Long Island. Continues his doctorate studies in Quantum Electronics at Berkeley, while attempting to pursue a graduate degree in art at the same university, a degree he abandons only eight months later to devote his efforts to making his own artwork.

1989
Moves to San Francisco, California. Works at Coherent Medical, a laser company. Patents four inventions on laser delivery systems. Publishes his first book of poetry, *Guthrie.*

1990
Unhappy with his experience within a corporate structure, Leaves Coherent. Moves to Oakland and supports himself by selling his artwork in the parks of San Francisco and modeling for fashion magazines.

1991
Travels to Africa and Europe with his friend, Brian Mountford. Publishes *Poems for the Bed.*

1992
Has his first solo exhibition at the Sunnyvale Art Center, California. Moves to Santa Barbara to attend the graduate art program at the University of California. Receives the Regents Fellowship and the Interdisciplinary Humanities Fellowship. Studies with artist Harry Reese. Mourns the death of two of his Berkeley professors, Joan Brown and Silvia Lark. Writes about his own work: "In the summer of 1992, I was trying to connect with my work by dismembering it. I slashed through canvases and created inventories of the findings. Then in regret, I would embrace the paintings and carefully sew them back together."[2] Destroys earlier work which includes the figurative and abandons such imagery in order to surpass the boundaries of conventional painting. Begins to make mixed

Öl- und Acrylfarben. Beginnt das erste seiner künstlerischen Skizzenbücher, von denen er jedes Jahr zwei mit Notizen über seine Arbeiten, seine Gedichte und seine Anregungen füllt.

1986
Besteht die Abschlussprüfung an der Cornell University und immatrikuliert sich für den Promotionsstudiengang der Quantenelektronik an der University of California in Berkeley. Der Vater beginnt zu malen. Die Leidenschaft seines Vaters für das Malen beschreibt er folgendermaßen: „Er malt mit festem Glauben an die Macht des Malens und mit Liebe für die Objekte und Themen, die er darstellt."[1]

1987
Arbeitet im Brookhaven National Laboratory auf Long Island. Setzt seine Promotion im Fachbereich Quantenelektronik in Berkeley fort, wobei er versucht, einen Abschluss in Kunst an derselben Universität zu erlangen. Diese Absicht gibt er schon acht Monate später auf, um sich ganz dem Schaffen der eigenen Kunstwerke zu widmen.

1989
Zieht nach San Francisco. Arbeitet bei der Laserfirma Coherent Medical. Meldet vier Patente für die Erfindung von Laserstrahlsystemen an. Veröffentlicht seinen ersten Gedichtband, *Guthrie.*

1990
Seine Erfahrungen innerhalb einer Firmenstruktur lösen Unzufriedenheit in ihm aus. Verlässt Coherent und zieht nach Oakland, wo er seinen Lebensunterhalt durch den Verkauf seiner Gemälde in den Parks von San Francisco und als Model für Modemagazine selbst bestreitet.

1991
Reist mit seinem Freund Brian Mountford nach Afrika und Europa. Veröffentlicht *Poems for the Bed/ Gedichte fur das Bett.*

1992
Erste Einzelausstellung im Sunnyvale Art Center in Kalifornien. Zieht nach Santa Barbara, um dort das Graduiertenstudium im Fachbereich Kunst an der University of California aufzunehmen. Erhält die Forschungsstipendien Regent Fellowship und Interdisciplinary Humanities Fellowship. Studiert bei dem Künstler Harry Reese. Beklagt den Tod zweier seiner Professoren an der Universität Berkeley, Joan Brown und

media works such as: *Sueños de Satin* (*Satin dreams*), 1992, oil, wax, thread, and paper on satin; *Pintura de un Caballito* (*A Little Horse Painting*), 1992, oil, fabric, burlap, tar, and thread on canvas; *El Ruiseñor* (*The Nightingale*), 1993, oil, wax, fabric and thread on canvas with plastic fruit. First interested in Joan of Arc, La Pucelle, the subject of a number of his later works.

1993
Is introduced to the writings of poet Paul Celan. Exhibits at Puerto Rico's Galeria Botello, San Juan. Begins the Black Paintings series which he explains as follows: "Beyond works of art, some paintings are devotional objects, not only a metaphoric space but a live source in themselves. This presence can only be summoned by an object made with love and through the object seen with love. For the observer this relationship would illustrate nothing in the conventional sense and yet, breathe a direct experience where metaphor and presence can coexist. This would be the natural conclusion of knowledge unmediated by doubt. I wanted to make paintings like that. Without the safeguard of cynicism or melodrama and that would overcome my own numbness. With this desire, I started the Black Paintings. I chose black because it is a demand to be present. ...Under the pressure of silence."[3] "The Black Paintings appeared as the fruit of these ideas. The vitality of black, flowers, and the small objects that emerged on the paintings were a way to undecorate by decorating and emptying by choosing what to put in. Trapped in these dichotomies, love, topical but controversial, became the main inspiration and the target to this series."[4] Develops an interest in Zen philosophy.

1994
Exhibits Black Paintings at the University Art Museum, Santa Barbara, California. Included are: *Siempre Más* (*Always More*); *Ballad for a Sprout*, *The Trouble with Memory*, *Water Can*, and *Miner's Lung*. Receives MFA from the University of California, Santa Barbara, California with honors and as recipient of the Art Affiliates Award. Attends Skowhegan School of Painting and Sculpture, Skowhegan, Maine where he meets Donald Baechler and Allen Ginsberg. Begins Paintings for Company series, which he describes as follows: "In them, the value of the particular and of silence remained, yet these works expected for me a new level of candor and intimacy. The handling of the paint became simpler, the color lighter and the compositions more aus-

Silvia Lark. Er schreibt über sein eigenes Schaffen: „Im Sommer 1992 habe ich versucht, durch Verstümmelung eine Verbindung zu meinen Werken herzustellen. Ich habe meine Leinwände aufgeschlitzt und Bestandsaufnahmen der Funde gemacht. Dies bedauernd, habe ich mich meiner Gemälde wieder angenommen und sie sorgfältig zusammengenäht."[2] Zerstört frühere Werke, einschließlich der figurativen Arbeiten, und wendet sich von dieser Bildwelt ab, um die Grenzen des konventionellen Malens zu überschreiten. Erste Werke aus verschiedenartigsten Materialien, wie zum Beispiel *Suenos de Satin*, 1992, Öl, Wachs, Garn und Papier auf Satin; *Pintura de un Caballito*, 1992, Öl, Gewebe, Sackleinen, Teer und Garn auf Leinwand; *El Ruiseñor*, 1993, Öl, Wachs, Gewebe und Garn auf Leinwand mit Plastikfrüchten. Erstes Interesse an der heiligen Johanna (Jungfrau von Orléans, Jeanne d'Arc, La Pucelle), die zum Thema späterer Arbeiten werden soll.

1993
Wird auf die Schriften des Dichters Paul Celan aufmerksam gemacht. Stellt in der Galeria Botello, San Juan, Puerto Rico, aus. Beginnt die Serie der Black Paintings/Schwarze Gemälde, die er folgendermaßen erläutert: „Einige Gemälde sind über Kunstwerke hinaus auch Gegenstände der Anbetung, nicht nur ein metaphorischer Bereich, sondern auch eine Lebensquelle in sich selbst. Dieser Zustand kann nur von einem Objekt hervorgerufen werden, das mit Liebe gemacht wurde, und der durch das Objekt mit Liebe betrachtet wird. Diese Beziehung beschreibt für den Betrachter weiter nichts im herkömmlichen Sinne, und doch ruft sie eine direkte Erfahrung dort hervor, wo Metapher und Gegenwart zusammen existieren können. Das wäre die natürliche Schlussfolgerung von Erkenntnis, nicht durch Zweifel vermittelt. Solche Gemälde wollte ich machen. Ohne den Schutz von Zynismus oder Melodrama und das würde meine eigene Gefühllosigkeit überkommen. Mit diesem Bedürfnis habe ich die Black Paintings begonnen. Ich habe Schwarz gewählt, weil es eine Forderung nach Anwesenheit darstellt ... Unter dem Druck der Stille."[3] „Die Black Paintings sind Früchte dieser Ideen. Die Vitalität des Schwarz, die Blumen und die kleinen Gegenstände, die auf den Gemälden erschienen, waren der Weg, durch Dekoration zu vereinfachen und durch die Auswahl, was hineinzunehmen sei, zu entleeren. In diesen Dichotomien gefangen, wurde Liebe, gegen-

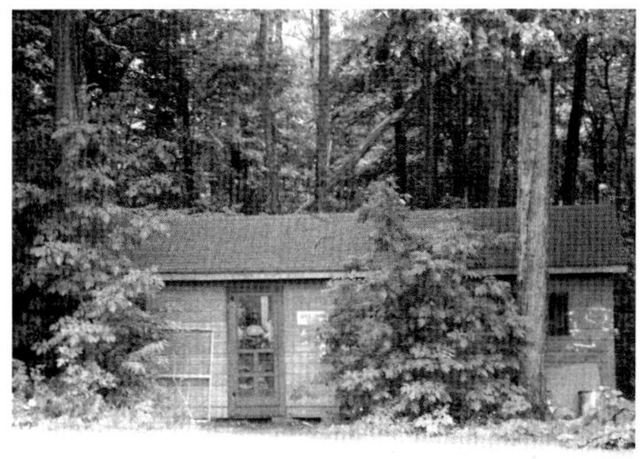

THE ARTIST'S STUDIO/DAS ATELIER DES KÜNSTLERS, SKOWHEGAN, MAINE, 1994

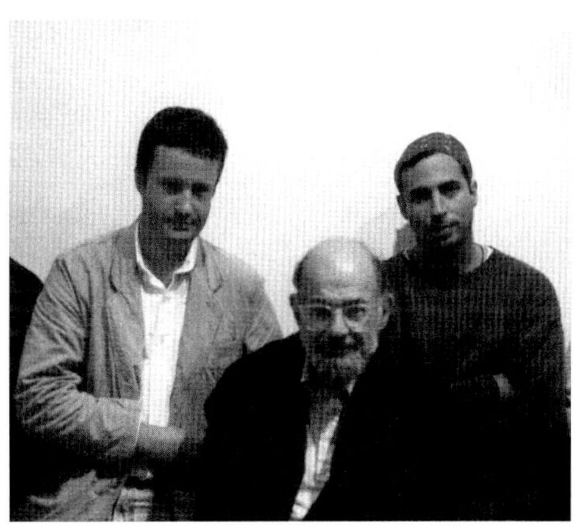

DONALD BAECHLER, ALLEN GINSBERG, AND MARTÍNEZ CELAYA, 1994

3. Enrique Martínez Celaya, *Black Paintings*, exhibition catalog/Ausstellungskatalog (Santa Barbara: University Art Museum, 1994).
4. Enrique Martínez Celaya, "About the Works" in *Presents & Proofs*, op. cit.

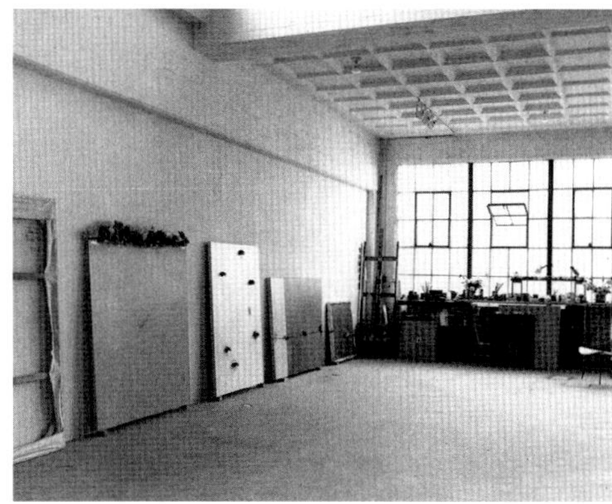

THE ARTIST'S STUDIO/DAS ATELIER DES KÜNSTLERS
POMONA, CALIFORNIA, 1995

facing page/gegenüberliegende Seite

PERFORMANCE DESTROYING ART WORK
/PERFORMANCE ZERSTÖRUNG VON KUNSTWERKEN
DANIEL ARVIZU GALLERY, SANTA ANA, CALIFORNIA, 1996

tere. The paintings were tempered by a poetry which was shyly but decidedly offered, and a certain quirkiness which prevented them from becoming overly severe. This series renewed my interest in paper, which became a way to navigate the distance from the verses to the silences. Patches lead to collages and materials found their way into the paper as grommets or tape. And by taping, patching and covering, the works on paper related presence and absence, echoing the concerns of my work for the past few years."[5] Works from this series include: *The Strawberry*, *The Wonderful Lies*, and *The Rope (for Cuba)*. Moves to Claremont, California. Accepts a position as Assistant Professor at Pomona College and transforms an old newspaper pressroom into his art studio.

1995
Joins Dorothy Goldeen Gallery where he exhibits for the first time his White Paintings. Frances K. Pohl describes the work in the exhibition's catalogue. She writes: "These paintings are silenced, rather than silent; they are brief attempts at communication quickly smothered by layers of dense whiteness, taut sheets upon which rest seemingly innocent, at times playful, objects but beneath which lie disturbing memories." Included in the exhibition are *Alibi*, *Sacrifice*, and *A Boy Named Sue*. A number of works from this series are also exhibited in a group show at the Newport Harbor Art Museum, Newport, California. Within this series of works, the head–an image central to the artist's work–first appears in *The Right Word*, 1994. Talks about the imagery of the work in a 1999 interview with Anne Trueblood Brodzky "...Are the heads self-portraits? Well, I think that in the work there are always coverings, stand-ins, and revelations. I think it is always my head, but it's my head as thought, or my head as remembered. It's not that important whether or not it looks like me. As a matter of fact, often when it looks like me I will change it. Some things have vestiges of self-portraiture. It's like the way a mirror works. I am purposely trying to distance them from me so I can see them."[6] Travels to New York City and visits with friends Donald Baechler and Pamela Fraser. Travels to London. Researches the history of Joan of Arc.

1996
Has first solo exhibition in New York at Tricia Collins•Grand Salon. A work is acquired by The Bronx Museum of the Arts, New York. Meets Ross Bleckner and Guillermo Kuitca. Becomes very interested in the iconog-

standsbezogen, aber umstritten, zur Hauptanregung und zum Ziel dieser Serie."[4] Interessiert sich für Zen-Philosophie.

1994
Austellung der Black Paintings im University of Art Museum, Santa Barbara, Kalifornien. Darunter sind: *Siempre Más/Immer mehr*, *Ballad for a Sprout/Ballade für einen Keimling*, *The Trouble with Memory/Das Problem mit dem Gedächtnis*, *Water Can/Gießkanne*, *Miner's Lung/Lunge eines Bergarbeiters*. Besteht sein Master of Fine Arts-Examen an der University of California, Santa Barbara, mit Auszeichnung und als Empfänger des Art Affiliates Award. Besucht die Skowhegan School of Painting and Sculpture, Skowhegan, Maine, wo er Donald Baechler und Allen Ginsberg begegnet. Erste Arbeiten der Serie Paintings for Company/Gemälde, um Gesellschaft zu haben, die er so beschreibt: „In ihnen blieb der Wert des Besonderen und der Stille erhalten, jedoch erwartete ich von ihnen eine neue Stufe Aufrichtigkeit und Intimität. Der Umgang mit der Farbe wurde einfacher, die Farbe heller und die Kompositionen strenger. Die Gemälde waren auch durch eine scheu, jedoch entschieden angebotene Poesie und eine gewisse Launigkeit bestimmt, was sie davon abhielt, übermäßig ernst zu werden. Mit dieser Serie erneuerte sich mein Interesse am Papier, das zu einem Medium wurde, die Entfernung von den Versen zur Stille zu überbrücken. Flicken entwickelten sich zu Collagen, andere Materialien wie Ösen und Klebestreifen gelangten ins Papier. Und durch Bekleben, Zusammenflicken und Abdecken vermittelten die Papierarbeiten Präsenz und Abwesenheit, was die Bemühungen meiner Arbeit der letzten Jahre widerspiegelt."[5] Werke dieser Serie sind: *The Strawberry/Die Erdbeere*, *The Wonderful Lies/Die wunderbaren Lügen* und *The Rope (for Cuba)/Das Seil (für Kuba)*. Zieht nach Claremont in Kalifornien. Nimmt eine Stellung als Assistant Professor am Pomona College an und baut eine alte Zeitungsdruckerei in ein Atelier um.

1995
Zusammenarbeit mit der Dorothy Goldeen Gallery, wo er das erste Mal seine White Paintings/Weiße Gemälde ausstellt. Im Katalog zu dieser Ausstellung beschreibt Frances K. Pohl diese Werke: „Diese Gemälde wurden eher zum Schweigen gebracht, als dass sie stumm sind; sie sind kurze Versuche zu kommunizieren, werden dann aber schnell durch Schichten von dichtem Weiß erstickt;

5. Enrique Martínez Celaya, "About the Works" in *Presents & Proofs*, op. cit.
6. Anne Brodzky, *Unbroken Poetry, the work of Enrique Martínez Celaya*, op. cit.

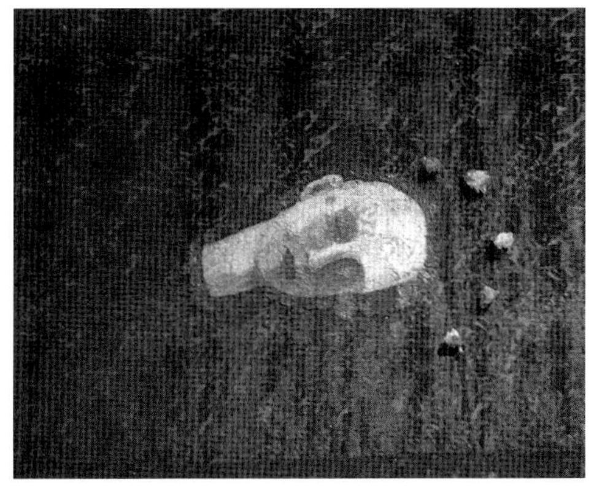
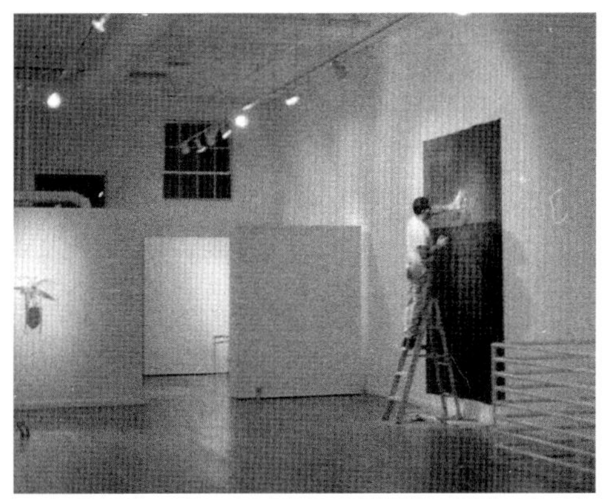
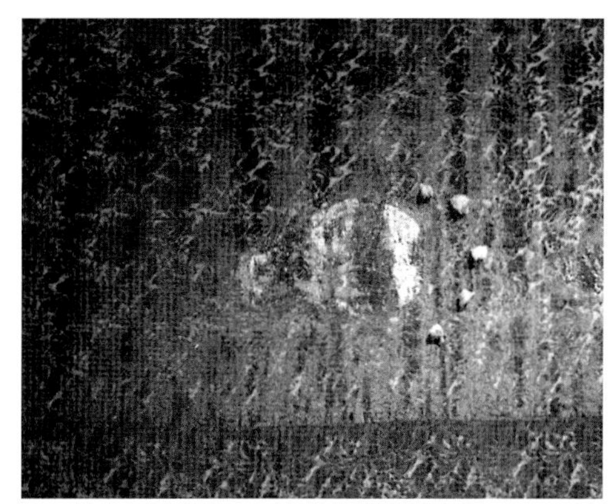
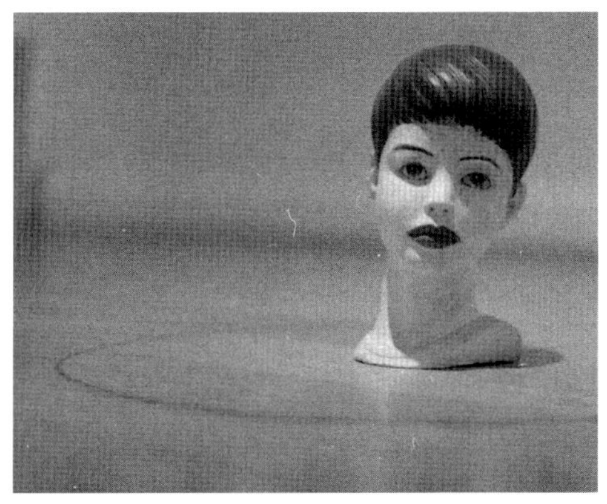
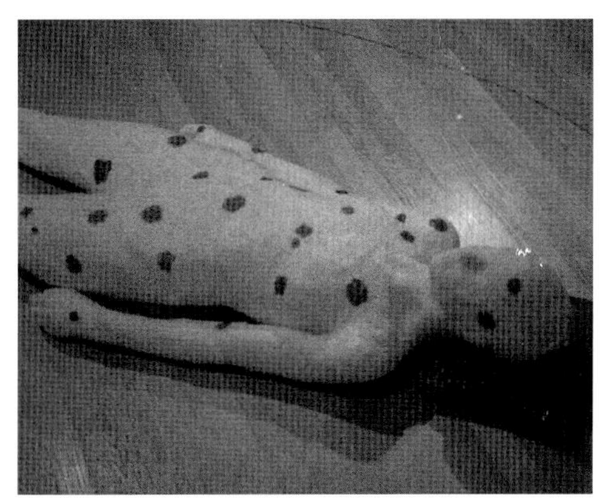
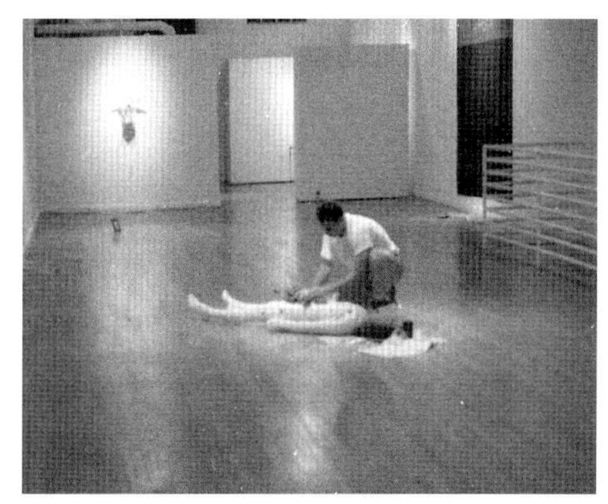
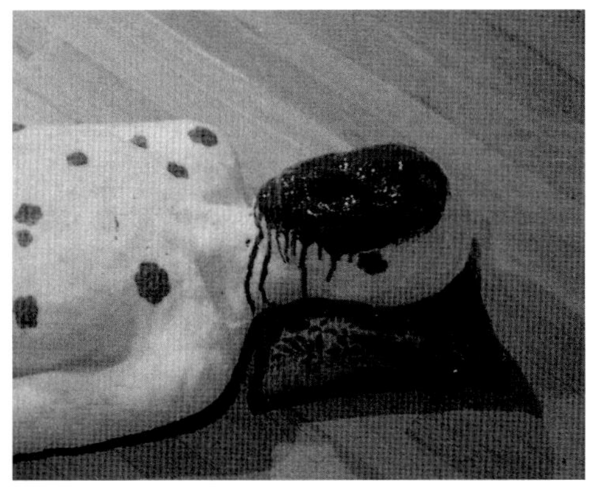
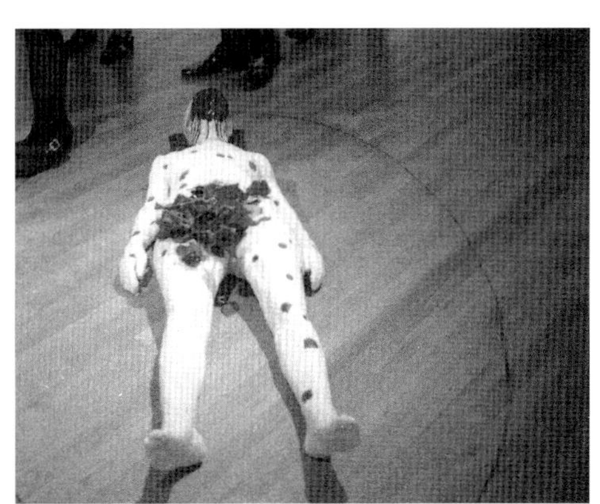
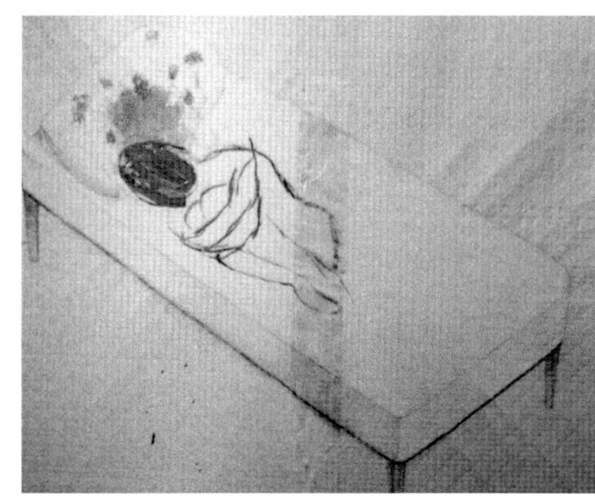
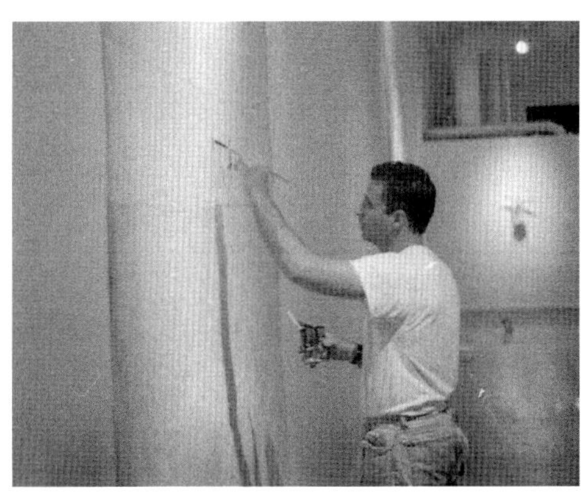
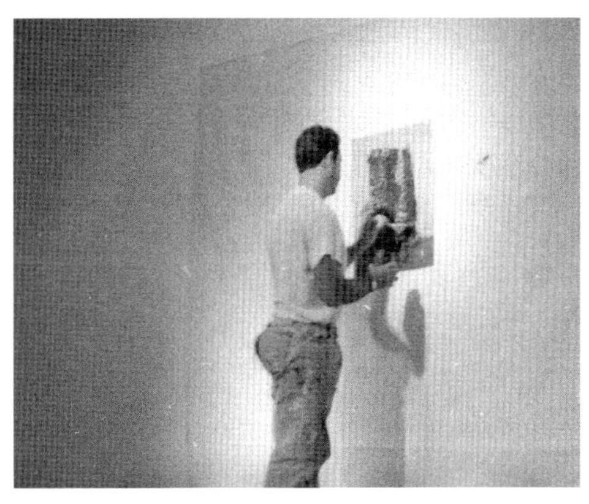
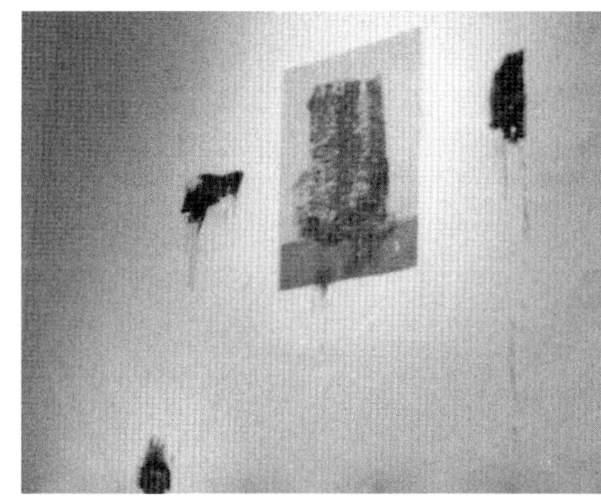

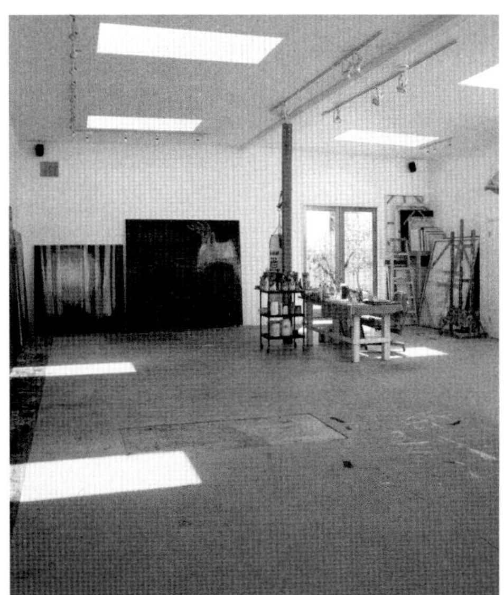

THE ARTIST'S STUDIO/DAS ATELIER DES KÜNSTLERS
VENICE, CALIFORNIA, 2001

raphy of martyred saints, and notions of sacrifice and redemption. Makes first works inspired by Joan of Arc, a series of twenty heart drawings beginning with *Destiny*, which in turn inspires his 'blankets' described as made "to prevent her [Jeanne d'Arc] from burning." In the catalogue accompanying his 1996 exhibition at Daniel Arvizu Gallery he states "Jeanne d'Arc is about the unknowable." Works from this series include: *Domremy*, *Orleans*, and *The Indictment*. Destroys all work related to Joan of Arc at the gallery where the work is exhibited. Moves to Venice, California.

1997

Is first inspired by the subject of St. Catherine. Reintroduces the figure in his work. Begins a series of etchings and monotypes. Works are acquired by the Arizona State University Art Museum and The Contemporary Museum, Honolulu, Hawaii. Meets Alexandra Williams. Joins his poetry and his artwork for the first time in an exhibition and catalogue in which he writes: "For me, these words and images weave a patchy fabric of displacement, history, and the tension between the personal and the impersonal.... In recent years I have wanted to fuse painting and poetry, to mix different forms of representation, in order to reach something more basic and more direct."[7] Joins Griffin Contemporary Exhibitions.

Example of poetry:

THE FIRST MEETING
Give me your stone,
I will bury mine and water yours.
Licking the aridness of your velvet
my tongue, your rag,
learning to make nothing of my teeth.

Visits Berlin and Hegel's tomb for first time. Describes the importance of Hegel to his work in an interview with M. A. Greenstein "I am interested in Hegel's ideas of reconciliation of opposites, the dialectic, which influences my disbelief in partial truths."[8] Makes a series of photographs inspired by a poem he wrote while in Berlin. Explains: "In the poem, as in the visual works, the question of reflection at the end of an epoch, doubt of reemergence, and displacement are present. The fragments, whether of bodies or architecture, are pieces lost or displaced by the evolution of time." Elaborates "I am trying to fix in time that which is inherently fugitive in time. These photographs are scattered pieces of events, memories and narratives"[9] The photographs include ink, tape and calligraphy.

gestraffte Papierbögen, auf denen, scheinbar unabsichtlich, zeitweise spielerisch, Objekte ruhen, unterhalb derer sich aber beunruhigende Erinnerungen befinden." Exponate dieser Ausstellung sind *Alibi*, *Sacrifice/Opfer* und *A Boy Named Sue/Ein Junge mit dem Namen Sue*. Einige dieser Werke werden auch in einer Gruppenausstellung im Newport Harbor Art Museum, Newport, Kalifornien, präsentiert. Innerhalb dieser Serie erscheint erstmalig der Kopf – ein zentrales Motiv im Werk des Künstlers – in *The Right Word/Das richtige Wort* aus dem Jahr 1994. 1999 spricht er in einem Interview mit Anne Trueblood Brodzky über die Metaphorik dieser Arbeit: „Sind die Köpfe Selbstporträts? Nun, ich glaube, dass es in meinen Arbeiten immer Verdeckung, Ersatz und Enthüllung gibt. Ich glaube, dass es immer mein Kopf ist, aber es ist mein Kopf als Gedanke oder mein Kopf als Erinnerung. Es ist nicht so wichtig, ob er aussieht wie ich oder nicht. Die Sache ist, wenn er so aussieht wie ich, ändere ich das oft. Einige Dinge haben eine Spur von Selbstporträts. Es funktioniert wie ein Spiegel. Ich versuche absichtlich, sie von mir zu entfernen, so dass ich sie sehen kann."[6] Reist nach New York City, wo er seine Freunde Donald Baechler und Pamela Fraser besucht. Reist nach London. Recherchiert die Geschichte der Johanna von Orléans.

1996

Erste Einzelausstellung in New York in Tricia Collins•Grand Salon. Eine Arbeit wird vom Bronx Museum of the Arts in New York erworben. Begegnet Ross Bleckner und Guillermo Kuitaca. Zeigt starkes Interesse an der Ikonographie von Märtyrerheiligen und an Vorstellungen von Aufopferung und Erlösung. Erste durch die Person der Johanna von Orléans angeregte Arbeiten; es entsteht eine Serie von zwanzig Herz-Zeichnungen, beginnend mit *Destiny/Schicksal*, das wiederum seine Blankets/Decken anregt, die als „um sie [Johanna von Orléans] vor dem Verbrennen zu schützen" gemacht beschrieben werden. Im Ausstellungskatalog der Daniel Arvizu Gallerie behauptet er 1996, dass „Jeanne d'Arc von dem Unfassbaren handelt". Werke der Serie sind: *Domremy*, *Orleans* und *The Indictment/Die Anklage*. Zerstört alle Arbeiten, die Johanna von Orléans thematisieren, in der Galerie, in der sie ausgestellt sind. Zieht nach Venice, Kalifornien.

7. Enrique Martínez Celaya, *Worksonpaperandsculptures*, exhibition catalog/Ausstellungskatalog (Venice: Griffin Contemporary and Old San Juan: Luigi Marrozzini Gallery, 1997).
8. M. A. Greenstein, "Why Hegel?" in *Berlin, the Fragility of Nearness* (Venice: William Griffin Editions, 1998).

Epilogue of *Berlin*:

We are all done.
We sit around a table,
shivering in between buildings
abandoned this afternoon,
and now with candles.
It is a long night and I have grown tired.
It is time to sleep.
I put my longing to your scars, Berlin,
my hope to your windows.
The earth burns bright
and we blow out the candles.
Cold, I lean against the brick wall,
my fingers playing with the wax,
and close my eyes to dream.
There are no angels
and no devils in Berlin.

1998
Has first solo exhibition in Europe at Galerie Bäumler, Regensburg, Germany. Receives the Los Angeles County Museum of Art Art Here and Now Award, for which a work is chosen for acquisition. Explains interest in the human body as a source of imagery, especially the expressionless human head and bird's heads which are portrayed with a sense of dignity, fatality and fragility. "These heads and the feelings they present, are my way to make images that insist or oppose that which the paintings establish. Sometimes they are intuitively produced and sometimes they are not, but they are always precipitated by the act of painting. Sometimes they hold together opposites, like violence and serenity, that seem to reconcile in the physical work. The compression of these opposites brings together different levels of awareness, and these in turn take physical form."[10]

1999
Marries Alexandra Williams. Explains imagery of work from 1999 in an interview with Anne Trueblood Brodzky. "I try to understand why the birds and all these other images came into my work. I think they came in because I didn't want to make figure paintings." "A fish, a very earthly thing, is very much bound in reality." "...the hummingbird itself is this sort of defiant little animal that when you hold it, it's as if there is nothing there. It is so insignificant in weight but its flight makes you very aware that it is very alive. Its definite presence of life, and its evanescent quality of weight, makes it a living metaphor for consciousness. So on one level the hummingbird is that. It can also become the manifestation of the spirit or a good way to suggest the spirit.... I like the fact

1997
Erstes Interesse am Thema der heiligen Katharina. Führt die Gestalt wieder in seine Arbeiten ein. Beginnt eine Serie Radierungen und Monotypien. Seine Arbeiten gelangen in die Sammlungen des Arizona State University Art Museums und des Contemporary Museums, Honolulu, Hawaii. Lernt Alexandra Williams kennen. Vereint erstmalig seine Gedichte und seine Kunstwerke in einer Ausstellung und einem Katalog, in dem er schreibt: „Für mich weben diese Worte und Bilder eine Flickenstruktur der Verdrängung, der Geschichte und der Spannung zwischen dem Persönlichen und dem Unpersönlichen ... In den letzten Jahren habe ich Malerei und Dichtung verschmelzen wollen, um unterschiedliche Formen der Darstellung zu mischen, um etwas Fundamentaleres und Direkteres zu erreichen."[7] Zusammenarbeit mit Griffin Contemporary Exhibitions.

Beispiel eines Gedichtes:

DIE ERSTE BEGEGNUNG
Gib mir deinen Stein,
Ich werde den meinen vergraben und
den deinen wässern.
Die Trockenheit deines Samtes leckend,
meine Zunge, dein Lappen,
lerne ich, nicht viel Wesen um meine
Zähne zu machen.

Besucht Berlin und das Grab Hegels zum ersten Mal. In einem Interview mit M.A. Greenstein beschreibt er den Einfluss Hegels auf sein Werk: „Ich bin an Hegels Idee der Aussöhnung von Gegensätzen, dem Dialektischen, interessiert, was Einfluss auf meinen Zweifel an Teilwahrheiten ausübt."[8] Es ensteht eine Serie von Photographien, angeregt durch ein Gedicht, das er während seines Aufenthaltes in Berlin schrieb. Er erklärt: „So wie in den visuellen Arbeiten sind auch im Gedicht die Frage nach dem Reflektieren am Ende einer Epoche, der Zweifel am Neuentstehen und der Aspekt der Verdrängung gegenwärtig. Die Fragmente, seien sie von Körpern oder von Architektur, sind Stücke, die durch die zeitliche Entwicklung verloren gingen oder verdrängt wurden." Er führt aus: „Ich versuche, in der Zeit das festzuhalten, was in der Zeit von Natur aus flüchtig ist. Diese Photographien sind verstreute Teile von Ereignissen, Erinnerungen und Erzählungen." Auf den Photographien werden Tinte, Klebeband und Kalligraphie verwendet.

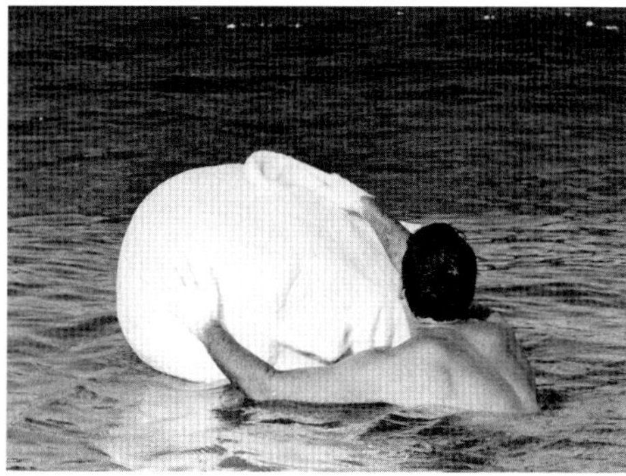

PERFORMANCE DOCUMENTATION/DOKUMENTATION DER PERFORMANCE MARINA DEL REY, CALIFORNIA, 1998

9. Enrique Martínez Celaya, "Notes" in *Berlin* (Los Angeles: Stephen Cohen Gallery and Venice: William Griffin Editions, 1998).
10. M.A. Greenstein, "Why Hegel?" in *Berlin, the Fragility of Nearness*, op. cit.

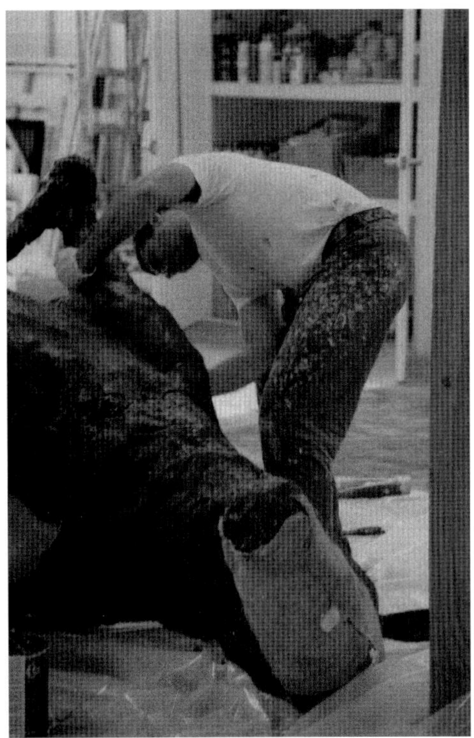

THE ARTIST IN HIS STUDIO/DER KÜNSTLER IN SEINEM ATELIER
VENICE, CALIFORNIA, 2000

that the juxtaposition of banality and seriousness can coexist within an image of a hummingbird."[11] "I often think of flowers, especially tulips, as symbols of decay and fungus."[12] Publishes notes regarding 1999 work. "In the new works (as in all the others) there is imagery that should be understood to be surrogates (Donald Baechler's word) of the figure and the spirit. These works are not about birds, or heads or flowers. Maybe this is true of many works. All these things are excuses, vehicles to get at specific moments that exist as artworks but that point beyond the artworks."[13] Works are aquired by The Museum of Fine Arts, Houston and The Frederick R. Weisman Art Museum, University of Minnesota.

2000
Continues to use the figure as a central part of his work and gives importance to landscape imagery. Works include: *El Bosque (Recuento)*, *Caminantes y la Nieve*, *Resolution*, and *Rain (The Wanderer)*. Shows work in solo gallery exhibitions in Los Angeles, San Francisco, New York, Seattle, and Monterrey, Mexico, and group exhibitions at the Los Angeles County Museum of Art and other museums.

2001
Exhibits sculptures, paintings, and photographs in inaugural show, *Coming Home*, at new space for Griffin Contemporary. All works in exhibition are acquired by Dieter and Si Rosenkranz, Berlin. Publishes first artist book, *October*, to accompany exhibition. Includes poem by the same name. Recent photographic works are acquired by the Hamburger Bahnhof, Museum für Gegenwart, Berlin, Germany; the Museum Ludwig, Cologne, Germany; the Museum of Photographic Arts, San Diego; the Oakland Museum of California, Oakland, California; The San Diego Museum of Contemporary Art, La Jolla, California and the Whitney Museum of American Art, New York. His work is the subject of a traveling museum exhibition organized by The Contemporary Museum, Honolulu, Hawaii, featuring work from 1992–2000. Introduces landscape imagery in most recent paintings. Receives the Hirsch Grant.

11. Anne Brodzky, *Unbroken Poetry, the work of Enrique Martínez Celaya*, op. cit.
12. Ibid.
13. Ibid.

Epilog zu *Berlin*:

Wir sind alle fertig.
Wir sitzen um einen Tisch herum,
zittern zwischen Gebäuden, die diesen
Nachmittag verlassen wurden,
und jetzt mit Kerzen.
Es ist eine lange Nacht und ich bin müde
geworden.
Es ist Zeit zu schlafen.
Ich setze meine Sehnsucht in deine
Narben, Berlin,
meine Hoffnung in deine Fenster.
Die Erde brennt hell
und wir blasen die Kerzen aus.
Kalt lehne ich an der Backsteinmauer,
meine Finger spielen mit dem Wachs,
und schließe meine Augen, um zu träumen.
Es gibt keine Engel
und keine Teufel in Berlin.

1998
Erste Einzelausstellung in Europa in der Galerie Bäumler in Regensburg, Deutschland. Erhält den Art Here and Now Award des Los Angeles County Museum of Art, im Zuge dessen ein Werk vom Museum erworben wird. Erklärt sein Interesse am menschlichen Körper als Quelle seiner Bildwelt, insbesondere des ausdruckslosen menschlichen Kopfes und der Vogelköpfe, die mit Sinn für Würde, Unabwendbarkeit und Zerbrechlichkeit abgebildet werden. „Diese Köpfe und die Gefühle, die sie darstellen, sind meine Art und Weise, Bilder zu machen, die auf dem bestehen oder dem widersprechen, was die Gemälde etablieren. Manchmal sind sie instinktiv hergestellt, manchmal auch nicht, aber sie werden immer durch den Akt des Malens beschleunigt. Manchmal halten sie Gegensätze wie Gewalt und Gelassenheit zusammen, die sich in den physischen Werken zu versöhnen scheinen. Die Verdichtung dieser Gegensätze bringt unterschiedliche Bewusstseinsebenen zusammen und diese nehmen eine gegenständliche Form an."[10]

1999
Heiratet Alexandra Williams. Erklärt die Bildsymbolik seiner seit 1999 entstandenen Werke in einem Interview mit Anne Trueblood Brodzky: „Ich versuche herauszufinden, warum die Vögel und all diese anderen Motive in mein Werk gelangten. Ich glaube, dass sie deswegen Eingang fanden, weil ich keine figurativen Bilder malen wollte." „Ein Fisch, ein sehr irdisches Wesen, ist der Realität sehr verhaftet." „... der Kolibri ist eine Art trotziges kleines Tier, so dass, wenn du es fest hältst, gar nichts vorhanden zu sein scheint. Sein Gewicht ist so unwesentlich, aber sein Flug

macht dir bewusst, dass er äußerst lebendig ist. Seine deutliche Lebenspräsenz und sein verschwindend geringes Gewicht machen ihn zu einer lebendigen Metapher des Bewusstseins. Das ist die eine Seite des Kolibris. Er kann aber auch Ausdruck des Geistes werden oder ein gutes Mittel, auf den Geist hinzuweisen. ... Ich mag es, dass Banalität und Seriosität im Bild des Kolibris koexistieren können."[11] „Ich betrachte Blumen, vor allem Tulpen, oft als Symbole für Verfall und Fungus."[12] Veröffentlicht Anmerkungen zu seinem 1999 entstandenen Werk: „Die neuen Arbeiten (wie auch all die anderen) enthalten eine Bildwelt, die als Surrogat (Donald Baechlers Wort) für die Gestalt und für den Geist verstanden werden sollte. Diese Werke handeln nicht von Vögeln oder Köpfen oder Blumen. Vielleicht gilt das für viele Arbeiten. All diese Dinge sind Ausreden, Vehikel, um zu bestimmten Momenten zu gelangen, die als Kunstwerke existieren, aber über sie hinaus weisen."[13] Einige seiner Arbeiten werden vom Museum of Fine Arts, Houston, und dem Frederick R. Weisman Art Museum, University of Minnesota, erworben

2000
Weiterhin stellt die Figur einen zentralen Bestandteil seines Werks dar und er misst Landschaftsmotiven Bedeutung zu. Einige Werke: *El Bosque (Recuento)*, *Caminantes y la Nieve*, *Resolution* und *Rain (The Wanderer)*. Zeigt Werke in Einzelausstellungen in Los Angeles, San Francisco, New York, Seattle und Monterrey, Mexiko, wie in Gruppenausstellungen im Los Angeles County Museum of Art und in anderen Museen.

2001
Zeigt Skulpturen, Gemälde und Photographien in *Coming Home*, der Eröffnungsausstellung des neuen Griffin Contemporary-Gebäudes. Alle Werke der Ausstellung werden von Dieter und Si Rosenkranz, Berlin, erworben. Begleitend erscheint in Amsterdam das erste Künstlerbuch, *October* mit dem gleichnamigen Gedicht. Neuere photographische Arbeiten werden vom Hamburger Bahnhof, Museum für Gegenwart, Berlin, dem Museum Ludwig, Köln, dem Museum of Photographic Arts, San Diego, dem Oakland Museum of California, dem San Diego Museum of Contemporary Art, La Jolla, und dem Whitney Museum of American Art, New York, angekauft. Sein Werk ist Thema einer vom Museum of Contemporary Art, Honolulu, organisierten Wanderausstellung für Museen, die Arbeiten von 1992 bis 2000 in den Mittelpunkt stellt. Führt Landschaftsmotive in seine neuesten Gemälde ein. Erhält den Hirsch Grant.

IT WAS NOT TIME OR CIRCUMSTANCE
that displaced your memory.
It was concentration.

Then the whole house filled with birds
flapping their wings
shaping the air into snowballs of sound
which they threw against corners
long ago left to silence.

The yard, abandoned to weeds,
had the flowers of laughter,
and the window flickered
light over the porcelain fish
which
jumped from the dark crystal table.

GERMAN TRANSLATION ON PAGE 282/DEUTSCHE ÜBERSETZUNG AUF SEITE 282

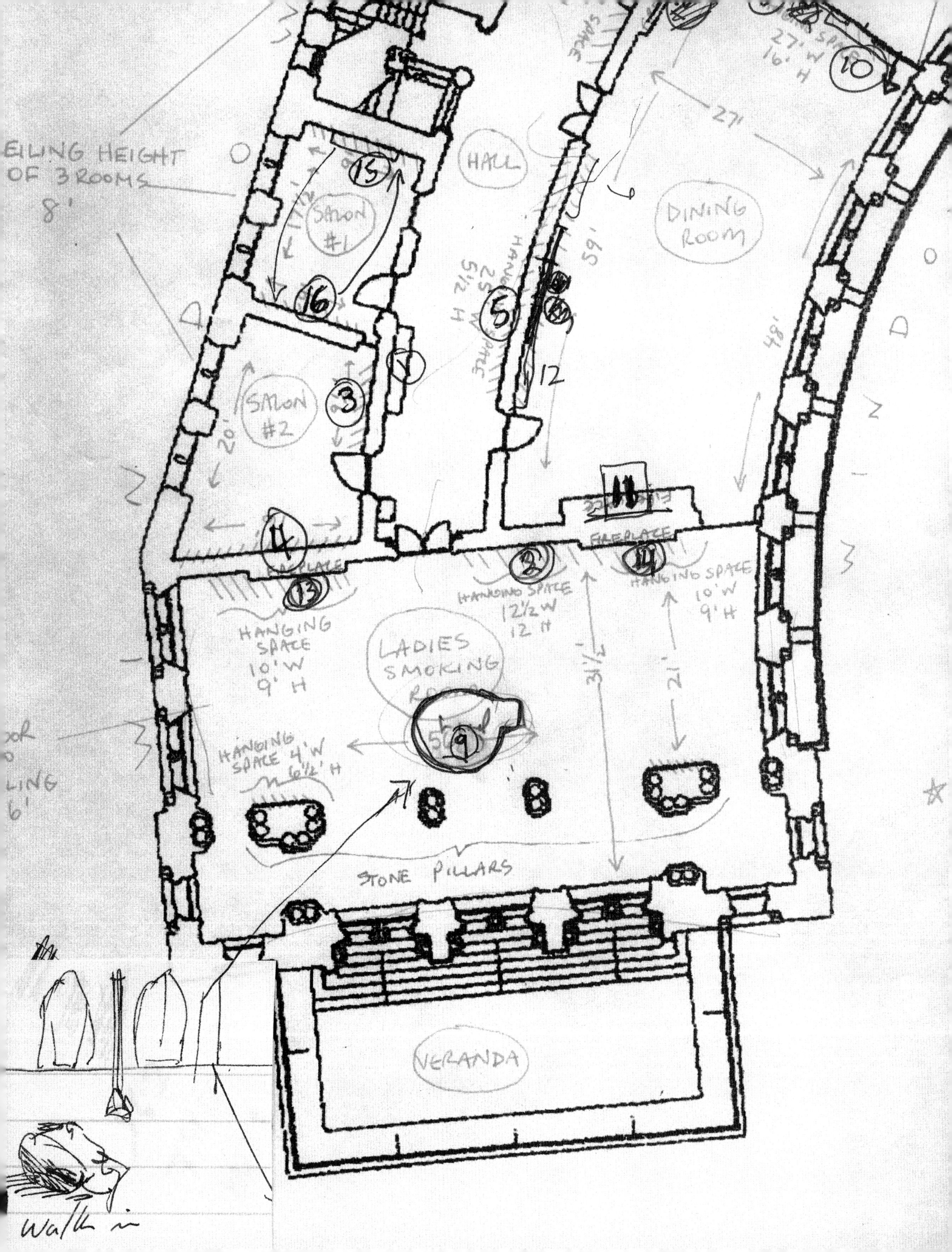

EILING HEIGHT OF 3 ROOMS 8'
HALL
DINING ROOM
27'
27' W
16' H
10
15
SALON #1
16
5
HANGING SPACE
12
59'
48'
SALON #2
3
20'
4
FIREPLACE
13
2
11
FIREPLACE
14
HANGING SPACE 10' W 9' H
HANGING SPACE 12 1/2 W 12 H
HANGING SPACE 10'W 9'H
LADIES SMOKING ROOM
31 1/2
21'
9
HANGING SPACE 4'W 6 1/2' H
STONE PILLARS
VERANDA
Walk in

BIBLIOGRAPHY AND EXHIBITION HISTORY /BIBLIOGRAPHIE UND AUSSTELLUNGSGESCHICHTE

PUBLICATIONS BY THE ARTIST /VERÖFFENTLICHUNGEN DES KÜNSTLERS

Guthrie, Albee Press, Berkeley, 1989;

Poems for the Bed, Albee Press, Berkeley, 1991;

Berlin, Stephen Cohen Gallery, Los Angeles, 1998;

Selections from Les Fleurs du Mal by Charles Baudelaire, Edited by Enrique Martínez Celaya, Whale and Star Press, Los Angeles, 2000;

October, Cinubia, Amsterdam, 2001.

BOOKS, SOLO EXHIBITION CATALOGUES /BÜCHER, KATALOGE VON EINZELAUSSTELLUNGEN

Enrique Martínez Celaya, Sunnyvale Arts Center, Sunnyvale, CA, 1992. Text by Patrice Wagner;

Enrique Martínez Celaya, Galeria Botello, PR, 1993. Text by Michael Darling;

The Black Paintings, University Art Museum, Santa Barbara, CA, 1994. Text by Enrique Martínez Celaya;

Presents and Proofs, Meridian Gallery, San Francisco, CA, and Ro Snell Gallery, Santa Barbara, CA, 1994. Text by Stephen Westfall;

Lions of Frosting, Dorothy Goldeen Gallery, Santa Monica, CA, 1995. Text by Frances Pohl;

Jeanne D'Arc, A Dress for her Marriage of Fire and Four Blankets to Prevent her from Burning, Daniel Arvizu Gallery, Santa Ana, CA, 1996. Text by Enrique Martínez Celaya;

Enrique Martínez Celaya, Tricia Collins • Grand Salon, New York, NY, 1996. Text by Charles A. Riley;

Works on Paper, Luigi Marrozini Gallery, San Juan, Puerto Rico and Griffin Contemporary Exhibitions, Venice, CA, 1997. Poems by Enrique Martínez Celaya;

Berlin, The Fragility of Nearness, Griffin Contemporary, Venice, CA, 1998. Texts by Abigail Solomon-Godeau, Peter Frank and M. A. Greeenstein;

Unbroken Poetry, the work of Enrique Martínez Celaya, Whale and Star Press, Venice, CA, 1999. Text by Anne Trueblood Brodzky and interviews with Amnon Yariv and Donald Baechler;

Paintings of Mercy, Rena Bransten Gallery, San Francisco, 2000. Text by Collette Chattopadhyay;

Enrique Martínez Celaya, Galeria Ramis Barquet, 2000. Text by Charles Merewether.

GROUP EXHIBITION BOOKS AND CATALOGUES /GRUPPENAUSSTELLUNGEN: BÜCHER UND KATALOGE

New American Talent, Laguna Gloria Art Museum, Austin, 1993. Text by Kerry Brougher;

Nature re(Contained), Irvine Fine Arts Center, Irvine, 1995. Text by Dorrit Rawlins;

Point, Counterpoint, Santa Barbara Museum of Art, Santa Barbara, 1995. Text by Diana Dupon;

Labyrinth of Multitude, Luckman Gallery, Los Angeles, 1999. Text by Susana Bautista;

Representing LA, The Frye Art Museum, Seattle, 2000;

Made in California: Art, Image, and Identity 1900–2000, Los Angeles County Museum of Art, University of California Press, Berkeley, 2000.

INTERVIEWS/INTERVIEWS

Christopher Miles, "A conversation with Enrique Martínez Celaya, painter," Art Week, December 1997, pp. 15–17;

M. A. Greenstein, "Why Hegel?," Berlin, The Fragility of Nearness, William Griffin Editions, Venice, 1998, pp. 73–80;

Amnon Yariv, "Compassion and Subjectivity," Unbroken Poetry, the work of Enrique Martínez Celaya, Whale and Star Press, Venice, 1999, pp. 67–75;

Donald Baechler, "Imagery and Process," Unbroken Poetry, the work of Enrique Martínez Celaya, Whale and Star Press, Venice, 1999, pp. 78–83;

Howard Fox, "Interview with Enrique Martínez Celaya," Modern and Contemporary Art Council of the Los Angeles County Museum of Art, at Griffin Contemporary, Venice, 1999;

Beatrice Foessel, "Interview with Enrique Martínez Celaya," www.templeflower.com, August, 2001.

ARTICLES AND REVIEWS/ARTIKEL UND KRITIKEN

"Estudiante construye láser," Departamento de Energiá, Revista, San Juan, Spring, 1982;

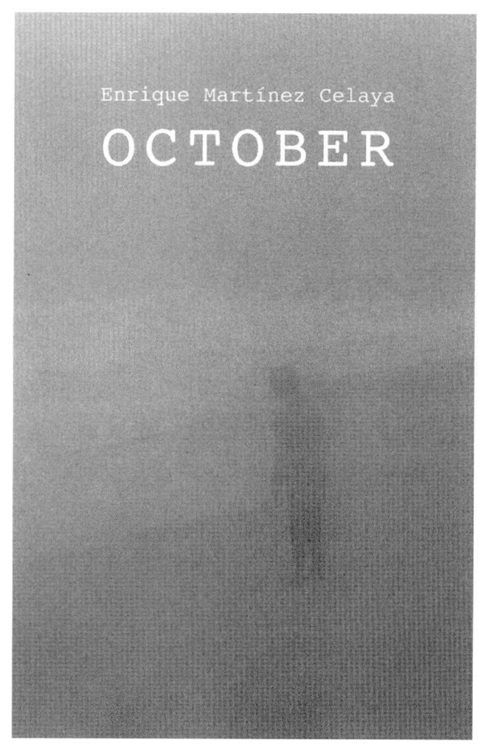

OCTOBER, ARTIST BOOK/KÜNSTLERBUCH, CINUBIA, AMSTERDAM, 2001

facing page/gegenüberliegende Seite

LAYOUT FOR/PLAN FÜR SAINT PANCRAS CHAMBERS LONDON, UNITED KINGDOM, 2000

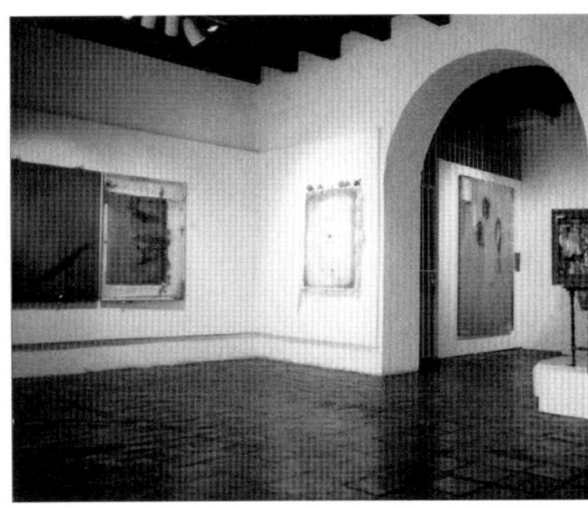

GALERIA BOTELLO
SAN JUAN, PUERTO RICO, 1993

Mario Alegre, "Profuso y cálido cromatismo en Martínez Celaya," El Nuevo Día, San Juan, June 28, 1991;

Stalks, Emeryville, 1991;

Derk Richardson, "Eight Days a Week," San Francisco Bay Guardian, San Francisco, 1992;

Dorothy Burkhart, "An Artist Worth Being Excited About," San Jose Mercury News, San Jose, March 18, 1992, p. 7D;

Pam O'Connell, "Arts Beat," Billboard Express, Berkeley, May 8, 1992, p. 33;

"Arte," El Nuevo Dia, San Juan, March 23, 1993;

Eneid Routte-Gomez, The San Juan Star, San Juan, March 23, 1993;

Manuel Álvarez Lezama, "Exhibit Asks Viewers to Question Boundaries," The San Juan Star, San Juan, April 7, 1993, p. F11;

Michael Darling, "An Unusually Rich Storehouse of Ideas," Scene Magazine, Santa Barbara, August 20, 1993;

Michael Darling, "Viewing Works Together, Singularly," Santa Barbara News Press, Santa Barbara, October 11, 1993;

Michael Darling, "The Graduate," Scene Magazine, Santa Barbara, April 29, 1994, pp. 23–24;

Chris George, Arts Week: Daily Nexus, Santa Barbara, May 19, 1994, p. 4;

Judith Callander, The Independent, Santa Barbara, May 19, 1994, p. 50;

Steven Jenkins, "An Open Heart," Artweek, November 17, 1994;

Joan Crowder, "Drawing the Viewers Into His Personal Drama," Santa Barbara News Press, Santa Barbara, November 25, 1994, p. 63;

Paul Von Froemming, "Gifts of Love," The Independent, Santa Barbara, December 1, 1994, p. 58;

David A. Greene, "Painting the Town," Los Angeles Reader, Los Angeles, September 29, 1995;

Joan Crowder, "A Vision with Two Views," Santa Barbara News Press, Santa Barbara, December 8, 1995, pp. 7–8;

Rebecca Schoenkopf, "A Marriage in Blood," OC Weekly, Orange County, August 9, 1996, p. 25;

P. Y., "Enrique Martínez Celaya," Buzz Weekly, Los Angeles, January 31–February 6, 1997, p. 14;

Eleanor Welles, "Enrique Martínez Celaya," ArtScene, February, 1997;

Nina Ellerman, "Self-portrait with Cup," Pomona College Magazine, Claremont, Spring, 1997, pp. 24–31;

Mario Alegre Barrios, El Nuevo Día, San Juan, September 2, 1997;

Enrique García Gutiérrez, "El artista en su laberinto," En Nuevo Día, Revista Domingo, San Juan, September 21, 1997, pp. 10–13;

Manuel Alvarez Lezama, San Juan Star, San Juan, October 3, 1997;

Armando Alvarez Bravo, El Nuevo Herald, Miami, November 2, 1997, p. 5E;

Rodolfo Windhausen, "Arte Latinoamericano," La Prensa, New York, November 23, 1997;

Art Scene, October 28–November 4, 1997;

Christopher Miles, "A conversation with Enrique Martínez Celaya, painter," Art Week, December, 1997, pp. 15–17;

Carol Damian, "Enrique Martínez Celaya," Art Nexus, January–March, 1998, pp. 132–133;

Peter Frank, "Enrique Martínez Celaya," ArtNews, 1998, February, p. 123;

Carrie Click, "Sultan, Celaya debut Baldwin's new space," Aspen Times, Aspen, February 14, 1998, p. 14B;

José Antonio Pérez Ruiz, "Enrique Martínez Celaya," Art Nexus, May, 1998, pp. 132–133;

T. W. Brown, The Argonaut, Venice, May 14, 1998, p. 23;

Mittelbayerische Zeitung, Regensburg, June 28, 1998, p. R6;

Claudia Böckel, "Er Will Bewegen: No Entertaining!" Mittelbayerische Zeitung, Regensburg, June 30, 1998;

Helmut Hein, "Atemwende oder Die Welt im Kopf," Mittelbayerische Zeitung, Regensburg, August 6, 1998;

Claudine Isé, "Visual Poetry," Los Angeles Times, Los Angeles, October 30, 1998, p. 30;

Dru Hilty, "Arts and Features," The Student Life, Claremont, October 30, 1998, p. 4;

Tricia Collins, "Tablet, the work of three poets," Zing Magazine, Winter, 1998, pp. 134–138;

Leah Ollman, "Meditation," Los Angeles Times, Los Angeles, December 25, 1998, p. F-40;

Art Scene, December 26, 1998;

Judy Perez, "Art on the Fringes," Claremont Courier, Claremont, April 10, p. 9;

Suvan Geer, "Enrique Martínez Celaya," Art Nexus, May–July, 1999, pp. 131–132;

Leah Ollman, "Enrique Martínez Celaya at Griffin Contemporary Exhibitions," Art in America, May, 1999, p. 166;

Neal Brown, "Enrique Martínez Celaya" The Independent, London, October 24, 1999;

Peter Frank, "Art Picks of the Week," LA Weekly, Los Angeles, October 29–November 4, 1999;

Walter Browning, "Terminal Thoughts," Hampstead and Highgate Express, London, November 5, 1999;

M. F., "Another Late Arrival," Highbury and Islington Express, London, November 12, 1999;

Eva Forgacs, "Enrique Martínez Celaya," Art Issues, Los Angeles, January/February, 2000, p. 49;

Clare McLean, "Artists as Vehicles for their own Ideas," www.artaccess.com, March, 2000, pp. 8–9;

Emily Hall, "New Developments: Photo Fact and Fiction," The Stranger, Seattle, March 23, 2000, p. 33;

Bertha Wario, "Encuentra en pintura respuesta a preguntas," El Norte, Monterrey, April 26, 2000;

David Hernandez, "De poesía, pintura y escultura," Diario de Monterrey, Monterrey, May 3, 2000, p. 38;

Leah Ollman, "Poetry in Pictures," Los Angeles Times, Los Angeles, May 26, 2000, p. F-21;

Bill Fark, "North County artists featured in museum exhibit," North County Times, June 2, 2000, pp. 3, 36;

Peter Frank, "Art Picks of the Week," LA Weekly, Los Angeles, June 2–8, 2000, p. 152;

Robert L. Pincus, "Next Wave shows the Versatility and Talent of Southern California Artists," The San Diego Union-Tribune, San Diego, June 8, 2000, pp. 32–33;

Bill Fark, "California artists show diversity in museum show," North County Times, June 9, 2000, pp. 33–34;

Noah Simblist, "Enrique Martínez Celaya at Eyre/Moore," Red Headed Step Child, Seattle, July, 2000, pp. 1–2;

Collette Chattopadhyay, "Enrique Martínez Celaya at Griffin Contemporary," Art Week, July/August, 2000, pp. 20–21;

Ions, Noetic Sciences Review, San Francisco, September–December, 2000, p. 25;

Barbara Thornburg, "Latin Quarters," Los Angeles Times Magazine, Los Angeles, September 24, 2000, pp. 32–35;

Calvin Tompkins, "Enrique Martínez Celaya," The New Yorker, December 11, 2000, p. 26;

Tom Breidenbach, "Enrique Martínez Celaya," Art Forum, February, 2001, p. 155;

Peter Frank, "Art Picks of the Week," LA Weekly, Los Angeles, February 16–22, 2001, p. 150;

Jeremy Rosenberg, "The Evolution of Enrique," Los Angeles Times, Los Angeles, March 6, 2001;

Carl Heyward, Art Papers, May/June, 2001, p. 53.

SOLO EXHIBITIONS/EINZELAUSSTELLUNGEN

1993

Galeria Botello, San Juan, Puerto Rico

1994

Ro Snell Gallery, Santa Barbara, California

Meridian Gallery, San Francisco, California

University Art Museum, Santa Barbara, California

1995

Dorothy Goldeen Gallery, Santa Monica, California

1996

Tricia Collins•Grand Salon, New York, New York

Rena Bransten Gallery, San Francisco, California

Bronx Museum of the Arts (with Alberto Rey), Bronx, New York

Daniel Arvizu Gallery, Santa Ana, California

1997

Burnett Miller Gallery, Santa Monica, California

Galeria Luigi Marrozzini, San Juan, Puerto Rico

Galerie Douyon, Miami, Florida

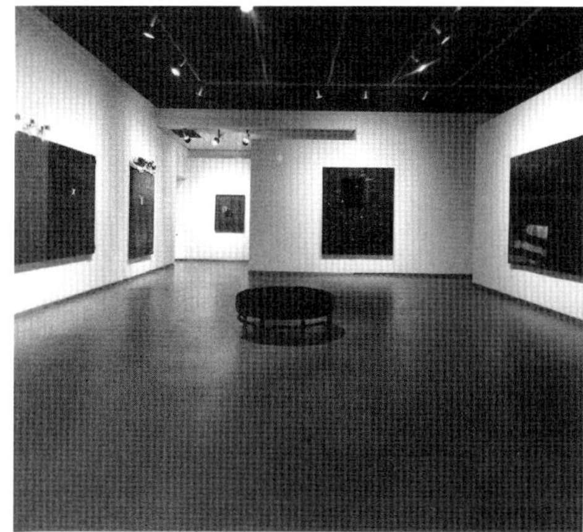

UNIVERSITY ART MUSEUM
SANTA BARBARA, CALIFORNIA, 1994

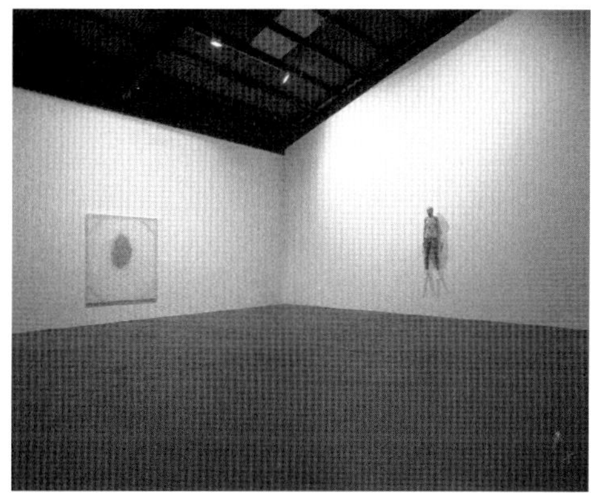

BURNETT MILLER GALLERY
SANTA MONICA, CALIFORNIA, 1997

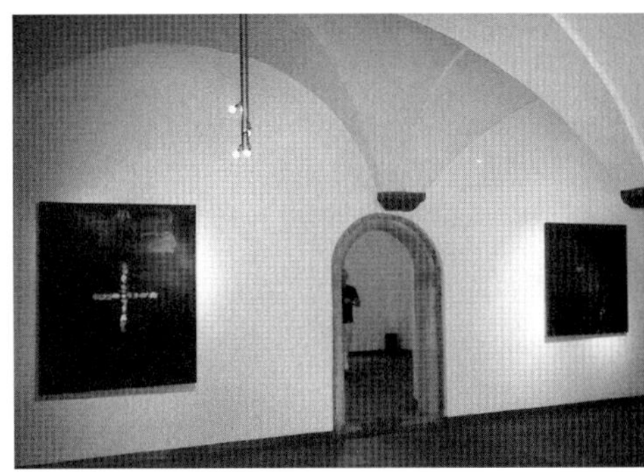

GALERIE BÄUMLER
REGENSBURG, GERMANY, 1998

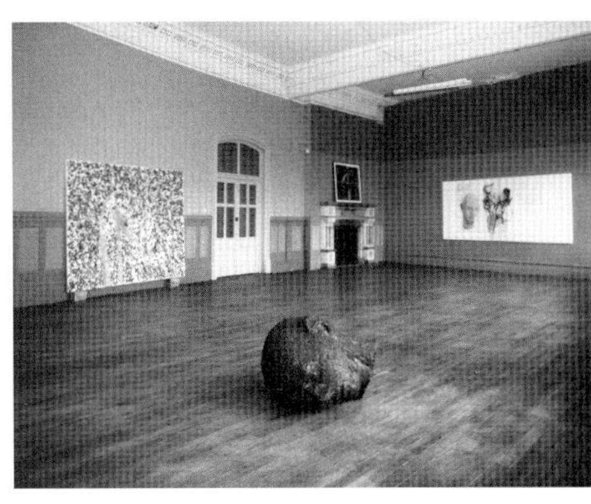

ANDREW MUMMERY GALLERY, INSTALLATION AT/EXPONATE IN DEN ST. PANCRAS CHAMBERS, LONDON, UNITED KINGDOM, 1998

Griffin Contemporary, Venice, California

1998

Galerie Bäumler, Regensburg, Germany

Griffin Contemporary, Venice, California

Baldwin Gallery, Aspen, Colorado

Stephen Cohen Gallery, Los Angeles, California

Rena Bransten Gallery, San Francisco, California

1999

Andrew Mummery Gallery, London, United Kingdom

ARCO, Cutting Edge, Madrid, Spain

Griffin Contemporary, Venice, California

2000

Galeria Ramis Barquet, New York, New York

Rena Bransten Gallery, San Francisco, California

Galeria Ramis Barquet, Monterrey, Mexico

Griffin Contemporary, Venice, California

Eyre/Moore Gallery, Seattle, Washington

2001

The Contemporary Museum, Honolulu, Hawaii

The Orange County Museum of Art, Newport Beach, California

Sandra and David Bakalar Gallery, Massachusetts College of Art, Boston, Massachusetts

FIAC 2001, Paris, France

Baldwin Gallery, Aspen, Colorado

Griffin Contemporary, Venice, California

GROUP EXHIBITIONS/GRUPPENAUSSTELLUNGEN

1979

Liga de Arte de San Juan, San Juan, Puerto Rico

1991

Corvallis Art Center, Corvallis, Oregon

Galeria Botello, San Juan, Puerto Rico

1992

Oakland Museum, Oakland, California

R.B. Stevenson Gallery, La Jolla, California

1993

Brown County Museum, Brownwood, Texas

Galeria Botello, San Juan, Puerto Rico

Ro Snell Gallery, Santa Barbara, California

Plainview Cultural Arts Council, Plainview, Texas

Atkinson Gallery, Santa Barbara, California

1994

Chattahoochee Valley Art Museum, *Lagrange XVIII National Biennial,* Lagrange, Georgia

Cheekwood Museum of Art, *National Contemporary Painting Exhibition,* Nashville, Tennessee

Contemporary Arts Forum, Santa Barbara, California

Laguna Gloria Art Museum, Austin, Texas

Texas A & M University Gallery, College Station, Texas

Los Angeles Municipal Art Gallery, Los Angeles, California

Ro Snell Gallery, Santa Barbara, California

1995

Santa Barbara Museum of Art, *Re-Inventing the Avant-Garde: Modernism and the Art of Latin America,* Santa Barbara, California

Newport Harbor Art Museum, Newport Beach, California

Museo Regional de Arte y Cultura, Palos, Cuba

Laguna Gloria Art Museum, *New American Talent: The Eleventh Exhibition,* Austin, Texas

Dorothy Goldeen Gallery, Santa Monica, California

Irvine Fine Arts Center, *Nature re(Contained),* Irvine, California

1996

Triton Museum of Art, *Drawings: Realism to Abstraction,* Santa Clara, California

Museum of Contemporary Art, Annual Auction, Santa Monica, California

Reed's Wharf Gallery, London, United Kingdom

Rena Bransten Gallery, San Francisco, California

Carla Stellweg Gallery, New York, New York

Griffin-Linton Contemporary Exhibitions, *Codpieces,* Venice, California

Tricia Collins • Grand Salon, New York, New York

Dorothy Goldeen Gallery, Santa Monica, California

1997

The Contemporary Museum, *The Permanent Collection*, Honolulu, Hawaii

Contemporary Arts Forum, Santa Monica, California

Andrew Mummery/33 Great Sutton Street, London, United Kingdom

George Adams Gallery, New York, New York

Tricia Collins • Grand Salon, *Conversions*, New York, New York

Rena Bransten Gallery, *Pool*, San Francisco, California

1998

Galerie T-19, Vienna, Austria

Fredric Snitzer Gallery, Miami, Florida

Weatherspoon Art Gallery, *Art on Paper*, University of North Carolina, Greensboro

Arkansas Art Center, *National Drawing Invitational*, Little Rock, Arkansas

Griffin Contemporary Exhibitions, Venice, California

Charles Cowles Gallery, New York, New York

Montgomery Gallery, *Interactions*, Claremont, California

Rare Gallery, *Pulse, Painting Now*, New York, New York

Rare Gallery, *California Current*, New York, New York

Luigi Marrozzini Gallery, *Pequeño Formato*, San Juan, Puerto Rico

1999

Los Angeles County Museum of Art, *Recent Acquisitions*, Los Angeles, California

Museo de las Americas, *Pequeño Formato 98.99*, San Juan, Puerto Rico

Griffin Contemporary Exhibitions, *Sculpture Show*, Venice, California

Luckman Fine Arts Gallery, California State University, *Contemporary Latin American Artists in Los Angeles*, Los Angeles, California

2000

California Center for the Arts, *Next Wave: New Painting in Southern California*, Escondido, California

Los Angeles County Museum of Art, *Made in California: Art, Image and Identity, 1900–2000*, Los Angeles, California

Frye Art Museum, *Representing LA*, Seattle, Washington

Eyre/Moore Gallery, *SelfDeveloped*, Seattle, Washington

Delaware Center for the Contemporary Arts, *Material and Ethereal*, Wilmington, Delaware

2001

Von der Heydt-Museum, *Nothing to Remember–Nothing to Forget*, Wuppertal, Germany

Momus Gallery, Tula Art Center, *Contemporary Latin American Art*, Atlanta, Georgia

Sheldon Memorial Art Gallery, *Surrealism in Photography*, University of Nebraska, Lincoln, Nebraska

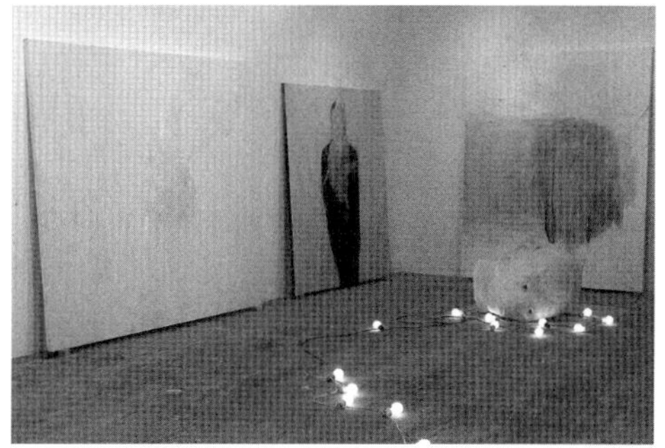

PICTURES OF MERCY, EXHIBITION ANNOUNCEMENT /BILDER DER GNADE, AUSSTELLUNGSANKÜNDIGUNG RENA BRANSTEN GALLERY, SAN FRANCISCO, CALIFORNIA, 2000

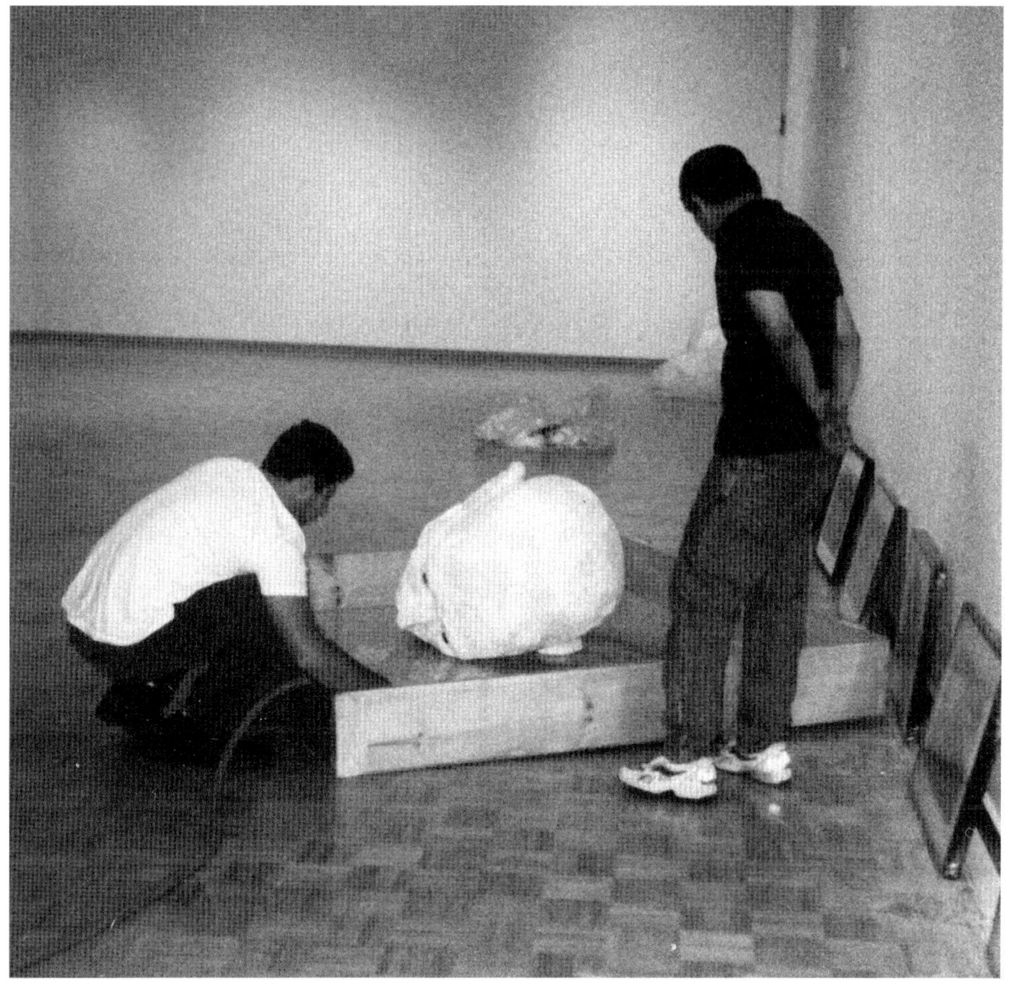

INSTALLING AT THE/AUFBAU IN DER LUCKMAN FINE ARTS GALLERY LOS ANGELES, CALIFORNIA, 1999

facing page/gegenüberliegende Seite

THE ARTIST'S STUDIO/DAS ATELIER DES KÜNSTLERS
VENICE, CALIFORNIA, 2001

SELECTED MUSEUM COLLECTIONS /AUSGEWÄHLTE SAMMLUNGEN (MUSEEN)

Arizona State University Art Museum, Tempe, Arizona

Arkansas Arts Center, Little Rock, Arkansas

The Bronx Museum of the Arts, Bronx, New York

The Contemporary Museum, Honolulu, Hawaii

Davenport Museum of Art, Davenport, Iowa

Frederick R. Weisman Art Museum, University of Minnesota, Minneapolis, Minnesota

German Centre of Photography, Berlin, Germany

Hamburger Bahnhof, Museum für Gegenwart, Berlin, Germany

Los Angeles County Museum of Art, Los Angeles, California

Museum Ludwig, Cologne, Germany

Montgomery Gallery, Pomona College, Claremont, California

Museo Extremeño Iberoamericano de Arte Contemporáneo (MEIAC), Badajoz, Spain.

Museum of Art, Fort Lauderdale, Florida

The Museum of Fine Arts, Houston, Texas

Museum of Photographic Arts, San Diego, California

Neues Stadtmuseum der Stadt Landsberg/Lech, Germany

Oakland Museum of California, Oakland, California

Palm Springs Desert Museum, Palm Springs, California

Sammlung und Privatmuseum Martin Scheuerer, Germany

San Diego Museum of Contemporary Art, La Jolla, California

Sheldon Memorial Art Gallery and Sculpture Garden, University of Nebraska, Lincoln, Nebraska

Whitney Museum of American Art, New York, New York

SELECTED CORPORATE COLLECTIONS /AUSGEWÄHLTE SAMMLUNGEN (FIRMEN)

The Capital Group, Los Angeles, California

MGM Grand, Las Vegas, Nevada

Microsoft Corporation, Seattle, Washington

Neuberger Berman, New York, New York

The Progressive Corporation, Cleveland, Ohio

RBC Dain Rauscher, Minneapolis, Minnesota

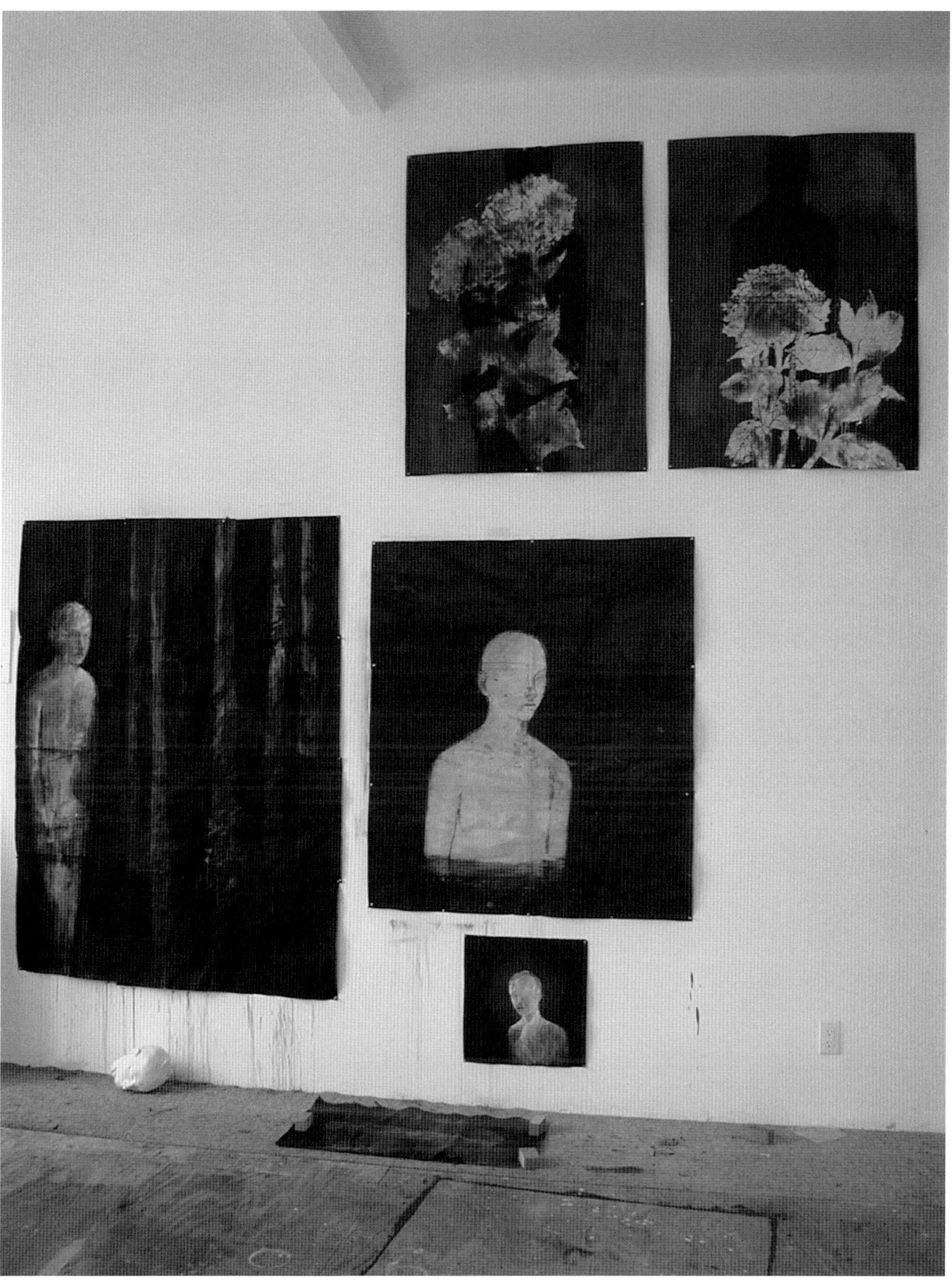

OCTOBER
black and white birches
open
and then dissolve
in the light of morning.
A morning of feathers,
of the frail water of snow.

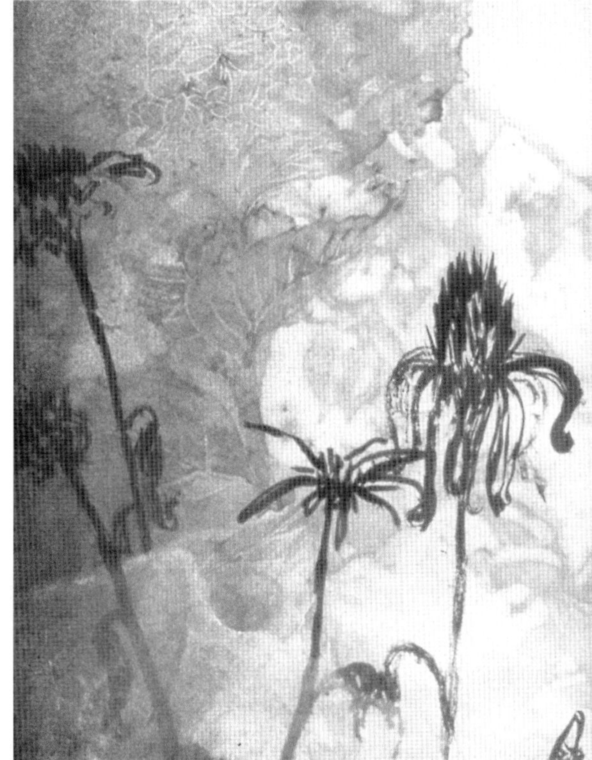

In the clearing
the merciful
raises his handless arm.
The architect of black bark
releases
a dove
of the lightest wood.
The wood of your exit.

All doors open to a withering garden
from which you will not return.

In the unspoken white
of the hour of angels
the remembered, bruised and restless,
collapses unheard
on icy leaves.
The mirror
that you placed on his antlers
rolls and softly etches a line and
when it comes to rest
it is all sky-unveiled, beyond mercy.

In the reflection
a dove
opens
and then dissolves
in the light of morning.
A morning of hunger,
of the coming of winter.

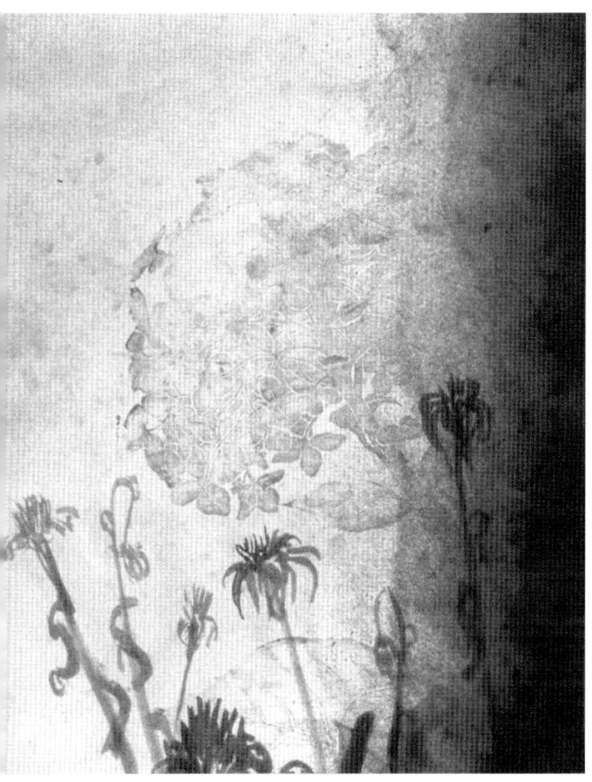

OKTOBER
schwarzweiße Birken
öffnen sich
und lösen sich dann auf
im Morgenlicht.
Ein Morgen der Federn,
des zarten Schneewassers.

In der Lichtung
erhebt der Gnadenvolle
seinen handlosen Arm.
Der Architekt der schwarzen Borke
gibt
eine Taube
aus leichtestem Holz frei.
Das Holz deines Ausgangs.

Alle Türen öffnen sich in den verwelkenden Garten,
aus dem du nicht zurückkehren wirst.

Im ungesprochenen Weiß
der Stunde der Engel
bricht der Erinnerte, Verletzte und Ruhelose
ungehört
auf eisigen Blättern zusammen.
Der Spiegel,
den du auf sein Geweih legtest,
rollt und ätzt weich eine Linie ein und
wenn er zur Ruhe kommt
ist der ganze Himmel jenseits der Gnade enthüllt.

In der Spiegelung
öffnet sich
eine Taube
und löst sich dann auf
im Morgenlicht.
Ein Morgen des Hungerns,
des kommenden Winters.

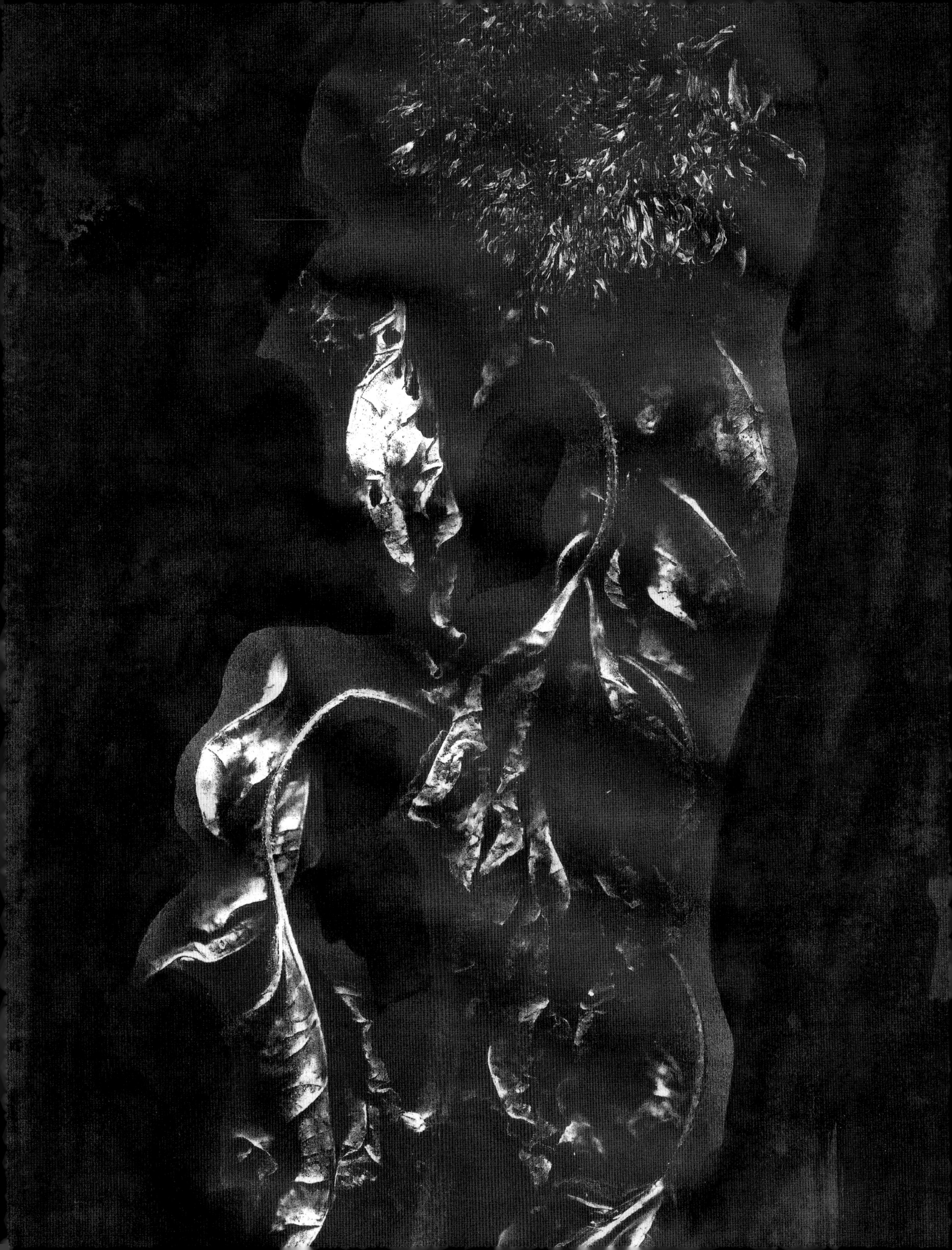

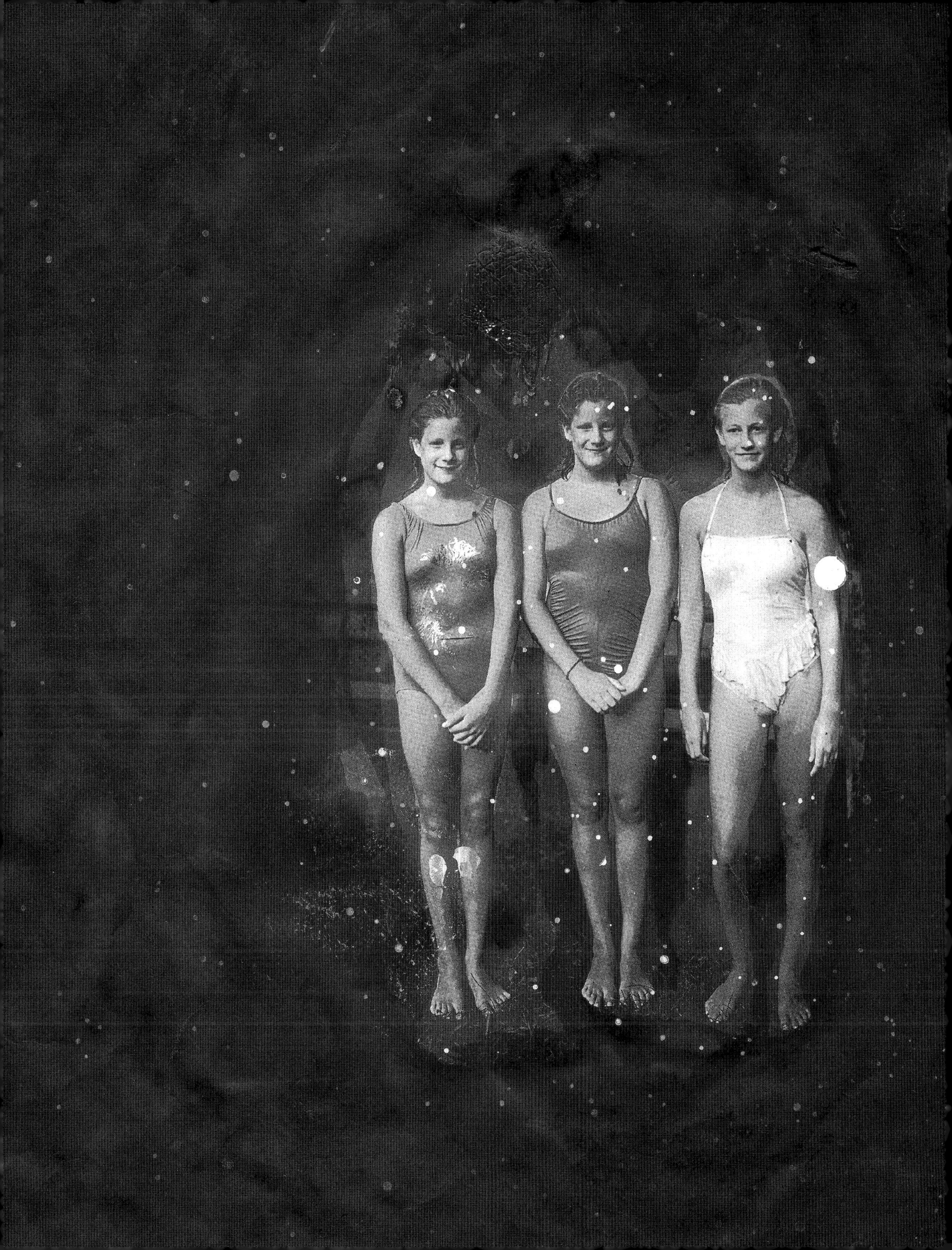

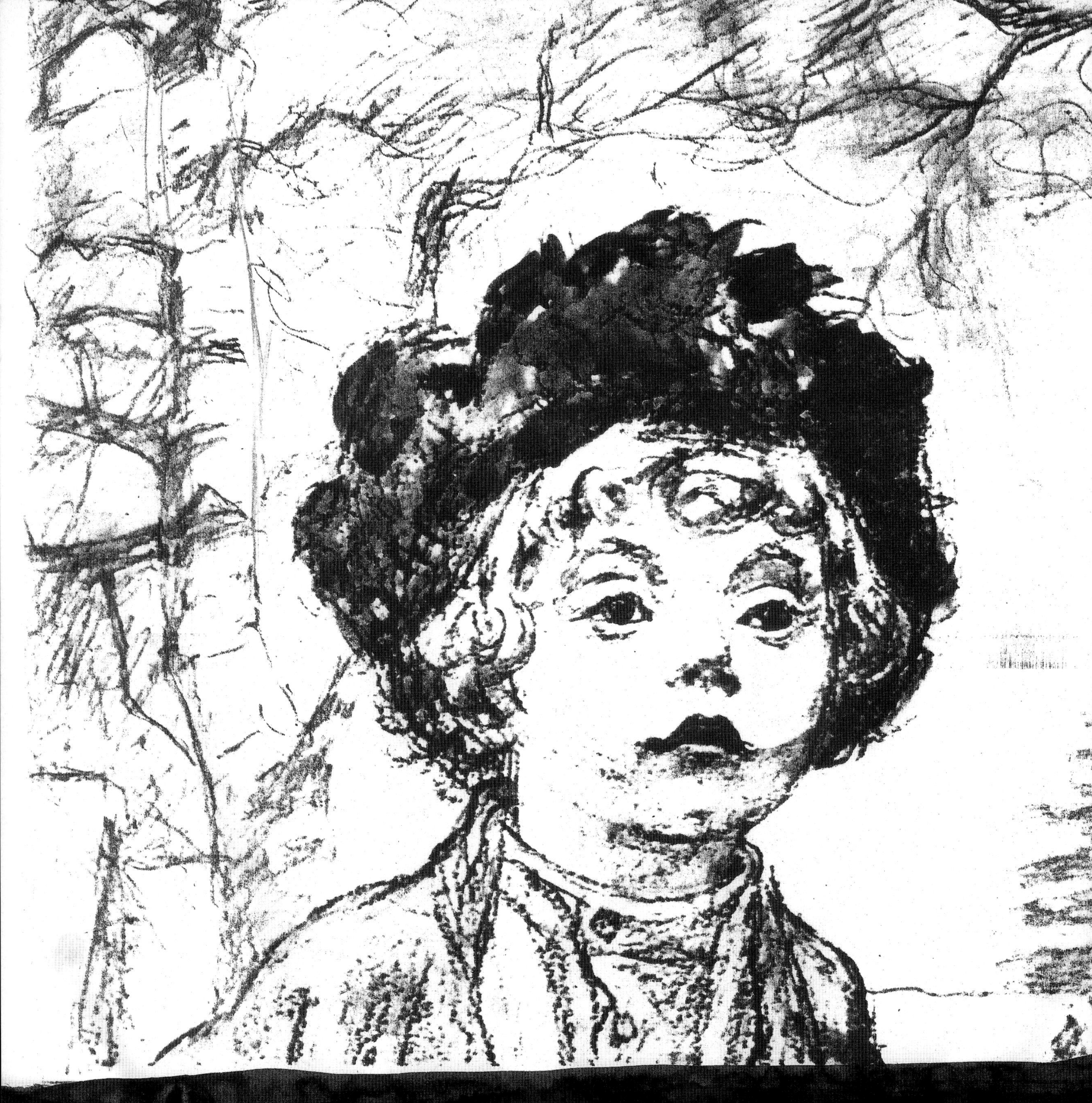

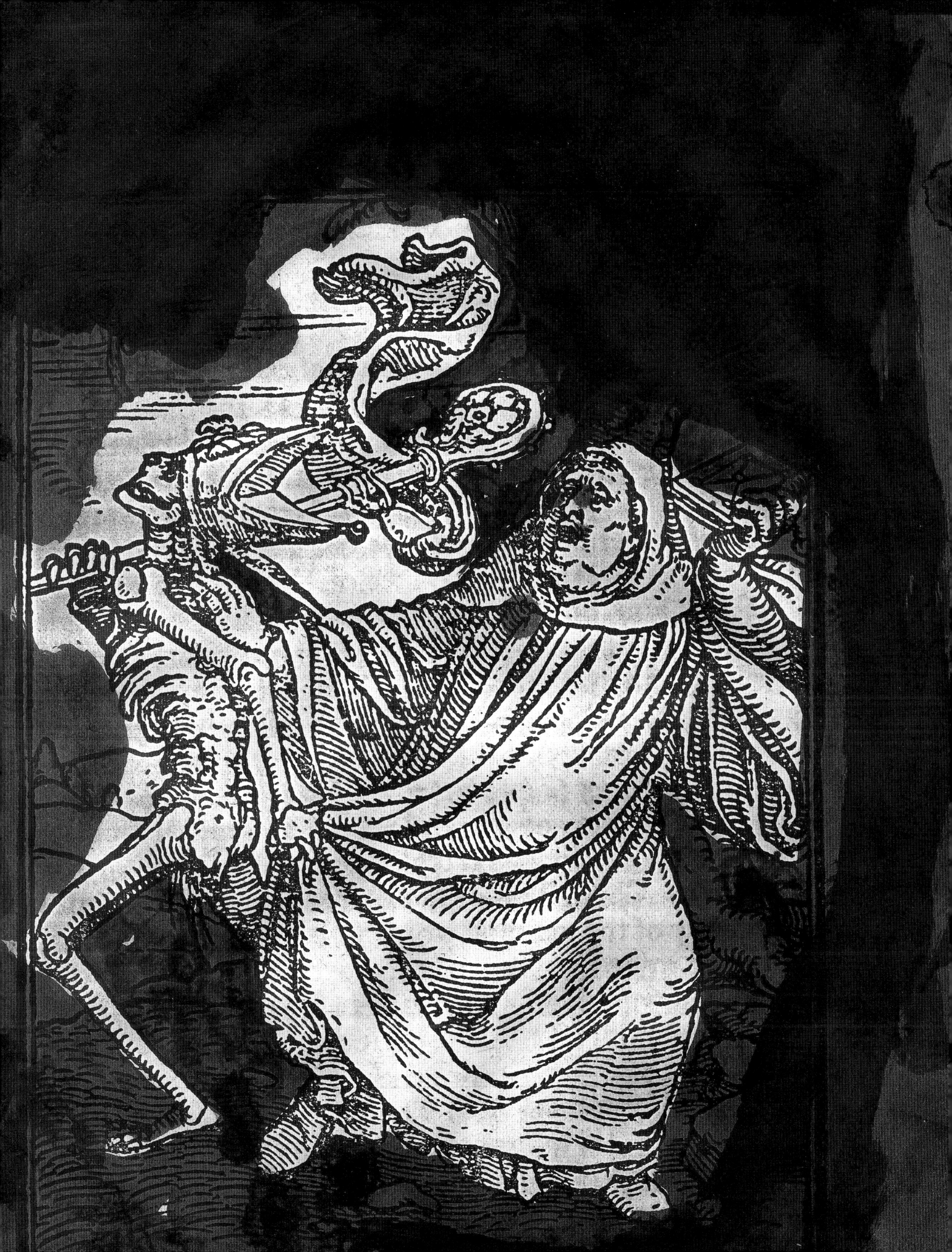

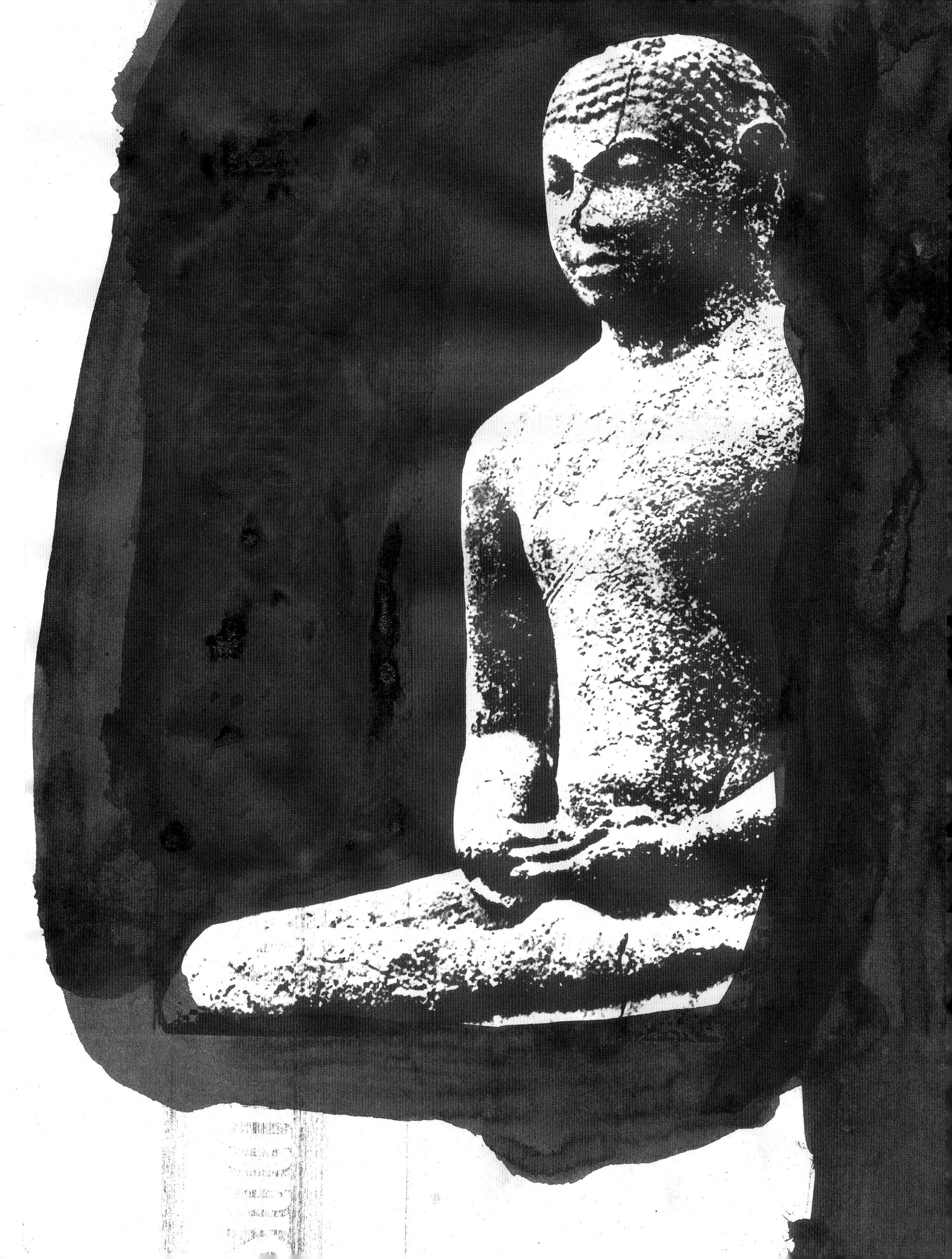

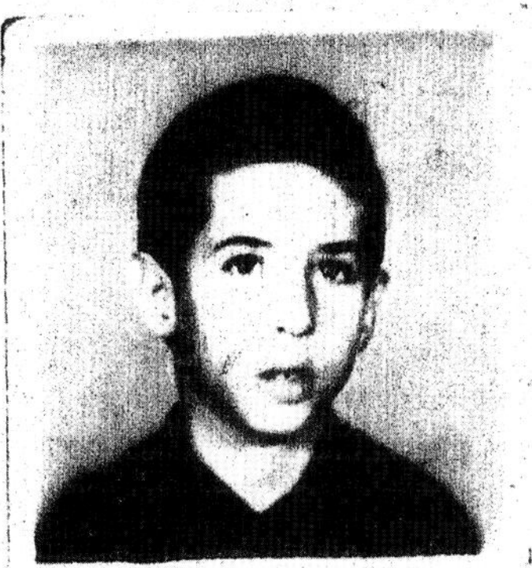

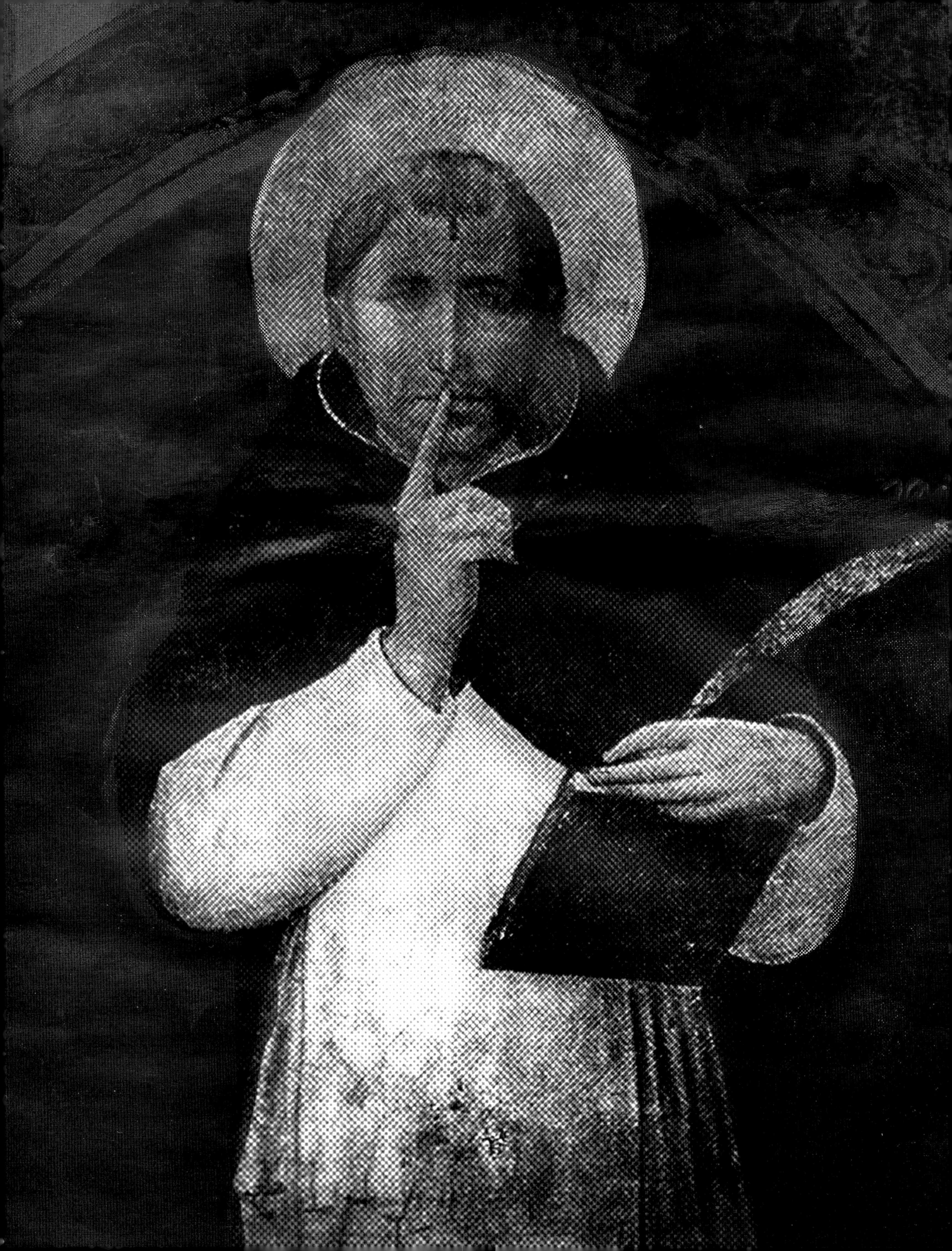

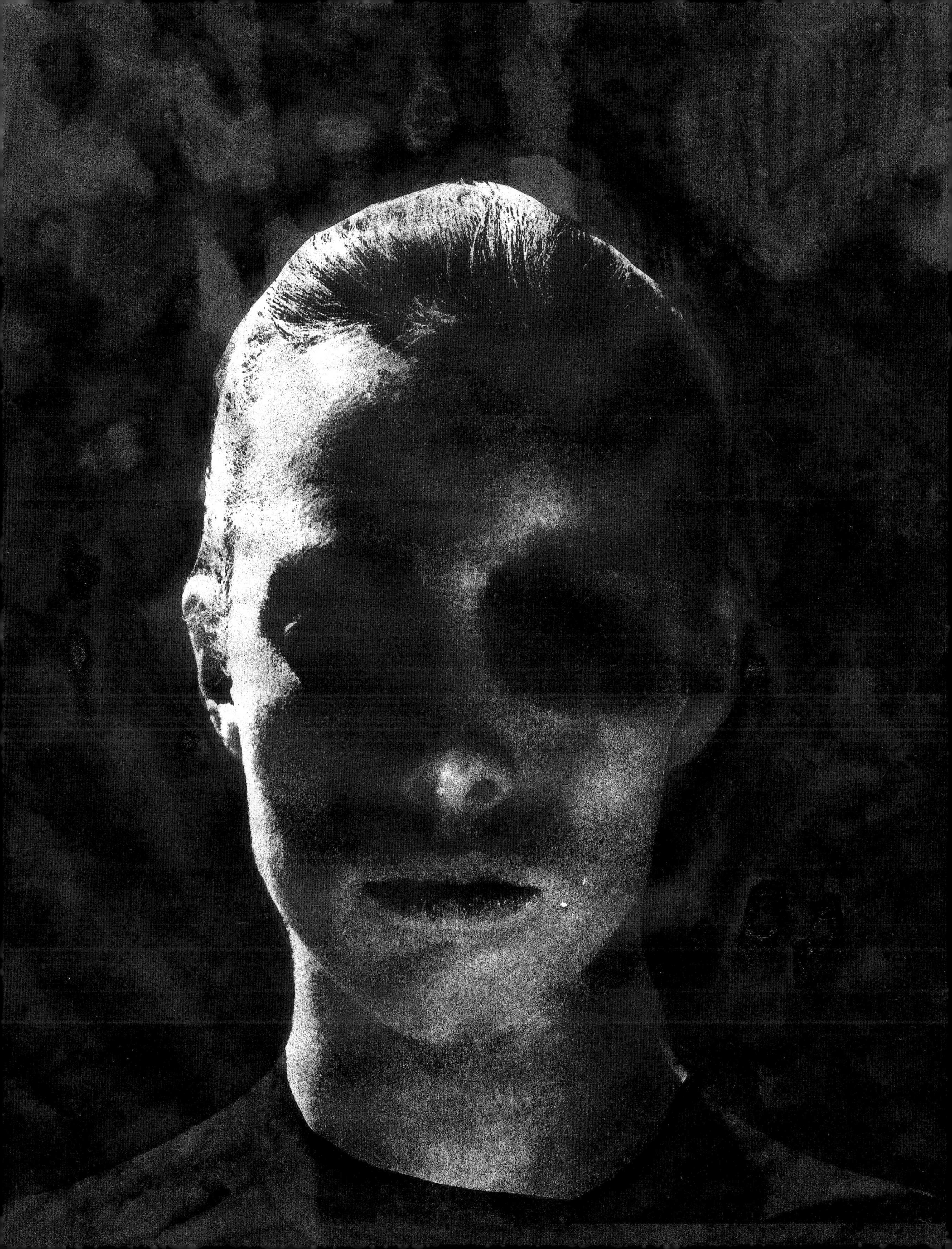

CONTRIBUTORS/AUTOREN

Charles Merewether is an art historian and Curator at the Getty Research Institute in Los Angeles. He has taught at Universidad Autonoma in Barcelona, the Ibero-Americana in Mexico City, the University of Sydney and University of Southern California. He has published extensively on the reconfiguration of modernism and the avant-garde in non-European cultures, especially Latin America, on aesthetics and violence and, more recently, on cultural memory, the archive and monuments. His publications include *A Marginal Body*, 1987; *The Remaining Evidence*, 2000; *Conditions of Uncertainty*, 2000 and *Anxieties of Revelation*, 2001. He has just completed a book of essays; *On the Trace*. He is presently writing a book on art in Japan and France during the immediate post World War II period. He is a regular contributor to and Advisory Editor of *Grand Street*.

Charles Merewether ist Kunsthistoriker und Kustos am Getty Research Institute in Los Angeles. Er hat an der Universidad Autonoma in Barcelona, der Ibero-Americana in Mexico City, der University of Sydney und der University of Southern California gelehrt. Unter seinen zahlreichen Publikationen sind Arbeiten über die Rekonfiguration des Modernismus und die Avantgarde in nichteuropäischen Kulturen, insbesondere in Lateinamerika, über Ästhetik und Gewalt sowie neuere Arbeiten über das kulturelle Erinnerungsvermögen, das Archiv und Monumente. Einige Titel seiner intensiven Veröffentlichungstätigkeit sind *A Marginal Body*, 1987, *The Remaining Evidence*, 2000; *Conditions of Uncertainty*, 2000, und *Anxieties of Revelation*, 2001. Charles Merewether hat soeben den Aufsatzband *On the Trace* fertiggestellt, zurzeit schreibt er ein Buch über die Kunst in Japan und Frankreich in der unmittelbaren Zeit nach dem Zweiten Weltkrieg. Er ist ein regelmäßiger Mitarbeiter und beratender Redakteur des Magazins *Grand Street*.

Abigail Solomon-Godeau (B.A., University of Massachusetts, Boston; Ph.D., Graduate Center, C.U.N.Y.) is a photography historian, a critic of contemporary art, and an art historian specializing in 19th-century French art, feminist and critical theory and contemporary art. She has recently received both a University of California President's Research Fellowship and a J. Paul Getty Fellowship. Her publications include *Photography at the Dock: Essays on Photographic History, Institutions and Practices*, 1991; *Male Trouble: A Crisis in Representation*, 1996, and essays in journals such as *Afterimage, Art in America, Camera Obscura, October, Parkett,* and *Screen* which have been anthologized frequently.

Abigail Solomon-Godeau (B.A., University of Massachusetts, Boston, Ph.D., Graduate Center, C.U.N.Y.) ist Photographie-Historikerin, Kritikerin zeitgenössischer Kunst und eine Kunsthistorikerin, die sich auf französische Kunst des 19. Jahrhunderts, feministische und kritische Theorie sowie zeitgenössische Kunst spezialisiert hat. Vor kurzem wurde sie mit den Stipendien University of California President's Research Fellowship und J. Paul Getty Fellowship ausgezeichnet. Einige Titel ihrer Veröffentlichungen sind: *Photography at the Dock: Essays on Photographic History, Institutions and Practices*, 1991; *Male Trouble: A Crisis in Representation*, 1996, und häufig in Anthologien aufgenommene Aufsätze in Zeitschriften wie *Afterimage, Art in America, Camera Obscura, October, Parkett* und *Screen*.

Howard N. Fox is Curator of Modern and Contemporary art at the Los Angeles County Museum of Art and a member of the humanities faculty of the Southern California Institute of Architecture. Prior to arriving in Los Angeles he was a curator at the Smithsonian Institution's Hirshhorn Museum and Sculpture Garden in Washington, D. C. He has written, lectured, taught extensively on issues of content and meaning in the art of our time. His exhibition catalogues on Lari Pittman (1996) and Eleanor Antin (1999) received annual achievement awards from the American chapter of the International Association of Art Critics.

Howard N. Fox ist Kustos für Moderne und Zeitgenössische Kunst am Los Angeles County Museum of Art und Mitglied der Fakultät für Geisteswissenschaften des Southern California Institute of Architecture. Vor seiner Ankunft in Los Angeles war er Kustos am Hirshhorn Museum and Sculpture Garden der Smithsonian Institution in Washington, D. C. Howard Fox hat viel über Inhalts- und Bedeutungsfragen in der Kunst unserer Zeit publiziert und gelehrt sowie zahlreiche Vorträge gehalten. Seinen Ausstellungskatalogen über Lari Pittman (1996) und Eleanor Antin (1999) wurden die jährlichen Auszeichnungen der amerikanischen Sektion der International Association of Art Critics verliehen.

Rosanna Albertini is a scholar of eighteenth-century philosophy who transferred her interest in human nature and history to contemporary art. She received her Laurea cum Laude in History of Philosophy in 1971 from the University of Milan. A former researcher in the Department of Philosophy of the University of Pisa, after two years in Paris at the Cité des Arts in 1990 and 1991, she moved to Los Angeles. She teaches at the UCLA Department of Art and is a correspondent for Art Press, Paris. She has done extensive research in new genre and contemporary art, lecturing in European museums, at video art festivals, and at art schools. From 1995 to 1999 she created and organized for the USC Annenberg Center for Communication the *Annenberg Dialogues*, multidisciplinary workshops about art, science and technology. Her most recent book is *Technological Rituals*, published by the Annenberg Center in 1999.

Rosanna Albertini hat sich zunächst auf die Philosophie des 18. Jahrhunderts spezialisiert und ihr Interesse an der menschlichen Natur und Geschichte auf die zeitgenössische Kunst übertragen. Sie erhielt ihre Laurea cum laude der Philosophiegeschichte 1971 von der Universität Mailand und forschte vor ihrem Umzug nach Los Angeles am Philosophischen Seminar der Universität Pisa und 1990/91 an der Cité des Arts in Paris. Sie lehrt am University of California, Los Angeles Department of Art und ist Korrespondentin für Art Press, Paris. Rosanna Albertini hat extensiv über New Genre und zeitgenössische Kunst gearbeitet, sie hielt Vorträge in europäischen Museen, auf Videokunst-Festivals und in Kunstschulen. Von 1995 bis 1999 konzipierte und organisierte sie die *Annenberg-Dialoge* für das University of Southern California Annenberg Center for Communication sowie interdisziplinäre Workshops über Kunst, Wissenschaft und Technologie. Ihr neuestes Buch trägt den Titel *Technological Rituals* und wurde 1999 vom Annenberg Center herausgegeben.

Judson J. Emerick is a Pennfield Scholar from the University of Pennsylvania, 1970–71. He is a Professor of Art History at Pomona College where he has been teaching since 1973. His publications include "The Early Sixth-Century Frescoes at S. Martino ai Monti in Rome", in *Römisches Jahrbuch für Kunstgeschichte*, 1984 and *The Tempietto del Clitunno near Spoleto*, 1998. He is currently studying Early Christian and Early Medieval liturgical furniture in Roman churches. His awards include the Samuel H. Kress Foundation Fellowship to the Bibliotheca Hertziana, Rome, 1971–73 and he was a Fellow of the National Endowment for the Humanities in 1981.

Judson J. Emerick ist Pennfield Scholar 1970/71 der University of Pennsylvania. Er ist Professor für Kunstgeschichte am Pomona College, wo er seit 1973 lehrt. Unter seinen Veröffentlichungen finden sich die Titel „The Early Sixth-Century Frescoes at S. Martino ai Monti in Rome" im *Römischen Jahrbuch für Kunstgeschichte*, 1984, und *The Tempietto del Clitunno near Spoleto*, 1998. Zurzeit studiert er das frühchristliche und frühmittelalterliche liturgische Mobiliar römischer Kirchen. 1971–73 war er Samuel H. Kress Foundation Fellow to the Bibliotheca Hertziana in Rom, 1981 wurde er als Fellow of the National Endowment for the Humanities ausgezeichnet.

Arden Reed received his Ph.D. in comparative literature at The Johns Hopkins University. Currently Professor of English at Pomona College, he wrote the prize-winning *Romantic Weather: The Climates of Coleridge and Baudelaire*, and edited a collection of essays *Romanticism and Language*. He has recently completed a study of Manet, Flaubert and the beginings of Modernism in France. He writes about art in Santa Fe and is a frequent contributor to *Art in America*.

Arden Reed promovierte in Vergleichender Literaturwissenschaft an der John Hopkins University. Zurzeit ist er Englischprofessor am Pomona College. Er schrieb das preisgekrönte Buch *Romantic Weather: The Climates of Coleridge and Baudelaire* und edierte die Aufsatzsammlung *Romanticism and Language*. Vor kurzem schloss er eine Studie über Manet, Flaubert und die Anfänge des Modernismus in Frankreich ab. Er schreibt über Kunst in Santa Fe und verfasst häufig Beiträge für *Art in America*.

Colette Dartnall is an independent curator and art historian. She has curated and co-organized numerous exhibitions at The Museum of Contemporary Art, Los Angeles, including *Catherine Opie* and *A Room of Their Own*. She is currently working on a number of other projects including forthcoming exhibitions *Matta in America: Paintings and Drawings from the 1940s* and *Post-Nature: Landscape and Land-use in Recent Los Angeles Art*. Dartnall has authored essays and has lectured widely on a variety of topics in modern and contemporary art.

Colette Dartnall arbeitet freiberuflich als Kuratorin und Kunsthistorikerin. Sie war Kuratorin und Mitorganisatorin einer beträchtlichen Anzahl von Ausstellungen des Museum of Contemporary Art in Los Angeles, u. a. *Catherine Opie* und *A Room of Their Own*. Zurzeit arbeitet sie an mehreren anderen Projekten wie. den künftigen Ausstellungen *Matta in America: Paintings and Drawings from the 1940s* und *Post-Nature: Landscape and Land-Use in Recent Los Angeles Art*. Colette Dartnall hat zahlreiche Aufsätze verfasst und Vorträge zu vielen Themen der modernen und zeitgenössischen Kunst gehalten.

LIST OF ILLUSTRATIONS
/VERZEICHNIS DER ABBILDUNGEN

The following listing is arranged by page number. We are providing detailed descriptions for those images not identified elsewhere. This list is intended as a representative survey of the artist's output over the past nine years. As such, it includes works not featured in the exhibition. Those works not included in the exhibition are designated with an asterisk (*). All photography by Gene Ogami, unless otherwise noted.

Die folgende Auflistung wurde nach Seitenzahlen geordnet und gibt detaillierte Angaben zu den nicht an anderer Stelle identifizierten Bildern Die Liste soll eine repräsentative Übersicht der Tätigkeit des Künstlers während der letzten neun Jahre bieten. Als solche schließt sie auch nicht in der Ausstellung präsentierte Werke ein. Die nicht ausgestellten Werke sind durch einen Stern (*) gekennzeichnet. Wenn nicht anderweitig vermerkt, sind die Photographien von Gene Ogami.

Front Cover/Umschlag
Frankness (Work of Mercy), detail/Offenheit (Werk der Gnade), Ausschnitt, 2000
(see p. 224/siehe S. 224)

Frontispieces/Einleitende Bildstrecke
1. Winter the Most Truthful, Release, detail/Winter der Wahrhaftigste, Befreiung, Ausschnitt, 2000*
(see p. 218/siehe S. 218)

4–5. Andrew Mummery Gallery, Installation at /Exponate in den St. Pancras Chambers, London, United Kingdom, 1998
Photograph by Adam Butler, London

6. Recollection (Dog), detail/Erinnerung (Hund), Ausschnitt, 2000*
Watercolor on paper/Aquarellfarbe auf Papier
11.5 x 11.5 inches (29 x 29 cm)
Collection/Sammlung Lydia Cheney, Birmingham, Alabama

7. October, detail/Oktober, Ausschnitt, 2000
(see p. 238/siehe S. 238)

8. Three Wounds, detail /Drei Wunden, Ausschnitt, 1995*
Oil, enamel and fabric on canvas/Öl, Emaille und Gewebe auf Leinwand
72 x 60 inches (183 x 152 cm)
Collection/Sammlung Lois and James Ukropina, San Marino, California
Photograph by Michael Honer, Claremont

9. Deep Water, detail /Tiefes Wasser, Ausschnitt, 1997*
Oil on canvas/Öl auf Leinwand
78 x 72 inches (198 x 183 cm)
Collection/Sammlung William Griffin Sr., Westfield, New Jersey

10–11. Coming Home/Heimkehr, 2000
(see p. 240/siehe S. 240)

12–13. Quiet Night (Ocean), Quiet Night (Marks), Quiet Night (Dirt)/Stille Nacht (Ozean), Stille Nacht (Markierungen), Stille Nacht (Erde), 1999
(see pp. 196–199/siehe S. 196–199)

14. The artist in his studio /Der Künstler in seinem Atelier, 2000
Photograph by Danny First, Los Angeles

24. Ausencia (Absence), detail/Ausencia (Abwesenheit), Ausschnitt, 1998*
Oil and pencil on paper/Öl und Bleistift auf Papier
25 x 19 inches (63.5 x 48 cm)
Collection/Sammlung Enrique and Alexandra Martínez Celaya

30. Vantage (Agua Removida [Murky Water]), detail/Standpunkt (Trübes Wasser), Ausschnitt, 2000*
Silver gelatin print/Silbergelatineabzug
42 x 57 inches (107 x 146 cm)
Courtesy of Enrique Martínez Celaya

33. Spoken For (the Merciful) /Fürgesprochene (die Gnadenvollen), 2000*
Oil on black velvet/Öl auf schwarzem Samt
96 x 108 inches (244 x 274 cm)
Museo Extremeño Iberoamericano de Arte Contemporáneo (MEIAC), Badajoz, Spain

34. Artist's photograph of bullet holes in a Berlin building/Künstlerphoto mit Kugellöchern in einem Berliner Gebäude, 1998
Photograph by Enrique Martínez Celaya

37. The Shore, iii/Das Ufer, iii, 2000*
Silver gelatin print/Silbergelatineabzug
5 x 7 inches (13 x 18 cm)
Private collection/Privatsammlung Brussels, Belgium

39. Reminder, detail/Mahnung, Ausschnitt, 2000*
Chromogenic print/Chromogenic print
42 x 42 inches (107 x 107 cm)
Courtesy of Baldwin Gallery, Aspen, Colorado

41. Acceptance of Longing /Akzeptanz der Sehnsucht, 1997
(see p. 146/siehe S. 146)

42. The Trouble with Memory /Das Problem mit dem Gedächtnis, 1993
(see p. 118/siehe S. 118)

45. Re-inventory/Re-inventur, 2000*
Rose stems, lavender, tar and oil on paper /Rosenstengel, Lavendel, Teer und Öl auf Papier
81.5 x 36 inches (207 x 92 cm)
Collection/Sammlung Dieter and Si Rosenkranz, Berlin, Germany

47. Figure (Resonance)/Gestalt (Resonanz), 2000*
Oil on black velvet/Öl auf schwarzem Samt
41 x 31.25 inches (104 x 79 cm)
Collection/Sammlung Jocelyn Grayson, Woodstock, Vermont

48–49 Installation at/Exponate in der Burnett Miller Gallery, Santa Monica, California, 1996

50. St. Catherine (Absolution)/Die heilige Katharina (Absolution), 1997
Polyester resin/Polyesterharz
7 x 9 x 9 inches (18 x 23 x 23 cm)
Collection/Sammlung Mary Paeng, San Francisco, California

52. The Wedding Dress/Das Hochzeitskleid, 1996*
Plaster, gauze, beeswax and oil /Gips, Gaze, Bienenwachs und Öl
12 x 70 x 22 inches (14.5 x 175 x 55 cm)
Private collection/Privatsammlung Paris, France

53. Sketchbook/Skizzenbuch, 1997

55. Water and Figure/Wasser und Gestalt, 2000*
Silver gelatin print/Silbergelatineabzug
60 x 30 inches (107 x 93 cm)
Whitney Museum of American Art, New York, New York

61. The House of Arms, detail
/Das Haus der Arme, Ausschnitt, 1998*
Wax and titanium powder/Wachs und Titanpuder
27 x 5 x 2.4 inches (69 x 13 x 6 cm)
Collection/Sammlung Stephen Cohen,
Los Angeles, California

63. Quiet Night (Dirt)/Stille Nacht (Erde), 1999
Photograph by Adam Butler, London
(see p. 196/siehe S. 196)

64. Powers and Dominions
/Mächte und Machtbereiche, 1997*
Oil, graphite and rose petals on paper
/Öl, Graphit und Rosenblütenblätter auf Papier
72 x 48 inches (183 x 122 cm)
Private Collection/Privatsammlung Naples, Florida

69. Circumstance/Umstand, 1997*
Oil on canvas/Öl auf Leinwand
84 x 96 inches (213 x 244 cm)
Collection/Sammlung Marano Elena Bowes,
London, United Kingdom

70. Sacrifice/Opfer, 1995*
Oil, enamel, paper, fabric and silkflowers on canvas/Öl, Emaille, Papier, Gewebe und Seidenblumen auf Leinwand
72 x 60 inches (183 x 152 cm)
Private Collection/Privatsammlung Virginia
Photograph by Michael Honer, Claremont

73. A Voice to Speak
/Eine Stimme zum Sprechen, 2000*
Watercolor, india ink and acrylic on paper/Aquarellfarbe, chinesische Tusche und Acryl auf Papier
69 x 35 inches (175 x 89 cm)
Microsoft Corporation, Seattle, Washington
Photograph by Spike Mafford, Seattle

74–75. Installation at/Exponate bei Griffin Contemporary, Venice, California, 1999

76. The artist in his studio
/Der Künstler in seinem Atelier, 2000
Photograph by Danny First, Los Angeles

81. The artist in his studio
/Der Künstler in seinem Atelier, 1999
Photographs by Danny First, Los Angeles

82. The artist in his studio
/Der Künstler in seinem Atelier, 1998
Photograph by Danny First, Los Angeles

85. The artist in his studio
/Der Künstler in seinem Atelier, 2000
Photograph by David Minnery, Los Angeles

90–91. Bed (the Creek)/Bett (der Bach), 1997
(see p. 138/siehe S. 138)

92. The artist in his studio
/Der Künstler in seinem Atelier, 1998
Photograph by Danny First, Los Angeles

95. Architecture/Architektur, 2001*
Chromogenic print/Chromogenic print
42 x 31 inches (107 x 79 cm)
Museum Ludwig, Cologne, Germany

96. tu voz entre las hojas (Your Voice among the Leaves)/tu voz entre las hojas (Deine Stimme unter den Blättern), 2000*
Ink and paper on chromogenic print
/Tinte und Papier auf Chromogenic print
42 x 43 inches (107 x 109 cm)
Collection/Sammlung Heidi Schneider, New York, New York

98. Joseph Beuys, Feltsuit/Filzanzug, 1978*
Photograph by Enrique Martínez Celaya
From the Happening at Basel, Switzerland that led to the work *Feuerstätte II*, now at the Kunstmuseum, Basel./Vom Happening in Basel, Schweiz, aus dem die Arbeit *Feuerstätte II* (jetzt im Kunstmuseum Basel) hervorging.

99. Figure in Boat (Judge)
/Figur in Boot (Richter), 2001*
Watercolor and india ink on paper
/Aquarellfarbe und chinesische Tusche auf Papier
15.5 x 17.5 inches (39 x 44 cm)
Courtesy of Baldwin Gallery, Aspen, Colorado
Photograph by Robert Wedemeyer, Los Angeles

101. Constellation IV, detail/Konstellation IV, Ausschnitt, 2001*
Tar, plaster, feathers and wig/Teer, Gips, Federn und Perücke
66 x 20 x 12 inches (168 x 51 x 31 cm)
Courtesy of Rena Bransten Gallery,
San Francisco, California
Photograph by Robert Wedemeyer, Los Angeles

102. Terror and Remains
/Schrecken und Überreste, 1998*
Oil and embroidery on canvas/Öl und Stickerei auf Leinwand
96 x 96 inches (245 x 245 cm)
Collection/Sammlung The Progressive Corporation, Cleveland, Ohio

105. The Forest V, Clearing
/Der Wald V, Lichtung, 1999
Watercolor on paper/Aquarellfarbe auf Papier
15 x 32 inches (38 x 81 cm)
Collection/Sammlung William Griffin,
Venice, California

106. Last Flower, detail
/Letzte Blume, Ausschnitt, 1998*
Silver gelatin print/Silbergelatineabzug
16 x 16 inches (40 x 40 cm)
Collection/Sammlung Enrique and Alexandra Martínez Celaya

108–109. The Shore, iv/Das Ufer, iv, 2000*
Silver gelatin print/Silbergelatineabzug
5 x 7 inches (13 x 18 cm)
Collection/Sammlung Dieter and Si Rosenkranz,
Berlin, Germany

116. A Little Horse Painting
/Gemälde eines kleinen Pferdes, 1992*
Oil, fabric, tar and thread on canvas with lights
/Öl, Tuch, Teer und Garn auf Leinwand, Lichter
51 x 60 inches (130 x 152 cm)
Collection/Sammlung Brian Mountford,
New York, New York
Photograph by Dave Folks, Santa Barbara

117. La Otra Prisión (The Other Prison)
/La Otra Prisión (Das andere Gefängnis), 1992,
Photograph by Dave Folks, Santa Barbara

119. The Trouble with Memory
/Das Problem mit dem Gedächtnis, 1993
Photograph by Dave Folks, Santa Barbara

121. Installation at Gallery 144/Installation in Gallery 144, Santa Barbara, California 1993
Photograph by the artist

121. No Doubt Good Writing/Zweifelsohne etwas gut Geschriebenes, 1995
Photograph by Michael Honer, Claremont

123. None of It Reminds Me of You
/Nichts davon erinnert mich an dich, 1995*
Photograph by Michael Honer, Claremont

124. Painting with Lion and Chair
/Gemälde mit Löwe und Stuhl, 1993*
Photograph by Dave Folks, Santa Barbara

125. The End of Tragedy
/Das Ende der Tragödie, 1995
Photograph by Michael Honer, Claremont

127. Unsafe/Nicht Sicher, 1996*

129. K, the Battlefield/K, das Schlachtfeld, 1996

131. The Habit of Hummingbirds
/Die Gewohnheit der Kolibris, 1996

133. Second Ornament/Zweite Verzierung, 1996

136. Head with Rabbit, detail/Kopf mit Kaninchen, Ausschnitt, 1997*
Watercolor, graphite and gold leaf on paper
/Aquarellfarbe, Graphit und Blattgold auf Papier
Collection/Sammlung Enrique and Alexandra Martínez Celaya

137. Thing and Deception
/Ding und Täuschung, 1997

138–139. Bed (the Creek)
/Bett (der Bach), 1997

140–141. Hopscotch/Himmel und Hölle, 1997*

143. The Burden of Your Hand
/Die Last deiner Hand, 1997*

145. The River/Der Fluss, 1997

146. Acceptance of Longing (study)
/Akzeptanz der Sehnsucht (Studie), 1997*
Oil on paper/Öl auf Papier
36 x 60 inches (91 x 152 cm)
Collection/Sammlung Dr. and Mrs. Stephen Kulvin, Coral Gables, Florida

147. Acceptance of Longing
/Akzeptanz der Sehnsucht, 1997

149. Stonewall/Steinmauer, 1997

153. Vanity and Redemption
/Eitelkeit und Erlösung, 1997

155. The Garden of Forgetfulness
/Der Garten der Vergesslichkeit, 1997

157. The Secrets/Die Geheimnisse, 1997
A Boy in his Room/Ein Knabe in seinem Zimmer, 1997

158. Snow and Time/Schnee und Zeit, 1998*
Wax, plaster and rose petals/Wachs, Gips und Rosenblütenblätter
15 x 7 x 10 inches (38 x 18 x 25 cm)
Courtesy of Griffin Contemporary, Venice California

159. Tu Brazo (Your Arm)
/Tu Brazo (Dein Arm), 1997

160, 161. The King's Shelter
/Der Zufluchtsort des Königs, 1997
Photograph by Robert Wedemeyer, Los Angeles

163. Map/Landkarte, 1998

165. Saint Catherine (Spirit)
/Die heilige Katharina (Geist), 1997

167. Saint Catherine (The Ethical Question)
/Die heilige Katharina (Die ethische Frage), 1997*

Saint Catherine (Absolution)
/Die heilige Katharina (Absolution), 1997

Saint Catherine (Culture)
/Die heilige Katharina (Kultur), 1997

Half Again, Flower
/Wieder halb, Blume, 1997

Saint Catherine (Pleasure)
/Die heilige Katharina (Vergnügen), 1997*

Saint Catherine (Beautiful Soul)
/Die heilige Katharina (Schöne Seele), 1997

169. First War/Erster Krieg, 1998

171. Second War/Zweiter Krieg, 1998

172. Sketchbook/Skizzenbuch, 1998

173. Accumulation of Tiredness
/Anhäufung der Müdigkeit, 1998

174. Fragility of Merit, detail/Die Zerbrechlichkeit des Verdienstes, Ausschnitt, 1998*
Oil, tar and velvet on canvas/Öl, Teer und Samt auf Leinwand
66 x 72 inches (168 x 183 cm)
Collection/Sammlung Bob and Sheryl Anderson, Newport Beach, California

175. Essential Equation
/Wesentliche Gleichung, 1998

177. Last Flower/Die letzte Blume, 1998*

178. The Size of a Wound
/Die Grösse einer Wunde, 1998

179. The Listener/Der Zuhörer, 1998

181. Fourth Flower for Paul Celan
/Die vierte Blume für Paul Celan, 1998

Capaz de lo más leve (Capable of the most subtle)/Capaz de lo más leve (Des Subtilsten fähig), 1998

Winter and Silk Flowers
/Winter und Seidenblumen, 1998

The Warden/Der Wächter, 1998

Heart and Bird/Herz und Vogel, 1998

184. untitled (Man and Forest), study for *Coming Home*/Ohne Titel (Mann und Wald), Studie für *Heimkehr*, 2000*

185. A Neck in Ashes/Ein Hals in Asche, 1999

186. Work in progress/Bei der Arbeit, 1999
Photograph by Danny First, Los Angeles

187. Pena (Sorrow)
/Pena (Schmerz), 1997–1999

188. Work in progress/Bei der Arbeit, 1999
Photograph by Danny First, Los Angeles

189 The Empty Garden/Der leere Garten, 1999

191. Unbroken Poetry (Herman Melville)
/Ungebrochene Dichtung (Herman Melville), 1999

193. The Field/Das Feld, 1999

194. Work in progress/Bei der Arbeit, 1999
Photograph by Danny First, Los Angeles

195. Quiet Night (Recollection) I
/Stille Nacht (Erinnerung) I, 1999

196. Installation at/Installation bei Griffin Contemporary, Venice, California 1999

197–199. Quiet Night/Stille Nacht
Quiet Night (Dirt)/Stille Nacht (Erde)

Quiet Night (Marks)/Stille Nacht (Markierungen)

Quiet Night Ocean)/Stille Nacht (Ozean), 1999

201. The Most Fragile/Das Verletzlichste, 1999

203. A Dry Bed/Ein trockenes Bett, 1999
The Imperfect Future
/Die unvollkommene Zukunft*

Must Find Me Extinguished
/Muss mich erloschen finden*

Trying to Make Sense
/Wenn ich versuche, den Sinn zu finden*

of Faults and Lack of Meaning
/von Fehlern und Bedeutungslosigkeit*

205. of Regrets
/des Bedauerns*

and People Inevitably Left Behind/und unvermeidlicherweise zurückgelassene Menschen*

and Irretrievable Moments with Them/und unwiederbringliche Momente mit ihnen*

This is Then the Past,/Das ist dann die Vergangenheit*

and I, the Counter./und Ich, der Zähler.*

(no text)/(kein Text)*

207. The Forest/Der Wald, 1999

The Forest I, Light/Der Wald I, Licht, 1999*

The Forest II, Bird/Der Wald II, Vogel, 1999*

The Forest IV, Lily/Der Wald IV, Lilie, 1999*

The Forest V, Clearing/Der Wald V, Lichtung, 1999

The Forest III, Tulip/Der Wald III, Tulpe, 1999*

209. Body in a Large Room (Beautiful Words)
/Körper in grossem Zimmer (Schöne Worte), 1999

211. Body at Rest (Renunciation)
/Ruhender Körper (Verzicht), 1999

213–215. Winter/Winter, 2000
Juegos Prohibidos (forbidden games)/Juegos Prohibidos (Verbotene Spiele), 2000

The Plains/Die Ebene, 2000

Wanderer (Night)/Wanderer (Nacht), 2000

Birch and Mountains/Birke und Berge, 2000

219, 221, 223. Elegias/Elegien, 2000–2001
Winter the Most Truthful, Release/Winter der Wahrhaftigste, Befreiung, 2000*

Traces and Marks (The River)/Spuren und Markierungen (Der Fluss), 2000*

Witness and Record/Zeuge und Protokoll, 2000*

220. Sketchbook/Skizzenbuch, 2000

222. Study for Traces and Marks
/Studie für Spuren und Markierungen, 2000*
Watercolor on paper/Aquarellfarbe auf Papier
11 x 11 inches (28 x 28 cm)
Courtesy of Enrique Martínez Celaya

225. Frankness (Work of Mercy)
/Offenheit (Werk der Gnade), 2000

227. Redemption/Erlösung, 2000

229, 231. Recent Watercolors
/Neue Aquarelle, 1999–2000

The Remembered/Der Erinnerte, 2000

Birches and Scabs/Birken und Schorf, 1999

Signal/Signal, 2000

Figure at Rest with Head
/Ruhende Figur mit Kopf, 2000

233 Transient (Oak Forest)
/Flüchtige Erscheinung (Eichenwald), 2000

235. Special Island (The Kiss)
/Die besondere Insel (Der Kuss), 2000*

237. The Blink/Der Augenblick, 2000

239. October/Oktober, 2000

240. untitled (Boy and Elk), detail
/Ohne Titel (Knabe und Hirsch), Ausschnitt, 2000*

241. Coming Home/Heimkehr, 2000

242. Work in progress/Unvollendete Arbeit, 2000*
Photograph by Danny First, Los Angeles

243. Dove and the Lightest Wood
/Taube und das leichteste Holz, 2000

244. Drawing with Birches and Red
/Zeichnung mit Birken und Rot, 2000*

245. The Opening/Die Öffnung, 2000

246–247. The artist's studio
/Das Atelier des Künstlers, 2000
Photograph by Danny First, Los Angeles

248. Me and My Brothers, detail
/Ich und meine Brüder, Ausschnitt, 1987*
Oil on canvas/Öl auf Leinwand
48 x 48 inches (122 x 122 cm)
Collection of /Sammlung Dr. Carlos Martínez, Long Beach

249. The artist/Der Künstler, 1994
Photographer unknown

250. Brookhaven National Laboratory, 1987
Photographer unknown

The artist's studio/Das Atelier des Künstlers, 1991
Photograph by the artist

Mezquita, Cordoba, Spain/Spanien, 1991
Photograph by the artist

251. The artist's studio/Das Atelier des Künstlers, 1994
Photograph by the artist

Donald Baechler, Allen Ginsberg, and Martínez Celaya, 1994
Photographer unknown

252 The artist's studio/Das Atelier des Künstlers, 1995
Photograph by Micheal Honer, Claremont

253. Performance destroying art work
/Performance Zerstörung von Kunstwerken
Daniel Arvizu Gallery, Santa Ana, California, 1996
Photographs by Walter James Christensen, Los Angeles

254. The artist's studio
/Das Atelier des Künstlers, 2001
Photograph by Robert Wedemeyer, Los Angeles

255. Performance documentation
/Dokumentation der Performance, 1998

256. The artist in his studio
/Der Künstler in seinem Atelier, 2000
Photograph by Danny First, Los Angeles

258. Layout for/Plan für Saint Pancras
Chambers, 2000

259. October, Artist book/Künstlerbuch, 2001

260. Galeria Botello, San Juan, Puerto Rico, 1993
Photograph by Juan Botello, San Juan

261. University Art Museum, 1994
Photograph by Richard Ross, Santa Barbara
Burnett Miller Gallery, 1997

262. Galerie Bäumler, 1998
Photograph by Alexandra Williams, Venice
Andrew Mummery Gallery, Installation at
/Exponate in den St. Pancras Chambers, 1998
Photograph by Adam Butler, London

263. Pictures of Mercy, exhibition announcement
/Bilder der Gnade, Ausstellungsankündigung, 2000
Installing at the/Aufbau in der
Luckman Fine Arts Gallery, 1999
Photograph by Susanna Bautista, Los Angeles

265. The artist's studio
/Das Atelier des Künstlers, 2000
Photograph by Danny First, Los Angeles

268–275. You Are Not the Others
/Du bist nicht die anderen, 2001*
8 x 10 inches (20 x 26 cm)
India ink on paper/Chinatinte auf Papier
Collection/Sammlung Enrique and Alexandra
Martínez Celaya

From p. 257/von S. 257

WEDER DIE ZEIT NOCH EIN UMSTAND
verdrängten deine Erinnerung.
Es war die Konzentration.

dann füllte sich das ganze Haus mit Vögeln
die ihre Flügel schlugen,
die Luft zu Schneebällen des Lautes formten,
welche sie an die Ecken warfen,
die längst der Stille überlassen waren.

Der Hof, dem Unkraut überlassen,
hatte die Blumen des Lachens
und das Fenster warf
Lichtstrahlen über den Porzellanfisch,
der von dem dunklen Kristalltisch sprang.